HOBBIES & CRAFTS

Leather Craft & Weaving

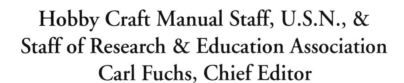

Hobby Craft Manual Staff, U.S.N., &
Staff of Research & Education Association
Carl Fuchs, Chief Editor

Research & Education Association
61 Ethel Road West
Piscataway, New Jersey 08854
Website: www.rea.com
Dr. M. Fogiel, Director

HOBBIES & CRAFTS™
LEATHER CRAFT & WEAVING

Printed in the United States of America

Library of Congress Control Number 2003090658

International Standard Book Number 0-87891-439-0

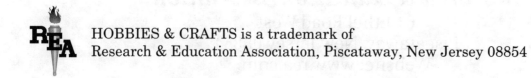
HOBBIES & CRAFTS is a trademark of
Research & Education Association, Piscataway, New Jersey 08854

What This Book Will Do For You

By combining both leatherworking and weaving into one volume, this unique "how-to book" is the ideal reference for these centuries-old crafts. Its comprehensive treatment of materials, tools and techniques makes it an invaluable handbook for creating beautiful designs. With a gallery of over 200 projects, you will become skilled in braiding, cutting, knotting, lacing, stitching, weaving, and color applications.

The section with design projects on leather craft cover the tanning process, preparation of leathers, leather classification, dyes and stains, and leather cutting. Each project specifies the tools, equipment and materials necessary to sew, dye, glue, and finish each design. Line drawings with detailed step-by-step instructions effectively illustrate methods used to create a variety of handbags, wallets, boxes, belts, briefcases, picture frames, and more.

The section with projects on weaving covers the origins of weaving, types of weaving, planning of patterns, dressing the loom, and weaving operations. Like the leather projects, each weaving design specifies tools and equipment, materials, and detailed instructions with illustrations for creating the projects.

About Research & Education Association

Research & Education Association (REA) is an organization of educators, scientists, and engineers specializing in various academic fields. REA was founded in 1959 with the purpose of disseminating the most recently developed scientific information to groups in industry, government, and universities. REA has since become a successful and highly respected publisher of study aids, handbooks, reference works, and test preparation books.

Created to extensively prepare students and professionals with the information they need, REA's Test Preparation series includes study guides for the Tests of Engineering (FE/EIT in General, Chemical, Civil, Industrial, and Mechanical Engineering), General Educational Development (GED), the Scholastic Assessment Tests (SAT I and SAT II), the Advanced Placement Exams (AP), the Test of English as a Foreign Language (TOEFL), as well as the Graduate Record Examinations (GRE), the Graduate Management Admission Test (GMAT), the Law School Admission Test (LSAT), and the Medical College Admission Test (MCAT).

REA's publications and educational materials are highly regarded and continually receive an unprecedented amount of praise from professionals, instructors, librarians, parents, and students. Our authors are as diverse as the fields represented in the books we publish. They are well-known in their respective disciplines and serve on the faculties of prestigious high schools, colleges, and universities throughout the United States and Canada.

Dr. M. Fogiel, Director
Carl Fuchs, Chief Editor

CONTENTS

Leather Craft

DESIGNS & PLANS FOR LEATHER CRAFT PROJECTS

DESIGNS & PLANS FOR LEATHER CRAFT PROJECTS

Weaving

DESIGNS & PLANS FOR WEAVING CRAFT PROJECTS

Leather Craft

Introduction

In recent years an increasing interest has developed in handicrafts. Despite the mechanical precision that has been attained in machine production, the beauty and charm of a handmade article is recognized by every art conscious individual.

In many instances the monetary value of an article is greatly increased if it has been made by hand. This has led many individuals to "set up shop" and make handmade articles to sell to the public. So, that which first expresses itself as a hobby may easily develop into a trade of profession.

One of the most popular hobbies is Leather Craft. The novice finds that even the most simple articles can be useful and attractive.

Furthermore, the initial outlay for materials is relatively low in cost and there is little waste as even scrap leather can be utilized for further projects.

The leather worker finds also that projects are easily portable during their working stages. Many of the actual operations can be continued outside of the shop or studio.

It is advisable for the novice to select comparatively simple articles as starting projects.

Increasing familiarity with tool usage, a greater knowledge of the adaptability of various leathers, and a perfecting of actual construction skills, will, in time, enable you to undertake even the most complicated projects.

Leather Craft

Early Tanning Methods Carried into Modern Times

The story of leather is as old as humanity itself. Early humans used pelts of animals, killed in the hunt, for body covering and also as sleeping mats on the earth and rock floors of caves.

Prehistoric tanners discovered that by rubbing animal fat into the skin of an animal, they could preserve the skin and render it pliable. The Inuit still practice this primitive process. The women of the tribe chew the skin to break down its fibrous stiffness, after which they rub it down with fat to preserve its pliability.

The earliest recorded use of leather dates back almost 5,000 years. From the hieroglyphics on ancient Egyptian stone tablets, we learn that they used it for items of clothing, furniture decoration and miscellaneous purposes. Many articles, dating back 3,000 years, have been perfectly preserved in the vaults of Egyptian tombs.

Bark Tanning Has Changed Little

Historic literature reveals that the Babylonians, the Greeks, and Romans were skilled in the processes of tanning, and accorded great value to leather. In this connection it is interesting to note that the word "pecuniary" is derived from "pecunia" money, and as used originally it denoted "property in cattle." It is evident from this, that leather was also used as a medium of exchange.

From the Latin word "tanare," meaning "oak bark," comes our own word "tanning."

The process of bark or vegetable tanning as we know it today is essentially the same as that used by the ancients. The bark of oak, hemlock, chestnut and other plant matter provides the tannic acid which reacts chemically on a raw hide, converting it into leather.

The Native Americans had developed a process of tanning leather. The same process is still used by them, and has been adopted by manufacturers with little variation, to produce what is known as "buckskin." (See Oil Tanning, pg. 3).

Process Used By Native Americans

The squaw was the tanner in the family unit. Individual tribes may have varied the procedure somewhat, but essentially the process was as follows:

First the pelt was soaked in a log trough filled with clear water. Wood ashes were sometimes added for the final soaking. When the hairs were loosened, the skin was stretched on a peeled log and unhaired with a sharpened rib bone. (The curve of the rib conformed to the contour of the log.) The brains of the animal were combined with other fatty parts to which was added hot water. This warm paste was applied to the skin and allowed to become partially dry. In this stage, it was stretched and pulled in every direction by hand. While the skin was still moist, the thickened or wrinkled areas were scraped with sharpened stones or shells to produce a uniform thickness.

New Tanning Methods Developed

The skin was then stretched on a frame and suspended over a slow smouldering fire that emitted a great deal of smoke. A small tepee was set up especially for that purpose. The wood chemicals in the smoke served as a preservative.

Buckskin, prepared in this way, was stronger and warmer than any cloth could have been.

In the 19th century additional methods of tanning were developed and many mechanical processes for the preparation of leather were devised. Leather can be produced from the skin of any animal, bird, reptile or fish. Obviously, some are preferred to others because of their texture and durability.

After the pelt is removed from the carcass, it must be salted or dried to prevent decomposition before it is sent to the tanner. Salting is the preferred method.

Pelts Soaked In Lime Solution

When the pelts reach the tannery, they are thoroughly soaked and washed in clear water or a weak chemical solution, to remove all blood, salt and dirt. They are then soaked in a lime solution to loosen the hairs. After the hairs have been removed by scraping, the skins go through a fleshing process to remove all fatty substances clinging to the flesh side of the hide. When this is accomplished, the lime is completely washed off the skins. They are then ready for tanning.

Tanning is the process by which the skin is preserved from putrefaction and rendered pliable. Pliability can also be increased with application of fats, oils and some chemical agents other than those found in the usual tanning agents. The word *tanning* originally applied to that method of leather preservation and preparation accomplished with tannic acid derived from vegetable material: bark, roots, fruit or berries. Now it covers all methods of preservation, whether the process involves vegetables, chemical or oil agents. These agents are known as *tannins*.

There are three methods of tanning:
(1) Vegetable tanning.
(2) Chemical tanning.
(3) Oil tanning.

Chemical Tanning Is Swift

For vegetable tanning, the skins are suspended on sticks, and submerged in vats containing a solution of water and extracts of oak, chestnut, hemlock or other vegetable matter. Additional extracts are added daily until the hides are thoroughly tanned. This process can sometimes extend over a period of months.

Chemical tanning, on the other hand, takes only a few hours. The skins are submerged in a solution of water, common salt and acid. This opens the pores to admit the penetration of the chrome salts when they are added to the solution.

After tanning, the leather is thoroughly washed and flattened in preparation for the splitting process. The hide is drawn by rollers against a wide horizontal blade that splits the leather to specified thicknesses. The skin or grain side is the top split, and layers lying next to it are stronger than those toward the flesh side of the leather.

Glass Roller Gives Gloss

The splits are then treated with oils and greases to make them pliable. They are polished in various ways. A high gloss is achieved by rubbing the leather with a glass roller; a dull finish is achieved by polishing the leather with roller brushes.

Leathers are embossed to simulate more expensive leathers, such as alligator, lizard, pigskin, by passing them through rollers that have been engraved with the grain of the leather. Presses, with engraved plates, are also used for embossing.

A suede finish is achieved by holding the flesh side of the leather against an emery wheel.

Oil tanning is used to produce buckskin and chamois. It results in a class of leather remarkable for its softness and velvety texture. Chamois is now made almost exclusively from the flesh splits of sheepskin. First, they are cleaned and washed thoroughly to remove all lime and other foreign matter. The splits are dried and thoroughly beaten by machines to soften them. Oil is then forced into the skin with additional beating. This oiling and beating is repeated two or three times until the skin has become a mustard color. After this, they are submitted to a heating process, never over 130 degrees F., to

oxidize the oil. When the oil has become completely oxidized, the skins are washed in hot water and squeezed in a hydraulic press. Any remaining oil is removed from the skin by washing in a solution of soda ash, which causes the fatty acids to saponify. Sulfuric acid solutions are used to neutralize the oils. A certain amount of oil remains in the skin to give them softness.

The dyes used by leather manufacturers are wood or coal tar products. The hides are dipped in a dye bath, or several coats of dye are sprayed or brushed on the surface of the leather.

LEATHER CLASSIFICATION

Leather classification conforms to the animal, reptile, or bird from which the hide or skin is taken, and in accordance with its tanning process.

ANIMAL HIDES: Cowhide is a heavy, comparatively coarse, grained leather. In its original thickness it is used for saddles, harness, sole leather and machine belting. After splitting, the grain or skin layer is used for luggage, belts, boots and miscellaneous cases.

The splits or layers cut from the remaining hide, are buffed and polished and often embossed to imitate the highly grained alligator, lizard and pigskin. Other splits are buffed to a velvet finish and used for suede articles.

This suede is more durable than sheep suede. The vegetable tanned, unembossed cowhide maybe used for tooling. It also takes color decoration.

Heavy cowhide, eight-nine ounces in weight and fully one-eighth inch thick, is suitable for carving.

One ounce leather is one sixty-fourth inch thick and one foot square.

Steerhide is similar to cowhide. It is prepared in the same way and used for the same purposes as cowhide. Next to calfskin it is the best tooling leather.

Calfskin is a close-grained, light weight leather, highly desirable for shoe uppers, fine handbags, wallets and bookbindings. It is ideal for tooling. "Russian" Calf, birch bark tanned, is considered the finest. American tanners have produced as fine a calf for tooling as that imported from Russia and in many instances the name is retained for commercial reasons.

Goatskin Ideal For Wallets

Horsehide or *colt* is extremely close-grained. It is stiff, and takes a high polish well. Commercially it is known as Cordovan leather. It does not take tooling.

Goatskin is a close-grained, tough skin. The finest, most durable goatskins are imported from the Alpine countries. Goatskin is associated with the Moroccans, who used it as far back at the 16th century for their book bindings. The finest Italian and Spanish leather articles are made of Morocco pin-grain goatskin. Its toughness and flexibility make it ideal for wallets, book bindings, box coverings, and linings.

Saffian goatskin is embossed with a linen-finish grain. *Levant* goatskin has an open grain, pebbly in appearance.

The smooth grained goatskins are toolable, and take stamp and wheel decoration. The highly grained or embossed textures are not toolable.

Pigskin Is Not Tooled

Pigskin comes in a wide range of naturally rippled grains. Its interesting texture and flexibility has increased its popularity in recent years. It is used for belts, gloves, handbags, luggage, wallets and miscellaneous cases. Its grain is not suitable for tooling.

Sheepskin is porous and more flexible than calf. When buffed to a velvet finish on the flesh side, it is known as *suede* sheepskin. Sheepskin *skiver* is the top split of the grain or skin layer of the hide. It is often embossed to imitate the grain of other leathers. A good top split, with glazed finish, is called *saddle sheepskin*. The one or one and one-half ounce weight can be used for linings, pockets, etc., in brief cases and luggage in place of lining calfskin. The two or two and one-half ounce weight can be used for handbags, wallets, and small cases.

Sheepskin is also embossed to resemble *Pin Seal* and, as such, it is used for wallets, handbags and small flexible cases.

Natural finish sheepskin is suitable for tooling.

Elkhide is comparatively smooth and close-grained, but flexible. It is generally used in its natural color for moccasins, belts, sporty casual-type handbags and flexible cases for sporting equipment.

Hides Used Effectively

Hair Hides. The hides of unborn and very young calves are tanned without removing the hair. Pony skin is also treated in this manner. Contemporary designers have utilized these hair hides very effectively in modern handbags, belts, and small cases.

Calfskin is most often used in combination with hair hide, although suede can also be used as an accent on belts and handbags. Lamp bases, chair backs and seats, hassocks and bookends, covered or accented with hair hide, are effective decorative notes in modern styled interiors.

Wool Sheepskin is also tanned with the wool on. The wool is sheared to an even length and is used for slippers, caps, jackets, and cases for breakable articles. All hair hides are cut from the flesh side of the skin.

REPTILE SKINS: *Alligator* skins are extremely durable, although there is a tendency for the leather to crack at the marking of a deep grain. The deepest markings should be placed away from the bending parts of an article. Genuine alligator skins are expensive, so it is suggested that amateurs develop sufficient skill in handling less expensive leathers before attempting to make wallets, handbags and belts with it. Calfskin and sheepskin are embossed with an alligator grain.

Lizard skins are durable and vary greatly in the size and roughness of scales. Skins are small, ranging from 9 inches wide to 17 inches long. This restricts their use to wallets, coin purses and small handbags, unless skins are pieced together.

BIRD SKIN: *Ostrich* is comparatively difficult to obtain, consequently it is expensive. It is used for wallets, handbags and coverings for small toilet articles and jewel boxes. An article made of ostrich is truly an item of distinction.

DYES AND STAINS

Many leathers are obtainable in assorted colors. They have been dyed by the manufacturer with wood or coal tar dyes.

There are times, however, when an individual wishes to dye his own leather. The dyeing of leather requires considerable skill, but the feat can be accomplished by anyone, provided it is done carefully and at the same time follows the correct, logical steps which are as follows:

    (1) Saturate the leather with water by use of a sponge. Be sure that the water penetrates evenly over the surface of the leather.

    (2) Apply the dye to the surface in the same manner as the water, and at the same time spread the dye with a sponge to eliminate "water rings."

    (3) Allow the leather to dry slowly at room temperature.

    (4) Wax leather.

Manufacturers furnish directions for the use of dyes. The following is a list of dyes than can be used most successfully on leather.

Spirit Dyes come in powder form, and they are soluble in alcohol. Unusual hues may be obtained with them by the mixture of two or more colors. They are applied with a sponge or sheepskin swab.

Apply Dye With Brush Or Sponge

Water Dyes are aniline dyes. They come in powder form and are soluble in hot water. The leather is completely immersed in a dye bath made with this solution. The dye may also be applied with a brush.

Oil Stains are used to produce antique or soft, blended effects. They are applied quickly with a cheese-cloth swab and wiped off immediately. The stain settles between the grain of the leather while the top surface of the grain is wiped clean. If a deeper stain is desired on the edges of the article, less of the stain is wiped off. Thin with turpentine if necessary.

If an article is to be tooled, always complete the tooling or stamping and punching of throng slits before it is dyed. Dye the lace at the same time. (See Leather Chart III, pg. 25). Sometimes the edges of an article will have a tendency to curl up after dyeing. Allow the piece to dry thoroughly, then put it under a smooth weight overnight. Rub it with a soft cloth, and complete lacing or stitching.

A design must first be outlined or modelled. Allow leather to dry thoroughly before applying the colored inks. If wet, the inks have a tendency to bleed beyond the outline. Apply the

ink with a No. 2, or No. 3 camel's hair water color brush.

Test Ink Before Using

Colored ink is effectively used to accent stamp and wheel designs on natural colored leathers. Often the depressed area of the stamp design does not show up the beauty of the intricate units of the design. If they are accented with a darker value of the leather color, or with a contrasting color, they show up to advantage.

Colored inks are also used to touch up the edges of colored leather where the cutting has exposed the raw leather.

In every case where dyes, stains or inks are used, the color should be tested on scrap leather before it is applied to the article being treated.

CRAFT LEATHER

Refer to the Leather Craft Material Chart for specific descriptions as to size, weight, thickness, tannage, finish and texture of the various leathers used by the craftsmen. The decorative possibilities, range of colors and list of suggested articles are also tabulated on the chart.

The "procedure" on each Project Sheet, pages 58 to 395, includes the suggested leather from which an article may be made. In the majority of cases, the individual need not feel restricted to the use of the particular leather designated. He may select others of similar weight, thickness and texture.

When a specific type of decoration is shown, such as carving, tooling or painting— and when the weight of a brief case, toilet kit, scuffies or sandals demand a heavy cowhide or sole leather— the article should be constructed of the leather specified for that item in the "procedure."

Keep Small Pieces Flat

The utmost care must be taken to keep the leather in good condition. Always roll it with the skin or grain side on the outside. If rolled otherwise, the skin side develops minute creases. Small pieces can be kept flat.

Place pieces of plain paper between leath-

ers that have a suede finish. Smooth them flat before rolling to avoid unnecessary creasing. Do not put a highly embossed leather, such as alligator or lizard, next to suede or a smooth surfaced leather, because it is apt to leave an impression on it.

Keep leather away from radiators and hot pipes, as heat dries out the oils and tends to make it brittle.

Vegetable tanned leathers are preferred for tooling, as the surface is firm, yet soft enough to absorb water. When tooled, the pores are easily compressed. On drying, the pores remain compressed, and the tooled design is retained indefinitely.

Chemical or chrome tanned leathers are practically waterproof. Consequently, they do not absorb sufficient moisture and it is more difficult to compress the pores for successful tooling. Tooling might be possible in some cases, but it is not recommended.

Avoid marking up smooth leather when handling it. Fingernail marks, pencil lines, knife or scissor scratches are impossible to eradicate.

Avoid Smudges On Leather

Cleanliness during each operation must be stressed. Dirty or oily hands leave smudges on leather. Tools should be free of rust, rubber cement and dye. Papers should be spread out on the working area during a cementing process, and destroyed when cementing is completed.

Utmost care should be taken when dyes are handled, so that clean leather will not become dye spotted.

TOOLS AND EQUIPMENT

Refer to the Leather Craft Tool Chart for a complete listing of tools and their descriptions. The chart includes tools used for all leather craft processes, ranging from simple to complex operations.

Novices will be concerned with those tools that are essential for constructing and decorating comparatively simple articles. They will often become interested enough to buy a set of tools of their own with which they can perform the basic leather operations.

The following is a list of essential tools:

Name of Tool	No. on Tool Chart, pg. 13-15
Bevel Point Skiving Knife	1
Steel Square	6
Tracer	13
Modeling Tool	9
Deerfoot and Double Edge Creaser	10
Metal Edge Creaser	27
Mallet	17
4-Prong Thonging Awl	4
1-Prong Thonging Awl	40
Awl (to pierce stitching holes)	25
Fid	26
Lacing Needle	18
6-Tube Revolving Punch	8
Snap Set	12
Eyelet Setter	14
Hardwood Board for Punching, etc.	32
Tooling Slab (plate glass or marble)	34

A jar with a screw cover, through which a brush is inserted, is ideal for rubber cement.

A regular nut pick can be used in place of a fid to tighten lacing. It can also be used for stippling background areas.

Care Of Tools Is Important

Tools must be cared for if they are to be kept in good condition for successful work. Prevent them from becoming rusty. Dry each modeling tool after its contact with moist leather. Rub the ends of modeling tools with an oily cloth occasionally. Store tools in a dry cabinet away from sweating walls.

Cutting tools need sharpening from time to time. A dull cutting edge chews the leather, and often shifts the position of the template. Dull punches cut irregular holes and cause the leather to stretch around the openings of the holes.

Sharpen a knife, thonging awl or scissors by rubbing the blade on any ordinary oil stone

to which has been applied a drop of light viscosity oil. Avoid developing a new angle on the blade. Rub lightly and slowly so as not to produce a feather edge.

CUTTING LEATHER

Refer to Leather Craft Chart I for specific, graphic suggestions on cutting procedure.

The beginner is urged to select articles from the prepared designs so as to become acquainted with general leather procedures. The patterns given on each job sheet are drawn to scale, unless otherwise noted. This makes it possible to enlarge the patterns to full size by photography or by projecting them on a screen from which they can be traced. In some cases, irregular patterns are drawn on plotting squares. This makes it possible to enlarge the patterns by a scaled drawing.

With an increasing familiarity with the possibilities of leather craft, individuals are anxious to develop their own ideas. In every case, they should be encouraged to experiment. Leather Craft provides an almost unlimited range of design and decoration.

Sketch Article For Guide

A knowledge of basic construction details concerning gussets, pockets, fasteners and straps (see Leather Chart IV, pages 28-30), enables an individual to create new patterns for handbags, wallets and miscellaneous cases.

An article should first be sketched to provide a visual guide for cutting the pattern. Measurements should be carefully planned as to proportions and function. Unless an article can serve a definite purpose it has little value. Therein lies the creed of the contemporary modern designer.

Functionalism should become the byword of every would-be designer. Function underlies all laws of proportion, materials and applied design.

Correct Measurements

After a sketch is complete with measurements, a pattern is drawn on heavy wrapping paper. The pattern is then cut out and tested for fit and overlap of flaps, etc. If gussets are used, they should be pinned or stapled in place.

Patterns should allow one eighth inch for lacing edges, and about one-quarter inch if edges are turned in for stitching. Every construction detail must be taken into account and measurements must be corrected if necessary. A final draft of the pattern is then drawn, cut out and transferred to the template.

Often, additional stiffness is required for the base, side or handles of an article and especially of handbags. Buckram is an ideal stiffener for handbags. It is cut one-eighth inch within the edges of the pattern of the outer leather so as not to interfere with the lacing or stitching.

Binder Board As Stiffener

Medium weight binder board or cardboard (not strawboard) is most satisfactory as a stiffener for the bottom and cover of toilet cases and cosmetic kits.

A few suggestions, in addition to those listed on Chart I, may be helpful.

The leather worker, in cutting larger pieces of leather, finds it difficult to hold a knife, to press on a steel square and to keep the hide in place all at the same time. A weight, made of a canvass bag filled with dry sand or small bird shot is excellent for holding the hide and pattern in position. Avoid weights that would leave straight-edged impressions on the leather.

Skived edges produce professional-like cemented edges. When a great amount of skiving has to be done, it become tedious and takes considerable time. Furthermore, there is always the danger of a skiving cut going through the leather. Skiving can be simplified and well regulated if it is done with the emery wheel of an I, electric driven hand grinder. (See Leather Chart III, Finishing, for an illustration of the grinder.)

SELECTION OF DESIGN

It is well to remember that an applied design can either *make or break* an article. The basic design (shape) may be functionally and proportionally perfect; the construction details may be on a professional level. All too often, however, the applied design ruins an otherwise perfect effect.

The beauty of the leather is marred by a scrawly naturalistic leaf and flower motif. A handsome portfolio is defaced by a resplendent sunset landscape in all its glowing colors. Such decoration is not in keeping with leather. A landscape or portrait belongs in a frame!

Many craft workers feel that an article must be heavily tooled or carved to bring it within the legitimate realm of leathercraft. The tendency of our professional contemporary designers is to simplify decoration so that it is definitely secondary to the functional lines and material of the article. Pleasing proportion and beauty of material, together with functional design, constitute perfection. "Nothing to excess" was the creed of the ancient Greeks, and the rule still holds in every phase of artistic creation.

Select Decorations Carefully

This point can be proved by a tour of the shops in any city. The more "gingerbread" that appears on an article, the cheaper it is apt to be. The simpler an article is, the more expensive it is apt to be.

The foregoing does not mean to imply that decoration should never be used. It is merely intended to stress the fact that elaborate decoration is not necessarily the best that an art has to offer, nor does it possess the greatest value.

Decoration, when used correctly, can enhance the beauty and texture of an article. For a study of superb applied designs on leather, one has only to study the beautiful tooled and colored designs on Italian and Spanish bookbindings of the 16th and 17th centuries. The leather work of those countries still ranks very high, although they are somewhat simpler today. Florentine gold tooling is unexcelled in the craft.

Ideas From Other Crafts

Designs from other crafts can often provide ideas of motifs and borders for leather articles. The wide range of plant, animal, and geometric designs can be adapted for use in either tooling or carving.

Research can be done from illustrations in the libraries, from observation of the actual articles in museums, and in finer shops throughout the country. This approach is practiced by every professional designer, who constantly jots down ideas suggested by research in similar fields. The source material listed above was selected because it lends itself easily to leather designs.

Conform To Shape Of Article

Select a design that conforms to the shape of the leather article. A curved flap on a handbag, for instance, calls for a motif that repeats the curve.

A triangular flap calls for a motif that has a triangular feeling to it. Large articles, such as portfolio covers or book jackets, are handsomely decorated with a border. Border designs are also used on belts.

Designs are classified as to style of treatment. There are four classifications of designs:

(1) Naturalistic—the design that is practically photographic in its adherence to the natural appearance of a flower, plant, bird or animal.

(2) Conventional—the design that simplifies the natural appearance of a flower, plant, bird or animal. The main lines of the motif are simplified and rearranged to form a unit that would be suitable as a design for a specific area. The motif is still recognized as a certain kind of flower, etc. For example, the twining leaves of grape vines and irregular outline of a bunch of grapes are rearranged to confine themselves to a triangular shape. In all cases, the motifs themselves are simplified.

(3) Geometric—the design that translates natural forms to their simplest geometric shapes; circle, semi-circle, square, rectangle, triangle, etc. These designs may still reveal the original source of the motif, but they are essentially geometric in feeling.

(4) Abstract—the design that has no relationship to any natural form whatsoever. Geometric shapes are arranged to form pleasing pattern balance, and space relationships.

The use of abstract design has passed through many stages. In the 1920's and 1930's, it was considered modern to literally throw tri-angles, circles and other forms together without any regard for harmony between the shapes. These designs are now labeled modernistic by designers of taste.

Harmony Should Exist

Today, geometric shapes are interlocked in a manner that conforms to the shape of the article designed. A circle is no longer thrust into a corner of a design, with triangular offshoots joining it to a square in the opposite corner.

Harmony should exist between the area of the article designed and the units within the motif.

Many articles have designs on both back and front— for instance, the flap and back of a handbag. Sometimes it is impossible to use the identical design on both surfaces. The same "theme" or motif must be used, with additional embellishments. For example, a naturalistic motif should never be combined with a geometric motif on the same article.

Monograms Should Harmonize

A word of warning can be issued concerning monograms. If borders or other designs are included with a monogram on an article, they should harmonize in theme. A bold, modern monogram would seem out of key with a naturalistic floral border.

The basic procedures for the varied applications of designs are illustrated and discussed on Leather Craft Chart II. Construction details are discussed on Chart IV.

PROCUREMENT OF MATERIALS

All retail art craft shops carry a selection of leather, but—as a rule—the quality and range are mediocre. Contact tanneries in your specific area. Order mill run lots in quantity to obtain lowest price quotations.

Consult the Leather Craft Material Chart for average size of skins available in calf, sheep, goat, etc. Most skins are sold by the entire hide, although prices are always listed per square foot. Large steer hides and cow hides are sometimes sold by the half-skin. Hides often have scars or other blemishes, but many articles can be cut within these defects. Save all scraps left after cutting for they can

be utilized for small articles. Scraps of heavy leather can be used for built-up leather projects.

Sole Leather Already Cut

Sole leather for making sandals or scuffies can be obtained already cut from shoe manufacturers or cobblers, if desired.

Calfskin and pigskin are apt to be most popular, so include a good range of these skins in your stock.

Lining calf is sometimes difficult to obtain, but one ounce saddle sheepskin or a good quality, glaze-finish, sheepskin skiver is an excellent substitute.

Leather lacing cannot be obtained from a tannery. Buy it by the bolt from art craft supply firms.

ADHESIVES: Do not stock the standard all-purpose rubber cement for leather work. Always buy the rubber cement specifically for leather cementing.

It is advisable to contact the suppliers for shoe concerns in your area. Order in gallon containers.

MISCELLANEOUS MATERIALS: Buckram, cotton batting, ribbons and buttons can be obtained from any dry goods store or from most hobby supply firms.

Summary

The preceding pages have been devoted to instructions in general relative to the craft of leather.

There is also a list of 161 items recommended for construction, as well as instructional charts necessary to make it possible to operate this program with a minimum of supervision.

They contain a wealth of information, and it is believed that by use of this material, the task of learning the hobby program in leather will be simplified.

LEATHER CRAFT

Item No.	Leather Tools (See Leather Tool Chart)
1	Bevel Point Skiving Knife
2	Push Beveler
3	Round Drive Punch
4	4-Prong Thonging Awl
5	Wood Edge Creaser
6	Steel Square
7	Eyelet Setting Punch
8	Revolving Punch
9	Modeler
10	Deerfoot and Creaser
11	Embossing Modeler
12	Snap Set
13	Tracer
14	Eyelet Setter
15	Embossing Holder and Wheels
16	Slitter Punch
17	Mallet
18	Lacing Needle
19	Skiving Knife
20	"C" Clamp
21	Bent Trimmers
22	Rocker Knife
23	Sewing Awl
24	Rivet Setter
25	Awl
26	Fid
27	Metal Edge Creaser
28	Spacing Wheel
29	Edge Beveler
30	Gauge Knife
31	Swivel Knife
32	Maple Cutting Board
33	Extension Blades and Handle
34	Tooling Slab
35	Beveling Modeler
36	Spatulated Modeler
37	Stippler
38	Assorted Stamps
39	Incising Knife
40	1-Prong Thonging Awl
41	Egg Eye Harness Needles
42	Curved Stitching Awl
43	Dividers
44	Assorted Carving Stamps

Item No.	Materials
1	Binders, Looseleaf Asst'd Sizes Doz
2	Non-Toxic Leather Dye, Red Pt
3	Yellow Pt.
4	Blue Pt.
5	Dark Brown Pt.
6	Black Pt.
7	Cement, AMCO Transparent #1499 2 Oz. Tube
8	Cement, Leather Rubber 1 Qt. #1494
9	Adhesive, Pinboard Plastic #20 (1 Gal.)
10	Buckram, 19" Wide, per Yd.
11	Buttons, Shank (for Animal Eyes) per Doz.
12	Cotton Batten (Kapok) Pkg.
13	Cement Rubber Qt.
14	Buckles 1" Doz.
15	1/4" Doz.
16	1 1/2" Doz.
17	1 1/4" Doz.
18	1 3/4" Doz.
19	1" Doz.
20	Edge Finish Bottle
21	Acid Crystals Oxalic Pkg.
22	Pin Backs (Gross)
23	Pin Backs (Gross)
24	Patterns, Folio, Special
25	Designs, Folio, Special
26	Designs, Folio
27	Designs, Leather Carving Set
28	Analine Dye, Red 1 Pt. Bottles
29	Orange 1 Pt. Bottles
30	Yellow 1 Pt. Bottles
31	Green 1 Pt. Bottles
32	Blue 1 Pt. Bottles
33	Violet 1 Pt. Bottles
34	Black 1 Pt. Bottles
35	Tooling Calf Asst'd. Colors 2 x 2 1/2 Oz. Sq. Ft.
36	Smooth Chrome Calf Asst'd. Colors 2 x 2 1/2 Oz. Sq. Ft.
37	Embossed Vegetable Calf, Alligator & Lizard Grain, 2 x 2 1/2 Oz. Sq. Ft.
38	Buckskin (per Sq. Ft.)
39	Calf, Hair (per Sq. Ft.)
40	Calf, Norwegian
41	Calf, Russia Tooling
42	Cowhide, Case
43	Cowhide, Embossed
44	Chamois
45	Elkskin
46	Goatskin, Saffian
47	Horsehide (Cordovan)
48	Kidskin
49	Sheepskin, Natural Tooling
50	Sheepskin, Wool
51	Sheepskin, Garment Suede
52	Suede, Blue
53	Suede, Lining
54	Steer Hide Mottle Brown, Brown and Natural Brown 2 x 2 1/2 Oz. (Sq. Ft.)
55	Natural Tooling Cowhide 2 x 2 1/2 Oz. (Sq. Ft.)
56	Natural Tooling Cowhide 5 Oz. (Sq. Ft.)
57	Carving Cowhide 8 Oz. (Sq. Ft.)
58	Hazel Pigskin 2 x 2 l/2 Oz. (Sq. Ft.)
59	Morocco Goat Asst'd. Colors 2 x 2 1/2 Oz. (Sq. Ft.)
60	Levant Grain Goat Asst'd. Colors 2 x 2 1/2 Oz. (Sq. Ft.)
61	Pinseal Sheepskin Asst'd. Colors (Sq. Ft.)
62	Natural Tooling Sheepskin (Sq. Ft.)
63	Saddle Sheepskin, Asst'd. Color (Sq. Ft.)
64	Sheepskin Skiver, Asst'd. Colors (Sq. Ft.)
65	Lining, Calf, Black and Brown (Sq. Ft.)
66	Calf and Goat Lacing, Asst'd. Colors 3/32" wide (G/Yds.)
67	Calfskin Lace, 3/32" (per 100 Yds.)
68	Florentine Lace, 3/16" (per 100 Yds.)
69	Florentine Lace, 3/8" (per 100 Yds.)
70	Rawhide Lace, 72" x 1/8, Indian Tan (per Doz.)
71	Rawhide Lace, 72" x 3/16", Indian Tan (per Doz.)
72	Rawhide Lace, 72" x 1/8", White (per Doz.)

73	Rawhide Lace, 72" x 3/16", White (per Doz.)
74	Craft Strip, 3/32", per M Yds.
75	Plastic Lace, 3/32", per M Yds.
76	Pyro, Cord, Round, 1/16" Dia. per M Yds.
77	Snap Buttons Asst'd. (Gross)
78	Snap Buttons Asst'd. (Gross)
79	Key Plates, 3 Hook (Gross)
80	Key Plates, 4 Hook (Gross)
81	Key Plates, 6 Hook (Gross)
82	Zippers 8" (Doz.)
83	Zippers 12" (Doz.)
84	Zippers 14" (Doz.)
85	Steel Binder Posts (Gross)

86	Rapid Rivets (Pkg.)
87	Swivel Snap (Gross)
88	Wrist Watch Strap Buckle (Doz.)
89	Center Bar Buckle 5/8" (Doz.)
90	Buckle Plain 1/2" (Doz.)
91	Buckle Brier Case 3/4" (Doz.)
92	Hinges, #2425, 3/4" Long, Doz. Pr.
93	Nails, Wire, Brass, Round-Head, Box 1/4" Long
94	Rivets #1467A (Nickel) 4 Doz. in Pkg. #1467B (Black) #1467C (Brown)
95	Buckles (per Doz.)

Leather Craft Tools

FOR CUTTING

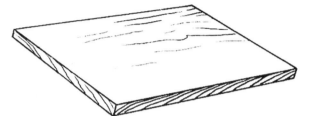

MAPLE CUTTING BOARD (32)
Use one side of board for cutting leather. Use reverse side for punching holes.

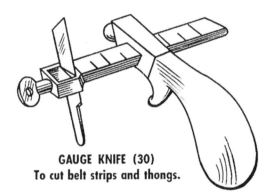

GAUGE KNIFE (30)
To cut belt strips and thongs.

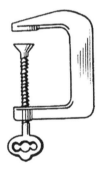

"C" CLAMP (20)
To hold work in place. Used also while braiding and cementing.

STEEL SQUARE (6)
To measure and lay out square and straight-edged patterns. Guide to cut leather with knife.

BEVEL POINT SKIVING KNIFE (1)
To cut, skive and trim edges of leather.

SKIVING KNIFE (19)
To skive edges of leather before cementing and stitching.

BEVEL

SHARP

LANCE

CURVE

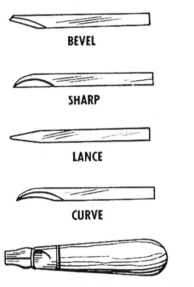

EXTENSION BLADES AND HANDLE (33)

ROCKER KNIFE (22)
To cut heavy cowhide and round off corners.

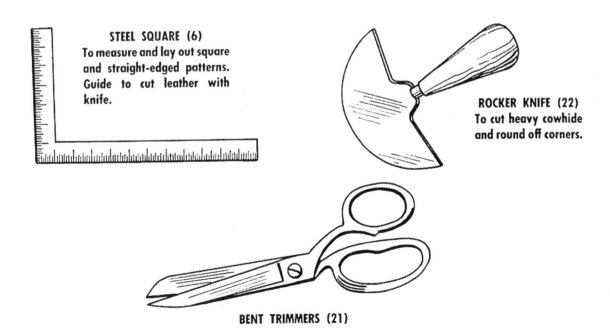

BENT TRIMMERS (21)

Leather Craft Tools

FOR TOOLING AND CARVING

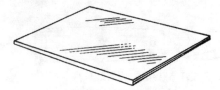

TOOLING SLAB (34)
A smooth marble or thick plate glass base for tooling leather.

EMBOSSING HOLDER AND WHEELS (15)

~~15-1	▮▮▮-4	⊃⊂⊃⊂-7
▮▮▮▮▮-2	⋁⋀⋁-5	⋈⋈-8
▮▮▮-3	⌇⌇⌇-6	∿∿∿-9

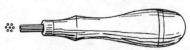

STIPPLER (37)
To stipple background areas.

TRACER (13)
To trace outline of design on dampened leather.

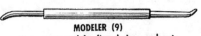

MODELER (9)
Use narrow end for line designs and outlining; wider end to tool small background areas.

SWIVEL KNIFE (31)
To cut outlines of all curved motifs in leather carving.

BEVELING MODELER (35)
For wide straight line designs and beveled edges of tooled areas.

EMBOSSING MODELER (11)
To emboss and stipple designs.

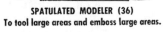

SPATULATED MODELER (36)
To tool large areas and emboss large areas.

DEERFOOT AND CREASER (10)
Use deerfoot end for small background areas in monograms, small floral designs and corners. Other end for edge creaser or border lines.

INCISING KNIFE (39)
To incise long, straight lines when carving leather. Blade is beveled to incise leather without cutting through.

WOOD EDGE CREASER (5)
To crease single or double edges of leather.

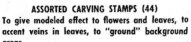

PUSH BEVELER (2)
To bevel long incised lines in leather carving for raised effect.

EDGE BEVELER (29)
Professional type to bevel and turn edges of leather.

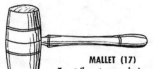

METAL EDGE CREASER (27)
To crease curves and straight lines on edges of leather. To mark stitching guide lines. Five sizes.

MALLET (17)
To strike stamps, lacing and stitching awls, round drive punch, eyelet setter, rivet setter and snap setter. To pound lacing flat.

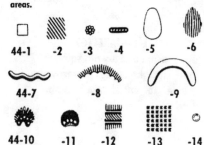

ASSORTED CARVING STAMPS (44)
To give modeled effect to flowers and leaves, to accent veins in leaves, to "ground" background areas.

44-1   -2   -3   -4   -5   -6

44-7   -8   -9

44-10   -11   -12   -13   -14

ASSORTED STAMPS (38)
Use singly or combine with other stamps or wheels for borders and all-over designs.

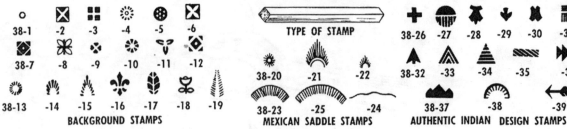

38-1   -2   -3   -4   -5   -6

38-7   -8   -9   -10   -11   -12

38-13   -14   -15   -16   -17   -18   -19

BACKGROUND STAMPS

TYPE OF STAMP

38-20   -21   -22

38-23   -25   -24

MEXICAN SADDLE STAMPS

38-26   -27   -28   -29   -30   -31

38-32   -33   -34   -35   -36

38-37   -38   -39

AUTHENTIC INDIAN DESIGN STAMPS

Leather Craft Tools

FOR LACING AND STITCHING

SPACING WHEEL (28)
To mark holes for stitching; 3 wheels: 5, 6, 7 spaces to inch.

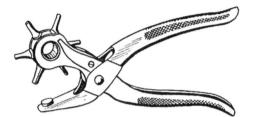

REVOLVING PUNCH (8)
To punch round holes in leather for lacing, snaps and rivets. Six tubes.

LACING NEEDLE (18)
With attached strip of thong for lacing. Note: Made of sheet metal.

**EGG EYE
HARNESS NEEDLES (41)**
To sew leather. Five sizes.

4-PRONG THONGING AWL (4)
To cut slits for lacing. Has 3/32" prongs.

1-PRONG THONGING AWL (40)
To cut slits for lacing around corners and curves where 4-prong awl is not suitable. Has 3/32" prong.

CURVED STITCHING AWL (42)
To make holes for stitching around gussets after they have been cemented.

FID (26)
To enlarge holes in leather. To tighten lacing and knots.

SLITTER PUNCH (16)
To make thong slits around corners. Special attachments.

AWL (25)
To pierce small holes for sewing.

SEWING AWL (23)
To sew leather by hand with lock stitch (like machine stitch).

FOR FASTENINGS

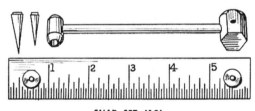

SNAP SET (12)
To attach snap fasteners and bag plates.

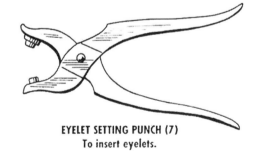

EYELET SETTING PUNCH (7)
To insert eyelets.

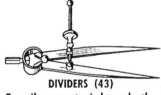

DIVIDERS (43)
To scribe accurate circles on leather, to space stitching holes not marked by spacing wheel, to mark spots for eyelets and snap fasteners.

EYELET SETTER (14)
To set eyelets where punch cannot reach. Spreads eyelet so it can be flattened with mallet.

**ROUND
DRIVE
PUNCH (3)**
To punch holes not within reach of revolving punch. Seven sizes; 3/64", 1/16", 5/64", 3/32", 1/8", 7/32", 1/4".

RIVET SETTER (24)
To set rivets on loose leaf binders, belts, straps, etc.

Leather Craft Material Chart

LEATHERS

CODE: A–VEGETABLE, B–CHROME, C–NATURAL UNFINISHED, D–ANILINE, E–PIGMENT, F–SMOOTH, G–EMBOSSED, H–WHOLE, I–HALF, J–QUARTER

NAME OF LEATHER	SIZES	WEIGHT AND THICKNESS	REMARKS
RUSSIA TOOLING CALFSKIN	6-13 SQ. FT.	2-2½ OZ.	MOST POPULAR FORM OF ALL-PURPOSE CRAFT LEATHER
CARVING AND TOOLING CALF	10-18 SQ. FT.	2-2½ OZ.	SUITABLE FOR SHALLOW CARVING
CHROME TANNED CALF	6-15 SQ. FT.	2-3 OZ.	A SOFT LEATHER AVAILABLE IN ALLIGATOR AND LIZARD GRAINS
HAIR CALF	2½-5 SQ. FT.		UNBORN CALF TANNED WITH HAIR ON
LINING CALF	6-12 SQ. FT.	1-1½ OZ.	USED MAINLY FOR LINING PURPOSES
NORWEGIAN CALF	9-15 SQ. FT.	2-3 OZ.	WIDELY USED FOR SHOES—SUITABLE FOR CRAFT USE ALSO
NATURAL TOOLING SHEEPSKIN	6-10 SQ. FT.	2 OZ.	INEXPENSIVE—MAY BE DYED—USED AS SUBSTITUTE FOR CALF
SADDLE SHEEPSKIN	6-10 SQ. FT.	2-2½ OZ.	LINING LEATHER WITH GLAZED FINISH
PIN SEAL SHEEPSKIN	6-10 SQ. FT.	2-2½ OZ.	RICH-LOOKING, INEXPENSIVE TOOLING LEATHER
WOOL SHEEPSKIN	7-11 SQ. FT.		TANNED WITH WOOL ON—TRIMMED TO DIFFERENT LENGTHS
SHEEPSKIN SKIVER	8-12 SQ. FT.	1 OZ.	USED FOR LINING PURPOSES ONLY
MOROCCO GOATSKIN	5-8 SQ. FT.	2-2½ OZ.	SUITABLE FOR SAME PURPOSE AS CALF
SAFFIAN GOAT	5-8 SQ. FT.	1½-2 OZ.	THIN EMBOSSED LEATHER—SUITABLE MAINLY FOR BILLFOLDS
LEVANT GRAINED GOATSKIN	6-8 SQ. FT.	2-2½ OZ.	EXCELLENT FOR BOOKBINDING—HAS NATURAL DECORATIVE GRAIN
STEERHIDE	18-26 SQ. FT.	2-2½ OZ.	SUBSTITUTE FOR CALF
TOOLING COWHIDE	18-26 SQ. FT.	3-6 OZ.	SOFTER THAN CARVING COWHIDE—COARSER THAN CALFSKIN
CARVING COWHIDE	18-26 SQ. FT.	6-10 OZ.	HEAVY WEIGHT, FINISHED FOR CARVING AND STAMPING
COWHIDE CASE LEATHER	18-26 SQ. FT.	5-6 OZ.	GLAZED, FINISHED COWHIDE—SUITABLE FOR STURDY ARTICLES
EMBOSSED COWHIDE	12-18 SQ. FT.	2-3 OZ.	AVAILABLE IN ALLIGATOR AND LIZARD GRAINS

1 OZ. LEATHER MEASURES BETWEEN 1/64" AND 1/32", DEPENDING ON COMPRESSION

Column categories across the chart: TANNAGE (A, B); FINISH (C, D, E); TEXTURE (F, G); SIDES; SKINS (H, I, J); DECORATION (TOOLING, CARVING, STAMPING); COLORS (NATURAL FINISH, BLACK, BROWN, DARK BROWN, ARMY RUSSET, GOLDEN BROWN, LONDON TAN, RED, GREEN, BLUE, WINE, GRAY, REDWOOD, WHITE); ARTICLES (BELTS, BOOK COVERS, BOOKENDS, BOXES, BILLFOLDS, BRIEF CASES, STURDY CASES, MISC. CASES, DESK ACCESS., GLOVES, MITTS, HANDBAGS, LAMP BASES, MOCCASINS, PICTURE FRAMES, SANDALS, STUFFED TOYS)

Leather Craft Material Chart

LEATHERS

CODE: A – VEGETABLE, B – CHROME, C – NATURAL UNFINISHED, D – ANILINE, E – PIGMENT, F – SMOOTH, G – EMBOSSED, H – WHOLE, I – HALF, J – QUARTER

NAME OF LEATHER	SIZES	WEIGHT AND THICKNESS	TANNAGE A	TANNAGE B	FINISH C	FINISH D	FINISH E	TEXTURE F	TEXTURE G	SIDES H	SIDES I	SKINS J	REMARKS
ELKSKIN	12-18 SQ. FT.	3-3½ OZ.		✓		✓	✓	✓		✓	✓		VERY SOFT AND FLEXIBLE
PIGSKIN	7-10 SQ. FT.	2-2½ OZ.	✓			✓			✓			✓	AVAILABLE IN NATURAL AND ARTIFICIAL GRAINS
GARMENT SUEDE SHEEPSKIN	6-8 SQ. FT.	2-2½ OZ.		✓		✓		✓				✓	SUEDED ON FLESH SIDE
BLUE SUEDE	6-8 SQ. FT.	2-2½ OZ.	✓			✓						✓	FIRMER THAN GARMENT SUEDE — SUEDED ON FLESH SIDE
LINING SUEDE	6-9 SQ. FT.	1 OZ.		✓		✓						✓	FINEST GRADE SUEDE, MOST SUITABLE FOR LININGS
BUCKSKIN	7-12 SQ. FT.	1-2 OZ.		✓		✓						✓	SOFT AND FLEXIBLE — WITH BUFFED FINISH
KIDSKIN	1½-6 SQ. FT.	1-2½ OZ.		✓		✓		✓				✓	GLAZED FINISH, RECOMMENDED FOR INFANTS' WEAR
CHAMOIS	3-7 SQ. FT.	1 OZ.		✓	✓			✓				✓	SOFT AND FLEXIBLE — WITH BUFFED FINISH
HORSEHIDE	14-25 SQ. FT.	2-5		✓		✓		✓				✓	SUITABLE FOR BASEBALL GLOVES AND OTHER SPORTS GOODS

DECORATION: TOOLING, CARVING, STAMPING

COLORS: NATURAL FINISH, BLACK, BROWN, DARK BROWN, ARMY RUSSET, GOLDEN BROWN, LONDON TAN, GOLDEN TAN, RED, GREEN, BLUE, WINE, GRAY, REDWOOD, WHITE

ARTICLES: BELTS, BOOK COVERS, BOOKENDS, BOXES, BILLFOLDS, BRIEF CASES, STURDY CASES, MISC. CASES, DESK ACCESS., GLOVES, MITTS, HANDBAGS, LAMP BASES, MOCCASINS, PICTURE FRAMES, SANDALS, STUFFED TOYS

1 OZ. LEATHER MEASURES BETWEEN 1/64" AND 1/32", DEPENDING ON COMPRESSION

LACING AND BRAIDING MATERIALS

LACING

GOATSKIN LACE — Imported India goatskin cut in continuous lengths. Edges are beveled, rolled and colored. WIDTH: 3/32"
COLORS: BLACK AND BROWN ONLY

CALFSKIN LACE — Cut from the finest tooling calf. Edges are beveled, rolled and colored. WIDTH: 3/32"
COLORS: BLACK, NATURAL AND ASSORTED

RAWHIDE LACE — Used where strength and durability are desired. Available greaseless or oiled. WIDTH: 72" x 1/8" AND 72" x 3/16"
COLORS: INDIAN TAN AND WHITE

FLORENTINE LACE — Soft, pliable kidskin, suitable for flat articles, portfolios and picture frames. WIDTH: 3/16" AND 3/8"
COLORS: BLACK, WHITE, NATURAL & ASSRTD.

PLASTIK LACE — Solid flexible plastic, color fast, washable, easily workable, for braiding, lacing and weaving. WIDTH: 3/32"
COLORS: BLACK, WHITE AND ASSORTED

PYRO-LACE — An imitation leather lace, flexible, strong and seamless. Beveled on both edges. WIDTH: 3/32"
COLORS: BLACK, WHITE, NATURAL & ASSRTD.

BRAIDING

PYRO-CORD — Round coated cord for braiding. Has bright finish. ABOUT 1/16" IN DIAMETER
COLORS: BLACK, WHITE AND ASSORTED

CRAFT STRIP — Seamless imitation leather lace, recommended for braiding. Has bright finish, beveled edges. WIDTH: 3/32"
COLORS: BLACK, WHITE AND ASSORTED

Leather Craft • Chart I • Cutting

HANDBAG

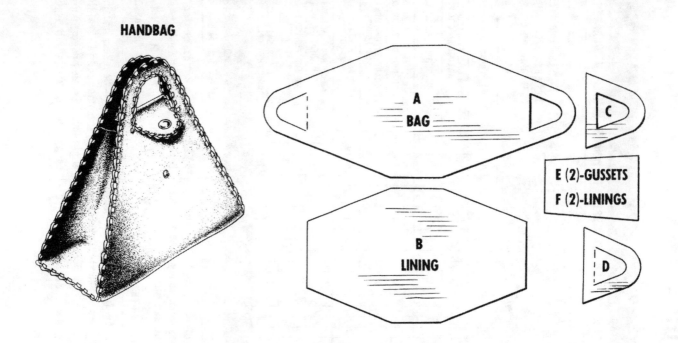

1. Enlarge patterns by scaled drawing or by photography.

2. Check measurements.

3. Cut paper patterns.

4. Fold parts to test fit.

5. Outline patterns on cardboard accurately.

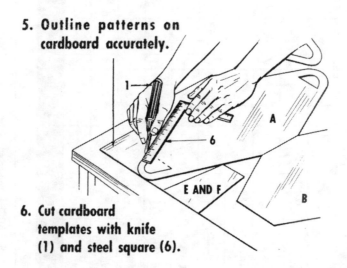

6. Cut cardboard templates with knife (1) and steel square (6).

Leather Craft • Chart I • Cutting

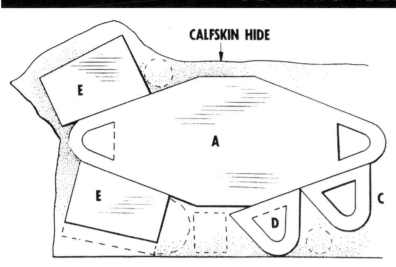

1. Lay cardboard templates on skin side of hide, away from thin edges.

2. Economize. Use one cutting line for two patterns, when possible.

3. Use scraps for small articles. See dotted lines.

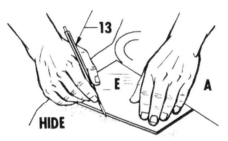

4. Outline templates with tracer (13).

5. Cut on outline with knife (1) using steel square as guide.

6. Cut away from corner.

7. Round off sharp corners for better fit in lacing or stitching gussets.

8. Cut curved edges using cardboard template for guide.

9. Outline templates with sharpened chalk, when marking suede. (Brush off chalk after suede is cut.)

10. Cut suede, 1-oz. lining calf and other thin leathers with scissors.

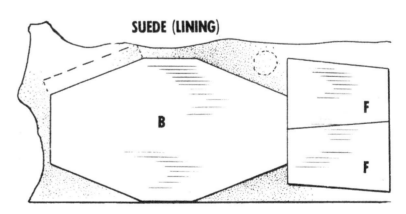

NOTE:

1. If additional stiffness or firmness is desired, cut a piece of buckram 1/8" within the pattern of outer leather.

2. Cement buckram to flesh side of outer leather.

3. Lining leather may extend beyond outer leather, but the excess may be trimmed after cementing lining to outer leather in final position.

Leather Craft • Chart I • Cutting

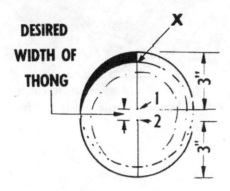

DESIRED WIDTH OF THONG

I. THONG DISC

1. Draw a circle, point (1) as center.

2. Draw second circle, point (2) as center.

3. Shaded area represents starting point of thong.

4. Dash-dot line represents cutting line for continuous thong.

5. A radius of 3″ or 4″ is preferable size for a disc. Avoid using one with a radius smaller than 2″.

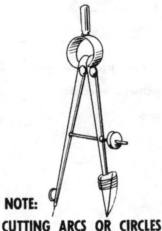

NOTE:
CUTTING ARCS OR CIRCLES

1. Secure part of razor blade or small blade to dividers or compass by soldering or taping and tying firmly in place.

2. Cement small strip of leather on center point of piece to be cut to avoid hole of compass on final piece. Remove strip.

II. CUTTING THONG DISC

1. Cut point of thong (shaded area in I).

2. Insert blade in gauge knife (30).

3. Adjust gauge knife to cut thong in width desired.

4. Insert the cut thong to point (X) between gauge and blade.

5. Hold disc in horizontal position.

6. Rotate disc slowly with its circumference against gauge.

7. Stop cutting when thong becomes too circular to stretch straight.

8. Stretch and wax thong.

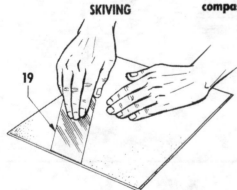

SKIVING

Skive edges of leather with skiving knife (19) when:

1. Overlapping edges of leather are to be cemented. (Leather covered boxes, billfold partitions, etc.)

2. A flexible edge is desired for stitching cowhide. (Brief cases, shaving kits, reel cases, etc.)

3. A hinge line is desired on heavy cowhide.

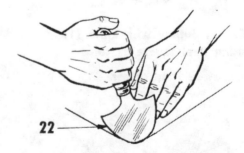

USING A ROCKER KNIFE (22)

1. Cut rounded corners with a rocker knife, (22).

2. Place knife on cutting line, and roll it forward.

3. Also use for cutting heavy leather.

Leather Craft • Chart II • Applied Design

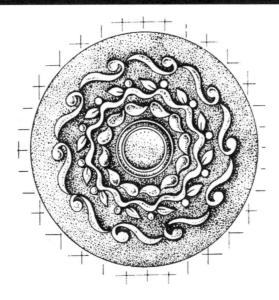

A design should harmonize with structural lines of article. Select a method of decoration suitable for leather used. (See Material Chart). Enlarge or reduce design to desired size by scaling or photography. Trace design to correct size on tracing paper. Cut pattern the exact size of article. Transfer design to paper pattern with carbon paper.

1. SPONGING LEATHER
Use cold water and clean sponge. Moisten entire piece of leather on flesh side. Leather darkens in color but should not ooze water.

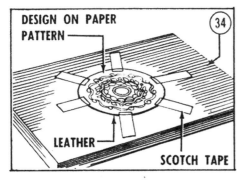

2. PLACING DESIGN
Lay leather on tooling slab (34), skin side up. Place carbon of design on leather, face down. Secure to slab with Scotch tape.

3. TRANSFER OF DESIGN
Transfer design to moist leather with tracer (13). Draw straight lines with steel square (6); curves freehand. Line designs are then outlined with tool (9).

Leather Craft • Chart II • Applied Design

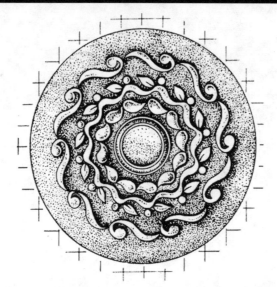

A. FLAT MODELING

1. Outline design with small end of modeling tool (9).

2. Press down background with wide end of tool (9) or (36).

4. Stipple with small end of (9) or (37). Use even pressure and spacing.

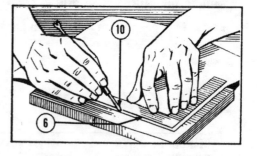

5. Tool broad straight lines using deerfoot (10) or beveler (35) with steel square (6).

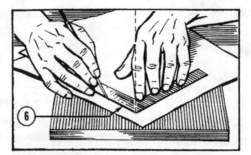

3. Outline straight edges with steel square (6) and (9). Press forward to corner; raise tool to vertical position.

Leather Craft • Chart II • Applied Design

B. EMBOSSING

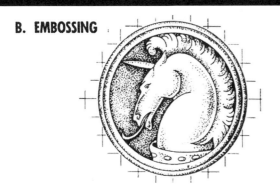

Circular design suitable for bookends, boxes, cigarette cases, scrapbooks or wallets.

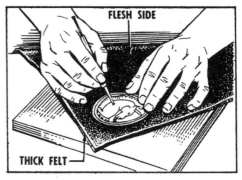

1. Outline and model as in (A). Depress flesh side of embossed area with embosser (11) and wide end of (9).

2. Fill depressed areas of flesh side with plaster of paris to background level. Cement buckram over plaster.

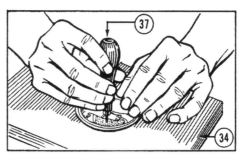

3. Turn leather skin side up. Stipple background as in (A-4). Note: Line all embossed articles.

C. CARVING

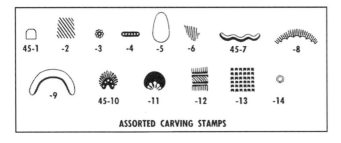

ASSORTED CARVING STAMPS

45-1 -2 -3 -4 -5 -6 45-7 -8 -9 45-10 -11 -12 -13 -14

1. Outline design with swivel knife (31), cutting 1/3 of leather thickness. Avoid crossing cuts in design.

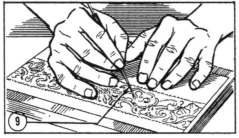

2. Open incised lines with small end of modeler (9). Depress background as in (A-2).

3. Accent leaves and flowers with assorted stamps (38) and (45). Stamp background with (45-3, -1) or (38-1).

Leather Craft • Chart II • Applied Design

METHODS OF DESIGN APPLICATION

D. STAMPING AND WHEELING

STAMP NOS.
38-10, -14, -15

Stamps and Wheels may be combined.

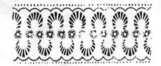

STAMP NOS. 38-14, -20
WHEEL NO. 15-9

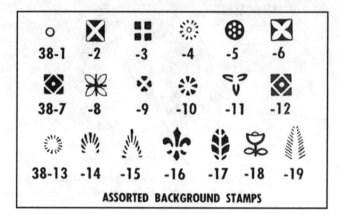

38-1	-2	-3	-4	-5	-6
38-7	-8	-9	-10	-11	-12
38-13	-14	-15	-16	-17	-18	-19

ASSORTED BACKGROUND STAMPS

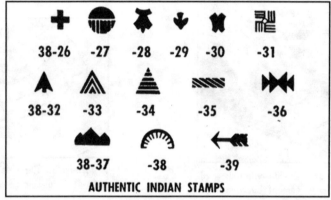

38-26	-27	-28	-29	-30	-31
38-32	-33	-34	-35	-36
38-37	-38	-39		

AUTHENTIC INDIAN STAMPS

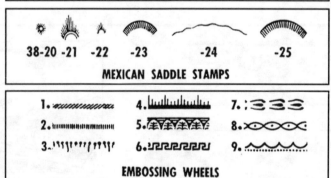

38-20 -21 -22 -23 -24 -25

MEXICAN SADDLE STAMPS

1. 4. 7.
2. 5. 8.
3. 6. 9.

EMBOSSING WHEELS

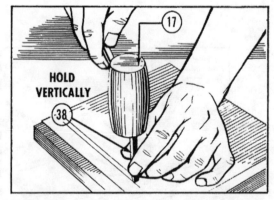

HOLD VERTICALLY

1. Mark line for stamp design. Strike stamp (38) with mallet (17).

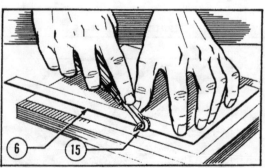

2. Roll wheel against steel square, away from you.

24

Leather Craft • Chart III • Color Application

I.

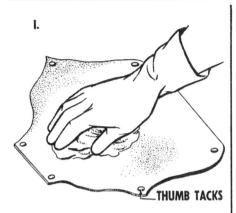

THUMB TACKS

1. Remove grime and finger prints before dyeing, using a solution of two tablespoons of oxalic acid crystals in one pint of warm water.
2. Tack hide to table.
3. Apply solution with sponge or cotton. (Wear rubber gloves.)
4. Wash off with clean warm water.
5. Allow to dry thoroughly and be sure all spots have been removed.

II.

Wear rubber gloves when using dyes.

SPONGE OR SHEEPSKIN SWAB

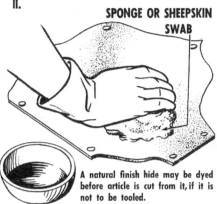

A natural finish hide may be dyed before article is cut from it, if it is not to be tooled.

1. Moisten leather if directions call for it.
2. Pour dye solution into glass or porcelain bowl.
3. Saturate sponge with dye.
4. Apply full sponge to leather in quick horizontal strokes, working from top to bottom.
5. Dry thoroughly. Polish with cloth.
6. Repeat process if darker color is desired.

III.

Complete tooling and punch all thong slits before dyeing. Proceed as in (II).

IV.

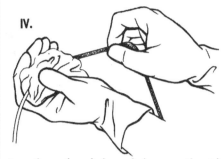

Draw thongs through dye-soaked sponge, if matching lacing is desired.

1. Paint small outlined areas, using colored inks and a No. 2 or 3 camel's hair brush.

2. Leather must be dry. The dye or colored ink will bleed beyond outline if leather is moist.

Apply colored inks to the depressed areas of stamp and wheel designs, if color accent is desired on natural leathers.

COLOR INLAY

I.

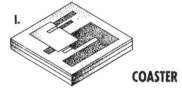

COASTER

Leather inlay is practical on non-flexible articles only. Bending causes a separation of pieces. The base is built up of heavy cowhide or wood.

II.

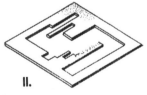

1. Enlarge design by scaled drawing or photography.
2. Trace design accurately. (See LEATHER CRAFT CHART II)
3. Transfer outline of entire cut-out area to top layer of leather.
4. Cut with thin-bladed knife (33).

III.

NOTE: Pieces in design must be same thickness. Adhere to base with rubber cement.

5. Transfer outlines of all units of design on their respective colors.
6. Cut all pieces with knife (33).

IV.

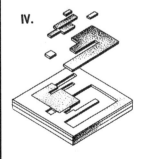

7. Cement top layer to base with rubber cement.
8. Cement largest pieces in cut-out area. Fit in smallest pieces last.
9. Shellac and wax. (See FINISHING VIII, page 27).

Leather Craft • Chart III • Color Application

I.

ARCHERY QUIVER

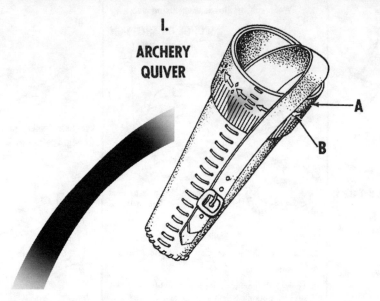

II.

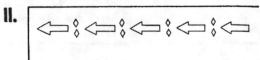

1. Draw the design in full size on paper, allowing enough space between cut-outs so background leather remains a firm band.

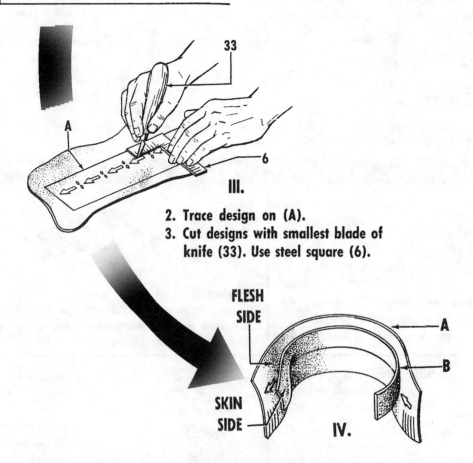

III.

2. Trace design on (A).
3. Cut designs with smallest blade of knife (33). Use steel square (6).

IV.

FLESH SIDE

SKIN SIDE

4. Cement skin side of (B) to flesh side of (A). Avoid getting cement on (B) where it is exposed through perforations.

Leather Craft • Chart III • Color Application

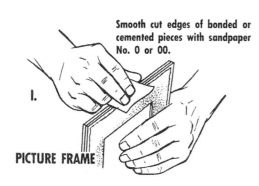

I. **PICTURE FRAME**

Smooth cut edges of bonded or cemented pieces with sandpaper No. 0 or 00.

ALTERNATE METHOD OF SANDING
Smooth cut edges of bonded or cemented pieces with emery wheel of electric hand grinder.

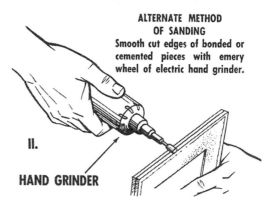

II. **HAND GRINDER**

III.

Clean article with a soft, white cloth moistened with commercially prepared leather cleaning solution to remove fingerprints or other marks.

IV. **WATER COLOR BRUSH**

Paint cut edges to match surface color with colored inks or left-over dye.

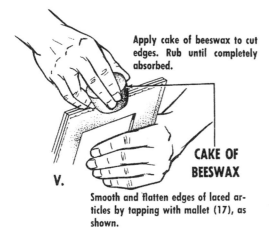

Apply cake of beeswax to cut edges. Rub until completely absorbed.

V. **CAKE OF BEESWAX**

Smooth and flatten edges of laced articles by tapping with mallet (17), as shown.

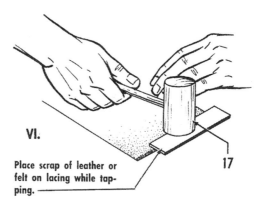

VI.

Place scrap of leather or felt on lacing while tapping.

17

VII.

Apply saddle soap or paste wax with soft cloth. Rub to gloss with clean soft cloth.

PLACE WAX WITHIN FOLDS.

Saddle Soap
or
Paste Wax

VIII.

Finish inlaid articles and coasters with thin white shellac before waxing. Sand lightly between coats of shellac. Wax to a high gloss.

Shellac

Leather Craft • Chart IV • Construction Details

GUSSETS

TIE GUSSET IN PLACE BEFORE FINAL STITCHING OR LACING.

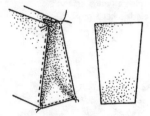 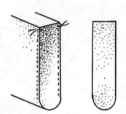  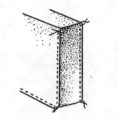

I. A gusset with a straight bottom edge is used for handbags and cases when a flat resting base is desired.

II. A gusset with a rounded bottom edge is used for camera cases and shoulder bags.

III. A triangular gusset is used for flat cases and envelope handbags.

IV. A gusset that forms a continuous band between 2 sides is used for sturdy, box-like cases.

LININGS

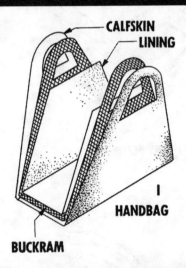

CALFSKIN
LINING

I
HANDBAG

BUCKRAM

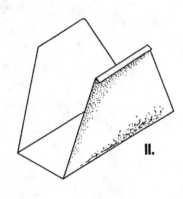

II.

1. Cut buckram ⅛" within all edges of outer leather if additional stiffness is desired.

2. Place lining within outer leather to test fit. (Fig. I.)

3. Skive and turn to flesh side all visible edges of lining if lightweight leather is used. This prevents fraying of edges. (Fig. II.)

4. Cut corners of lining to fold a neat mitered corner on square article. (Fig. III.)

See LEATHER CRAFT CHART I

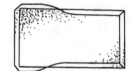

III.
See MATERIAL CHART for Lining Leathers

POCKETS

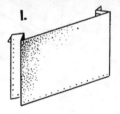 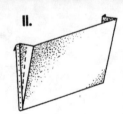 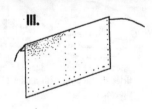

I. **II.** **III.**

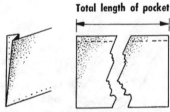

Total length of pocket

I. Cut a rectangular piece, adding desired length for inverted fold of gusset at each end.

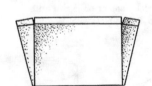

II. Add triangular piece at each end of pocket, for gussets.

III. Cut rectangular piece; insert wire or cord under folded top edge for reinforcement of edge. Stitch to lining, forming pockets of desired width.

Always sew pockets to linings before cementing lining.

Leather Craft • Chart IV • Construction Details

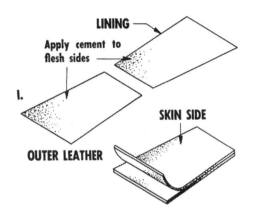

LINING

Apply cement to flesh sides

I.

OUTER LEATHER

SKIN SIDE

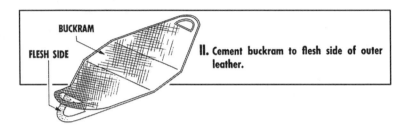

BUCKRAM

FLESH SIDE

II. Cement buckram to flesh side of outer leather.

1. Apply rubber cement to flesh surfaces of lining and outer leather.

2. Allow cement to dry before combining pieces. Use caution in exact placement of pieces.

3. Trim edges of lining if necessary.

4. Cement edges only of parts to be stitched. Ex.: Wallet partitions.

5. Cement edges of zipper tape to leather before stitching. (See LEATHER CHART VI)

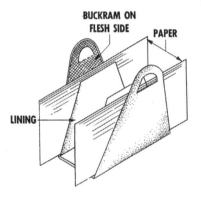

BUCKRAM ON FLESH SIDE

PAPER

LINING

III. 1. Apply cement to flesh surface of lining and buckram side of outer leather.

2. Place sheets of paper on sides of bag to cover all but bottom area of bag.

3. Cement lining to bottom area only. The papers prevent lining from adhering to sides.

4. Raise sides of bag in vertical position as shown. (Fig. III.)

5. Slowly remove paper from one side, cementing lining smoothly against buckram as paper is raised. This prevents wrinkling of lining at fold line.

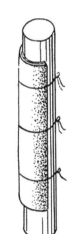

IV.

1. Form a curved back for book by cementing lining to outer leather on a rounded form. Use a mailing tube, folded magazine or rounded object for form.

2. Tie around form to set curve while cement dries thoroughly.

Bond layers of heavy leather with Pliobond Plastic Adhesive if article is to be nonflexible. Example:

CRIBBAGE BOARD

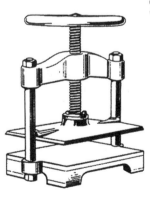

V.

1. Sandpaper all skin surfaces to be bonded.

2. Apply Pliobond to both surfaces.

3. Dry until tacky, (about 5 minutes).

4. Bond pieces. Put in press or under weight for 18-24 hours.

Leather Craft • Chart IV • Construction Details

BUCKLES

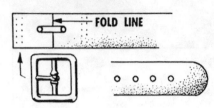

1. Punch holes with revolving punch (8) for prong of buckle in rounded end of belt.
2. Punch 2 holes with same sized punch in square end of belt to mark slot for prong of buckle.
3. Cut slot between holes punched.

4. Insert buckle in slot; fold.
5. Cement end for stiching.
6. Punch stitching holes with awl (25) as marked.
7. Sew with saddler's stitch.
   Note: A rivet may be used instead of stitching.

SNAP BUTTONS

CAP   EYELET   SPRING   POST

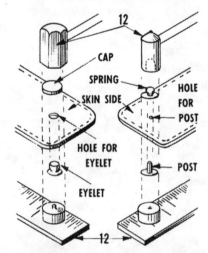

1. Attach cap and eyelet as shown.
2. Mark position of spring and post by pressing cap firmly.
3. Attach spring and post as shown.

EYELETS

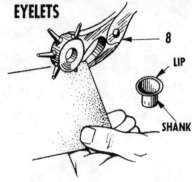

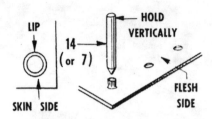

1. Punch hole with revolving punch (8), or drive punch (3), for shank of eyelet. Punch hole same size as shank.

2. Insert eyelet with lip on skin side; shank rising to flesh side.
3. Strike eyelet setter (7) with mallet (17).

RIVETS

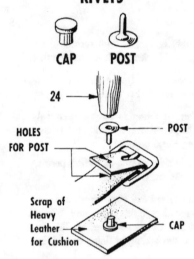

1. Punch holes with revolving punch (8) to fit size of post in parts to be riveted.
2. Insert post from back of article.
3. Fit cap on post on right side.
4. Place article with cap resting on heavy leather. Strike rivet setter (24) with mallet (17) to secure rivet.

ZIPPERS

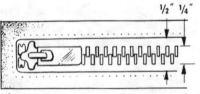

I. Cut zipper opening in heavy leather. Allow ½″ space for ¼″ teeth; ⅜″ for 3/16″ teeth.

II. Cut thin leather as shown. Fold and cement edges to create opening for zipper.

III. Adjust zipper and inner gusset strip to curve of outer strip. Use on brief cases for sturdiness.

See LEATHER CRAFT CHART VII — STITCHING

Leather Craft • Chart V • Lacing

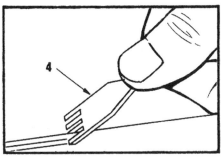

Mark light guide line for thong slits on edge of leather with 4-prong thonging awl (4).

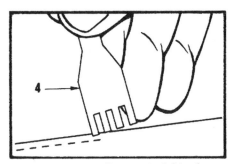

Punch thong slits on straight edge with 4-prong thonging awl (4) and mallet (17). Use last slit as guide for even spacing.

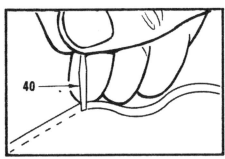

Punch thong slits on a curved edge with 1-prong thonging awl (40) and mallet (17). Slitter punch (16) can also be used.

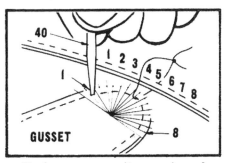

Mark a corresponding number of spaces on a curved edge as there are slits on the matching straight edge. Draw radii. Punch thong slits between radii.

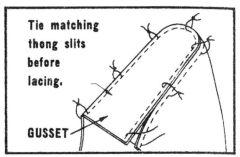

Punch the same number of thong slits along the matching edge of each piece to be laced together.

Leather Craft • Chart V • Lacing

TYPES OF LACING

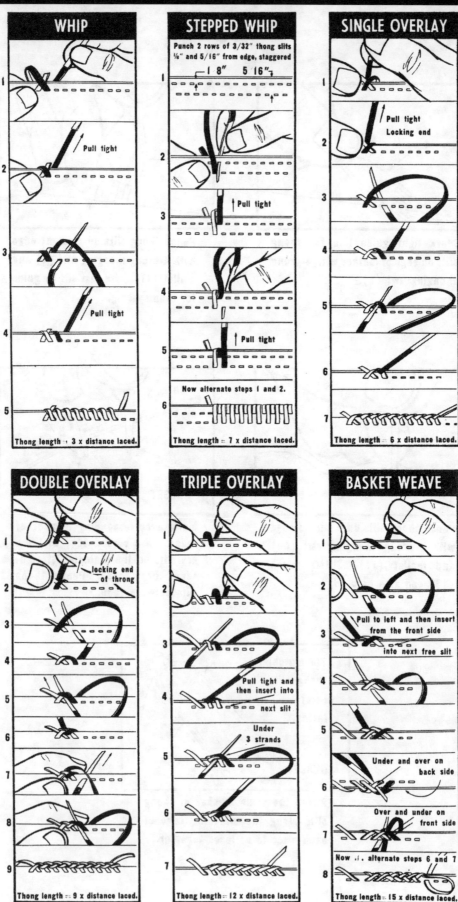

WHIP

1
2   Pull tight
3
4   Pull tight
5

Thong length = 3 x distance laced.

STEPPED WHIP

Punch 2 rows of 3/32" thong slits 1/8" and 5/16" from edge, staggered

⌐ 1 8"   5 16" ⌐

1
2
3   Pull tight
4
5   Pull tight

Now alternate steps 1 and 2.

6

Thong length = 7 x distance laced.

SINGLE OVERLAY

1
2   Pull tight   Locking end
3
4
5
6
7

Thong length = 6 x distance laced.

DOUBLE OVERLAY

1
2   locking end of throng
3
4
5
6
7
8
9

Thong length = 9 x distance laced.

TRIPLE OVERLAY

1
2
3
4   Pull tight and then insert into next slit
5   Under 3 strands
6
7

Thong length = 12 x distance laced.

BASKET WEAVE

1
2
3   Pull to left and then insert from the front side into next free slit
4
5
6   Under and over on back side
7   Over and under on front side

Now ..i. alternate steps 6 and 7.

8

Thong length = 15 x distance laced.

Leather Craft • Chart V • Lacing

Terminate thongs as shown, when lacing is continuous and ending point meets starting point.
1. Pull out loop and thong slit
2. Cement thong between pieces

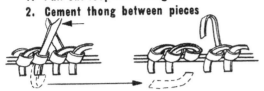

3. Insert free end through loop and thong slit. Cement between pieces

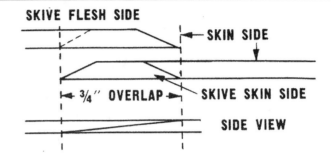

SKIVE FLESH SIDE — SKIN SIDE

3/4" OVERLAP — SKIVE SKIN SIDE

SIDE VIEW

Lengthen thong by splicing.
1. Skive 3/4" of each end
2. Cement

Joining should be no thicker than original thong.

Start with one whip stitch and cement end as shown, when lacing is not continuous.

Terminate lacing by cementing thong between pieces laced.

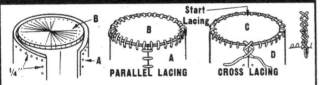

Pass thong twice through each corner thong slit, when lacing around a corner.

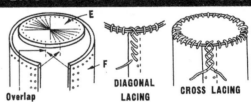

THONG SLITS USED TWICE

LACING BUTT EDGES

PARALLEL LACING   CROSS LACING

1/4"

1. Mark holes 1/4" apart on edges of (A).
2. Draw a corresponding number of lines on circumference of (B).
3. Draw radius lines on (B), from marks on circumference.
4. Punch a 3/32" hole, with revolving punch (8), 1/8" from circumference on each radius line of (B) and along marked edges of (A).
5. For PARALLEL LACING start at corner of (A) and lace (B) to (A) with a whip stitch. Continue the lacing to completion through parallel holes of (A).
6. FOR CROSS LACE start lacing of (C) to (D) at point opposite vertical seam, using both ends of thong. Continue the lacing to completion with both ends of thong by joining together edges of (D) with CROSS LACE.

LACING OVERLAP EDGES

Overlap   DIAGONAL LACING   CROSS LACING

1. Punch holes in (E) and top edge of (F) as directed for (A) (B) in Fig. 16.
2. Punch a double row of 3/32" matching holes in (F) 1/8" and 3/8" respectively from edge and 1/4" apart with revolving punch (8). And (B) in Fig. 16.
3. For DIAGONAL LACING proceed as directed for (A) and (B) in Fig. 16, but pass lace through diagonal holes on overlapped edges.
4. For CROSS LACING use procedure for (C) and (D), Fig. 16.

FLORENTINE LACING

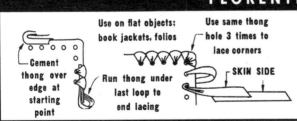

Use on flat objects: book jackets, folios

Use same thong hole 3 times to lace corners

Cement thong over edge at starting point

Run thong under last loop to end lacing

SKIN SIDE

1. Starting from corners punch 3/32" holes 1/4" apart and 1/8" from edges.
2. Lace as shown with whip stitch, using 3/8" Florentine thong. Edges should be completely covered. Length of thong is 2 1/2 times distance laced. NOTE: Punch holes 1/8" apart and use 3/16" Florentine thong on small articles.
3. Cement 3/4" overlap of skived ends, to splice thong.

SUGGESTIONS FOR LACING PROCEDURE:

1. Apply saddle soap to thong for smoother handling.
2. Keep thong from twisting; 2 yards or less is best length.
3. Cut thong end to a point and apply ivory soap or paste wax to the skin side, if lacing needle (18) can't be used.
4. Enlarge thong holes with fid (26), if necessary.
5. Use fid to tighten loops and get an even tension, when lacing.
6. Lay a completely laced article flat, with no overlapping of laced edges. Place felt on laced edge and flatten with mallet (17).

Leather Craft • Chart Ⅵ • Stitching

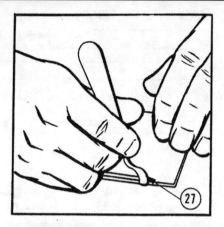

Mark guide line for stitching holes on edge of article with edge creaser (27).

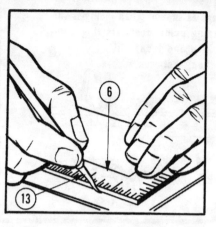

Mark guide line for stitching holes with tracer (13) and steel square (6), when edge creaser is not practicable.

Mark 1/4" and 1/8" spaced stitching holes with fid (26) and steel square (6).

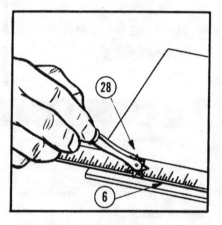

Mark 1/5", 1/6" and 1/7" spaced stitching holes with spacing wheel (28) and steel square (6).

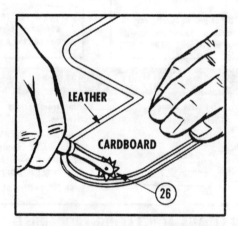

Mark stitching holes on curved edges with a cardboard template cut to size within stitching line as guide.

Leather Craft • Chart VI • Stitching

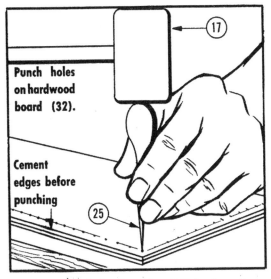

Punch holes on hardwood board (32).

Cement edges before punching

Punch stitching holes through HEAVY leathers, (cowhide, calfskin) or several thicknesses of thin leather, with awl (25) and mallet (17).

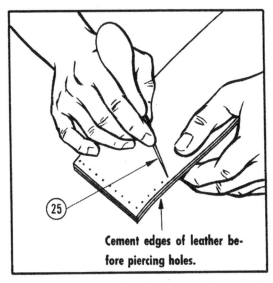

Cement edges of leather before piercing holes.

Pierce stitching holes through LIGHT leathers (suede, lining calf, goatskin) with awl (25).

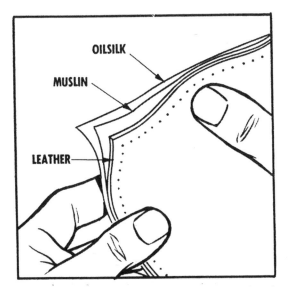

OILSILK

MUSLIN

LEATHER

Punch holes in heavy leather only, when it is combined with oilsilk, muslin, 1-oz. suede, or 1-oz. lining calf. Punched holes will guide stitching of all parts.

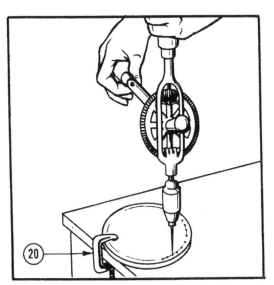

Drill holes in built-up leather articles with 1/16" hand drill. Hold article in place with "C" clamp (20). Drill holes 3/16" from edge; 1/5" apart.

SADDLE STITCH

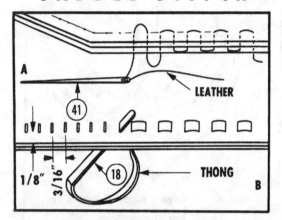

Saddle stitch, sewn with linen thread, is used on LIGHT leathers, bearing no great strain. See (A). Cut thong slits as shown (B), when lacing thong is used for saddle stitching.

"SADDLER'S" STITCH

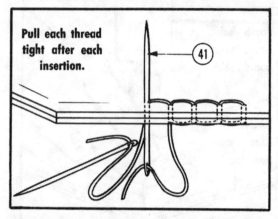

Use "Saddler's" stitch, sewn with linen thread, on HEAVY leathers, and those bearing weight or strain. Stitch with 2 needles (41), inserting thread in same hole in opposite directions.

BACK STITCH

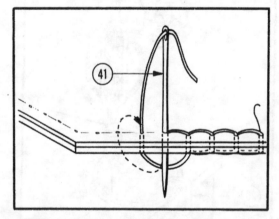

Use back stitch, sewn with linen thread, on LIGHT leathers. Use only when underside of stitch is not exposed, as in stitching a pocket to a lining.

LOCK STITCH

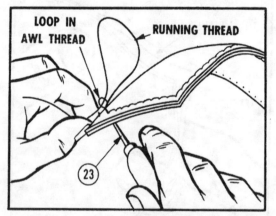

Lock stitch resembles machine stitch. Push threaded awl (23) through leather 5/8". Withdraw awl to form loop in thread at needle point. Insert running thread in loop.

Leather Craft • Chart VI • Stitching

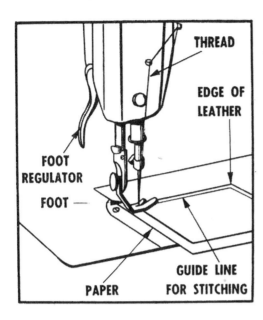

STARTING TO STITCH

1. Thread machine according to manufacturer's directions.

2. Regulate to 9 stitches per inch for thin leather; 6 stitches for heavy leather.

3. Cement edges to be sewed, to prevent their slipping while being stitched.

4. Mark guide line for stitching.

5. Place article on paper to prevent its stretching while stitching.

6. Place under raised foot, so first stitch falls on leather.

7. Lower foot for stitching position.

8. Stitch slowly and evenly on guide line.

9. Raise foot to end stitching. Release threads; cut and knot.

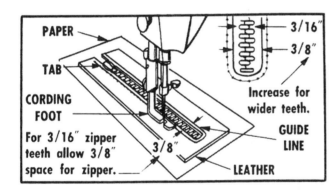

STITCHING A ZIPPER

1. Cement zipper tape to leather.
2. Mark guide line for stitching.
3. Regulate stitch. (See STARTING TO STITCH.)
4. Keep zipper closed; flat.
5. Start stitching at "tab" end.
6. Stitch end tapes.

GENERAL SUGGESTIONS

THREADS AND NEEDLES

A. HAND STITCHING

1. Use No. 18 cotton with No. 5 needle.

2. Use No. 20 linen with No. 3 or 5 needle for small and medium articles.

3. Use No. 18 linen for large articles.

4. Use No. D nylon for all purposes.

B. MACHINE STITCHING

1. Use No. 24 cotton with No. 13 needle.

2. Use No. E shoe-twist machine-silk with No. 19 needle.

3. Use No. D nylon with No. 12 needle, with cotton thread in bobbin.

C. MISCELLANEOUS HINTS

1. Pass cotton and linen thread over cake of beeswax to prevent fraying of thread when handstitching.

2. Color white thread after stitching with Higgins colored inks if matching leather color is desired.

Leather Craft • Chart VII • Braiding

THONG PLATING ROUND

GROUP A – FOUR-PLAIT ROUND, DIAMOND PATTERN

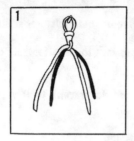 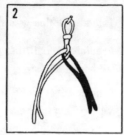 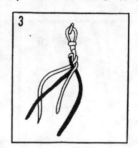

1. Grasp hanging thongs with last three fingers of each hand and manipulate with thumbs and forefingers.

  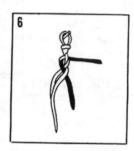

2. Follow the steps illustrated, keeping an even tension on all thongs.

 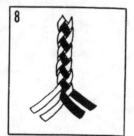

3. Keep braid tight while changing thongs from hand to hand.

GROUP B – FOUR-PLAIT ROUND, SPIRAL PATTERN

 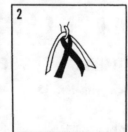 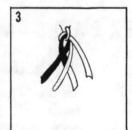 

1. Grasp and manipulate thongs as described above.   2. Follow steps illustrated.

THONGS NEED NOT BE COLORED. THEY ARE SO ILLUSTRATED TO CLARIFY THE PROCEDURE. USE EITHER PATTERN FOR TAGS, LEASHES AND CROPS.

Leather Craft • Chart VII • Braiding

FLAT BRAIDING

GROUP C

Four-thong:

Over 1, under 1

Seven-thong:

Over 2, under 2

Nine-thong:

Under 2, over 1,

under 1, over 2

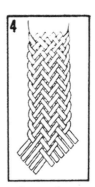

Eleven-thong:

Under 2, over 2,

under 2, over 2

GROUP D

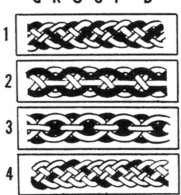

Use vari-colored thongs for the different
designs, if so desired. Secure ends as shown
in Group F.

GROUP E

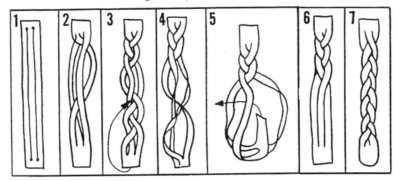

Follow braiding steps shown in Figs. 2, 3. Untangle
the lower section of straps, as shown in Figs. 3, 4,
5, 6. Repeat the steps until the straps ends are too short
for further braiding. Adjust braid to distribute slack. Fig. 7.

GROUP F

1

2

Cut thongs in a strap that is more than twice the width desired for a finished belt, leaving one end as shown in Fig. 1. Fold uncut end flesh to flesh and stitch or cement together. Braid thongs in any desired pattern. Cut slot and attach buckle. Fig. 2.

GROUP G

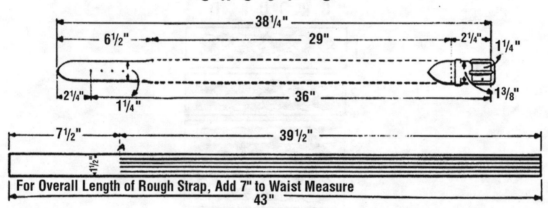

38¼"

6½" • 29" • 2¼" • 1¼"

2¼" • 1¼" • 36" • 1³⁄₈"

7½" • 39½"

1½"

For Overall Length of Rough Strap, Add 7" to Waist Measure

43"

The length and width of finished flat braids will be 2/3 the original sizes of the material used. Add 7" to waist measurement for cutting unbraided belt. This allows 5" to be taken up in braiding, and 1" at each end to trim belt ends.

GROUP H

1

2

Cut pieces for tabs and buckle, if braided section of belt has loose thong ends. Place flattened thong ends between flesh sides of pieces and cement. Cut slot and stitch buckle in place.

THONG PLAITING - SQUARE

GROUP J — FOUR PLAIT — SQUARE

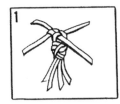  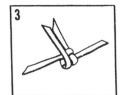  

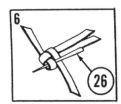  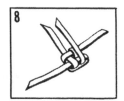 

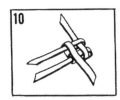  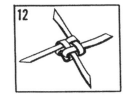 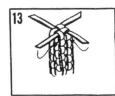 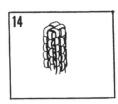

USE EITHER PATTERN FOR HANDLES, CHAINS AND LEASHES.

1. Knot four thongs together, then form a crown. Fig. 1.
2. Continue forming one crown upon another. Figs. 2 through 12.
3. Terminate thongs by tucking ends under next lowest crown. Trim excess. Figs. 13, 14.

GROUP K — FOUR-PLAIT SPIRAL REVERSE

  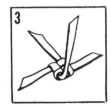  

 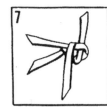 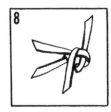  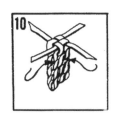

Follow steps illustrated in Figs. 1 through 10

Leather Craft • Chart VIII • Knotting

GAUCHO KNOTS

GROUP A -- SINGLE GAUCHO, BASKET WEAVE PATTERN

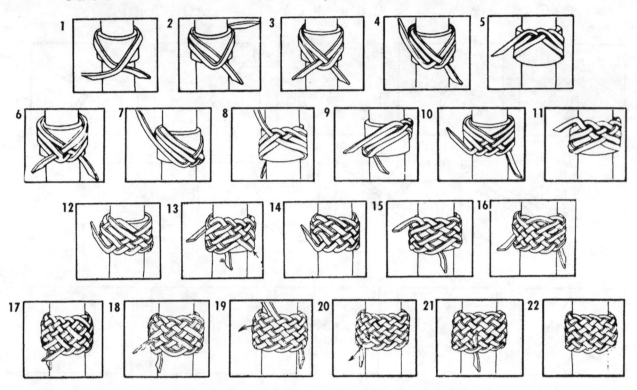

GROUP B -- DOUBLE GAUCHO, HERRINGBONE PATTERN, SINGLE

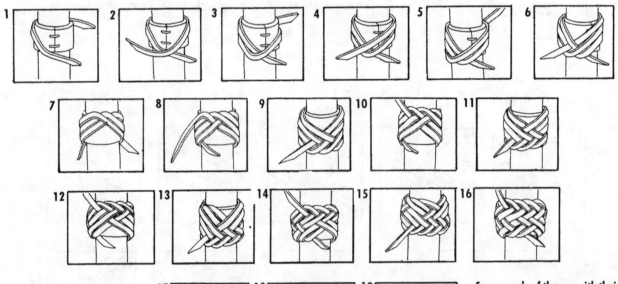

Fit a piece of scrap leather tightly around part to be covered and sew ends together. Edge of tube holds thong in place while forming knot. See Figs. 1.

Secure ends of thongs with their junction near the center of knot, when weaving is completed. Adjust length of loops and tighten slack with fid. Trim ends. Roll knot under a board to smooth it.

BOTH PATTERNS USED FOR SLIDING AND ORNAMENTAL KNOTS OR TERMINALS

Leather Craft • Chart VIII • Knotting

GROUP C -- TWO-BIGHT KNOT

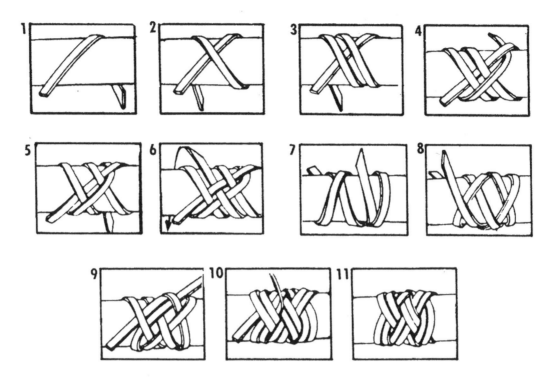

Form sliding knot over a single core, such as a cane or whip handle.

GROUP D -- THREE-BIGHT KNOT

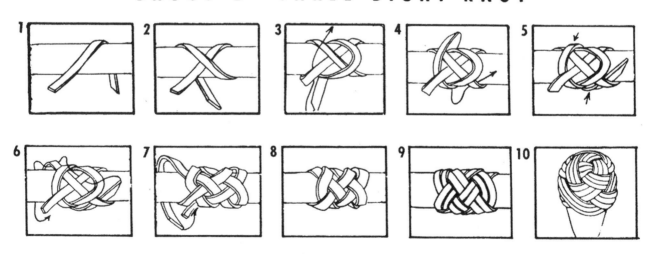

1. The knot in single thong structure is shown in Fig. 8.

2. The thongs may be doubled as in Fig. 9 or tripled as in Fig. 10, to cover more space.

GROUP E -- FOUR-BIGHT KNOT.
USE AS AN ORNAMENT ON CROPS
OR TO CONCEAL JUNCTIONS

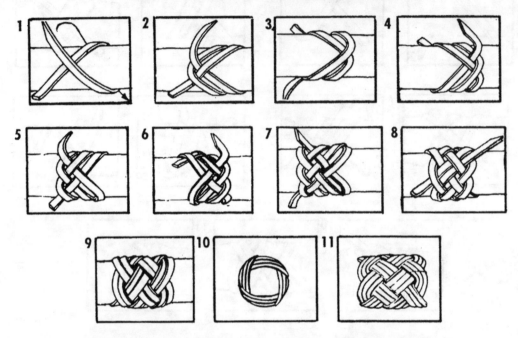

May be made with a single wide thong or with double or triple narrow thongs. A double thong structure can be converted into a triple strand structure, for the closing of open spaces.

GROUP F -- FIVE-BIGHT KNOT

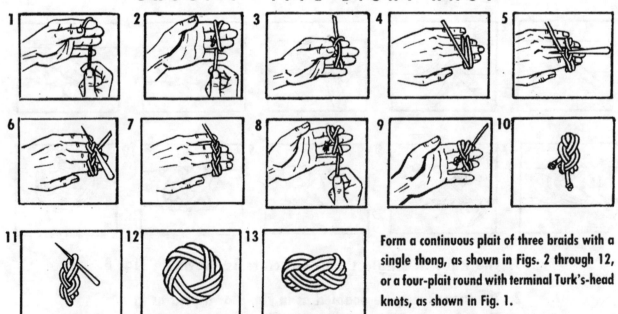

Form a continuous plait of three braids with a single thong, as shown in Figs. 2 through 12, or a four-plait round with terminal Turk's-head knots, as shown in Fig. 1.

USE TURK'S HEAD SLIDES FOR NECKERCHIEFS

Leather Craft • Chart VIII • Knotting

GROUP G -- CROWN BUTTON

 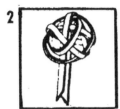

1. Construction details.
2. Cup into shape.
3. Tighten
4. Top view.

GROUP H -- CROWN AND TERMINAL TURK'S-HEAD

CROWN TERMINAL, SQUARE

Form a succession of crown on a terminal Turk's-head. See Leathercraft Chart VIII for square braiding.

SUGGESTIONS:

1. Wax ends of thongs.
2. Use either 3/32″ plastic or leather thongs, cut wider thongs from leather discs, as shown on Leathercraft Chart I.

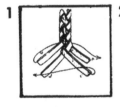 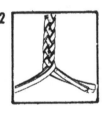  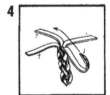 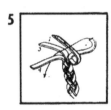

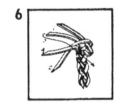 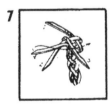 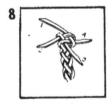 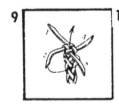 

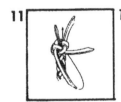 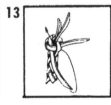  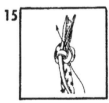 

1. Form crowns as shown in Figs. 1 through 8.
2. Form Turk's-head knots as shown in Figs. 9 through 16.
3. Terminate knot by leaving ends short, in fringe form or by pulling down through the center of knot with fid and cutting ends short.

USE THIS KNOT AS A TERMINAL ON BRAIDS.

Border Designs

Apply these designs to belts and straps, and wherever decorative borders are desired.
Enlarge or reduce by means of photography. Dash lines indicate repeat of motif.

Native American Symbols

 38-26   38-27   38-28   38-29   38-30   38-31   38-32   38-33

38-34   38-35   38-36   38-37   38-38   38-39

 THUNDERBIRD, Sacred bearer of Happiness unlimited

 LIGHTNING SNAKE

 RAIN CLOUDS, Good Prospects

 ARROW, Protection

SNAKE, Defiance, Wisdom

 LIGHTNING AND LIGHTNING ARROW, Swiftness

 CROSSED ARROWS, Friendship

 THUNDERBIRD TRACK, Bright Prospects

 DAYS AND NIGHTS, Time

 ARROWHEAD, Alertness

 DEER TRACK, Plenty Game

 MORNING STARS, Guidance

 4 AGES, Infancy, Youth, Middle and Old Age

 BEAR TRACK, Good Omen

 SUN SYMBOLS, Happiness

 CACTUS, Sign of the Desert

 RATTLESNAKE JAW, Strength

 RUNNING WATER, Constant Life

 GILA MONSTER, Sign of the Desert

 SUN RAYS, Constancy

 RAINDROP-RAIN, Plentiful Crops

 CACTUS FLOWER, Courtship

 HEADDRESS, Ceremonial Dance

 HOGAN, Permanent Home

 HORSE-Journey

 BUTTERFLY, Everlasting Life

 TEPEE, Temporary Home

 SADDLE BAGS, Journey

 COYOTE TRACKS

 SKY BAND, Leading To Happiness

 BIRD, Carefree, Light-hearted

 MAN, Human Life

 MOUNTAIN RANGE

 MEDICINE MAN'S EYE, Wise, Watchful

 PATHS CROSSING

 LASSO, Captivity

 BIG MOUNTAIN, Abundance

 WARDING OFF EVIL SPIRITS

 EAGLE FEATHERS, Chief

 FENCE, Guarding Good Luck

 HOUSE OF WATER

 ENCLOSURE FOR CEREMONIAL DANCES

Authentic Native American stamps (38-26 through -39) can be combined.
Use native American symbols singly or combined as on following page. Execute designs in
Line or Modeling. See Leather Chart II. Enlarge or reduce by photography.

Native American Symbol Combinations

Bright Prospects
Wise
Good Prospects

Wise   Time Guidance
Wisdom   Constant Life

Lighthearted   Friendship
Carefree   Courtship
Guarding Good Luck Plentiful Crops

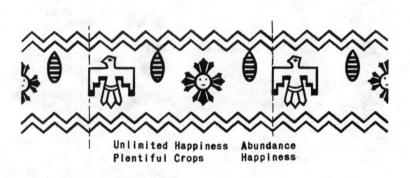

Unlimited Happiness Abundance
Plentiful Crops   Happiness

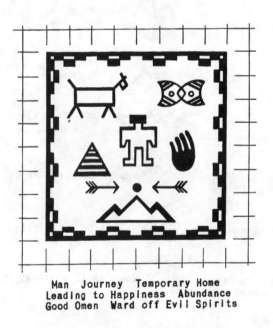

Man Journey Temporary Home
Leading to Happiness Abundance
Good Omen Ward off Evil Spirits

Good Omen   Protection
Happiness   Strength

Specimen designs made by combining the Native American symbols shown on preceding page. Execute designs in Line, Modeling or Embossing. (See Leather Chart II). Enlarge or reduce by scale lines or photography. Dash lines indicate repeat of motif.

Navajo Designs

Enlarge or reduce to desired size by scale lines or photography. Dash lines indicate repeat of motif.

Stamp and Wheel Designs

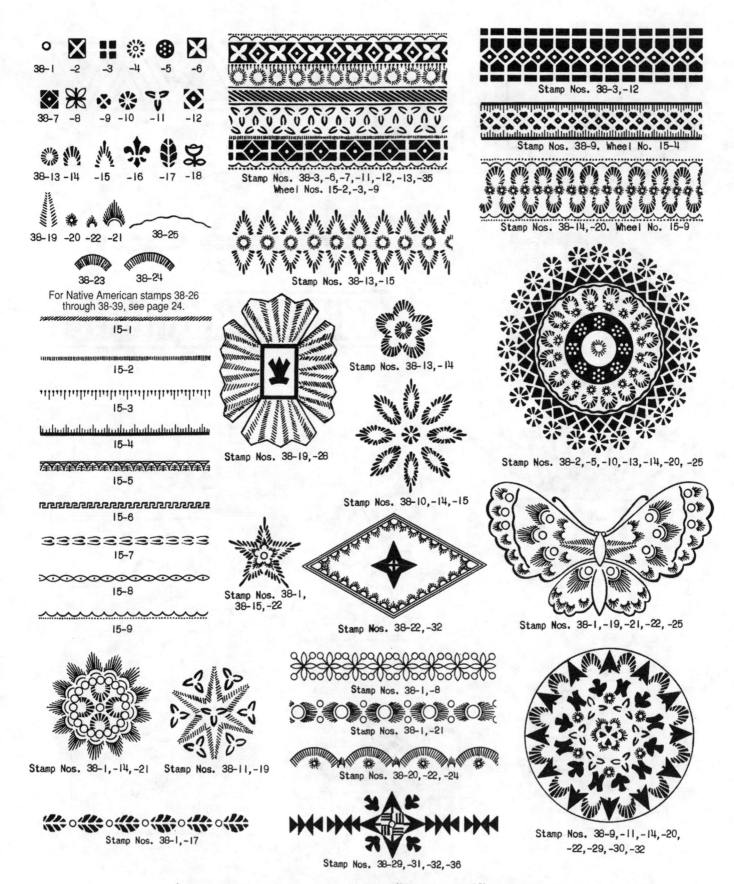

38-1 -2 -3 -4 -5 -6
38-7 -8 -9 -10 -11 -12
38-13 -14 -15 -16 -17 -18
38-19 -20 -22 -21 38-25
38-23 38-24

For Native American stamps 38-26 through 38-39, see page 24.

15-1
15-2
15-3
15-4
15-5
15-6
15-7
15-8
15-9

Stamp Nos. 38-3, -6, -7, -11, -12, -13, -35
Wheel Nos. 15-2, -3, -9

Stamp Nos. 38-13, -15

Stamp Nos. 38-19, -28

Stamp Nos. 38-13, -14

Stamp Nos. 38-10, -14, -15

Stamp Nos. 38-1, 38-15, -22

Stamp Nos. 38-22, -32

Stamp Nos. 38-3, -12

Stamp Nos. 38-9. Wheel No. 15-4

Stamp Nos. 38-14, -20. Wheel No. 15-9

Stamp Nos. 38-2, -5, -10, -13, -14, -20, -25

Stamp Nos. 38-1, -19, -21, -22, -25

Stamp Nos. 38-1, -14, -21   Stamp Nos. 38-11, -19

Stamp Nos. 38-1, -17

Stamp Nos. 38-1, -8

Stamp Nos. 38-1, -21

Stamp Nos. 38-20, -22, -24

Stamp Nos. 38-29, -31, -32, -36

Stamp Nos. 38-9, -11, -14, -20, -22, -29, -30, -32

Specimen designs made by combining stamps (38-1 through -39) and wheels (15-1 through -9). See page 24 and Leather Chart 11 for stamping procedure.

Monograms & Signs of the Zodiac

AQUARIUS
Jan.20 to Feb.18

LEO
July 23 to Aug.22

PISCES
Feb.19 to Mar.20

VIRGO
Aug.23 to Sept.22

ARIES
Mar.21 to Apr.19

LIBRA
Sept.23 to Oct.22

TAURUS
Apr.20 to May 20

Stamp No. 38-22

SCORPIO
Oct.23 to Nov.22

Wheel No. 15-1

GEMINI
May 21 to June 20

Wheel No. 15-2

SAGITTARUS
Nov.23 to Dec.22

CANCER
June 21 to July 22

Stamp No. 38-22

CAPRICORN
Dec.23 to Jan.19

Zodiac Signs

Zodiac Signs

Various monograms and Signs of the Zodiac. Enlarge or reduce by photography.

51

Stamp No. 38-I

Stamp No. 38-I

Enlarge or reduce to desired size by scale lines or photography. Dash lines in borders indicate repeat of motif. Tool Nos. (9), (13). See Leather Chart II for Line Decoration.

Design for Modeling

Design for Knitting Bag

Design for Stationery Folder

Design for Knitting Bag

Design for Desk Paper Clamp

Enlarge or reduce to desired size by scale lines or photography. Dash lines indicate repeat of motif. Tool Nos. 9, 10, 11, 13, 36. See Leather Chart II for Modeling procedure.

Designs for Embossing

Design used on Drum Pouch Bag
Dash lines indicate repeat of motif

Enlarge or reduce to desired size by scale lines or photography. Tool Nos.
(9), (10), (11), (13), (36). See Leather Chart II for Embossing Procedure.

Designs for Carving

Stamp Nos. 38-22, -19; 45-5, -8, -14.

45-1

45-2

45-3

45-4

45-5

45-6

45-7

1. Tap Beveler
2. Ribbed Tap Beveler
3. Round Grounder
4. Bar Grounder
5. Pear Shader
6. Ribbed Shader
7. Veiner

Stamp Nos. 45-13
Wheel 15-14

Stamp No. 45-14

Stamp Nos. 45-5, -6, -10; 14.

45-8

45-9

45-10   45-11

45-12   45-13

45-14

8. Barker
9. Crowner
10. Sun Burst
11. Dot and Flare
12. Basket
13. Waffle
14. Seed, 1/8"

Stamp Nos. 45-3, -5, -8. Dash lines indicate repeat of Motif.

Enlarge or reduce to desired size by scale lines or photography. Tool Nos. (2), (31), (39), (44-1 through 14.)
Stamps No. 38 can be used also. See Leather Chart II for carving procedure.

Enlarge or reduce by scale lines or photography. Dash lines indicate
repeat of motif. Tool No. 33. See Leather Chart III for inlay procedure.

Designs for Painting

Design used on Earring Box

Design used on Child's "Treasure Chest" Coin Bank

Enlarge or reduce to desired size by scale lines or photography. Dash lines in borders indicate repeat of motif. Tool Nos. (9), (13). See Leather Chart III for painting procedure.

Archery Arm Guard

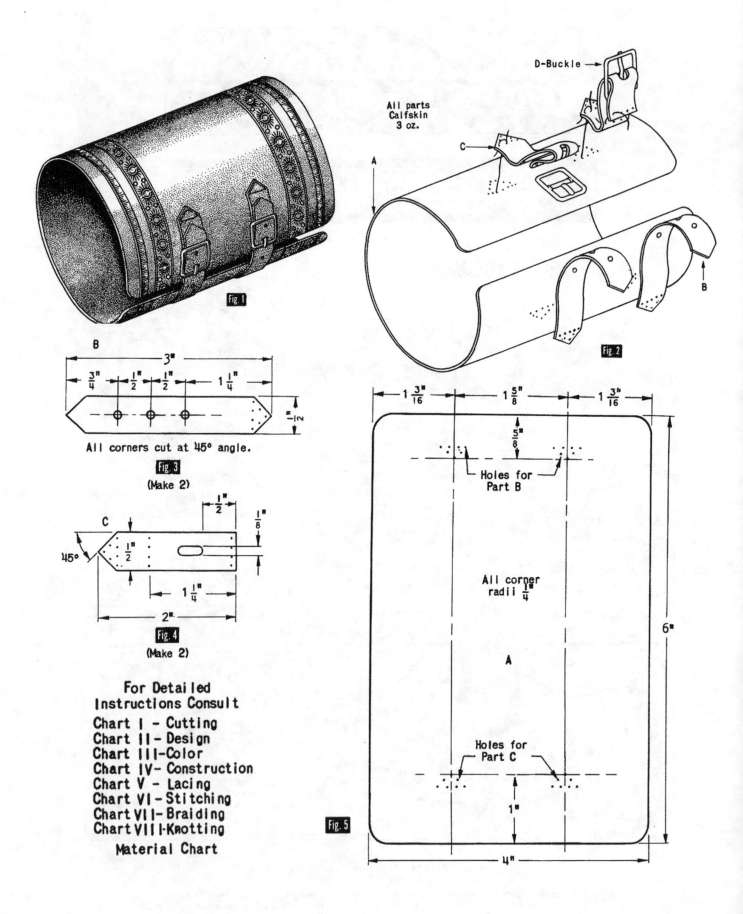

All parts
Calfskin
3 oz.

D-Buckle

Fig. 1

Fig. 2

B

3"

3/4"   1/2"   1/2"   1 1/4"

1/2"

All corners cut at 45° angle.

Fig. 3
(Make 2)

C

45°

1/2"

1/2"

1/8"

1 1/4"

2"

Fig. 4
(Make 2)

For Detailed
Instructions Consult
Chart I - Cutting
Chart II - Design
Chart III - Color
Chart IV - Construction
Chart V - Lacing
Chart VI - Stitching
Chart VII - Braiding
Chart VIII - Knotting
Material Chart

1 3/16"   1 5/8"   1 3/16"

5/8"

Holes for
Part B

All corner
radii 1/4"

A

6"

Holes for
Part C

1"

Fig. 5

4"

PROCEDURE: (CONSULT LEATHER CRAFT PROCESSING CHARTS)

1. Cut and prepare parts (A), (B), (C). Figs. 1, 2, 3, 4, 5.
2. Cut slit in parts (C) for buckle prongs. Fig. 4.
3. With awl punch stitching holes for buckles in (C) at matching points designated. Fig. 4.
4. Attach buckles to (C) with saddler's stitch. Figs. 1, 2.
5. Punch 3 buckle holes $\frac{1}{2}"$ apart, in (B), using revolving punch. Figs. 1, 2, 3.
6. With awl punch stitching holes in matching parts of (A), (B), (C). Figs. 2, 3, 4, 5.
7. Attach parts (B) and (C) to part (A) with saddler's stitch. Figs. 1, 2.

MATERIALS:

Calfskin

Two $\frac{1}{2}"$ **Center** bar buckles

Heavy linen thread

TOOLS:

(1), (6), (25), (41)

Belt Pouch (Archery)

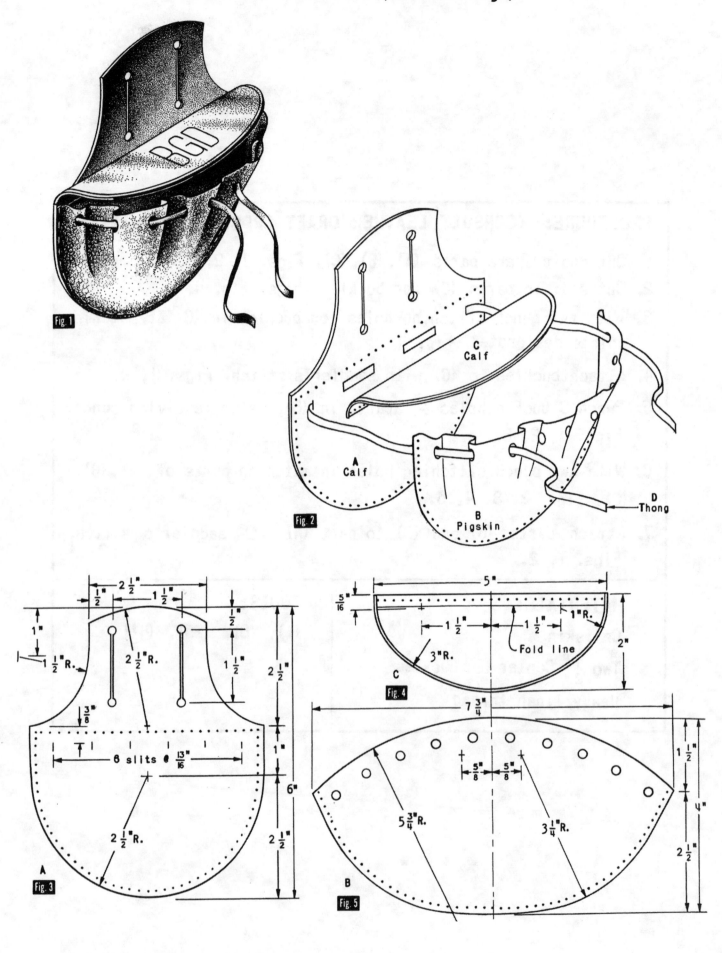

Fig. 1

Fig. 2
C Calf
A Calf
B Pigskin
D Thong

Fig. 3
A
2 1/2"
1 1/2"
1/2"
1"
1 1/2" R.
2 1/2" R.
3/8"
1 1/2"
1 1/2"
2 1/2"
6 slits @ 13/16"
1"
6"
2 1/2"
2 1/2" R.

Fig. 4
C
5"
5/16"
1 1/2"
1 1/2"
1" R.
Fold line
3" R.
2"

Fig. 5
B
7 3/4"
5/8"
5/8"
5 3/4" R.
3 1/4" R.
1 1/2"
4"
2 1/2"

PROCEDURE: (CONSULT LEATHER CRAFT PROCESSING CHARTS)

1. Cut and prepare parts (A), (B), (C). Figs. 3, 4, 5.

2. With No. 4 tube, punch 4 holes in part (A) and connect with 1/16" slots, as shown. Fig. 3.

3. With edge creaser, mark rounded edge and fold of (C). Fig. 4.

4. With awl, punch 1/7" stitching holes, 1/8" from edge of (C), in matching parts of (A) and (C). Figs. 2, 3, 4.

5. Sew (C) to (A) with saddler's stitch. Fig. 2.

6. With awl, punch 6 equi-spaced thong slits in (A), 1/8" below edge of (C). Fig. 3.

7. With No. 4 tube, punch 10 equi-spaced holes 3/8" from top edge of part (B). Fig. 5.

8. With awl, punch 1/7" stitching holes 1/8" from edge, in matching parts of (AC) and (B). Figs. 2, 3, 5.

9. Sew (B) to (AC) with saddler's stitch. Figs. 1, 2.

10. Insert drawstring thong (D) through thong slits of (AC) and holes of (B). Figs. 1, 2.

MATERIALS:

Calfskin, 4-5 oz.

Pigskin, lightweight

Calfskin lace 3/32", 20" long

TOOLS:

(5), (6), (8), (18), (25), (28), (33), (40), (41).

For Detailed
Instructions Consult

Chart I - Cutting
Chart II - Design
Chart III - Color
Chart IV - Construction
Chart V - Lacing
Chart VI - Stitching
Chart VII - Braiding
Chart VIII - Knotting

Material Chart

Archery Belt Pouch

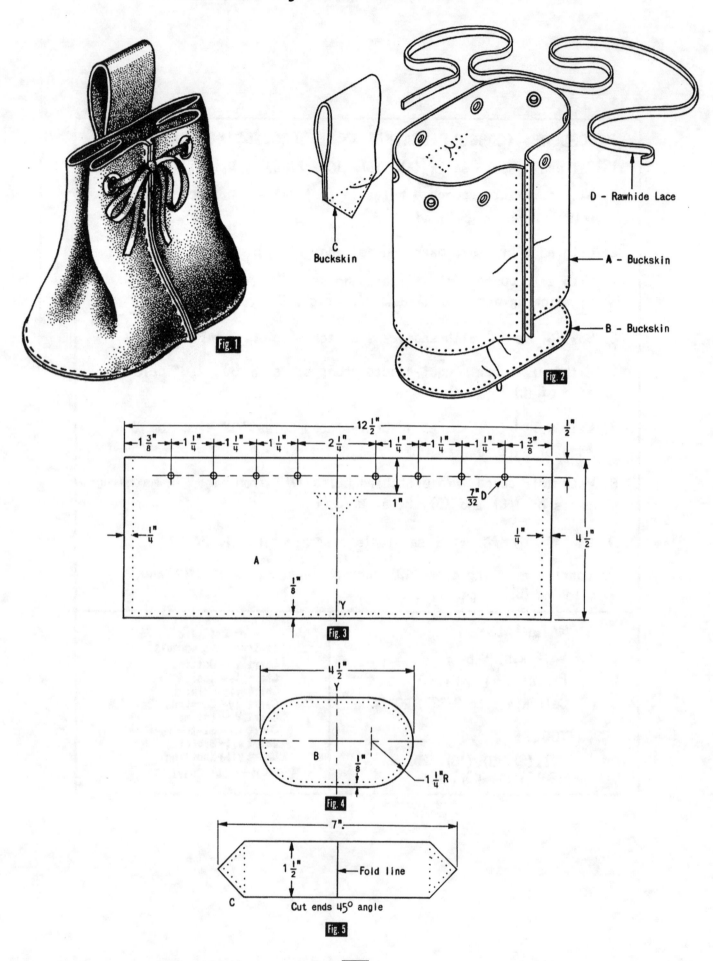

Fig. 1

Fig. 2

C
Buckskin

D – Rawhide Lace

A – Buckskin

B – Buckskin

Fig. 3

12 $\frac{1}{2}$"

$\frac{1}{2}$"

1 $\frac{3}{8}$" 1 $\frac{1}{4}$" 1 $\frac{1}{4}$" 1 $\frac{1}{4}$" 2 $\frac{1}{4}$" 1 $\frac{1}{4}$" 1 $\frac{1}{4}$" 1 $\frac{1}{4}$" 1 $\frac{3}{8}$"

1"

$\frac{7}{32}$" D

$\frac{1}{4}$"

$\frac{1}{4}$"

4 $\frac{1}{2}$"

A

$\frac{1}{8}$"

Y

Fig. 4

4 $\frac{1}{2}$"

Y

B

$\frac{1}{8}$"

1 $\frac{1}{4}$" R

Fig. 5

7"

1 $\frac{1}{2}$"

Fold line

C

Cut ends 45° angle

62

PROCEDURE: (CONSULT LEATHER CRAFT PROCESSING CHARTS)

1. Cut parts (A), (B) and (C). Figs. 3, 4, 5.

2. Punch eight $\frac{7"}{32}$ holes $\frac{1"}{2}$ from top edge of (A). Fig. 3.
   Insert No. 6 K eyelets.

3. Fold (C). With awl, punch holes $\frac{1"}{8}$ apart, $\frac{1"}{8}$ from edge in matching parts (C) and (A). Figs. 2, 3, 5.

4. Sew (C) to (A) with saddler's stitch. Fig. 2.

5. Match point (Y) of (A) to point (Y) of (B). With awl, punch holes in matching parts of (A) and (B), working each side from point (Y) around to center front seam. Figs. 2, 3, 4.

6. Sew (A) to (B) with saddle stitch. Fig. 2.

7. With awl, punch holes $\frac{1"}{8}$ apart in ends of (A) for center seam. Sew with saddle stitch. Fig. 2.

8. Insert drawstring (D). Fig. 2.

MATERIALS:
Suede finish buckskin
Rawhide lace $\frac{1"}{8}$, 25" long
Heavy linen thread
Eight No. 6 K eyelets

TOOLS:
(1), (3), (6), (14), (25), (41).

For Detailed
Instructions Consult

Chart I – Cutting
Chart II – Design
Chart III – Color
Chart IV – Construction
Chart V – Lacing
Chart VI – Stitching
Chart VII – Braiding
Chart VIII – Knotting
Material Chart

Archery Shooting Glove

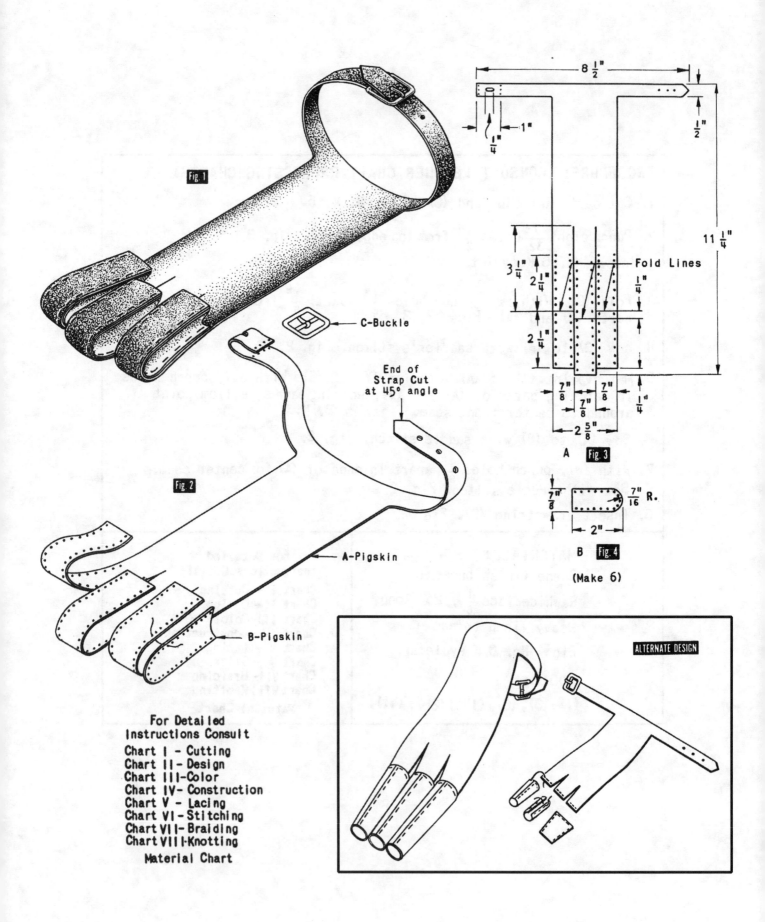

Fig.1

C-Buckle

End of
Strap Cut
at 45° angle

Fig 2

A-Pigskin

B-Pigskin

8 1/2"

1"

1/4"

11 1/4"

1/2"

Fold Lines

3 1/4"

2 1/4"

1/4"

2 1/4"

7/8"

7/8"

7/8"

1/4"

2 5/8"

A   Fig. 3

7/8"   7/16" R.

2"

B   Fig. 4

(Make 6)

ALTERNATE DESIGN

For Detailed
Instructions Consult
Chart I – Cutting
Chart II – Design
Chart III – Color
Chart IV – Construction
Chart V – Lacing
Chart VI – Stitching
Chart VII – Braiding
Chart VIII – Knotting
Material Chart

64

PROCEDURE: (CONSULT LEATHER CRAFT PROCESSING CHARTS)

1. Cut and prepare parts (A),(B). Use edge creaser for fold lines. Figs. 3, 4.

2. With 1/7" spacing wheel, mark stitching holes in matching parts of (A) and (B), 1/8" from edges. Figs. 2, 3, 4.

3. With awl punch all stitching holes.

4. Attach buckle, using saddler's stitch. Figs. 2, 3.

5. Saddle stitch parts (B) to part (A). Figs. 1, 2.
   Note: Dimensions of alternate design are essentially the same.

MATERIALS:

Pigskin ($2\frac{1}{2}$ oz.)

Buckle, $\frac{1}{2}$", center bar

Heavy Linen Thread

TOOLS:

(5), (6), (8), (25), (33), (41).

Archery Shooting Tabs

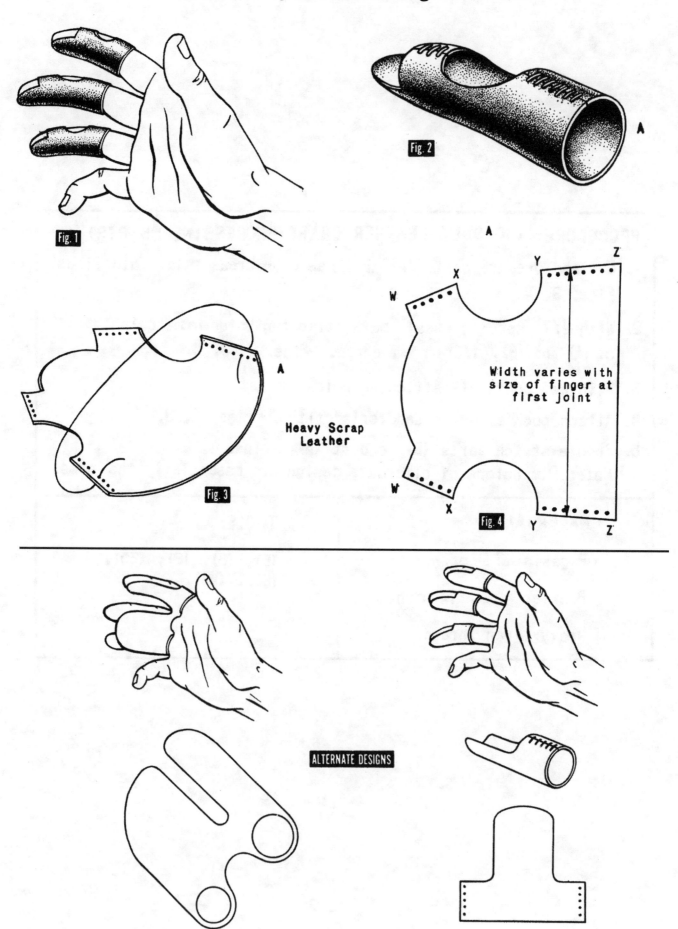

Fig. 1

Fig. 2

A

A

Heavy Scrap Leather

Fig. 3

W   X   Y   Z

Width varies with
size of finger at
first joint

W
    X   Y   Z

Fig. 4

ALTERNATE DESIGNS

PROCEDURE: (CONSULT LEATHER CRAFT PROCESSING CHARTS)

1. Cut parts (A) to fit fingers.

2. With awl, punch holes simultaneously, $\frac{1}{8}"$ apart, $\frac{1}{8}"$ from edge on matching lines (WX) and (YZ).

3. Whip stitch (WX) and (YZ) together.

MATERIALS:

Heavy scrap leather

Heavy linen thread

TOOLS:

(1), (6), (17), (25), (41).

For Detailed
Instructions Consult

Chart I – Cutting
Chart II – Design
Chart III – Color
Chart IV – Construction
Chart V – Lacing
Chart VI – Stitching
Chart VII – Braiding
Chart VIII – Knotting
Material Chart

Archery Quiver

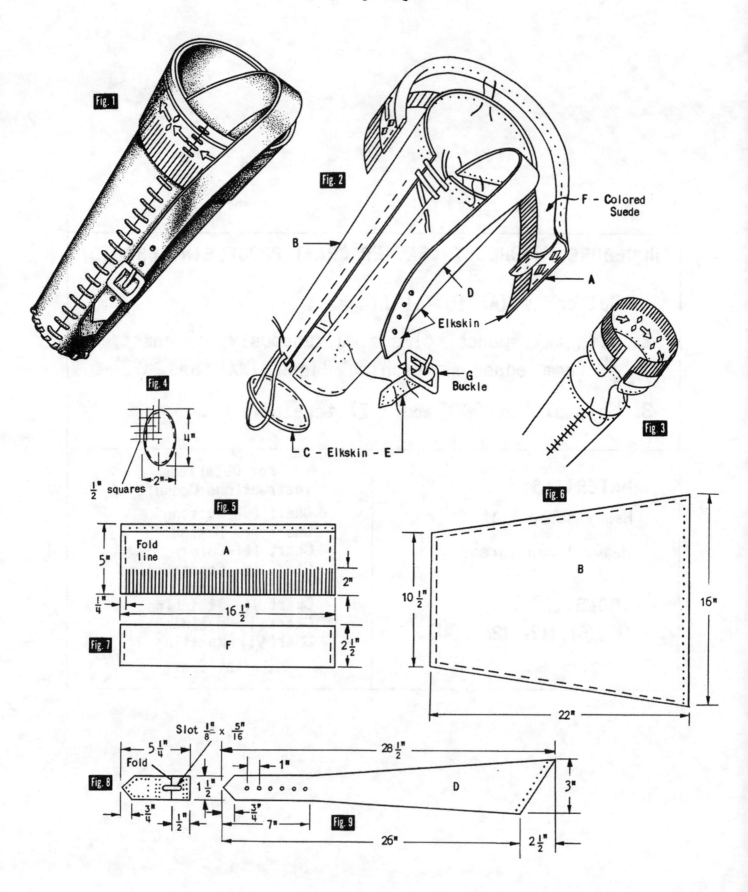

Fig. 1

Fig. 2

F – Colored Suede

B

D

Elkskin

A

G Buckle

Fig. 3

C – Elkskin – E

Fig. 4

4"

2"

½" squares

Fig. 5

Fold line

A

5"

2"

¼"

16½"

Fig. 7

F

2½"

Fig. 6

B

10½"

16"

22"

Slot ⅛" x 5/16"

Fold

5¼"

Fig. 8

1½"

¾"

½"

1"

¾"

7"

Fig. 9

D

28½"

3"

26"

2½"

PROCEDURE: (CONSULT LEATHER CRAFT PROCESSING CHARTS)

1. Cut and prepare parts (A), (B), (C), (D), (E), (F). Figs. 4, 5, 6, 7, 8, 9.

2. With awl, punch matching $\frac{1}{8}"$ thong slits $\frac{3}{16}"$ from side and bottom edges of (B) and (C). Figs. 2, 4, 6.

3. With awl, punch $\frac{1}{8}"$ stitching holes in matching parts of (B) and (E), and (B) and (D) as shown. Figs. 2, 6, 8, 9.

4. Fold (E); insert buckle (G) in slot. Punch double row of $\frac{1}{8}"$ stitching holes through fold of (E). Figs. 2, 8.

5. Sew fold with saddler's stitch. Fig. 2.

6. Sew (E) to (B) with saddler's stitch. Fig. 2.

7. Beginning at top, lace seam of (B) with whip stitch; with same thong continue to lace (C) to (B). Fig. 2.

8. Sew wide end of (D) to (BC) with saddler's stitch. Fig. 2.

9. Cement skin side of (F) to flesh side of perforated band of (A), $\frac{1}{2}"$ from edge of (A). Figs. 2, 5, 7.

10. With awl, punch $\frac{1}{8}"$ thong slits on ends of (AF), $\frac{3}{16}"$ from edge. Figs. 2, 5, 7.

11. Place skin side of (A) against skin side of (BCD) with $\frac{1}{2}"$ overlap. With awl, punch $\frac{1}{8}"$ stitching holes $\frac{3}{8}"$ from edge of (AF), simultaneously through (AF) and (BCD). Fig. 3.

12. Sew (AF) to (BCD) with saddle stitch. Turn down (AF) over (BCD) to form cuff. Figs. 2, 3.

13. Join ends of (AF) with whip stitch. Figs. 1, 2.

MATERIALS:

Elkskin

Suede of contrasting color, (2 oz.)

Rawhide lace, Indian tan, $\frac{1}{8}"$ wide.

Heavy linen thread

Rubber cement

Buckle, $1\frac{1}{2}"$

TOOLS:

(1), (4), (6), (17), (18), (21), (25), (27), (33), (40), (41), (43).

See Leather Chart V for punching thong slits

For Detailed Instructions Consult

Chart I – Cutting
Chart II – Design
Chart III – Color
Chart IV – Construction
Chart V – Lacing
Chart VI – Stitching
Chart VII – Braiding
Chart VIII – Knotting

Material Chart

Archery Quiver

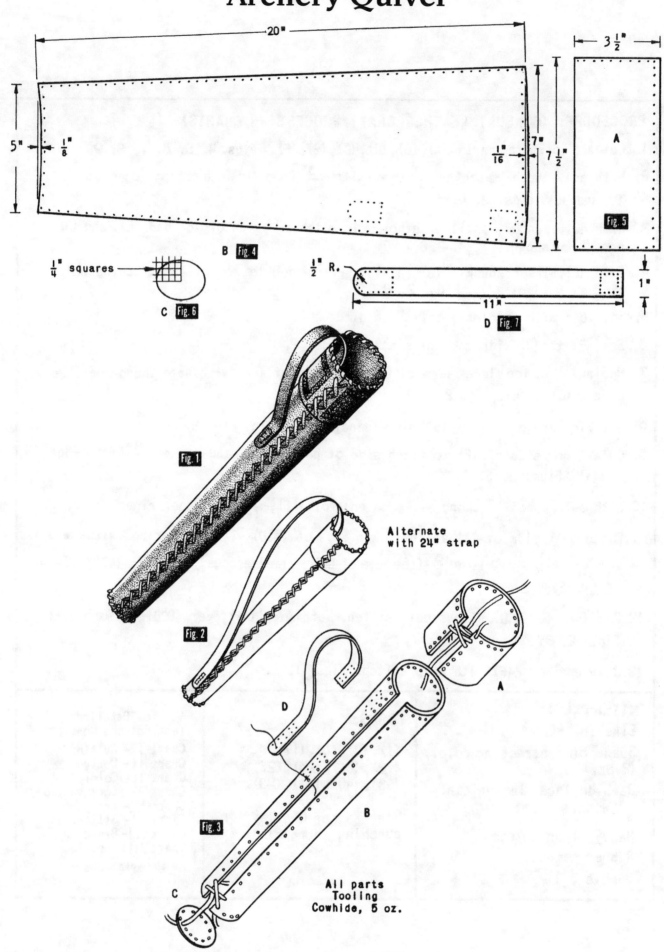

20"

5" ⅛"

7"

7 ½"

3 ½"

A

Fig. 5

B Fig. 4

¼" squares →

C Fig. 6

½" R.

11"

1"

D Fig. 7

Fig. 1

Fig. 2

Alternate
with 24" strap

A

D

B

Fig. 3

C

All parts
Tooling
Cowhide, 5 oz.

PROCEDURE: (CONSULT LEATHER CRAFT PROCESSING CHARTS)

1. Cut and prepare parts (A), (B), (C), (D). Figs. 4, 5, 6, 7.

2. With No. 1 tube, punch matching holes $\frac{3}{8}''$ apart, $\frac{1}{8}''$ from side and bottom edges of (B). Figs. 3, 4.

3. With No. 1 tube, punch matching holes in (C), $\frac{1}{8}''$ from edge. Figs. 3, 6.

4. With awl, punch matching holes in (D) and (B) as shown, $\frac{1}{8}''$ from edge of (D). Figs. 3, 4, 7.

5. Sew (D) to (B) with saddler's stitch. Fig. 3.

6. Beginning at bottom midpoint of (B), lace (C) to (B) with whip stitch. Fig. 3.

7. Without terminating thong, lace seam of (B) with cross stitch. Fig. 3 and Chart V.

8. With No. 1 tube, punch matching holes on short ends of (A), $\frac{3}{8}''$ apart, $\frac{1}{8}''$ from edges. Figs. 3, 5.

9. Place (A) in position on (BCD). With No. 1 tube, punch holes $\frac{3}{8}''$ apart, $\frac{1}{4}''$ from top edge, through matching parts of (A) and (BCD). Figs. 3, 4, 5.

10. Starting at bottom of cuff (A), lace ends of (A) with cross stitch. Continue with same thong to lace (A) to (BCD) with whip stitch. Fig. 3.

MATERIALS:

Heavy tooling cowhide, 5 oz.

Calfskin lace, $\frac{3}{32}''$

Heavy linen thread

TOOLS:

(1), (6), (8), (17), (18), (25), (41).

See Leather Chart V for punching holes in (C).

For Detailed Instructions Consult
Chart I - Cutting
Chart II - Design
Chart III - Color
Chart IV - Construction
Chart V - Lacing
Chart VI - Stitching
Chart VII - Braiding
Chart VIII - Knotting
Material Chart

Archery Arm Guard

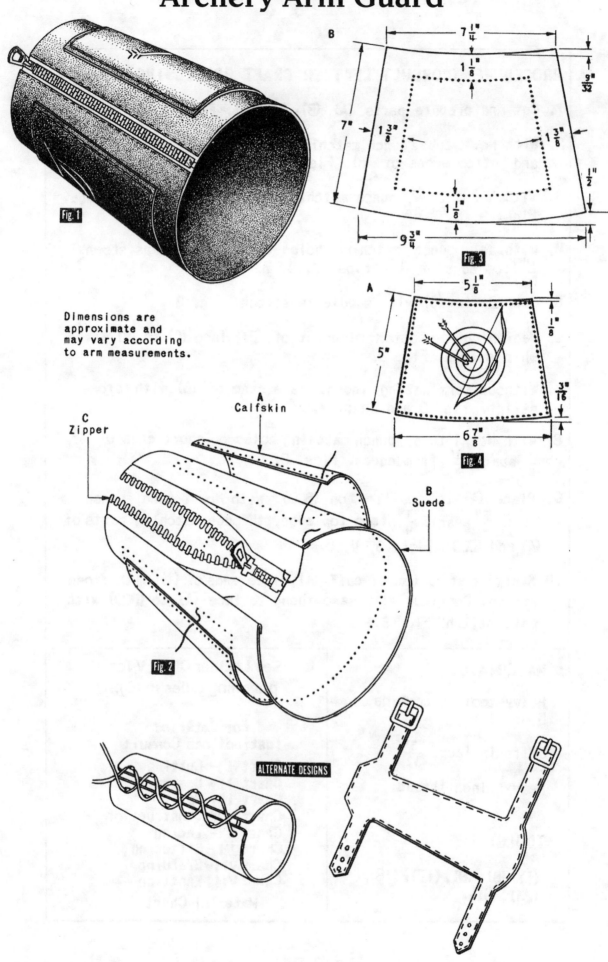

Fig. 1

B

$7\frac{1}{4}$"

$1\frac{1}{8}$"

$\frac{9}{32}$"

7" $1\frac{3}{8}$" $1\frac{3}{8}$"

$\frac{1}{2}$"

$1\frac{1}{8}$"

$9\frac{3}{4}$"

Fig. 3

A

$5\frac{1}{8}$"

$\frac{1}{8}$"

5"

$\frac{3}{16}$"

$6\frac{7}{8}$"

Fig. 4

Dimensions are approximate and may vary according to arm measurements.

A
Calfskin

C
Zipper

B
Suede

Fig. 2

ALTERNATE DESIGNS

72

PROCEDURE:
(CONSULT LEATHER CRAFT PROCESSING CHARTS)

1. Cut and prepare parts (A) and (B). Figs. 3, 4.

2. Cement (A) in position on (B). Fig. 2.

3. With awl, punch stitching holes, 7 to the inch, $\frac{1}{8}''$ from edge of (A), simultaneously through matching edge of (A) and (B). Figs. 3, 4.

4. Sew (A) to (B) with saddler's stitch. Fig. 2.

5. Turn back straight edges of (B) 1/4", and cement. Cement zipper (C) to (AB). Fig. 2.

6. Stitch (C) to (AB) on sewing machine.

MATERIALS:
Russia tooling calfskin $2\frac{1}{2}$ oz.

Suede, 2 oz.

Zipper, 7"

Heavy linen thread

Rubber cement

TOOLS:
(1), (6), (25), (28), (41).

For Detailed
Instructions Consult
Chart I – Cutting
Chart II – Design
Chart III – Color
Chart IV – Construction
Chart V – Lacing
Chart VI – Stitching
Chart VII – Braiding
Chart VIII – Knotting
Material Chart

Baby Halter

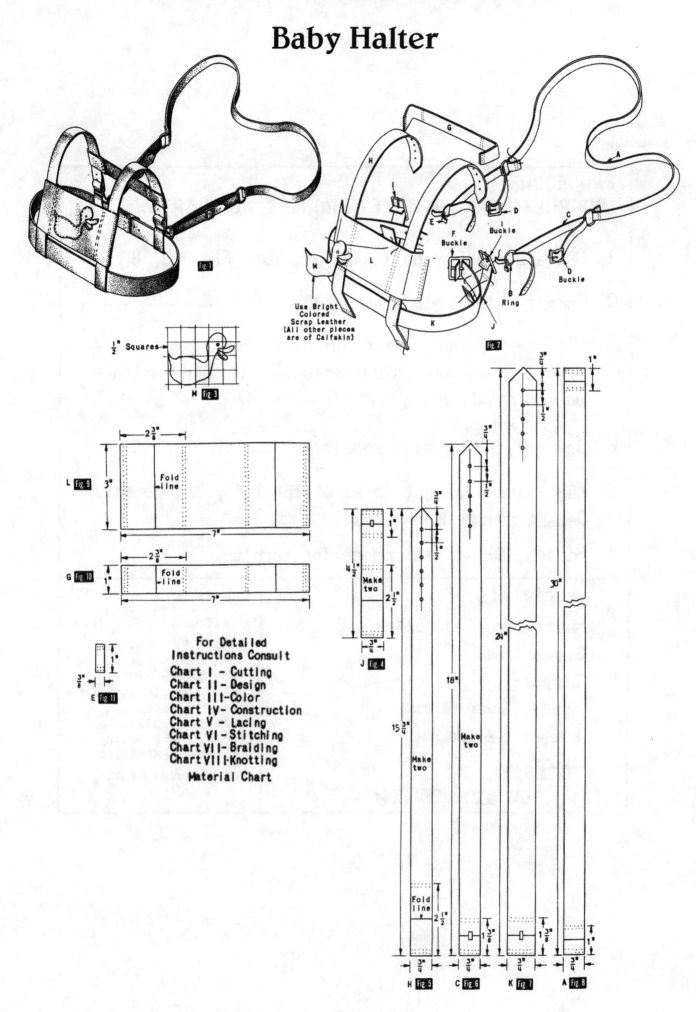

Fig. 1

Fig. 2

Use Bright
Colored
Scrap Leather
(All other pieces
are of Calfskin)

½" Squares

M Fig. 3

L Fig. 9

3"

2 ⅜"

Fold line

7"

G Fig. 10

2 ⅜"

1"

Fold line

7"

E Fig. 11

3/8"

1"

For Detailed
Instructions Consult

Chart I – Cutting
Chart II–Design
Chart III–Color
Chart IV–Construction
Chart V – Lacing
Chart VI–Stitching
Chart VII–Braiding
Chart VIII–Knotting

Material Chart

J Fig. 4

4 ½"

2 ½"

1"

3/4"

Make two

H Fig. 5   C Fig. 6   K Fig. 7   A Fig. 8

15 ¾"

18"

24"

30"

Make two

Make two

Fold line

2 ½"

1 ¾"   1 ¾"   1"

3/4"   3/4"   3/4"   3/4"

PROCEDURE: (CONSULT LEATHER CRAFT PROCESSING CHARTS)

1. Cut parts (A),(C),(E),(G),(H),(J),(K),(L),(M). Figs. 3, 4, 5, 6, 7, 8, 9, 10, 11.

2. Outline edges of all parts with edge creaser. Figs. 3, 4, 5, 6, 7, 8, 9, 10, 11.

3. Cement (M) to (L). Figs. 2, 3.

4. Punch closely spaced stitching holes through (ML) on crease line of (M). Fig. 2.

5. Sew (M) to (L) with saddle stitch. Figs. 1, 2.

6. Cut slots for prongs of buckles (I),(F) and (D) in square ends of (J),(K) and (C) respectively. Figs. 4, 6, 7.

7. Punch holes with revolving punch for prongs of (I),(F) and (D) in pointed ends of (H),(K) and (C) respectively. Figs. 5, 6, 7.

8. Insert (I),(F) and (D) in folded ends of (J),(K) and (C). Punch double row of stitching holes, 1/8" apart, through folded ends of (J),(K) and (C). Figs. 4, 6, 7.

9. Sew with saddler's stitch. Fig. 2.

10. Fold ends of (LM) and (G) over parts (H). Fig. 2.

11. Mark stitching holes with 1/7" spacing wheel, 1" from folded edge, on (LM) and (G). Figs. 9, 10.

12. Punch stitching holes through folded (LM) and (G). Figs. 9, 10.

13. Sew with saddler's stitch. Fig. 2.

14. Fold ends of parts (H) and (J) over (K). Fig. 2.

15. Mark closely spaced stitching holes 1-3/8" from folded edge of (H) and (J). Figs. 4, 5.

16. Punch stitching holes through folds of (H) and (J). Figs. 4, 5.

17. Sew with saddler's stitch. Fig. 2.

18. Place parts (E) in position on (K), allowing fullness to accommodate rings (B). Figs. 2, 11.

19. Punch double row of closely spaced stitching holes through (K) and ends of (E). Figs. 7, 11.

20. Insert (B); stitch parts (E) to (K) with saddler's stitch. Fig. 2.

21. Fold ends of (A). Punch double row of closely spaced stitching holes through folded ends, 1/2" from folded edge. Figs. 2, 8.

22. Insert (B); stitch ends of (A) with saddler's stitch. Fig. 2.

23. Insert parts (C) through rings (B) on ends of (A) and rings attached to (K) by (E). Fig. 2.

24. Fasten all buckles. Figs. 1, 2.

MATERIALS:

Calfskin, 3 - 3-1/2 oz.

Scrap leather, bright color for duck

Rubber cement

Heavy linen thread

Four metal rings, 1" diameter

Buckles, 4 - 3/4", 1 - 1", center bar

TOOLS:

(1), (6), (8), (25), (27), (28), (30), (41).

Toy Belt and Holster

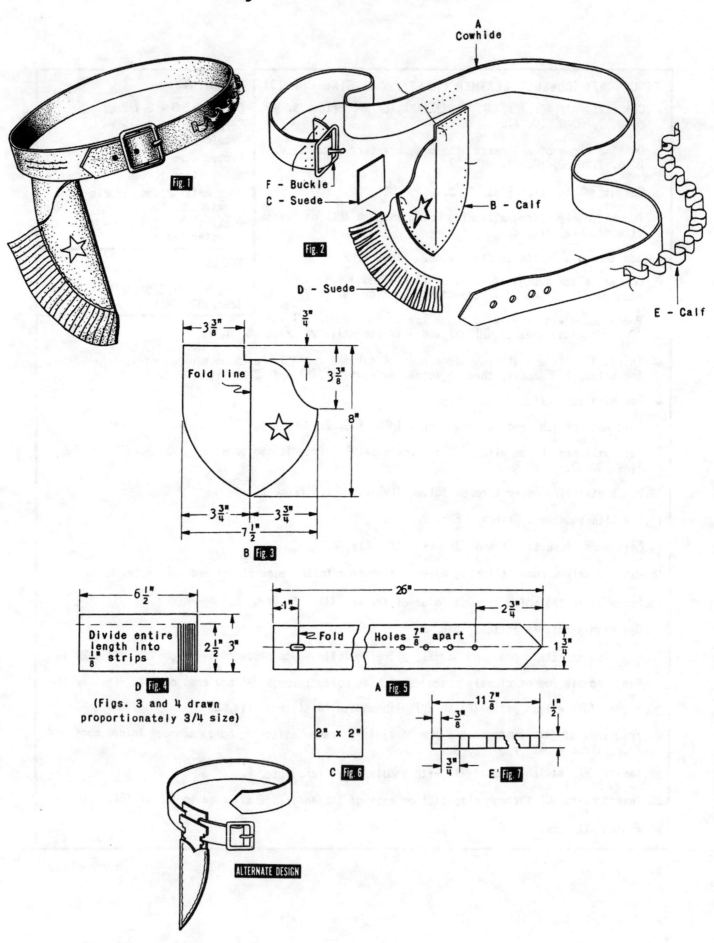

A
Cowhide

Fig. 1

F - Buckle
C - Suede

Fig. 2

B - Calf

D - Suede

E - Calf

3 3/8"

3/4"

3 3/8"

Fold line

8"

★

3 3/4"   3 3/4"

7 1/2"

B Fig. 3

6 1/2"

Divide entire
length into
1/8" strips

2 1/2"   3"

D Fig. 4

(Figs. 3 and 4 drawn
proportionately 3/4 size)

26"

1"

Fold   Holes 7/8" apart

2 3/4"

1 3/4"

A Fig. 5

2" x 2"

C Fig. 6

11 7/8"

1/2"

3/8"

3/4"

E Fig. 7

ALTERNATE DESIGN

PROCEDURE: (CONSULT LEATHER CRAFT PROCESSING CHARTS)

1. Cut parts (A), (B), (C), (D) and (E). Figs. 3, 4, 5, 6, 7.

2. Mark fold lines with edge creaser on (E). Fig. 7.

3. Adjust folds of (E) on (A), using paper clips to hold (E) to (A) between cartridge loops. Fig. 2.

4. Punch closely spaced stitching holes through (E) and (A) on fold lines. Fig. 2.

5. Sew with saddler's stitch in one continuous operation. Fig. 2.

6. Make cut-out of star in (B). Fig. 3.

7. Cement (C) of contrasting color to flesh side of edges of star cutout in (B). Fig. 2.

8. Cut fringe strips 2-1/2" long, 1/8" wide, on edge of (D). Fig. 4.

9. Cement uncut edge of (D) between curved edges of (B) and cement top end of (B) to (A). Fig. 2.

10. Mark stitching holes with 1/7" spacing wheel, 1/8" from edge of (B) on (D) and around end of (B) on flesh side of (A). Fig. 2.

11. Punch stitching holes with awl through (AE) and (BD). Fig. 2.

12. Sew with saddler's stitch. Fig. 2.

13. Cut slot for prong of buckle (F) in square end of (A), and punch holes in pointed end for prong. Fig. 5.

14. Insert (F) in slot and fold (A). Fig. 2.

15. Punch double row of closely spaced stitching holes through folded (A). Fig. 2.

16. Sew (A) with saddler's stitch. Fig. 2.

MATERIALS:	TOOLS:	For Detailed Instructions Consult
Cowhide, 5 oz.	(1), (6), (8), (17), (21), (25), (28), (30), (33), (41), (43).	Chart I - Cutting
Calf, 2 oz.		Chart II - Design
Suede, contrasting color		Chart III - Color
Buckle, center bar, 1-3/4"		Chart IV - Construction
Heavy linen thread		Chart V - Lacing
Rubber cement		Chart VI - Stitching
		Chart VII - Braiding
		Chart VIII - Knotting
		Material Chart

Western Belt & Cuff Set

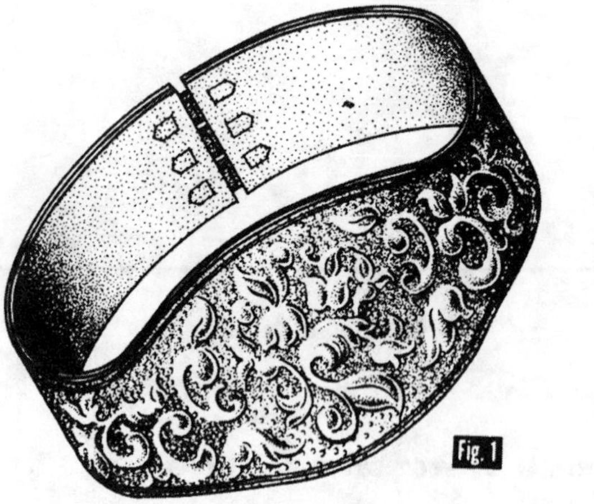

Fig. 1

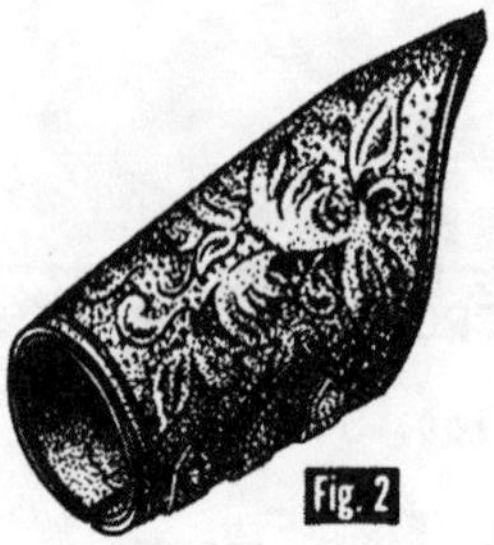

Fig. 2

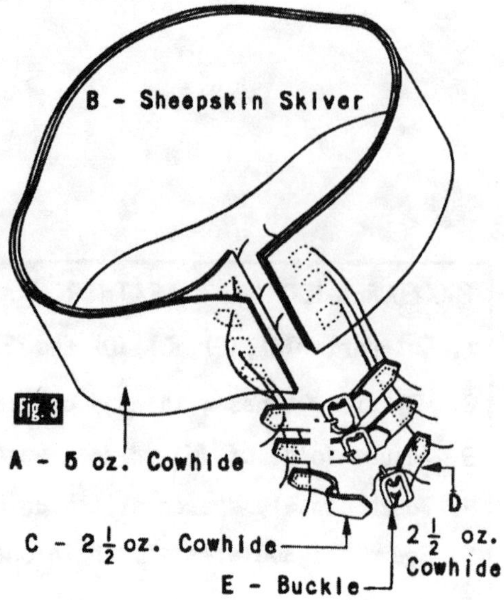
B - Sheepskin Skiver
A - 5 oz. Cowhide
D
C - 2 1/2 oz. Cowhide
2 1/2 oz. Cowhide
E - Buckle

Fig. 3

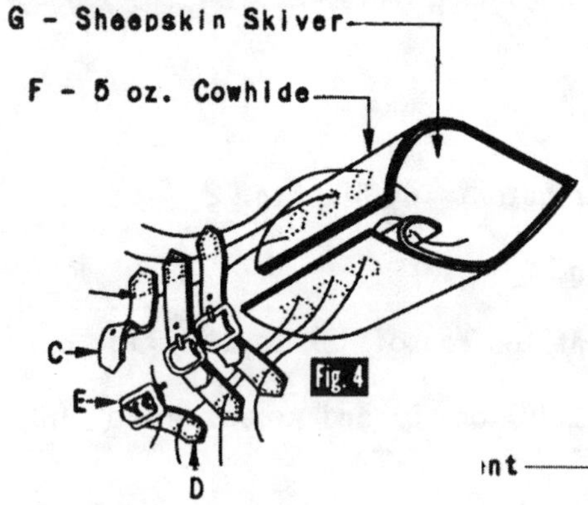
G - Sheepskin Skiver
F - 5 oz. Cowhide
C
E
D

Fig. 4

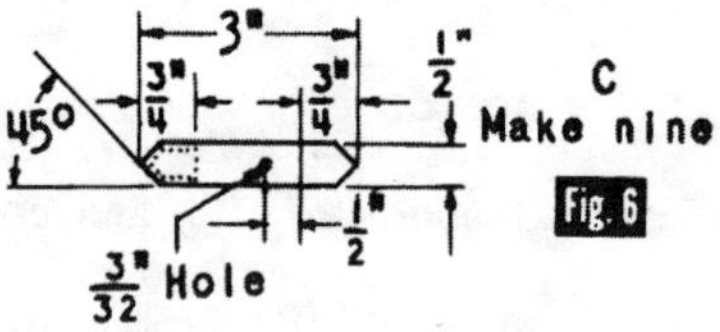
3"
3/4"
3/4"
1/2"
45°
C
Make nine
1/2"
3/32" Hole

Fig. 6

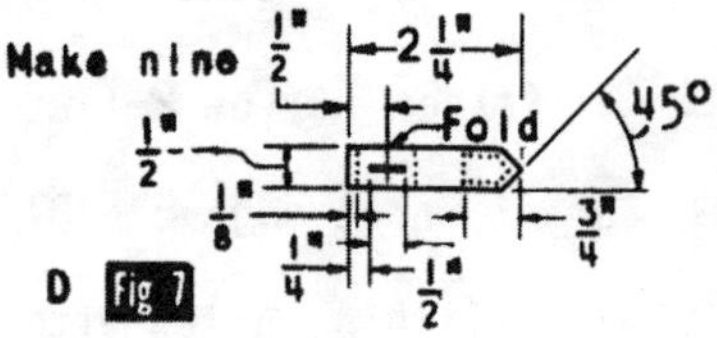
Make nine 1/2"
2 1/4"
1/2"
Fold
45°
1/8"
3/4"
1"/4
1/2"
D

Fig 7

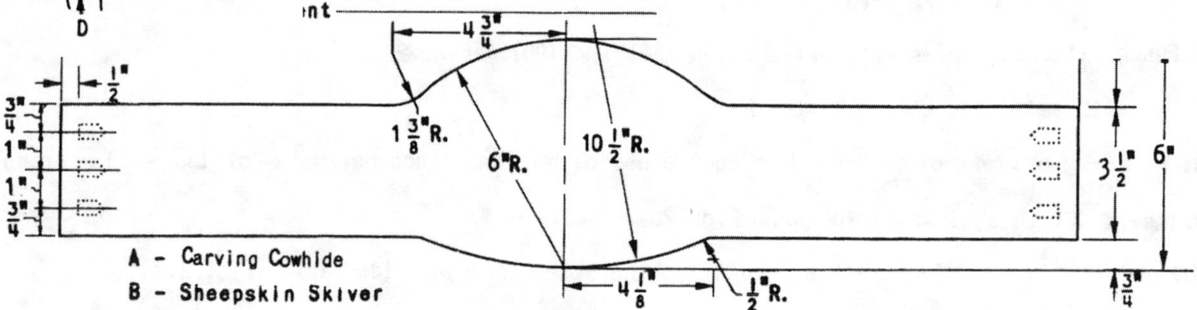
4 3/4"
1/2"
3/4"
1"
1"
3/4"
1 3/8"R.
6"R.
10 1/2"R.
3 1/2"
6"
4 1/8"
1/2"R.
3/4"
A - Carving Cowhide
B - Sheepskin Skiver

Fig. 5

Note: Cut linings (B) and (G) for (A) and (F) after carving is completed.

Design pattern for belt and cuffs

F - Carved Cowhide (Make two
G - Sheepskin Skiver of each)

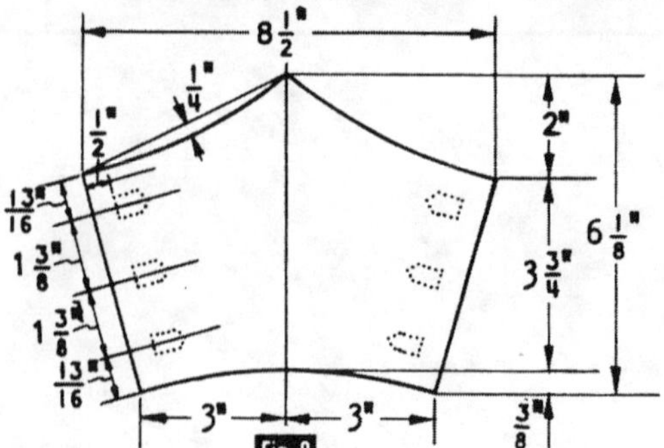
8 1/2"
1/4"
1/2"
2"
13/16"
1 3/8"
1 3/8"
13/16"
3 3/4"
6 1/8"
3"
3"
3/8"

Fig. 8

PROCEDURE:
(CONSULT LEATHER CRAFT PROCESSING CHARTS)

1. Cut and prepare parts (A), (B), (C), (D), (F), (G). Figs. 5, 6, 7, 8.

2. Bevel all edges of (A) and (F). Figs. 5, 8.

3. Cement (B) to (A) and (G) to (F). Figs. 3, 4.

4. Make slit in (D) for prong of buckle (E). Fig. 7.

5. Insert (E) in (D). Fold back end of (D). Figs. 3, 4.

6. With awl, punch double row of closely spaced stitching holes through fold of (D). Fig. 7.

7. Sew fold of (D) with saddler's stitch. Figs. 3, 4.

8. Place (C) and (D) in position on (AB) and (GF). Figs. 3, 4, 5, 8.

9. With awl, punch closely spaced stitching holes simultaneously through matching parts of (C) and (D) on (AB) and (GF). Figs. 5, 6, 7, 8.

10. Sew (C) and (D) to (AB) and (GF) with saddler's stitch. Figs. 3, 4.

11. With revolving punch, punch holes in (C) to fit prong of (E). Figs. 3, 4, 6.

MATERIALS:

Carving cowhide, 5 oz.

Cowhide, 2-1/2 oz. for straps

Sheepskin skiver

Nine 3/4" buckles

Rubber cement

Heavy linen thread

TOOLS:

(1), (6), (8), (17), (21), (25) (29), (30), (33), (41), (43).

For Detailed Instructions Consult

Chart I - Cutting
Chart II - Design
Chart III - Color
Chart IV - Construction
Chart V - Lacing
Chart VI - Stitching
Chart VII - Braiding
Chart VIII - Knotting

Material Chart

Woman's Belt

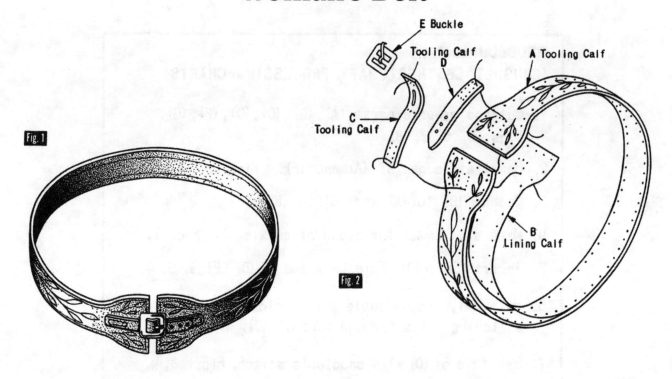

Fig. 1

Fig. 2

E Buckle
Tooling Calf
A Tooling Calf
D
C
Tooling Calf
B
Lining Calf

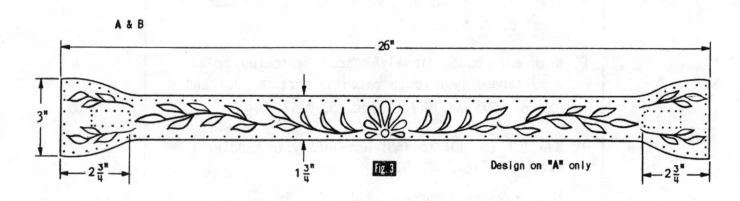

A & B

26"

3"

2 3/4"

1 3/4"

Fig. 3

Design on "A" only

2 3/4"

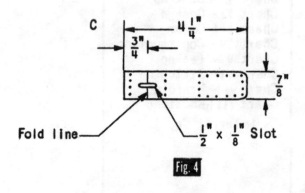

C

4 1/4"

3/4"

7/8"

Fold line

1/2" x 1/8" Slot

Fig. 4

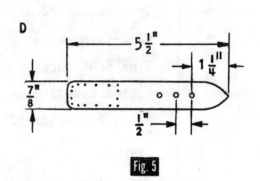

D

5 1/2"

1 1/4"

7/8"

1/2"

Fig. 5

PROCEDURE: (CONSULT LEATHER CRAFT PROCESSING CHARTS)

1. Cut and prepare parts (A), (B), (C) and (D). Figs. 3, 4, 5.

2. Cement (B) to (A). Fig. 2.

3. With $\frac{1}{7}''$ spacing wheel, mark stitching holes $\frac{1}{8}''$ from edge around all edges of (AB). Fig. 3.

4. With awl, punch stitching holes on (AB). Fig. 3.

5. Sew (AB) with saddler's stitch. Fig. 2.

6. Turn back to flesh side $\frac{3}{4}''$ buckle end of (C). Cut slot on fold for prong of (E). Fig. 4.

7. With awl, punch $\frac{1}{8}''$ stitching holes $\frac{1}{8}''$ from edge where buckle fold is sewn. Fig. 4.

8. Insert (E) and sew in place with saddler's stitch. Fig. 2.

9. With No. 3. tube, punch holes for prong of (C) in (D). Fig. 5.

10. Place (CE) and (D) in position on (AB). With $\frac{1}{7}''$ spacing wheel, mark stitching holes on (CE) and (D) where they are sewn to (AB). Figs. 3, 4, 5.

11. With awl, punch stitching holes simultaneously through (CE) and (AB), and (D) and (AB). Figs. 3, 4, 5.

12. Sew (CE) and (D) to (AB) with saddler's stitch. Fig. 2.

MATERIALS:	TOOLS:
Russia tooling calf	(1), (6), (8), (17), (20), (21), (25), (28), (30), (41).
Lining calf	
Rubber cement	**For Detailed Instructions Consult**
1" buckle, center bar	Chart I – Cutting
Heavy linen thread	Chart II – Design
	Chart III – Color
	Chart IV – Construction
	Chart V – Lacing
	Chart VI – Stitching
	Chart VII – Braiding
	Chart VIII – Knotting
	Material Chart

Woman's Crushed Belt

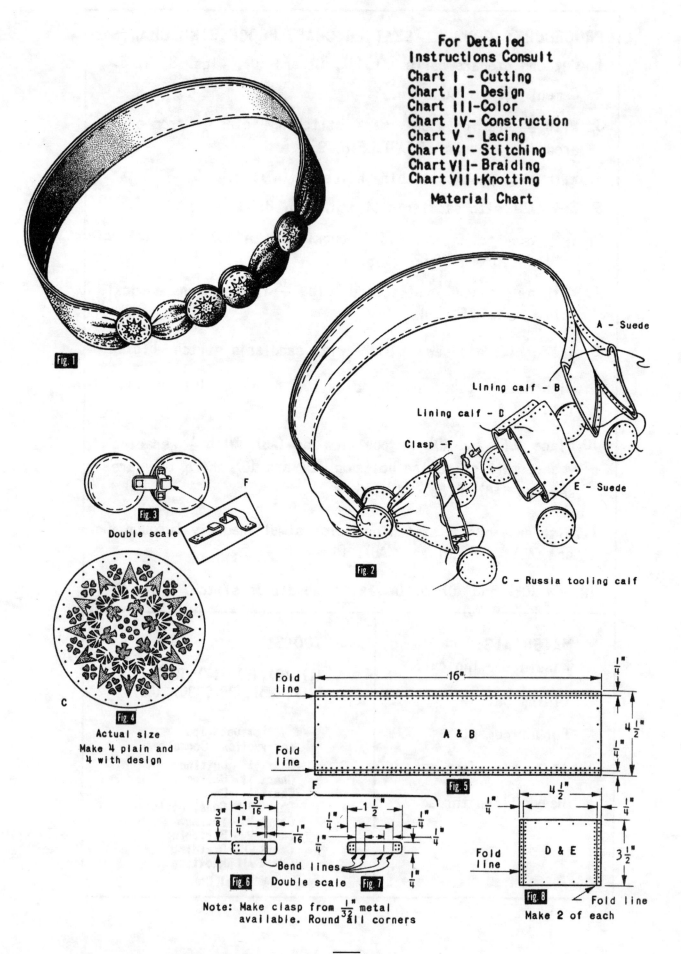

For Detailed
Instructions Consult
Chart I - Cutting
Chart II - Design
Chart III - Color
Chart IV - Construction
Chart V - Lacing
Chart VI - Stitching
Chart VII - Braiding
Chart VIII - Knotting
Material Chart

Fig. 1

A - Suede

Lining calf - B

Lining calf - D

Clasp - F

E - Suede

Fig. 2

C - Russia tooling calf

Fig. 3
Double scale

F

C

Fig. 4
Actual size
Make 4 plain and
4 with design

Fold line

16"

A & B

Fold line

Fig. 5

4½"

¼"

¼"

¼"

F

⅜"

1 5/16"

¼"

1/16"

¼"

1½"

¼"

¼"

¼"

Bend lines

Fig. 6   Double scale   Fig. 7

¼"

Note: Make clasp from 1/32" metal
available. Round all corners

¼"

4½"

¼"

Fold line

D & E

3½"

Fig. 8

Fold line

Make 2 of each

PROCEDURE:
(CONSULT LEATHER CRAFT PROCESSING CHARTS)

1. Cut and prepare (A), (B), (C), (D) and (E). Figs. 4, 5, 8.

2. Turn back 1/4" on long sides of (A) and (B), and short sides of (D) and (E). Figs. 5, 8.

3. Place (A) to (B) and (E) to (D) with turned back edges facing. Cement. Fig. 2.

4. With 1/7" spacing wheel, mark stitching holes 1/8" from top and bottom edges of (A) on (B) and (E) on (D). Figs. 2, 5, 8.

5. With awl, punch stitching holes through marked edges of (A) and (B), and (E) and (D). Figs. 5, 8.

6. Sew (A) to (B) and (E) to (D) with saddle stitch. Fig. 2.
   Note: If saddle stitching is not desired, stitch on sewing machine without punching holes with awl.

7. Gather ends of (AB) and (DE) with short running stitch to a width of 1-1/4". Figs. 1, 2.

8. Sew (F) to skin side of 2 plain (C) for front fastening. Figs. 2, 3, 6, 7.

9. Place stamped (C) to matching plain (C), flesh sides together. Mark 1/8" stitching holes 1/8" from edge of stamped (C). Fig. 4.

10. With awl, punch stitching holes on (C). Fig. 4.

11. Sew (C) to (C) with saddle stitch, including the inserted ends of (AB) and (DE) at their respective positions. Fig. 2.

MATERIALS:	TOOLS:
Suede, light-weight	(6), (21), (25), (28), (33), (41).
Lining calf, 1 oz.	Stamps: 38-1, -9, -14, -28, -31
Russia tooling calf, 2-1/2" oz.	
One metal clasp	
Linen thread	

Woman's Belt

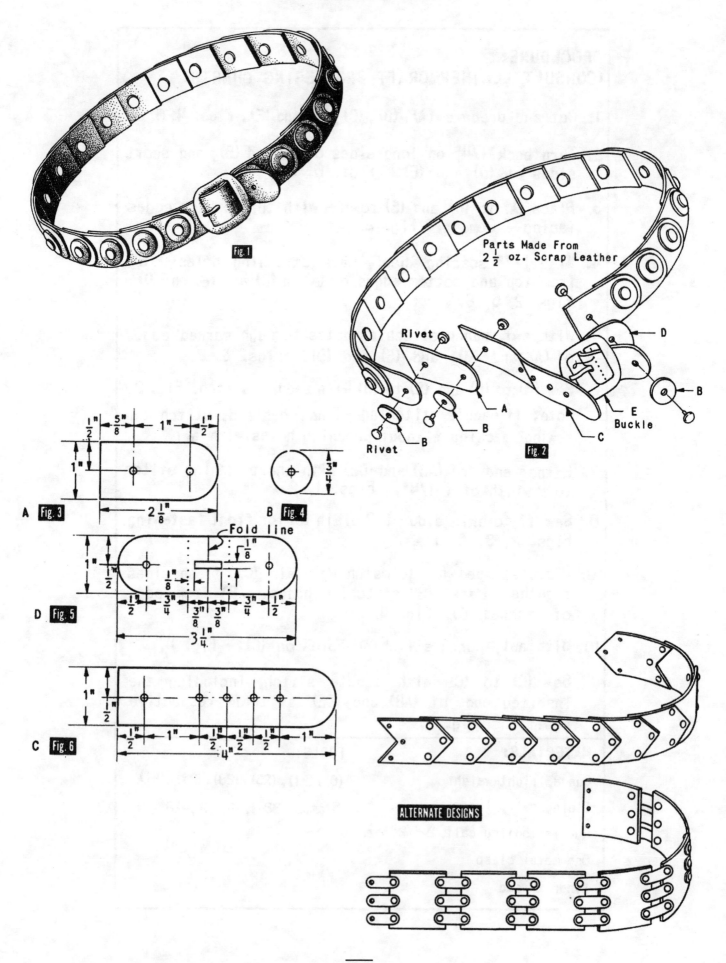

Fig.1

Parts Made From
2½ oz. Scrap Leather

Rivet

Rivet

A

B

B

C

D

E
Buckle

B

Fig. 2

A **Fig. 3**

B **Fig. 4**

Fold line

D **Fig. 5**

C **Fig. 6**

ALTERNATE DESIGNS

PROCEDURE: (CONSULT LEATHER CRAFT PROCESSING CHARTS)

1. Cut parts (A), (B), (C), (D). Figs. 3, 4, 5, 6.

2. Cement (B) to (A) on all links. Figs. 3, 4.

3. With No. 4 tube, punch holes for prong of buckle (E) in (C). Fig. 6.

4. Place (AB) in position on (C). With drive punch, punch hole for rivet in size desired through matching parts of (AB) and (C). Figs. 2, 6.

5. Insert rivet through (AB) and (C). Fig. 2.

6. With drive punch, punch hole for rivets through each (AB) and succeeding (AB). Figs. 2, 3.

7. Rivet links (AB) together. Continue to desired length of belt. Fig. 2.

8. Cut slot in (D) for prong of (E). Fig. 5.

9. Insert (E) in (D), and fold. Figs. 2, 5.

10. With awl, punch 1/8" stitching holes through folded parts of (D).

11. Sew (D) with saddler's stitch. Fig. 2.

12. Place (DE) in position on last (AB) and attach with rivet as before. Fig. 2.

For Detailed
Instructions Consult
Chart I – Cutting
Chart II – Design
Chart III – Color
Chart IV – Construction
Chart V – Lacing
Chart VI – Stitching
Chart VII – Braiding
Chart VIII – Knotting
Material Chart

MATERIALS:

Scrap leather

calfskin 2-1/2 oz.

sheepskin 2-1/2 oz.

cowhide 2-1/2-3 oz.

Rivets, size optional

Buckle, 1" center bar

TOOLS:

(3), (6), (8), (17), (24), (25), (30), (33), (41), (43).

Man's Belt

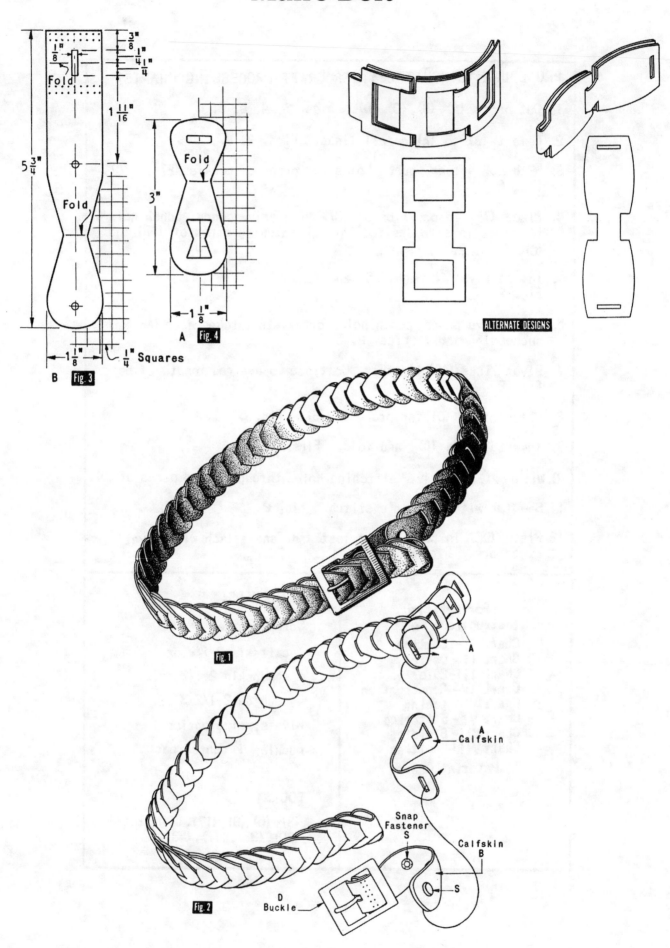

$\frac{3}{8}$"
$\frac{1}{8}$"
$\frac{1}{4}$"
$\frac{1}{4}$"

Fold

$1\frac{11}{16}$"

$5\frac{3}{4}$"

Fold

3"

Fold

$1\frac{1}{8}$"

A   **Fig. 4**

$1\frac{1}{8}$" $\frac{1}{4}$" Squares

B   **Fig. 3**

ALTERNATE DESIGNS

Fig. 1

A

A
Calfskin

Snap
Fastener
S

Calfskin
B

S

D
Buckle

Fig. 2

PROCEDURE:
(CONSULT LEATHER CRAFT PROCESSING CHARTS)

1. Cut parts (A) and (B). Count eight complete links (A) for 6" span of belt. Figs. 3, 4.

2. Cut slot in (B) for prong of buckle (D). Fig. 3.

3. Fold back end of (B). With awl, punch 1/8" stitching holes through fold of (B). Figs. 2, 3.

4. Insert (D) in (B) and sew with saddler's stitch. Fig. 2.

5. Insert snap fastener (S) in (B). Figs. 2, 3.

6. Fold (A), flesh sides facing, with single slot meeting top of large cutout. Fig. 4.

7. Insert second link (A) through opening formed by slot and top of cutout of first part (A). Fold in place. Fig. 2.

8. Insert third link (A) through opening formed by slot and cutout of second link (A) and bottom of cutout of first link (A). Fig. 2.

9. Continue in turn with rest of links (A). Fig. 2.

10. When desired length is reached, insert (B) through opening of last two links and snap in place. Figs. 2, 3.

MATERIALS:

Calfskin, 2-1/2 oz.
(Scrap leather of one color or assorted)

Buckle, 1-1/8",
center bar

Snap fastener

Heavy linen thread

TOOLS:

(1), (6), (8), (12), (17), (25), (33), (41).

For Detailed
Instructions Consult
Chart I - Cutting
Chart II - Design
Chart III - Color
Chart IV - Construction
Chart V - Lacing
Chart VI - Stitching
Chart VII - Braiding
Chart VIII - Knotting
Material Chart

Woman's Belt

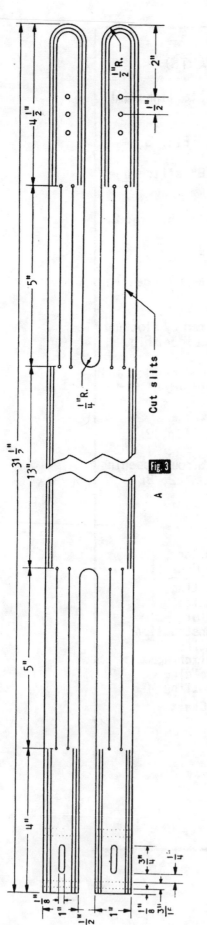

4½"

2"

1"R.
2

1½"

5"

Cut slits

1"R.
4

31½"

13"

A

Fig. 3

5"

4"

3"
4

1¼"

1"
8 4

1"
2

1"
2

1"

1"
8

3"
4

Fig. 1

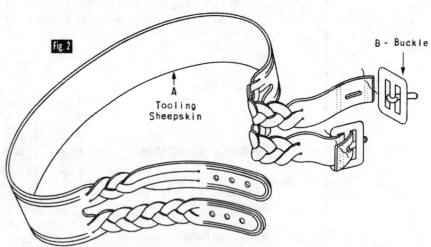

Fig. 2

A
Tooling
Sheepskin

B - Buckle

This belt is for a 26" waist.

For larger waists increase 13" dimension.

PROCEDURE: (CONSULT LEATHER CRAFT PROCESSING CHARTS)

1. Cut (A). Fig. 3.

2. Using double-edged creaser, outline all unbraided edges of (A). Figs. 2, 3.

3. Cut 5" slits in (A) as shown. Fig. 3.

4. Braid slit sections of (A). Figs. 2, 3 and **Leather** Chart VII.

5. Using No. 3 tube, punch holes for prongs of buckles (B) in rounded ends of (A). Fig. 3.

6. Cut slits in square ends of (A) for prongs of (B). Fig. 3.

7. Insert (B) and fold back end of (A). Figs. 2, 3.

8. With awl, punch double row of closely spaced stitching holes through folded end of (A). Fig. 3.

9. Sew with saddler's stitch. Fig. 2.

MATERIALS:

Tooling Sheepskin $2\frac{1}{2}$ oz.

Two buckles, 1", center bar

Heavy linen thread

TOOLS:

(6), (8), (20), (25), (27), (30), (33), (41).

See **Leather** Chart VII for details of braid.

For Detailed
Instructions Consult
Chart I - Cutting
Chart II - Design
Chart III - Color
Chart IV - Construction
Chart V - Lacing
Chart VI - Stitching
Chart VII - Braiding
Chart VIII - Knotting
Material Chart

Woman's Belt

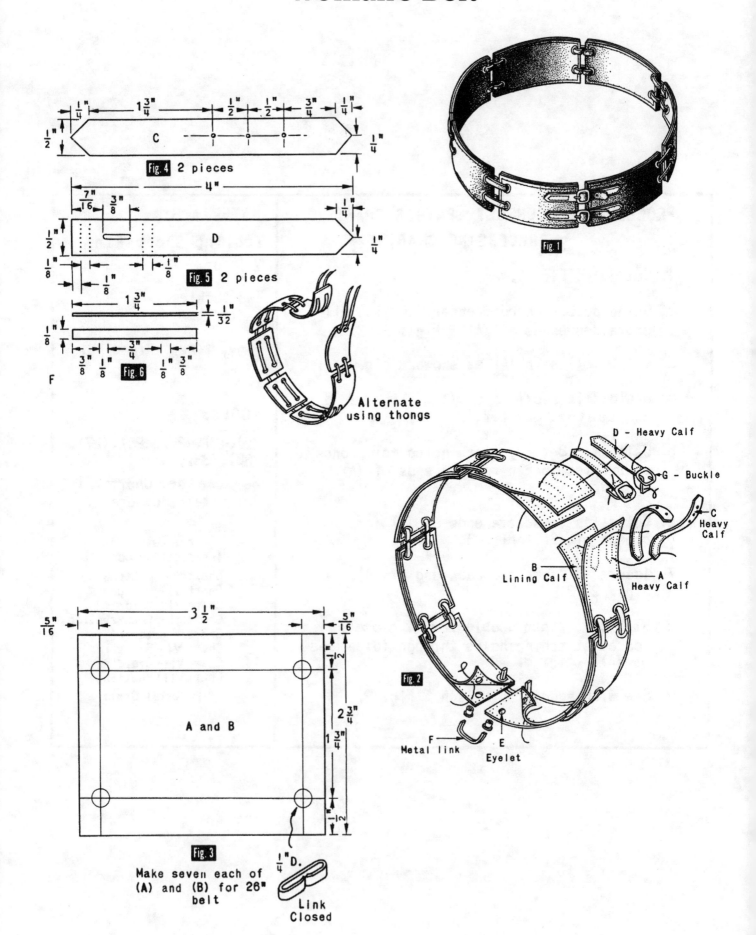

Fig. 4 2 pieces

C

Fig. 5 2 pieces

D

Fig. 6

F

Alternate using thongs

Fig. 1

D – Heavy Calf

G – Buckle

C Heavy Calf

B Lining Calf

A Heavy Calf

Fig. 2

F → Metal link

E Eyelet

A and B

Fig. 3

Make seven each of (A) and (B) for 26" belt

Link Closed

¼" D.

PROCEDURE: (CONSULT LEATHER CRAFT PROCESSING CHARTS)

1. Cut parts (A), (B), (C) and (D). Figs. 3, 4, 5.

2. Cement parts (B) to parts (A). Fig. 2.

3. With edge creaser, outline all edges of (A), (C) and (D). Fig. 2.

4. Using crease lines for guide, stitch (A) to (B) on sewing machine. Fig. 2.

5. Mark eyelet holes in (AB). Using a drive punch, punch holes as marked. Figs. 2, 3.

6. Set eyelets (E) in punched holes. Fig. 2.

7. Attach metal links (F) to eyelets. Figs. 1, 2.

8. Cut slot for prong of buckle (G) in square end of (D). Insert (G) in place. Fig. 5.

9. Fold end of (D). With awl, punch double row of closely spaced stitching holes through folded parts of (D). Figs. 2, 5.

10. Sew fold of (D) with saddler's stitch. Fig. 2.

11. With revolving punch, punch holes in one end of (C) for prong of (E). Fig. 4.

12. Place (C) and (D) in position on (AB). Using crease lines as guide, sew (C) and (D) to (AB) on sewing machine. Fig. 2

MATERIALS:

Heavy calfskin

Lining calf

24 No. 6 K eyelets

2 - 1/2" buckles , center bar

12 - 5/8" metal belt loops or links

TOOLS:

(1), (3, No. 7), (6), (14), (17), (25), (27), (30), (33), (41), (43).

For Detailed
Instructions Consult
Chart I - Cutting
Chart II - Design
Chart III - Color
Chart IV - Construction
Chart V - Lacing
Chart VI - Stitching
Chart VII - Braiding
Chart VIII - Knotting
Material Chart

Woman's Belt

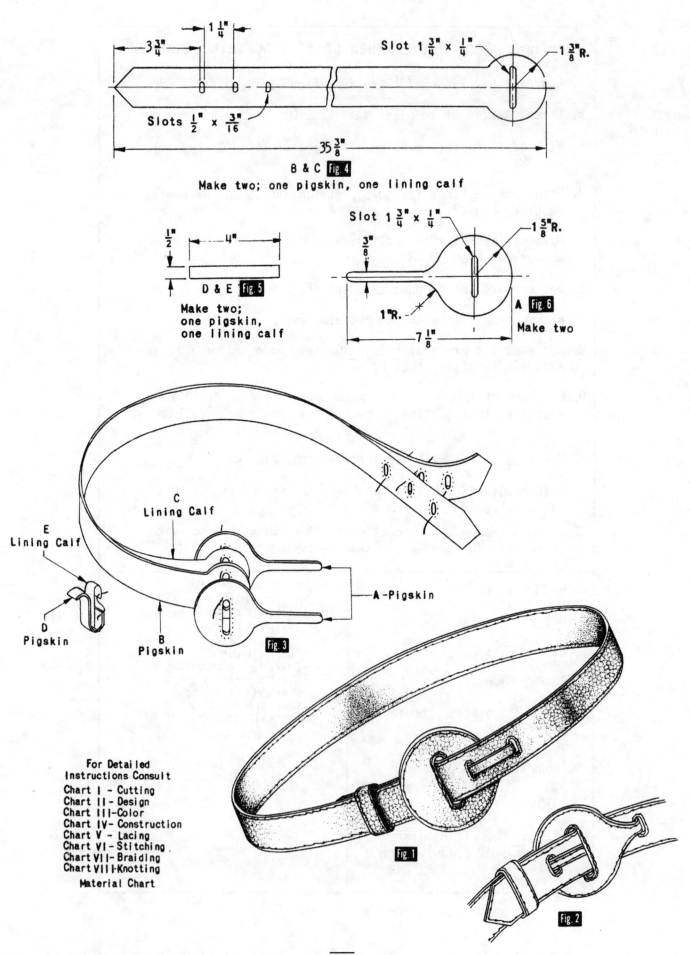

3 3/4"

1 1/4"

Slot 1 3/4" x 1/4"

1 3/8" R.

Slots 1/2" x 3/16"

35 3/8"

B & C **Fig. 4**

Make two; one pigskin, one lining calf

1/2"

4"

D & E **Fig. 5**

Make two;
one pigskin,
one lining calf

Slot 1 3/4" x 1/4"

1 5/8" R.

3/8"

1" R.

7 1/8"

A **Fig. 6**

Make two

C
Lining Calf

E
Lining Calf

D
Pigskin

B
Pigskin

A-Pigskin

Fig. 3

For Detailed
Instructions Consult
Chart I – Cutting
Chart II – Design
Chart III – Color
Chart IV – Construction
Chart V – Lacing
Chart VI – Stitching
Chart VII – Braiding
Chart VIII – Knotting
Material Chart

Fig. 1

Fig. 2

PROCEDURE:

(CONSULT LEATHER CRAFT PROCESSING CHARTS)

1. Cut parts (C), (D) and (E). Figs. 4, 5, 6.

2. Cement (C) to (B) and (E) to (D) flesh sides together. Fig. 3.

3. Cement parts (A) to (BC). Cement tabs of (A) together, skirt sides out. Fig. 3.

4. Mark slot on (A) and slots for tab of (A) on (BC). Figs. 3, 4, 6.

5. Cut slots marked on (A) and (BC). Figs. 3, 4, 6.

6. Outline slots and all edges to be stitched with edge creaser, including edges of (DE). Fig. 1.

7. Mark 1/7" stitching holes around all slots. Fig. 3.

8. Punch stitching holes around slots with awl. Fig. 3.

9. Stitch around all slots with saddler's stitch. Figs. 1, 3.

10. Stitch all remaining edges, and (DE) on sewing machine, using creased line as guide. Figs. 1, 2, 3.

11. Overlap ends of (DE) and stitch with saddler's stitch. Fig. 3.

12. Slip (DE) over length of belt toward (A), for belt loop. Figs. 1, 3.

MATERIALS:

Pigskin or calfskin, 2-1/2 oz.
Lining calf, 1-1/2 oz.
Rubber cement
Linen thread

TOOLS:

(1), (6), (17), (25), (27), (28), (33), (41), (43).

Book Jacket

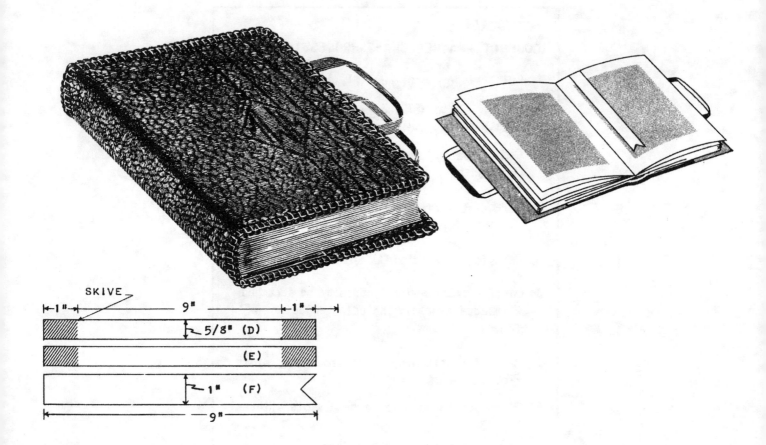

SKIVE

1" ← 9" → 1"

5/8" (D)

(E)

1" (F)

9"

PROCEDURE:
HAVING PREPARED THE SIX SEPARATE
PARTS...
(1) LOCATE AND CEMENT (D)&(E) ON
    FLESH SIDE OF (A)
(2) LOCATE (B)&(C) ON (A) FLESH
    SIDES TOGETHER, AND SLIGHTLY
    ROUND CORNERS.
(3) PUNCH 3/32" THONG SLITS 1/8"
    FROM EDGES AND LACE.

TOOLS:
(1)(2)(4)(5)(6)(9)(10)(11)(13)
(15)(17)

MATERIALS:
CONSULT LEATHER CHART
RUBBER CEMENT

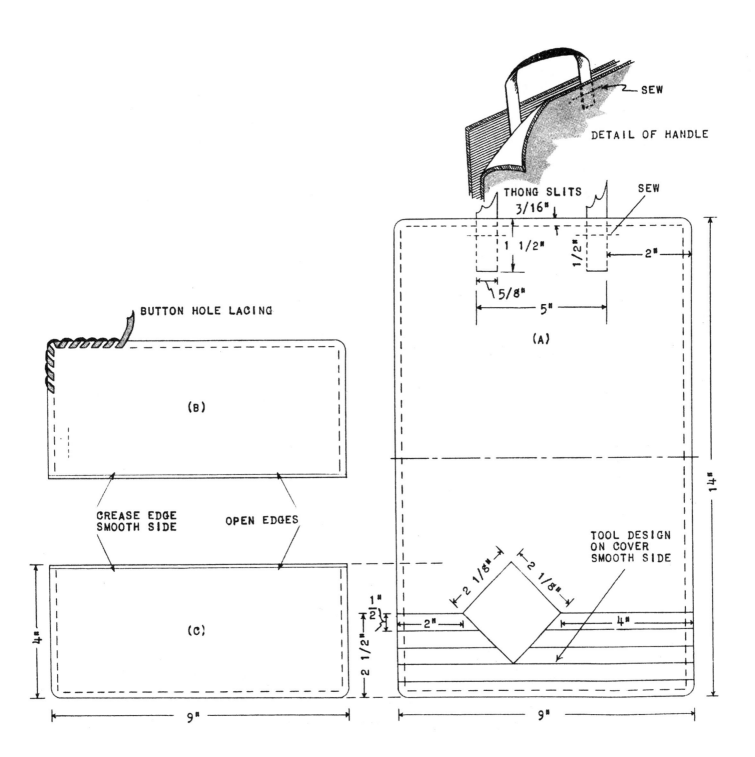

DETAIL OF HANDLE

SEW

THONG SLITS
3/16"

SEW

1 1/2"

1/2"

2"

5/8"

5"

(A)

BUTTON HOLE LACING

(B)

CREASE EDGE
SMOOTH SIDE

OPEN EDGES

(C)

TOOL DESIGN
ON COVER
SMOOTH SIDE

2 1/8"

2 1/8"

1"

2 1/2"

2"

4"

4"

9"

14"

9"

Book Ends

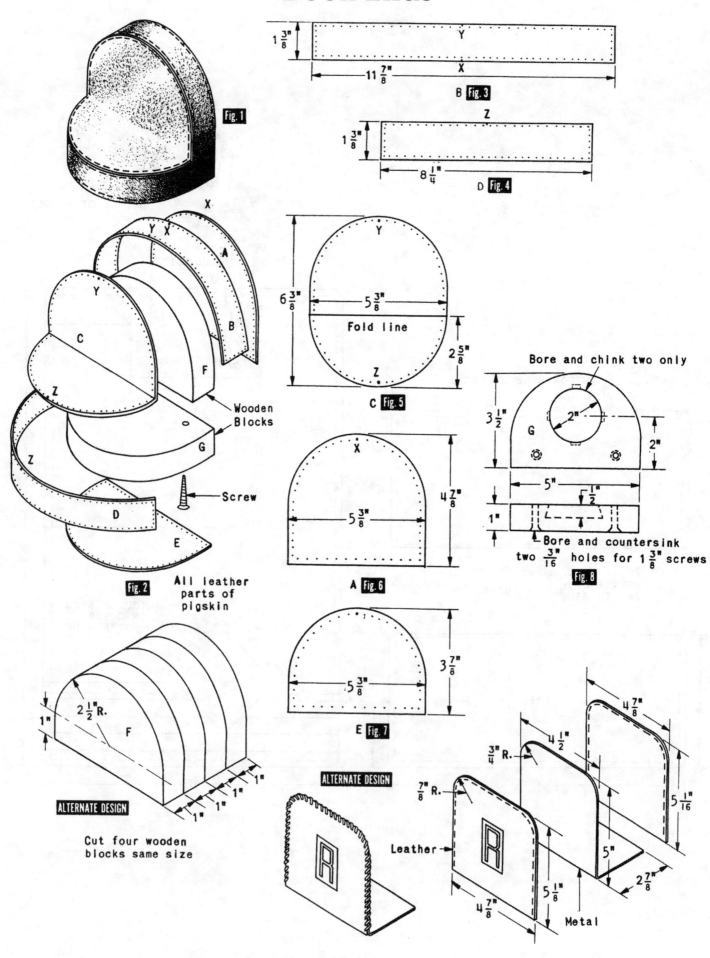

Fig. 1

B Fig. 3

$1\frac{3}{8}"$

Y

X

$11\frac{7}{8}"$

Z

$1\frac{3}{8}"$

$8\frac{1}{4}"$

D Fig. 4

X

Y X

A

B

F

Y

C

Z

Wooden Blocks

Z

G

Screw

D

E

Fig. 2

All leather parts of pigskin

Y

$6\frac{3}{8}"$

$5\frac{3}{8}"$

Fold line

$2\frac{5}{8}"$

Z

C Fig. 5

X

$5\frac{3}{8}"$

$4\frac{7}{8}"$

A Fig. 6

$5\frac{3}{8}"$

$3\frac{7}{8}"$

E Fig. 7

Bore and chink two only

$3\frac{1}{2}"$

G

$2"$

$2"$

$5"$

$\frac{1}{2}"$

$1"$

Bore and countersink two $\frac{3}{16}"$ holes for $1\frac{3}{8}"$ screws

Fig. 8

$2\frac{1}{2}"$ R.

$1"$

F

ALTERNATE DESIGN

$1"$ $1"$ $1"$ $1"$

Cut four wooden blocks same size

ALTERNATE DESIGN

R

$\frac{7}{8}"$ R.

Leather

$\frac{3}{4}"$ R.

$4\frac{1}{2}"$

$4\frac{7}{8}"$

$5\frac{1}{16}"$

$5"$

$5\frac{1}{8}"$

$4\frac{7}{8}"$

$2\frac{7}{8}"$

Metal

PROCEDURE:
(CONSULT LEATHER CRAFT PROCESSING CHARTS)

1. Cut parts (A), (B), (C), (D) and (E).
   Figs. 3, 4, 5, 6, 7.

   Note: Construct weighted wooden forms (F) and (G).

2. Mark stitching holes with 1/7" spacing wheel, 1/8" from edge on all matching parts.
   Figs. 3, 4, 5, 6, 7, and Leather Chart V.

3. Punch holes with awl simultaneously through all matching parts. Fig. 2.

4. Saddle stitch top edge of (D) to front edge of (C) with points (Z) coinciding. Fig. 2.

5. Saddle stitch front edge of (B) to top edge of (C) with points (Y) coinciding. Fig. 2.

6. Saddle stitch back edge of (B) to (A) with points (X) coinciding. Fig. 2.

7. Fit assembled parts (ABCD) over book end form (FG). Fig. 2.

8. Saddle stitch (E) to (ABCD), sewing straight edge first. Fig. 2.

MATERIALS:

Pigskin, natural, 2-1/2 oz.

Heavy linen thread

TOOLS:

(1), (6), (25), (28), (41).

For Detailed
Instructions Consult

Chart I - Cutting
Chart II - Design
Chart III - Color
Chart IV - Construction
Chart V - Lacing
Chart VI - Stitching
Chart VII - Braiding
Chart VIII - Knotting
Material Chart

Book Marks

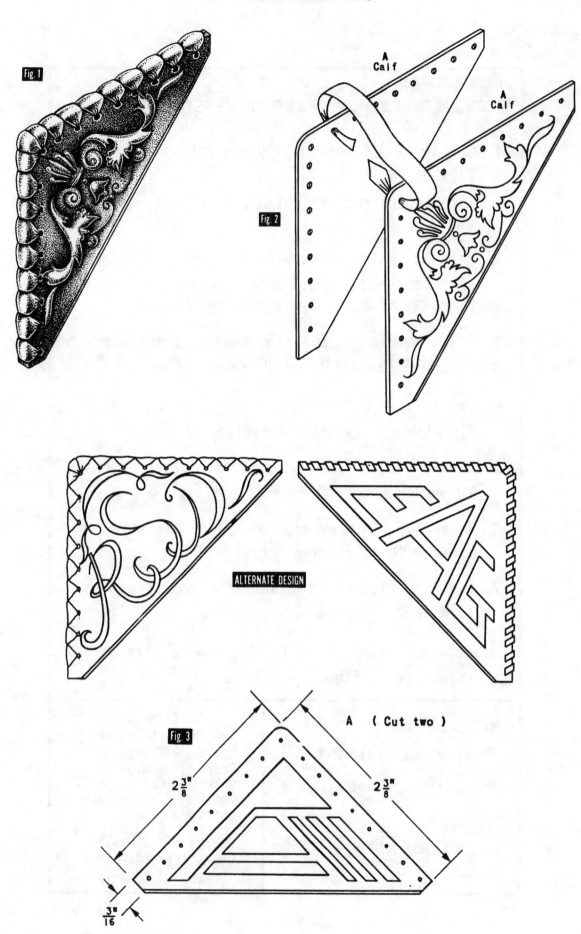

Fig. 1

Fig. 2

A
Calf

A
Calf

ALTERNATE DESIGN

Fig. 3

A (Cut two)

$2\frac{3}{8}$"

$2\frac{3}{8}$"

$\frac{3}{16}$"

PROCEDURE: (CONSULT LEATHER CRAFT PROCESSING CHARTS)

1. Cut and prepare (A), Fig. 3.

2. With edge creaser, outline diagonal edge of (A). Fig. 3.

3. Place (A) to (A), flesh sides together. Mark thong holes $\frac{1}{8}"$ from edge, $\frac{1}{4}"$ apart around square corner. Figs. 2, 3.

4. With $\frac{3}{32}"$ tube, punch thong holes in (A). Fig. 2.

5. Stitch (A) to (A) with Florentine lacing. Figs. 1, 2.

MATERIALS:

Russia tooling calf (scraps)

Florentine lacing, $\frac{3}{8}"$, 14" per corner

TOOLS:

(1), (6), (8).

For Detailed
Instructions Consult
Chart I - Cutting
Chart II - Design
Chart III - Color
Chart IV - Construction
Chart V - Lacing
Chart VI - Stitching
Chart VII - Braiding
Chart VIII - Knotting
Material Chart

Book Ends

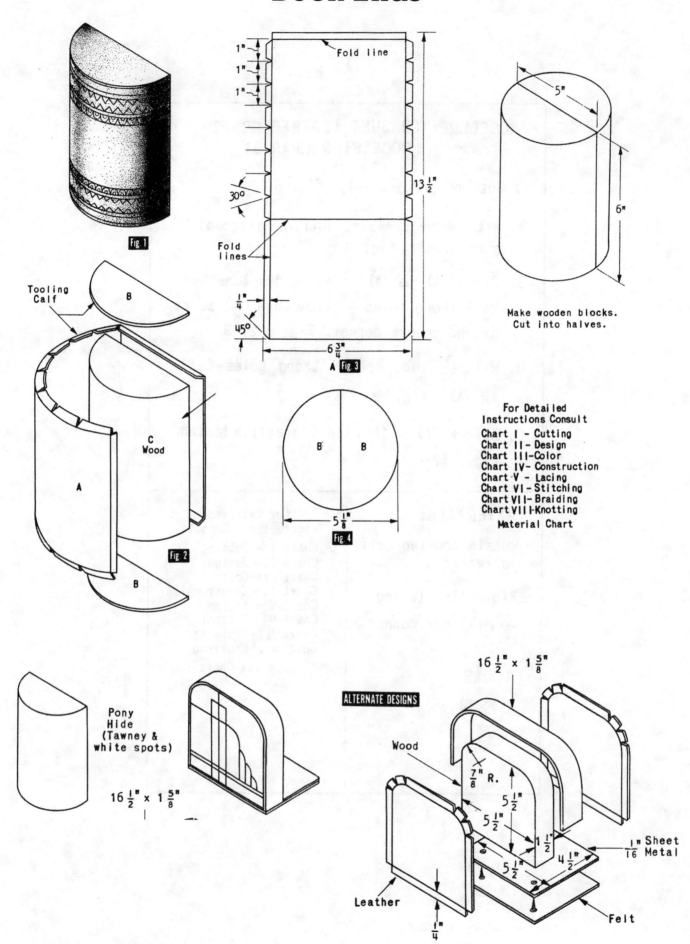

Fig. 1

Fold line

1"
1"
1"

30°

Fold lines

1/4"

45°

13 1/2"

6 3/4"

A Fig. 3

Tooling Calf

B

C
Wood

A

B

Fig. 2

B   B

5 1/8"

Fig. 4

5"

6"

Make wooden blocks.
Cut into halves.

For Detailed
Instructions Consult
Chart I – Cutting
Chart II – Design
Chart III – Color
Chart IV – Construction
Chart V – Lacing
Chart VI – Stitching
Chart VII – Braiding
Chart VIII – Knotting
Material Chart

Pony
Hide
(Tawney &
white spots)

16 1/2" x 1 5/8"

ALTERNATE DESIGNS

16 1/2" x 1 5/8"

Wood

7/8" R.

5 1/2"

5 1/2"

1 1/2"

5 1/2"

4 1/2"

1/16" Sheet Metal

Leather

1/4"

Felt

PROCEDURE:
(CONSULT LEATHER CRAFT PROCESSING CHARTS)

1. Cut and prepare parts (A) and (B). Figs. 3, 4.
   Note: Construct weighted wooden semi-cylindrical forms (C).

2. Skive all edges of (A) and (B). Figs. 3, 4.

3. Mark fold lines with edge creaser on (A).
   Outline edges of parts (B). Figs. 3, 4.

4. Cement 1/4" fold of (A), between notched edges, to vertical back edge of book end (C). Fig. 2.

5. Continue to cement (A) to rounded surface and back of (C), overlapping the 1/4" fold. Fig. 2.

6. Fold and cement top and bottom edges of (A) to top and base of (C). Fig. 2.

7. Cement parts (B) to top and base of (C). Fig. 2.

MATERIALS:
Russia tooling calfskin, 2 oz.

Pliobond cement

TOOLS:
(1), (6), (19), (27).

Brief Case

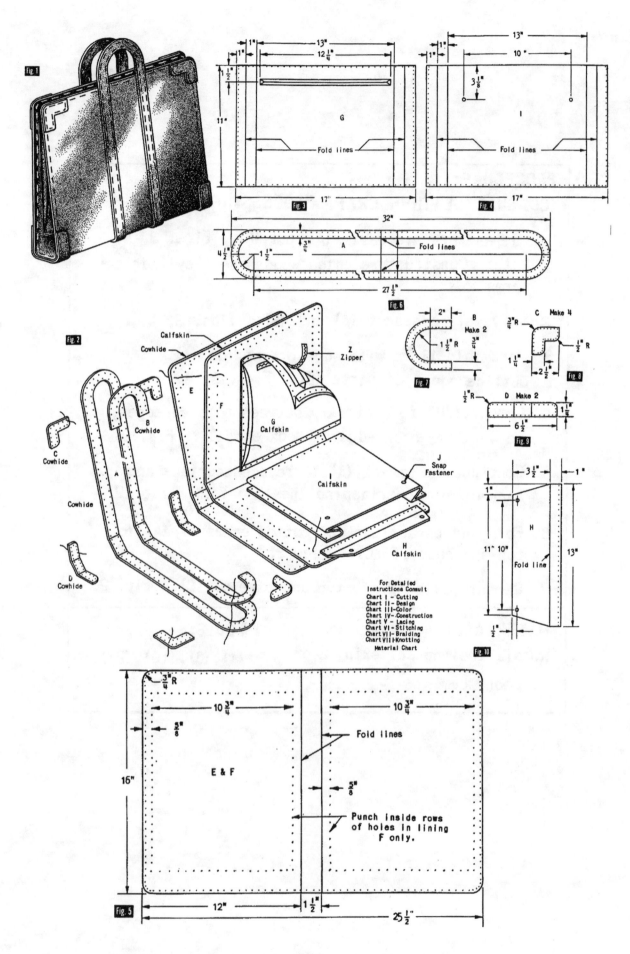

Fig. 1

Fig. 3

Fig. 4

Fig. 6

G

Fold lines

17"

I

Fold lines

17"

13"
12 1/4"
1"
1"
1 1/2"
11"

13"
10"
1"
1"
3 1/8"

32"
4 1/2"
1 1/2"
3/4"
A
Fold lines
27 1/2"

Fig. 7

B
Make 2
2"
1 1/2" R
3/4"

Fig. 8

C   Make 4
3/4" R
1/2" R
1 1/4"
2 1/2"

Fig. 9

D   Make 2
1/2" R
6 1/2"
1 1/8"

Fig. 2

Calfskin

Cowhide

Z
Zipper

E

F

G
Calfskin

I
Calfskin

B
Cowhide

A

Cowhide

C
Cowhide

D
Cowhide

J
Snap
Fastener

H
Calfskin

For Detailed
Instructions Consult
Chart I - Cutting
Chart II - Design
Chart III - Color
Chart IV - Construction
Chart V - Lacing
Chart VI - Stitching
Chart VII - Braiding
Chart VIII - Knotting
Material Chart

Fig. 10
3 1/2"
1"
1"
H
11" 10"
Fold line
13"
1/2"

Fig. 5
3/4" R
10 3/4"
10 3/4"
5/8"
Fold lines
5/8"
16"
E & F
Punch inside rows
of holes in lining
F only.
12"
1 1/2"
25 1/2"

PROCEDURE: (CONSULT LEATHER CRAFT PROCESSING CHARTS)

1. Cut and prepare parts (A), (B), (C), (D), (E), (F), (G), (H) and (I). Figs. 3, 4, 5, 6, 7, 8, 9, 10.

2. With edge creaser, mark folds in parts (A), (D), (E), (F), (G), (H) and (I). Figs. 2, 3, 4, 5, 6, 9, 10.

3. Cement parts (B) to part (A), and parts (AB), (C) and (D) to part (E). With $\frac{1}{7}$" spacing wheel, mark stitching holes, $\frac{1}{8}$" from inside edges of (C) and (D). Figs. 2, 8, 9.

4. With awl, punch stitching holes on inside edges only of parts (C) and (D). Figs. 2, 8, 9.

5. Saddle stitch these portions of (C) and (D) to (E). Fig. 2.

6. With $\frac{1}{7}$" spacing wheel, mark stitching holes, $\frac{1}{8}$" from edges on (ABE). With awl, punch stitching holes as marked. Figs. 2, 5, 6, 7.

7. Sew (ABE) together with saddle stitch. Figs. 1, 2.

8. Fold under edges of zipper slot in (G) and attach zipper (Z) with sewing machine. Figs. 2, 3.

9. Insert caps of snap fasteners (J) in (H). Figs. 2, 10.

10. Place (G) with gussets folded in place, on (F). With $\frac{1}{7}$" spacing wheel, mark stitching holes $\frac{1}{8}$" from edges of (G) as shown. With awl, punch stitching holes simultaneously through (G) and (F). Figs. 2, 3, 5.

11. Sew (G) to (F) with saddler's stitch or on sewing machine. Fig. 2.

12. With $\frac{1}{7}$" spacing wheel, mark stitching holes, $\frac{1}{8}$" from edge, in (H). Place (H) in position on (F) and punch stitching holes simultaneously through both parts. Figs. 2, 5, 10.

13. Sew (H) to (F) with saddler's stitch or on sewing machine. Fig. 2.

14. Place (I) with gussets folded in place, on (F). With $\frac{1}{7}$" spacing wheel, mark stitching holes $\frac{1}{8}$" from edges of (I). With awl, punch stitching holes simultaneously through (I) and (F) as marked. Figs. 2, 4, 5.

15. Sew (I) to (F) with saddler's stitch or on sewing machine. Fig. 2.

16. Hold snap fastener caps in (H) in place, and mark positions of post sections on (I). With awl, punch holes in (I) and insert posts and springs. Figs. 2, 4.

17. Cement (FGHI) to (E). Fig. 2.

18. With $\frac{1}{7}$" spacing wheel, mark stitching holes, $\frac{3}{16}$" from edges of (E), including outer edges of (C) and (D). With awl punch stitching holes through matching parts of (CDE) and (F). Figs. 2, 5, 8, 9.

19. Sew (CDE) to (F) with saddle stitch. Fig. 2.

MATERIALS:

Cowhide case leather

Calfskin, 1 oz.

12" zipper

Two snap fasteners

Rubber cement

Heavy linen thread

TOOLS:

(1), (5), (6), (8), (12), (17), (22), (25), (27), (28), (30), (41), (43).

Brief Case

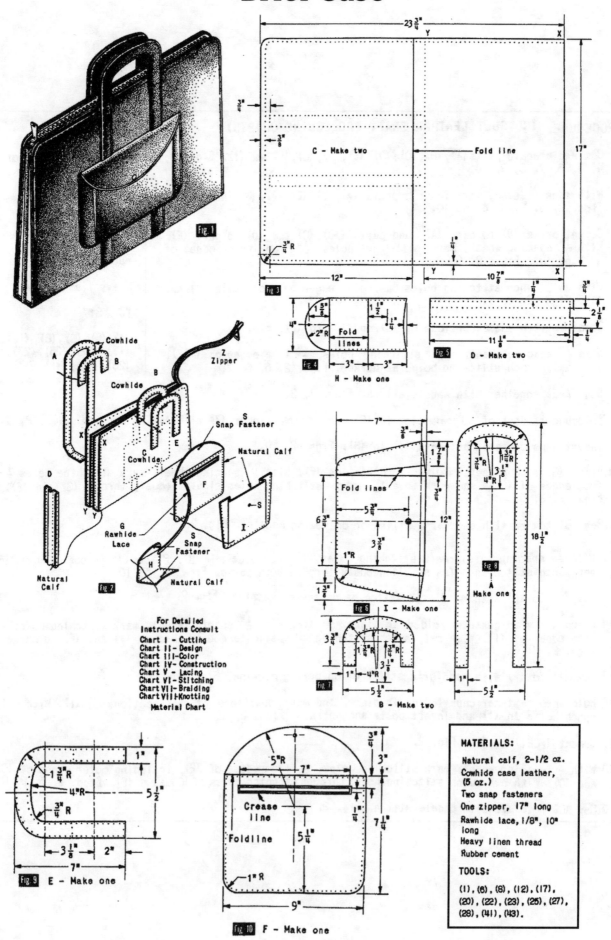

Fig. 1

23 3/4"
Y   X

4 1/4"
3 3/8"

C - Make two   Fold line   17"

3/4" R

12"   Y   10 7/8"   X

Fig. 3

1/4"   4 1/4"   3/4"

Fig. 4
H - Make one

1 5/8"   1 1/2"
4"   1 1/4"
Fold lines
2"   3"   3"

11 1/4"   2 1/8"
1/4"

Fig. 5
D - Make two

A   B
Cowhide

B   Z
Cowhide   Zipper

X
X   C   E
Cowhide   S
Snap Fastener

D   Y   Y   Natural Calf
F   S
G
Rawhide   I
Lace   H   S
Snap
Fastener

Natural
Calf   **Fig. 2**   Natural Calf

**For Detailed
Instructions Consult**
Chart I - Cutting
Chart II - Design
Chart III - Color
Chart IV - Construction
Chart V - Lacing
Chart VI - Stitching
Chart VII - Braiding
Chart VIII - Knotting
Material Chart

7"   3/8"
1 7/8"
3 1/4"
Fold lines   3/4" R   1 1/4" R
3" R
6 3/4"   5 3/4"   4" R
3 3/4"   12"   18 1/2"
1" R
1 3/8"
Fig. 6
I - Make one   1"   4" R
Fig. 8
A
Make one

3 1/4" R   5 1/2"
3" R   1 1/4" R   3/4" R
3" R
1"   4" R   3 3/8"
Fig. 7
5 1/2"
B - Make two

1"
1 3/4" R
4" R   5 1/2"
3/4" R

3 1/8"   2"
7"
Fig. 9   E - Make one

5" R   7"   3/4"
3"
Crease
line   1 1/4"
Foldline   5 1/4"
7 1/4"

9"   1" R
Fig. 10   F - Make one

MATERIALS:

Natural calf, 2-1/2 oz.
Cowhide case leather,
(5 oz.)
Two snap fasteners
One zipper, 17" long
Rawhide lace, 1/8", 10"
long
Heavy linen thread
Rubber cement

TOOLS:

(1), (6), (8), (12), (17),
(20), (22), (23), (25), (27),
(28), (41), (43).

PROCEDURE: (CONSULT LEATHER CRAFT PROCESSING CHARTS)

1. Cut parts (A), (B), (C), (D), (E), (F), (H) and (I). Figs. 3, 4, 5, 6, 7, 8, 9, 10.

2. Fold parts (C) and place together, skin sides facing. With 1/7" spacing wheel, mark stitching holes between points (Y) on flesh side of (C). Figs. 2, 3.

3. With awl, punch stitching holes between points (Y) on (C). Fig. 3.

4. Sew (C) to (C) with saddler's stitch. Fig. 2.

5. Cement edges of (C) to (C) between points (X) and (Y). Fig. 2.

6. Fold (D) in half, skin side out. Cement fold of (D) over 1/4" of edge (XY) of (C). Figs. 2, 5.

7. With 1/7" spacing wheel, mark stitching holes 1/4" from folded edge of (D) over (XY) of (C). Figs. 2, 5.

8. With awl, punch stitching holes simultaneously through folded edge of (D) over (XY) of (C). Fig. 2.

9. Sew (D) to (C) with saddler's stitch. Fig. 2.

10. Cement one part (B) to (A) and second part (B) to (E), flesh sides together. Fig. 2.

11. Place (AB) and (BE) in position on (CD). With 1/7" spacing wheel, mark stitching lines 1/8" from edge on (AB) and (BE). Figs. 2, 7, 8, 9.

12. With awl, punch stitching holes simultaneously through matching parts of (AB) and (BE) on (CD). Figs. 2, 3.

13. Sew (AB) and (BE) to (CD) with saddler's stitch. Fig. 2.

14. Cut slot in (F). Outline edge of slot and flap with edge creaser. Fig. 10.

15. With edge creaser, mark folding lines of (I). Fold in place. Figs. 2, 6.

16. Attach snap fasteners (S) to (F), (H) and (I). Figs. 2, 4, 6, 10.

17. With edge creaser, mark folding lines on (H). Fold in place. Fig. 4.

18. Cement lace (G) between edges of (H) to be stitched. Fig. 2.

19. With 1/7" spacing wheel, mark stitching holes 1/8" from edge of (H). Fig. 4.

20. With awl, punch stitching holes simultaneously through matching edges of (H). Fig. 4.

21. Sew (H) with saddler's stitch. Fig. 2.

22. Cement end of (G) on back of (F) in line with edge of (F) to be stitched to (C). Fig. 2.

23. With 1/7" spacing wheel, mark stitching holes 1/8" from edge of (I). Fig. 6.

24. Place (F) and (I) in position on (C). With awl, punch stitching holes simultaneously through (I), (F), and (C). Figs. 2, 6, 10.

25. Sew (I) and (F) to (C) with saddler's stitch. Fig. 2.

26. With 1/7" spacing wheel, mark stitching holes 3/8" from edge on top edges of (C). Fig. 3.

27. With sewing awl, lock stitch (Z) to (C) where stitching holes occur. Fig. 2.

28. With 1/7" spacing wheel, mark stitching holes 1/4" from outer edges of (D). Fig. 5.

29. With awl, punch stitching holes simultaneously through matching edges of (C) and (D). Fig. 2.

30. Sew (D) to (C) with saddler's stitch. Fig. 2.

Brief Case

Fig. 1

For Detailed
Instructions Consult
Chart I – Cutting
Chart II – Design
Chart III – Color
Chart IV – Construction
Chart V – Lacing
Chart VI – Stitching
Chart VII – Braiding
Chart VIII – Knotting
Material Chart

$1\frac{1}{2}$" $1\frac{1}{2}$" $\frac{1}{2}$" $\frac{3}{8}$" $\frac{3}{8}$" $\frac{1}{2}$"

$10\frac{1}{8}$"

$\frac{1}{2}$"

B Fig. 5

Make two

12"

16"

E Fig. 3

$3\frac{1}{4}$" $1\frac{5}{8}$"

$\frac{1}{4}$" $\frac{1}{4}$"

Fold lines

D Fig. 4

Make two

$1\frac{1}{4}$" $2\frac{1}{2}$"

B
C Cowhide
Y
X
X
Y
D
E
Cowhide
D
Calfskin
F
Buckle F
A
Cowhide
Goatskin Lace
Fig. 2

$\frac{3}{8}$"
$1\frac{3}{8}$"
$\frac{5}{8}$"
$\frac{5}{8}$"
$\frac{5}{8}$"
$\frac{5}{8}$"

$1\frac{1}{4}$"

$31\frac{3}{4}$"

Fold line

$\frac{3}{16}$"
$\frac{1}{2}$"
$\frac{7}{8}$"

A Fig. 6

Make two

16"

$3\frac{1}{4}$"

Fold line

$3\frac{3}{8}$" Y X X Y

Position of (B) on (C)
before punching holes

30"

$4\frac{1}{8}$"

$7\frac{1}{4}$"

C Fig. 7

PROCEDURE: (CONSULT LEATHER CRAFT PROCESSING CHARTS)

1. Cut and prepare parts (A), (B), (C), (D) and (E). Figs. 3, 4, 5, 6, 7.

2. Mark all folding lines with edge creaser and outline top edge of (E). Figs. 3, 4, 6, 7.

3. Cement (B) to (B) flesh sides together. Fig. 5.

4. Mark stitching holes with 1/7" spacing wheel, 1/8" from all edges of (B). Punch stitching holes with awl. Fig. 5.

5. Sew (BB) with saddler's stitch. Fig. 2.

6. Place (BB) in position on (C). Allow fullness for hand grip between points (X) and (X), and fullness for straps between points (X) and (Y). Figs. 1, 2, 5, 7.

7. Punch with awl triple row of closely spaced stitching holes through matching points of (BB) and (C). Figs. 2, 5, 7.

8. Sew (BB) to (C) with saddler's stitch. Fig. 2.

9. Cut slit for prong of buckle (F) in square end of (A). Insert (F) in (A). Fig. 6.

10. Fold back, end of (A). Punch with awl double row of closely spaced stitching holes through fold of (A). Fig. 6.

11. Sew fold with saddler's stitch. Fig. 2.

12. Place (A) in position on (C). With awl, punch double row of closely spaced stitching holes through matching parts of (A) and (C). Figs. 2, 6, 7.

13. Sew (A) to (C) with saddler's stitch. Fig. 2.

14. Place center fold of (D) over short end of (E). Mark stitching holes, 1/4" from folded edge, with 1/7" spacing wheel. Figs. 2, 3, 4.

15. Punch stitching holes with awl through fold of (D) over (E). Figs. 2, 4.

16. Sew (D) to (E) with saddler's stitch. Fig. 2.

17. Punch 3/32" thong slits with awl, 3/16" from edge, on inner top edge of (C). Continue punching thong slits simultaneously through matching edges of (C) and (D) and flap edge of (C). Fig. 2.

18. Lace parts with double overlay stitch. Fig. 1.

19. Close briefcase to determine position of holes in (A) for prong of (F). Mark position of holes. Figs. 2, 6.

20. With No. 4 tube, punch holes in (A). Figs. 2, 6.

MATERIALS:

Cowhide case leather, 5-6 oz.

Calfskin, 2-1/2 oz.

2 - 1-1/4" buckles., center bar

Goatskin lacing, 3/32"

Heavy linen thread

Rubber cement

TOOLS:

(1), (4), (6), (8), (17), (18), (25), (26), (27), (28), (30), (40), (41), (43).

Brief Case

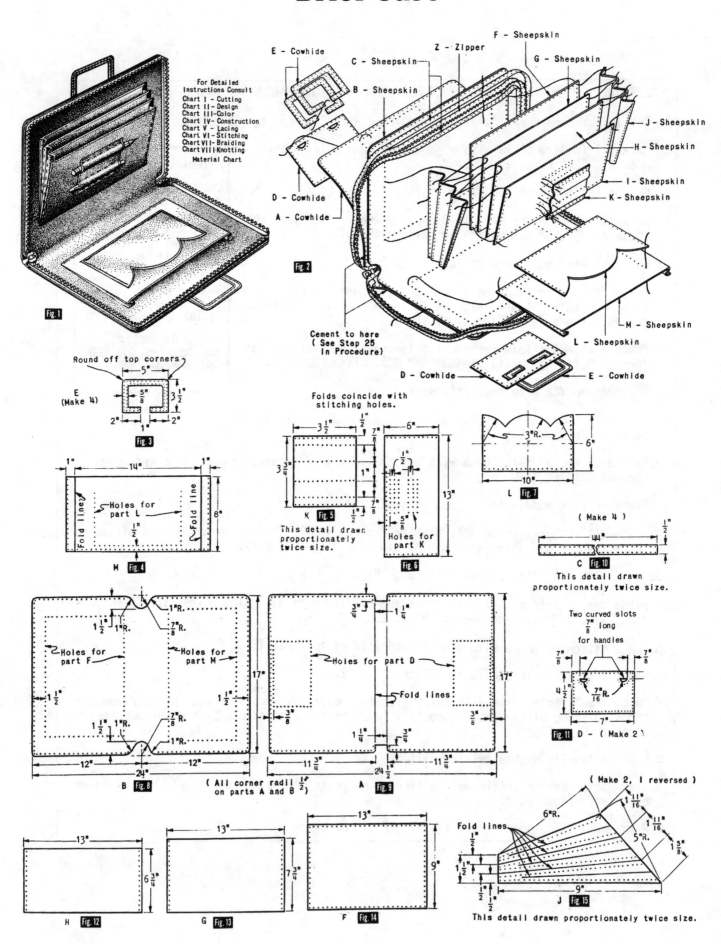

For Detailed
Instructions Consult
Chart I – Cutting
Chart II – Design
Chart III – Color
Chart IV – Construction
Chart V – Lacing
Chart VI – Stitching
Chart VII – Braiding
Chart VIII – Knotting
Material Chart

Fig. 1

E – Cowhide
C – Sheepskin
B – Sheepskin
Z – Zipper
F – Sheepskin
G – Sheepskin
J – Sheepskin
H – Sheepskin
I – Sheepskin
K – Sheepskin

D – Cowhide
A – Cowhide

Cement to here
(See Step 25
In Procedure)

M – Sheepskin
L – Sheepskin

D – Cowhide
E – Cowhide

Fig. 2

Round off top corners
E (Make 4)
5"
5/8"
3 1/2"
2"   1"   2"
Fig. 3

Folds coincide with
stitching holes.
3 1/2"   1/2"   6"
7/8"
3 3/4"   1"   13"
1/2"
7/8"
5/8"
K   **Fig. 5**   Holes for part K
This detail drawn
proportionately
twice size.
Fig. 6

3"R.   6"
10"
L   **Fig. 7**

(Make 4)
44"   1/2"
C   **Fig. 10**
This detail drawn
proportionately twice size.

1"   14"   1"
Fold line   Holes for part L   Fold line   8"
1/2"
M   **Fig. 4**

Two curved slots
7/8" long
for handles
7/8"   7/8"
4 1/2"   7/16"R.
7"
Fig. 11 D – (Make 2)

1"R.
1 1/2"   1"R.
7/8"R.
Holes for part F   Holes for part M
17"
1 1/2"   1 1/2"
1 1/2"   1"R.
7/8"R.
1"R.
12"   12"
24"
B   **Fig. 8**
(All corner radii 1/2"
on parts A and B)

3/4"   1 1/4"
Holes for part D
17"
Fold lines
3/8"   3/8"
1 1/4"   3/4"
11 3/4"   11 3/4"
24"
A   **Fig. 9**

13"
6 3/4"
H   **Fig. 12**

13"
7 3/4"
G   **Fig. 13**

13"
9"
F   **Fig. 14**

(Make 2, 1 reversed)
1 11/16"
6"R.
1 11/16"
Fold lines
1/2"
1 1/2"   5"R.
1 5/8"
1/2"
9"
J   **Fig. 15**
This detail drawn proportionately twice size.

PROCEDURE: (CONSULT LEATHER CRAFT PROCESSING CHARTS)

1. Cut (A),(B),(C),(D),(E),(F),(G),(H),(I),(J),(K),(L) and (M). Figs. 3 through 15.

2. Cement (E) to (E) flesh sides facing. Fig. 2.

3. With 1/7" spacing wheel, mark stitching holes 1/8" from edge on all edges of (EE). With awl, punch stitching holes as marked. Fig. 3.

4. Sew (EE) with saddler's stitch, and stitch around slots of (D). Fig. 2.

5. Insert ends of (EE) through slots in (D) and place in position on (A). Figs. 2, 9.

6. With 1/7" spacing wheel, mark stitching holes 1/8" from all edges of (D). With awl, punch stitching holes through matching parts of (D) and (A). Figs. 9, 11.

7. Sew (D) to (A) with saddler's stitch. Fig. 2.

8. Cement zipper (Z) between parts (C) (skin sides out). On sewing machine sew (Z) to (C), allowing room for movement of zipper. Fig. 2.

9. With 1/7" spacing wheel, mark stitching holes 1/8" from outer edges of (CC). Fig. 10.

10. With edge creaser, crease top edges of (F),(G),(H),(I),(J),(K),(L), and (M). Figs. 1, 2.

11. With creaser, mark folding lines on (A),(J),(K) and (M). Fold as shown. Figs. 4, 5, 9, 15.

12. Place (K) in position on (I). With 1/7" spacing wheel, mark stitching holes on (K). With awl, punch stitching holes simultaneously through matching parts of (K) and (I). Figs. 2, 5, 6.

13. Sew (K) to (I) with saddler's stitch. Fig. 2.

14. With 1/7" spacing wheel, mark stitching holes on folds of (J) that match with (G) and (H), 1/4" from edge of fold. With awl, punch stitching holes through (J) and (G), and (J) and (H). Figs. 1, 12, 13, 15.

15. Sew (J) to (G) and (J) to (H) with saddler's stitch. Fig. 2.

16. With 1/7" spacing wheel, mark stitching holes on (IK), 1/4" from edge where (IK) matches front fold of (J). With awl, punch stitching holes through (J) and (IK). Figs. 2, 6, 15.

17. Sew (J) to (IK) with saddler's stitch. Fig. 2.

18. Place back end fold of (J) on (F). With 1/7" spacing wheel, mark stitching holes 3/16" from edge of (J) on (F), along top edge of (F) and along bottom edge of (I). Figs. 2, 6, 14, 15.

19. Place (F,G,H,I,K,J) in position on (B). With awl, punch stitching holes simultaneously through matching parts of (F), (I) and (J) on (B). Figs. 2, 6, 14, 15.

20. Sew the entire partitioned pocket to (B) with saddler's stitch. Fig. 2.

21. With 1/7" spacing wheel, mark stitching holes 1/8" from edges, along straight sides of (L). With awl, punch stitching holes through matching parts of (L) and (M). Figs. 2, 4, 7.

22. Sew (L) to (M) with saddler's stitch. Fig. 2.

23. With 1/7" spacing wheel, mark stitching holes 3/16" from edge of sides and bottom of (LM). With awl, punch stitching holes simultaneously through matching parts of (LM) and (B), including bottom of gusset fold. Figs. 2, 4, 8.

24. Sew (LM) to (B) with saddler's stitch. Fig. 2.

25. Cement (B) to (A) to points indicated. Fig. 2.

26. Mark stitching holes on all sides of (AB), (excepting indented curve of (B)), to correspond to stitching holes punched in (CZC). Figs. 8, 9, and Leather Chart V.

27. With awl, punch stitching holes in (AB). Figs. 8, 9.

28. Sew (CZC) to (AB) with saddler's stitch. Fig. 2.

29. Cement ends of (Z) to (A) by lifting curved, uncemented edge of (B) away from (A). Fig. 2.

MATERIALS:

Cowhide case leather, 5 oz.

Sheepskin, 1 oz.

Zipper, 41" (Special Order)

Heavy linen thread

Rubber cement

TOOLS:

(1),(2),(6),(17),(22), (25),(27),(28),(30), (41).

See Leather Chart V for spacing stitching holes on curve.

Scrap Book

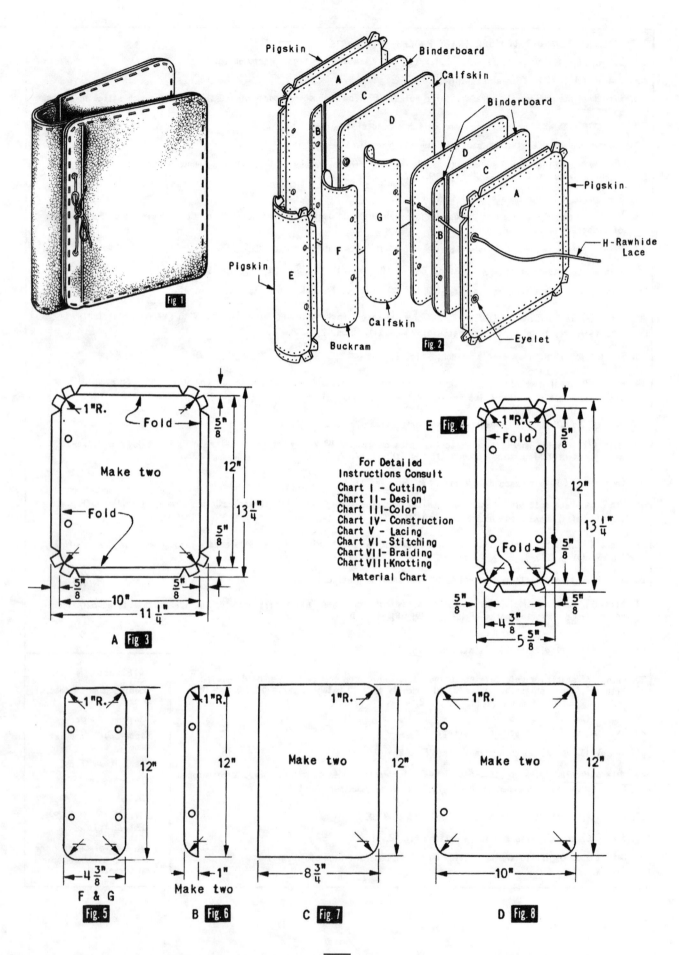

Fig. 1

Pigskin
Binderboard
Calfskin
Binderboard

A
C
D
B
D
C
A

Pigskin
E
F
G
B

Pigskin

H - Rawhide Lace

Eyelet

Calfskin

Buckram

Fig. 2

1"R.
Fold
$5\frac{5}{8}$"
12"
$13\frac{1}{4}$"
Fold
$5\frac{5}{8}$"
$\frac{5}{8}$"
$\frac{5}{8}$"
10"
$11\frac{1}{4}$"
Make two

A Fig. 3

E Fig. 4

For Detailed
Instructions Consult
Chart I - Cutting
Chart II - Design
Chart III - Color
Chart IV - Construction
Chart V - Lacing
Chart VI - Stitching
Chart VII - Braiding
Chart VIII - Knotting
Material Chart

1"R.
Fold
$5\frac{5}{8}$"
12"
$13\frac{1}{4}$"
Fold
$5\frac{5}{8}$"
$\frac{5}{8}$"
$\frac{5}{8}$"
$4\frac{3}{4}$"
$5\frac{5}{8}$"

1"R.
12"
$4\frac{3}{8}$"
F & G
Fig. 5

1"R.
12"
1"
Make two
B Fig. 6

1"R.
Make two
12"
$8\frac{3}{4}$"
C Fig. 7

1"R.
Make two
12"
10"
D Fig. 8

110

PROCEDURE: (CONSULT LEATHER CRAFT PROCESSING CHARTS)

1. Cut parts (A), (B), (C), (D), (E), (F) and (G). Figs. 3, 4, 5, 6, 7, 8.

2. Skive all edges of parts (A), (D), (E) and (G). Figs. 3, 8.

3. Cement (B) and (C) to (A), leaving 1/4" between (B) and (C). Fig. 2.

4. Fold edges of (A) and cement over (B) and (C). Fig. 2.

5. Cement (D) to (ABC). Fig. 2.

6. Cement (F) to (E). Fig. 2.

7. Fold edges of (E) over (F) and cement. Cement (G) to (EF) and adjust leathers over a rounded object, such as a mailing tube or folded magazine, while cement is drying. Fig. 2 and Leather Chart IV.

8. Punch holes with drive punch for eyelets in all parts. Figs. 2, 3, 4, 5, 6, 8.

9. Insert eyelets. Fig. 2.

10. Mark 1/4" stitching holes, 1/4" from all 4 edges of all parts. Figs. 2.

11. Punch all stitching holes with awl. Fig. 2.

12. Saddle stitch with heavy linen thread. Figs. 1, 2.

13. Insert lace (H) through eyelets and tie. Figs. 1, 2.

MATERIALS:

Pigskin

Hard-rolled binder board Light weight.

Calfskin

Buckram

Rawhide lace

8 Eyelets, No. 6 K

Pliobond Plastic Adhesive

Heavy linen thread, brown

TOOLS:

(1), (3 No. 7), (6), (14), (17), (19), (25), (41).

See Leather Chart IV for cementing rounded parts.

Bracelet

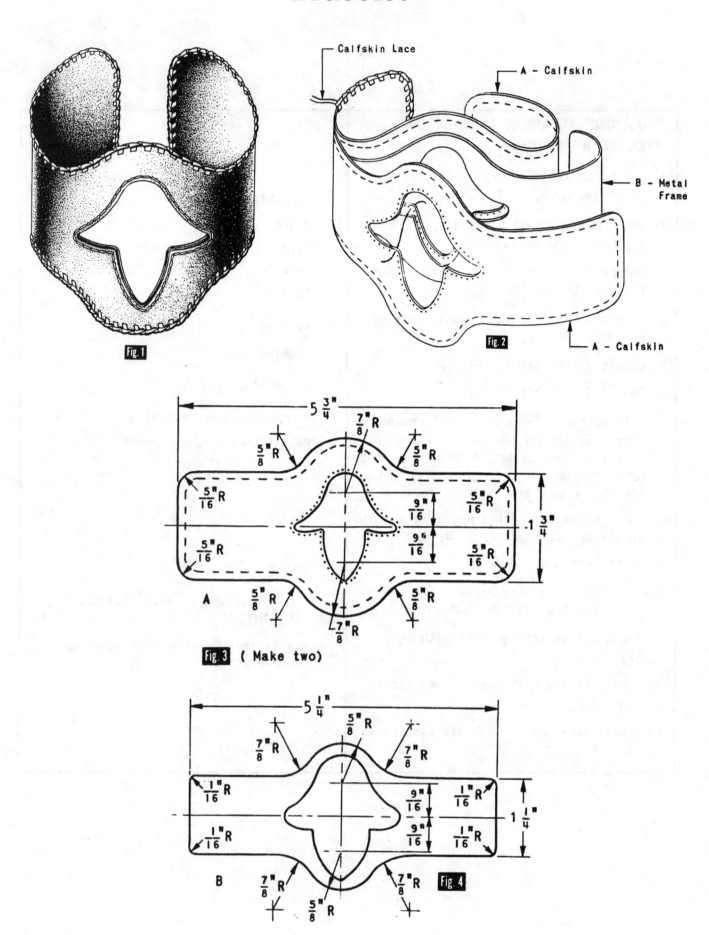

Calfskin Lace

A – Calfskin

B – Metal Frame

A – Calfskin

Fig. 1

Fig. 2

5 3/4"

7/8" R

5/8" R   5/8" R

5/16" R   5/16" R

9/16"

9/16"

1 3/4"

5/16" R   5/16" R

A   5/8" R   5/8" R

7/8" R

Fig. 3 (Make two)

5 1/4"

7/8" R   5/8" R   7/8" R

1/16" R   1/16" R

9/16"

9/16"

1 1/4"

1/16" R   1/16" R

B   7/8" R   7/8" R   **Fig. 4**

5/8" R

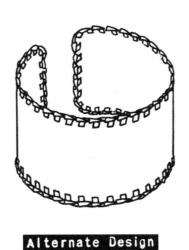

Alternate Design

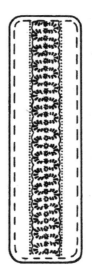

PROCEDURE:(CONSULT LEATHER CRAFT PROCESSING CHARTS)	MATERIALS:

PROCEDURE:(CONSULT LEATHER CRAFT PROCESSING CHARTS)

1. Cut and prepare parts (A). Fig. 3.

2. Place (A) to (A), flesh sides together, over frame (B). Fig. 2.

3. With awl, punch 3/32" thong slits, 1/8" from edge, simultaneously through matching edges of (A), retaining curve of (B). Trim ends of inner (A). Figs. 2, 3.

4. Lace top edges of (A) to (A) with single overlay stitch. Do not terminate thong. Fig. 2.

5. Insert (B) between (A) and (A). Finish lacing all edges. Figs. 1, 2.

6. With awl, punch closely spaced stitching holes around inner cut in (A). Stitch with saddler's stitch. Figs. 1, 2, 3.

MATERIALS:

Russia tooling calfskin

Calfskin lace, 3/32"x 8'

TOOLS:

(1), (4), (6), (17), (18), (25), (26), (33), (40).

For Detailed
Instructions Consult
Chart I - Cutting
Chart II - Design
Chart III-Color
Chart IV- Construction
Chart V - Lacing
Chart VI - Stitching
Chart VII-Braiding
Chart VIII-Knotting
Material Chart

Bracelet

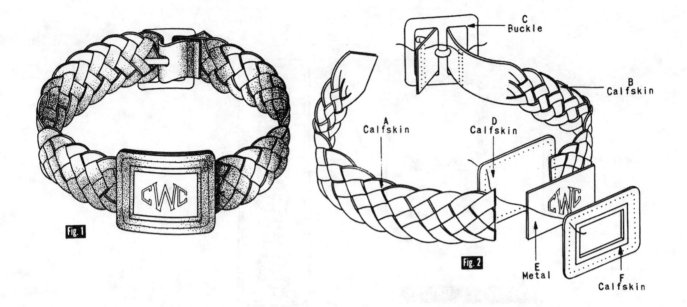

Fig. 1

Fig. 2

C Buckle
B Calfskin
A Calfskin
D Calfskin
E Metal
F Calfskin

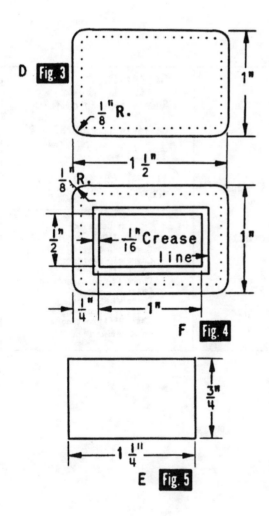

D Fig. 3

1"

$\frac{1}{8}$" R.

1 $\frac{1}{2}$"

$\frac{1}{8}$" R.

1"

$\frac{1}{2}$"

$\frac{1}{16}$" Crease line

$\frac{1}{4}$"

1"

F Fig. 4

$\frac{3}{4}$"

1 $\frac{1}{4}$"

E Fig. 5

ALTERNATE DESIGN

For Detailed
Instructions Consult
Chart I – Cutting
Chart II – Design
Chart III – Color
Chart IV – Construction
Chart V – Lacing
Chart VI – Stitching
Chart VII – Braiding
Chart VIII – Knotting

Material Chart

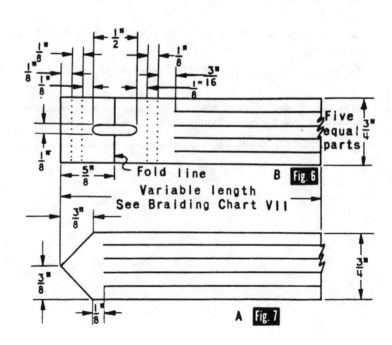

$\frac{1}{8}$"
$\frac{1}{8}$"
$\frac{1}{8}$"
$\frac{1}{2}$"
$\frac{1}{8}$"
$\frac{3}{16}$"
$\frac{1}{8}$"

$\frac{1}{8}$"

$\frac{5}{8}$"

Fold line

Variable length
See Braiding Chart VII

Five equal parts

$\frac{3}{4}$"

B Fig. 6

$\frac{3}{8}$"

$\frac{3}{8}$"

$\frac{1}{8}$"

$\frac{1}{4}$"

A Fig. 7

PROCEDURE: (CONSULT LEATHER CRAFT PROCESSING CHARTS)

1. Cut parts (A), (B), (D) and (F). Figs. 3, 4, 6, 7.

2. Braid strands of (A) and (B). Figs. 2, 6, 7, and **Leather Chart VII.**

3. Outline edge of cut-out in (F) with edge creaser. Fig. 4.

4. Skive ends of braid strands of (A) and (B). Figs. 6, 7.

5. Arrange and cement strands singly in braided sequence on (D), flesh sides together. Fig. 2.

6. Place (F) in position on (ABD). Mark closely spaced stitching holes 3/32" from outside edge of (F). Figs. 2, 4.

7. Punch stitching holes with awl simultaneously through matching parts of (ABD) and (F). Figs. 2, 3, 4.

8. Sew top and ends of (F) to (ABD) with saddler's stitch. Without terminating threads, insert (E) between (DF). Finish stitching bottom edges. Fig. 2.

9. Cut slot for prong of buckle (C) in straight end of (B). Insert (C). Figs. 2, 6.

10. Fold back end of (B) and mark closely spaced stitching holes through fold. Figs. 2, 6.

11. Sew (B) with saddler's stitch. Fig. 2.

12. Fasten (A) in buckle by inserting prong in any space between braided strands. Fig. 1.

MATERIALS:

Calfskin

Metal initial plate

Buckle, 3/4", center bar

Heavy linen thread

Rubber cement

TOOLS:

(1), (6), (17), (20), (25), (41).

See Leather Chart VII for details of braid and lengths.

Buttons

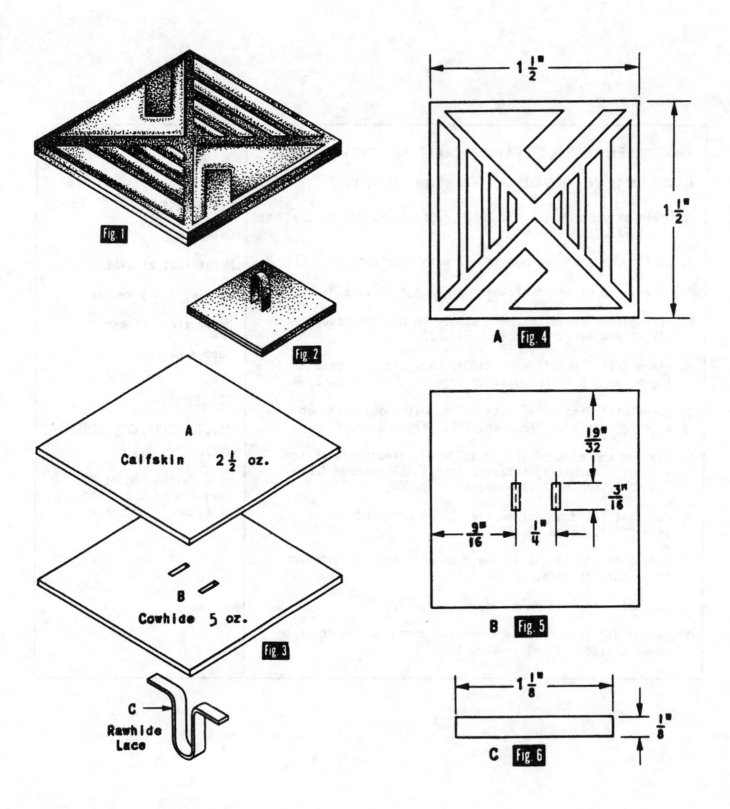

Fig. 1

Fig. 2

Fig. 3

A

Calfskin   2½ oz.

B

Cowhide 5 oz.

C → Rawhide Lace

A   Fig. 4

1½"

1½"

B   Fig. 5

19"/32

3"/16

9"/16

¼"

C   Fig. 6

1⅛"

⅛"

PROCEDURE: (CONSULT LEATHER CRAFT PROCESSING CHARTS)

1. Cut and prepare parts (A), (B) and (C). Figs. 4, 5, 6.

2. Punch with awl two 1/8" thong slits for (C) in (B). Fig. 5.

3. Skive ends of (C) to be cemented to (B). Fig. 6.

4. Insert (C) in (B) with skin side exposed in loop. Cement 1/4" ends of (C) to flesh side of (B). Figs. 2, 3.

5. Cement (A) to (BC). Figs. 2, 3.

MATERIALS:

Russia tooling calfskin scraps, 2-1/2 oz.
Cowhide scraps, 5 oz.
Rawhide lace, 1/8"
Rubber cement

TOOLS:

(17), (33), (40).

For Detailed
Instructions Consult
Chart I - Cutting
Chart II - Design
Chart III - Color
Chart IV - Construction
Chart V - Lacing
Chart VI - Stitching
Chart VII - Braiding
Chart VIII - Knotting
Material Chart

Buttons

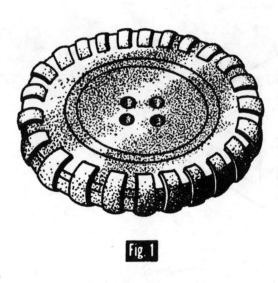

Fig. 1

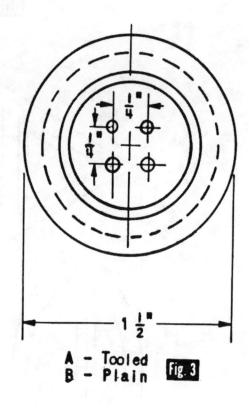

A - Tooled
B - Plain   Fig. 3

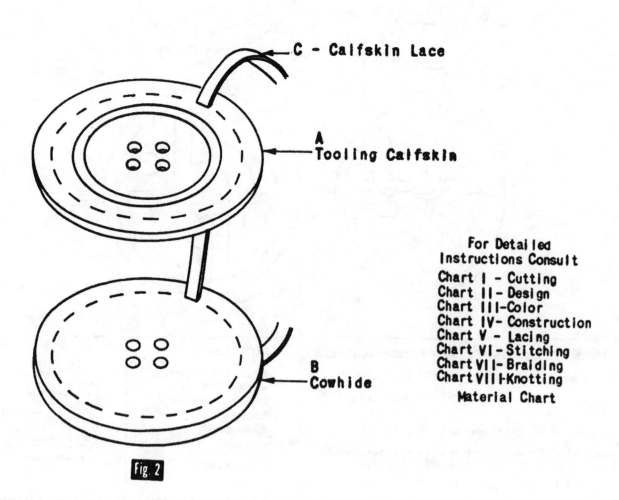

C - Calfskin Lace

A
Tooling Calfskin

B
Cowhide

Fig. 2

For Detailed
Instructions Consult
Chart I - Cutting
Chart II - Design
Chart III - Color
Chart IV - Construction
Chart V - Lacing
Chart VI - Stitching
Chart VII - Braiding
Chart VIII - Knotting
Material Chart

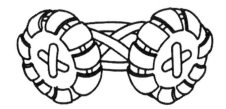

 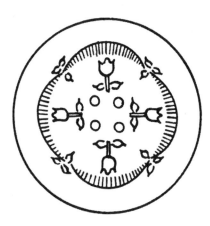 

PROCEDURE: (CONSULT LEATHER CRAFT PROCESSING CHARTS)

1. Cut and prepare parts (A) and (B). Fig. 3.

2. Cement (A) to (B) flesh sides together. Fig. 2.

3. Punch 4 equidistant holes in (AB) with No. I tube. Fig. 3.

4. Punch with awl, 3/32" thong slits, 1/8" from edge of (AB). Fig. 3.

5. Lace (AB) with whip-stitch. Figs. I, 2.

MATERIALS:

Russia tooling calfskin scraps, 2-1/2 oz.
Cowhide scraps, 5 oz.
Rubber cement
Calfskin lace

TOOLS:

(4), (8), (17), (18), (33), (43).

Baby's Bottle Carrier

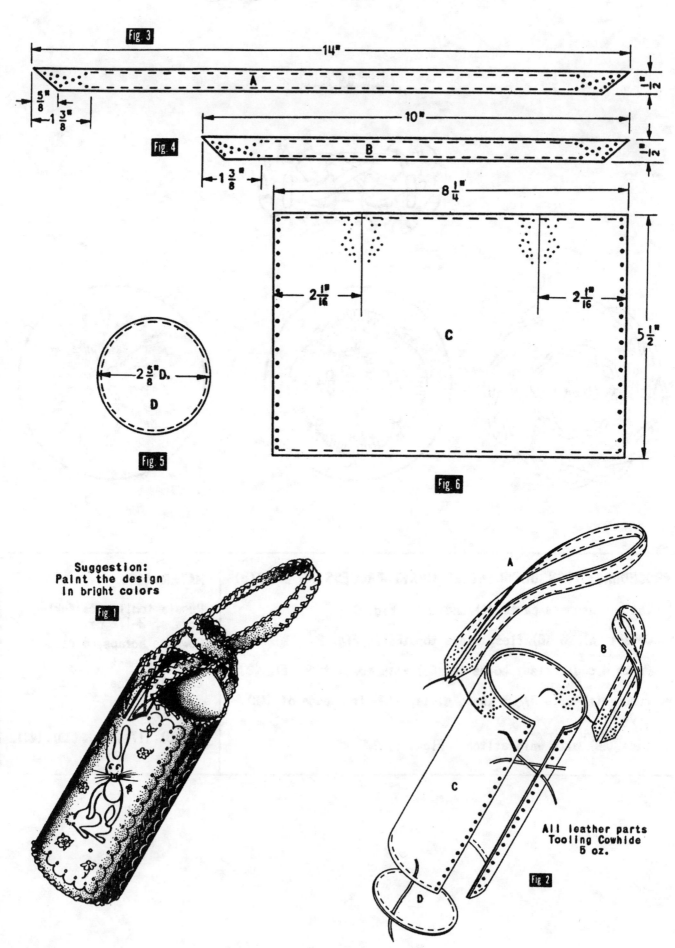

Fig. 3

14"

A

5/8"

1 3/8"

1/2"

Fig. 4

10"

B

1 3/8"

1/2"

8 1/4"

2 1/16"

2 1/16"

C

5 1/2"

2 5/8" D.

D

Fig. 5

Fig. 6

Suggestion:
Paint the design
in bright colors

Fig 1

A

B

C

D

All leather parts
Tooling Cowhide
5 oz.

Fig 2

PROCEDURE: (CONSULT LEATHER CRAFT PROCESSING CHARTS)

1. Cut and prepare parts (A), (B), (C) and (D). Figs. 3, 4, 5, 6.

2. With No. 1 tube, punch $\frac{1}{4}''$ matching thong holes, $\frac{1}{8}''$ from edges, simultaneously on short sides of (C). Fig. 6.

3. With awl, punch $\frac{3}{32}''$ thong slits, $\frac{1}{8}''$ from edges on long sides of (C), and on sides of (A) and (B) as shown. Figs. 3, 4, 6.

4. Place (A) and (B) in position on (C). With awl, punch $\frac{1}{7}''$ stitching holes through matching parts of (A) and (C) and (B) and (C) as shown. Figs. 2, 3, 4, 6.

5. Sew (A) and (B) to (C) with saddler's stitch. Fig. 2.

6. With awl, punch $\frac{3}{32}''$ thong slits, $\frac{1}{8}''$ from edge of (D). Figs. 2, 5, and Leather Chart V.

7. Lace (D) to (ABC) with whip stitch. With same thong, lace vertical seam of (C) with cross stitch. Cut and terminate only one thong. Fig. 2, and Leather Chart V.

8. With the one thong left from cross stitching, lace with single overlay stitch in one continuous operation top edge of (C) and outside edges of (A) and (B). Figs. 1, 2.

9. Lace inner edges of (A) and (B) with single overlay stitch. Figs. 1, 2.

MATERIALS:

Tooling cowhide, 5 oz., light natural color

Goatskin lace, $\frac{3}{32}''$, 23'.

TOOLS:

(1), (4), (6), (8), (17), (18), (25), (28), (40), (41).

For Detailed
Instructions Consult
Chart I – Cutting
Chart II – Design
Chart III – Color
Chart IV – Construction
Chart V – Lacing
Chart VI – Stitching
Chart VII – Braiding
Chart VIII – Knotting
Material Chart

Child's "Chick" Purse

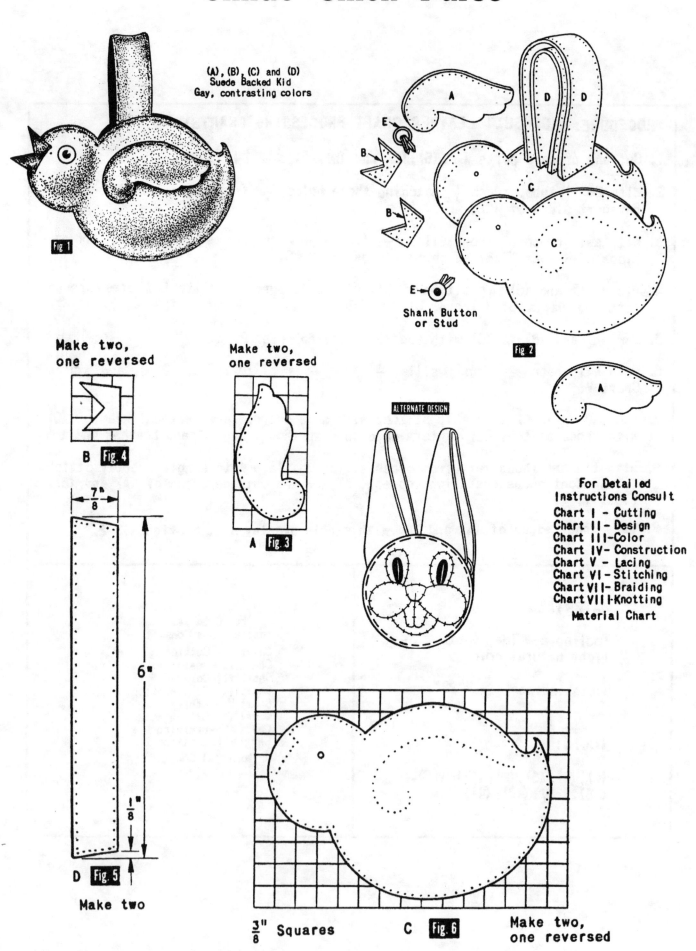

(A), (B), (C) and (D)
Suede Backed Kid
Gay, contrasting colors

Fig. 1

E
Shank Button
or Stud

Fig. 2

A

Make two,
one reversed

B Fig. 4

Make two,
one reversed

A Fig. 3

7"/8

6"

1"/8

D Fig. 5

Make two

ALTERNATE DESIGN

For Detailed
Instructions Consult
Chart I - Cutting
Chart II - Design
Chart III - Color
Chart IV - Construction
Chart V - Lacing
Chart VI - Stitching
Chart VII - Braiding
Chart VIII - Knotting
Material Chart

3/8" Squares   C Fig. 6   Make two,
one reversed

122

PROCEDURE:(CONSULT LEATHER CRAFT PROCESSING CHARTS)

1. Cut parts (A), (B), (C) and (D). Reverse duplicate patterns. Figs. 3, 4, 5, 6.

2. Cement parts (A) on (C), and (D) to (D). Figs. 2, 5, 6.

3. Mark 1/7" stitching holes close to edge of (A) where shown, and along all edges of (DD). Figs. 3, 5.

4. Punch stitching holes with awl as marked. Fig. 2.

5. Saddle stitch (A) to (C), and edges of (DD). Fig. 2.

6. Cement ends of (DD) to back of parts (AC). Figs. 1, 2.

7. Mark 1/7" stitching holes around one entire (C) and open edge of second (C). Figs. 2, 6.

8. Punch stitching holes with awl on edges of purse opening. Figs. 2, 6.

9. Attach eyes (E) to (C). Fig. 2.

10. Assemble parts (AC) and (D). Punch stitching holes through matching edges of (C). Figs. 2, 6.

11. Sew (C) to (C) with saddle stitch, including (D). Start at head end of opening and stitch one side of opening, and around tail, bottom edge and head. Complete stitching other side of opening, including (D). Fig. 2.

12. Mark stitching holes on all edges of one part (B). Fig. 4.

13. Cement (B) to (B) in position on (C). Punch stitching holes with awl through all matching parts. Fig. 2.

14. Sew with saddle stitch. Fig. 2.

MATERIALS:

Suede backed kid, 2 oz.
Shank buttons or studs, 2
Linen thread
Rubber cement

TOOLS:

(6), (21), (25), (28), (33), (41).

Child's Bean Bag

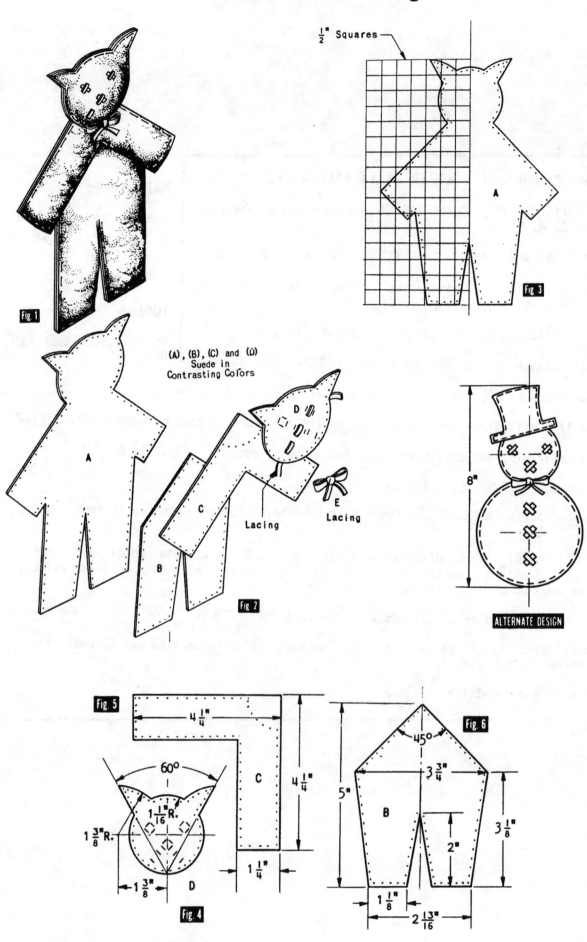

½" Squares

Fig. 1

Fig. 3

A

(A), (B), (C) and (D)
Suede in
Contrasting Colors

A

C

B

D

E
Lacing

Lacing

Fig. 2

8"

ALTERNATE DESIGN

Fig. 5

4 ¼"

4 ¼"

C

1 ¼"

60°

1 1/16" R.

1 3/8" R.

1 3/8"

D

Fig. 4

Fig. 6

45°

3 ¾"

5"

B

2"

3 1/8"

1 1/8"

2 13/16"

PROCEDURE:(CONSULT LEATHER CRAFT PROCESSING CHARTS)

1. Cut parts (A),(B),(C) and (D). Figs. 3, 4, 5, 6.

2. Punch 3/32" thong slits in (D) for eyes, nose and mouth. Fig. 4.

3. Insert cross stitches in (D) with one continuous lacing, cementing ends to back of (D). Figs. 2, 4.

4. Place (D), (C) and (B) in position to fit on (A). Mark 1/7" stitching holes 1/8" from edges that overlap. Figs. 2, 3, 4, 5, 6.

5. Remove (A). Punch stitching holes simultaneously on overlapping edges of (D), (C) and (B). Figs. 2, 4, 5, 6.

6. Saddle stitch (D), (C) and (B). Figs. 1, 2.

7. Tie lacing (E) in bow. Sew on seam of (DC). Figs. 1, 2.

8. Place (DCB) in position on (A). Cement all edges except top edge between ears. Figs. 1, 2.

9. Mark 1/7" stitching holes 1/8" from entire outer edge of assembled parts. Fig. 2.

10. Punch stitching holes with awl. Fig. 2.

11. Sew edge with saddle stitch, starting at point of ear and continuing around body to other ear. Do not terminate thread. Fig. 2.

12. Insert beans. Finish stitching top of head. Figs. 1, 2.

MATERIALS:
Suede, contrasting colors
Rubber cement   Goat lacing
Linen thread   Beans

TOOLS:
(6),(17),(21),(25),(28), (33),(40),(41).

Child's Shoulder Bag

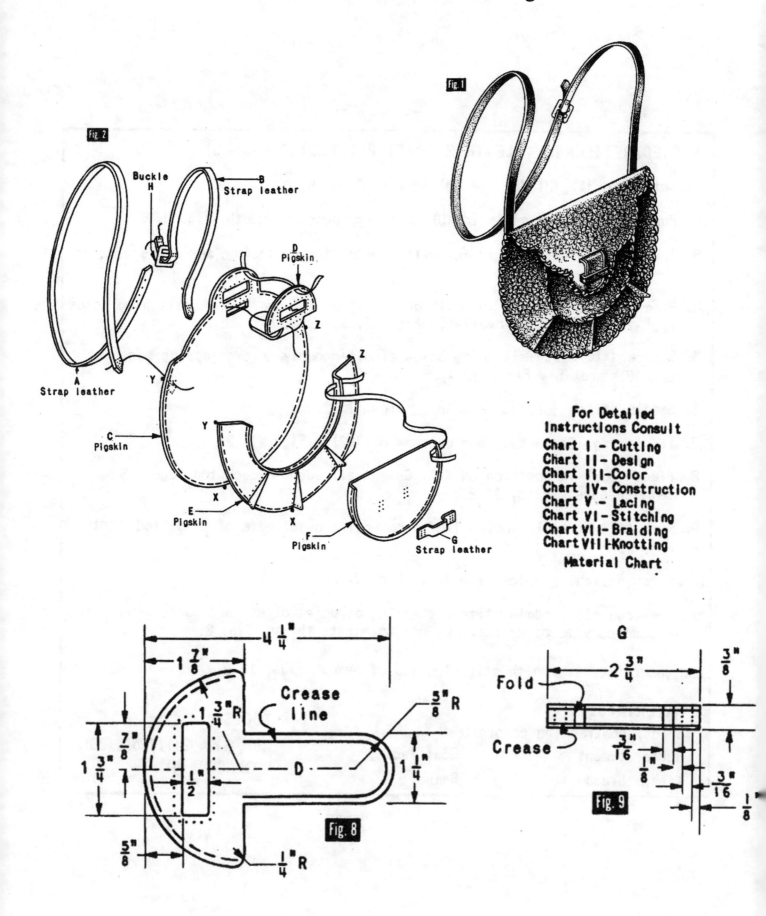

Fig. 2

Buckle
H

Strap leather B

Strap leather A

D Pigskin

Z

Z

Y

Y

C Pigskin

E Pigskin

X

X

F Pigskin

G
Strap leather

Fig. 1

For Detailed
Instructions Consult
Chart I - Cutting
Chart II - Design
Chart III - Color
Chart IV - Construction
Chart V - Lacing
Chart VI - Stitching
Chart VII - Braiding
Chart VIII - Knotting
Material Chart

$4\frac{1}{4}''$

$1\frac{7}{8}''$

Crease line

$\frac{5}{8}''$ R

$1\frac{3}{4}''$ R

1

$\frac{7}{8}''$

$1\frac{3}{4}''$

$\frac{1}{2}''$

D

$1\frac{1}{4}''$

$\frac{5}{8}''$

$\frac{1}{4}''$ R

Fig. 8

G

Fold

$2\frac{3}{4}''$

$\frac{3}{8}''$

Crease

$\frac{3}{16}''$

$\frac{1}{8}''$

$\frac{3}{16}''$

$\frac{1}{8}''$

Fig. 9

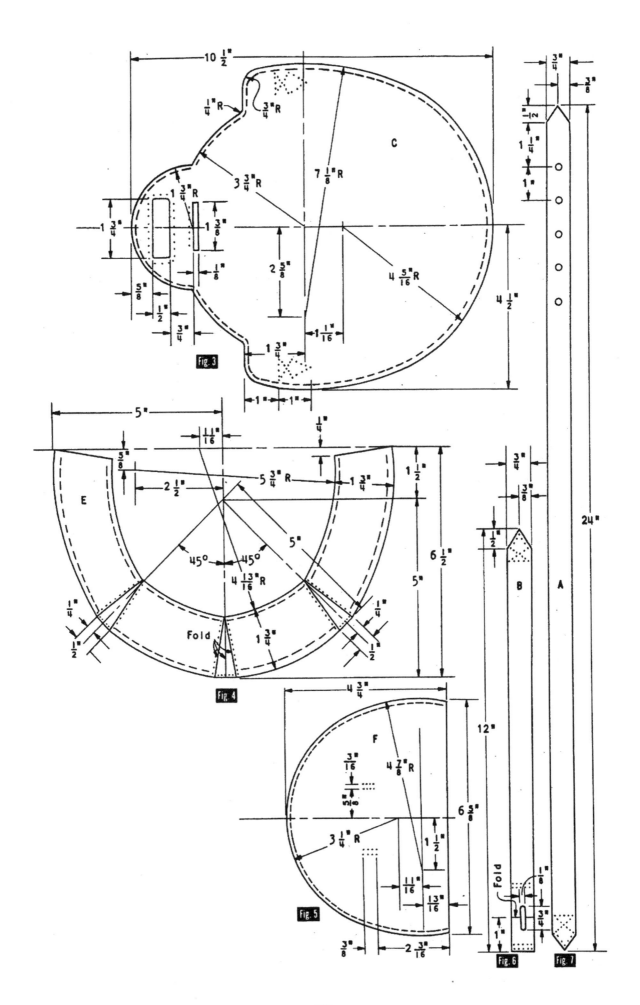

10 1/2"

1/4" R   3/4" R

C

7 1/8" R

3 3/4" R

1 3/4" R

1 3/4"   1 3/8"

1 3/4"   1"

4 5/16" R

4 1/2"

2 5/8"

1"

5/8"   1/2"   3/4"

1 1/8"

1 3/4"   1 3/8"

1"   1"

Fig. 3

5"

1 1/16"

1/4"

5/8"

5 3/4" R   1 3/4"

1 1/2"

2 1/2"

E

45°   45°   5"

4 13/16" R

6 1/2"

5"

Fold   1 3/4"

1/4"   1/2"

1/4"   1/2"

Fig 4

4 3/4"

F

3/16"

5/8"

4 7/8" R

6 5/8"

3 1/4" R

1 1/2"

1 1/16"

13/16"

3/8"   2 3/16"

Fig. 5

3/4"

1/2"

1 1/4"

1"

24"

3/4"

3/8"

1 1/2"

B   A

12"

3/4"

3/8"

1/2"

Fold

1"

1"

1/8"

3/4"

Fig. 6   **Fig. 7**

127

PROCEDURE: (CONSULT LEATHER CRAFT PROCESSING CHARTS)

1. Cut parts (A), (B), (C), (D), (E), (F), and (G). Figs. 3, 4, 5, 6, 7, 8, 9.

2. Place (A) and (B) in position on (C), skin sides facing. Mark 1/8" stitching holes, 1/8" from edge on (A) and (B) as shown. Figs. 2, 6, 7.

3. With awl, punch stitching holes simultaneously through (A), (B) and (C). Figs. 3, 6, 7.

4. Sew (A) and (B) to (C) with saddler's stitch. Fig. 2.

5. With edge creaser, mark folds on (E). Fig. 4.

6. Fold tucks of (E). With 1/7" spacing wheel, mark stitching holes for tucks. Figs. 2, 4.

7. With awl, punch stitching holes on (E) as marked. Fig. 4.

8. Sew tucks with saddle stitch. Fig. 2.

9. With edge creaser, outline edges of tab of (D) and (G). Mark folds on (G). Fold. Figs. 8, 9.

10. Place (G) on (F). With awl, punch closely spaced stitching holes simultaneously through matching parts of (G) and (F). Figs. 5, 9.

11. Sew (G) to (F) with saddler's stitch. Fig. 2.

12. Cut 1/8" slit in (C). Fig. 3.

13. Cement (D) to (C) flesh sides together, up to 1/8" slit in (C). Fig. 2.

14. With 1/7" spacing wheel, mark one row of stitching holes on (C), 1/8" below edge of slit. Figs. 2, 3.

15. With awl, punch stitching holes simultaneously through matching parts of (C) and (D) as marked. Fig. 2.

16. Sew (D) to (C) below slit with saddler's stitch. Fig. 2.

17. Cut 1/2" slot in (CD). Figs. 2, 3, 8.

18. Pull tongue of (D) through slit in (C). Fig. 2.

19. With 1/7" spacing wheel, 1/8" from edge of slot in (CD), mark stitching holes in (CD). Figs. 2, 3, 8.

20. With awl, punch stitching holes as marked. Fig. 2.

21. Sew around slot in (CD) with saddler's stitch. Fig. 2.

22. With awl, punch 3/32" thong slits, 1/8" from edge, along flap edge of (CD) and along matching edges of (E) and (F). Figs. 2, 3, 4, 5.

23. Place point (X) of (E) on point (X) of (C). With awl, punch 3/32" thong slits, 1/8" from edge, simultaneously through matching edges of (E) and (C). Punch from (X) to (Y); then (X) to (Z). Figs. 2, 3, 4.

24. With double overlay stitch, lace (F) to (E); then (FE) to (C). Fig. 2.

25. With No. 4 tube, punch five 1/8" holes in (A). Fig. 7.

26. Cut slot for prong of buckle (H) in (B). Figs. 2, 6.

27. With awl, punch double row of stitching holes through folded end of (B). Figs. 2, 6.

28. Insert buckle (H) in fold and sew with saddler's stitch. Fig. 2.

MATERIALS:

Pigskin, 2 oz.
Strap leather
3/32" x 11-1/2 yd. goat-skin lacing
3/4" center bar buckle
Heavy linen thread
Rubber cement

TOOLS:

(1), (4), (5), (6), (8), (17), (18), (25), (26), (28), (30), (33), (40), (41).
See Leather Chart V for punching slits on curve.

Child's Treasure Chest Bank

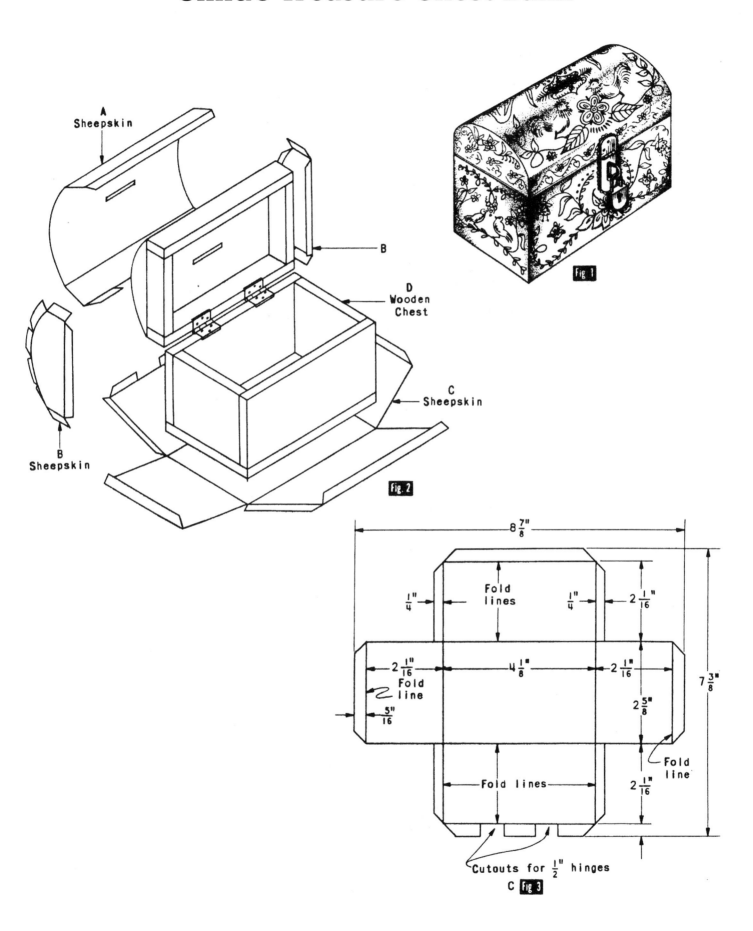

A
Sheepskin

B

D
Wooden
Chest

C
Sheepskin

B
Sheepskin

Fig. 2

Fig 1

$8\frac{7}{8}$"

Fold
lines

$\frac{1}{4}$" $\frac{1}{4}$" $2\frac{1}{16}$"

$2\frac{1}{16}$" $4\frac{1}{8}$" $2\frac{1}{16}$"

Fold
line

$2\frac{5}{8}$" $7\frac{3}{8}$"

$\frac{5}{16}$"

Fold
line

$2\frac{1}{16}$"

Fold lines

Cutouts for $\frac{1}{2}$" hinges

C   Fig 3

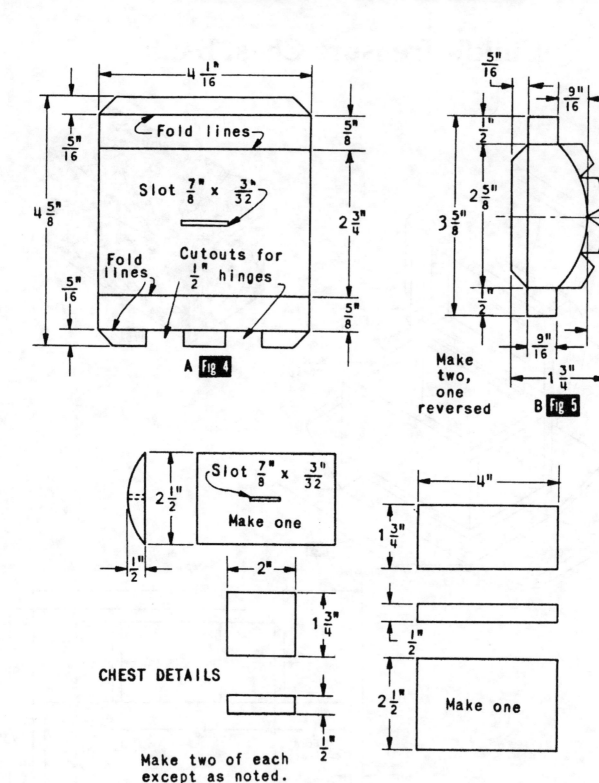

Fold lines

$4\frac{1}{16}$"

$\frac{5}{16}$"

$\frac{5}{8}$"

$4\frac{5}{8}$"

Slot $\frac{7}{8}$" x $\frac{3}{32}$"

$2\frac{3}{4}$"

Fold lines

Cutouts for $\frac{1}{2}$" hinges

$\frac{5}{16}$"

$\frac{5}{8}$"

A **Fig 4**

$\frac{5}{16}$"

$\frac{9}{16}$"

$\frac{1}{2}$"

$2\frac{5}{8}$"

$3\frac{5}{8}$"

$\frac{1}{2}$"

$\frac{5}{16}$"

$\frac{9}{16}$"

$1\frac{3}{4}$"

Make two, one reversed

B **Fig 5**

Slot $\frac{7}{8}$" x $\frac{3}{32}$"

$2\frac{1}{2}$"

Make one

$\frac{1}{2}$"

2"

$1\frac{3}{4}$"

4"

$1\frac{3}{4}$"

$\frac{1}{2}$"

$2\frac{1}{2}$"

Make one

CHEST DETAILS

$\frac{1}{2}$"

Make two of each except as noted.

For Detailed
Instructions Consult
Chart I - Cutting
Chart II - Design
Chart III - Color
Chart IV - Construction
Chart V - Lacing
Chart VI - Stitching
Chart VII - Braiding
Chart VIII - Knotting
Material Chart

PROCEDURE:(CONSULT LEATHER CRAFT PROCESSING CHARTS)

1. Cut and prepare parts (A),(B) and (C). Figs. 3, 4, 5.

   Note: Construct wooden chest with hinged cover and lock of 1/4" plywood.

2. Skive all edges to be cemented. Fig. 2.

3. Cement parts (B) to lid of chest (D). Fig. 2.

4. Cement (A) on (D), with coin slots coinciding. Fig. 2.

5. Cement long sides and bottom of (C) to (D), with folded flaps cemented to ends of (D). Fig. 2.

6. Cement ends of (C) to ends of (D) covering cemented side flaps of (C) at corner. Fig. 2.

MATERIALS:	TOOLS:
Tooling sheepskin, 1-1/2 oz., light natural color	(1), (6).
Rubber cement	See Leather Chart III for painting of design.

Coasters

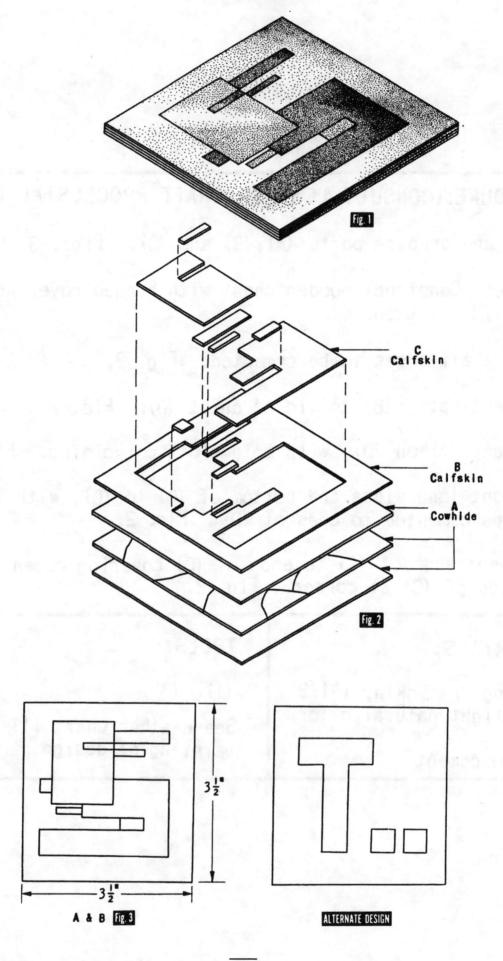

Fig. 1

C
Calfskin

B
Calfskin

A
Cowhide

Fig. 2

3½"

3½"

A & B Fig. 3

ALTERNATE DESIGN

PROCEDURE: (CONSULT LEATHER CRAFT PROCESSING CHARTS)

1. Cut top and bottom parts (A) and part (B). Figs. 2, 3.

2. Cut up scraps of leather to form inner (A). Piece tightly fitted scraps together, jig-saw fashion. Fig. 2.

3. Sandpaper skin sides of all layers to be cemented. Fig. 2.

4. Cement scrap leather (A) to bottom (A), flesh sides together, with pliobond plastic adhesive. Fig. 2.

5. Cement flesh side of top (A) to scrap (A) with pliobond plastic adhesive. Fig. 2.

6. Place cemented layers of (A) under weight and allow to dry for 18- 24 hours. Fig. 2.

7. Cut out area for inlay design in (B). Fig. 3.

8. Cut design units (C) of contrasting colors to fit in respective areas of cut-out in (B). Figs. 2, 3.

9. Test fit of pieces and evenness of edges. Cement (B) to (A) with rubber cement. Figs. 2, 3.

10. Cement design motifs (C) in place with rubber cement. Fig. 2.

11. Place (AB) under weight over night. Fig. 2.

12. Sandpaper cut edges of (AB) until smooth. Figs. 1, 2.

13. Apply several coats of Johnson's paste wax to edges and all surfaces of (AB). Rub until glossy. Fig. 1.

MATERIALS:	TOOLS:	For Detailed Instructions Consult
Cowhide, 6 oz. Russian calfskin, assorted colors Pliobond plastic adhesive Rubber cement Sandpaper, No. 00 Johnson's paste wax	(1), (6), (33). See Leather Chart III for Leather Inlay	Chart I - Cutting Chart II - Design Chart III - Color Chart IV - Construction Chart V - Lacing Chart VI - Stitching Chart VII - Braiding Chart VIII - Knotting Material Chart

Coasters

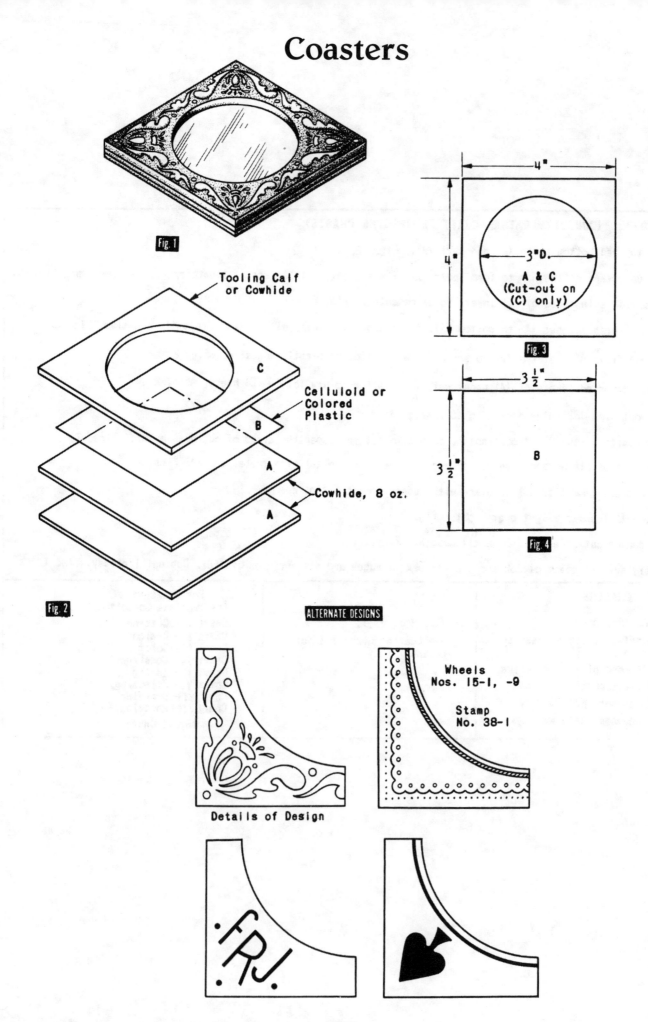

Fig. 1

Tooling Calf
or Cowhide

Celluloid or
Colored
Plastic

Cowhide, 8 oz.

C

B

A

A

Fig. 2

4"

4"

3"D.

A & C
(Cut-out on
(C) only)

Fig. 3

3 1/2"

3 1/2"

B

Fig. 4

ALTERNATE DESIGNS

Details of Design

Wheels
Nos. 15-1, -9

Stamp
No. 38-1

.FRJ.

PROCEDURE: (CONSULT LEATHER CRAFT PROCESSING CHARTS)

1. Cut and prepare parts (A), (B) and (C). Figs. 3, 4.

2. Cement part (A) to (A) flesh sides together. Fig. 2.

3. Cement edges of (B), centering (B) on (A). Fig. 2.

4. Sandpaper skin side of (A) extending beyond (B). Fig. 2.

5. Cement (C) to (AB). Put assembled pieces under weight. Allow to dry for 18-24 hours. Fig. 2.

6. Sandpaper cut edges until smooth. Fig. 1.

7. Color cut edges to match color used for (C). Fig. 1.

8. Apply Johnson's paste wax to sanded, colored edges and rub until polished. Fig. 1.

MATERIALS:

Cowhide, scraps, 8 oz.

Tooling calf or cowhide, assorted colors

Celluloid or colored plastic

Pliobond plastic adhesive

Sandpaper No. 0

Higgin's colored inks

Johnson's paste wax

TOOLS:

(1), (6).

For Detailed
Instructions Consult
Chart I - Cutting
Chart II - Design
Chart III - Color
Chart IV - Construction
Chart V - Lacing
Chart VI - Stitching
Chart VII - Braiding
Chart VIII - Knotting

Material Chart

Coasters

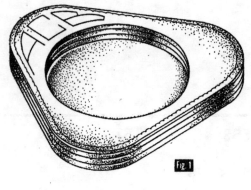

Fig. 1

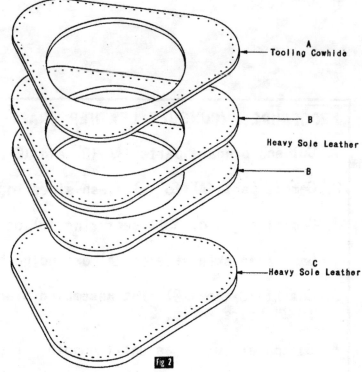

A — Tooling Cowhide

B

Heavy Sole Leather

B

C
Heavy Sole Leather

Fig 2

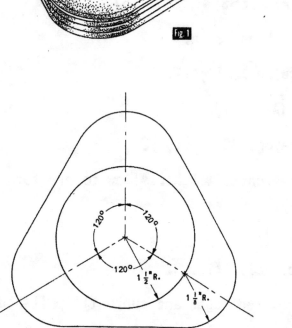

120°   120°

120° $1\frac{1}{2}$" R.

$1\frac{1}{8}$" R.

A, B & C
(C without hole)

Fig. 3

**For Detailed
Instructions Consult**
Chart I – Cutting
Chart II – Design
Chart III – Color
Chart IV – Construction
Chart V – Lacing
Chart VI – Stitching
Chart VII – Braiding
Chart VIII – Knotting
Material Chart

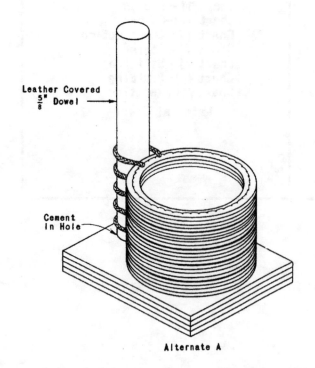

Leather Covered
$\frac{5}{8}$" Dowel

Cement
In Hole

Alternate A

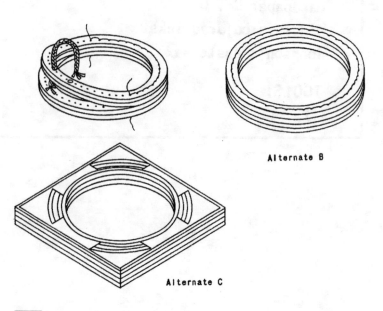

Alternate B

Alternate C

PROCEDURE: (CONSULT LEATHER CRAFT PROCESSING CHARTS)

1. Cut and prepare parts (A), (B) and (C). Fig. 3.
   Use 3" diameter die cut.

2. Sandpaper all skin surfaces to be cemented. Fig. 2.

3. Cement together parts (B); cement (B) to skin side of
   (C); cement (A) to (BC). Fig. 2.

4. Place under weight and allow to dry for 24 hours.

5. Sandpaper all cut edges to smooth surface.

6. Burnish edges on burnishing wheel to obtain hard finish.

7. Shellac all surfaces and allow to dry. Sandpaper surfaces
   lightly. Repeat this procedure three times.

8. Apply Johnson's paste wax to all surfaces. Rub to glossy finish.

9. Mark stitching holes on (A) with 1/5" spacing wheel, 3/16" from outer edge. Fig. 2.

10. Drill 1/16" stitching holes with hand drill as marked. Fig. 2.

11. Sew edges of (ABC) with saddler's stitch. Figs. 1, 2.

PROCEDURE: - Alternate Designs

A Make wooden cylinder. Cover with leather in color to match braided craftstrip
   handles on coaster.

C This design differs from described procedure in shape only.

MATERIALS:

Heavy sole leather
Tooling cowhide, 2-1/2 - 3 oz.
Pliobond plastic adhesive
Heavy linen thread
Sandpaper, No. 00
White shellac
Johnson's paste wax

TOOLS:

(1), (6), (41), and brush
for shellac.
Arbor press and burnishing
tools,
Hand drill.

Cosmetic Case

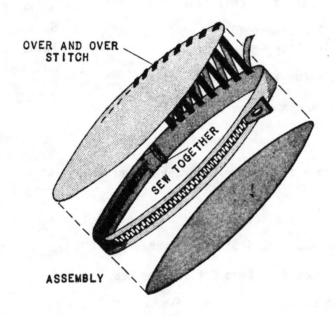

OVER AND OVER
STITCH

SEW TOGETHER

ASSEMBLY

PROCEDURE:

HAVING PREPARED THE THREE SEPARATE PIECES...
(1) PUNCH 3/32" THONG SLITS 1/8" IN FROM
    EDGES AS SHOWN IN DRAWINGS.
(2) SEW IN 8" ZIPPER INTO (C) AND SEW ENDS
    OF (C) TOGETHER, 1/8" IN FROM EDGES.
(3) LACE (A),(B) AND (C) TOGETHER.

TOOLS: (1) (2) (4) (6), (13), (17) (18)
FOR TOOLING ADD (9) (10) (11)

MATERIALS: CONSULT LEATHER CHART,
            8" ZIPPER

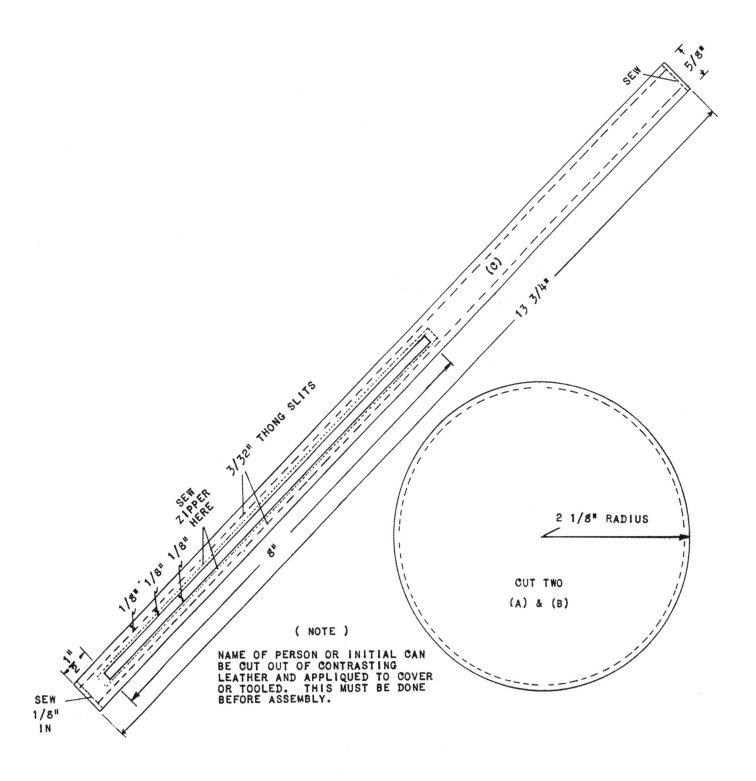

SEW

5/8"

(C)

13 3/4"

3/32" THONG SLITS

2 1/8" RADIUS

CUT TWO
(A) & (B)

SEW
ZIPPER
HERE

1/8" 1/8" 1/8"

8"

1"
2"

SEW
1/8"
IN

(NOTE)

NAME OF PERSON OR INITIAL CAN
BE CUT OUT OF CONTRASTING
LEATHER AND APPLIQUED TO COVER
OR TOOLED. THIS MUST BE DONE
BEFORE ASSEMBLY.

Comb & Nail File Case

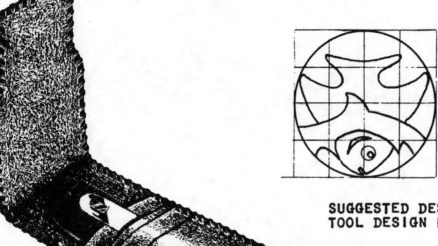

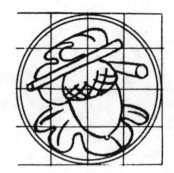

SUGGESTED DESIGNS FOR FLAP
TOOL DESIGN BEFORE ASSEMBLY

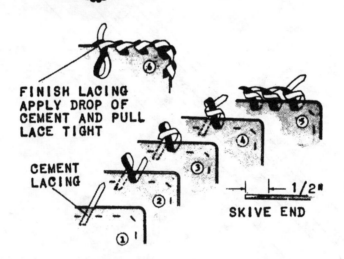

FINISH LACING
APPLY DROP OF
CEMENT AND PULL
LACE TIGHT

CEMENT
LACING

1/2"

SKIVE END

HOW TO MAKE
BUTTONHOLE
STITCH

PROCEDURE:
HAVING PREPARED THE FOUR SEPARATE PIECES...
(1) LOCATE (D)(C)(B) ON (A), SEE ASSEMBLY, AND
    CEMENT EDGES TO HOLD PIECES IN PLACE.
(2) PUNCH 3/32" THONG SLITS 1/8" IN FROM EDGES,
    AS INDICATED, AND LACE TOGETHER.

TOOLS: (1)(2)(4)(6)(16)(17)
FOR TOOLING, ADD (9)(10)(11)(13)

MATERIALS: CONSULT LEATHER CHART, RUBBER CEMENT.

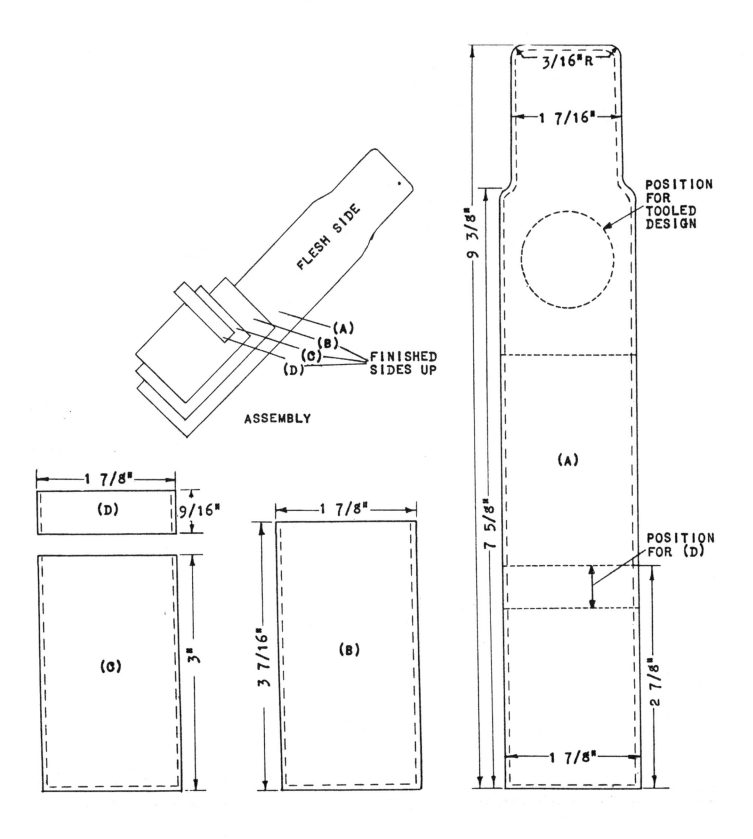

FLESH SIDE

(A)
(B)
(C)
(D)

FINISHED
SIDES UP

ASSEMBLY

1 7/8"

(D)

9/16"

(C)

3"

1 7/8"

(B)

3 7/16"

3/16"R

1 7/16"

POSITION
FOR
TOOLED
DESIGN

9 3/8"

(A)

7 5/8"

POSITION
FOR (D)

2 7/8"

1 7/8"

Combination Eyeglass Case

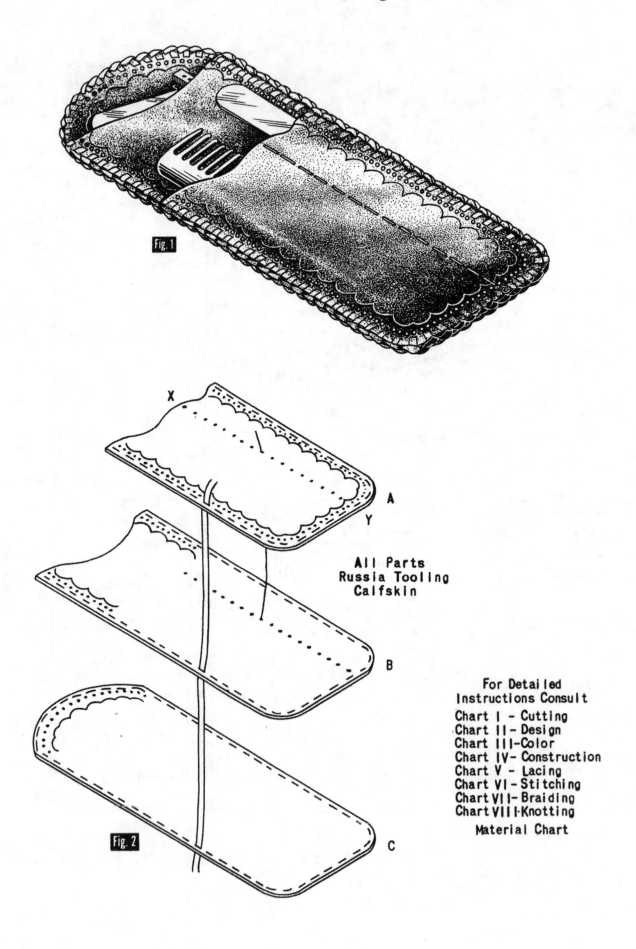

Fig. 1

Fig. 2

X

Y

A

B

C

All Parts
Russia Tooling
Calfskin

For Detailed
Instructions Consult
Chart I - Cutting
Chart II- Design
Chart III-Color
Chart IV- Construction
Chart V - Lacing
Chart VI-Stitching
Chart VII- Braiding
Chart VIII-Knotting
Material Chart

142

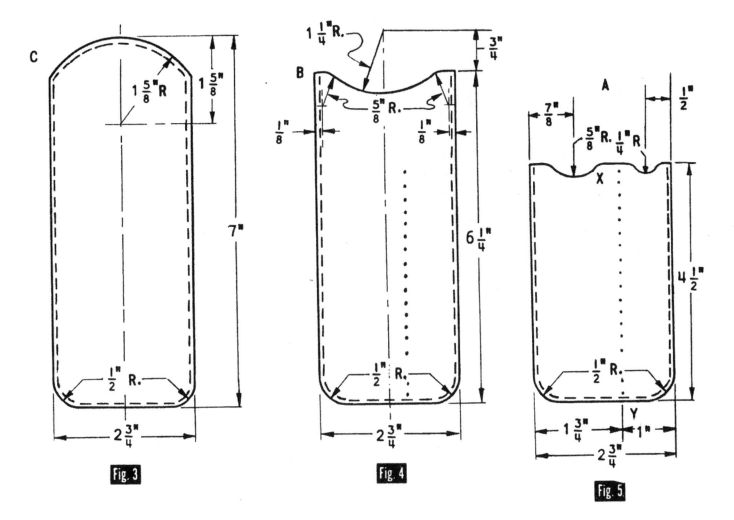

Fig. 3

Fig. 4

Fig. 5

PROCEDURE: (CONSULT LEATHER CRAFT PROCESSING CHARTS)

1. Cut and prepare parts (A), (B) and (C). Figs. 3, 4, 5.

2. Place (A) in position on (B). With awl, punch 1/8" stitching holes simultaneously through (A) and (B) along line (XY). Figs. 2, 4, 5.

3. Cement (A) to (B), 3/16" from matching edges. Fig. 2.

4. Saddle stitch (A) to (B) along line (XY). Fig. 2.

5. Cement (AB) to (C), 3/16" from matching edges. Fig. 2.

6. With awl, punch 3/32" thong slits, 1/8" from edges, in (ABC). Figs. 2, 3, 4, 5.

7. Lace edges of (ABC) with single overlay stitch. Figs. 1, 2.

MATERIALS:

Russia tooling calfskin

Goatskin lacing, 10'

Rubber cement

Heavy linen thread

TOOLS:

(1), (4), (15 No. 9), (18), (25), (26), (40), (41).

Coin Purse

Robert Towell

FIG.1

FOLD TOGETHER
COUNTER CLOCKWISE

FIG.2

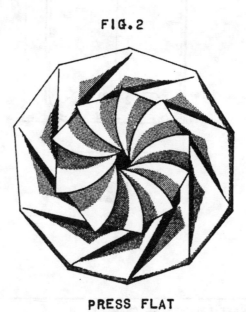

PRESS FLAT

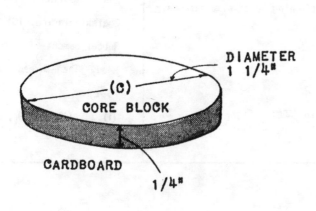

DIAMETER
1 1/4"

(C)
CORE BLOCK

CARDBOARD

1/4"

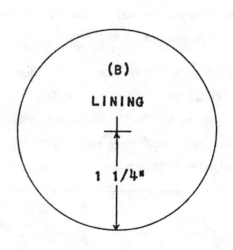

(B)

LINING

1 1/4"

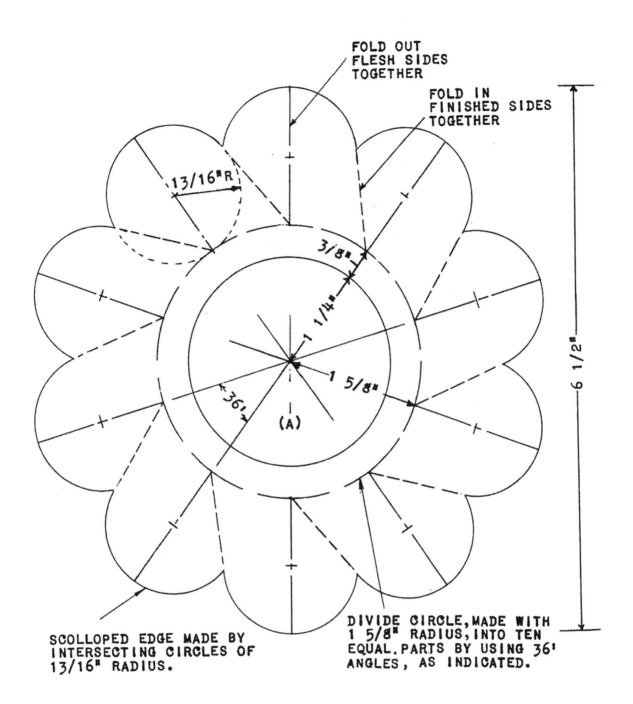

FOLD OUT
FLESH SIDES
TOGETHER

FOLD IN
FINISHED SIDES
TOGETHER

13/16"R

3/8"

1 1/4"

1 5/8"

36'

(A)

6 1/2"

SCOLLOPED EDGE MADE BY
INTERSECTING CIRCLES OF
13/16" RADIUS.

DIVIDE CIRCLE, MADE WITH
1 5/8" RADIUS, INTO TEN
EQUAL PARTS BY USING 36'
ANGLES, AS INDICATED.

PROCEDURE:
HAVING PREPARED THE THREE SEPARATE PARTS...
(1) LOCATE AND CEMENT PART (B) TO (A), FLESH SIDES TOGETHER.
(2) MOISTEN FLESH SIDE OF (A) WITH WATER UNTIL LEATHER DARKENS
      ON FINISHED SIDE.
(3) CENTER CORE, (C) OVER (B).
(4) START AT ANY CONVENIENT PLACE AND FOLD SCOLLOPED EDGE OVER
      CORE AS INDICATED IN FIG.1. PRESS FLAT AS IN FIG.2. PLACE
      IN CLAMP TO KEEP FOLDS DOWN UNTIL COMPLETELY DRY. WHEN DRY,
      REMOVE CORE.

TOOLS: (1)(6)(20)

MATERIALS:

CONSULT LEATHER CHART,
RUBBER CEMENT, CARDBOARD,
TEMPLATE PAPER.

Coin and Bill Purse

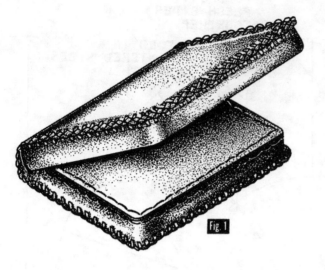

Fig. 1

For Detailed
Instructions Consult
Chart I - Cutting
Chart II - Design
Chart III - Color
Chart IV - Construction
Chart V - Lacing
Chart VI - Stitching
Chart VII - Braiding
Chart VIII - Knotting
Material Chart

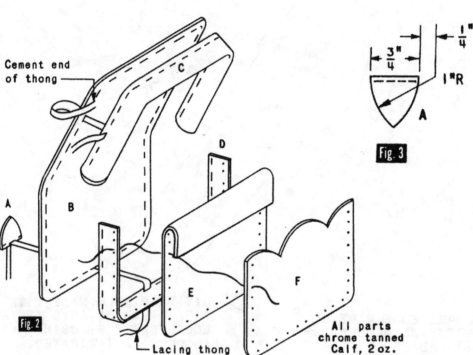

Cement end of thong

Fig. 2

Lacing thong

All parts chrome tanned Calf, 2 oz.

Fig. 3

PROCEDURE: (CONSULT LEATHER CRAFT PROCESSING CHARTS)

1. Cut parts (A), (B), (C), (D), (E), (F). Figs. 3, 4, 5, 6, 7, 8.

2. Fold (C) on center and cement sides together. Fig. 7.

3. With awl punch holes $\frac{1}{8}$" apart, $\frac{1}{8}$" from edges, simultaneously on (D), (E), (F), while in assembled position. Fig. 2.

4. Punch $\frac{3}{32}$" thong slits $\frac{1}{8}$" from edges, simultaneously on (A), (B), (C), (D) while in assembled position. Fig. 2.

5. Sew (D), (E), (F), using saddler's stitch. Fig. 2.

6. Assemble (A), (B), (C) and assembly (DEF), using single overlay lacing stitch. Fig. 2.

MATERIALS:

Chrome tanned calf (2 oz.)

Goatskin lacing $\frac{3}{32}$" wide, 10' long

Heavy linen thread

Rubber cement

TOOLS:

(4), (5), (6), (17), (18), (25), (26), (33), (40), (41).

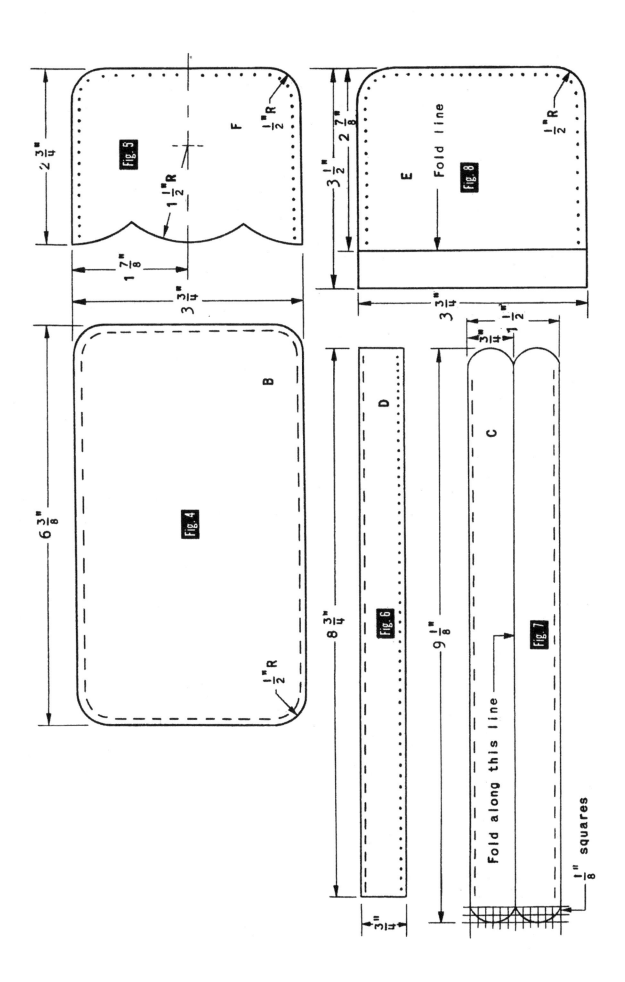

Fig. 5

F

$2\frac{3}{4}$"

$\frac{1}{2}$"R

$1\frac{1}{2}$"R

$1\frac{7}{8}$"

$3\frac{3}{4}$"

B

Fig. 4

$6\frac{3}{8}$"

$\frac{1}{2}$"R

E

Fold line

Fig. 8

$3\frac{1}{2}$"

$2\frac{7}{8}$"

$\frac{1}{2}$"R

$3\frac{3}{4}$"

D

Fig. 6

$8\frac{3}{4}$"

$\frac{3}{4}$"

$1\frac{1}{2}$"

$\frac{3}{4}$"

1"

C

Fig. 7

$9\frac{1}{8}$"

Fold along this line

$\frac{1}{8}$" squares

147

Dog Leash and Collar

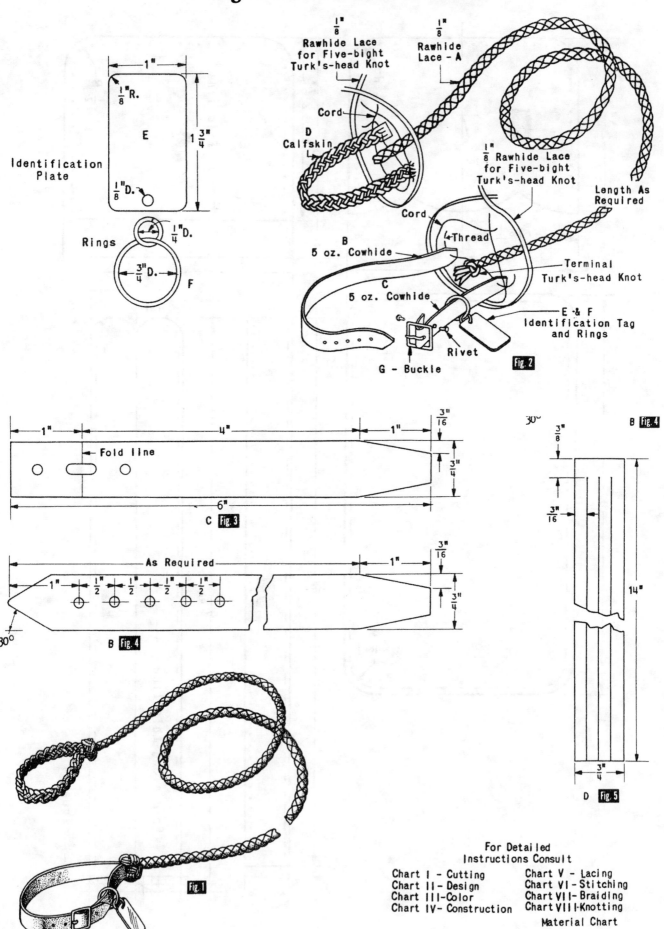

Identification Plate

1"
1/8"R.
E
1 3/4"
1/8"D.

Rings
1/4"D.
3/4"D.
F

1/8 Rawhide Lace for Five-bight Turk's-head Knot

1/8 Rawhide Lace - A

Cord

D Calfskin

1/8 Rawhide Lace for Five-bight Turk's-head Knot

Length As Required

Cord

B 5 oz. Cowhide

Thread

Terminal Turk's-head Knot

C 5 oz. Cowhide

E & F Identification Tag and Rings

Rivet

G - Buckle

Fig. 2

Fold line
1"   4"   1"   3/16"   3/4"
6"
C   Fig. 3

As Required   1"   3/16"
1"   1/2" 1/2" 1/2" 1/2"   3/4"
30°
B   Fig. 4

30°   B   Fig. 4
3/8"
3/16"
14"
3/4"
D   Fig. 5

Fig. 1

For Detailed Instructions Consult
Chart I - Cutting   Chart V - Lacing
Chart II- Design   Chart VI-Stitching
Chart III-Color   Chart VII-Braiding
Chart IV- Construction   Chart VIII-Knotting
                    Material Chart

148

PROCEDURE: (CONSULT LEATHER CRAFT PROCESSING CHARTS)

1. Cut (B),(C) and (D). Figs. 3, 4, 5.

2. Cut slot for prong of buckle (G) in (C), and punch holes for prong in (B). Figs. 3, 4.

3. Insert (G) in (C). Fold (C) and insert rivet. Fig. 2.

4. Attach identification plate (E) to (C) with rings (F). Fig. 2.

5. Braid leash (A) with four-plait round, diamond pattern, with double thong structure. Fig. 2.

6. End (A) with terminal Turk's-head knot. Fig. 2.

7. Cement ends of (B) and (C) to (A). Sew several reinforcing stitches through (A) and ends of (B) and (C). Tie firmly with cord. Fig. 2.

8. Make five-bight Turk's-head knot over junction of (ABC). Fig. 2.

9. Make a four-plait flat braid of (D) for hand strap. Figs. 2, 5.

10. Cement ends of (D) over (A). Sew several reinforcing stitches through (D) and (A). Tie firmly with cord. Fig. 2.

11. Make five-bight Turk's-head knot over junction of (DA). Fig. 2.

MATERIALS:

Cowhide, 5 oz., natural

Calfskin, 2 oz.

Rawhide lace, 1/8", natural

Rubber cement

Heavy linen thread

Twine

Rivet

Buckle, center-bar, 1"

TOOLS:

(1), (6), (8), (17), (20), (24), (26), (41).

See Leather Charts VII and VIII for braiding and knotting.

Lamp Base and Shade

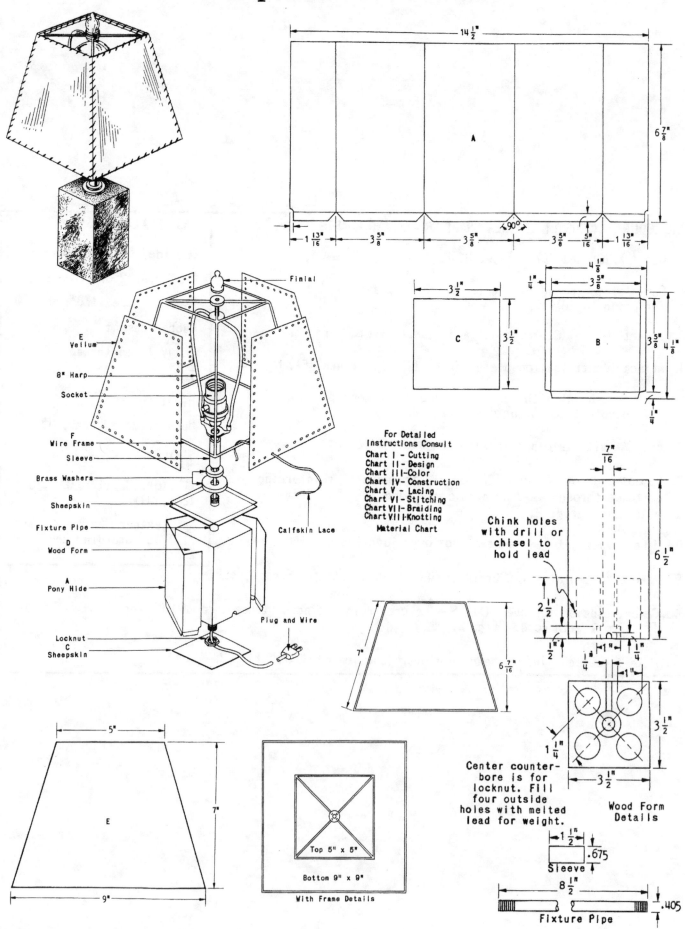

A

14 1/2"

6 7/8"

1 13/16" 3 5/8" 3 5/8" 3 5/8" 5/16" 1 13/16"

90°

Finial

E
Vellum

8" Harp

Socket

F
Wire Frame

Sleeve

Brass Washers

B
Sheepskin

Fixture Pipe

D
Wood Form

A
Pony Hide

Locknut
C
Sheepskin

Calfskin Lace

Plug and Wire

For Detailed
Instructions Consult
Chart I - Cutting
Chart II - Design
Chart III - Color
Chart IV - Construction
Chart V - Lacing
Chart VI - Stitching
Chart VII - Braiding
Chart VIII - Knotting
Material Chart

3 1/2"

C

3 1/2"

4 1/8"

1/4"

3 5/8"

B

3 5/8" 4 1/8"

1/4"

7/16"

Chink holes
with drill or
chisel to
hold lead

6 1/2"

2 1/2"

1/2" 1/4" 1" 1/4"

1"

3 1/2"

1 1/4"

3 1/2"

Center counter-
bore is for
locknut. Fill
four outside
holes with melted
lead for weight.

Wood Form
Details

7"

6 7/16"

5"

7"

E

9"

Top 5" x 5"

Bottom 9" x 9"

With Frame Details

1 1/2"

.675

Sleeve

8 1/2"

.405

Fixture Pipe

150

PROCEDURE: (CONSULT LEATHER CRAFT PROCESSING CHARTS)

1. Cut parts (A),(B),(C) and (E). Figs. 3, 4, 5, 6.

2. Skive all edges of (B). Skive and shear 1/4" bottom edge of (A). Figs. 3, 5.

3. Mark all fold lines with edge creaser on (A) and (B). Figs. 3, 5.

4. Cut corners of (A) and hole in (B) for wiring as shown. Figs. 3, 5.

5. Cement (B) to wood form (D). Fig. 2.

6. Cement (A) around (D). Fig. 2.

7. Assemble harp, sleeve, washers, fixture pipe, locknut, socket, plug and wire on (ABD) as shown. Fig. 2.

8. Cement (C) to (ABD), covering wire in groove. Fig. 2.

9. Mark holes 3/8" apart, 1/4" from edge, on all sides of one part (E). Figs. 2, 6.

10. Place marked part (E) on top of three remaining parts (E). Clip firmly together to prevent slipping.

11. Punch 3/32" holes with revolving punch on all sides of (E) through 4 parts simultaneously.

12. Lace corner edges of (E) to frame (F), using parallel whip stitch. Then lace (E) to (F) along top and bottom edges of shade. Fig. 2.

13. Attach shade to lamp with finial.

MATERIALS:

Pony hide (tawny and white)
Saddle sheepskin, 2 oz.
Vellum
Calfskin lace
Pliobond adhesive

TOOLS:

(1),(6),(8),(19),(33).

Lamp Base and Shade

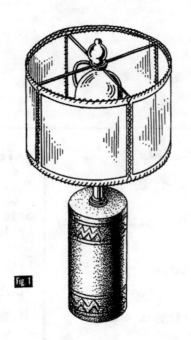

Fig. 1

For Detailed
Instructions Consult
Chart I - Cutting
Chart II - Design
Chart III - Color
Chart IV - Construction
Chart V - Lacing
Chart VI - Stitching
Chart VII - Braiding
Chart VIII - Knotting
    Material Chart

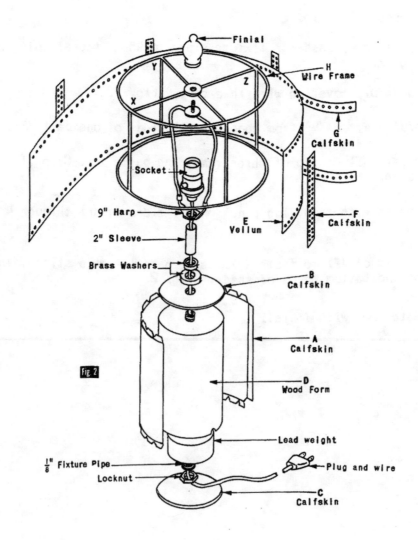

Fig 2

- Finial
- H Wire Frame
- G Calfskin
- Socket
- 9" Harp
- 2" Sleeve
- E Vellum
- F Calfskin
- Brass Washers
- B Calfskin
- A Calfskin
- D Wood Form
- Lead weight
- 1/8" Fixture Pipe
- Locknut
- Plug and wire
- C Calfskin

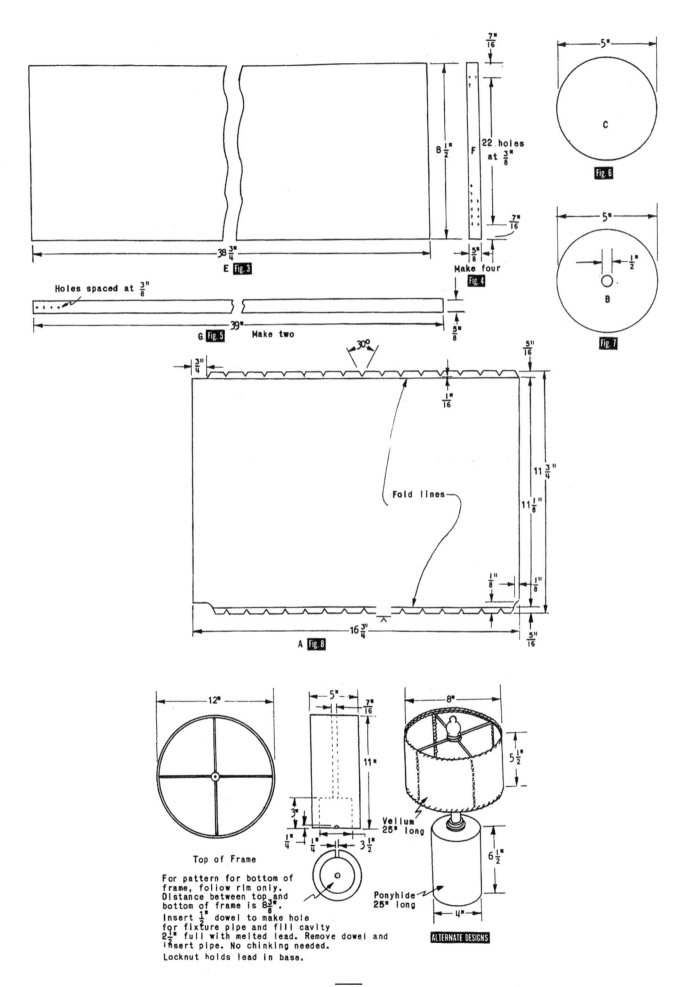

8½"

38¾"

E Fig. 3

7/16"

F

22 holes
at 3/8"

7/16"

5/8"

Make four

Fig. 4

5"

C

Fig. 6

5"

B

Fig. 7

½"

Holes spaced at 3/8"

G Fig. 5   Make two

39"

5/8"

30°

¾"

5/16"

1/16"

11¾"

11⅛"

Fold lines

1/8"

1/8"

1/8"

5/16"

16¾"

A Fig. 8

12"

Top of Frame

For pattern for bottom of
frame, follow rim only.
Distance between top and
bottom of frame is 8⅜".
Insert ½" dowel to make hole
for fixture pipe and fill cavity
2½" full with melted lead. Remove dowel and
insert pipe. No chinking needed.
Locknut holds lead in base.

5"

7/16"

11"

3"

¼"

¼"   3½"

O

Vellum
25" long

Ponyhide
25" long

8"

5½"

6½"

4"

ALTERNATE DESIGNS

153

PROCEDURE: (CONSULT LEATHER CRAFT PROCESSING CHARTS)

1. Cut and prepare parts (A), (B), (C), (E), (F) and (G). Figs. 3, 4, 5, 6, 7, 8.

2. Skive all edges of (A), (B) and (C). Figs. 6, 7, 8.

3. Mark fold lines with edge creaser on (A). Fig. 8.

4. Notch long edges of (A) about 1/16" from fold line to avoid exposing cut notches where (A) is folded over top and base of (D). Fig. 8.

5. Cement (A) to (D), overlapping skived ends in line with opening for wiring. Fig. 2.

6. Fold over and cement notched edges of (A) to top and base of (D). Fig. 2.

7. Cement part (B) to (D). Fig. 2.

8. Assemble harp, sleeve, washers, fixture pipe, locknut, socket plug and wire on (ABD) as shown. Fig. 2.

9. Cement (C) to (ABD) covering wire in groove. Fig. 2.

10. Place (E) around frame (H) to determine exact overlap of ends of (E) and placement of parts (F) on (E) at vertical wires of (H). Fig. 2.

11. Skive ends of parts (F) and (G). Figs. 4, 5.

12. Cement parts (F) on (E). Fig. 2.

13. Mark double row of parallel holes 3/8" apart, 1/8" from sides of parts (F), and single row of holes 1/4" apart on center line of parts (G). Figs. 2, 4, 5.

14. Punch all holes as marked through (EF) with 3/32" drive punch. Fig. 2.

15. Lace (EF) to (H) at (X), (Y) and (Z) with cross stitch. Fig. 2.

16. Cement overlapping ends of (E). Caution: Be sure that double row of holes punched in (EF) coincide at overlap. Fig. 2.

17. Cement parts (G) to (E) overlapping skived ends. Fig. 2.

18. Punch 3/32" holes with revolving punch, through (GE) at points marked on (G).

19. Beginning at point (Y) opposite overlapped ends of (E), lace top (GE) to (H) with whip stitch, meeting at overlap of (E). Without terminating thongs, cross stitch overlapped edge (EF) to (H). Still using same thongs, whip stitch bottom (GE) to (H), terminating thongs below point where lacing was started at point (Y). Fig. 2.

20. Attach shade to lamp with finial.

MATERIALS:

Russia tooling calfskin
Vellum
Calfskin lace, 12 yds.
Leather cement

TOOLS:

(1), (3), (6), (8), (19), (30).

Lamp Base and Shade

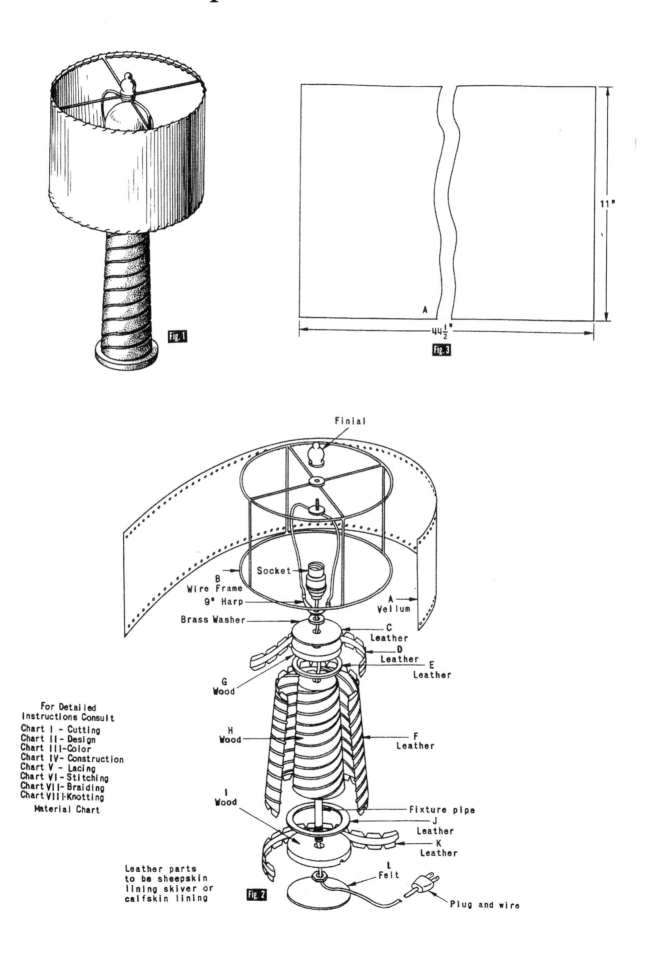

Fig.1

Fig.3

11"

44½"

A

Finial

B
Wire Frame

Socket

9" Harp

Brass Washer

A
Vellum

C
Leather

D
Leather

E
Leather

G
Wood

H
Wood

F
Leather

I
Wood

Fixture pipe

J
Leather

K
Leather

L
Felt

Plug and wire

For Detailed
Instructions Consult
Chart I – Cutting
Chart II – Design
Chart III – Color
Chart IV – Construction
Chart V – Lacing
Chart VI – Stitching
Chart VII – Braiding
Chart VIII – Knotting
    Material Chart

Leather parts
to be sheepskin
lining skiver or
calfskin lining

Fig. 2

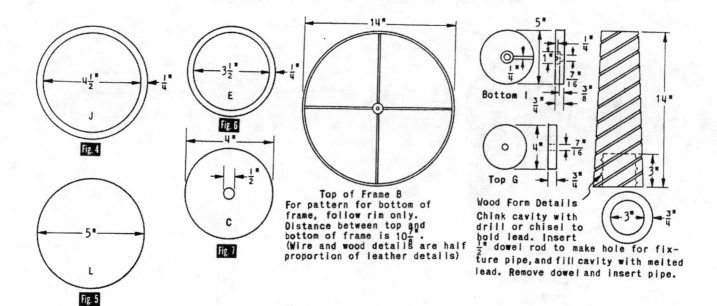

Fig. 4 — J — $4\frac{1}{2}$" — $\frac{1}{4}$"

Fig. 6 — E — $3\frac{1}{2}$" — $\frac{1}{4}$"

Fig. 5 — L — 5"

4" — C — $\frac{1}{2}$" **Fig. 7**

14"

Top of Frame B
For pattern for bottom of
frame, follow rim only.
Distance between top and
bottom of frame is $10\frac{1}{2}$".
(Wire and wood details are half
proportion of leather details)

5"
Bottom I — $\frac{1}{4}$" — 1" — $\frac{7}{16}$" — $\frac{3}{8}$" — $\frac{3}{4}$" — $\frac{1}{4}$"

Top G — 4" — $\frac{7}{16}$" — $\frac{3}{4}$"

14"

3"

3" — $\frac{3}{4}$"

Wood Form Details
Chink cavity with
drill or chisel to
hold lead. Insert
$\frac{1}{2}$" dowel rod to make hole for fixture pipe, and fill cavity with melted
lead. Remove dowel and insert pipe.

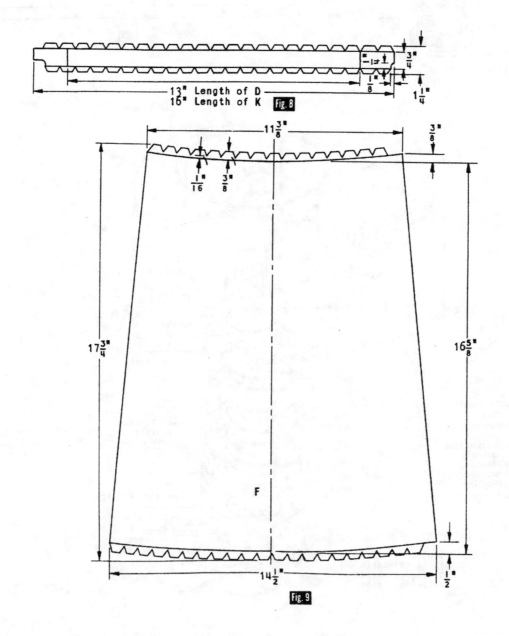

13" Length of D
16" Length of K   **Fig. 8**

$\frac{3}{4}$"
$1\frac{1}{4}$"
$\frac{1}{8}$"
$1 \pm \frac{1}{4}$"

$11\frac{3}{8}$"
$\frac{3}{8}$"

$\frac{1}{16}$" $\frac{3}{8}$"

$17\frac{3}{4}$"

$16\frac{5}{8}$"

F

$14\frac{1}{2}$"
$\frac{1}{2}$"

Fig. 9

PROCEDURE: (CONSULT LEATHER CRAFT PROCESSING CHARTS)

1. Cut parts (A), (C), (D), (E), (F), (J), (K), and (L). Figs. 3, 4, 5, 6, 7, 8, 9.

2. Moisten (F); place in position around (H), using thumb tacks to hold overlapping edges in place. Figs. 2, 9.

3. Fasten heavy cords, 1/8" diameter, to base of (H) with thumb tacks, at points where 4 spirals start.

4. With leather moist enough, adjust cords into respective grooves, and tack cords to top of (H). Press leather into position while moist. Allow leather to dry overnight with cords in grooves.

5. Remove tacks and cords, retaining as much of the stretched shape of leather as possible. Trim and skive overlapping edges if necessary.

6. Cement (F) to (H) with indentations made in leather corresponding to grooves. Press leather into grooves with embossing tool. Cement overlapping vertical edge. Fig. 2.

7. Cement notched edges of (F) to top and bottom of (H). Fig. 2.

8. Cement (D) to (G) and (K) to (I) with notched edges on top and bottom. Overlap ends in line with groove for wire outlet in (I). Fig. 2.

9. Cement (C) and (E) to (G), covering notched edges of (D). Fig. 2.

10. Cement (J) to (I) covering notched edges of (K). Fig. 2.

11. With lead weight in (H), cement (CDEG) and (IJK) to (FH). Fig. 2.

12. Assemble harp, washer, fixture pipe, locknut, socket, plug and wire to the base.

13. Cement felt (L) to bottom of base, covering wire in groove. Fig. 2.

14. Punch 3/32" holes with revolving punch, 3/8" apart, 1/4" from edge, on long sides of (A). Fig. 2.

15. Place (A) in position around wire frame (B), tying temporary threads through holes and around wire to keep (A) in position for lacing. Place (A) so overlapping ends coincide with a vertical wire of (B).

16. Cement overlapping ends of (A).

17. Lace (A) over wire of (B) with whip stitch. Remove temporary tying threads. Figs. 1, 2.

MATERIALS:

Sheepskin lining skiver or calfskin lining

Use smooth, thin, flexible leather that will stretch over base without tearing. Dye any desired color

Calfskin lace, 3/32", 6 yds.

Parchment vellum

Felt

Rubber cement

Cord

Thumbtacks

TOOLS:

(1), (6), (8), (11), (21).

Fishing Leader Book

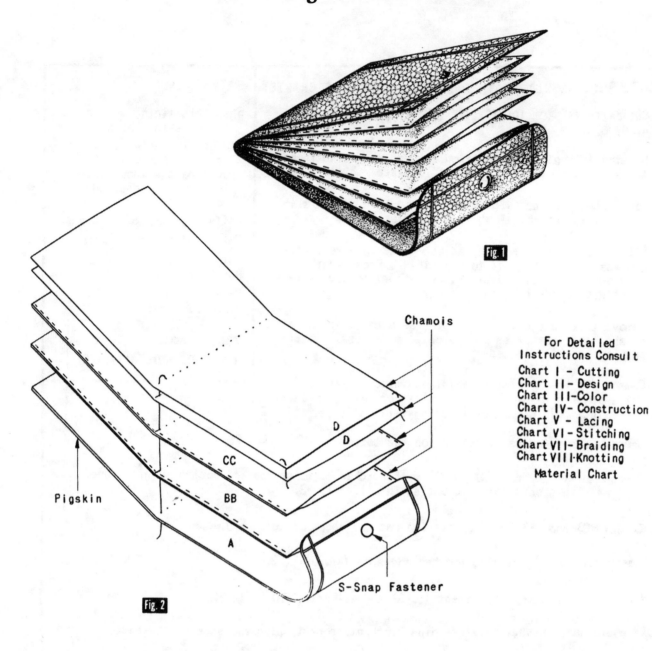

Fig. 1

Chamois

Pigskin

D
D
CC
BB
A

S-Snap Fastener

Fig. 2

For Detailed
Instructions Consult
Chart I - Cutting
Chart II - Design
Chart III - Color
Chart IV - Construction
Chart V - Lacing
Chart VI - Stitching
Chart VII - Braiding
Chart VIII - Knotting
Material Chart

PROCEDURE: (CONSULT LEATHER CRAFT PROCESSING CHARTS)

1. Cut and prepare parts (A), (B), (C) and (D). Figs. 3, 4.

2. Place (B) to (B), (C) to (C), and (D) to (D). Stitch along sides 1/8" from edges on sewing machine. Figs. 2, 4.

3. Place (BB), (CC) and (DD) in position on (A). Leave in open position. Fig. 2.

4. Mark stitching holes with 1/7" spacing wheel on center fold line of (A). Fig. 3.

5. Punch stitching holes simultaneously through parts (A), (BB), (CC) and (DD). Fig. 2.

6. Stitch with saddler's stitch. Fig. 2.

7. Attach cap of snap fastener (S) to flap of (A). Fig. 3.

8. Fold book to determine position of post of snap fastener. Insert post. Fig. 2.

MATERIALS:

Pigskin, natural grain, toolable

Chamois

Linen thread

1 snap fastener

TOOLS:

(1), (6), (8), (9), (12), (17), (21). (25), (41), (43).

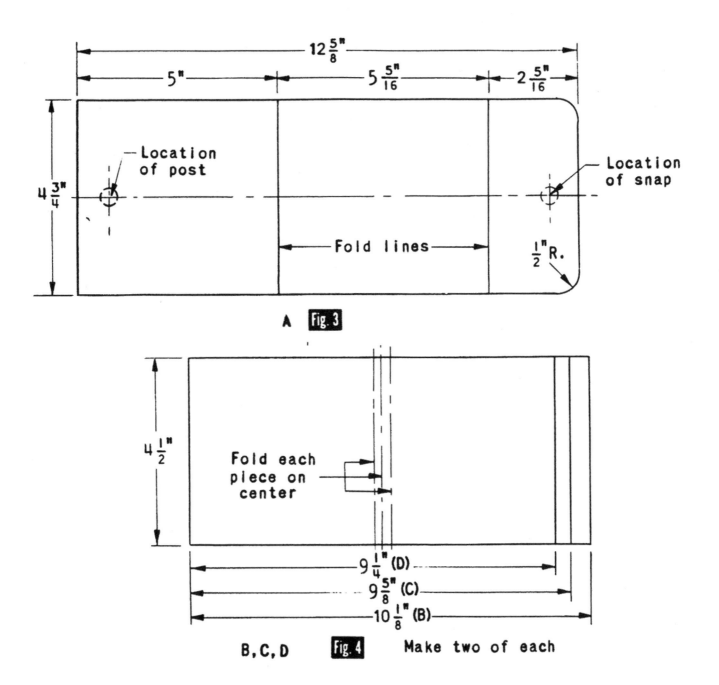

12 5/8"

5"   5 5/16"   2 5/16"

Location of post

4 3/4"

Location of snap

Fold lines

1/2" R.

A   **Fig. 3**

4 1/2"

Fold each piece on center

9 1/4" (D)

9 5/8" (C)

10 1/8" (B)

B, C, D   **Fig. 4**   Make two of each

Fishing Tackle Box

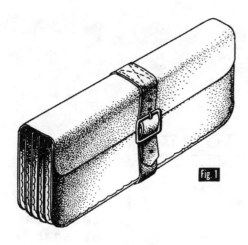

Fig.1

For Detailed
Instructions Consult
Chart I – Cutting
Chart II – Design
Chart III – Color
Chart IV – Construction
Chart V – Lacing
Chart VI – Stitching
Chart VII – Braiding
Chart VIII – Knotting
Material Chart

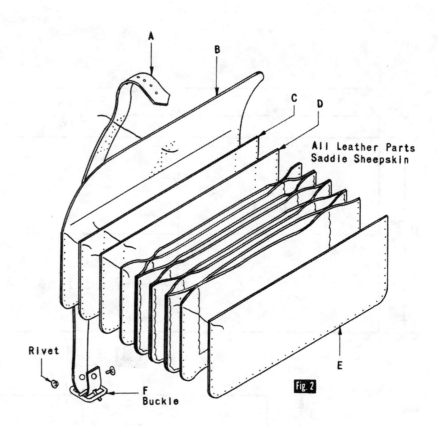

A

B

C

D

All Leather Parts
Saddle Sheepskin

Rivet

F
Buckle

E

Fig. 2

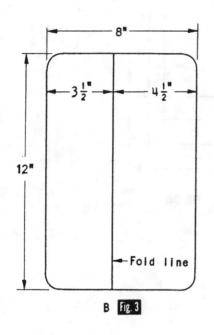

8"

3 1/2"   4 1/2"

12"

Fold line

B   Fig. 3

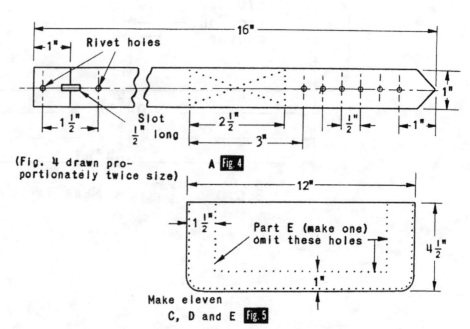

16"

1"

Rivet holes

Slot
1/2" long

1 1/2"

2 1/2"

3"

1 1/2"

1"

1"

(Fig. 4 drawn pro-
portionately twice size)

A   Fig. 4

12"

1 1/2"

Part E (make one)
omit these holes

4 1/2"

1"

Make eleven
C, D and E   Fig. 5

PROCEDURE: (CONSULT LEATHER CRAFT PROCESSING CHARTS)

1. Cut parts (A),(B),(C),(D) and (E). Figs. 3, 4, 5.

2. Outline all edges with edge creaser. Figs. 3, 4, 5.

3. Mark stitching holes with 1/7" spacing wheel on each (D) as shown, and outer edge of each (C). Figs. 2, 5.

4. Place parts (D) on (C) flesh sides together. Punch stitching holes with awl through (D) and (C) simultaneously on inner line only. (This results in 5 prs. of (DC)). Figs. 2, 5.

5. Sew (D) to (C) with saddler's stitch. Fig. 2.

6. Place (E) on one (DC). Mark stitching holes with 1/7" spacing wheel on crease line of (E). Fig. 2.

7. Punch stitching holes through (E) and matching edges of (D) only. Fig. 2.

8. Sew (E) to (D) with saddler's stitch. Fig. 2.

9. Place (EDC) on second pair (DC). Punch stitching holes through (C) of first pair (DC) and (D) of second pair (DC), as marked in step (3). Fig. 2.

10. Sew with saddler's stitch. Fig. 2.

11. Finish sewing succeeding pairs of (DC) to one another. Fig. 2.

12. Place assembled series of (DC) with (E) on flesh side of (B). Punch stitching holes through last (C) and (B), as marked in step (3). Figs. 2, 3.

13. Sew (B) to assembled (EDC) with saddler's stitch. Fig. 2.

14. Cut slot for prong of buckle (F) in square end of (A), and punch holes for prong with revolving punch in pointed end of (A). Fig. 4.

15. Insert (F); fold end of (A). Fig. 2.

16. Insert rivet through folded end of (A). Fig. 2.

17. Cement section of (A) to be stitched to (B). Punch stitching holes with awl through (AB) as shown. Figs. 1, 3, 4.

18. Sew with saddler's stitch. Fig. 2.

MATERIALS:

Saddle sheepskin, 2 oz.
1 Buckle, center bar, 1"
1 Rivet
Rubber cement
Heavy linen thread

TOOLS:

(1), (6), (8), (17), (24), (25), (28), (41), (43).

Surf Rod Belt

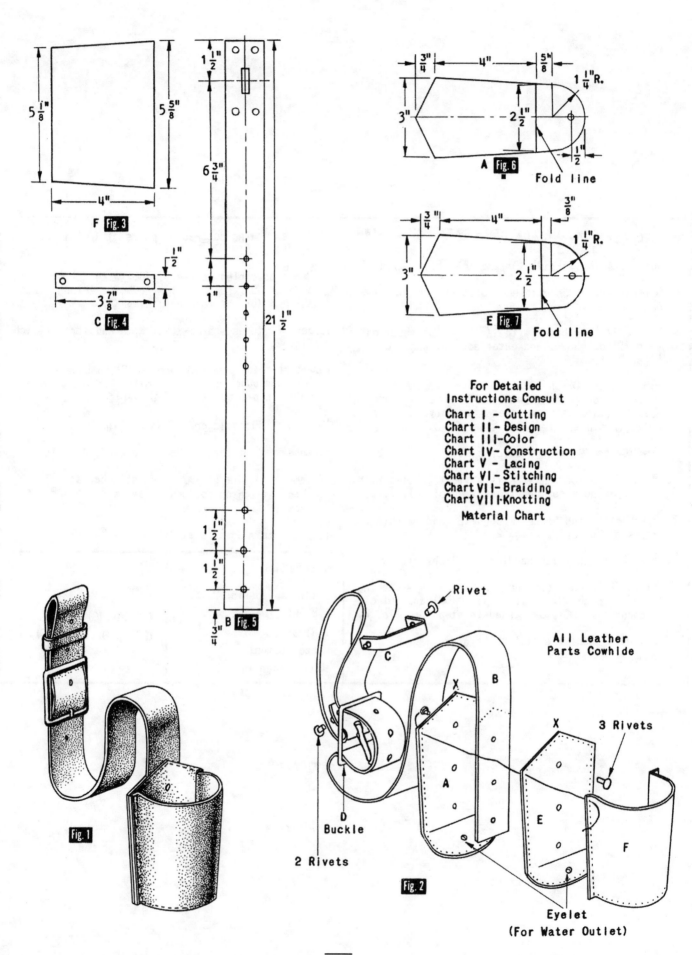

F Fig. 3

C Fig. 4

B Fig. 5

A Fig. 6

E Fig. 7

Fold line

For Detailed
Instructions Consult
Chart I – Cutting
Chart II – Design
Chart III – Color
Chart IV – Construction
Chart V – Lacing
Chart VI – Stitching
Chart VII – Braiding
Chart VIII – Knotting
Material Chart

All Leather
Parts Cowhide

Rivet

3 Rivets

Buckle

2 Rivets

Eyelet
(For Water Outlet)

D

Fig. 1

Fig. 2

PROCEDURE: (CONSULT LEATHER CRAFT PROCESSING CHARTS)

1. Cut parts (A), (B), (C), (E) and (F). Figs. 3, 4, 5, 6, 7.

2. Skive flesh side of all stitching edges on (A), (E) and (F); skive fold lines on (A) and (E), and end of (B) to be inserted between (A) and (E). Figs. 2, 6, 7.

3. Cut slot in buckle end of (B) for prong of (D), and punch holes with revolving punch for prong of (D) in (B) as shown. Figs. 2, 5.

4. Insert (D) in (B); fold end of (B). Fig. 2.

5. Insert rivets through folded end of (B). Fig. 2.

6. Pull (B) through (D) to make loop for belt. Fig. 2.

7. Adjust (C) around loop to determine to exact width when tightly fitted. Insert rivet through overlapped ends of (C). Fig. 2.

8. Slide (C) over folded end of (B). Fig. 2.

9. Cement (B) between flesh sides of (A) and (E), and bottom of (E) on (A) to form base of rod holder. Fig. 2.

10. Insert eyelet in bottom of (AE) as shown. Fig. 2.

11. Insert three rivets along center line of (ABE). Fig. 2.

12. Outline all stitching edges with edge creaser on (E), (F) and skin side of circular bottom edge of (A). Fig. 2.

13. Mark stitching holes with 1/7" spacing wheel on guide lines of (F) and top edge of (E). Fig. 2.

14. Mark stitching holes on skin side of rounded edge of (A) to correspond with matching bottom edge of (F). Fig. 2.

15. Punch stitching holes with awl through matching vertical edges of (F) and (AE) simultaneously. Fig. 2.

16. Punch matching stitching holes in bottom edge of (F) and corresponding edge of (AE). Fig. 2.

17. Sew (F) to (ABE) with saddler's stitch. starting and ending at point (X) of (AE). Figs. 1, 2.

MATERIALS:

Cowhide 5-6 oz.
6 Rivets
1 Buckle, center bar 1-1/2"
1 No. 6 K eyelet
Rubber cement
Heavy linen thread

TOOLS:

(1), (6), (7), (8), (17), (19), (24), (25), (27), (28), (30), (41), (43).

Trolling Rod Belt

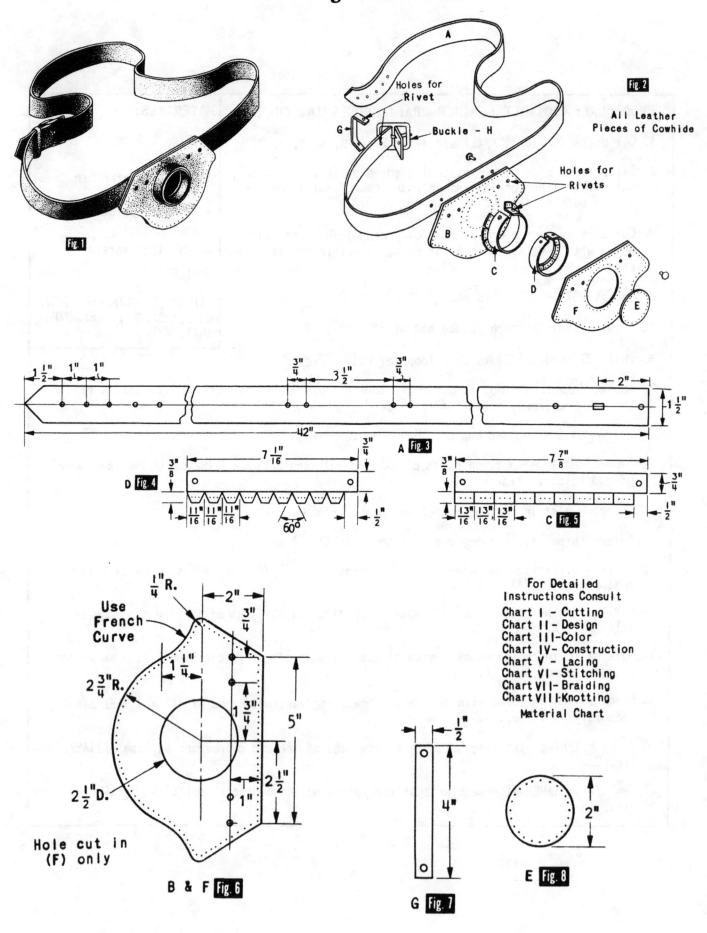

Fig. 1

Fig. 2

Holes for Rivet

Buckle - H

G

A

All Leather Pieces of Cowhide

Holes for Rivets

B

C

D

F

E

A Fig. 3

1 1/2"   1"   1"   3/4"   3 1/2"   3/4"   2"   1 1/2"

42"

D Fig. 4

3/8"   7 1/16"   3/4"

11/16"   11/16"   11/16"   60°   1/2"

C Fig. 5

3/8"   7 7/8"   3/4"

13/16"   13/16"   13/16"   1/2"

1/4" R.
Use French Curve
2 3/4" R.
2 1/2" D.

2"   3/4"
1 1/4"
1   3/4"
5"
2 1/2"
1"

Hole cut in (F) only

B & F Fig. 6

For Detailed Instructions Consult
Chart I - Cutting
Chart II - Design
Chart III - Color
Chart IV - Construction
Chart V - Lacing
Chart VI - Stitching
Chart VII - Braiding
Chart VIII - Knotting
Material Chart

1/2"
4"

G Fig. 7

2"

E Fig. 8

PROCEDURE: (CONSULT LEATHER CRAFT PROCESSING CHARTS)

1. Cut parts (A),(B),(C),(D),(E),(F) and (G). Figs. 3, 4, 5, 6, 7, 8.

2. Cut slot for prong of buckle (H) in square end of (A) and punch holes with revolving punch for prong of (H) in pointed end of (A). Fig. 3.

3. Insert (H) in (A). Fold end of (A); place (G) around fold, and insert rivet through folded ends of (A) and (G). Fig. 2.

4. Skive all stitching edges of (B),(C),(D),(E),(F), and notched edges of (C) and (D). Figs. 4, 5, 6, 8.

5. Mark size of circle cut in (F) on flesh side of (B). Figs. 2, 6.

6. Adjust (C), skin side out, to form circular wall within circle marked on (B). Cement overlapping ends of (C). Fig. 2.

7. Cement slit edge of (C) to (B). Fig. 2.

8. Adjust (D) to fit close within (C), flesh sides together. Cement together overlapping ends of (D). Fig. 2.

9. Cement (D) within (C), with notched edges lying on (B) within circular cut, and end seams of (C) and (D) in line for riveting. Fig. 2.

10. Insert rivet through end seams of (CD). Fig. 2.

11. Outline outer and inner edges of (F) and edge of (E) with edge creaser. Figs. 6, 8.

12. Mark stitching holes with 1/7" spacing wheel on crease lines of (F) and (E). Figs. 6, 8.

13. Cement (F) to (B) and (E) to (BD). Fig. 2.

14. Punch stitching holes through assembled parts, as marked. Fig. 2.

15. Sew with saddler's stitch. Fig. 2.

16. Cement assembled rod rest to (A). Insert rivets through (ABF) where shown. Fig. 2.

MATERIALS:
Cowhide, 6-7 oz.
6 Rivets
1 Buckle, center bar 1-1/2"
Heavy linen thread
Rubber cement

TOOLS:
(1), (6), (8), (17), (18), (24), (25), (27), (28), (30), (41), (43).

Fishing Reel Case

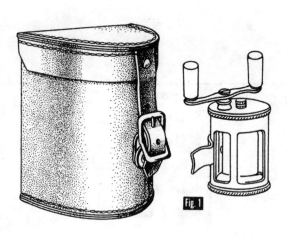

Fig. 1

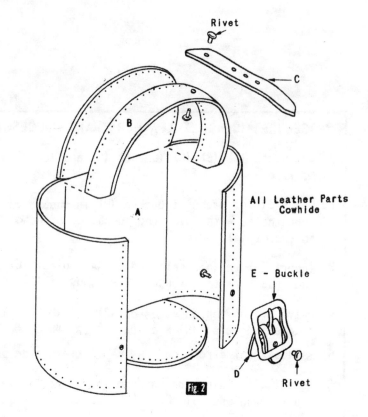

Rivet

C

All Leather Parts
Cowhide

E - Buckle

D

Rivet

Fig. 2

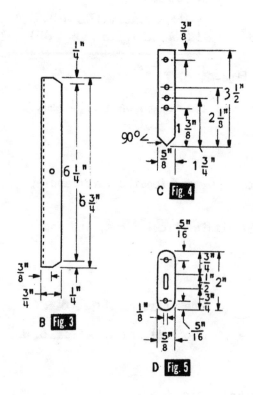

$\frac{1}{4}$"

$6\frac{1}{4}$"

$6\frac{3}{4}$"

$\frac{3}{8}$"

$\frac{3}{4}$"

$\frac{1}{4}$"

B Fig. 3

$\frac{3}{8}$"

90°

$3\frac{1}{2}$"

$2\frac{1}{8}$"

$1\frac{3}{8}$"

1

$\frac{5}{8}$"

$1\frac{3}{4}$"

C Fig. 4

$\frac{5}{16}$"

$\frac{3}{4}$"

$\frac{1}{2}$"

$\frac{3}{4}$"

2"

$\frac{1}{8}$"

$\frac{5}{8}$"

$\frac{5}{16}$"

D Fig. 5

For Detailed
Instructions Consult
Chart I - Cutting
Chart II - Design
Chart III - Color
Chart IV - Construction
Chart V - Lacing
Chart VI - Stitching
Chart VII - Braiding
Chart VIII - Knotting
Material Chart

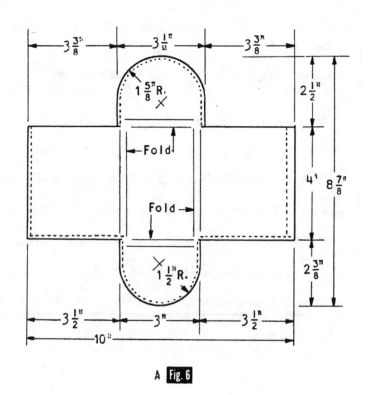

$3\frac{3}{8}$" $3\frac{1}{4}$" $3\frac{3}{8}$"

$1\frac{5}{8}$" R.

Fold

Fold

$1\frac{1}{2}$" R.

$3\frac{1}{2}$" 3" $3\frac{1}{2}$"

$2\frac{1}{2}$"

4"

$2\frac{3}{8}$"

$8\frac{7}{8}$"

10"

A Fig. 6

PROCEDURE: (CONSULT LEATHER CRAFT PROCESSING CHARTS)

1. Cut parts (A), (B), (C) and (D). Figs. 3, 4, 5, 6.

2. Skive the flesh side of (A) to a width of 1/4" on fold lines to facilitate bending. Fig. 6.

3. Skive two overlapping front edges of (A). Figs. 2, 6.

4. Skive the rounded edges of (A) and the matching bottom edges of the wall of (A), and top edge of (B) to form flexible stitching edges. Figs. 2, 3, 6.

5. Mark stitching line with edge creaser on all edges to be stitched on (A) and (B), and a crease line to finish all other unstitched edges. Fig. 2.

6. Mark stitching holes with 1/7" spacing wheel on all edges to be stitched except rounded top and bottom edges of (A). Figs. 3, 6.

7. Mark stitching holes on rounded top and bottom edges of (A) to correspond to matching straight edges. Figs. 2, 6.

8. Punch all stitching holes except front vertical seam. Fig. 2.

9. Cement overlapping front edges of (A). Insert small block of wood for punching holes. Fig. 2.

10. Punch stitching holes through cemented edges of (A). Fig. 2.

11. Sew vertical seam with saddler's stitch. Fig. 2.

12. Sew (B) to (A), and bottom seam of (A) with saddler's stitch. Fig. 2.

13. Cut slot for prong of buckle (E) in (D), and holes for prong of (E) in (C). Figs. 4, 5.

14. Fold (D); insert (E). Fig. 2.

15. Attach ends of (D) to (A) and end of (C) to (B) with rivets. Figs. 2, 3, 6.

MATERIALS:
Cowhide, 6-7 oz.
Buckle, center bar, 5/8"
Two Rivets
Heavy linen thread
Rubber cement

TOOLS:
(1),((6),(8),(17),(19),(24),
(25),(28),(41).

See Leather Chart V for punching holes on circular edge.

Fishing Reel Case

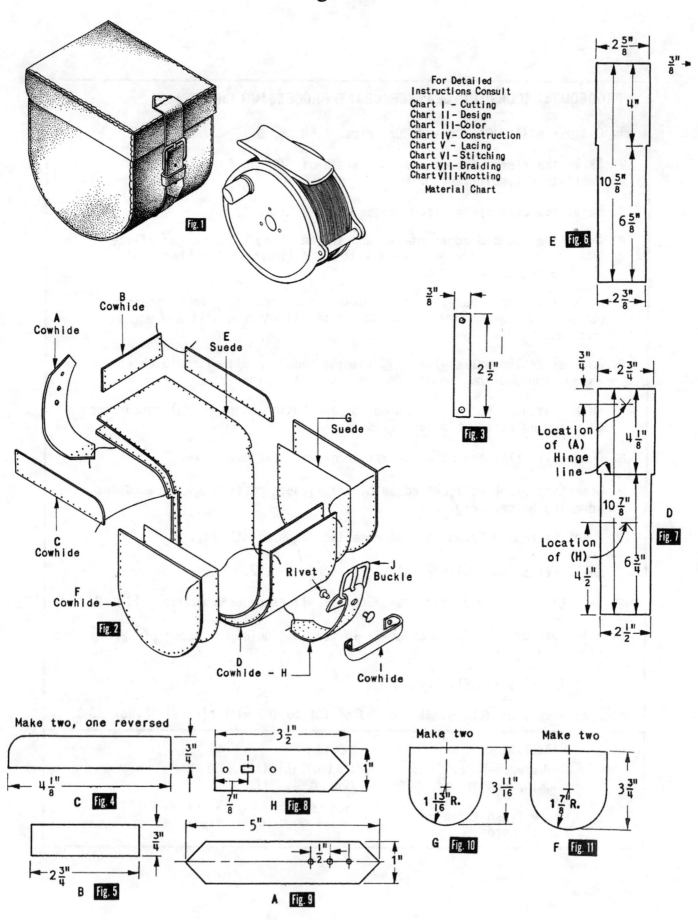

For Detailed
Instructions Consult
Chart I – Cutting
Chart II – Design
Chart III-Color
Chart IV- Construction
Chart V – Lacing
Chart VI- Stitching
Chart VII- Braiding
Chart VIII-Knotting
Material Chart

Fig. 1

A
Cowhide

B
Cowhide

E
Suede

G
Suede

C
Cowhide

F
Cowhide

Fig. 2

Rivet

J
Buckle

D
Cowhide – H

I
Cowhide

Fig. 3

2 5/8"

3/8"

4"

10 5/8"

6 5/8"

2 3/8"

E Fig. 6

2 1/2"

3/8"

3/4"

2 3/4"

Location
of (A)
Hinge
line

4 1/8"

10 7/8"

Location
of (H)

6 3/4"

4 1/2"

2 1/2"

D
Fig. 7

Make two, one reversed

3/4"

4 1/8"

C Fig. 4

3/4"

2 3/4"

B Fig. 5

3 1/2"

1"

7/8"

H Fig. 8

5"

1/2"

1"

A Fig. 9

Make two

3 11/16"

1 13/16" R.

G Fig. 10

Make two

3 3/4"

1 7/8" R.

F Fig. 11

168

PROCEDURE: (CONSULT LEATHER CRAFT PROCESSING CHARTS)

MATERIALS:

Cowhide, 8 oz.
Suede, 1 oz.
1 Buckle, 1"
1 Rivet
Heavy linen thread
Rubber cement

TOOLS:

(1), (6), (8), (17), (19), (24),
(25), (27), (28), (30), (41).

1. Cut parts (A), (B), (C), (D), (E), (F), (G), (H) and (I). Figs. 3, 4, 5, 6, 7, 8, 9, 10, 11.

2. Outline all edges of (A), (B), (C), (D), (F), (H) and (I) with edge creaser. Figs. 3, 4, 5, 7, 8, 9, 11.

3. Skive to a width of 1/4", the hinge line on flesh side of (D). Skive all stitching edges of (B), (C), (D) and (F) to make flexible stitching edges. Figs. 2, 7.

4. Cut slot for prong of buckle (J) in (H); punch holes for prong of (J) in (A). Figs. 8, 9.

5. Insert (J) in (H). Fold end of (H) and cement. Fig. 2.

6. Place (I) in position around folded (H). Insert rivet through overlapping ends of (I) and fold of (H). Fig. 2.

7. Cement pointed end of (H) and end of (A) in position on (D). Figs. 2, 7.

8. Mark stitching holes on crease lines of (H) and (A) with 1/7" spacing wheel, where (A) and (H) are to be stitched to (D). Fig. 2.

9. Punch stitching holes with awl through (AD) and (HD). Fig. 2.

10. Sew with saddler's stitch. Fig. 2.

11. Cement parts (G) to flesh sides of parts (F); cement (E) to flesh side of (D) taking into account curve and hinge edge of (D). Fig. 2.

12. Mark stitching holes with 1/7" spacing wheel on all edges of (D) to be stitched. Fig. 2.

13. Mark corresponding stitching holes in matching edges of (B), (C), and (F). Fig. 2.

14. Punch stitching holes with awl, on edges of (B), (C), (F) and (D), simultaneously on straight edges when possible. Fig. 2.

15. Sew parts together with saddler's stitch. Start at left front corner of (DF); stitch around base, continue around cover; finish with right front corner of (DF). Fig. 2.

Flashlight Case

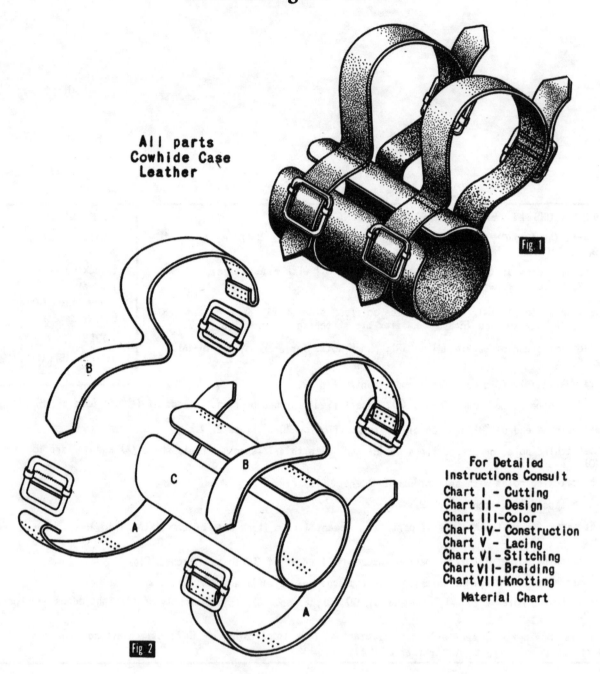

All parts
Cowhide Case
Leather

Fig. 1

B

B

C

A

A

Fig 2

For Detailed
Instructions Consult
Chart I - Cutting
Chart II- Design
Chart III-Color
Chart IV- Construction
Chart V - Lacing
Chart VI- Stitching
Chart VII-Braiding
Chart VIII-Knotting
Material Chart

PROCEDURE: (CONSULT LEATHER CRAFT PROCESSING CHARTS)	MATERIALS:

PROCEDURE: (CONSULT LEATHER CRAFT PROCESSING CHARTS)

1. Cut parts (A), (B), (C). Figs. 3, 4, 5.

2. Fold back ends of (A) and (B) $\frac{5}{8}$" and with awl punch stitching holes at matching points designated. Figs. 4, 5.

3. Place buckles in position and sew with saddler's stitch. Figs. 1, 2.

4. Punch stitching holes in parts (A) and (B) and matching holes in part (C). Figs. 1, 2, 3, 4, 5.

5. Sew (A) and (B) to part (C) with saddler's stitch. Figs. 1, 2.

MATERIALS:

Cowhide case leather

Heavy linen thread (tan)

4 saw-tooth edged buckles

TOOLS:

(1), (6), (17), (25), (30), (41).

170

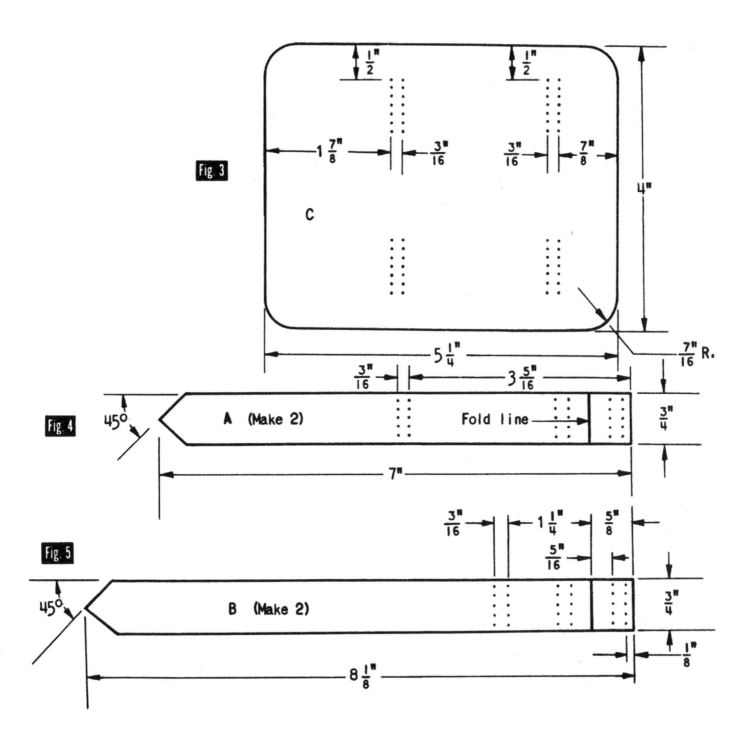

Fig. 3

C

Fig. 4

A (Make 2)   Fold line

45°

7"

Fig. 5

B (Make 2)

45°

8 1/8"

Scuffies

DESIGN FOR STRAPS (C)&(D)

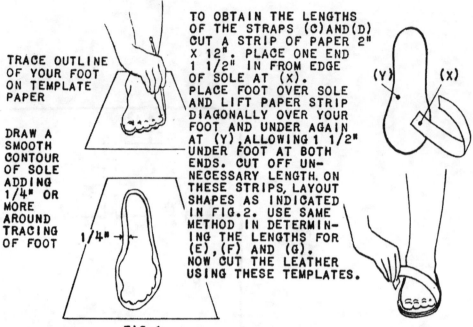

TRACE OUTLINE OF YOUR FOOT ON TEMPLATE PAPER

DRAW A SMOOTH CONTOUR OF SOLE ADDING 1/4" OR MORE AROUND TRACING OF FOOT

1/4"

TO OBTAIN THE LENGTHS OF THE STRAPS (C) AND (D) CUT A STRIP OF PAPER 2" X 12". PLACE ONE END 1 1/2" IN FROM EDGE OF SOLE AT (X). PLACE FOOT OVER SOLE AND LIFT PAPER STRIP DIAGONALLY OVER YOUR FOOT AND UNDER AGAIN AT (Y), ALLOWING 1 1/2" UNDER FOOT AT BOTH ENDS. CUT OFF UN- NECESSARY LENGTH. ON THESE STRIPS, LAYOUT SHAPES AS INDICATED IN FIG.2. USE SAME METHOD IN DETERMIN- ING THE LENGTHS FOR (E), (F) AND (G). NOW CUT THE LEATHER USING THESE TEMPLATES.

(Y)   (X)

FIG.1
PROCEDURE FOR DETERMINING LENGTHS

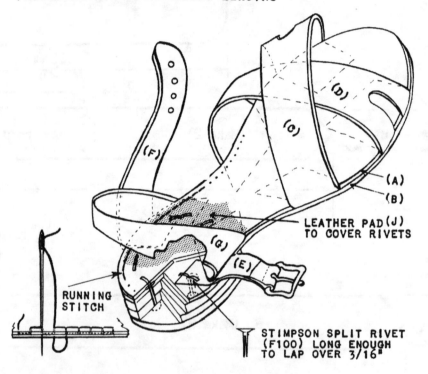

RUNNING STITCH

LEATHER PAD (J) TO COVER RIVETS

STIMPSON SPLIT RIVET (F100) LONG ENOUGH TO LAP OVER 3/16"

PROCEDURE:
HAVING PREPARED THE ELEVEN PIECES FOR EACH SHOE...
(1) APPLY RUBBER CEMENT TO THE FLESH SURFACES OF (A)&(B). SKIVE ALL ENDS OF STRAPS (C)(D)(E)(F) AND G, LOCATE AND CEMENT ON (B). INSERT (A) THRU STRAPS OVER (B) AND HAMMER TOGETHER.
(2) PUNCH HOLES WITH AWL 5 STITCHES PER INCH 1/8" FROM EDGE AND HAND STITCH.
(3) LOCATE AND CEMENT (H) TO (B) AND RIVET TOGETHER.
(4) LOCATE AND CEMENT PAD (J)
TOOLS: (1)(2)(5)(6)(8)(9)(10)(11)(13)(14)(17)
MATERIALS: CONSULT LEATHER CHART. TWO BUCKLES, RUB- BER CEMENT. THREAD, STITCHING NEEDLE AND TEN RIVETS.

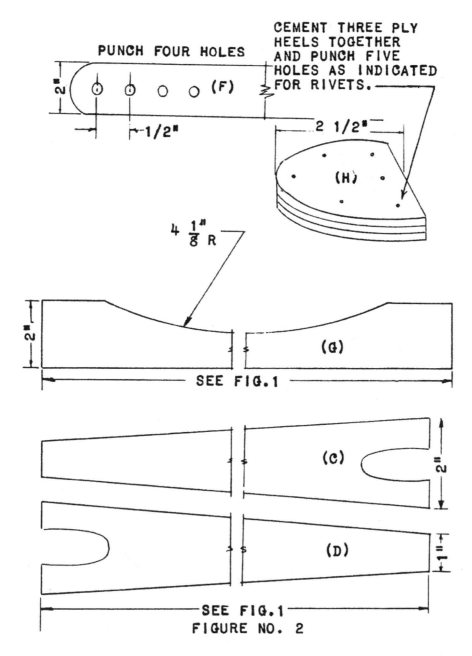

PUNCH FOUR HOLES

2"

1/2"

(F)

CEMENT THREE PLY
HEELS TOGETHER
AND PUNCH FIVE
HOLES AS INDICATED
FOR RIVETS.

2 1/2"

(H)

4 $\frac{1}{8}$" R

2"

(G)

SEE FIG.1

(C)

2"

(D)

1"

SEE FIG.1

FIGURE NO. 2

SKIVE, INSERT BUCKLE,
CEMENT AND SEW

(E)

1"

Indian Moccasins

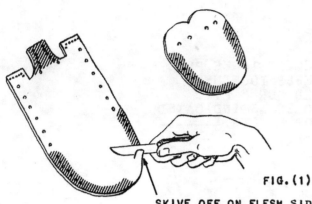

SKIVE OFF ON FLESH SIDE
OF LEATHER ON TOE, HEEL
AND TONGUE AS INDICATED.

FIG. (1)

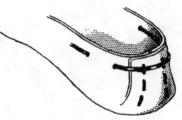

KNOT LACING
ON INSIDE

FIG. (2)

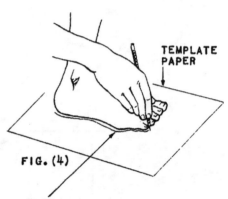

FIG. (3)   METHOD OF
LACING HEEL

TEMPLATE
PAPER

FIG. (4)

DRAW AROUND CONTOUR OF
FOOT, THEN ADD 1/4" ALL
AROUND; SMOOTHING OUT
IRREGULARITIES TO OBTAIN
FINAL SHAPE.

FIG. (6)

START, OVER AND OVER
LACING, AT CENTER OF
TOE AND LACE TOWARD
END OF EACH SIDE.

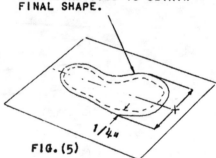

1/4"

FIG. (5)

PROCEDURE:
(1) PREPARE A TEMPLATE FOR PART (A)
ACCORDING TO FIG. (4) & FIG. (5).
COMPLETE TEMPLATE BY LAYING OUT
PART (A) AS INDICATED IN DRAW-
ING, INCLUDING POINTS FOR HOLES.
MAKE TEMPLATE FOR PART (B) AS
INDICATED.
(2) CUT TWO PIECES OF LEATHER LARGE
ENOUGH FOR PART (A), PLACE TO-
GETHER, FLESH SIDES IN. USING
TEMPLATE (A) CUT THE PARTS OUT
AND PUNCH HOLES WITH NO. 2 PUNCH.
(3) PREPARE TWO PARTS (B) USING SAME
PROCEDURE.
(4) LACE PARTS (A)&(B) TOGETHER,-
FLESH SIDES IN, AS SHOWN IN FIG.
(2)(3)(6).

TOOLS: (1)(2)(6)(8)

MATERIALS: CONSULT LEATHER CHART,
TEMPLATE PAPER.

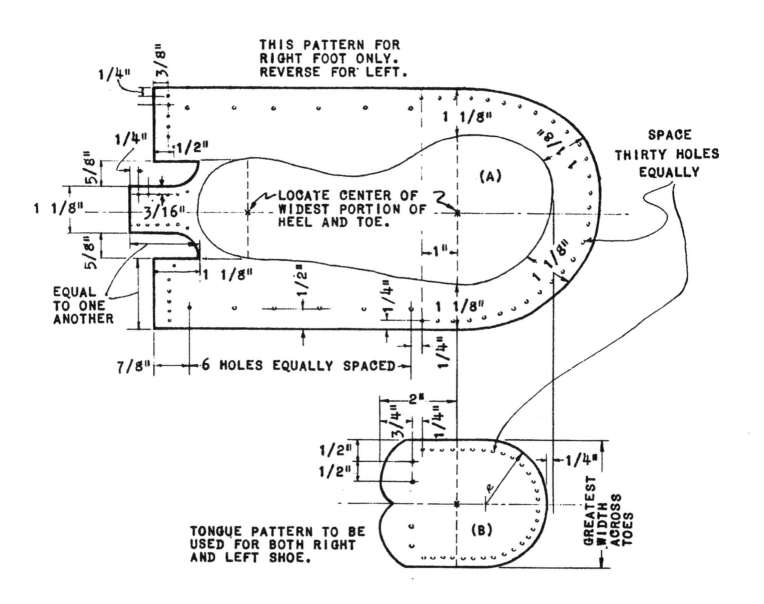

THIS PATTERN FOR
RIGHT FOOT ONLY.
REVERSE FOR LEFT.

1/4"

3/8"

1 1/8"

1/8 1 1

SPACE
THIRTY HOLES
EQUALLY

1/4"

1/2"

5/8"

LOCATE CENTER OF
WIDEST PORTION OF
HEEL AND TOE.

(A)

1 1/8"

3/16"

1"

1 1/8"

1 1/8"

5/8"

1 1/8"

1/2"

1/4"

1 1/8"

EQUAL
TO ONE
ANOTHER

1/4"

1/4"

7/8"

6 HOLES EQUALLY SPACED

2"

3/4"

1/4"

1/2"

1/4"

1/2"

1/4"

GREATEST WIDTH ACROSS TOES

TONGUE PATTERN TO BE
USED FOR BOTH RIGHT
AND LEFT SHOE.

(B)

Baby's Booties

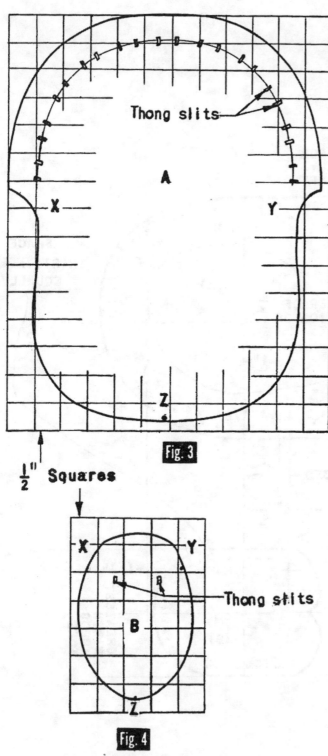

Thong slits

A

X   Y

Z

Fig. 3

½" Squares

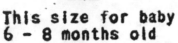

X   Y

Thong slits

B

Z

Fig. 4

This size for baby
6 - 8 months old

Fig. 1

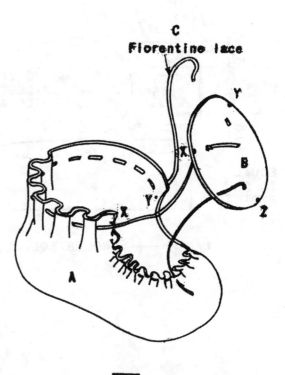

C
Florentine lace

Y

X

B

Y'

X'

Z

A

Fig. 2

For Detailed
Instructions Consult
Chart I - Cutting
Chart II- Design
Chart III-Color
Chart IV- Construction
Chart V - Lacing
Chart VI- Stitching
Chart VII- Braiding
Chart VIII-Knotting
Material Chart

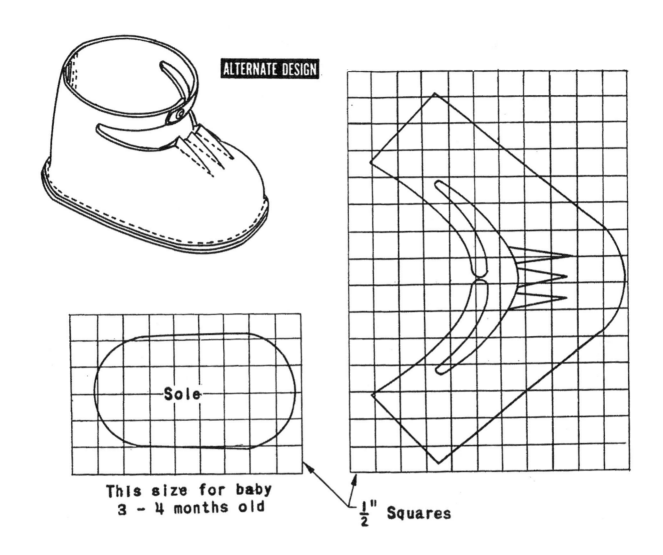

ALTERNATE DESIGN

-Sole-

This size for baby
3 - 4 months old

$\frac{1}{2}$" Squares

PROCEDURE: (CONSULT LEATHER CRAFT PROCESSING CHARTS)

1. Cut parts (A) and (B). Figs. 3, 4.

2. Punch with awl, 1/8" thong slits on (A) and (B) as shown. Figs. 2, 3, 4.

3. Sew one row of running stitches on (A), 1/7" apart, 1/8" from edges, between points (X) and (Y). Fig. 3.

4. Tack point (Z) of (B) to point (Z) of (A) with straight pin. Gather (A) between points (Z) and (Y) and (Z) and (X) to match points (Z) and (Y) and (Z) and (X) of (B). Spread gathers evenly, and tack (A) to (B) with straight pins. Figs. 2, 3, 4.

5. Sew (B) to (A) with small stitches. Fig. 2.

6. Insert lace (C) through (B) and (A), and draw to desired size. Tie ends in bow. Figs. 1, 2.

MATERIALS:
Soft white suede or kid

Florentine lace, white, 3/16"

Heavy linen thread

TOOLS:
(17), (21), (28), (40), (41), (43).

Woman's Lounging Slippers

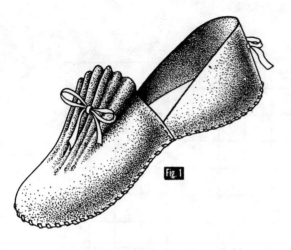

Fig. 1

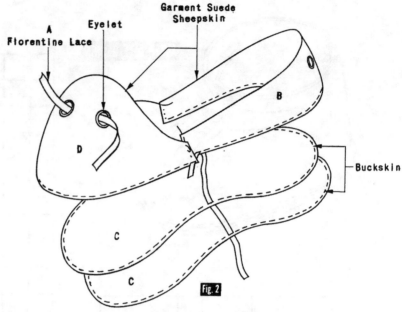

A
Florentine Lace

Eyelet

Garment Suede
Sheepskin

B

D

Buckskin

C

C

Fig. 2

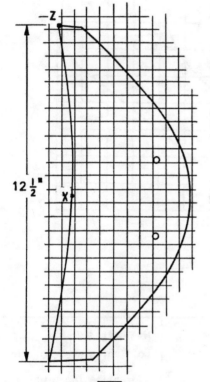

Z

12½"

X

B Fig. 3

Make two,
one reversed

For Detailed
Instructions Consult
Chart I - Cutting
Chart II - Design
Chart III - Color
Chart IV - Construction
Chart V - Lacing
Chart VI - Stitching
Chart VII - Braiding
Chart VIII - Knotting

Material Chart

Y

9¼" for size 5
10 " for size 6
10½" for size 7

Z

X

C Fig. 4   ½" Squares

Make four, two reversed

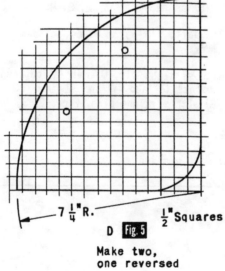

7¼"R.   ½"Squares

D Fig. 5

Make two,
one reversed

PROCEDURE:(CONSULT LEATHER CRAFT PROCESSING CHARTS)

1. Cut parts (B),(C),and (D). Figs. 3, 4, 5.

2. Punch holes for lace (A) in (B) and (D). Insert eyelets. Figs. 3, 5.

3. Cement (C) to (C), back to back. Fig. 2.

4. Place point (X) of (B) on point (X) of (C). Clip together. Punch with awl, 3/32" thong slits, 1/8" apart, 3/16" from edge, simultaneously through matching parts of (B) and (C). Work along edge of heel to either side of point (X). Fig. 2.

5. Place point (Y) of (D) on point (Y) of (C). Clip together. Punch with awl, 3/32" thong slits, 1/8" apart, simultaneously through matching parts of (C) and (D). Be sure to match thong slits where (D) overlaps (B). Fig. 2.

6. Sew (B) and (D) to (C) with whip stitch, starting and ending at point (Z). Figs. 1, 2, 3.

7. Punch stitching holes with awl, 1/8" apart, 3/16" from edge of (D), in (B) and (D) in vertical overlap. Fig. 2.

8. Sew vertical overlaps of (B) and (D) with saddler's stitch. Figs. 1, 2.

9. Insert lace (A) through eyelets in (B) and (D) and tie. Figs. 1, 2.

MATERIALS:

Heavy buckskin, (suede finish)

Garment suede sheepskin, 2-1/2 oz., green

8 No. 6 K eyelets (per pair)

Calfskin lace, 3/32" wide, 12' long (per pair)

Florentine lace, green, 3/16" wide, 4' (per pair)

Rubber cement

Heavy linen thread

TOOLS:

(3 No. 7), (14), (17), (18), (21), (25), (33), (40), (41), (43).

Woman's House Slippers

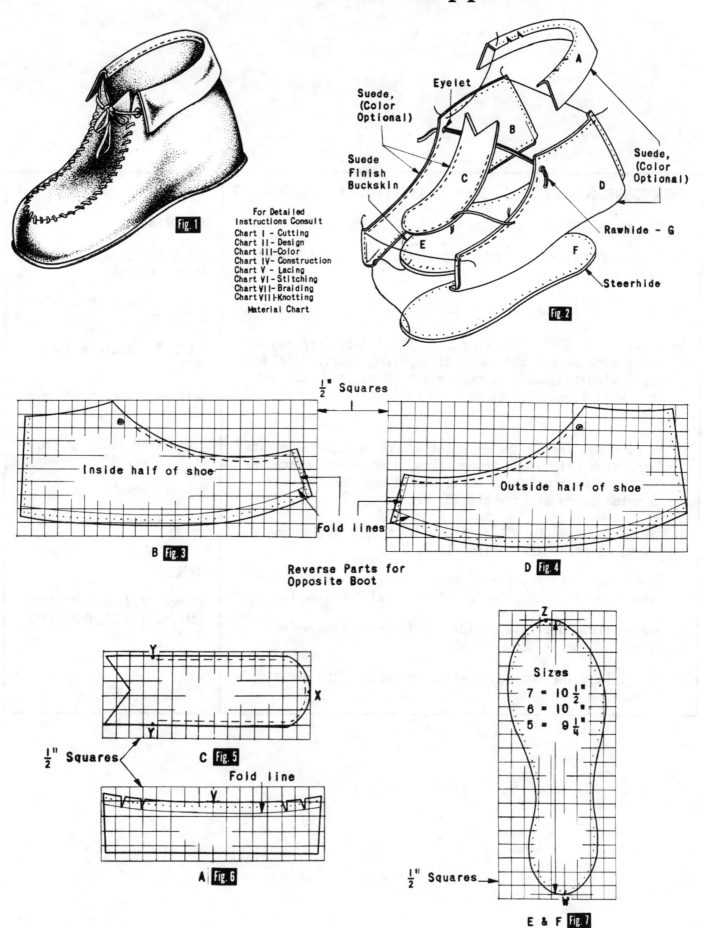

Fig. 1

For Detailed
Instructions Consult
Chart I - Cutting
Chart II - Design
Chart III - Color
Chart IV - Construction
Chart V - Lacing
Chart VI - Stitching
Chart VII - Braiding
Chart VIII - Knotting
Material Chart

Eyelet

Suede,
(Color
Optional)

Suede
Finish
Buckskin

Suede,
(Color
Optional)

A

B

C

D

E

F

Rawhide - G

Steerhide

Fig. 2

½" Squares

Inside half of shoe

Fold lines

B **Fig. 3**

Outside half of shoe

D **Fig. 4**

Reverse Parts for
Opposite Boot

Y
Y
X

½" Squares

C **Fig. 5**

Fold line

A **Fig. 6**

Z

Sizes
7 = 10 ½"
6 = 10 "
5 = 9 ¼"

½" Squares

E & F **Fig. 7**

PROCEDURE: (CONSULT LEATHER CRAFT PROCESSING CHARTS)

1. Cut parts (A), (B), (C), (D), (E) and (F). Figs. 3, 4, 5, 6, 7.

2. Punch holes for drawstring (G) in (B) and (D). Insert eyelets. Figs. 3, 4.

3. Punch stitching holes with awl, 1/8" apart, 3/16" from edge, simultaneously on matching heel and toe seams of (B) and (D). Figs. 3, 4.

4. Sew (B) to (D) with saddler's stitch. Fig. 2.

5. Place point (X) of (C) on toe seam of (BD). Fasten with clip. Fig. 2.

6. Punch 3/32" thong slits with awl, 1/8" apart, 1/8" from edge, simultaneously through matching parts of (BD) and (C). Work from point (X) along either side to points (Y). Figs. 2, 5.

7. Turn under 3/8" of curved edge of (A). Place point (V) of (A) at heel seam of (BD) with 3/8" overlap. Fasten with clip. Fig. 2.

8. Punch stitching holes with awl, 1/8" apart, 3/16" from edge of (A), through matching parts of (A) and (BD). Work from point (V) along either side to ends of (A). Figs. 2, 6.

9. Sew (A) to (BD) with lock stitch. Fig. 2.

10. Turn under 3/8" of sole edge of (ABD). Place (ABD) on (E) with heel and toe seams co inciding with points (W) and (Z) of (E) respectively. Figs. 2, 7.

11. Punch stitching holes with awl, 1/4" apart, 3/16" from edge of (ABD), through matching parts of (E) and (ABD). Fig. 2.

12. Sew (E) to (ABD) with saddler's stitch. Fig. 2.

13. Cement (F) to (ABDE). Fig. 2.

14. Sew (C) to (ABDEF) with whip stitch. Figs. 1, 2.

15. Insert drawstring (C). Fig. 1.

MATERIALS:

Steerhide, heavy
Buckskin, suede finish
Suede, color optional
4 No. 6 K eyelets
Goatskin lace, 3/32"
Rawhide lace, 1/8", 24"
  long (per pair)
Heavy linen thread
Rubber cement

TOOLS:

(1), (3 No. 7), (14), (17), (18), (21), (23), (25), (33), (40), (41), (43).

Man's Scuffies

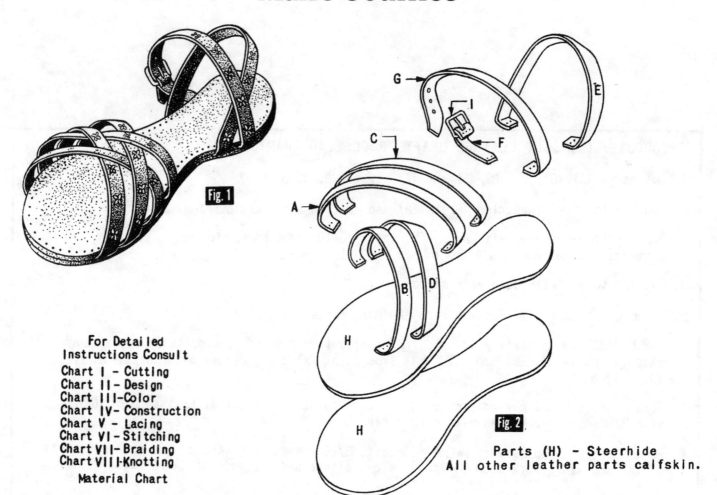

Fig. 1

For Detailed
Instructions Consult
Chart I – Cutting
Chart II – Design
Chart III – Color
Chart IV – Construction
Chart V – Lacing
Chart VI – Stitching
Chart VII – Braiding
Chart VIII – Knotting
    Material Chart

Fig. 2

Parts (H) – Steerhide
All other leather parts calfskin.

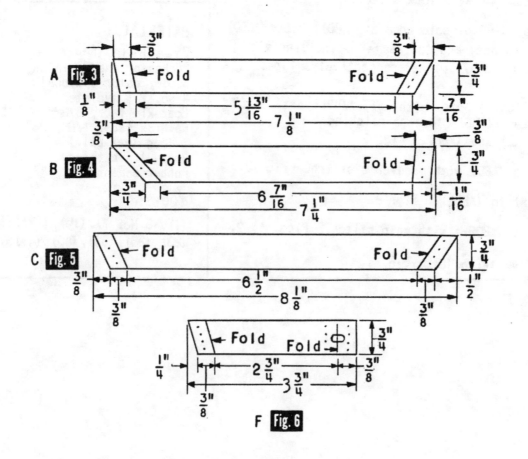

A Fig. 3

B Fig. 4

C Fig. 5

F Fig. 6

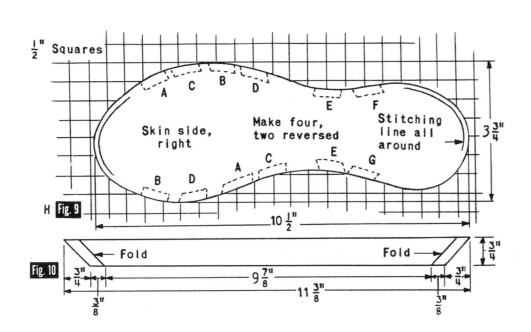

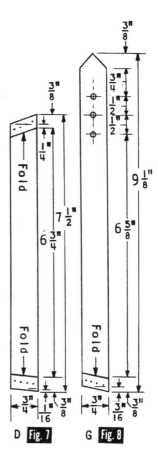

½" Squares

Skin side, right

Make four, two reversed

Stitching line all around

3¾"

10½"

H **Fig. 9**

Fig. 10

Fold   Fold

¾"   9⅞"   ¾"

11⅜"

⅜"   ⅜"   ¾"

Fold

Fold

⅜"

⅜"

¼"

6¾"

7½"

⅜"

1/16"   ⅜"

¾"

D **Fig. 7**

⅜"

¾"

½"

9⅛"

6⅝"

⅜"

1/16"   ⅜"

¾"

G **Fig. 8**

PROCEDURE: (CONSULT LEATHER CRAFT PROCESSING CHARTS)

1. Cut and prepare parts (A), (B), (C), (D), (E), (F), (G) and (H). Letter each part on flesh side to avoid confusion in assembling. Figs. 3 through 10.

2. Outline edges and mark fold lines on all parts indicated, with edge creaser. Fold. Figs. 3, 4, 5, 6, 7, 8, 10.

3. Skive all ends to be cemented between (H). Fig. 2.

4. Cement all parts to flesh side of inner sole (H) as marked. Figs. 2, 9.

5. Cement inner sole (H) to bottom sole (H) flesh sides together. Fig. 2.

6. Mark stitching holes with 1/5" spacing wheel, 1/8" from edge of (H). Fig. 2.

7. Punch stitching holes with awl through all cemented parts. Fig. 2.

8. Sew with saddler's stitch. Fig. 2.

9. Cut slot in (F) for prong of buckle (I). Insert (I). Fold back (F). Figs. 2, 6.

10. Punch with awl closely spaced stitching holes in folded (F). Fig. 6.

11. Sew fold of (F) with saddler's stitch. Fig. 2.

12. Punch holes in (G) for prong of (I) with No. 4 tube. Fig. 8.

MATERIALS:
Steerhide, 6 oz.

Russia tooling calfskin, 2 oz.

Heavy linen thread

Rubber cement

2 Buckles, 3/4", center bar

TOOLS:
(1), (6), (8), (17), (25), (27), (30), (41), (43).

183

Man's Scuffies

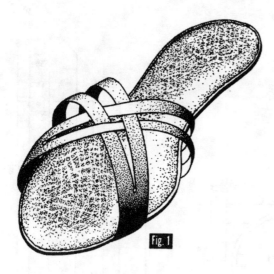

Fig. 1

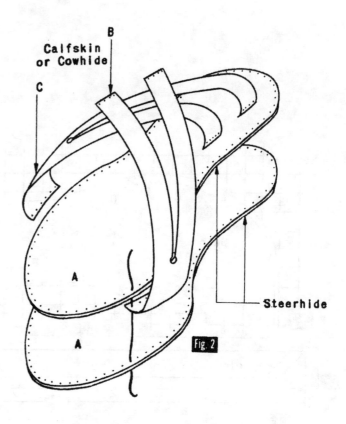

Calfskin
or Cowhide

B

C

A

A

Steerhide

Fig. 2

For Detailed
Instructions Consult
Chart I - Cutting
Chart II- Design
Chart III-Color
Chart IV- Construction
Chart V - Lacing
Chart VI - Stitching
Chart VII - Braiding
Chart VIII-Knotting
Material Chart

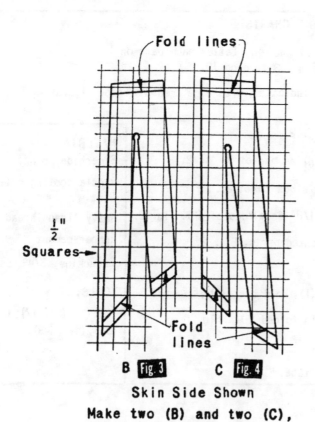

Fold lines

$\frac{1}{2}$"

Squares→

Fold
lines

B Fig. 3   C Fig. 4

Skin Side Shown

Make two (B) and two (C),
one of each reversed

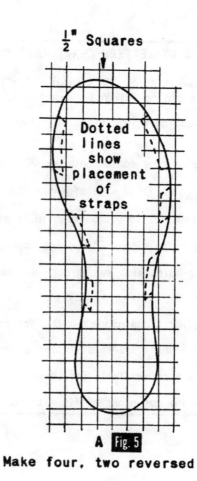

$\frac{1}{2}$" Squares

Dotted
lines
show
placement
of
straps

A Fig. 5

Make four, two reversed

184

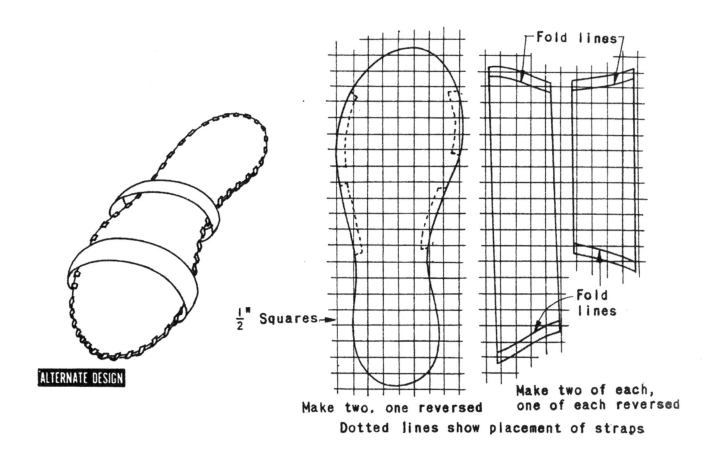

ALTERNATE DESIGN

½" Squares →

Fold lines

Fold lines

Make two, one reversed

Make two of each, one of each reversed

Dotted lines show placement of straps

PROCEDURE: (CONSULT LEATHER CRAFT PROCESSING CHARTS)

1. Cut and prepare parts (A), (B) and (C). Figs. 3, 4, 5.

2. Mark folding lines on (B) and (C) with edge creaser. Fold. Figs. 3, 4.

3. Skive ends of (B) and (C) to be inserted between (A). Figs. 2, 3, 4, 5

4. Cement (B) and (C) to flesh side of inner sole (A), where indicated. Figs. 1, 2, 5.

5. Cement bottom sole (A) to (ABC) flesh sides together. Fig. 2.

6. Mark stitching holes with 1/5" spacing wheel, 1/8" from edge of (A). Fig. 2.

7. Punch stitching holes with awl through cemented parts (ABC). Fig. 2.

8. Sew (ABC) with saddler's stitch. Figs. 1, 2.

MATERIALS:

Steerhide, 6 oz.

Natural tooling calfskinn, or cowhide, 3 oz.

Heavy linen thread

Rubber cement

TOOLS:

(1), (17), (22), (25), (27), (30), (41), (43).

Woman's Sandals

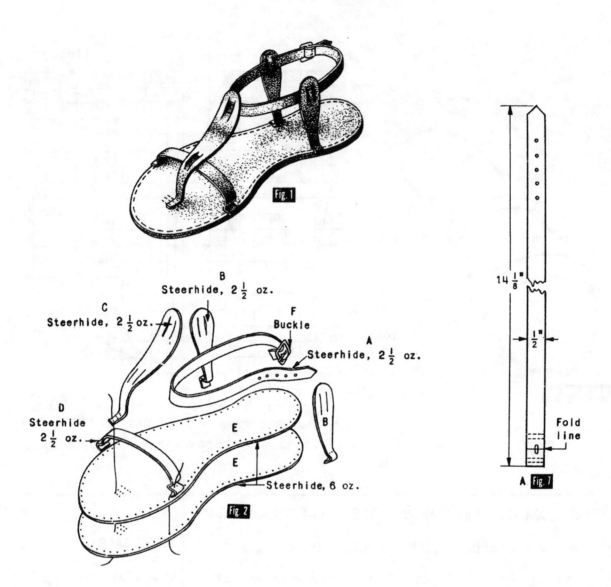

Fig. 1

B
Steerhide, 2½ oz.

C
Steerhide, 2½ oz.

F
Buckle

A
Steerhide, 2½ oz.

D
Steerhide
2½ oz.

E

E

B

Steerhide, 6 oz.

Fig. 2

14⅛"

½"

Fold line

A Fig. 7

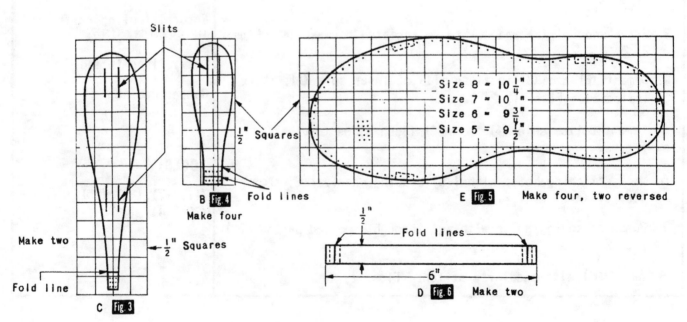

Slits

½" Squares

½" Squares

B Fig. 4   Fold lines

Make four

Make two

Fold line

C Fig. 3

Size 8 = 10¼"
Size 7 = 10"
Size 6 = 9¾"
Size 5 = 9½"

E Fig. 5   Make four, two reversed

½"

Fold lines

6"

D Fig. 6   Make two

PROCEDURE:(CONSULT LEATHER CRAFT PROCESSING CHARTS)

1. Cut parts (A), (B), (C), (D) and (E). Figs. 3, 4, 5, 6, 7.

2. Outline edges and mark fold lines on all parts indicated with edge creaser. Figs. 4, 6.

3. Skive all ends to be cemented between top and bottom soles (E). Figs. 2, 4, 6.

4. Cut slits in (B) and (C). Outline slits with edge creaser. Figs. 3, 4.

5. Insert (D) in (C). Fig. 1.

6. Cement ends of (D) and (B) to flesh side of top (E), and (C) to skin side of top (E). Figs. 2, 5.

7. Punch stitching holes with awl through matching parts of (C) on (E). Figs. 3, 5.

8. Sew with saddler's stitch. Figs. 1, 2.

9. Cement (E) to (E) flesh sides together. Fig. 2.

10. Mark stitching holes with 1/5" spacing wheel, 3/16" from edge of (E), including (D) and (B) on (E). Fig. 5.

11. Punch stitching holes with awl through all cemented parts. Fig. 2.

12. Sew with saddler's stitch. Fig. 2.

13. Cut slot in straight end of (A) for prong of buckle (F). Insert (F). Fold back (A). Figs. 2, 7.

14. Punch with awl double row of closely spaced stitching holes in folded (A). Fig. 7.

15. Sew fold with saddler's stitch. Fig. 2.

16. Punch holes with revolving punch for prong of (F) in pointed end of (A). Fig. 7.

17. Insert (A) through (B) and (C). Fig. 1.

MATERIALS:

Steerhide, 6 oz.
Steerhide, 2-1/2 oz
2 Buckles, 1/2",
center bar

Heavy linen thread
Rubber cement

TOOLS:

(1), (6), (8), (17), (25), (27), (28), (30), (41).

For Detailed
Instructions Consult
Chart I - Cutting
Chart II - Design
Chart III-Color
Chart IV- Construction
Chart V - Lacing
Chart VI -Stitching
Chart VII- Braiding
Chart VIII-Knotting

Material Chart

Woman's Sandals

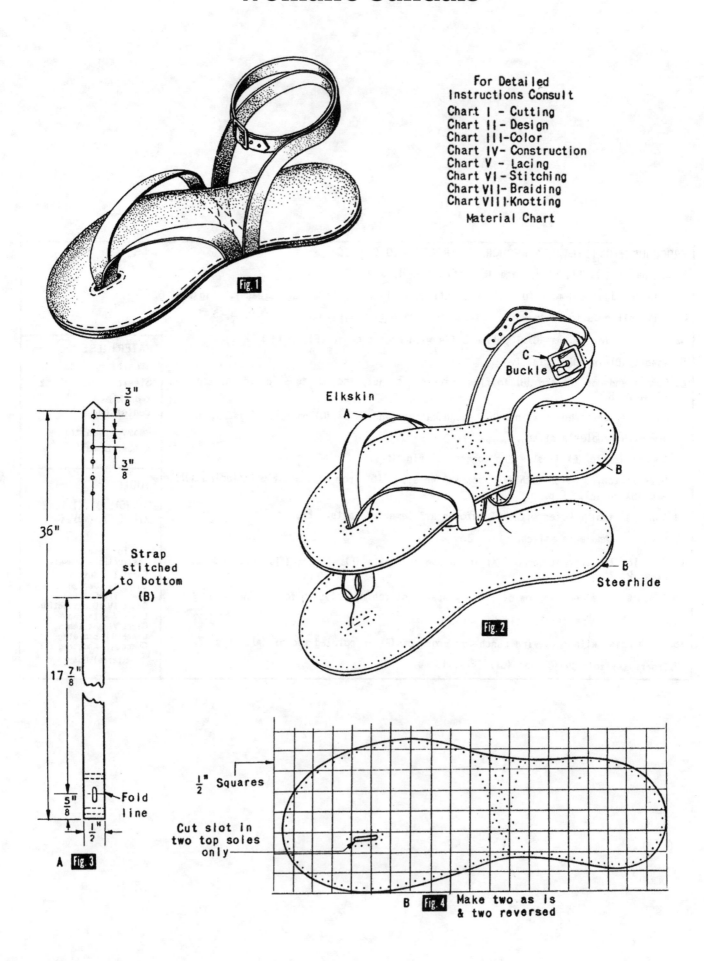

Fig. 1

For Detailed
Instructions Consult
Chart I – Cutting
Chart II – Design
Chart III – Color
Chart IV – Construction
Chart V – Lacing
Chart VI – Stitching
Chart VII – Braiding
Chart VIII – Knotting
Material Chart

Elkskin
A

C
Buckle

B

B
Steerhide

Fig. 2

$\frac{3}{8}$"

$\frac{3}{8}$"

36"

Strap
stitched
to bottom
(B)

17 $\frac{7}{8}$"

$\frac{5}{8}$"

$\frac{1}{2}$"

Fold
line

A Fig. 3

$\frac{1}{2}$" Squares

Cut slot in
two top soles
only

B Fig. 4 Make two as is
& two reversed

PROCEDURE: (CONSULT LEATHER CRAFT PROCESSING CHARTS)

1. Cut parts (A) and (B). Figs. 3, 4.

2. Outline edge and mark folding lines of (A) with edge creaser. Fig. 3.

3. Cut slot in top (B) with skin side up. Mark slot on flesh side of corresponding bottom (B). Fig. 4.

4. Insert folded (A) thru slot in top (B). Match (A) to slot mark of bottom (B), flesh sides facing. Figs. 2, 3, 4.

5. Punch closely spaced stitching holes with awl, through (A) and bottom (B). Figs. 2, 4.

6. Stitch (A) to bottom (B) with saddler's stitch. Fig. 2.

7. Arrange crossing of (A) to flesh side of top (B). Skive (A) at crossing and cement. Fig. 2.

8. Cement (AB) to flesh side of bottom (B). Fig. 2.

9. Mark stitching holes with 1/5" spacing wheel, 3/16" from edge of (B), around slot of (B) and where (A) crosses under instep between (B) and (B). Figs. 2, 4.

10. Punch stitching holes with awl, through matching parts of (A) and (B). Fig. 2.

11. Sew with saddler's stitch. Fig. 2.

12. Cut slot in straight end of (A) for prong of buckle (C). Insert (C). Fold back (A). Figs. 2, 3.

13. Punch with awl, double row of closely spaced stitching holes in folded (A). Fig. 3.

14. Sew fold with saddler's stitch. Fig. 2.

15. Punch holes with revolving punch for prong of (C) in pointed end of (A). Fig. 3.

MATERIALS:

Steerhide, 6 oz.

Elkskin, 3-1/2 oz.

2 Buckles, 1/2" center bar

Heavy linen thread

Rubber cement

TOOLS:

(1), (8), (17), (25), (27), (28), (30), (41).

Traveling Slippers and Case

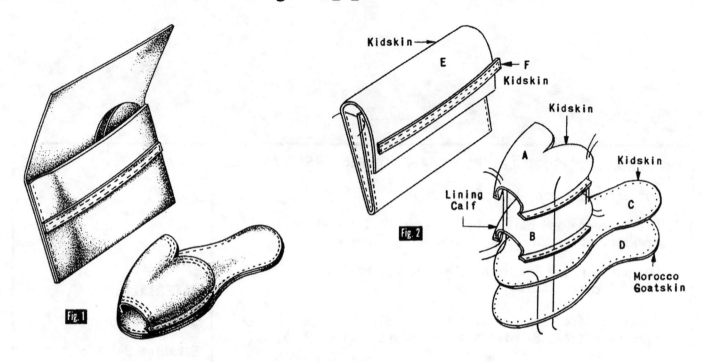

Kidskin

E

F

Kidskin

Kidskin

A

Kidskin

Lining Calf

B

C

D

Morocco Goatskin

Fig. 2

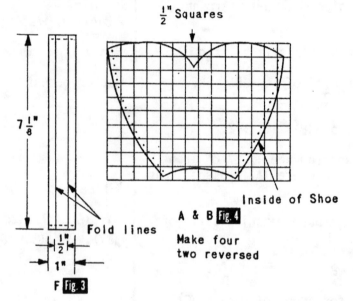

$\frac{1}{2}$" Squares

$7\frac{1}{8}$"

$\frac{1}{2}$"

1"

Fold lines

F Fig. 3

Inside of Shoe

A & B Fig. 4

Make four
two reversed

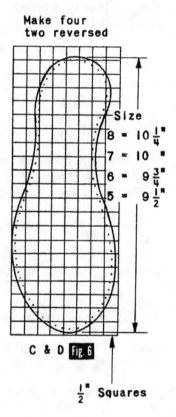

Make four
two reversed

Size	
8 =	$10\frac{1}{4}$"
7 =	10"
6 =	$9\frac{3}{4}$"
5 =	$9\frac{1}{2}$"

C & D Fig. 6

$\frac{1}{2}$" Squares

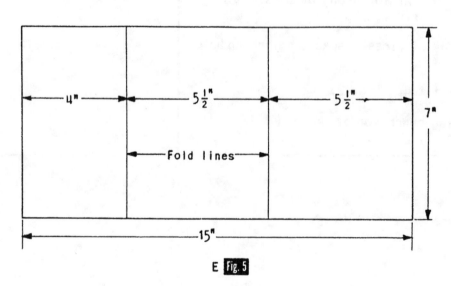

4"

$5\frac{1}{2}$"

$5\frac{1}{2}$"

7"

Fold lines

15"

E Fig. 5

PROCEDURE: (CONSULT LEATHER CRAFT PROCESSING CHARTS)

1. Cut parts (A), (B), (C), (D), (E), and (F). Figs. 3, 4, 5, 6.

2. Cement (A) to (B) and (C) to (D) flesh sides together. Figs. 4, 6.

3. Sew on sewing machine double row of stitching at toe and instep edges of (AB). Fig. 2.

4. Place (AB) in position on (CD). Mark stitching holes with 1/7" spacing wheel, 1/8" from outer edge of entire slipper. Figs. 2, 4, 6.

5. Punch stitching holes through matching parts, working from toe toward heel. Figs. 2, 4, 6.

6. Sew with saddler's stitch. Fig. 2.

7. Fold (E) to form case. Figs. 2, 5.

8. Fold (F) along fold lines, and cement flesh sides together. Fig. 3.

9. Stitch edges of (F) on sewing machine. Fig. 2.

10. Place ends of (F) flush with edges of (E) to be stitched. Figs. 1, 2.

11. Sew ends of (E), including (F) on sewing machine. Figs. 1,2.

MATERIALS:

Kidskin

Lining calf

Morocco goatskin

Heavy linen thread

Rubber cement

TOOLS:

(1), (6), (17), (21), (25), (28), (33), (41).

For Detailed Instructions Consult

Chart I – Cutting
Chart II – Design
Chart III – Color
Chart IV – Construction
Chart V – Lacing
Chart VI – Stitching
Chart VII – Braiding
Chart VIII – Knotting

Material Chart

Wool Sheepskin Moccasins

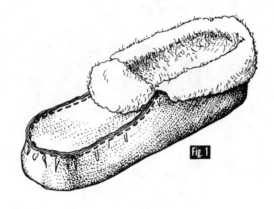

Fig. 1

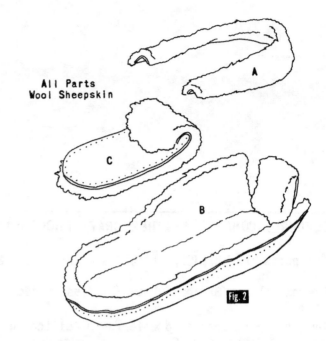

All Parts
Wool Sheepskin

A

C

B

Fig. 2

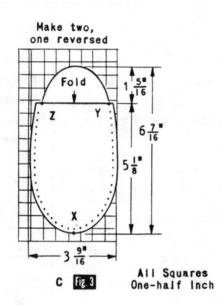

Make two,
one reversed

Fold

Z   Y

$1\frac{5}{16}"$

$6\frac{7}{16}"$

$5\frac{1}{8}"$

X

$3\frac{9}{16}"$

C   Fig. 3

All Squares
One-half Inch

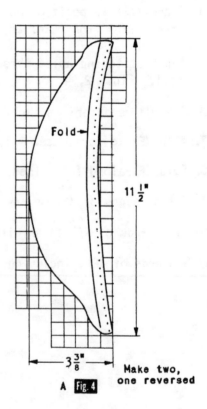

Fold

$11\frac{1}{2}"$

$3\frac{3}{8}"$

Make two,
one reversed

A   Fig. 4

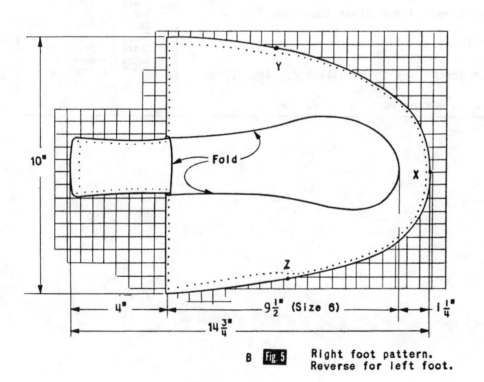

Y

Fold

X

10"

Z

4"

$9\frac{1}{2}"$ (Size 6)

$1\frac{1}{4}"$

$14\frac{3}{4}"$

B   Fig. 5   Right foot pattern.
Reverse for left foot.

PROCEDURE:(CONSULT LEATHER CRAFT PROCESSING CHARTS)

1. Cut parts (A), (B) and (C) on flesh side so as not to shear wool. Figs. 3, 4, 5.

2. Match points (X), (Y), (Z) of (C) to points (X), (Y), (Z) of (B). Make one temporary stitch at each point to hold (B) and (C) in place. Figs. 3, 5.

3. Sew (C) to (B) with saddle stitch, about 1/8" from edge. Begin sewing at point (Z). Gather (B) for toe fullness to fit edge of (C). Fig. 2.

4. Adjust two heel seams of (B) for individual fit. Sew seams with saddle stitch. Fig. 2.

5. Center (A) to center of heel, with wool side of (A) against wool of (B). Make a temporary stitch to hold (A) to (B). (Cuff will be turned down inside of heel.) Fig. 2.

6. Sew edges of (A) to (B) with saddle stitch. Pull cuff up and turn over sides and heel of moccasin. Fig. 2.

MATERIALS:

Wool sheepskin
Heavy linen thread

TOOLS:

(1 or 33), (41)

For Detailed
Instructions Consult
Chart I – Cutting
Chart II – Design
Chart III – Color
Chart IV – Construction
Chart V – Lacing
Chart VI – Stitching
Chart VII – Braiding
Chart VIII – Knotting
Material Chart

Baby's Mittens

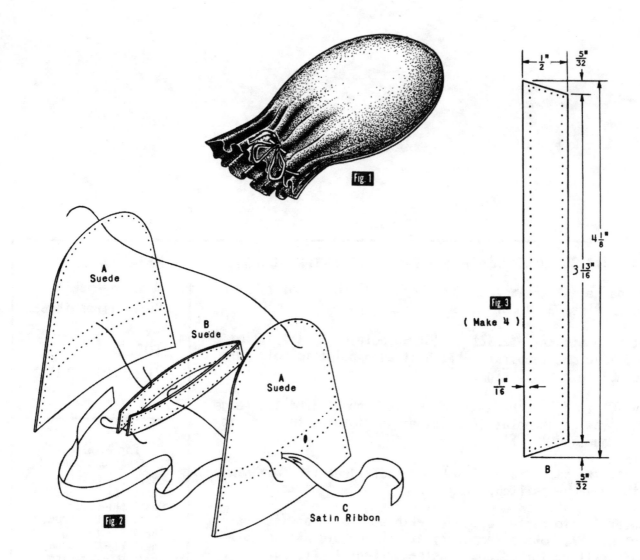

Fig. 1

Fig. 2

Fig. 3
(Make 4)

PROCEDURE: (CONSULT LEATHER CRAFT PROCESSING CHARTS)

1. Cut parts (A) and (B). Figs. 3, 4.

2. With awl, punch $\frac{1}{8}$" slits in one part (A). Fig. 4.

3. Place (A) to (A), flesh sides together. With spacing wheel, mark $\frac{1}{7}$" stitching holes approximately $\frac{3}{32}$" from rounded edge of (A).

4. Sew (A) to (A) with saddle stitch. Fig. 2.

5. Sew (B) to (B) at ends to make circular band. Figs. 2, 3.

6. Turn (AA) inside out. Place (BB) over (AA), $\frac{5}{8}$" down from straight edge of (AA), with end seams of (BB) facing seams of (AA). Fig. 2.

7. Stitch (BB) to (AA) with short running stitches. Turn mitten right side out. Fig. 2.

8. Insert lacing ribbon (C) as shown. Figs. 1, 2.

MATERIALS:

Soft white suede or kid

White satin ribbon $\frac{1}{2}$", 30" long (per pair)

White nylon thread No. D

TOOLS:

(6), (17), (21), (28), (40), (41).

For Detailed Instructions Consult

Chart I - Cutting
Chart II - Design
Chart III - Color
Chart IV - Construction
Chart V - Lacing
Chart VI - Stitching
Chart VII - Braiding
Chart VIII - Knotting
Material Chart

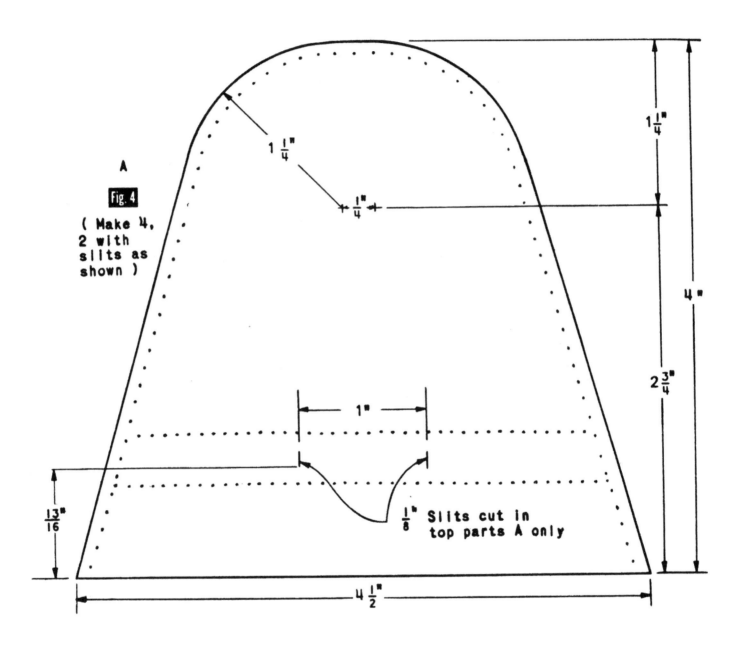

A

Fig. 4

(Make 4,
2 with
slits as
shown)

$1\frac{1}{4}$"

$\frac{1}{4}$"

$1\frac{1}{4}$"

4"

$2\frac{3}{4}$"

1"

$\frac{13}{16}$"

$\frac{1}{8}$" Slits cut in
top parts A only

$4\frac{1}{2}$"

Woman's Mittens

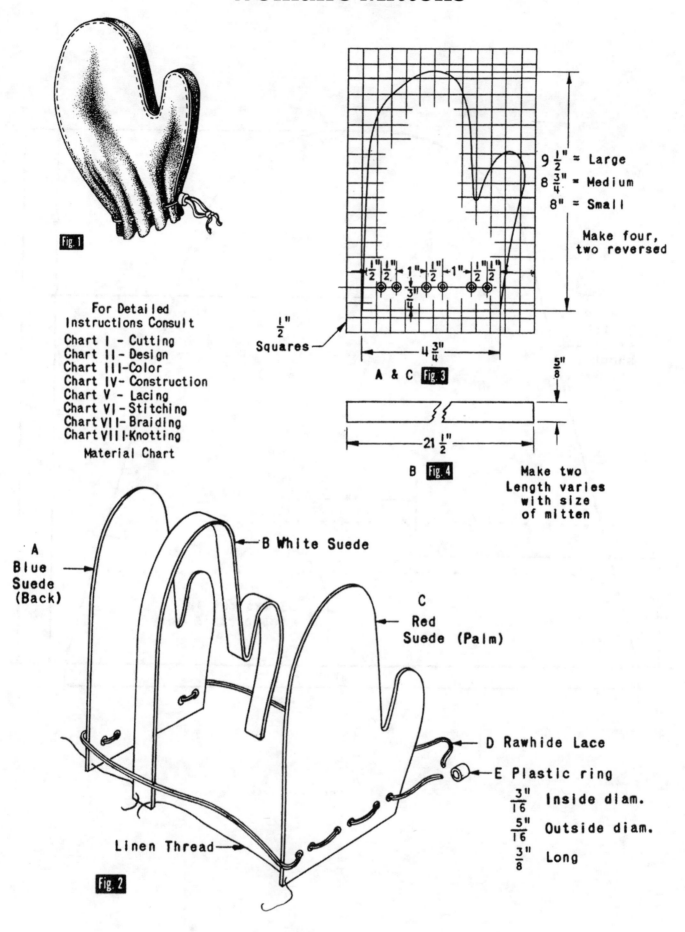

Fig. 1

For Detailed
Instructions Consult
Chart I - Cutting
Chart II - Design
Chart III - Color
Chart IV - Construction
Chart V - Lacing
Chart VI - Stitching
Chart VII - Braiding
Chart VIII - Knotting
Material Chart

$9\frac{1}{2}$" = Large
$8\frac{3}{4}$" = Medium
8" = Small

Make four,
two reversed

$\frac{1}{2}$" $\frac{1}{2}$" 1" $\frac{1}{2}$" 1" $\frac{1}{2}$" $\frac{1}{2}$"
$\frac{3}{4}$"

$\frac{1}{2}$"
Squares

$4\frac{3}{4}$"

A & C **Fig. 3**

$\frac{5}{8}$"

$21\frac{1}{2}$"

B **Fig. 4**

Make two
Length varies
with size
of mitten

A
Blue
Suede
(Back)

B White Suede

C
Red
Suede (Palm)

D Rawhide Lace

E Plastic ring

$\frac{3}{16}$" Inside diam.

$\frac{5}{16}$" Outside diam.

$\frac{3}{8}$" Long

Linen Thread

Fig. 2

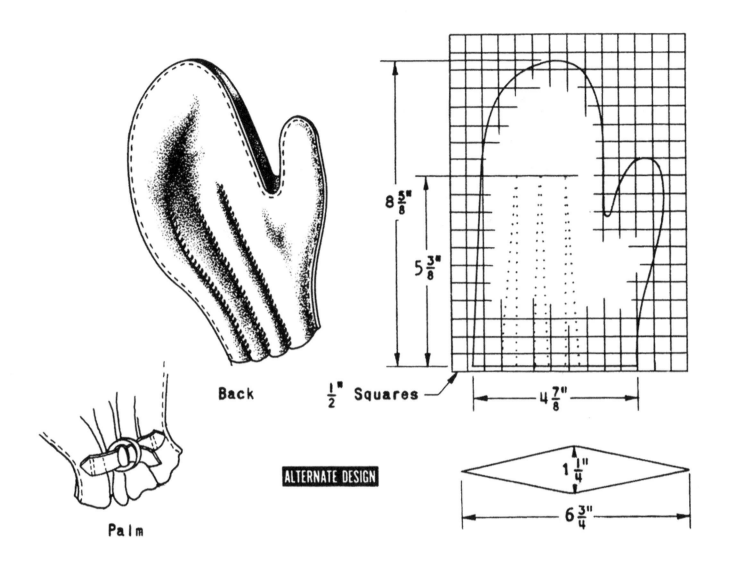

Back

$\frac{1}{2}$" Squares

$8\frac{5}{8}$"

$5\frac{3}{8}$"

$4\frac{7}{8}$"

Palm

ALTERNATE DESIGN

$1\frac{1}{4}$"

$6\frac{3}{4}$"

PROCEDURE: (CONSULT LEATHER CRAFT PROCESSING CHARTS)

1. Cut parts (A), (B), and (C). Figs. 3, 4.

2. Punch holes in (A) and (C) for eyelets. Insert eyelets in place. Figs. 2, 3.

3. Place (C) against (B), flesh sides together. Sew (B) to (C) with short, equi-spaced running stitches. Fig. 2.

4. Place (A) against (BC). Sew (A) to (BC) with same running stitch. Fig. 2.

5. Insert lace (D) through eyelets. Slip ring (E) in place over ends of (D). Knot ends of (D). Figs. 1, 2.

MATERIALS:

Suede (red, white and blue)

Rawhide lace, $\frac{1}{8}$"

Small eyelets, 24 per pair

Small plastic ring

Linen thread

TOOLS:

(6), (7), (8), (21), (41), (43)

Glove Box

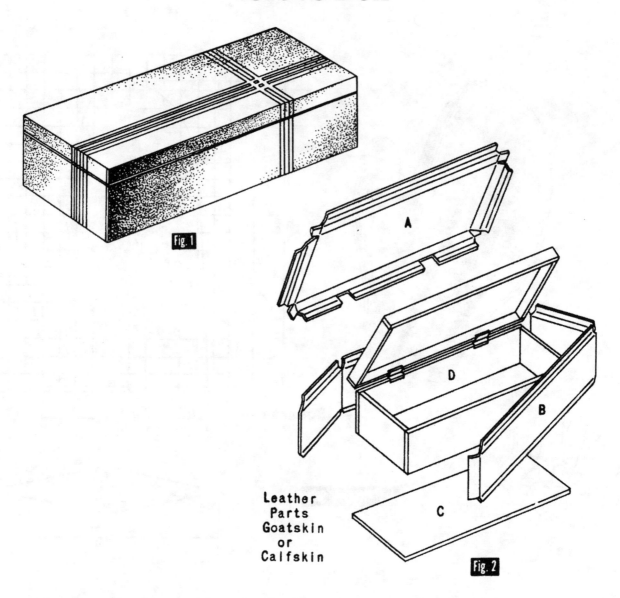

Fig. 1

Leather
Parts
Goatskin
or
Calfskin

Fig. 2

PROCEDURE: (CONSULT LEATHER CRAFT PROCESSING CHARTS)

1. Cut and prepare parts (A), (B) and (C). Figs. 3, 4, 5.

2. Make cut-outs in (A) and (B) to accommodate size of box hinges used. Figs. 3, 4.

3. Skive all edges to be cemented. Fig. 2.

4. Cement (A) to cover of box (D), covering edges of cover and turning down 1/4" within edges. Fig. 2.

5. Cement (B) to sides of (D) with ends meeting in an over-lapped seam at back corner, and flap edges turned over to bottom of (D). Fig. 2.

6. Cement (C) to bottom of (D). Fig. 2.

MATERIALS:

Tooling morocco goatskin if stamping wheel or line design is used

Tooling calfskin if modeled design is used

Rubber cement

TOOLS:

(1), (6), (19).

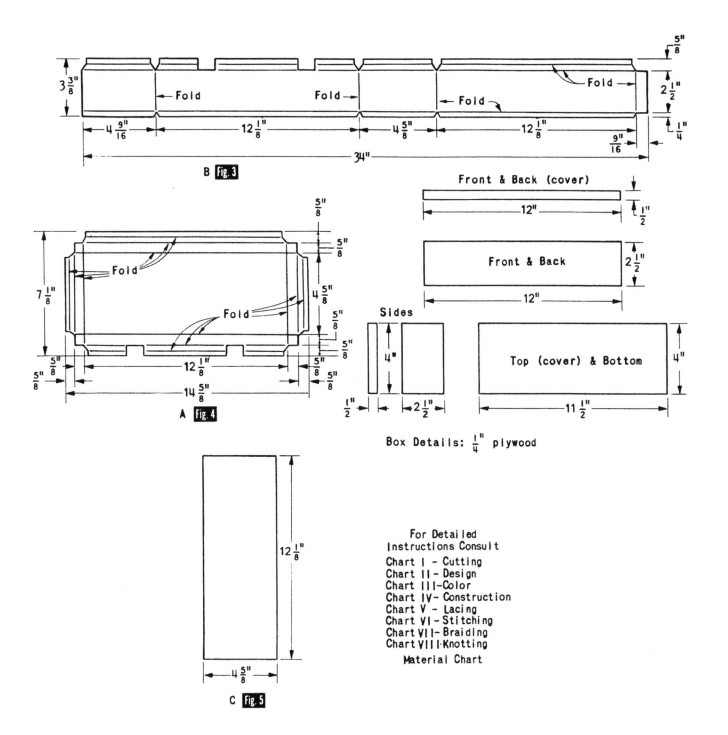

B **Fig. 3**

Front & Back (cover)

12"

Front & Back

12"

Sides

Top (cover) & Bottom

11 1/2"

Box Details: 1/4" plywood

Fold

A **Fig. 4**

C **Fig. 5**

For Detailed
Instructions Consult
Chart I – Cutting
Chart II– Design
Chart III–Color
Chart IV– Construction
Chart V – Lacing
Chart VI–Stitching
Chart VII–Braiding
Chart VIII·Knotting
Material Chart

Woman's Gloves

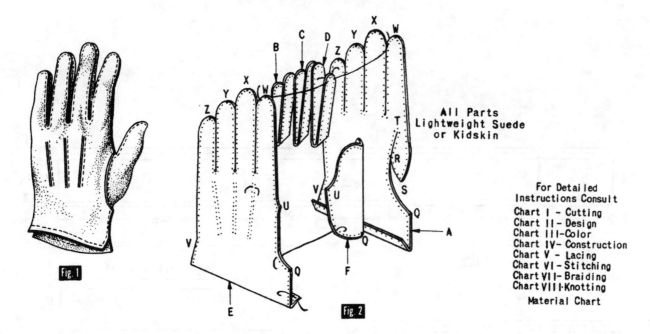

Fig. 1

Fig. 2

All Parts
Lightweight Suede
or Kidskin

For Detailed
Instructions Consult
Chart I – Cutting
Chart II – Design
Chart III – Color
Chart IV – Construction
Chart V – Lacing
Chart VI – Stitching
Chart VII – Braiding
Chart VIII – Knotting
Material Chart

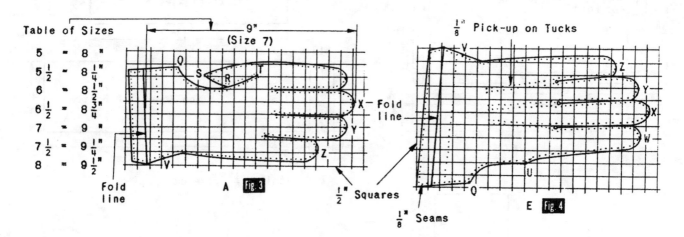

Table of Sizes

5	=	8"
5 1/2	=	8 1/4"
6	=	8 1/2"
6 1/2	=	8 3/4"
7	=	9"
7 1/2	=	9 1/4"
8	=	9 1/2"

9"
(Size 7)

Fold line

Fold line

A   Fig. 3

1/2" Squares

1/8" Pick-up on Tucks

X – Fold line

1/8" Seams

1/2" Squares

E   Fig. 4

PATTERNS SHOWN ARE FOR LEFT HAND
REVERSE FOR RIGHT HAND

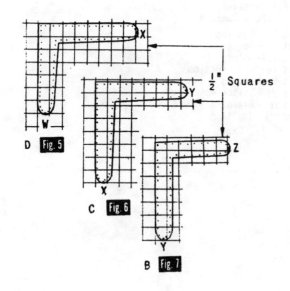

1/2" Squares

D   Fig. 5

C   Fig. 6

B   Fig. 7

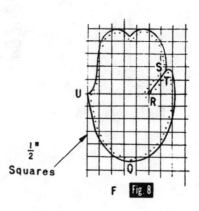

1/2" Squares

F   Fig. 8

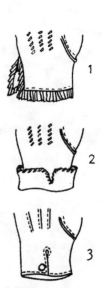

1

2

3

ALTERNATE DESIGNS

PROCEDURE: (CONSULT LEATHERCRAFT PROCESSING CHARTS)

1. Cut parts (A), (B), (C), (D), (E) and (F). Figs. 3, 4, 5, 6, 7, 8.

2. Sew tucks on parts (E) with short saddle stitches, taking up 1/8" for each tuck. Fig. 4.

3. Turn under 5/8" on cuff opening on parts (A) and (E). Sew open ends of fold and hem edge with short saddle stitches. Figs. 2, 3, 4.

4. Sew (A) to (E) starting at point (V). Allow 1/8" seams on all edges when sewing. Stop at (Z), without terminating thread. Figs. 2, 3, 4.

5. Insert (B) with points (Z) and (Y) of (B) coinciding with (Z) and (Y) of (A) and (E). Fig. 2.

6. Saddle stitch (B) to (A) and (E), in one continuous stitching line. Fig. 2.

7. Repeat steps (5) and (6) in sewing (C) and (D) to their respective points on (A) and (E). Fig. 2.

8. Sew (A) to (E) from point (W) to (U). Figs. 2, 3, 4.

9. Sew thumb (F) to (E) between points (U) and (O). Finish seam by sewing cuff edge of (A) to (E). Figs. 2, 4, 8.

10. Sew (F) to (A) between points (O) and (T); continue along points from (T) through (R) and (S); then from (S) to (U). Figs. 2, 3, 8.

11. Finish sewing folded (F) at top of thumb. Fig. 2.

MATERIALS:

Suede, light weight or Kidskin, light weight
Linen thread

TOOLS:

(1), (6), (21), (41).

201

Cribbage Board

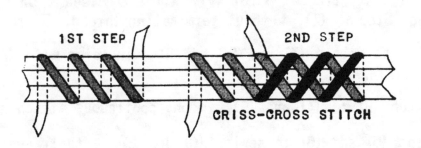

1ST STEP   2ND STEP

CRISS-CROSS STITCH

PROCEDURE:
HAVING PREPARED THE SIX SEPARATE PARTS...
(1) CEMENT (E) IN PLACE ON (A)
(2) CEMENT 2 PIECES (B) TOGETHER, PUNCH
NO. 3 PEG HOLES AS INDICATED. TOOL AND
CUT IN HALF, MAKING 2 PIECES 2" X 4 3/16",
PLACE IN POSITION ON (A) LOOSELY; FOLD
OVER BOTH ENDS TO LOCATE POSITION OF
SNAP BUTTON
(3) REMOVE PARTS (B) AND SET SNAP BUTTON
(4) LOCATE AND SEW (D) ON (C), THEN
CEMENT IN PLACE ON (A) - CEMENT PARTS (B)
ON (A)
(5) PUNCH 3/32" SLITS 1/8" FROM EDGES
(6) DYE ALL EDGES AND LACE

TOOLS:
(1) (2) (6) (9) (10) (11) (12) (8) (17) (16)

MATERIALS:
CONSULT LEATHER CHART
TEMPLATE PAPER
RUBBER CEMENT
3/8" SNAP BUTTON
WOOD OR PLASTICS FOR PEGS

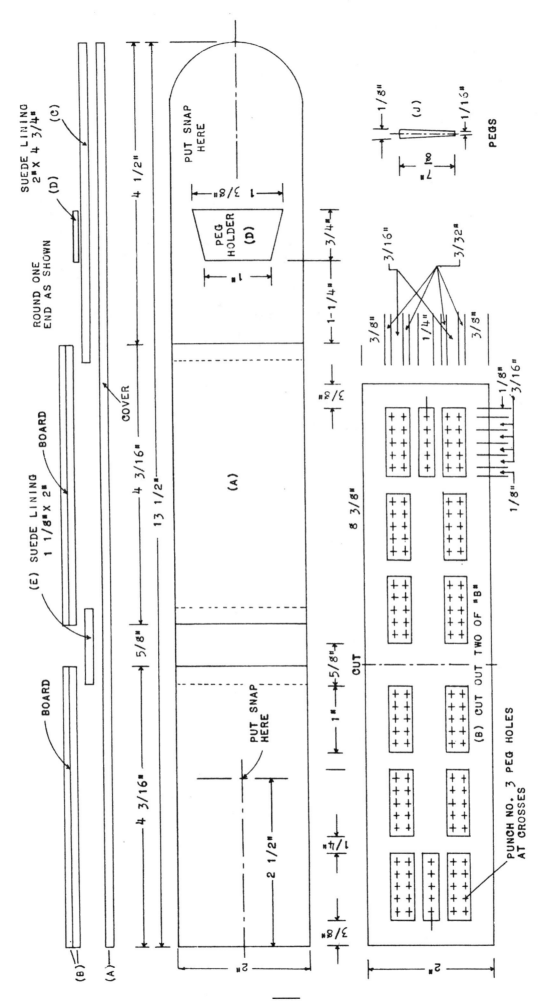

SUEDE LINING 2" X 4 3/4" (C)

(D)

ROUND ONE END AS SHOWN

COVER

BOARD

(E) SUEDE LINING 1 1/8" X 2"

BOARD

(B)

(A)

PUT SNAP HERE

PEG HOLDER (D)

1 3/8"

1"

4 1/2"

4 3/16"

13 1/2"

5/8"

4 3/16"

(A)

3/8"

1 1/4"

3/4"

PUT SNAP HERE

2 1/2"

1"

5/8"

CUT

1/4"

3/8"

2"

(J)

PEGS

1/8"

1/16"

7"

8

3/16"

3/32"

3/8"

1/4"

3/8"

1/8"

3/16"

8 3/8"

(B) CUT OUT TWO OF "B"

1/8"

PUNCH NO. 3 PEG HOLES AT CROSSES

2

Pocket Checkerboard

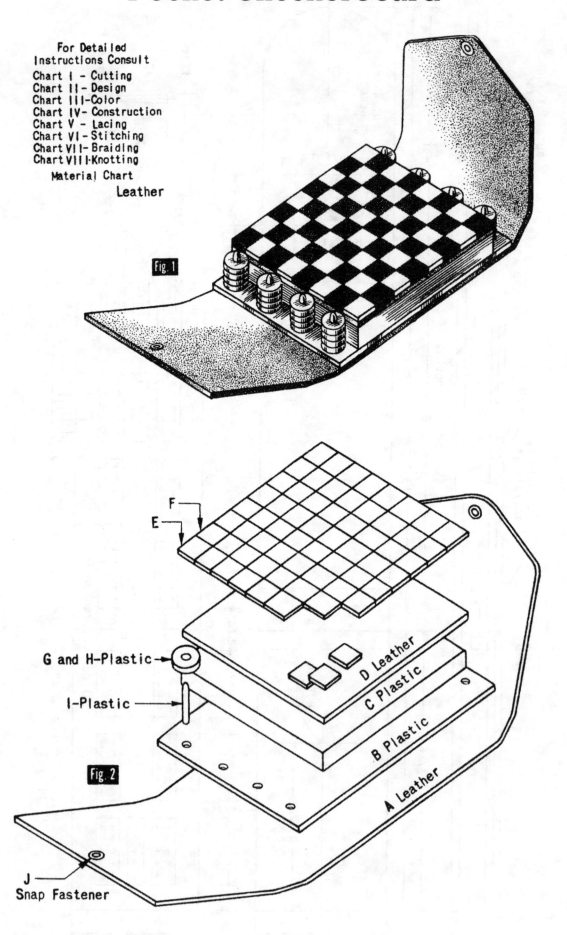

For Detailed
Instructions Consult
Chart I - Cutting
Chart II - Design
Chart III - Color
Chart IV - Construction
Chart V - Lacing
Chart VI - Stitching
Chart VII - Braiding
Chart VIII - Knotting
    Material Chart
            Leather

Fig. 1

F
E

G and H-Plastic →

I-Plastic →

D Leather
C Plastic
B Plastic
A Leather

Fig. 2

J
Snap Fastener

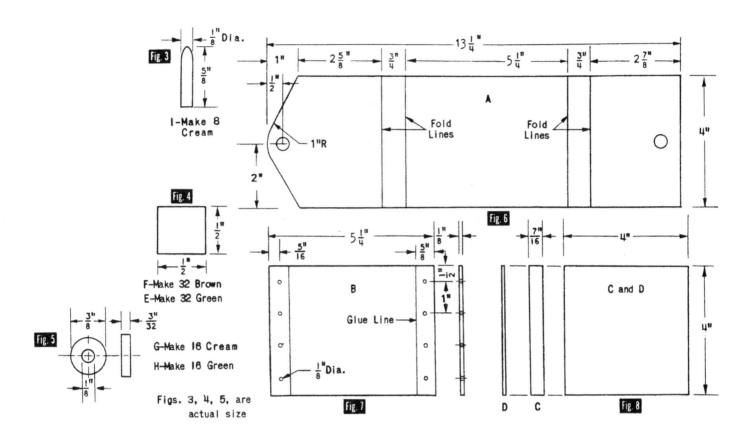

Fig. 3
$\frac{1}{8}$"Dia.
$\frac{5}{8}$"

I-Make 8
Cream

Fig. 4
$\frac{1}{2}$"
$\frac{1}{2}$"

F-Make 32 Brown
E-Make 32 Green

Fig. 5
$\frac{3}{8}$"
$\frac{3}{32}$"

G-Make 16 Cream

H-Make 16 Green

$\frac{1}{8}$"

Figs. 3, 4, 5, are
actual size

1"
2$\frac{5}{8}$"
$\frac{3}{4}$"
13$\frac{1}{4}$"
5$\frac{1}{4}$"
$\frac{3}{4}$"
2$\frac{7}{8}$"
$\frac{1}{2}$"
A
Fold Lines
Fold Lines
4"
1"R
2"
Fig. 6

5$\frac{1}{4}$"
$\frac{5}{16}$"
$\frac{1}{8}$"
$\frac{5}{8}$"
$\frac{1}{2}$"
B
1"
Glue Line
$\frac{1}{8}$"Dia.
Fig. 7

$\frac{7}{16}$"
4"
C and D
4"
D   C
Fig. 8

PROCEDURE: (CONSULT LEATHER CRAFT PROCESSING CHARTS)

1. Cut leather parts (A), (D), (E), (F). Figs. 4, 6, 8.

2. Cut and prepare plastic parts (B), (C), (G), (H), (I). Figs. 2, 3, 5, 7, 8.

3. Attach cap section of snap fastener (J) to part (A). Figs. 2, 6.

4. Cement the 64 brown and green squares, parts (E) and (F), to part (D), in the pattern shown. Fig. 2.

5. Cement part (B) to part (A). Fig. 2.

6. Cement the 8 pegs, parts (I), into the holes previously prepared in part (B). Fig. 2.

7. Cement part (C) to assembly (AB). Fig. 2.

8. Cement assembly (DEF) to assembly (ABC). Fig. 2.

9. Place the 32 checkers, parts (G) and (H), over pegs (I). Figs. 1, 2.

10. Close case to determine position and attach post section of snap fastener (J) to part (A). Figs. 2, 6.

MATERIALS:

Russia tooling calfskin (natural)

Levant grained goatskin (British brown and green)

Catalin: cream & green

$\frac{7}{16}$" diam. snap fastener

Rubber cement

TOOLS:

(1), (3), (5), (6), (12), (43).

Tennis Racket Case

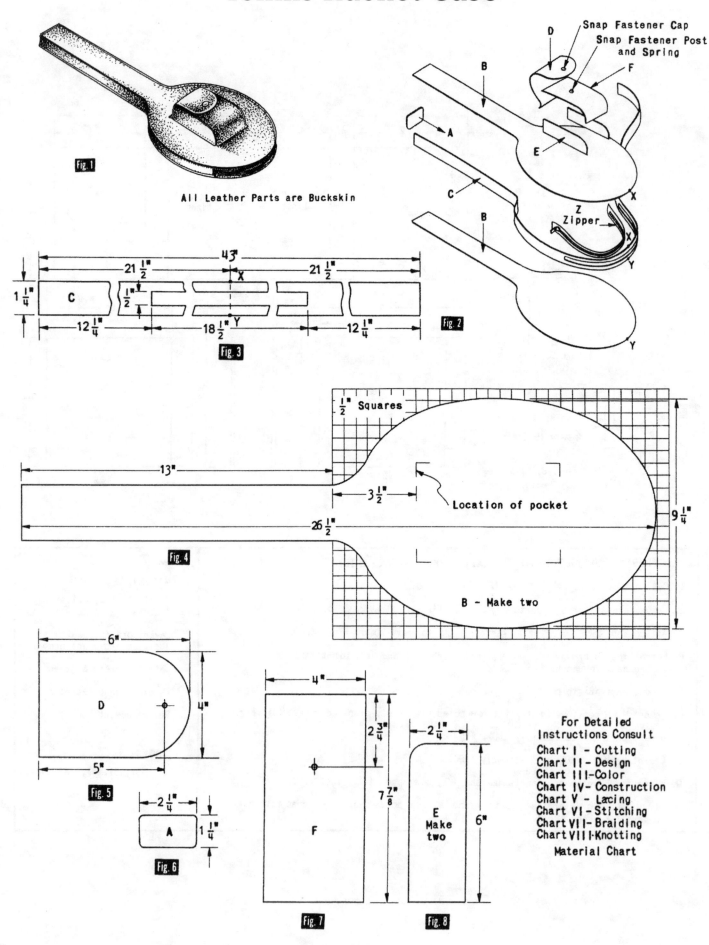

All Leather Parts are Buckskin

Snap Fastener Cap
Snap Fastener Post and Spring

Fig. 1
Fig. 2
Fig. 3
Fig. 4
Fig. 5
Fig. 6
Fig. 7
Fig. 8

All Leather Parts are Buckskin

43"
21 1/2"
21 1/2"
1 1/4"
C
1/2"
12 1/4"
18 1/2"
12 1/4"

1/2" Squares
13"
3 1/2"
Location of pocket
26 1/2"
9 1/4"
B - Make two

6"
D
4"
5"

4"
2 3/4"
F
7 7/8"

2 1/4"
E
Make two
6"

2 1/4"
A
1 1/4"

For Detailed
Instructions Consult
Chart I - Cutting
Chart II - Design
Chart III - Color
Chart IV - Construction
Chart V - Lacing
Chart VI - Stitching
Chart VII - Braiding
Chart VIII - Knotting
Material Chart

PROCEDURE: (CONSULT LEATHER CRAFT PROCESSING CHARTS)

1. Cut parts (A), (B), (C), (D), (E) and (F). Figs. 3, 4, 5, 6, 7, 8.

2. Cut slot for zipper (Z) in (C). Fig. 3.

3. Cement tape edges of (Z) to back edges of slot in (C). Fig. 2.

4. Sew (Z) to (C) on sewing machine. Fig. 2.

5. Sew parts (E) to (F). Fig. 2.

6. Attach cap of snap fastener to (D) and post and spring of snap fastener to (F). Figs. 2, 5, 7.

7. Sew straight edge of (D) and pocket edges of (EF) to top (B). Figs. 2, 4.

8. Fit (C) to top (B) with points (X) coinciding. Sew a few temporary stitches to hold edges of (C) and (B) together. Fig. 2.

9. Sew top (B) to (C) on sewing machine. Fig. 2.

10. Fit bottom (B) to (BC) with points (Y) coinciding. Make temporary stitches on edges. Fig. 2.

11. Sew bottom (B) to (BC) on sewing machine. Fig. 2.

12. Punch closely spaced stitching holes with awl through matching edges of (A) and (BBC). Fig. 2.

13. Sew (A) to (BBC) with saddler's stitch. Fig. 2.

MATERIALS:

Buckskin
1-18" zipper
1-snap fastener
Rubber cement
Thread

TOOLS:

(1), (6), (8), (12), (17), (21), (25), (41).

Golf Club Covers

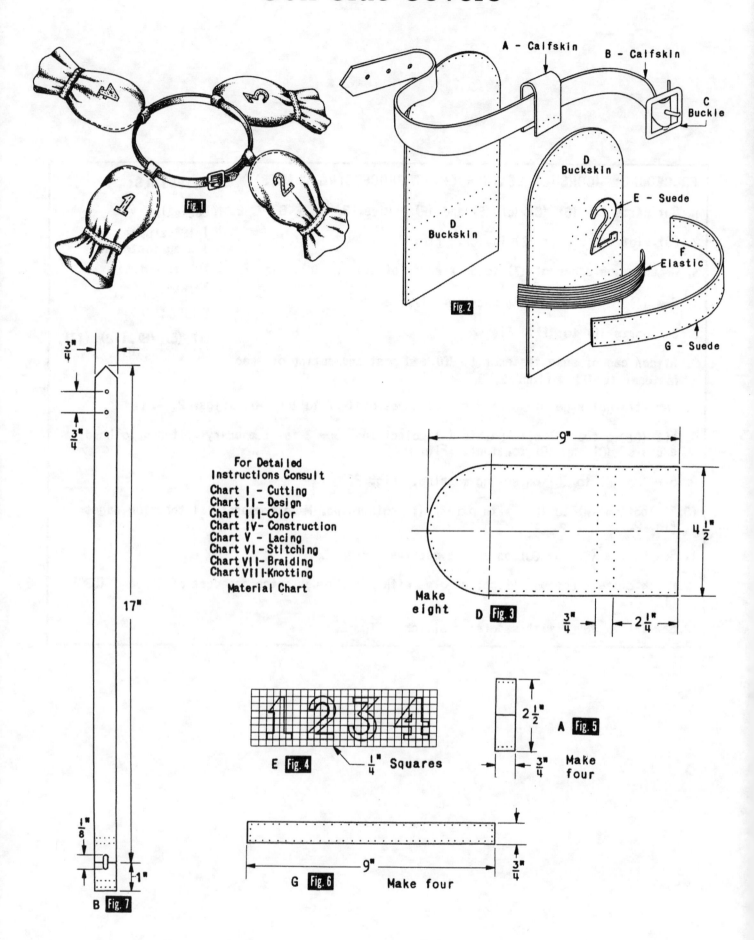

Fig. 1

A - Calfskin
B - Calfskin
C - Buckle
D - Buckskin
D - Buckskin
E - Suede
F - Elastic
G - Suede

Fig. 2

For Detailed
Instructions Consult
Chart I - Cutting
Chart II - Design
Chart III - Color
Chart IV - Construction
Chart V - Lacing
Chart VI - Stitching
Chart VII - Braiding
Chart VIII - Knotting
Material Chart

9"

4 1/2"

Make eight   D **Fig. 3**

3/4"   2 1/4"

3/4"

3/4"

E **Fig. 4**   1/4" Squares

2 1/2"   A **Fig. 5**
3/4"   Make four

17"

1/8"

1"

B **Fig. 7**

9"

3/4"

G **Fig. 6**   Make four

PROCEDURE: (CONSULT LEATHER CRAFT PROCESSING CHARTS)

1. Cut parts (A),(B),(D),(E – 1,2,3,4), (F) and (G). Figs. 3, 4, 5, 6, 7.

2. Cement parts (E – 1,2,3,4) on 4 parts (D). Fig. 2.

3. Mark closely spaced stitching holes through (E – 1,2,3,4) and (D). Fig. 2.

4. Punch stitching holes with awl. Fig. 2.

5. Sew (E – 1,2,3,4) to parts (D) with saddle stitch. Fig. 2.

6. Fold (A). Insert between (DE) and plain (D). Figs. 2, 5.

7. Cement 1/8" of edges of (DE) to plain (D). Fig. 2.

8. Mark stitching holes with 1/7" spacing wheel 1/8" from edge of (D). Figs. 2, 3.

9. Punch stitching holes through (D) and (DE), including (A). Fig. 2.

10. Sew (D) to (DE) with saddle stitch. Fig. 2.

11. Place (G) around (DDE). Sew long edges of (G) to (DDE), leaving ends free at seam on edge of (D). Fig. 2.

12. Insert elastic (F) through opening left at ends of (G). Sew ends of (F) together, and stitch ends of (G). Fig. 2.

13. Cut slot in square end of (B) for prong of buckle (C). Fig. 7.

14. Insert buckle. and punch double row of closely spaced stitching holes through folded end of (B). Fig. 7.

15. Stitch fold of (B) with saddler's stitch. Fig. 2.

16. Punch holes for prong of (C) in pointed end of (B). Fig. 7.

17. Run (B) through loops (A) on covers. Fasten buckle. Figs. 1, 2.

MATERIALS:

Buckskin

Calfskin, 3 oz.

Suede, 1 oz.

Elastic, 18", 3/8" wide

Linen thread

Buckle, 3/4" center bar

Rubber cement

TOOLS:

(1), (6), (8), (17), (21), (25), (28), (30), (33), (41).

Cribbage Board

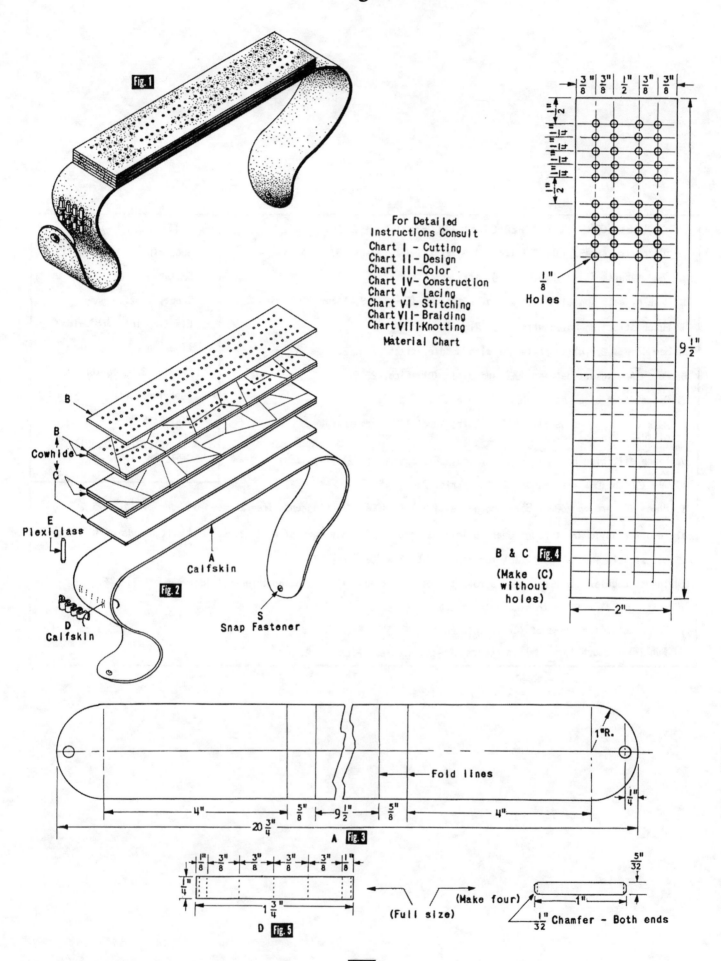

Fig. 1

For Detailed
Instructions Consult
Chart I - Cutting
Chart II- Design
Chart III-Color
Chart IV- Construction
Chart V - Lacing
Chart VI - Stitching
Chart VII- Braiding
Chart VIII-Knotting
  Material Chart

B

B
Cowhide

C

E
Plexiglass

A

Calfskin

Fig. 2

D
Calfskin

Snap Fastener

$\frac{3}{8}$" $\frac{3}{8}$" $\frac{1}{2}$" $\frac{3}{8}$" $\frac{3}{8}$"

$\frac{1}{2}$"
$1\frac{1}{4}$"
$1\frac{1}{4}$"
$1\frac{1}{4}$"
$\frac{1}{2}$"

$\frac{1}{8}$"
Holes

$9\frac{1}{2}$"

B & C **Fig. 4**
(Make (C)
without
holes)

2"

1"R.

Fold lines

$\frac{1}{4}$"

4" $\frac{5}{8}$" $9\frac{1}{2}$" $\frac{5}{8}$"   4"

$20\frac{3}{4}$"

A **Fig. 3**

$\frac{1}{8}$" $\frac{3}{8}$" $\frac{3}{8}$" $\frac{3}{8}$" $\frac{3}{8}$" $\frac{1}{8}$"

$\frac{5}{32}$"

$\frac{1}{4}$"

$1\frac{3}{4}$"

(Make four)

(Full size)

1"

$\frac{1}{32}$" Chamfer - Both ends

D **Fig. 5**

PROCEDURE: (CONSULT LEATHER CRAFT PROCESSING CHARTS)

1. Cut (A), surface layer of (B), bottom layer of (C), and (D). Figs. 3, 4, 5.

2. Cut up scraps of leather to form inside layers of (B) and (C). Build up (BB) and (CC) to a height of 1/4" each by piecing together, jig-saw fashion, tightly fitted leather scraps of same thickness. Fig. 2.

3. Sandpaper all skin surfaces to be cemented. Fig. 2.

4. Assemble and cement inner layers of (B) and (C) to outer (B) and (C) respectively. Place under weight and allow to dry 18-24 hours. Do not cement (B) to (C). Fig. 2.

5. Drill 1/8" holes with hand drill for pegs (E) through (B) as shown. Figs. 2, 4.

6. Cement section (B) to section (C). Place under weight and allow to dry as before. Fig. 2.

7. Sandpaper all cut edges of (BC) to a smooth surface. Apply successive coats of Johnson's paste wax, rubbing thoroughly to achieve a smooth, waxed finish. Fig. 2.

8. Outline edges of (A) with edge creaser. Fig. 3.

9. Sew (D) in position on flesh side of (A) with saddler's stitch. Figs. 2, 3.

10. Cement (BC) to flesh side of (A). Place under weight and allow to dry as before. Fig. 2.

11. Fold (A) in position to determine position of snap fastener (S). Attach parts of snap fastener to (A). Figs. 2, 3.

MATERIALS:

Cowhide, 6-8 oz.
Scrap cowhide, 6-8 oz.
Calfskin, 3 oz.
Pliobond Plastic Adhesive
1 - Snap fastener
Sandpaper, No. 00.
Johnson's paste wax

TOOLS:

(1), (6), (8), (12), (17), (25), (27), (41).

$\frac{1}{8}$" Drill

Outdoor Card Game Board

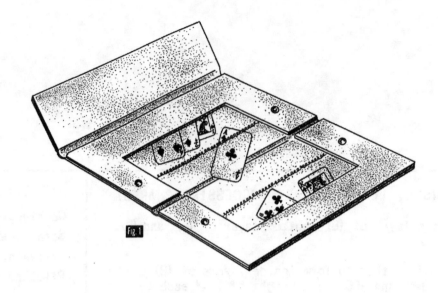

Fig. 1

B⟵ Rivet (4 Req.)

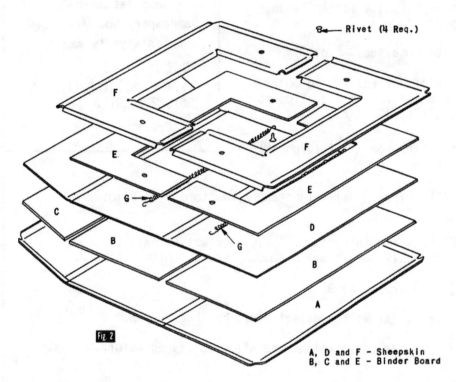

F

F

E

E

C

B

D

B

A

G

G

Fig. 2

A, D and F - Sheepskin
B, C and E - Binder Board

For Detailed
Instructions Consult
Chart I - Cutting
Chart II - Design
Chart III - Color
Chart IV - Construction
Chart V - Lacing
Chart VI - Stitching
Chart VII - Braiding
Chart VIII - Knotting

Material Chart

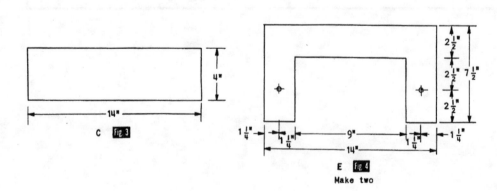

4"

14"

C Fig. 3

2 1/2"
2 1/2" 7 1/2"
2 1/2"

1 1/4" 1 1/4" 9" 1 1/4" 1 1/4"
14"

E Fig. 4
Make two

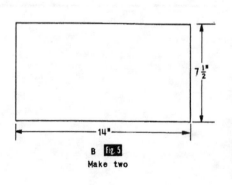

7 1/2"

14"

B Fig. 5
Make two

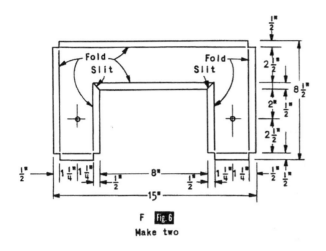

F **Fig. 6**
Make two

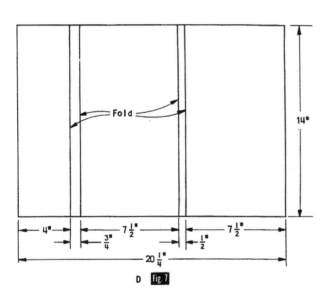

D **Fig. 7**

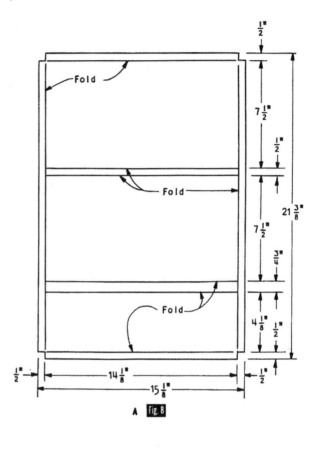

A **Fig. 8**

PROCEDURE: (CONSULT LEATHERCRAFT PROCESSING CHARTS)

1. Cut parts (A), (B), (C), (D), (E) and (F). Figs. 3, 4, 5, 6, 7, 8.
   Note: Construct coiled springs (G).

2. Skive all edges of (A), (D) and (F). Figs. 6, 7, 8.

3. Mark fold lines on (A) and (F) with edge creaser. Figs. 6, 8.

4. Cement parts (B) and (C) to flesh side of (A). Fig. 2.

5. Fold flap edges of (A) and cement to (B) and (C). Fig. 2.

6. Cement (D) to (ABC) Fig. 2.

7. Cement parts (E) to flesh side of parts (F). Figs. 2, 4, 6.

8. Fold flap edges of (F) and cement to (E). Figs. 2, 6.

9. Insert rivets through (EF), with last coils of spring (G) wound around stems of rivets on cardboard side. Figs. 2, 4, 6.

10. Cement 1" of outside edge of (EF) to (ABD), including short ends of (EF). Fig. 2.

MATERIALS:
Sheepskin skiver, 1 oz.
Hard-rolled binder board
(Millboard) .093"
4 - Button rivets
Rubber cement

TOOLS:
(1), (6), (8), (17), (19), (24).

Handbag

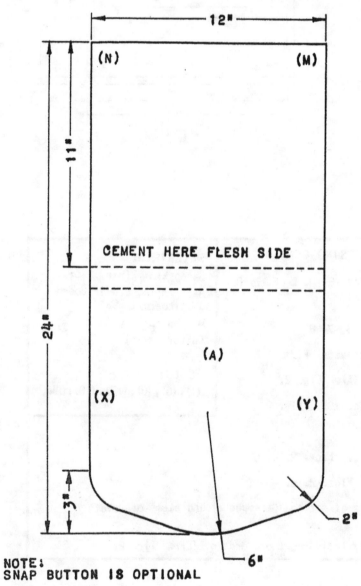

12"

(N) (M)

11"

CEMENT HERE FLESH SIDE

24"

(A)

(X) (Y)

3"

2"

6"

NOTE:
SNAP BUTTON IS OPTIONAL

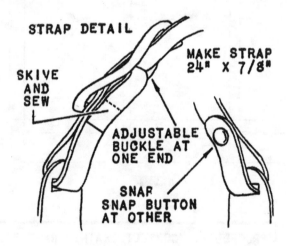

STRAP DETAIL

SKIVE
AND
SEW

MAKE STRAP
24" X 7/8"

ADJUSTABLE
BUCKLE AT
ONE END

SNAP
SNAP BUTTON
AT OTHER

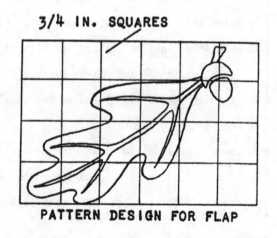

3/4 IN. SQUARES

PATTERN DESIGN FOR FLAP

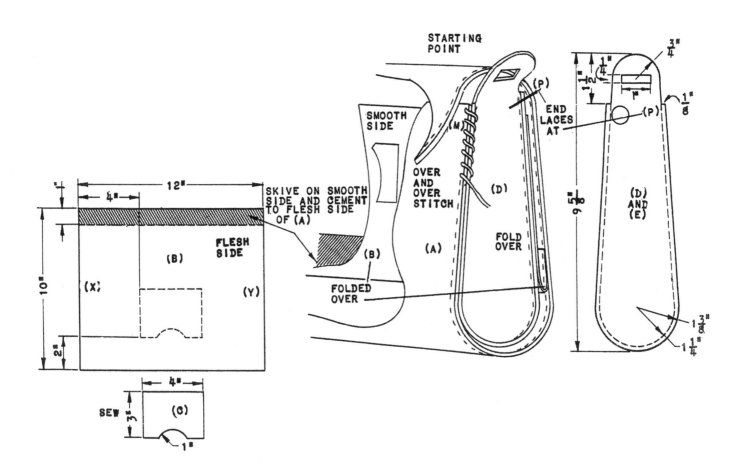

STARTING
POINT

SMOOTH
SIDE

OVER
AND
OVER
STITCH

(M)

(A)

(B)

FOLDED
OVER

SKIVE ON SMOOTH
SIDE AND CEMENT
TO FLESH SIDE
OF (A)

FLESH
SIDE

(B)

(X)

(B)

(Y)

12"

4"

10"

2"

SEW

4"

(C)

3"

1"

(D)

FOLD
OVER

(P)

END
LACES
AT

(P)

3"
4

1"
4

1"
2

1"

(D)
AND
(E)

9 5"
8

1"
8

1 3"
8

1 1"
4

PROCEDURE:

HAVING PREPARED THE SIX SEPARATE PARTS...
(1) SEW (C) TO (B) ON SMOOTH SIDE
(2) SKIVE EDGE OF (B) LOCATE AND CEMENT
    TO FLESH SIDE OF (A) STARTING AT (M)
    PUNCH 3/32" THONG SLITS 1/8" FROM
    EDGES ON (A) AND (B) WHICH IS FOLDED
    OVER. ALSO PUNCH SLITS IN (D) AND (E)
(3) LACE, STARTING AT POINTS (M) AND (N)
    SIMULTANEOUSLY AND END AT (P)
(4) LOCATE AND SET 3/8" SNAP BUTTONS ON FLAP AND STRAP

TOOLS: (1)(2)(3)(4)
(6)(8)(9)(12)(13)(16)

MATERIALS:
CONSULT LEATHER CHART
RUBBER CEMENT
TWO 3/8" SNAP BUTTONS
ONE ADJUSTABLE BUCKLE

Handbag

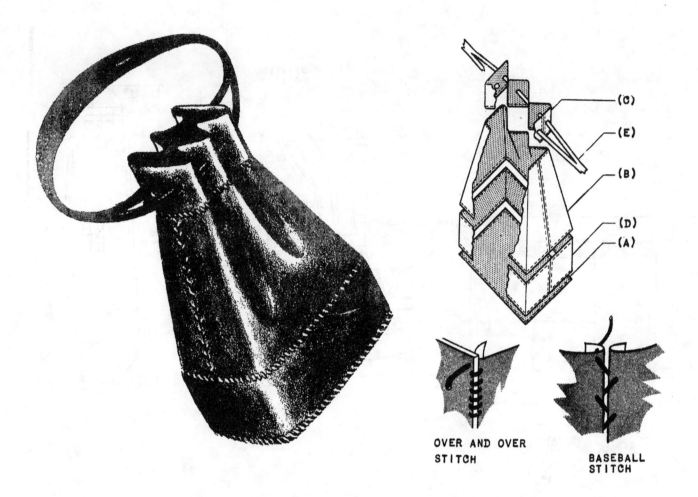

OVER AND OVER
STITCH

BASEBALL
STITCH

PROCEDURE:
HAVING PREPARED THE FOUR SEPARATE PIECES,(SEVEN IF
STIFFNER AND LINING ARE USED IN BOTTOM)...
(1) SLIGHTLY ROUND CORNERS OF (A) AND PUNCH 3/32"
    THONG SLITS 3/16" IN FROM EDGES. LIKEWISE,PUNCH
    SLITS IN (B)(C)(D) AS INDICATED BY DOTTED LINES.
(2) LACE TOGETHER AS SHOWN IN ASSEMBLY DRAWING.
(3) INSERT STRINGS (E) AND TIE ENDS TOGETHER.
    IF STIFFNER AND LINING ARE USED IN BOTTOM, THEY
    SHOULD BE CEMENTED TOGETHER BEFORE THONG SLITS
    ARE PUNCHED.

TOOLS: (1)(2)(4)(6)(8)(16)

MATERIALS: CONSULT LEATHER CHARTS, RUBBER CEMENT.

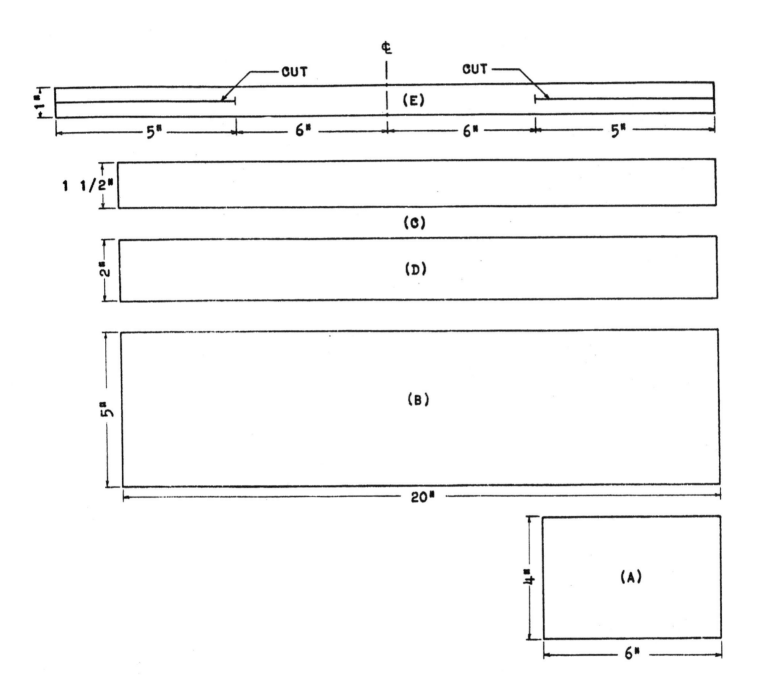

White Handbag

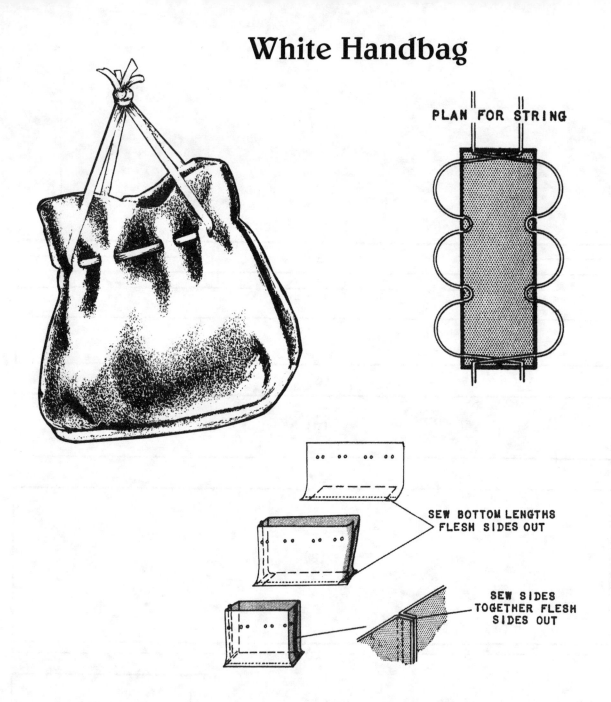

PLAN FOR STRING

SEW BOTTOM LENGTHS
FLESH SIDES OUT

SEW SIDES
TOGETHER FLESH
SIDES OUT

PROCEDURE:
HAVING PREPARED THE THREE SEPERATE PIECES OF WHITE CALFSKIN...

(1) PUNCH 1/4" HOLES AS INDICATED.

(2) USING SEWING MACHINE, SEW (A) TO (C) FROM POINT (X) TO (Y), FLESH SIDES OUT.
LIKEWISE, SEW (B) TO (C). THEN COMPLETE THE SEWING ALONG THE BOTTOM EDGES.

(3) SEW SIDES TOGETHER FROM POINT (W) TO (Z).

(4) TURN BAG INSIDE OUT. LACE THE TWO 1/4" X 18" STRINGS THRU THE HOLES AS SHOWN
IN ILLUSTRATION AND TIE KNOT.

TOOLS: (1) (3) (6)   MATERIALS: WHITE CALFSKIN.

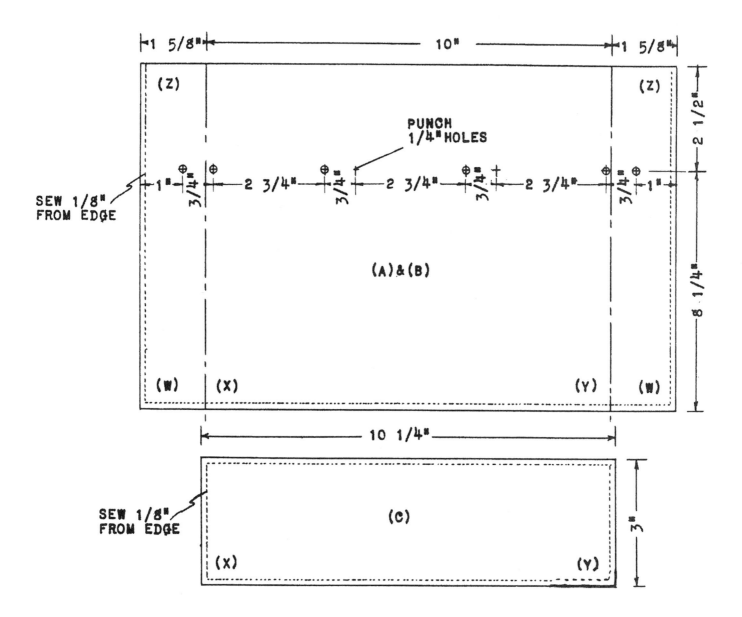

Handbag

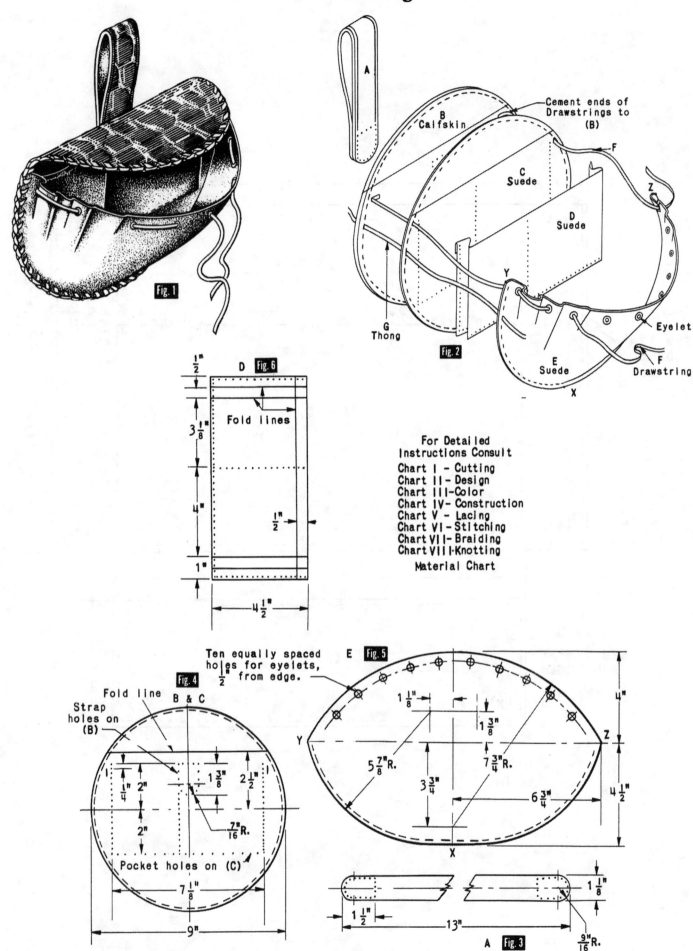

Fig. 1

Fig. 2
- B Calfskin
- Cement ends of Drawstrings to (B)
- C Suede
- D Suede
- F
- Z
- Y
- Eyelet
- F Drawstring
- G Thong
- E Suede
- X

A

Fig. 6 D
- $\frac{1}{2}$"
- Fold lines
- $3\frac{1}{8}$"
- 4"
- $\frac{1}{2}$"
- 1"
- $4\frac{1}{2}$"

For Detailed Instructions Consult
Chart I - Cutting
Chart II - Design
Chart III - Color
Chart IV - Construction
Chart V - Lacing
Chart VI - Stitching
Chart VII - Braiding
Chart VIII - Knotting
Material Chart

Fig. 4
- Fold line B & C
- Strap holes on (B)
- $\frac{1}{4}$"
- 2"
- 2"
- $1\frac{3}{8}$"
- $2\frac{1}{2}$"
- $\frac{7}{16}$"R.
- Pocket holes on (C)
- $7\frac{1}{8}$"
- 9"

Fig. 5 E
- Ten equally spaced holes for eyelets, $\frac{1}{2}$" from edge.
- $1\frac{1}{8}$"
- $1\frac{3}{8}$"
- Y
- $5\frac{7}{8}$"R.
- $7\frac{3}{4}$"R.
- $3\frac{3}{4}$"
- $6\frac{3}{4}$"
- Z
- 4"
- $4\frac{1}{2}$"
- X

Fig. 3 A
- $1\frac{1}{2}$"
- 13"
- $1\frac{1}{8}$"
- $\frac{9}{16}$"R.

PROCEDURE: (CONSULT LEATHER CRAFT PROCESSING CHARTS)

1. Cut parts (A),(B),(C),(D) and (E). Figs. 3, 4, 5, 6.

2. Outline edge of (A) and mark folding line of (B) with edge creaser. Figs. 2, 4.

3. Mark stitching holes 1/8" apart, in one end of (A) as shown. Fig. 3.

4. Fold (A) in half and place in position on (B). With awl, punch stitching holes simultaneously in both ends of (A) and in matching area of (B). Figs. 2, 3, 4.

5. Sew (A) to (B) with saddler's stitch. Fig. 2.

6. With #7 tube, punch eyelet holes in (E) and insert eyelets. Fig. 5.

7. Fold back top edge of (D) 1/2" and cement in place. Fig. 6.

8. With spacing wheel, mark sewing lines on part (D). Fig. 6.

9. Fold ends of (D) in place and sew to (C) on sewing machine. Figs. 2, 4, 6.

10. Cut holes for drawstrings (F) in (C). Pass (F) through holes and cement ends to (B) as shown. Cement (CD) to (B). Figs. 2, 4.

11. Place part (E) on assembly (ABCD). Starting from point (X), punch 3/32" thongs slits, 1/8" from edge, in (E) and (BC), simultaneously, to point (Y). Return to point (X) and repeat operation to point (Z) and balance of (BC). Figs. 2, 4, 5.

12. Lace part (E) to assembly (ABCD) with single overlay stitch. Fig. 2.

13. Insert drawstring (F) through eyelets and tie. Fig. 2.

MATERIALS:

Calfskin, alligator grain

Suede, matching color

10-6K eyelets

Rawhide lace for drawstring

Calfskin lace, 3/32", 14'

Rubber cement

Heavy linen thread

TOOLS:

(1), (3, No. 7), (4), (6), (8), (14), (17), (18), (21), (25), (26), (27), (28), (30), (40), (41), (43).

Handbag

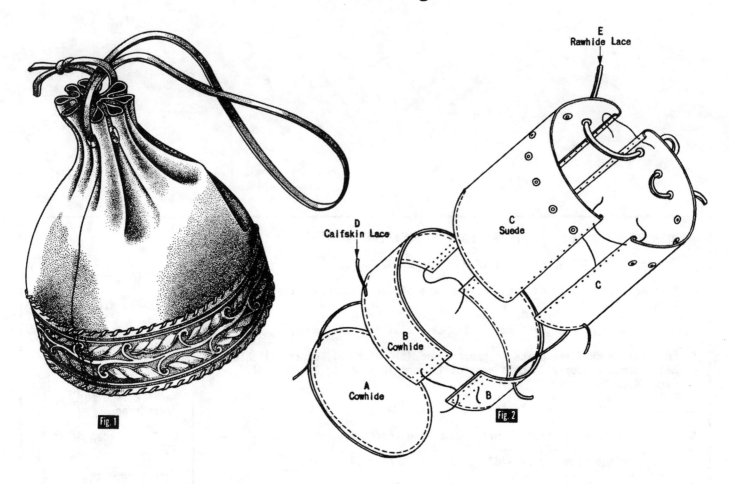

Fig. 1

E
Rawhide Lace

D
Calfskin Lace

C
Suede

C

B
Cowhide

A
Cowhide

B

Fig. 2

PROCEDURE: (CONSULT LEATHER CRAFT PROCESSING CHARTS)

1. Cut and prepare parts (A), (B), (C). Figs. 3, 4, 5.

2. Cut $\frac{3}{32}$" thong slits in matching parts of (A), (B) and (C), $\frac{1}{8}$" from edges. Figs. 2, 3, 4, 5.

3. Punch holes and insert metal eyelets in parts (C).

4. With sewing awl stitch together the two sections of (C), with seams inside. Figs. 2, 3.

5. With awl punch a double row of stitching holes in the two sections of part (B). Figs. 1, 2, 4.

6. Sew parts (B) with saddler's stitch lapping one end over the other. Figs. 1, 2.

7. Lace part (A) to (B) and part (AB) to (C) with (D) using whipstitch. Figs. 1, 2.

8. Insert drawstring thong through eyelets and tie. Figs. 1, 2.

MATERIALS:

Heavy tooling cowhide

Garment suede sheepskin

Calfskin lace $\frac{3}{32}$" wide, 28" long

Rawhide lace $\frac{3}{16}$" wide, 28" long

16 metal eyelets, No. 6 K

TOOLS:

(1), (4), (6), (14), (17), (18), (21), (23), (40).

See Leather Chart V for thong slits

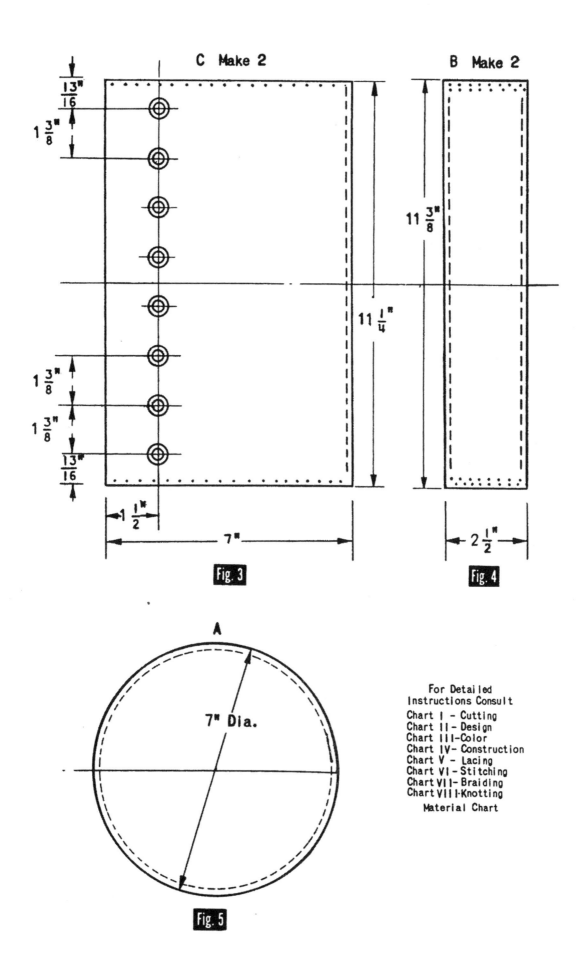

C Make 2

$\frac{13"}{16}$

$1\frac{3}{8}"$

$11\frac{3}{8}"$

$11\frac{1}{4}"$

$1\frac{3}{8}"$

$1\frac{3}{8}"$

$\frac{13"}{16}$

$1\frac{1}{2}"$

7"

Fig. 3

B Make 2

$2\frac{1}{2}"$

Fig. 4

A

7" Dia.

Fig. 5

For Detailed
Instructions Consult
Chart I – Cutting
Chart II – Design
Chart III–Color
Chart IV– Construction
Chart V – Lacing
Chart VI – Stitching
Chart VII–Braiding
Chart VIII·Knotting

Material Chart

223

Handbag

Fig. 1

For Detailed
Instructions Consult
Chart I - Cutting
Chart II- Design
Chart III-Color
Chart IV- Construction
Chart V - Lacing
Chart VI- Stitching
Chart VII- Braiding
Chart VIII-Knotting
Material Chart

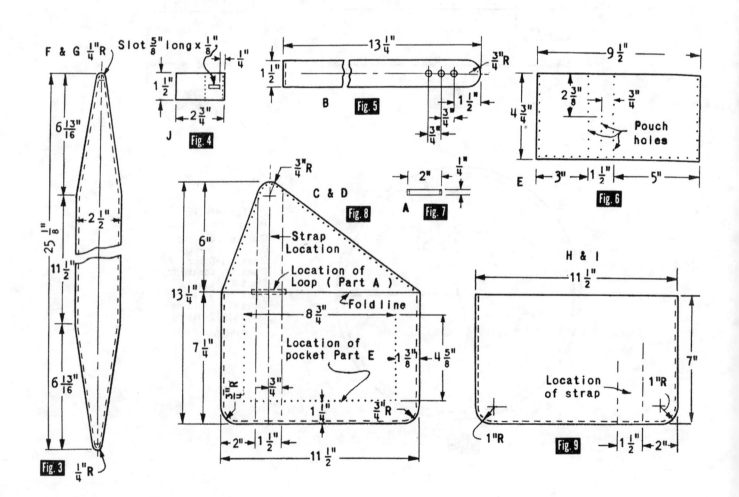

A Calfskin
B Calfskin
C Calfskin
D Lining Calf
E Lining Calf
Cement thong
F Calfskin
G Lining Calf
H Lining Calf
I Calfskin
J Calfskin
K

Fig. 2

F & G $\frac{1}{4}$"R

25 $\frac{1}{8}$"

6 $\frac{13}{16}$"
11 $\frac{1}{2}$"
6 $\frac{13}{16}$"
2 $\frac{1}{2}$"

Fig. 3 $\frac{1}{4}$R

Slot $\frac{5}{8}$" long x $\frac{1}{8}$"
1 $\frac{1}{4}$"
1 $\frac{1}{2}$"
2 $\frac{3}{4}$"
J   Fig. 4

13 $\frac{1}{4}$"
1 $\frac{1}{2}$"
$\frac{3}{4}$"R
B   Fig. 5
$\frac{3}{4}$"   1 $\frac{1}{2}$"
$\frac{3}{4}$"

2" $\frac{1}{4}$"
A   Fig. 7

9 $\frac{1}{2}$"
2 $\frac{3}{8}$" $\frac{3}{4}$"
Pouch holes
4 $\frac{3}{4}$"
E   3"   1 $\frac{1}{2}$"   5"   Fig. 6

$\frac{3}{4}$"R
C & D   Fig. 8
6"
13 $\frac{1}{4}$"
Strap Location
Location of Loop (Part A)
Foldline
8 $\frac{3}{4}$"
7 $\frac{1}{4}$"
Location of pocket Part E
1 $\frac{3}{8}$"   4 $\frac{5}{8}$"
$\frac{3}{4}$"R
$\frac{3}{4}$"
1 $\frac{1}{4}$" $\frac{3}{4}$"R
2"   1 $\frac{1}{2}$"
11 $\frac{1}{2}$"

H & I
11 $\frac{1}{2}$"
Location of strap
1"R
7"
1"R   Fig. 9   1 $\frac{1}{2}$"   2"

PROCEDURE: (CONSULT LEATHER CRAFT PROCESSING CHARTS)

1. Cut parts (A), (B), (C), (D), (E), (F), (G), (H), (I), (J). Figs. 3 through 9. Reverse pattern when cutting lining (D). Fig. 8.

2. Punch holes with awl, and saddle stitch belt loop (A) to skin side of (C). Figs. 2, 7, 8.

3. Punch holes and saddle stitch (E) to (D), being sure to pouch $1\frac{1}{2}"$ section to $1"$. Stitch up bottom center of pouch $2\frac{3}{8}"$. Figs. 2, 6.

4. Cement end of thong to (C) as shown. Cement (D) to (C), (G) to (F), (H) to (I). Fig. 2.

5. Cut slit in (J) for buckle prong. Stitch buckle (K) in place with saddler's stitch. Figs. 2, 4.

6. Punch holes in (B) large enough for buckle prong. Fig. 5.

7. Punch $\frac{3}{32}"$ thong slits in all matching parts, $\frac{1}{8}"$ from edges. Starting at cemented end, lace all matching parts together with single overlay stitch, attaching (B) and (J) in their proper places. Figs. 2, 8, 9.

8. Punch holes along flap of (CD), $\frac{3}{16}"$ apart, and sew with saddler's stitch. Fig. 2.

MATERIALS:

Heavy calfskin

Lining calf

Calfskin lace $\frac{3}{32}"$ 26' long

Buckle with center bar $1\frac{1}{2}"$

Rubber cement

TOOLS:

(1), (4), (6), (8), (17), (18), (21), (25), (26), (33), (40), (41), (43).

Handbag

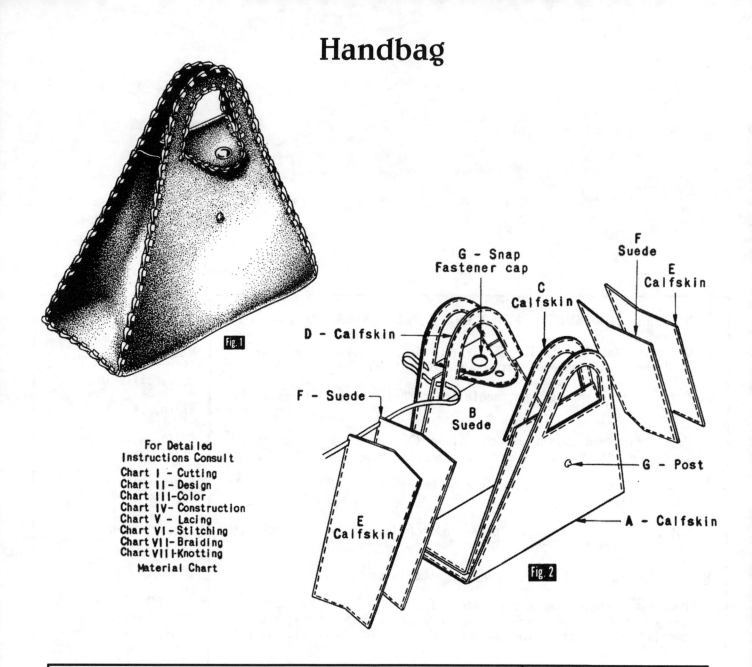

Fig. 1

For Detailed
Instructions Consult
Chart I - Cutting
Chart II - Design
Chart III - Color
Chart IV - Construction
Chart V - Lacing
Chart VI - Stitching
Chart VII - Braiding
Chart VIII - Knotting
Material Chart

G - Snap
Fastener cap

D - Calfskin

C
Calfskin

F
Suede

E
Calfskin

F - Suede

B
Suede

G - Post

E
Calfskin

A - Calfskin

Fig. 2

PROCEDURE: (CONSULT LEATHER CRAFT PROCESSING CHARTS)

1. Cut and prepare parts (A), (B), (C), (D), (E), (F). Use edge creaser for fold lines. Figs. 3, 4, 5, 6, 7.

2. Cement parts (B), (C) and (D) to part (A), and parts (E) to parts (F).

3. With awl punch $\frac{3"}{32}$ lacing slits in matching parts of (ABCD) and (EF) $\frac{1"}{8}$ from edges. Before cement dries insert end of lace between (A) and (B), as shown Fig. 2.

4. Lace parts together with single overlay stitch. Fig. 1.

5. Attach snap fastener (G) to (AD) and (AB) as shown. Figs. 1, 2.

MATERIALS:

Chrome tanned calfskin
(heaviest weight)

Suede lining

Goat lacing $\frac{3"}{32}$
x 12 yds.

$\frac{7"}{16}$ Snap fastener

TOOLS:

(1), (3), (4), (5), (6),
(12), (17), (18), (21),
(26), (40).

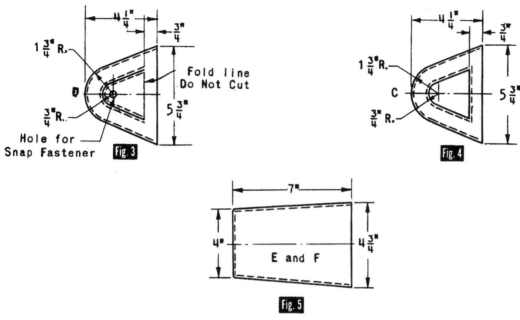

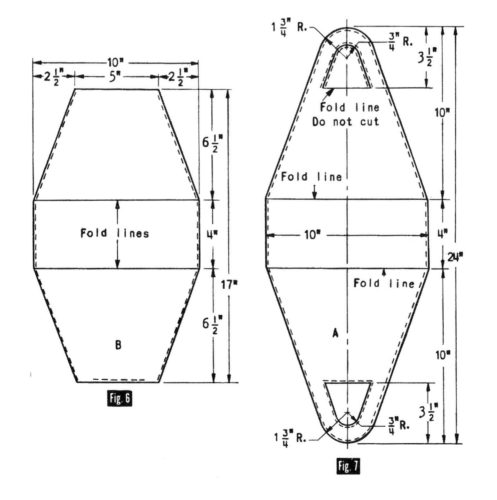

(Make 4: 2 calfskin, 2 suede)

Handbag

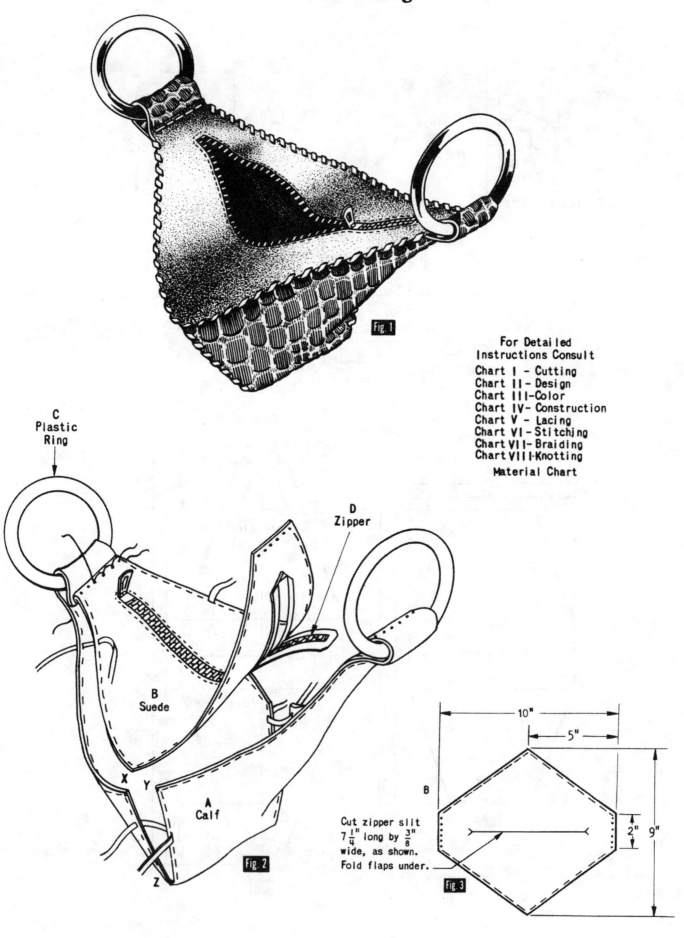

Fig. 1

For Detailed
Instructions Consult
Chart I – Cutting
Chart II – Design
Chart III – Color
Chart IV – Construction
Chart V – Lacing
Chart VI – Stitching
Chart VII – Braiding
Chart VIII – Knotting
Material Chart

C
Plastic
Ring

D
Zipper

B
Suede

X Y

A
Calf

Fig. 2

B

10"

5"

2" 9"

Cut zipper slit
7 $\frac{1}{4}$" long by $\frac{3}{8}$"
wide, as shown.
Fold flaps under.

Fig. 3

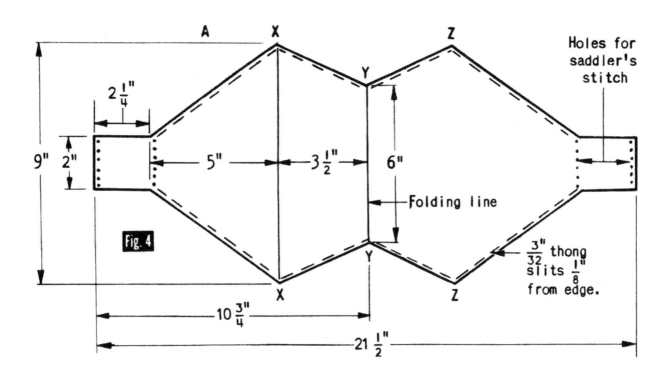

Fig. 4

PROCEDURE: (CONSULT LEATHER CRAFT PROCESSING CHARTS)

1. Cut parts (A) and (B). Figs. 3, 4.

2. Punch $\frac{3}{32}$" thong slits in matching parts of (A) and (B), simultaneously, $\frac{1}{8}$" from edges. Figs. 2, 3, 4.

3. Fold (A) and lace together section (XYZ). Figs. 2, 4.

4. Fold under flaps of zipper slit in part (B). Use sewing machine and stitch zipper (D) in place. Fig. 2.

5. Fold ends of part (A) over rings (C) and punch stitching holes with awl in parts (A) and (B), simultaneously, allowing $\frac{1}{8}$" seam. Figs. 2, 4.

6. Sew rings (C) in place, using saddler's stitch. Fig. 2.

7. Complete lacing of part (A) to (B). Figs. 1, 2.

MATERIALS:

Red alligator grain calfskin

Black goat lacing $\frac{3}{32}$" wide, 15' long

Black garment suede sheepskin

7" zipper

Two 4" diam. plastic rings

Black thread

TOOLS:

(1), (4), (6), (17), (18), (21), (25), (40), (41).

Knapsack Bag

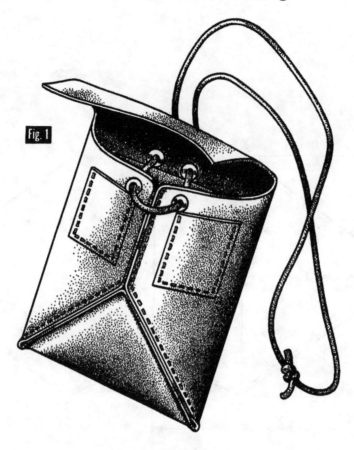

Fig. 1

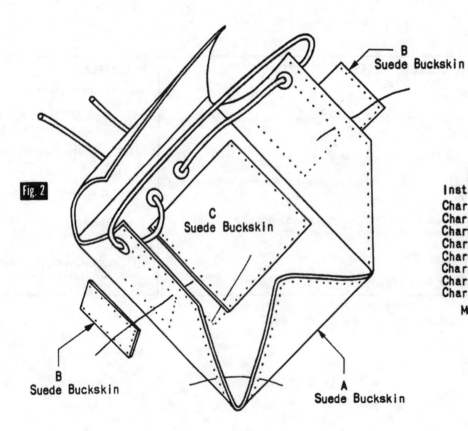

Fig. 2

B
Suede Buckskin

C
Suede Buckskin

B
Suede Buckskin

A
Suede Buckskin

For Detailed
Instructions Consult
Chart I - Cutting
Chart II - Design
Chart III - Color
Chart IV - Construction
Chart V - Lacing
Chart VI - Stitching
Chart VII - Braiding
Chart VIII - Knotting
Material Chart

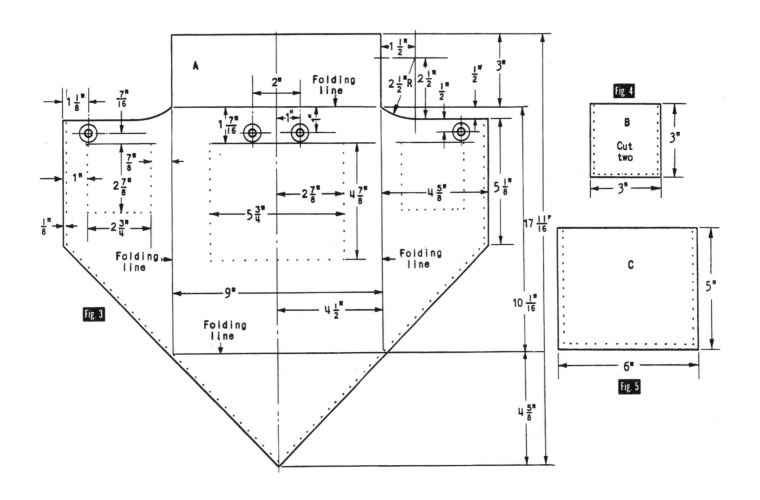

Fig. 3

Fig. 4

B
Cut
two

Fig. 5

C

PROCEDURE: (CONSULT LEATHER CRAFT PROCESSING CHARTS)

1. Cut and prepare parts (A), (B), (C). Figs. 3, 4, 5.

2. Punch holes in part (A) and insert metal eyelets. Fig. 3.

3. Put in folding lines as indicated, with edge creaser. Fig. 3.

4. With 1/7" spacing wheel, mark stitching holes on parts (A), (B), (C). Punch with awl. Figs. 2, 3, 4, 5.

5. Saddle stitch part (C) to the flesh side of part (A). Figs. 2, 3.

6. Saddle stitch parts (B) to the skin side of part (A). Fig. 2.

7. Saddle stitch matching edges of part (A), Figs. 1, 2.

8. Insert rawhide lace and tie. Fig. 1.

MATERIALS:

Suede buckskin (natural)

4 No. 6K metal eyelets

Heavy linen thread

Rawhide lace $\frac{3"}{16}$ x 3' long

TOOLS:

(3), (5), (14), (21), (25), (41), (43).

Handbag

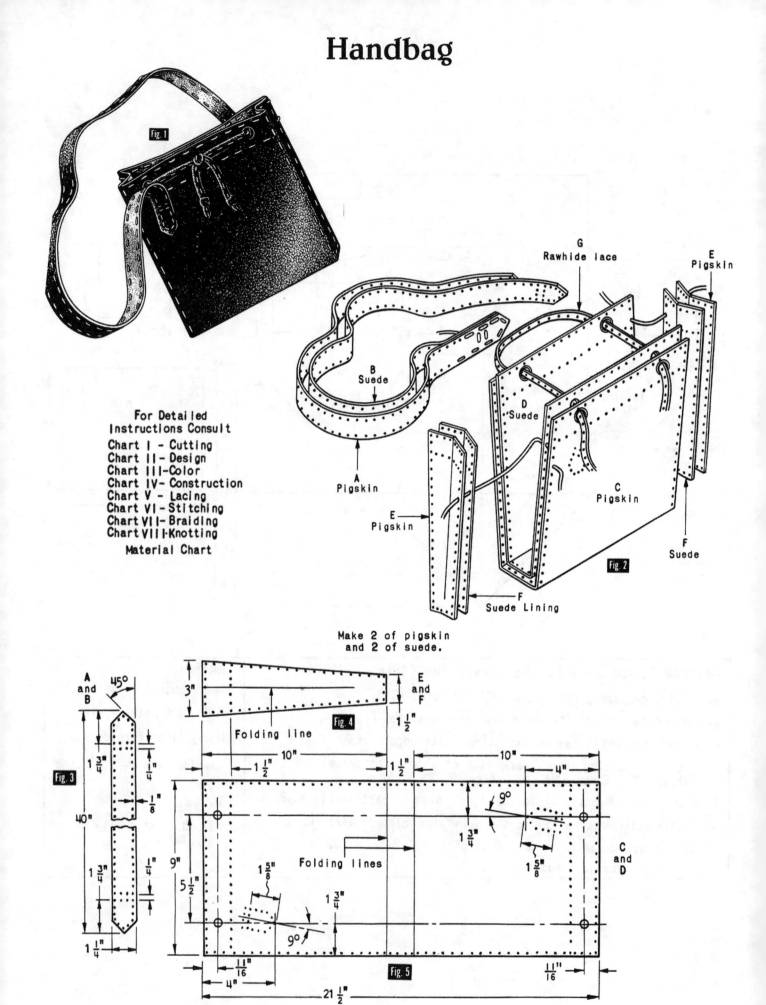

Fig. 1

Fig. 2

G
Rawhide lace

E
Pigskin

B
Suede

D
Suede

A
Pigskin

E
Pigskin

C
Pigskin

F
Suede

F
Suede Lining

For Detailed
Instructions Consult
Chart I - Cutting
Chart II - Design
Chart III - Color
Chart IV - Construction
Chart V - Lacing
Chart VI - Stitching
Chart VII - Braiding
Chart VIII - Knotting
Material Chart

Make 2 of pigskin
and 2 of suede.

A
and
B

45°

Fig. 3

1 $\frac{3}{4}$"

$\frac{1}{4}$"

$\frac{1}{8}$"

40"

1 $\frac{3}{4}$"

$\frac{1}{4}$"

1 $\frac{1}{4}$"

Fig. 4

3"

Folding line

E
and
F

1 $\frac{1}{2}$"

10"

1 $\frac{1}{2}$"

1 $\frac{1}{2}$"

10"

4"

9°

9"

5 $\frac{1}{2}$"

Folding lines

1 $\frac{5}{8}$"

1 $\frac{3}{4}$"

9°

1 $\frac{3}{4}$"

1 $\frac{5}{8}$"

C
and
D

$\frac{11}{16}$"

$\frac{11}{16}$"

4"

Fig. 5

21 $\frac{1}{2}$"

232

PROCEDURE: (CONSULT LEATHER CRAFT PROCESSING CHARTS)

1. Cut parts (A), (B), (C), (D), (E), (F). Figs 2, 3, 4, 5.

2. Make crease lines on parts (C) and (E). Figs. 2, 4, 5.

3. Cement part (A) to part (B). Fig. 2.

4. With 1/5" spacing wheel, mark stitching holes 1/8" from edges of (AB). Figs. 2, 3, 5.

5. With awl, punch stitching holes in (AB) and in matching parts of (C) where ends of (AB) are attached. Figs. 2, 3, 5.

6. With white thread saddle stitch ends of (AB) to (C) and continue stitching along edges of (AB). Figs. 1, 2, 3, 5.

7. Cement part (C) to part (D) and parts (E) to parts (F). Fold parts (EF). Figs. 2, 4.

8. Punch holes and insert eyelets in (CD). Figs. 2, 5.

9. With 1/5" spacing wheel, mark stitching holes on long sides of (CD), (EF) and along center of (G). Figs. 2, 4, 5.

10. Mark two rows of holes 1/8" and 1 1/2", respectively, from top edges of (CD) and (EF), as indicated. Figs. 2, 4, 5.

11. With awl, punch all stitching holes, as marked. Figs. 2, 4, 5.

12. With brown thread, saddle stitch matching edges of (CD) and (EF). Figs. 1, 2.

13. With white thread, saddle stitch top rows of (CD) and (EF) and center of (G). Figs. 1, 2.

14. Insert thong (G) through eyelets and tie knot in each end. Figs. 1, 2.

MATERIALS:

Dark brown pigskin
Beige suede lining
Four metal eyelets, No. 6 K
Heavy white thread
Heavy brown thread
Rawhide lace 1/4", 24" long

TOOLS:

(1), (3), (5), (6), (14), (17), (21), (25), (41), (43).

Handbag

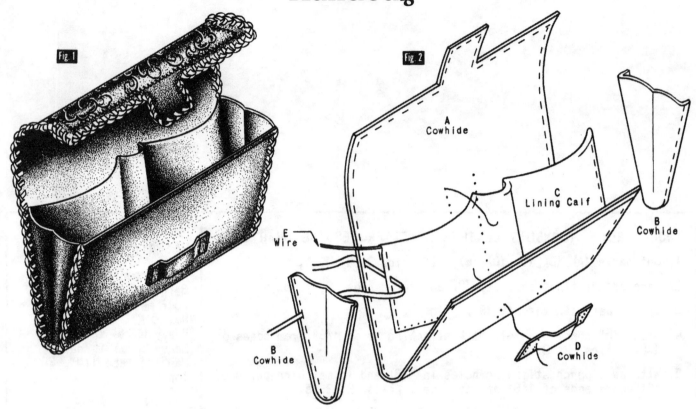

Fig. 1

Fig. 2

A Cowhide

C Lining Calf

B Cowhide

E Wire

B Cowhide

D Cowhide

For Detailed
Instructions Consult
Chart I - Cutting
Chart II - Design
Chart III - Color
Chart IV - Construction
Chart V - Lacing
Chart VI - Stitching
Chart VII - Braiding
Chart VIII - Knotting
Material Chart

Crease line

A

$\frac{3}{32}$" Thong slits

$\frac{1}{8}$"

4"

2"

10"

4"

Fold

$3\frac{1}{4}$"

$6\frac{7}{8}$"

$7\frac{1}{8}$"

4"

18"

20"

Fig. 3

C

13"

$4\frac{1}{2}$"

$4\frac{1}{2}$"

$\frac{3}{8}$"

Fold

5"

$1\frac{1}{2}$"

3"

10"

Fig. 4

B

$2\frac{1}{2}$"

Make 2

$6\frac{1}{4}$"

1"R.

Fig. 5

D

4"

1"

$\frac{1}{2}$"

$\frac{1}{8}$"

Fig. 6

PROCEDURE: (CONSULT LEATHER CRAFT PROCESSING CHARTS)

1. Cut and prepare parts (A), (B), (C), (D). Figs. 3, 4, 5, 6.

2. With edge creaser, mark folding lines on (A), (B), (C), (D). Figs. 3, 4, 5, 6.

3. Fold (C), insert wire (E) under fold, and cement in place. Figs. 2, 4.

4. With $\frac{1}{7}"$ spacing wheel, mark stitching holes on bottom edge and two vertical pocket lines of (C). Fig. 4.

5. With awl, punch stitching holes simultaneously in matching parts of (A) and (C). Fig. 2.

6. Sew (C) to (A) with saddler's stitch. Fig. 2.

7. With awl, punch holes simultaneously in matching parts of (A) and (D). Figs. 2, 6.

8. Sew (D) to (A) with saddler's stitch. Fig. 2.

9. With awl, punch $\frac{3}{32}"$ thong slits $\frac{1}{8}"$ from edges of (A), (B), (C). Figs. 2, 3, 4, 5.

10. Lace matching parts of (A), (B), (C), and flap of (A) with double overlay stitch. Fig. 2.

MATERIALS:

Carving cowhide

Calfskin lace $\frac{3}{32}"$ 17'

Lining calf

Heavy linen thread

Wire

TOOLS:

(1), (4), (5), (6), (17), (18), (22), (25), (26), (28), (40), (41)

"Patchwork" Pouch Bag

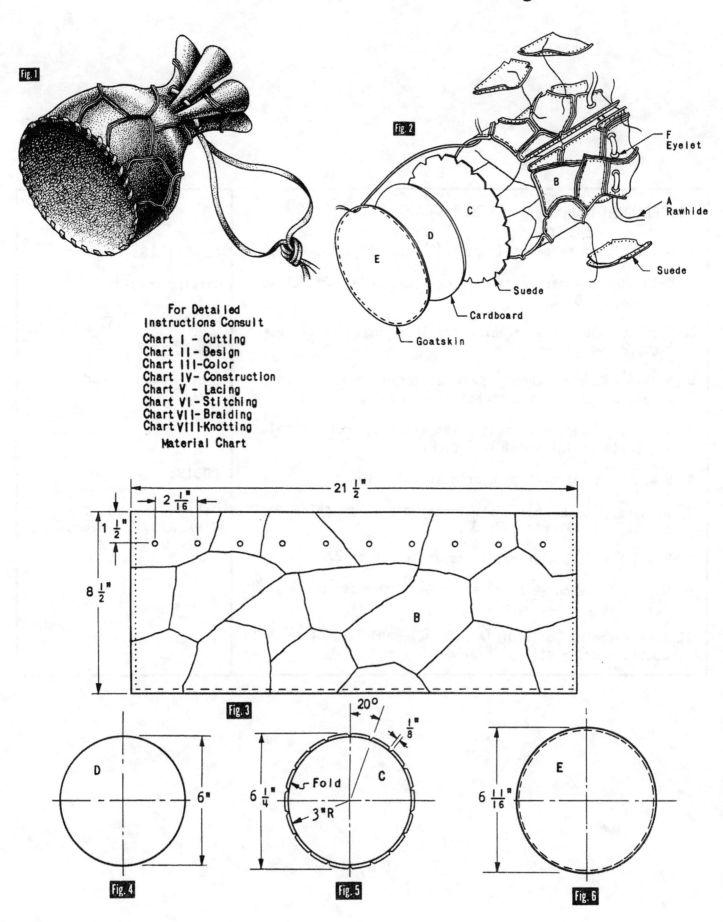

Fig. 1

Fig. 2

F Eyelet

A Rawhide

Suede

Suede

Cardboard

Goatskin

C

D

E

B

For Detailed
Instructions Consult
Chart I – Cutting
Chart II – Design
Chart III – Color
Chart IV – Construction
Chart V – Lacing
Chart VI – Stitching
Chart VII – Braiding
Chart VIII – Knotting
Material Chart

21 ½"

2 1/16"

1 ½"

8 ½"

B

Fig. 3

D

6"

Fig. 4

20°

⅛"

6 ¼"

Fold

3"R

C

Fig. 5

6 11/16"

E

Fig. 6

PROCEDURE: (CONSULT LEATHER CRAFT PROCESSING CHARTS)

1. Using vari-colored scraps of suede, fit pieces and sew together with short saddle stitch and 1/8" seams to make (B). Fig. 3.

2. Cut (C), (D) and (E). Figs. 4, 5, 6.

3. With No. 7 punch, cut lacing holes in (B), 2-1/16" between centers. Insert eyelets (F). Figs. 2, 3.

4. With awl, punch 3/32" thong slits, 1/8" from bottom edge of (B). Punch corresponding thong slits 1/8" from edge of (E). Figs. 2, 3, 5, and Lacing Chart V.

5. Sew together short ends of (B) with saddle stitch. Figs. 2, 3.

6. Sew (B) to (E) with whip stitch. Fig. 2.

7. Cement flesh side of (C) to (D). Fig. 2.

8. Turn under notched edge of (C), and cement to back of (D). Cement (CD) in bottom of (BE). Fig. 2.

9. Insert lace (A) in (BCDE). Figs. 1, 2.

MATERIALS:

Goatskin (2-1/2" oz.)

Scraps of suede

Ten No. 6 K eyelets

Rawhide lace, 3/16", 22" long

Goatskin lace 3/32", 5' - 3" long

Heavy cardboard

Rubber Cement

Linen thread

TOOLS:

(3 No.7), (4), (6), (14), (17), (18), (21), (26), (33), (40), (41), (43).

See **Leather Chart V** for punching thong slits

Handbag

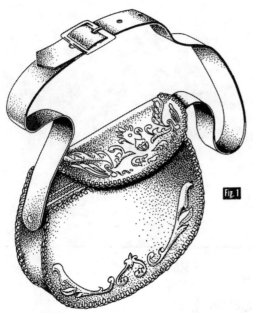

Fig. 1

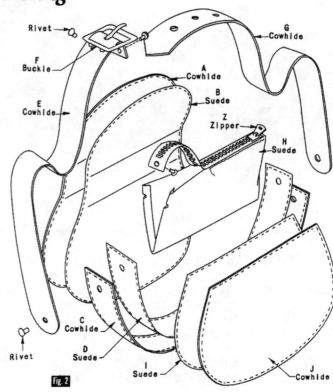

Rivet
F
Buckle
E
Cowhide
A
Cowhide
B
Suede
Z
Zipper
G
Cowhide
H
Suede
C
Cowhide
D
Suede
Rivet
I
Suede
J
Cowhide
Fig. 2

For Detailed
Instructions Consult
Chart I - Cutting
Chart II- Design
Chart III-Color
Chart IV- Construction
Chart V - Lacing
Chart VI- Stitching
Chart VII-Braiding
Chart VIII-Knotting
Material Chart

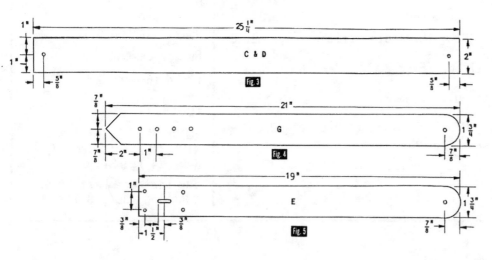

1"
25 1/4"
1"
C & D
2"
5/8"
5/8"
Fig. 3

7/8"
21"
G
1 3/4"
7/8"
2"
1"
7/8"
Fig. 4

19"
1"
E
1 3/4"
3/8"
1 1/2"
3/8"
7/8"
Fig. 5

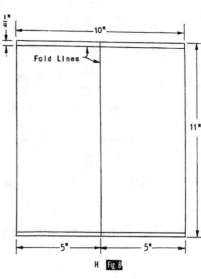

1/4"
10"
Fold Lines
11"
5"
5"
H
Fig. 8

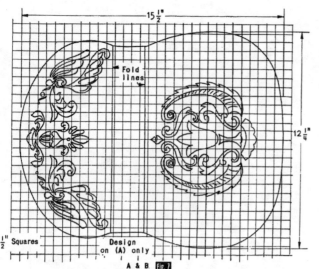

15 1/2"
Fold lines
12 1/4"
1/2" Squares
Design on (A) only
A & B
Fig. 7

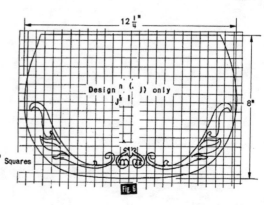

12 1/4"
Design on (J) only
J
8"
1/2" Squares
Fig. 6

238

MATERIALS:

Tooling cowhide, 4-5 oz.
Suede, 1 oz.
1 buckle, 1-3/4" center bar
4 Rivets
1 Zipper, 10"
Calfskin lace, 3/32", 8 yds.
Heavy linen thread

TOOLS:

(1), (4), (6), (8), (17), (18), (21), (23), (24), (26), (27), (30), (40).

PROCEDURE: (CONSULT LEATHER CRAFT PROCESSING CHARTS)

1. Cut and prepare parts (A), (B), (C), (D), (E), (G), (H), (I) and (J). Figs. 3, 4, 5, 6, 7, 8.

2. Outline with edge creaser all edges of (E) and (G). Figs. 3, 4, 5, 6, 7.

3. Cement (B) to (A); (D) to (C); and (I) to (J). Fig. 2.

4. Punch 3/32" thong slits 1/8" from all edges of (CD) and corresponding slits in matching edges of (AB) and (IJ). Punch slits around flap of (AB). Fig. 2.

5. Lace (IJ) and (AB) to (CD) with double overlay stitch. Finish lacing flap of (AB). Figs. 1, 2.

6. Cut slot in square end of (E) for prong of buckle (F); punch holes in pointed end of (G) for prong of (F). Figs. 4, 5.

7. Insert buckle in slot of (E). Fold end of (E) and punch rivet holes through fold. Insert rivets. Figs. 2, 5.

8. Fold (H) to form case. Stitch ends on sewing machine, 1/4" from edges. Turn seams inside. Figs. 2, 8.

9. Cement edges of zipper (Z) tapes under top edges of (H). Cement loose ends of tapes against flattened end seams inside of (H). Fig. 2.

10. Stitch (Z) to (H) on sewing machine, or with sewing awl. Fig. 2.

11. Cement rounded ends of (E) and (G) against outside of gusset, as shown. Figs. 1, 2.

12. Punch rivet holes through (ECU) and (GCD) with revolving punch. Fig. 2.

13. Place (HZ) within bag with top end seams in position against rivet holes in gusset. Top edge of zipper should come at least 1/4" below top edge of gusset ends. Fig. 2.

14. Mark and punch rivet holes in (HZ). Fig. 2.

15. Attach (HZ) to (ECD) and (GCD) with rivets. Figs. 1, 2.

Handbag

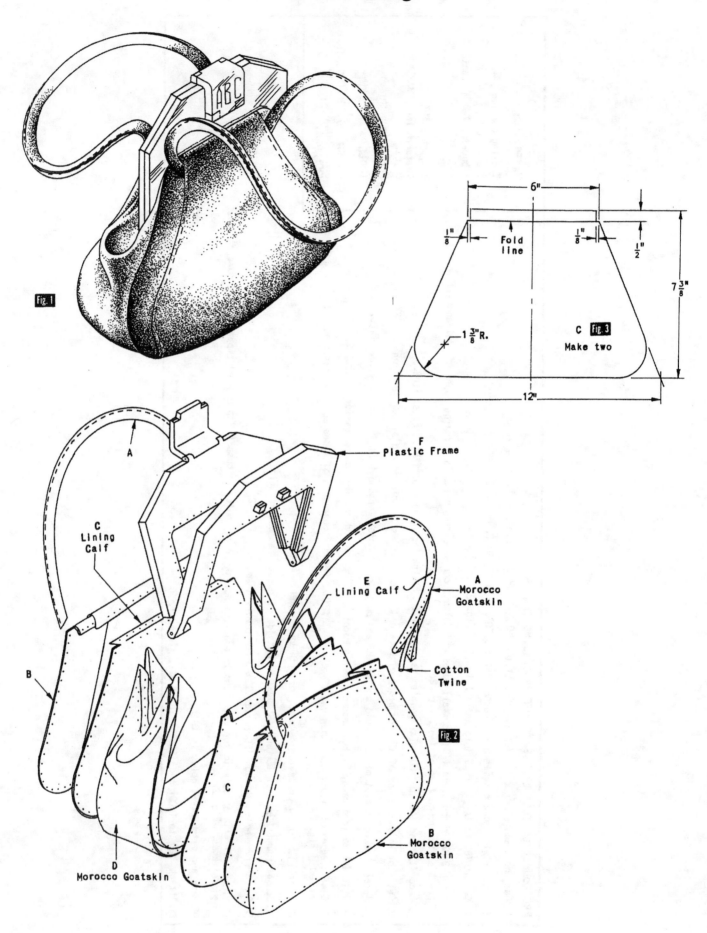

Fig. 1

6"

Fold line

$\frac{1}{8}$"

$\frac{1}{8}$"

$\frac{1}{2}$"

$7\frac{3}{8}$"

$1\frac{3}{8}$"R.

C   Fig. 3

Make two

12"

A

F
Plastic Frame

C
Lining
Calf

E
Lining Calf

A
Morocco
Goatskin

B

Cotton
Twine

Fig. 2

C

B
Morocco
Goatskin

D
Morocco Goatskin

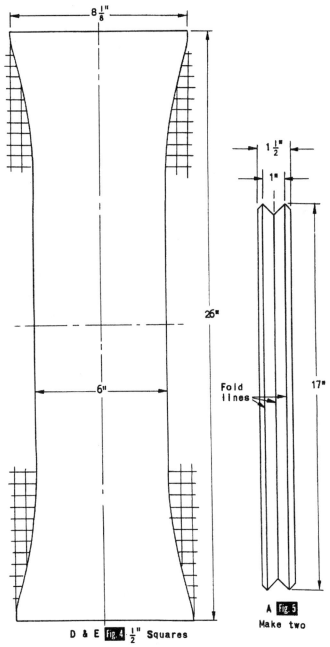

$8\frac{1}{8}"$

$26"$

$6"$

D & E **Fig. 4** $\frac{1}{2}"$ Squares

$1\frac{1}{2}"$

$1"$

$17"$

Fold lines

A **Fig. 5**
Make two

For Detailed
Instructions Consult
Chart I - Cutting
Chart II - Design
Chart III - Color
Chart IV - Construction
Chart V - Lacing
Chart VI - Stitching
Chart VII - Braiding
Chart VIII - Knotting
Material Chart

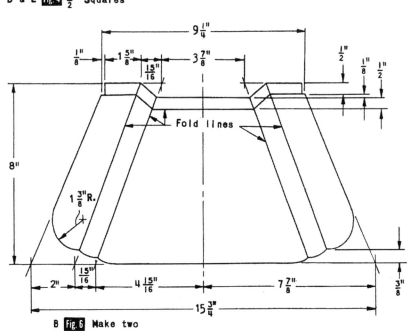

$9\frac{1}{4}"$

$\frac{1}{8}"$

$1\frac{5}{8}"$

$\frac{15}{16}"$

$3\frac{7}{8}"$

$\frac{1}{2}"$

$\frac{1}{8}"$ $1"$

Fold lines

$8"$

$1\frac{3}{8}"R.$

$2"$

$\frac{15}{16}"$

$4\frac{15}{16}"$

$7\frac{7}{8}"$

$\frac{3}{8}"$

$15\frac{3}{4}"$

B **Fig. 6** Make two

PROCEDURE: (CONSULT LEATHER CRAFT PROCESSING CHARTS)

1. Cut parts (A), (B), (C), (D) and (E). Figs. 3, 4, 5, 6.

2. Fold handles (A) lengthwise. Turn in 1/4" of long edges to wrong side. Cement fold of edge. Fig. 5.

3. Place heavy cotton twine for filler within fold of (A) away from stitching edges. Fig. 2.

4. Stitch cemented edges of (A) with closely spaced saddle stitch in contrasting color. Figs. 1, 2.

5. Fold gusset of (B) as shown. Mark stitching holes with 1/7" spacing wheel 1/4" from folded edge of (B). Figs. 2, 6.

6. Cement ends of (A) in position within folded tucks of (B), with inner end of handles 1/4" below top fold line of (B). Fig. 2.

7. Sew through gusset folds of (B), including ends of (A), with saddle stitch. Fig. 2.

8. Stitch parts (B) to (D) on sewing machine, with 1/8" seams, flesh sides out. Fig. 2.

9. Turn (BD) with seams inside. Fig. 2.

10. Stitch parts (C) to (E) on sewing machine with 1/8" seams, flesh sides out. Fig. 2.

11. Place (CE) within (BD), raw seams facing. Fig. 2.

12. Fold 1/2" of all top edges of (CE) and (BD) to seam sides. Cement folded edges of (CE) to (BD), concealing all raw edges. Fig. 2.

13. Place stitching edges of (BDCE) in position within stitching groove of plastic frame (F). Fig. 2.

14. Sew (BDCE) to (F) with saddler's stitch; also stitch spans of gussets that are not stitched to (F) at hinge. Figs. 1, 2.

MATERIALS:
Morocco goatskin, 1-1/2 oz.

Lining calf, 1 oz.
Cotton twine, 3'
Heavy linen thread
Rubber cement

TOOLS:
(1), (6), (21), (28), (41).

Handbag

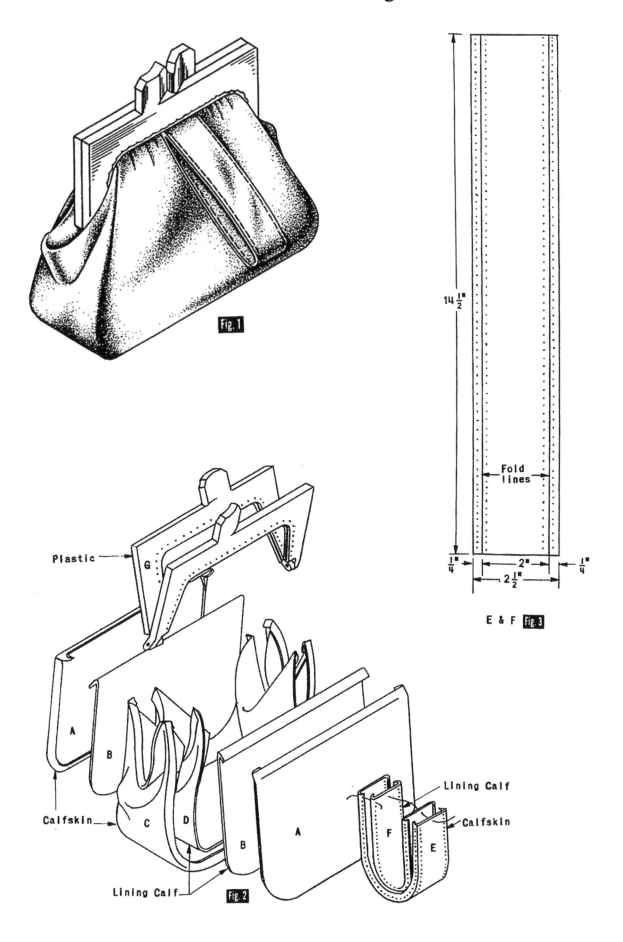

Fig. 1

Plastic

G

A

B

C

D

B

A

Calfskin

Lining Calf

Fig. 2

Lining Calf

Calfskin

F

E

$14\frac{1}{2}$"

Fold lines

$\frac{1}{4}$" 2" $\frac{1}{4}$"

$2\frac{1}{2}$"

E & F **Fig. 3**

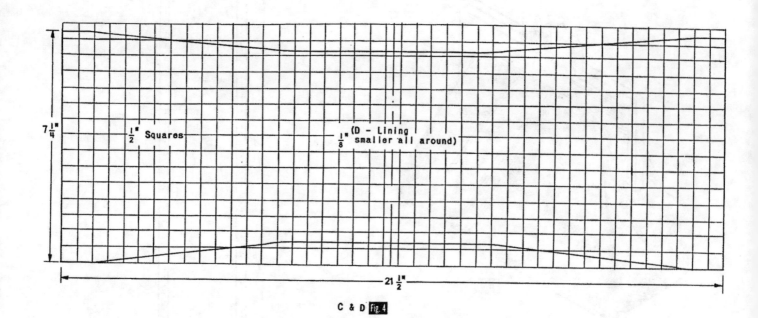

7¼"

½" Squares

⅛" (D – Lining smaller all around)

21½"

C & D **Fig. 4**

For Detailed
Instructions Consult

Chart I – Cutting
Chart II – Design
Chart III – Color
Chart IV – Construction
Chart V – Lacing
Chart VI – Stitching
Chart VII – Braiding
Chart VIII – Knotting

Material Chart

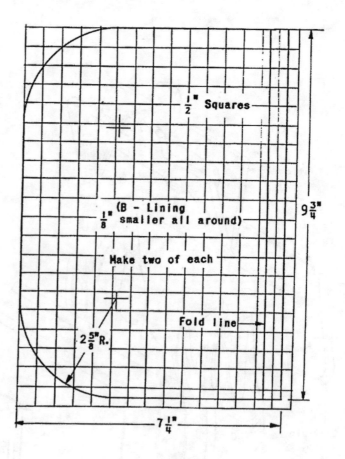

½" Squares

⅛" (B – Lining smaller all around)

9¾"

Make two of each

Fold line →

2⅝" R.

7¼"

A & B **Fig. 5**

PROCEDURE: (CONSULT LEATHER CRAFT PROCESSING CHARTS)

1. Cut parts (A),(B),(C),(D),(E) and (F). Figs. 3, 4, 5.
   Note: Construct frame (G) of 3/8" plastic.

2. Skive all edges of (A),(C) and (E). Figs. 3, 4, 5.

3. Fold 1/4" of long edges of (E) and (F) to flesh sides. Cement folded edges. Fig. 3.

4. Cement (E) to (F) flesh sides together. Fig. 2.

5. Mark stitching holes with 1/7" spacing wheel, 1/8" from edges of (EF). Figs. 2, 3.

6. Punch stitching holes with awl through edge of (EF). Fig. 2.

7. Sew (EF) with saddler's stitch. Fig. 2.

8. Stitch parts (A) to (C) on sewing machine, with 1/8" seams, skin sides together. Fig. 2.

9. Turn (AC) with seams inside. Fig. 2.

10. Stitch parts (B) to (D) on sewing machine, with 1/8" seams, skin sides together. Fig. 2.

11. Place (BD) within (AC), raw seams facing. Fig. 2.

12. Fold 1/2" of all top edges of (BD) and (AC) to seam sides. Cement folded edges of (BD) to (AC), concealing all raw edges. Fig. 2.

13. Gather top edge of (AB) with short running stitch to fit span of horizontal stitching edge of frame (G). Fig. 2.

14. Fold (EF) with (E) outside. Cement ends of (EF) together. Cement ends of (EF) to (A) for stitching to (G). Fig. 2.

15. Place stitching edges of (ABCDEF) within stitching groove of (G). Fig. 2.

16. Sew bag to (G) with saddler's stitch; also stitch spans of gussets that are not stitched to (G) at hinge. Figs. 1, 2.

MATERIALS:
Calfskin,
1-1/2 - 2 oz.
Lining calf, 1 oz.
Heavy linen thread
Rubber cement

TOOLS:
(1),(6),(17),(19),
(21),(25),(28),(41).

Handbag

Fig. 1

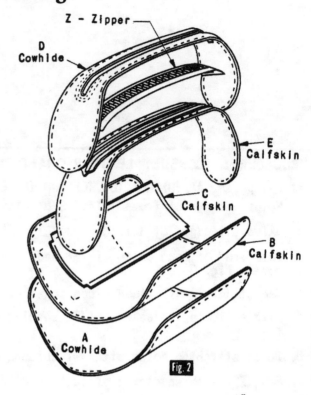

Z – Zipper

D
Cowhide

E
Calfskin

C
Calfskin

B
Calfskin

A
Cowhide

Fig. 2

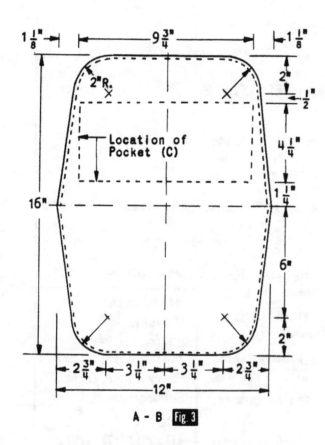

1 1/8"

9 3/4"

1 1/8"

2" R.

2"

1/2"

Location of
Pocket (C)

4 1/4"

1 1/4"

16"

6"

2"

2 3/4"

3 1/4"

3 1/4"

2 3/4"

12"

A – B   Fig. 3

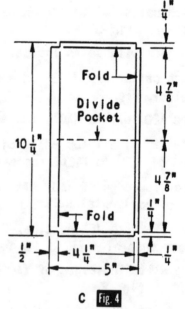

1/4"

Fold

4 7/8"

Divide
Pocket

10 1/4"

4 7/8"

1/4"

Fold

1/2"

4 1/4"

1/4"

5"

C   Fig. 4

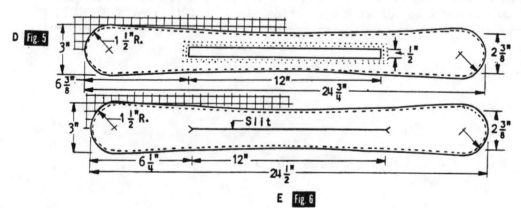

D   Fig. 5

3"

1 1/2" R.

1/2"

2 3/8"

6 3/8"

12"

24 3/4"

3"

1 1/2" R.

Slit

2 3/8"

6 1/4"

12"

24 1/2"

E   Fig. 6

For Detailed
Instructions Consult
Chart I – Cutting
Chart II– Design
Chart III–Color
Chart IV– Construction
Chart V – Lacing
Chart VI –Stitching
Chart VII–Braiding
Chart VIII–Knotting
Material Chart

PROCEDURE: (CONSULT LEATHER CRAFT PROCESSING CHARTS)

1. Cut and prepare parts (A), (B), (C), (D) and (E). Figs. 3, 4, 5, 6.

2. Skive all edges of (C). Fig. 4.

3. Outline all fold lines of (C) with edge creaser. Fig. 4.

4. Fold and cement all edges of (C). Figs. 2, 4.

5. Place (C) in position on skin side of (B). Stitch (C) to (B) on sewing machine forming divided pocket as shown. Figs. 2, 3.

6. Make cuts in (D) and (E) for zipper (Z). Figs. 5, 6.

7. Outline cut in (D) with edge creaser. Fig. 5.

8. Cement (Z) to flesh side of edges of cut in (D). Fig. 2.

9. Turn back to flesh side the edge of the cut made for (Z) in (E). Cement edges. Figs. 2, 6.

10. Cement (E) to (DZ) flesh sides together; cement (BC) to (A), flesh sides together, taking into account curved shape of parts. Fig. 2.

11. Mark double row of stitching holes with 1/7" spacing wheel around cut for (Z) in (D). Use crease line for inner row; 1/4" between rows. Figs. 2, 5.

12. Punch stitching holes with awl through (DEZ). Fig. 2.

13. Sew (DEZ) with saddler's stitch. Fig. 2.

14. Punch 3/32" thong slits on all edges of (AB) and corresponding thong slits on matching edges of (DE). Figs. 2, 3, 5, 6.

15. Lace (AB) to (DE) with triple overlay stitch. Figs. 1, 2.

MATERIALS:
Carving cowhide, 6 oz.
Lining calf, 1 - 1-1/2 oz.
Calf lacing, 3/32", 8 yds.
Zipper, 1/4" teeth, 12" long
Heavy linen thread
Rubber cement

TOOLS:
(1), (4), (6), (17), (19), (25), (26), (27), (28), (40), (41).

See Leather Chart V for Lacing, and Chart II for carving and tools.

Hankerchief Box

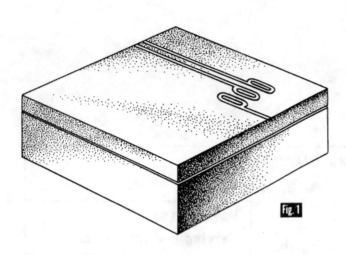

Fig. 1

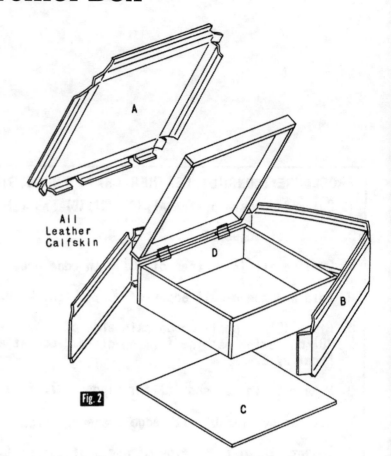

All
Leather
Calfskin

Fig. 2

For Detailed
Instructions Consult
Chart I - Cutting
Chart II - Design
Chart III-Color
Chart IV- Construction
Chart V - Lacing
Chart VI-Stitching
Chart VII-Braiding
Chart VIII-Knotting
Material Chart

PROCEDURE:(CONSULT LEATHER CRAFT PROCESSING CHARTS)

1. Cut and prepare parts (A),(B) and (C). Figs. 3, 4, 5.

   Note: Construct wooden box (D) of 1/4" plywood. Paint inside any desired color.

2. Make cut-outs in (A) and (B) to accommodate size of hinges used. Figs. 3, 4.

3. Skive all edges to be cemented. Fig. 2.

4. Cement (A) to cover of box (D), covering edges and turning down 1/4" within edges. Fig. 2.

5. Cement (B) to sides of (D) with ends meeting in an over-lapped seam at back corner and flap edges turned over to bottom of (D). Fig. 2.

6. Cement (C) to bottom of (D). Fig. 2.

MATERIALS:

Tooling calfskin, 2 oz., for modeled monogram

Rubber cement

TOOLS:

(1), (6), (19)

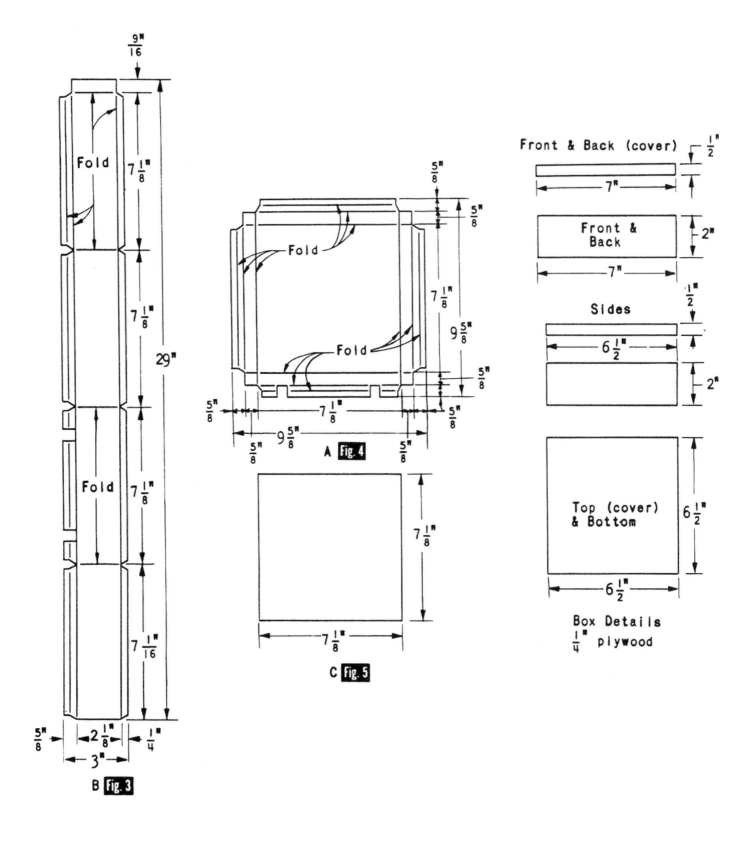

$\frac{9"}{16}$

Fold

$7\frac{1}{8}"$

$7\frac{1}{8}"$

29"

Fold

$7\frac{1}{8}"$

$7\frac{1}{16}"$

$\frac{5"}{8}$ $2\frac{1}{8}"$ $\frac{1"}{4}$

3"

B **Fig. 3**

$\frac{5"}{8}$

$\frac{5"}{8}$

Fold

$7\frac{1}{8}"$

$9\frac{5}{8}"$

Fold

$\frac{5"}{8}$

$\frac{5"}{8}$ $7\frac{1}{8}"$ $\frac{5"}{8}$

$9\frac{5}{8}"$

$\frac{5"}{8}$ $\frac{5"}{8}$

A **Fig. 4**

$7\frac{1}{8}"$

$7\frac{1}{8}"$

C **Fig. 5**

Front & Back (cover)

$\frac{1"}{2}$

7"

Front & Back

2"

7"

Sides

$\frac{1"}{2}$

$6\frac{1}{2}"$

2"

Top (cover) & Bottom

$6\frac{1}{2}"$

$6\frac{1}{2}"$

Box Details
$\frac{1"}{4}$ plywood

Stud Box

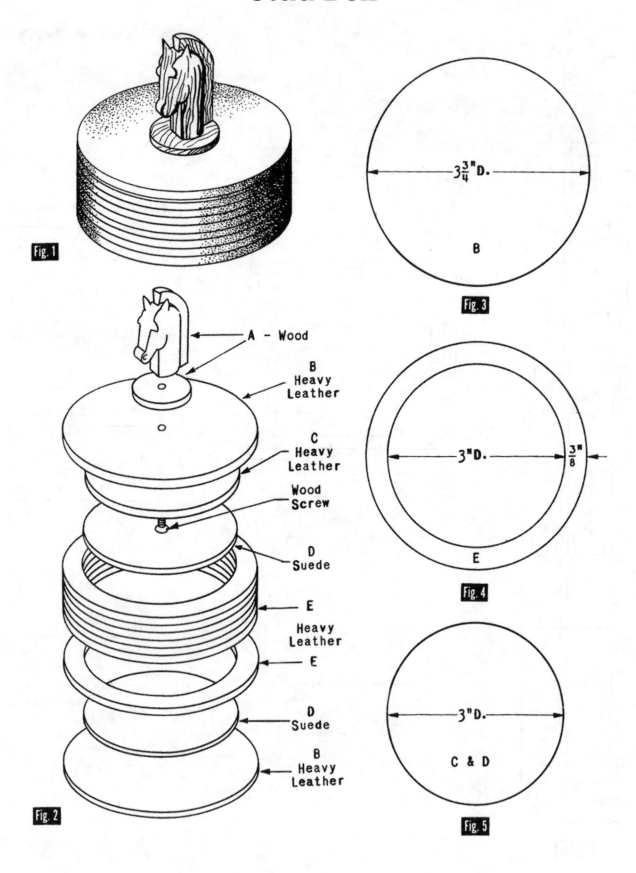

Fig. 1

Fig. 3

$3\frac{3}{4}"$D.

B

A - Wood

B
Heavy
Leather

C
Heavy
Leather

Wood
Screw

D
Suede

E
Heavy
Leather

E

D
Suede

B
Heavy
Leather

Fig. 2

Fig. 4

$3"$D.

$\frac{3}{8}$

E

Fig. 5

$3"$D.

C & D

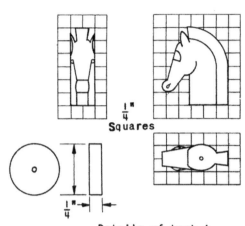

1"
¼
Squares

Details of knob **A**

For Detailed
Instructions Consult
Chart I – Cutting   Chart V – Lacing
Chart II– Design   Chart VI –Stitching
Chart III–Color   Chart VII– Braiding
Chart IV– Construction Chart VIII·Knotting
Material Chart

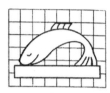

Alternate
Knobs

PROCEDURE: (CONSULT LEATHER CRAFT PROCESSING CHARTS)

1. Follow steps (1) through (6) to build (BE) to an approximate height of 1-1/8".

   Note: Construct knob (A) of sugar pine.

2. Cut circle for cover (B). Fig. 3.

3. Cut (C) and sandpaper edges to fit within walls of (E). Fig. 5.

4. Cement (C) to cover (B), flesh sides together. Fig. 2.

5. Place (BC) under weight and allow to dry for 24 hours.

6. Drill 3/16" hole through (BC) for screw attachment to knob (A). Fig. 2.

7. Sandpaper all cut edges of (BC) and (BE) to smooth surface. Fig. 2.

8. Burnish edges of (BC) and (BE) on burnishing wheel to obtain hard finish.

9. Shellac all surfaces and allow to dry. Sandpaper surfaces lightly. Repeat this procedure three times.

10. Apply Johnson's paste wax to all surfaces except inside of base (B) and (C). Rub to glossy finish.

11. Insert screw through hole drilled in (BC) and attach knob (A). Fig. 2.

12. Cut parts (D) and cement to (C) and inside of base (E) with suede side up.

MATERIALS:

Heavy sole leather
   (3/16"-1/4" thick)
Suede, 1-1/2" oz.
Pliobond plastic adhesive
Sandpaper No. 00
White shellac
Johnson's paste wax
Screw, 1" flat-head, wood

TOOLS:

(21), and brush for shel-
   lac

Jewel Box

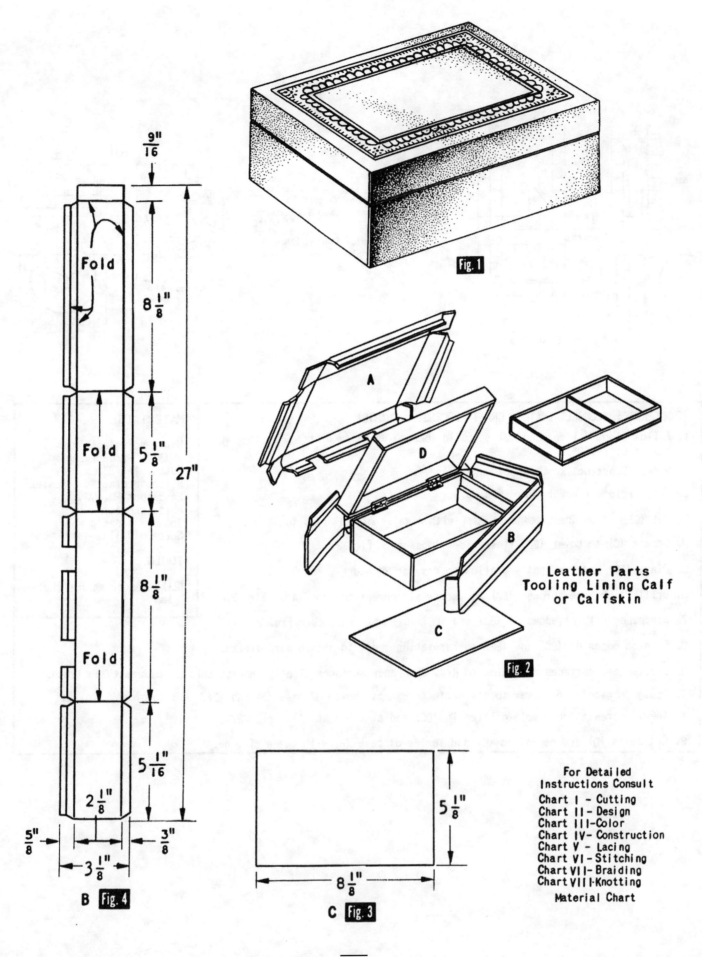

Fig. 1

Fig. 2

Leather Parts
Tooling Lining Calf
or Calfskin

B **Fig. 4**

C **Fig. 3**

For Detailed
Instructions Consult

Chart I – Cutting
Chart II – Design
Chart III – Color
Chart IV – Construction
Chart V – Lacing
Chart VI – Stitching
Chart VII – Braiding
Chart VIII – Knotting

Material Chart

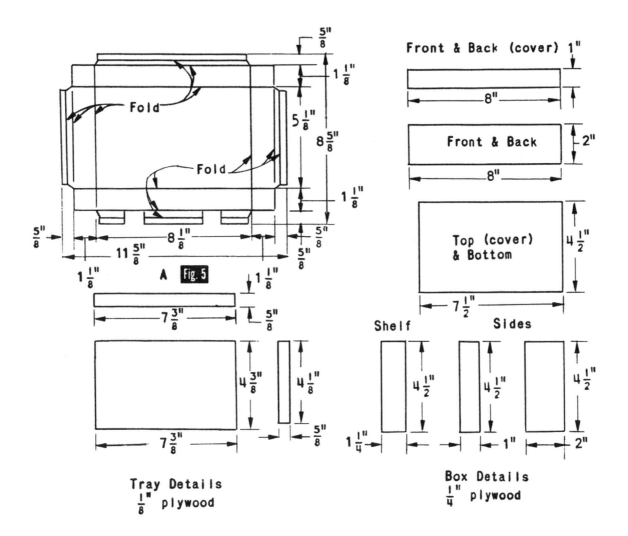

A **Fig. 5**

Front & Back (cover) 1"
8"

Front & Back 2"
8"

Top (cover) & Bottom 4 1/2"
7 1/2"

Shelf 4 1/2" 1 1/4"
Sides 4 1/2" 1"
4 1/2" 2"

Box Details
1/4" plywood

Tray Details
1/8" plywood

PROCEDURE: (CONSULT LEATHER CRAFT PROCESSING CHARTS)

1. Cut and prepare (A),(B) and (C). Figs. 3, 4, 5.

   Note: Construct wooden box (D) with divided tray of 1/4" plywood. Paint inside of box any desired color.

2. Make cut-outs in (A) and (B) to accommodate size of hinges used. Figs. 4, 5.

3. Skive all edges to be cemented. Fig. 2.

4. Cement (A) to cover of box (D), covering edges, and turning down 1/4" within edges. Fig. 2.

5. Cement (B) to sides of (D) with ends meeting in an overlapped seam at back corner, and flap edges turned over to bottom of (D). Fig. 2.

6. Cement (C) to bottom of (D). Fig. 2.

MATERIALS:

Tooling lining calf 1-1/2 oz., for stamping or wheel design
or
Tooling calfskin, 2 oz., for modeled design

Rubber cement

TOOLS:

(1),(6),(19),(15-1,-2,-5).

Earring Box

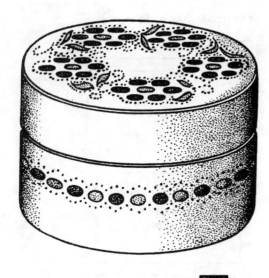

Fig. 1

For Detailed
Instructions Consult
Chart I – Cutting
Chart II – Design
Chart III – Color
Chart IV – Construction
Chart V – Lacing
Chart VI – Stitching
Chart VII – Braiding
Chart VIII – Knotting
Material Chart

All Leather Parts
Kidskin or Calfskin

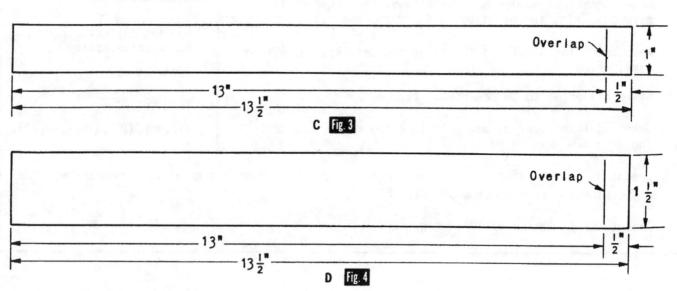

Fig. 2

Overlap
1"
13"
13 1/2"
1/2"
C **Fig. 3**

Overlap
1 1/2"
13"
13 1/2"
1/2"
D **Fig. 4**

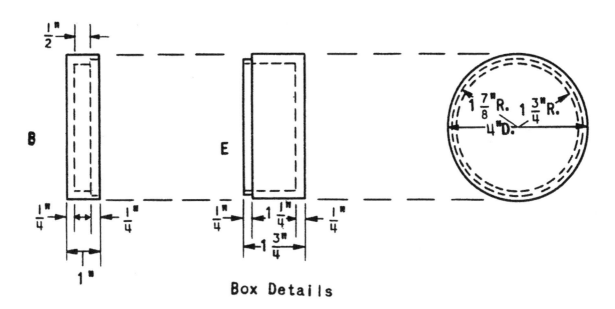

Box Details

PROCEDURE: (CONSULT LEATHER CRAFT PROCESSING CHARTS)	MATERIALS:

PROCEDURE: (CONSULT LEATHER CRAFT PROCESSING CHARTS)

1. Cut and prepare parts (A), (C) and (D). Figs. 3, 4, 5.

   Note: Construct wooden box (E) with cover (B) of pine wood.

2. Skive all edges to be cemented. Fig. 2.

3. Cement top (A) to box cover (B), with notched edges cemented to sides of (B). Fig. 2.

4. Cement (C) to (B) covering notched edges of (A). Cement overlapping skived ends of (C). Fig. 2.

5. Cement bottom (A) to box (E) with notched edges cemented to sides of (E). Fig. 2.

6. Cement (D) to (E) covering notched edges of (A). Cement overlapping skived ends of (D). Fig. 2.

MATERIALS:

Kidskin, white or natural, 1 oz.

or

Tooling calfskin, 1-1/2 oz., natural

Rubber cement

Johnson's paste wax

TOOLS:

(1), (6), (19).

Cuff Links

Fig. 1

A Calfskin

C Calfskin

B Goatskin

Fig. 2

ABCDEFGHI
JKLMNOPQR
STUVWXYZ

Fig. 3   Alphabet – Actual Size

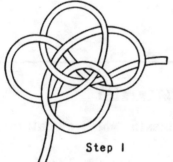

Step 1

Step 2

Top

Side

Step 3

Crown Detail

Step 4

Fig. 4

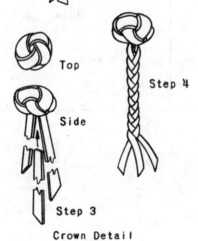

Calfskin horseshoes with saddler's stitch

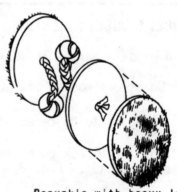

Ponyskin with heavy leather backing punched for crown Cement together

Clovers with backing punched for crown

PROCEDURE: (CONSULT LEATHER CRAFT PROCESSING CHARTS)

1. Cut parts (A) and (C) (your first and last initials or last only). Figs. 2, 3.

2. Make crown (B). Do not cut thong ends. Fig. 4.

3. Insert end of second thong in (B) and cement in place. Fig. 4.

4. Braid thongs to length desired for link. Cut off extra length. Fig. 4.

5. Skive thong ends and cement each end flat against flesh side of (A), (first letter). Fig. 2.

6. Cement (AB) to (A), flesh sides together. Fig. 2.

7. With awl, punch closely spaced stitching holes in (AB). Fig. 2.

8. Sew (AB) to (A) with saddle stitch. Fig. 2.

9. Repeat procedure for (C), (second letter). Fig. 2.

MATERIALS:

Calfskin, scrap leather

Goatskin lacing, $\frac{3"}{32}$, 3' per pair

Heavy linen thread

Rubber cement

TOOLS:
(6), (25), (33), (41).

For Detailed
Instructions Consult
Chart I – Cutting
Chart II – Design
Chart III – Color
Chart IV – Construction
Chart V – Lacing
Chart VI – Stitching
Chart VII – Braiding
Chart VIII – Knotting
Material Chart

Man's Tie Clip & Cuff Links

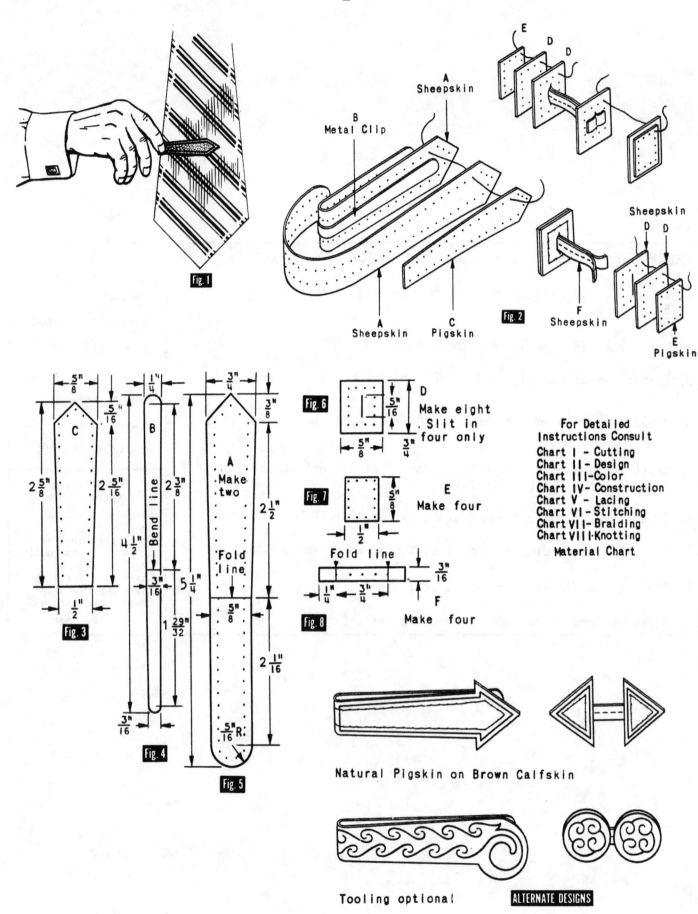

Fig. 1

B
Metal Clip

A
Sheepskin

Fig. 2

A
Sheepskin

C
Pigskin

E
D
D

Sheepskin
D D

F
Sheepskin

E
Pigskin

Fig. 3
C
$\frac{5}{8}$"
$2\frac{5}{8}$"
$\frac{1}{2}$"

Fig. 4
B
Bend line
$\frac{1}{4}$"
$\frac{5}{16}$"
$2\frac{5}{16}$"
$2\frac{3}{8}$"
$4\frac{1}{2}$"
$\frac{3}{16}$"
$\frac{3}{16}$"

Fig. 5
A
Make two
Fold line
$\frac{3}{4}$"
$\frac{3}{8}$"
$2\frac{1}{2}$"
$5\frac{1}{4}$"
$1\frac{29}{32}$"
$\frac{5}{8}$"
$2\frac{1}{16}$"
$\frac{5}{16}$"R.

Fig. 6
D
Make eight
Slit in four only
$\frac{5}{16}$"
$\frac{3}{4}$"
$\frac{5}{8}$"

Fig. 7
E
Make four
$\frac{5}{8}$"
$\frac{1}{2}$"

Fig. 8
F
Make four
Fold line
$\frac{3}{16}$"
$\frac{1}{4}$"
$\frac{3}{4}$"

For Detailed
Instructions Consult
Chart I – Cutting
Chart II – Design
Chart III – Color
Chart IV – Construction
Chart V – Lacing
Chart VI – Stitching
Chart VII – Braiding
Chart VIII – Knotting
   Material Chart

Natural Pigskin on Brown Calfskin

Tooling optional

ALTERNATE DESIGNS

PROCEDURE:(CONSULT LEATHER CRAFT PROCESSING CHARTS)

1. Cut and prepare parts (A),(C),(D) and (E). Figs. 3, 5, 6, 7.

2. Cement (C) to skin side of one part (A) as shown. Fig. 2.

3. Place second (A) to (AC) flesh sides together. With 1/7" spacing wheel, mark stitching holes 1/8" from all edges of (AC). Fig. 5.

4. Punch stitching holes with awl through matching edges of (A) and (AC). Figs. 3, 5.

5. Lock stitch with sewing awl, leaving narrow end open. Do not terminate thread. Fig. 2.

6. Insert metal clip (B). Finish sewing narrow end. Fig. 2.

7. Cement (E) to skin side of one (D). Fig. 2.

8. Skive ends of (F); cement (F) to (F) flesh sides together. Figs. 2, 8.

9. Punch stitching holes with awl, 1/8" apart, on center line of (F). Fig. 8.

10. Saddle stitch (F) to (F). Fig. 2.

11. Cut slit in second (D) for (F). Figs. 2, 6.

12. Insert (F) in slit of (D). Separate ends and cement to flesh side of (D). Fig. 2.

13. Cement (DF) to (DE), flesh sides together. Fig. 2.

14. Mark stitching holes with 1/7" spacing wheel, 1/8" from all edges of (DE). Figs. 6, 7.

15. Punch stitching holes with awl in (DEF). Figs, 6, 7.

16. Sew with saddler's stitch. Fig. 2.

MATERIALS:

Pigskin, hazel, 2 oz., pliable

Pin seal sheepskin, 2 oz.

Rubber cement

Metal clip
Linen thread

TOOLS:

(6),(25),(28),(33),(41).

Knitting Case

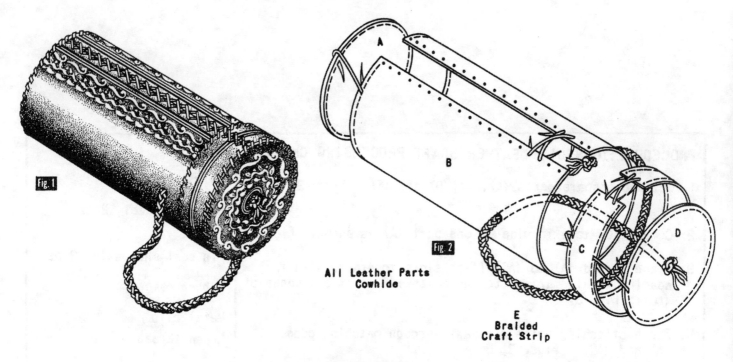

Fig. 1

Fig. 2

All Leather Parts
Cowhide

E
Braided
Craft Strip

For Detailed
Instructions Consult
Chart I - Cutting
Chart II- Design
Chart III-Color
Chart IV- Construction
Chart V - Lacing
Chart VI- Stitching
Chart VII- Braiding
Chart VIII-Knotting
Material Chart

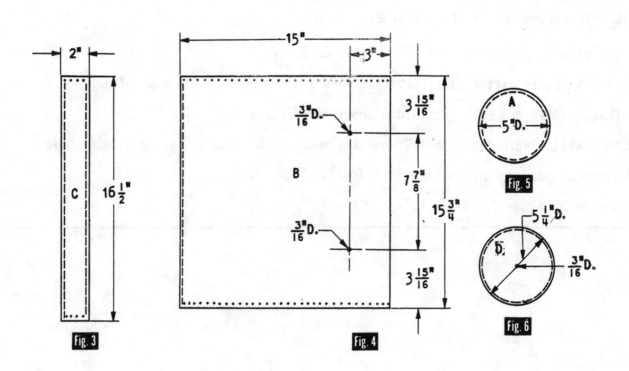

2"

C

16 ½"

Fig. 3

15"

3"

$\frac{3"}{16}$D.

B

$\frac{3"}{16}$D.

$3\frac{15"}{16}$

$7\frac{7}{8}"$

$15\frac{3"}{4}$

$3\frac{15"}{16}$

Fig. 4

A

5"D.

Fig. 5

$5\frac{1"}{4}$D.

D.

$\frac{3"}{16}$D.

Fig. 6

PROCEDURE: (CONSULT LEATHER CRAFT PROCESSING CHARTS)

1. Cut and prepare (A), (B), (C) and (D). Figs. 3, 4, 5, 6.

2. With No. 7 punch, cut holes in (B) and (D) for (E). Figs. 2, 4, 6.

3. With awl, punch thong slits, 1/8" from edge, on long sides of (C) and bottom edge of (B). Figs. 2, 3, 4.

4. With awl, punch thong slits in (A) and (D), 1/8" from edge. Figs. 2, 5, 6 and Leather Chart V.

5. With No. 1 tube, punch holes at 3/8" intervals, 1/8" from edge, on short ends of (C) and seam of (B). Figs. 2, 3, 4.

6. Lace (A) to (B) with whip stitch. Continue with same lace to cross stitch seam of (B). Fig. 2.

7. Lace (D) to (C) with whip stitch. Continue with same lace to cross stitch short edge of (C), and finish off bottom edge of (C) with whip stitch. Figs. 1, 2 and Leather Chart V.

8. Using Four Plait Round, braid (E) 33" long. Finish one end with a Crown and Terminal Turk's-head knot. Figs. 2, and Leather Chart VI.

9. Insert (E) through (CD) and (AB) with Turk's-head knot on outside of (CD). Make Turk's-head knot where (E) ends within (AB). Fig. 2.

MATERIALS:

Heavy tooling cowhide (5 oz.)

Calfskin lace, 3/32" 20' long

Craft strip (gimp)

TOOLS:

(1), (3 No. 7), (4), (6), (8), (17), (18), (20), (22), (26), (40), (43).

See Leather Chart V for punching thong slits.

Leather Tool Kit

INDEX TO TOOLS:

1. Modeling tool
2. 1 and 4 prong awl
3. Eyelet setter
4. Tracer
5. Deerfoot and double-crease
6. X-acto knife
7. Embossing tool
8. Spatulated modeler
9. Rivet setter
10. #7 Drive punch

Fig. 1

Fig. 2

C Lining Calf

D Steerhide F

Snap Fastener

Snap Fastener

B Lining Calf

A E Steerhide

Fig. 3
4 1/2"
7 1/2"
D - Make two

Fig. 4
Fold line
8"
1/2"
4 1/2"
C

Fig. 5
1/8"
1"
1"
1 1/8"
7/8"
15/16"
7/8"
13/16"
1 1/4"
1 7/8"
10"
Fold lines
1/8"
1 1/2"
E

Fig. 6
12 3/4"
3 1/2"   4 3/4"   4 1/2"
1/2"
1/4" 9/16"
1 3/4"
Location of part (F) (on part (B) only)
3/16" 7/16" 7/16" 1/2" 3/8" 7/16" 3/8" 7/16" 15/16" 7/16" 3/16"
Location of part (E) (on part (B) only)
8"
1/2"
3"
1 1/2"
Fold lines
A & B

For Detailed Instructions Consult

Chart I - Cutting	Chart V - Lacing
Chart II - Design	Chart VI - Stitching
Chart III - Color	Chart VII - Braiding
Chart IV - Construction	Chart VIII - Knotting
	Material Chart

Fig. 7
1 1/4"
1"
F

PROCEDURE: (CONSULT LEATHER CRAFT PROCESSING CHARTS)

1. Cut parts (A), (B), (C), (D), (E) and (F). Figs. 3, 4, 5, 6, 7.

2. Mark stitching lines with edge creaser on (E) and (F), and fold line and stitching lines on (C). Figs. 4, 5, 6.

3. Sew (E) and (F) to (B), with closely spaced saddler's stitch at points designated to form loops for tools. Figs. 2, 6.

4. Fold (C) and cement to flesh side. Figs. 3, 4.

5. Cement (B) to (A); cement stitching edges of (C) to one (D) flesh sides together. Fig. 2.

6. Mark stitching holes with 1/7" spacing wheel on stitching lines of (CD). Fig. 2.

7. Punch stitching holes with awl, and sew edges of (CD) with saddler's stitch. Fig. 2.

8. Cement lacing edges of (CD) and (D) in closed position on open (AB). Fig. 2.

9. Punch 3/32" thong slits around all edges of (AB) including ends of (CD) and (D). Figs. 1, 2.

10. Lace with double overlay stitch. Figs. 1, 2.

11. Insert cap of snap fasteners to top flap of (AB). Fold kit, allowing fullness for tools, to determine position of post of fastener. Insert posts and springs. Figs. 1, 2.

MATERIALS:

Steerhide, 2 oz.
Lining calf
Goatskin lace, 3/32", 10 yds.
2 Snap fasteners
Linen thread
Rubber cement

TOOLS:

(1), (4), (6), (8), (12), (17), (18), (25), (26), (27), (28), (40), (41).

Carry-All Kit

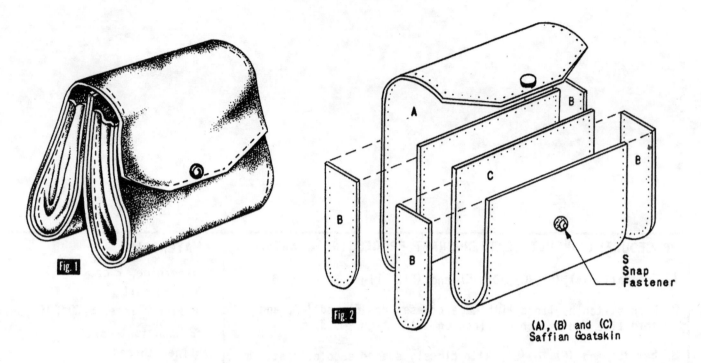

Fig. 1

Fig. 2

S
Snap
Fastener

(A), (B) and (C)
Saffian Goatskin

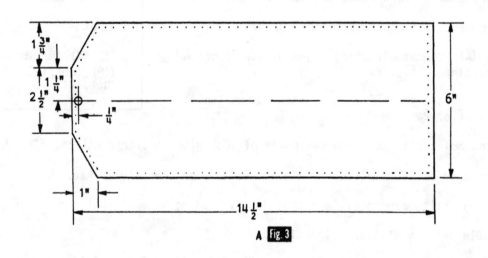

1 3/4"

1 1/4"

2 1/2"

1/4"

6"

1"

14 1/2"

A Fig. 3

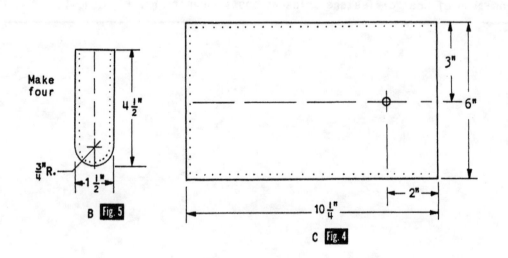

Make
four

4 1/2"

3/4" R.

1 1/2"

B Fig. 5

3"

6"

2"

10 1/4"

C Fig. 4

For Detailed
Instructions Consult
Chart I - Cutting
Chart II - Design
Chart III - Color
Chart IV - Construction
Chart V - Lacing
Chart VI - Stitching
Chart VII - Braiding
Chart VIII - Knotting
Material Chart

PROCEDURE:(CONSULT LEATHER CRAFT PROCESSING CHARTS)

1. Cut parts (A),(B) and (C). Figs. 3, 4, 5.

2. Outline all edges of (A),(B) and (C) with edge creaser. Figs. 3, 4, 5.

3. Mark 1/7" stitching holes, using creased line as guide, on flap end and long sides of (A) and on long sides of (C). Figs. 3, 4.

4. Mark stitching holes in four parts (B) to correspond to matching edges of (A) and (C). Figs. 2, 5 and Leather Chart V.

5. Punch stitching holes with awl in matching edges of (A) and (B); (C) and (B). Fig. 2.

6. Saddle stitch one part (B) to (A); continue to stitch around flap of (A); then stitch second (B) to (A). Fig. 2.

7. Saddle stitch parts (B) to (C). Fig. 2.

8. Mark 1/7" stitching holes on "partition" seam of (A) and (C). Figs. 2, 3, 4.

9. Punch stitching holes with awl through (A) and (C).

10. Sew with saddler's stitch. Fig. 2.

11. Attach snap fastener (S) to (A) and (C). Figs. 2, 3, 4.

MATERIALS:

Saffian goatskin

Snap fastener

Heavy linen thread

TOOLS:

(1),(6),(8),(12),(17), (25),(27),(28),(41),(43).

See Leather Chart V for marking stitching holes on curve.

Key Identification Chain

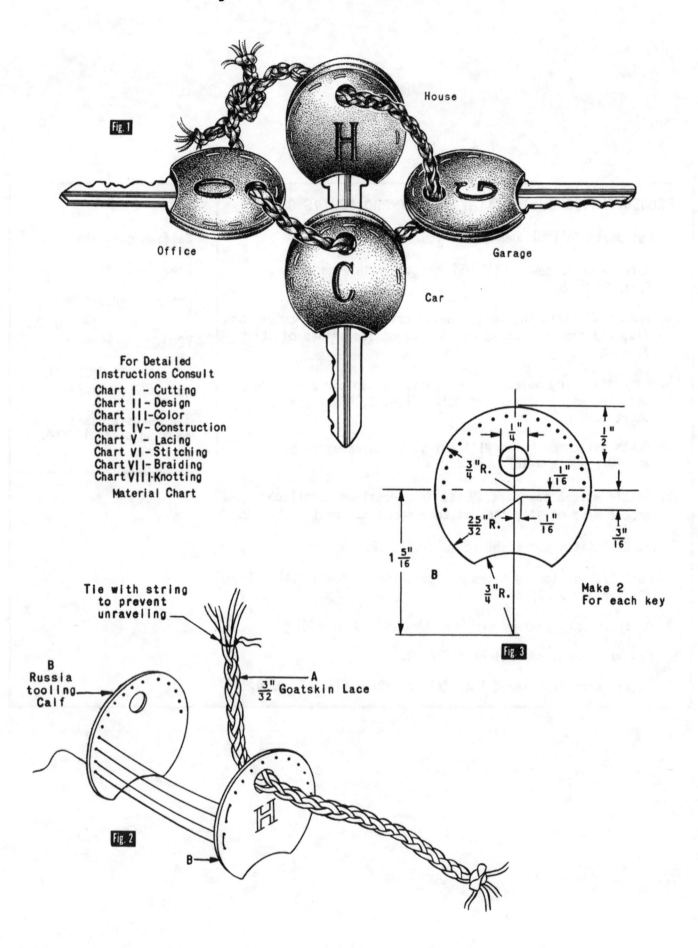

Fig. 1

House

Office

Garage

Car

For Detailed
Instructions Consult
Chart I – Cutting
Chart II – Design
Chart III – Color
Chart IV – Construction
Chart V – Lacing
Chart VI – Stitching
Chart VII – Braiding
Chart VIII – Knotting
Material Chart

$\frac{1}{4}$"

$\frac{1}{2}$"

$\frac{3}{4}$"R.

$\frac{1}{16}$"

$\frac{25}{32}$"R.

$\frac{1}{16}$"

$\frac{3}{16}$"

$1\frac{5}{16}$"

B

$\frac{3}{4}$"R.

Make 2
For each key

Fig. 3

Tie with string
to prevent
unraveling

A

$\frac{3}{32}$" Goatskin Lace

B
Russia
tooling
Calf

H

B

Fig. 2

PROCEDURE: (CONSULT LEATHER CRAFT PROCESSING CHARTS)

1. Cut and prepare (B), eight pieces. Fig. 3.

2. Mark 1/8" stitching holes, 3/32" from edge on four parts of (B). Fig. 3.

3. Place four marked parts of (B) flesh to flesh with four unmarked parts of (B). With awl, punch stitching holes as marked. Fig. 2.

4. Sew (B) to (B) with saddle stitch. Fig. 2.

5. With No. 7 drive punch, punch holes for chain in each (BB). Figs. 2, 3.

6. Make four plait round braid of (A). Terminate one end of (A) in small knot. Fig. 2.

7. Insert keys into respective (BB). Fig. 1.

8. Insert unknotted end of (A) through holes in (BB). Figs. 1, 2.

9. Terminate other end of (A). Fig. 2.

10. Tie ends of (A) in square knot. Fig. 1.

MATERIALS:

Russia tooling calf

3/32" goatskin lace

Heavy linen thread

TOOLS:

(3 No. 7), (9), (20), (25), (33), (41).

See **Leather** Chart VII for details of braid.

Magazine Rack

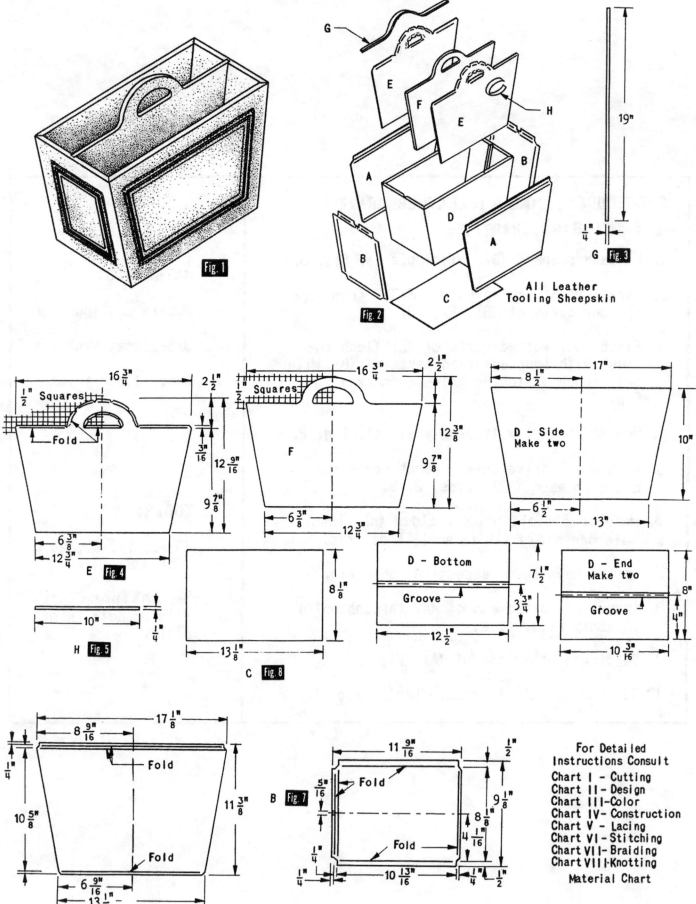

Fig. 1

Fig. 2

G Fig. 3

All Leather
Tooling Sheepskin

G — 19" — 1/4"

H — 10" — 1/4" **H Fig. 5**

E Fig. 4
Squares 1/2"
Fold
16 3/4"
2 1/2"
3/16"
12 9/16"
9 7/8"
6 3/8"
12 3/4"

F
Squares 1/2"
16 3/4"
2 1/2"
12 3/8"
9 7/8"
6 3/8"
12 3/4"

D — Side
Make two
17"
8 1/2"
10"
6 1/2"
13"

D — Bottom
Groove
7 1/2"
3 3/4"
12 1/2"

D — End
Make two
Groove
8"
4"
10 3/16"

C Fig. 8
8 1/8"
13 1/8"

A Fig. 6 Make two
17 1/8"
8 9/16"
Fold
1/4"
11 3/8"
10 5/8"
Fold
6 9/16"
13 1/8"

B Fig. 7
11 9/16"
Fold
5/16"
9 1/8"
8 1/8"
4 1/16"
Fold
1/4"
1/4"
1/2"
10 13/16"
1/2"

For Detailed
Instructions Consult
Chart I - Cutting
Chart II - Design
Chart III - Color
Chart IV - Construction
Chart V - Lacing
Chart VI - Stitching
Chart VII - Braiding
Chart VIII - Knotting
Material Chart

PROCEDURE: (CONSULT LEATHERCRAFT PROCESSING CHARTS)

1. Cut and prepare parts (A), (B), (C), (E), (G) and (H). Figs. 3, 4, 5, 6, 7.

   Note: Construct magazine rack (DF). Paint inside of (D) only. Partition to be left free for covering.

2. Mark all fold lines on (A), (B) and (E). Figs. 4, 6, 7.

3. Skive all edges to be cemented. Fig. 2.

4. Cement parts (B) to (D) with 1/2" overlap cemented to top edge, bottom, and sides of (D). Fig. 2.

5. Cement parts (A) to (D) with 1/2" overlap cemented over corners of (B) on top and bottom edges of (D), and sides of (A) covering overlapped edges of (B) at corners of (D). Fig. 2.

6. Cement (C) to bottom of (D). Fig. 2.

7. Cement parts (E) to (F) with 1/8" notched overlap on top edge. Fig. 2.

8. Cement (G) and (H) to (F), covering notched edges of (E) on (F). Fig. 2.

9. Cement groove at ends of (D) and insert covered (F). Fig. 2.

MATERIALS:
Tooling sheepskin, 1-1/2oz

Rubber cement

TOOLS:
(1), (6), (15-1 and -5), (19)

Necklace

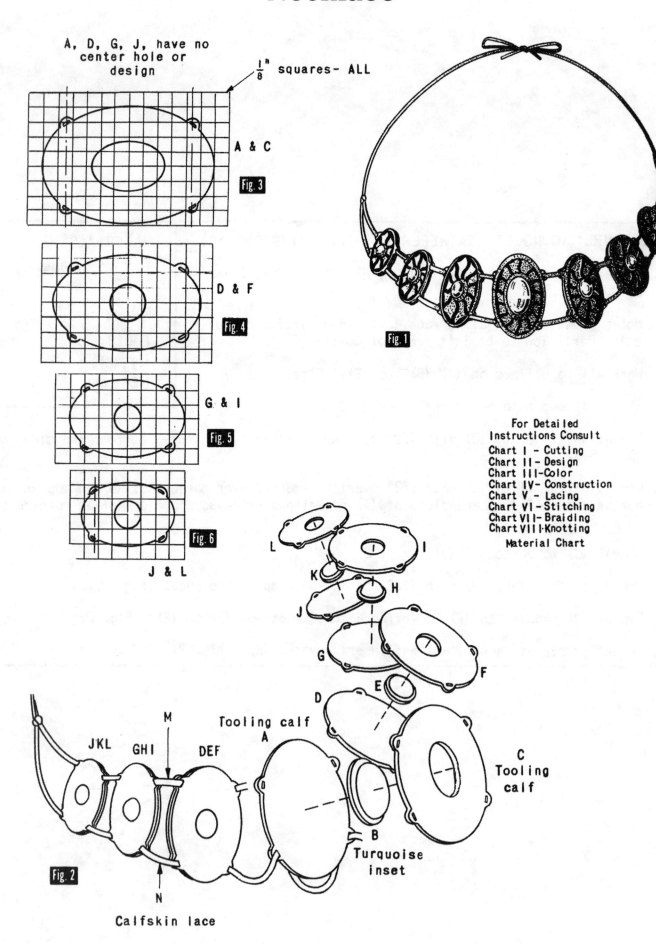

A, D, G, J, have no center hole or design

$\frac{1}{8}"$ squares- ALL

A & C

Fig. 3

D & F

Fig. 4

G & I

Fig. 5

J & L

Fig. 6

Fig. 1

For Detailed Instructions Consult

Chart I – Cutting
Chart II – Design
Chart III – Color
Chart IV – Construction
Chart V – Lacing
Chart VI – Stitching
Chart VII – Braiding
Chart VIII – Knotting
Material Chart

L

K

J

I

H

G

F

E

D

C
Tooling calf

B
Turquoise inset

M

JKL   GHI   DEF

Tooling calf
A

Fig. 2

N

Calfskin lace

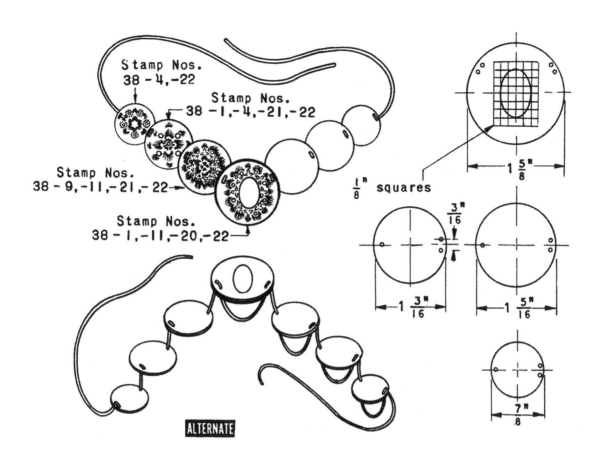

Stamp Nos.
38 -4,-22

Stamp Nos.
38 -1,-4,-21,-22

Stamp Nos.
38 -9,-11,-21,-22

Stamp Nos.
38 -1,-11,-20,-22

$\frac{1}{8}$" squares

$1\frac{5}{8}$"

$\frac{3}{16}$"

$1\frac{3}{16}$"

$1\frac{5}{16}$"

$\frac{7}{8}$"

ALTERNATE

PROCEDURE: (CONSULT LEATHER CRAFT PROCESSING CHARTS)

1. Cut and prepare parts (A),(C),(D),(F),(G),(I),(J) and (L).
   Figs. 3, 4, 5, 6.
   Note: (B),(E),(H) and (K) are cut and polished by Lapidary.

2. Locate (B),(E),(H) and (K) on flesh sides of (A),(D),(G) and (J)
   respectively. Cement in place. Figs. 2, 3, 4, 5, 6.

3. Skive inner edge of (C),(F),(I) and (L) to fit over (B),(E),(H) and (K).
   Skive flesh side of all thong tabs. Fig. 2.

4. Cement (C),(F),(I) and (L) to (A),(D),(G) and (J) respectively. Fig. 2.

5. Punch 3/32" thong slits with awl in thong tabs of
   all cemented parts. -Figs. 2, 3, 4, 5, 6.

6. Insert laces (M) and (N) in respective thong slits, allowing greater circumference for (N)
   so that necklace lies flat. Cement thongs to back of each unit. Fig. 2.

7. Knot (M) and (N) about 1-1/4" above (JKL). Figs. 1, 2.

8. Cement (M) to (N), flesh sides together, for remaining length. Tie in bow at back. Figs. 1, 2.

MATERIALS:
Russia tooling calf
Turquois insets
Calfskin lace, 3/32"
Pliobond plastic adhesive

TOOLS:
(1),(17),(18),(33),(40),
(43).
Design tools: (9),(13)

Necklace

Fig. 1

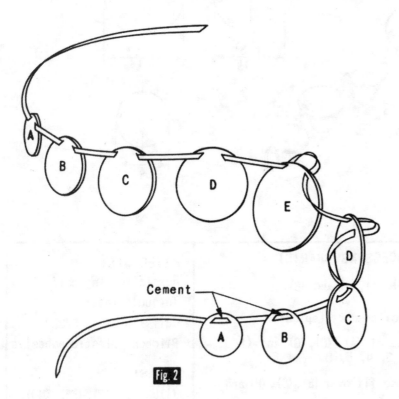

Cement

Fig. 2

E

1" Dia.
Stamp Nos.
152,C,B
38-10,
-14,-15
Make One

Fig. 3

D

$\frac{7}{8}$" Dia.
Stamp Nos.
38-20,-22,-25
Make Two

Fig. 4

$\frac{3}{4}$" Dia.
Stamp Nos.
38-1,-30
Make Two

Fig. 5

C

$\frac{5}{8}$" Dia.
Stamp Nos.
38-21,-23
Make Two

Fig. 6

B

A

$\frac{1}{2}$" Dia.
Stamp No. 38-8
Make Two

Fig. 7

For Detailed
Instructions Consult
Chart I - Cutting
Chart II - Design
Chart III-Color
Chart IV- Construction
Chart V - Lacing
Chart VI-Stitching
Chart VII- Braiding
Chart VIII-Knotting
   Material Chart

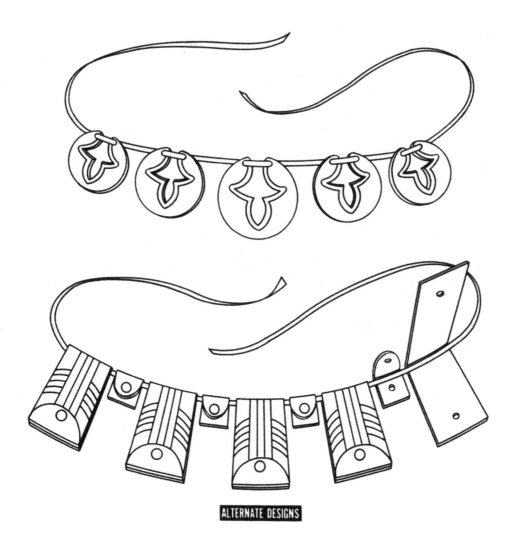

ALTERNATE DESIGNS

PROCEDURE: (CONSULT LEATHER CRAFT PROCESSING CHARTS)	MATERIALS:
1. Cut and prepare parts (A), (B), (C), (D) and (E). Figs. 3, 4, 5, 6, 7. 2. Punch thong slits with awl in (A), (B), (C), (D) and (E) for lace (G). Figs. 3, 4, 5, 6, 7. 3. Skive (G) between points spanning (A) to (A). Fig. 2. 4. Insert (G) through thong slits of discs (A) to (A). 5. Space discs. Cement skin side of (G) to flesh side of matching disc. Fig. 2. 6. Tie thong ends in bow. Fig. 1.	Tooling cowhide, 5 oz. Calfskin lace, 3/32" Rubber cement **TOOLS:** (17), (18), (33), (40)

Credentials Wallet

PROCEDURE:
HAVING PREPARED THE SIX
SEPARATE PARTS...
1. SEW (C) TO (D), THEN...
   (C) (D) TO (A) AS IN-
   DICATED.
2. SEW (F) TO (E) AS IN-
   DICATED.
3. CEMENT EDGES (X) (Y),
   FLESH SIDE, OF (E)
   TO EDGES (X) (Y),
   SMOOTH SIDE, OF (A).
4. PLACE (A) OVER (B)
   FLESH SIDE TOGETHER,
   SLIGHTLY ROUND COR-
   NERS, MAKE 3/32"
   THONG SLITS 1/8"
   FROM EDGES (X) (Y) (Z)
   AND LACE.

TOOLS:
(6) (1) (4) (2) (16)

MATERIALS:
CONSULT LEATHER CHARTS,
THREAD, RUBBER CEMENT

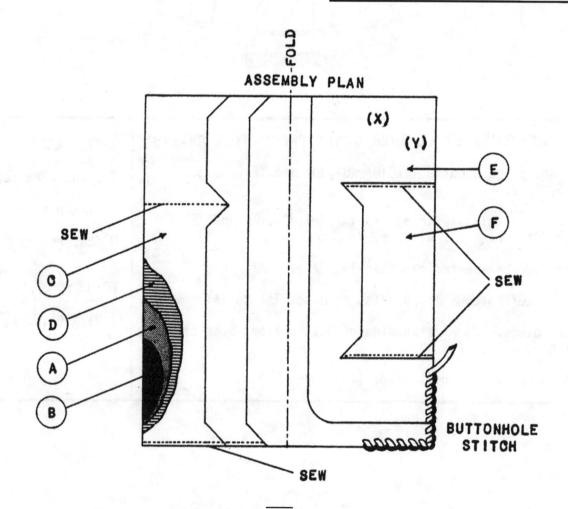

ASSEMBLY PLAN

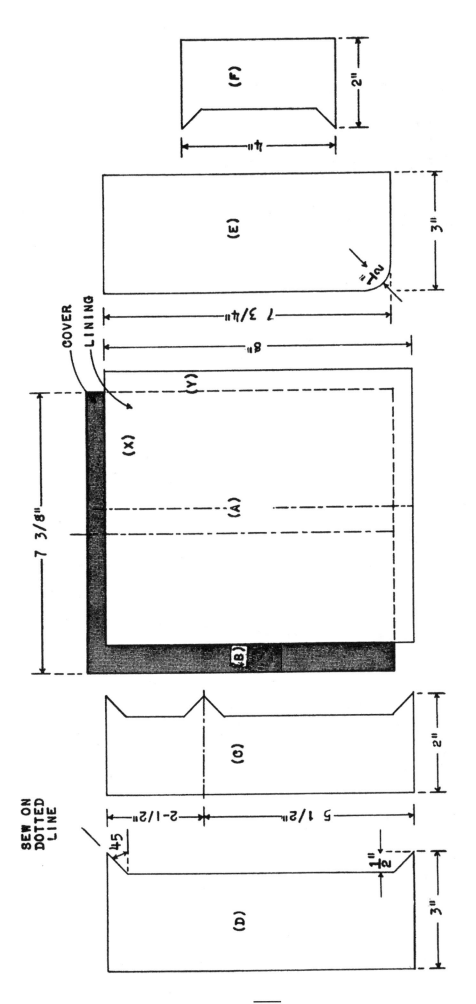

(F)

2"

4"

(E)

3"

2"

7 3/4"

8"

COVER

LINING

(X)

(Y)

(A)

7 3/8"

(B)

(C)

2"

2-1/2"

5 1/2"

SEW ON
DOTTED
LINE

45°

1/2"

(D)

3"

275

Billfold

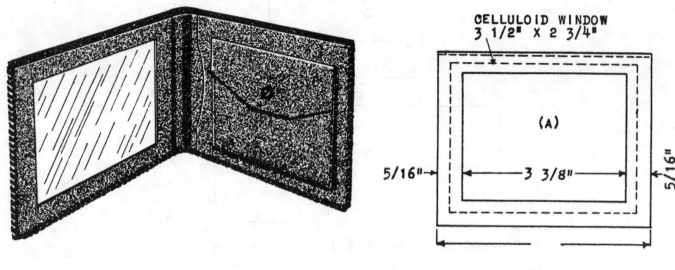

CELLULOID WINDOW
3 1/2" X 2 3/4"

(A)

5/16" → ← 5/16"

3 3/8"

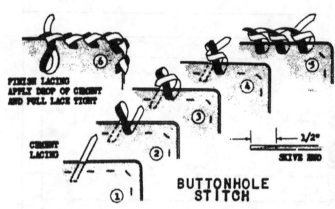

FINISH LACING
APPLY DROP OF CEMENT
AND PULL LACE TIGHT

CEMENT
LACING

BUTTONHOLE
STITCH

1/2"

SKIVE END

PROCEDURE:
HAVING PREPARED THE SEVEN SEPARATE PARTS...
(1) CEMENT AND SEW (D) ON (E) THEN (F) ON (E)
(2) LOCATE (E) OVER SMOOTH SIDE OF (B) AND SEW
(3) PLACE (A) IN POSITION ON (B) AND SEW
(4) PUT (B) AND (C) TOGETHER, FLESH SIDES IN,
    SLIGHTLY ROUND THE CORNERS AND MAKE 3/32"
    THONG SLITS 1/8" IN FROM EDGES OF SIDES X,
    Y AND Z AND LACE TOGETHER
(5) FOLD FLAP (D) OVER (F) LOCATE POSITION OF
    SNAP BUTTON AND SET
(6) INSERT CELLULOID WINDOW

TOOLS:
(1) (2) (3) (4) (5) (6) (8) (12) (16)

MATERIALS:
CONSULT LEATHER CHARTS
CELLULOID
RUBBER CEMENT
ONE 3/8" SNAP BUTTON

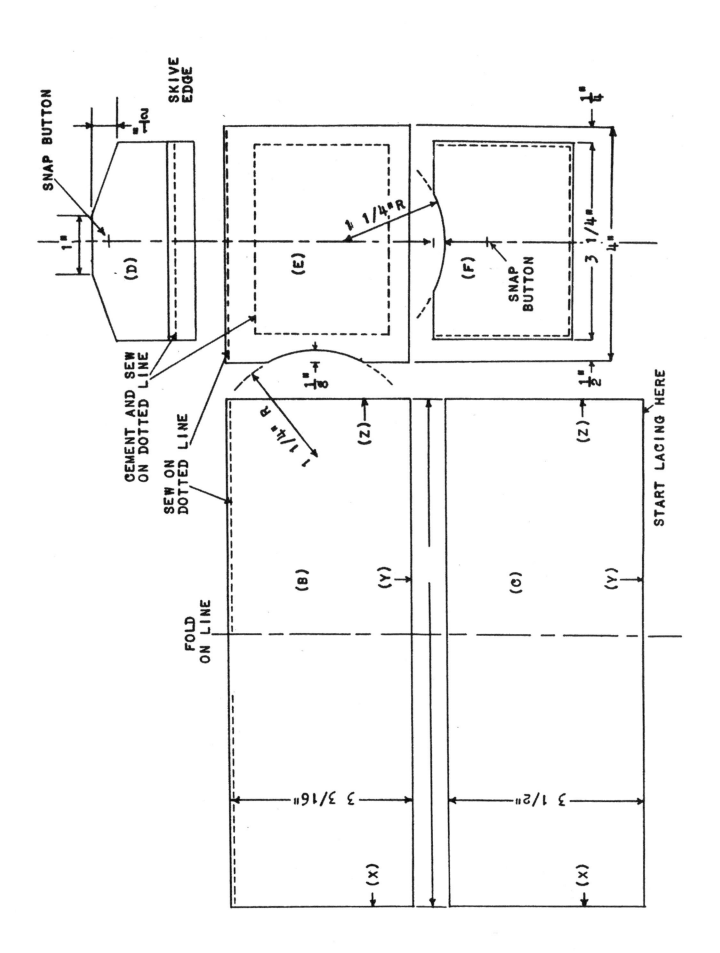

SNAP BUTTON

SKIVE EDGE

(D)

$\frac{1}{2}$"

1"

CEMENT AND SEW ON DOTTED LINE

(E)

1 1/4"R

(F)

SNAP BUTTON

3 1/4"

4"

$\frac{1}{4}$"

SEW ON DOTTED LINE

$\frac{1}{8}$"

1 1/4"R

(Z)

(Z)

$\frac{1}{2}$"

FOLD ON LINE

(B)

(Y)

(C)

(Y)

START LACING HERE

3 3/16"

3 1/2"

(X)

(X)

Billfold

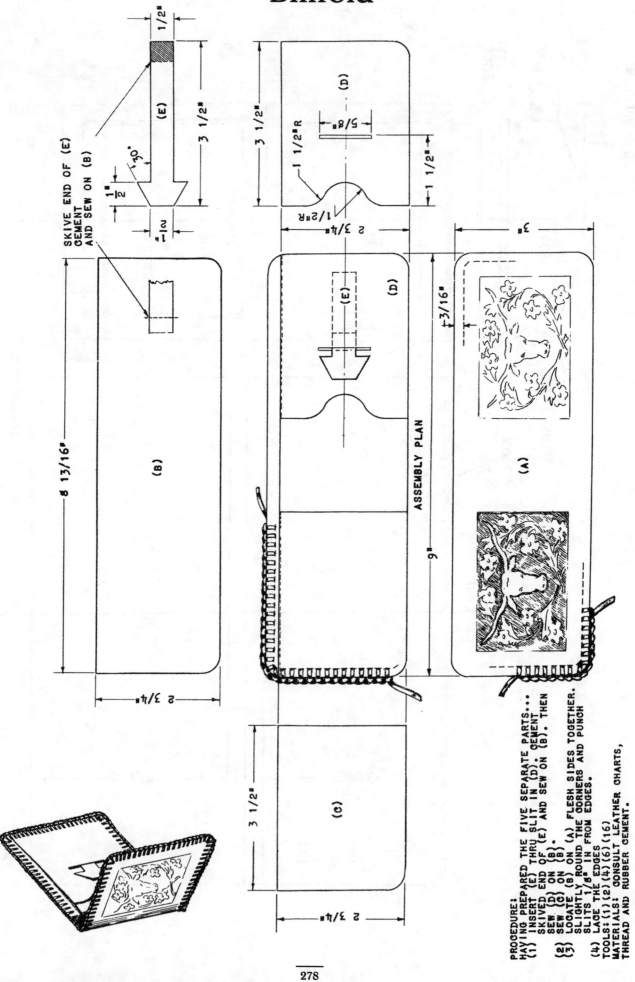

SKIVE END OF (E)
CEMENT
AND SEW ON (B)

1/2"

(E)

3 1/2"

30°

1/2"

1/2"

(B)

8 13/16"

2 3/4"

(D)

5/8"

1 1/2"R

1/2"R

3 1/2"

1 1/2"

2 3/4"

(E)

(D)

ASSEMBLY PLAN

9"

(C)

3 1/2"

2 3/4"

3"

3/16"

(A)

PROCEDURE:
HAVING PREPARED THE FIVE SEPARATE PARTS...
(1) INSERT (E) THRU SLIT IN (D). CEMENT
SKIVED END OF (E) AND SEW ON (B). THEN
(2) SEW (D) ON (B).
(3) SEW (C) ON (B).
(3) LOCATE (B) ON (A) FLESH SIDES TOGETHER.
SLIGHTLY ROUND THE CORNERS AND PUNCH
SLITS 1/8" IN FROM EDGES.
(4) LACE THE EDGES.
TOOLS: (1)(2)(4)(6)(16)
MATERIALS: CONSULT LEATHER CHARTS,
THREAD AND RUBBER CEMENT.

278

Business Card Holder

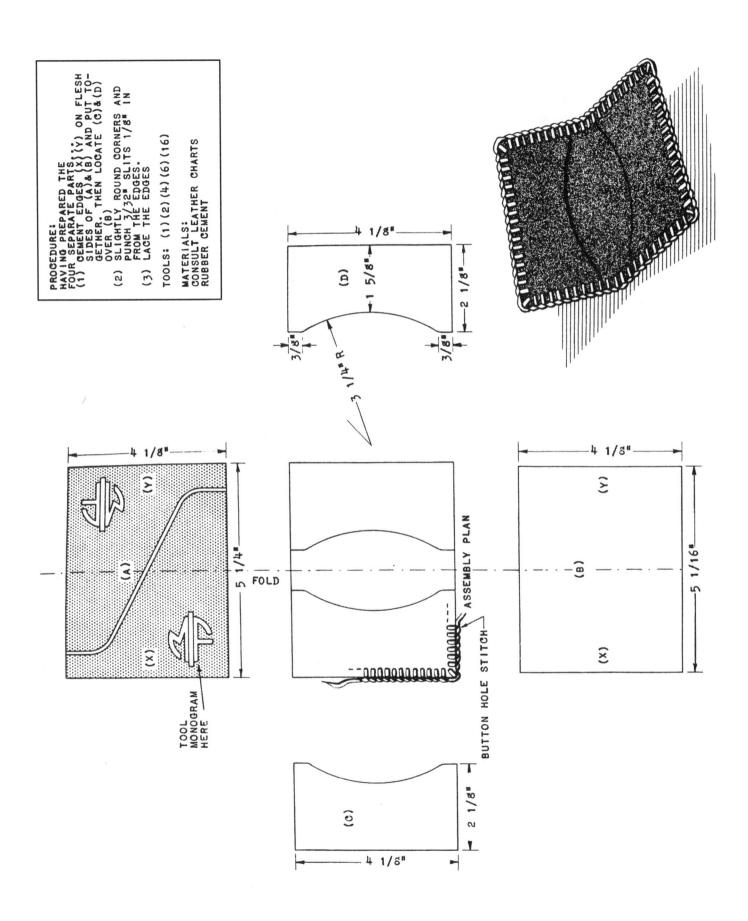

PROCEDURE:
HAVING PREPARED THE
FOUR SEPARATE PARTS (X)(Y) ON FLESH
(1) CEMENT EDGES (X)&(B)
SIDES OF (A)&(B) AND PUT TO-
GETHER. THEN LOCATE (C)&(D)
OVER (B).
(2) SLIGHTLY ROUND CORNERS AND
PUNCH 3/32" SLITS 1/8" IN
FROM THE EDGES.
(3) LACE THE EDGES

TOOLS: (1)(2)(4)(6)(16)

MATERIALS:
CONSULT LEATHER CHARTS
RUBBER CEMENT

4 1/8"

(D)

1 5/8"

2 1/8"

3/8"   3/8"

3 1/4" R

4 1/8"

(Y)

(A)

5 1/4"

(X)

FOLD

TOOL
MONOGRAM
HERE

ASSEMBLY PLAN

BUTTON HOLE STITCH

(C)

2 1/8"

4 1/8"

4 1/8"

(Y)

(B)

5 1/16"

(X)

Wallet

NOTE:
NAME OF PERSON OR INITIALS CAN BE CUT OUT OF
CONTRASTING LEATHER AND APPLIQUED TO COVER OR
TOOLED. THIS MUST BE DONE BEFORE ASSEMBLY.

CORNER DETAIL OF
OVER & OVER STITCH

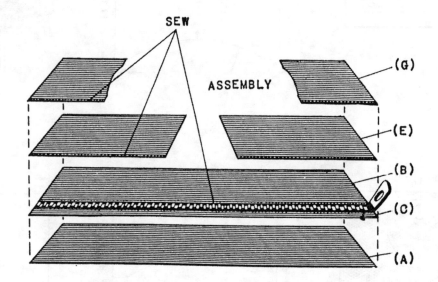

SEW

ASSEMBLY

(G)
(E)
(B)
(C)
(A)

PROCEDURE:
HAVING PREPARED THE SEVEN SEPARATE PIECES...
(1) SEW ZIPPER TO (C)
(2) LOCATE (D)(E)(F)&(G) ON (B) FINISHED SIDES UP, AS IN
    ASSEMBLY, AND CEMENT EDGES TO HOLD THEM TOGETHER, WHILE
    SEWING ZIPPER TO INDICATED SIDE OF THESE PIECES.
(3) SEE NOTE. LOCATE FLESH SIDE OF (B) OVER FLESH SIDE OF (A).
    SLIGHTLY ROUND CORNER AND PUNCH 3/32" THONG SLITS 1/8" IN
    FROM EDGES AND LACE.

TOOLS: (1)(2)(4)(6)
FOR TOOLING, ADD (9)(10)(11)(13)(17)

MATERIALS: CONSULT LEATHER CHARTS, RUBBER CEMENT, 8" ZIPPER.

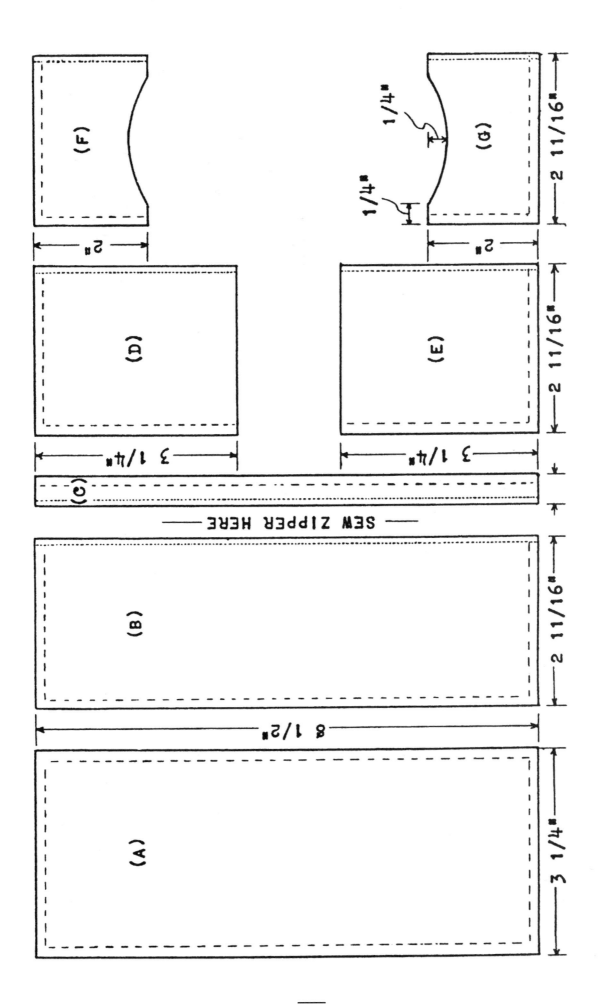

SEW ZIPPER HERE

(A)

(B)

(C)

(D)

(E)

(F)

(G)

3 1/4"

8 1/2"

2 11/16"

2 11/16"

2 11/16"

2 11/16"

3 1/4"

3 1/4"

2"

2"

1/4"

1/4"

Belt Purse

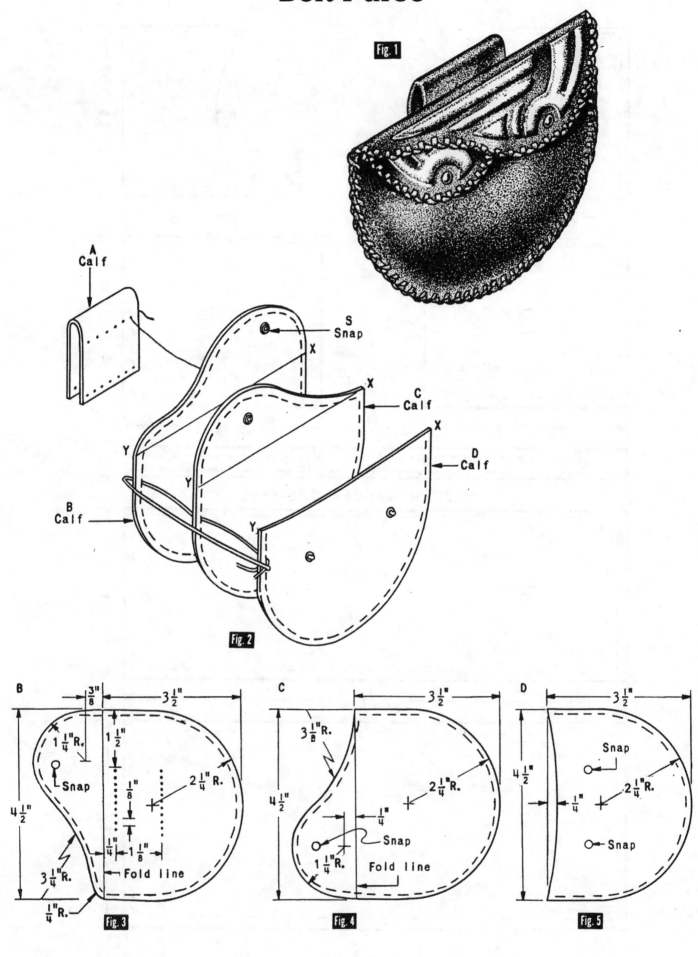

Fig. 1

A
Calf

S
Snap

X

X

C
Calf

X

D
Calf

Y

Y

B
Calf

Y

Fig. 2

B

3/8"   3 1/2"

1 1/4"R.   1 1/2"

1/8"

2 1/4" R.

Snap

4 1/2"

1/4"   1 1/8"

3 1/4"R.   Fold line

1/4"R.

Fig. 3

C

3 1/2"

3 1/8"R.

2 1/4"R.

4 1/2"

1/4"

Snap

1 1/4"R.   Fold line

Fig. 4

D

3 1/2"

Snap

2 1/4"R.

4 1/2"

1/4"

Snap

Fig. 5

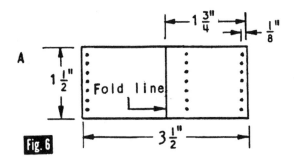

Fig. 6

A
$1\frac{1}{2}''$
Fold line
$1\frac{3}{4}''$ $\frac{1}{8}''$
$3\frac{1}{2}''$

For Detailed
Instructions Consult
Chart I - Cutting
Chart II - Design
Chart III - Color
Chart IV - Construction
Chart V - Lacing
Chart VI - Stitching
Chart VII - Braiding
Chart VIII - Knotting
Material Chart

PROCEDURE: (CONSULT LEATHER CRAFT PROCESSING CHARTS)

1. Cut and prepare parts (A), (B), (C) and (D). Figs. 3, 4, 5, 6.

2. Attach snap fasteners (S) to (B), (C) and (D). Figs. 2, 3, 4, 5.

3. Fold (A) on center line. With awl, punch $\frac{1}{8}''$ stitching holes, $\frac{1}{2}''$ from folded edge, on side of fold to be attached to (B). Punch matching holes $\frac{1}{4}''$ from folded edge of (B). Figs. 2, 3, 6.

4. Sew (A) to (B), skin to skin side, with saddler's stitch. Fig. 2.

5. Fold (A) in position against (B). With awl, punch $\frac{1}{8}''$ stitching holes, $\frac{1}{8}''$ from cut edge of (A), in matching parts of (A) and (B). Figs. 2, 3, 6.

6. Sew (A) to (B) with saddler's stitch. Fig. 2.

7. With awl, punch $\frac{3}{32}''$ thong slits, $\frac{1}{8}''$ from flap edges of (AB) and (C). Figs. 2, 3, 4.

8. Place (AB), (C) and (D) in position. With awl, punch $\frac{3}{32}''$ thong slits, $\frac{1}{8}''$ from edge, simultaneously through matching edges. Figs. 2, 3, 4, 5.

9. Lace together (AB), (C) and (D) with single overlay stitch. First lace flap of (C) from point (X) to point (Y); then lace together round edges of (AB), (C) and (D). Without cutting thong, lace flap of (B) from point (X) to point (Y). Fig. 2.

MATERIALS:

Russia tooling calfskin

Two snap fasteners , $\frac{7}{16}''$

Goatskin lace, $\frac{3}{32}'' \times 11'$

TOOLS:

(1), (4), (6), (12), (17), (18), (25), (26), (40), (41).

Woman's Evening Billfold

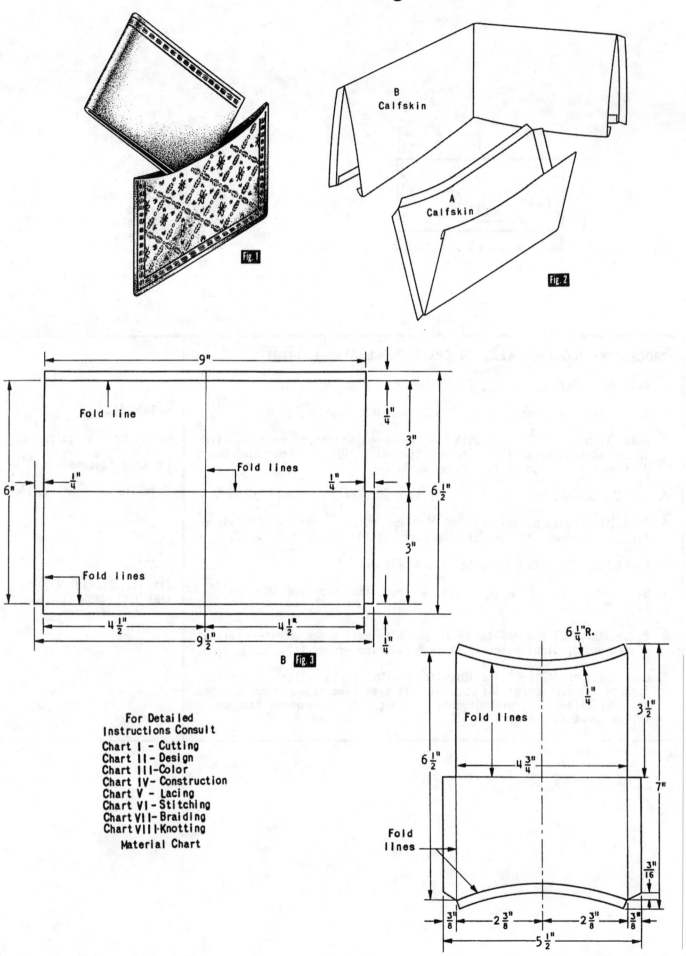

Fig. 1

B
Calfskin

A
Calfskin

Fig. 2

9"

Fold line

1/4"

3"

1/4"   Fold lines   1/4"

6"   6 1/2"

3"

Fold lines

4 1/2"   4 1/2"

9 1/2"

1/4"

B   Fig. 3

For Detailed
Instructions Consult
Chart I – Cutting
Chart II– Design
Chart III–Color
Chart IV– Construction
Chart V – Lacing
Chart VI–Stitching
Chart VII–Braiding
Chart VIII–Knotting
Material Chart

6 1/4"R.

1/4"

Fold lines

3 1/2"

6 1/2"   4 3/4"

7"

Fold
lines

3/16"

3/8"   2 3/8"   2 3/8"   3/8"

5 1/2"

PROCEDURE: (CONSULT LEATHER CRAFT PROCESSING CHARTS)

1. Cut and prepare parts (A) and (B). Figs. 3, 4.

2. Mark fold lines on (A) and (B) with edge creaser. Figs. 3, 4.

3. Skive long edges and flap ends of (A) and (B). Figs. 3, 4.

4. Fold down curved edges of (A) and long edges of (B) to flesh side. Cement in place. Fig. 2.

5. Fold (A) and (B) on horizontal center lines. Figs. 2, 3, 4.

6. Fold down flap ends of (A) and (B). Cement in place. Figs. 2, 3, 4.

7. Crease all edges of (A) and (B) with edge creaser. Figs. 2, 3, 4.

MATERIALS:
Lining calf, 1-1/2 oz., tooling
Rubber Cement

TOOLS:
(1), (6), (27)
Wheel (15-7)
Stamps 38-1,-8, -17,-22

Woman's French Purse

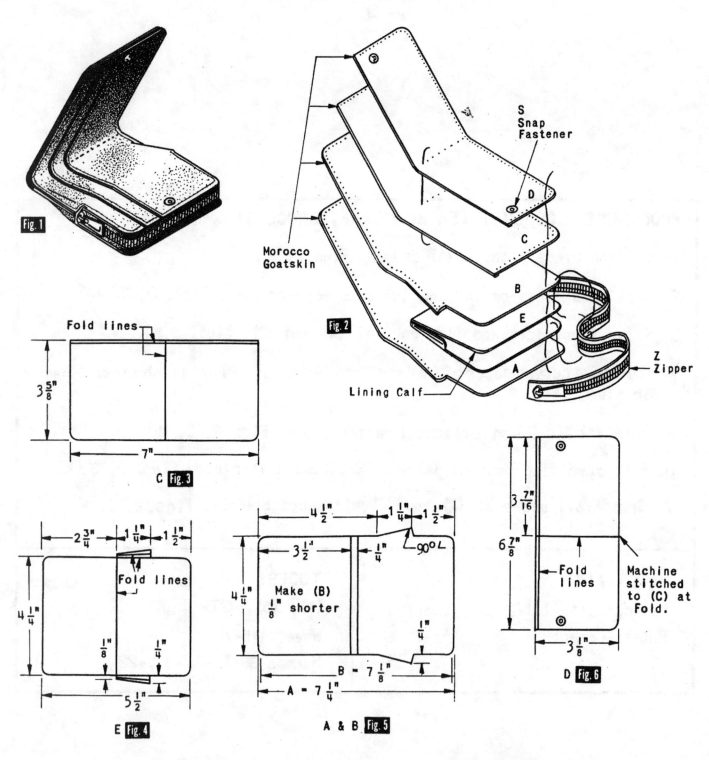

Fig. 1

Fig. 2

S
Snap
Fastener

D

C

B

E

A

Z
Zipper

Morocco
Goatskin

Lining Calf

Fold lines

$3\frac{5}{8}"$

$7"$

C **Fig. 3**

$2\frac{3}{4}"$ $1\frac{1}{4}"$ $1\frac{1}{2}"$

Fold lines

$4\frac{1}{4}"$

$\frac{1}{8}"$ $\frac{1}{4}"$

$5\frac{1}{2}"$

E **Fig. 4**

$4\frac{1}{2}"$ $1\frac{1}{4}"$ $1\frac{1}{2}"$

$3\frac{1}{2}"$ $\frac{1}{4}"$ $90°L$

$4\frac{1}{4}"$

Make (B)
$\frac{1}{8}"$ shorter

$\frac{1}{4}"$

$B = 7\frac{1}{8}"$

$A = 7\frac{1}{4}"$

A & B **Fig. 5**

$3\frac{7}{16}"$

$6\frac{7}{8}"$

Fold
lines

Machine
stitched
to (C) at
Fold.

$3\frac{1}{8}"$

D **Fig. 6**

For Detailed
Instructions Consult
Chart I - Cutting
Chart II - Design
Chart III - Color
Chart IV - Construction
Chart V - Lacing
Chart VI - Stitching
Chart VII - Braiding
Chart VIII - Knotting
Material Chart

PROCEDURE: (CONSULT LEATHER CRAFT PROCESSING CHARTS)

1. Cut parts (A), (B), (C), (D) and (E). Figs. 3, 4, 5, 6.

2. Skive all edges of (A), (B), (C) and (D). Figs. 3, 5, 6.

3. Turn down to flesh side free edges of (C) and (D). Cement. Figs. 3, 6.

4. Stitch folded edges of (C) and (D), close to edge, on sewing machine. Fig. 2.

5. Stitch (D) to (C) on sewing machine at center fold line to form pockets. Fig. 2.

6. Attach cap of snap fastener (S) to flesh side of (D) at zipper end. Fold (D) to determine position of post of snap fastener. Attach post. Figs. 2, 6.

7. Fold (E), skin sides together. Stitch diagonal gusset edge on sewing machine to matching edge at back of (E) to form coin purse. Fig. 2.

8. Place (E) in position with (A) and (B), flesh sides facing. Fig. 2.

9. Cement edges of (E) to those edges of (A) and (B) to which zipper (Z) is to be attached. Fig. 2.

10. Stitch (Z) to (A) and (B) on sewing machine; cement tape ends to edges of (A) and (B). Fig. 2.

11. Cement 1/8" stitching edges of (D) to (C); then (CD) to (B); then (BCD) to (A). Fig. 2.

12. Mark stitching holes with 1/7" spacing wheel on (A), 1/8" from edge. Fig. 2.

13. Punch stitching holes with awl through (ABCD). Figs. 1, 2.

14. Sew around edges of (ABCD), with saddler's stitch, beginning and ending by stitching (Z) to (ABE) at short ends of zipper opening. Figs. 1, 2.

MATERIALS:

Morocco goatskin
Lining calf, 1-1/2 oz.
Zipper, 7"
Snap fastener
Linen thread
Rubber cement

TOOLS:

(1), (6), (8), (12), (17), (19), (25), (28), (41).

Identification Billfold

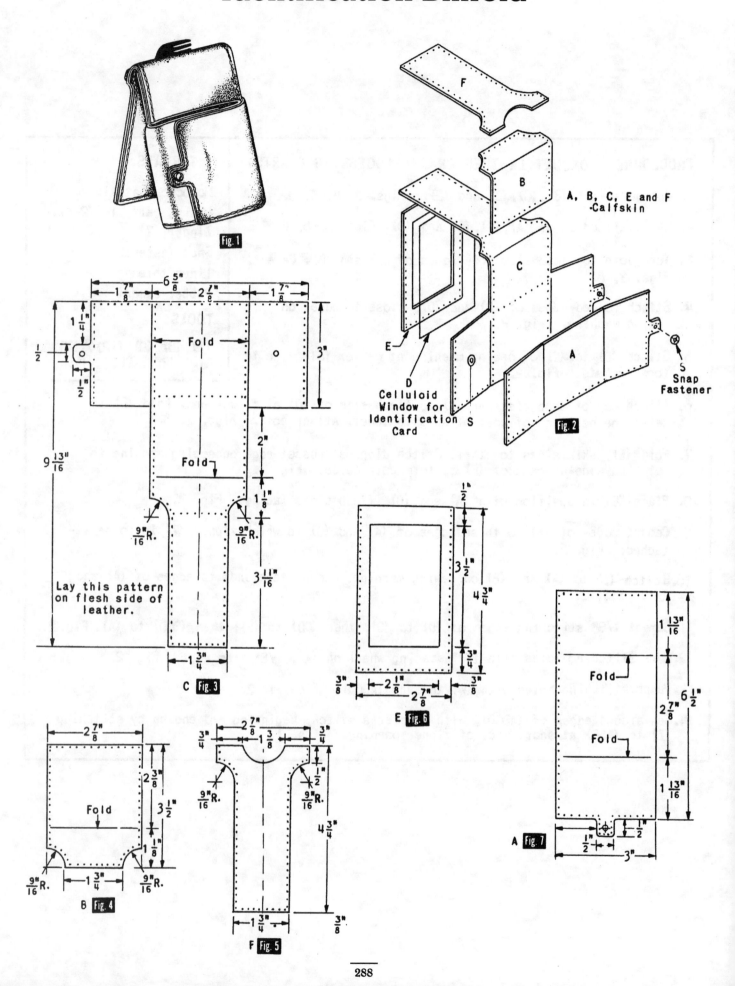

Fig. 1

F

A, B, C, E and F
Calfskin

B

C

E

D

Celluloid
Window for
Identification
Card

S

A

S
Snap
Fastener

Fig. 2

$6\frac{5}{8}$"
$1\frac{7}{8}$" $2\frac{7}{8}$" $1\frac{7}{8}$"

$1\frac{1}{4}$"

Fold

$\frac{1}{2}$

$\frac{1}{2}$

3"

Fold

2"

$9\frac{13}{16}$"

$1\frac{1}{8}$"

$\frac{9}{16}$"R. $\frac{9}{16}$"R.

$3\frac{11}{16}$"

Lay this pattern
on flesh side of
leather.

$1\frac{3}{4}$"

C   Fig. 3

$\frac{1}{2}$"

$3\frac{1}{2}$" $4\frac{3}{4}$"

$\frac{3}{4}$"

$\frac{3}{8}$" $2\frac{1}{8}$" $\frac{3}{8}$"
$2\frac{7}{8}$"

E   Fig. 6

$1\frac{13}{16}$"

Fold

$2\frac{7}{8}$" $6\frac{1}{2}$"

Fold

$1\frac{13}{16}$"

$\frac{1}{2}$"

$\frac{1}{2}$"

A   Fig. 7

3"

$2\frac{7}{8}$"

$2\frac{3}{8}$"

Fold $3\frac{1}{2}$"

$1\frac{1}{8}$"

$\frac{9}{16}$"R. $1\frac{3}{4}$" $\frac{9}{16}$"R.

B   Fig. 4

$\frac{3}{4}$ $2\frac{7}{8}$" $\frac{3}{4}$
$1\frac{3}{8}$

$\frac{1}{2}$"

$\frac{9}{16}$"R. $\frac{9}{16}$"R.

$4\frac{3}{4}$"

$1\frac{3}{4}$" $\frac{3}{8}$"

F   Fig. 5

288

PROCEDURE: (CONSULT LEATHER CRAFT PROCESSING CHARTS)

1. Cut parts (A), (B), (C), (D), (E) and (F). Figs. 3, 4, 5, 6, 7.

2. Skive all edges to be stitched. Figs. 3, 4, 5, 6, 7.

3. Mark all fold lines with edge creaser. Figs. 3, 4.

4. Cement (E) to (C), flesh sides together. Allow fullness in (E) to bend over (C). Figs. 2, 3, 4.

5. Cement 1/8" stitching edges of (F) to (BC), and (E) to (C), leaving top edge of (E) free for insertion of celluloid (D) and Identification Card. Fig. 2.

6. Mark stitching holes with 1/7" spacing wheel, 1/8" from edge, around (F) on (BC) and (E) on (C). Figs. 2, 3, 5, 6.

7. Punch stitching holes with awl. Fig. 2.

8. Sew with saddler's stitch. Fig. 2.

9. Attach post of snap fastener (S) to skin side of (C) in position for cap of snap on tab. Figs. 2, 3.

10. Cement 1/8" stitching edges and tab of (A) to (BC). Fig. 2.

11. Mark stitching holes with 1/7" spacing wheel, 1/8" from ends and bottom edge of (A) on (BC). Figs. 2, 7.

12. Punch stitching holes with awl through (ABC). Fig. 2.

13. Sew with saddler's stitch. Fig. 2.

14. Attach cap of snap fastener to tab of (AC). Figs. 2, 3, 7.

15. Insert celluloid (D). Fig. 2.

MATERIALS:

Calfskin, 2-1/2 oz.

Celluloid, 2-5/8" x 4-1/2"

1 Snap fastener

Linen thread

Rubber cement

TOOLS:

(1), (6), (8), (12), (17), (25), (27), (41).

For Detailed
Instructions Consult
Chart I - Cutting
Chart II - Design
Chart III - Color
Chart IV - Construction
Chart V - Lacing
Chart VI - Stitching
Chart VII - Braiding
Chart VIII - Knotting
Material Chart

Billfold

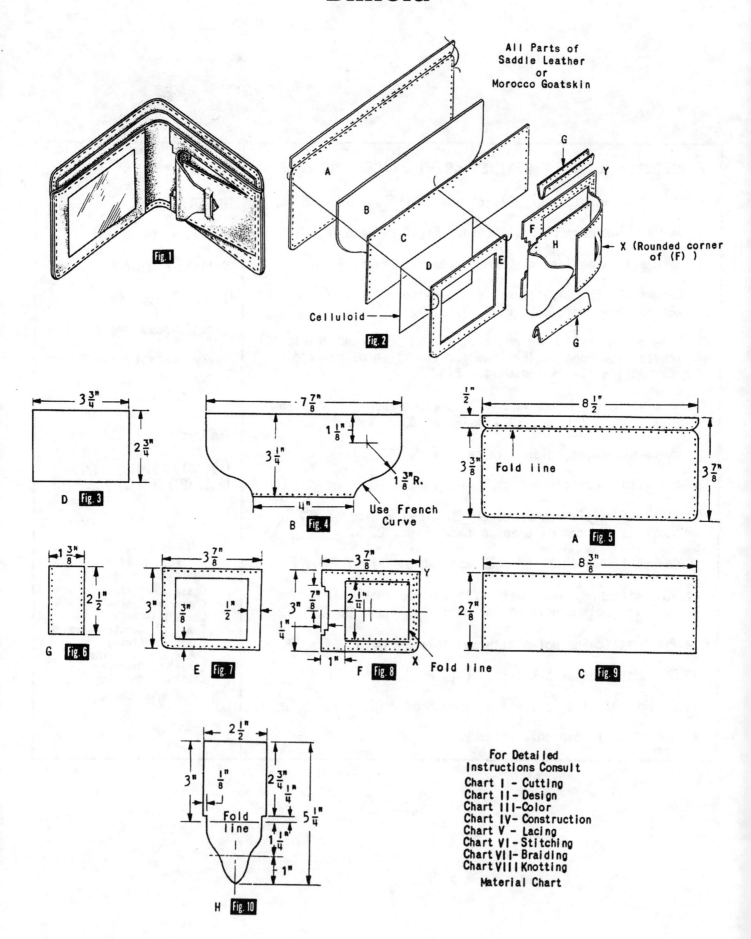

All Parts of
Saddle Leather
or
Morocco Goatskin

A

B

G

Y

C

F

D

E

H

X (Rounded corner
of (F))

Celluloid

Fig. 1

Fig. 2

3 3/4" 2 3/4"

D Fig. 3

7 7/8" 3 1/4" 1 1/8" 1 3/8" R.
4"
Use French Curve

B Fig. 4

1/2" 8 1/2" 3 3/8" Fold line 3 7/8"

A Fig. 5

1 3/8" 2 1/2"

G Fig. 6

3 7/8" 3" 3/8" 1/2"

E Fig. 7

3 7/8" 7/8" 3" 2 1/4" 1/4" 1" Y X Fold line

F Fig. 8

8 3/8" 2 7/8"

C Fig. 9

2 1/2" 3" 1 1/8" 2 3/4" 1/4" Fold line 1 1/4" 5 1/4" 1"

H Fig. 10

For Detailed
Instructions Consult
Chart I - Cutting
Chart II - Design
Chart III - Color
Chart IV - Construction
Chart V - Lacing
Chart VI - Stitching
Chart VII - Braiding
Chart VIII Knotting
Material Chart

PROCEDURE: (CONSULT LEATHER CRAFT PROCESSING CHARTS)

Note: If lightweight leather is used, all seams can be stitched on sewing machine, 1/16" from edges.

1. Cut parts (A), (B), (C), (D), (E), (F), (G), (H). Figs. 3, 4, 5, 6, 7, 8, 9, 10.

2. Outline all unstitched edges with edge creaser. Fig. 2.

3. Place parts (G) in position with (F), flesh sides together. Stitch front edge of (G) to front edge of (F) on sewing machine. Fig. 2.

4. Insert (H) in cut made in (F), with notched edge of (H) under corner of cut. Fig. 2.

5. Place back edges of parts (G) under side cuts in (F) on top of (H). Fig. 2.

6. Stitch along cut edges of (F) through (F), (G) and (H), and secure flap (H) of pocket by stitching it to (F) in an open position (flesh side up). Fig. 2.

7. Place (E) and (FGH) in position on (C). Stitch along top compartment edge only. Fig. 2.

8. Fold and cement 1/2" free edge of (A). Figs. 2, 5.

9. Assemble all parts. Fig. 2.

10. Stitch all parts together, around entire outer edge. Start stitching at point (X), across to (Y), around cemented flap edge of (A) and around to (X). Reinforce coin compartment edge by stitching between points (X) and (Y) a second time, 1/16" apart. Fig. 2.

MATERIALS:

Saddle leather, 1-1/2 oz.
or
Morocco goatskin, 1-1/2 oz.
Celluloid
Rubber cement
Linen thread

TOOLS:

(1), (6), (27).

Card Case

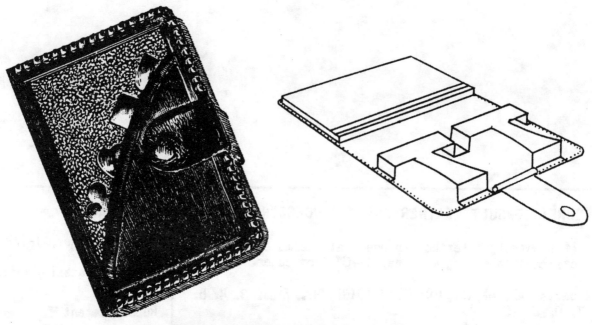

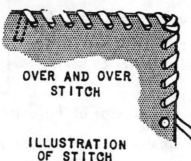

OVER AND OVER
STITCH

PASS THRU
CORNER HOLES
THREE TIMES

ILLUSTRATION
OF STITCH

PROCEDURE:
HAVING PREPARED THE FIVE SEPARATE
PARTS...
(1) LOCATE POSITION OF SNAP BUTTON
AND SET.
(2) PUNCH HOLES IN (A) AND (B) AND
LACE (B) TO (A) AT POINT (X)
(3) CEMENT (D) AND (F) IN POSITION
INDICATED BY DOTTED LINES, ON
FLESH SIDE OF (C)
(4) CEMENT (A) TO (C), FLESH SIDES
TOGETHER, SMOOTHING OUT ALL
WRINKLES.
(5) SLIGHTLY ROUND THE CORNERS...
PUNCH HOLES 1/8" IN FROM EDGES
LOCATING (E), (B), (G) AND PENCIL
TAB DURING PROCESS...THEN LACE.
TOOLS:
(1) (3) (5) (6) (8) (10) (12) (13)
MATERIALS:
CONSULT LEATHER CHARTS
ONE 3/8" SNAP BUTTON, CARDBOARD
AND RUBBER CEMENT

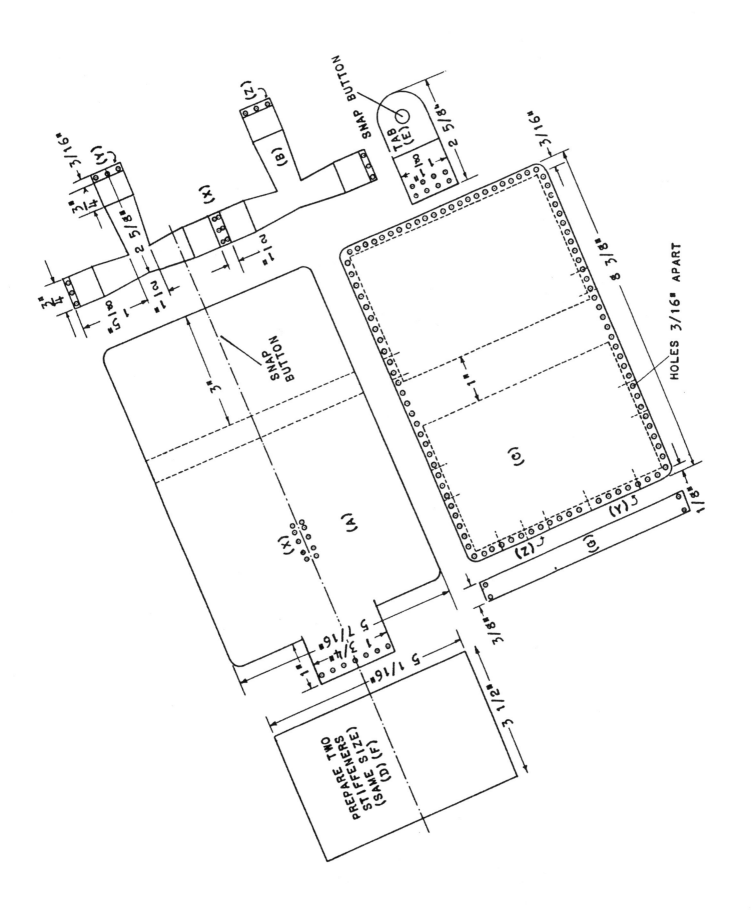

SNAP BUTTON

TAB (E)

SNAP BUTTON

3/16"

(Y)

3"/4

2 5/8"

3"/4

1/8"

1/2

1/2

(Z)

(B)

(X)

1"/2

3"

SNAP BUTTON

(A)

(X)

5 7/16"

3"/4

1"

5 7/16"

3/8"

3 1/2"

PREPARE TWO STIFFENERS (SAME SIZE)
(D) (F)

2 5/8"

3/16"

8 3/8"

1"

(C)

(Z)

(Y)

(G)

1/8"

HOLES 3/16" APART

Card and Score Case

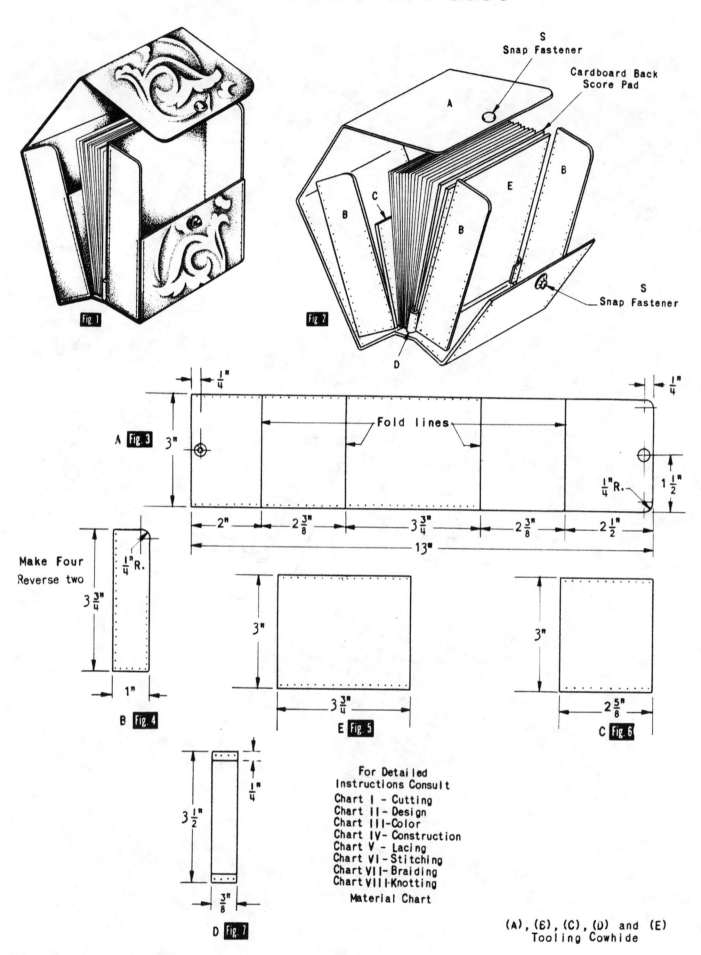

S
Snap Fastener

Cardboard Back
Score Pad

A

B

C

B

E

B

D

S
Snap Fastener

Fig. 1

Fig. 2

Fold lines

A Fig. 3

3"

1"
4

1"
4

1 1"
2

1"
4 R.

2"

2 3"
8

3 3"
4

2 3"
8

2 1"
2

13"

Make Four
Reverse two

1"
4 R.

3 3"
4

1"

B Fig. 4

3"

3 3"
4

E Fig. 5

3"

2 5"
8

C Fig. 6

1"
4

3 1"
2

3"
8

D Fig. 7

For Detailed
Instructions Consult
Chart I - Cutting
Chart II- Design
Chart III-Color
Chart IV- Construction
Chart V - Lacing
Chart VI- Stitching
Chart VII- Braiding
Chart VIII-Knotting
Material Chart

(A), (B), (C), (D) and (E)
Tooling Cowhide

PROCEDURE: (CONSULT LEATHER CRAFT PROCESSING CHARTS)

1. Cut and prepare parts (A),(B),(C),(D) and (E). Figs. 3, 4, 5, 6, 7.

2. Outline edges of all parts with edge creaser. Figs. 3, 4, 5, 6, 7.

3. Mark 1/7" stitching holes on following, using creased line as guide: vertical edges of (C) and matching edges of parts (B); long straight edges of (B) and matching edges of (A) and (E); vertical edges of front compartment (A) and matching edges of parts (B). Figs. 2, 3, 4, 5, 6.

4. Punch all stitching holes with awl as marked, simultaneously when possible. Include ends of (D) in punching holes through (B) and (E). Figs. 2, 4, 5, 7.

5. Sew parts with saddler's stitch in following sequence: (E) and (D) to parts (B); (C) to parts (B). Fig. 2.

6. Punch with awl closely spaced stitching holes in matching edges of (A) and square ends of parts (B). Figs. 2, 3, 4.

7. Attach snap fastener (S) to (A). Figs. 2, 3.

8. Complete assembly by sewing edges of (A) to matching edges of (BDE) and (BC). Fig. 2.

MATERIALS:

Tooling cowhide

Snap fastener

Linen thread

TOOLS:

(1),(6),(8),(12),(17), (25),(27),(28),(41).

Double-Deck Card Case

Fig. 1

B   Fig. 4

1"R.

1"

3 3/4"

Make two, one reversed

Fig. 2

SCORE

1"

3 5/8"

1/4"

F   Fig. 5

1/4"

1 3/4"

D   Fig. 6

C

B

A

E

Fig. 3

D

F

All Leather Parts Calfskin

**For Detailed
Instructions Consult**

Chart I - Cutting
Chart II - Design
Chart III - Color
Chart IV - Construction
Chart V - Lacing
Chart VI - Stitching
Chart VII - Braiding
Chart VIII - Knotting

Material Chart

3 1/2"

2 5/8"

3/4"

1 1/2"   6 3/4"

2 5/8"

**Fold
lines**

C   Fig. 7

11 7/8"

3 11/16"   1"   3 3/4"   1"   2 7/16"

1 1/4"

**Fold
lines**

**Center part
(D) here**

**Fold
lines**

5 3/4"

3/4"

3 1/2"

5/8"

1"

E   Fig. 8

**Center part
(E) here**

A   Fig. 9

Figs. 7, 8, 9 are drawn proportionately two-thirds size of other details.

296

PROCEDURE: (CONSULT LEATHER CRAFT PROCESSING CHARTS)

1. Cut parts (A), (B), (C), (D), (E) and (F). Figs. 4, 5, 6, 7, 8, 9.

2. Mark all fold lines on (A) and (C) and outline all unstitched edges with edge creaser. Figs. 3, 7, 9.

3. Place (D), (E) and (F) in position on (A). Punch closely spaced stitching holes 1/8" from edges of (D), (E) and (F) through matching parts of (A) as shown. Figs. 3, 5, 6, 8, 9.

4. Sew (D), (E) and (F) to (A) with saddler's stitch. Fig. 2.

5. Fold (C) on center fold, flesh sides together. Cement fold to form partition 5/8" high. Cut one end of fold to correspond to curved end of (B). Figs. 3, 7.

6. Mark stitching holes with 1/7" spacing wheel at bottom of partition fold in (C). Fig. 3.

7. Punch stitching holes with awl as marked. Fig. 3.

8. Sew fold with saddler's stitch. Fig. 3.

9. Cement (C) to flesh side of (A). Fig. 3.

10. Mark stitching lines with edge creaser on edges of (A) and (B) to be stitched together. Fig. 3.

11. Mark stitching holes with 1/7" spacing wheel on guide lines of (A). Mark corresponding holes on matching edges of (B). Fig. 3.

12. Punch stitching holes with awl in (A) and (B). Fig. 3.

13. Sew (B) to (A) with saddler's stitch. Figs. 1, 2, 3.

MATERIALS:

Calfskin, 3-1/2 oz.

Linen thread

Rubber cement

TOOLS:

(1), (6), (25), (27), (28), (41)

Double-Deck Card Holder

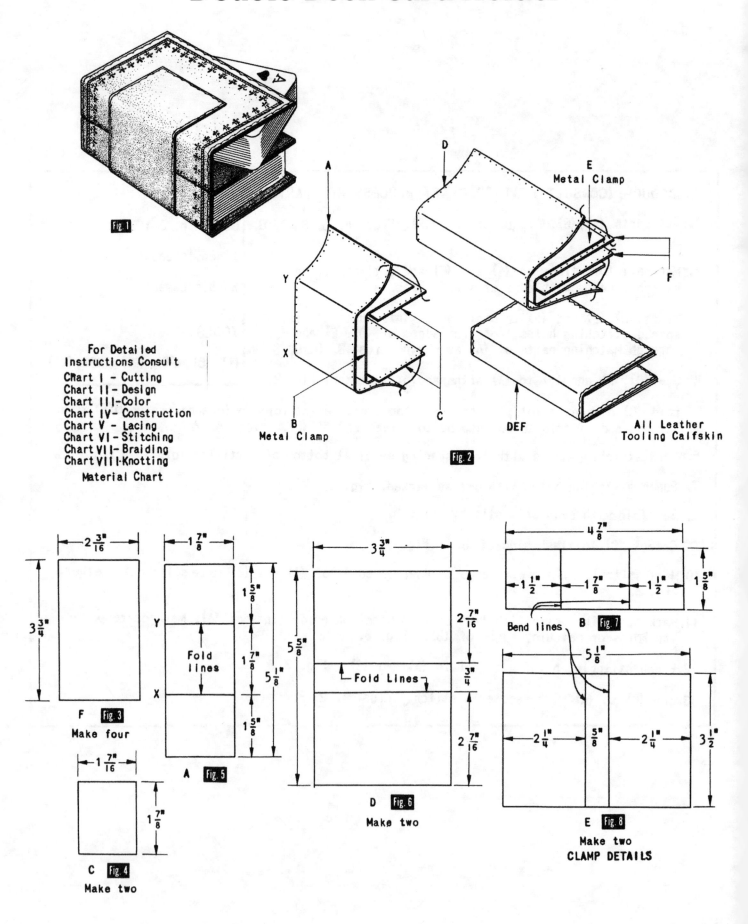

Fig. 1

For Detailed
Instructions Consult
Chart I – Cutting
Chart II – Design
Chart III – Color
Chart IV – Construction
Chart V – Lacing
Chart VI – Stitching
Chart VII – Braiding
Chart VIII – Knotting
    Material Chart

Metal Clamp

A

Y

X

B
Metal Clamp

C

D

E
Metal Clamp

F

DEF

All Leather
Tooling Calfskin

Fig. 2

F   Fig. 3
Make four

C   Fig. 4
Make two

A   Fig. 5

Fold
lines

D   Fig. 6
Make two

Fold Lines

Bend lines   B   Fig. 7

Bend lines

E   Fig. 8
Make two
CLAMP DETAILS

PROCEDURE: (CONSULT LEATHER CRAFT PROCESSING CHARTS)

MATERIALS:

Higgins colored inks

Tooling calfskin, 2 – 2-1/2 oz., natural

Heavy linen thread

TOOLS:

(1), (6), (15-1), (17), (25), (27), (28), (38-16), (41).

See Leather Chart III for painting procedure and tools.

1. Cut and prepare parts (A), (C), (D) and (F). Figs. 3, 4, 5, 6.

   Note: Construct 3 metal clamps (E) and (B) of light gauge spring steel (.015").

2. Outline all edges with edge creaser. Figs. 3, 4, 5, 6.

3. Mark stitching holes with 1/7" spacing wheel on all edges to be stitched. Fig. 2.

4. Place parts (C) in position on (A), flesh sides together. Figs. 2, 4, 5.

5. Punch stitching holes with awl through (A) and (C) simultaneously; also punch holes in edges of (A) that cover back of clamp (B). Fig. 2.

6. Saddle stitch edge of (A) from point (X) to (Y); continue stitching edges of top (C) to (A); finish stitching edge of (A) opposite (XY). Do not terminate threads. Fig. 2.

7. Insert (B) in (AC). Place free end of (A) and bottom (C) in position on (B). Fig. 2.

8. Continue stitching bottom (C) to (A) enclosing (B). Fig. 2.

9. Repeat steps (4) through (8) to complete assembling parts (D) and (F) with clamp (E). Figs. 2, 3, 6.

10. Insert parts (DEF) within (ABC). Fig. 1.

Picture Frame

Mark Finfer

PROCEDURE:	TOOLS:
HAVING PREPARED THE SEVEN SEPARATE PARTS...	(6) (1) (4) (2) (16)

PROCEDURE:
HAVING PREPARED THE SEVEN SEPARATE PARTS...
1. CEMENT (B) AND (C), USING BUCKRAM OR
   CARDBOARD STIFFENERS, TO FLESH SIDE OF
   (A), AS INDICATED BY DOTTED LINES.
2. CEMENT (E) OVER (C).
3. CEMENT (D) OVER (B), SMOOTH OUT WRINKLES.
4. CEMENT EDGES X,Y,Z OF (F) TO EDGES X,Y,Z
   OF (E).
5. SLIGHTLY ROUND THE CORNERS--MAKE 3/32"
   THONG SLITS 1/8" IN FROM EDGES AND LACE.
6. INSERT CELLULOID WINDOW (G)

TOOLS:

(6) (1) (4) (2) (16)

MATERIALS:

CONSULT LEATHER CHARTS
CARDBOARD
CELLULOID
AND RUBBER CEMENT

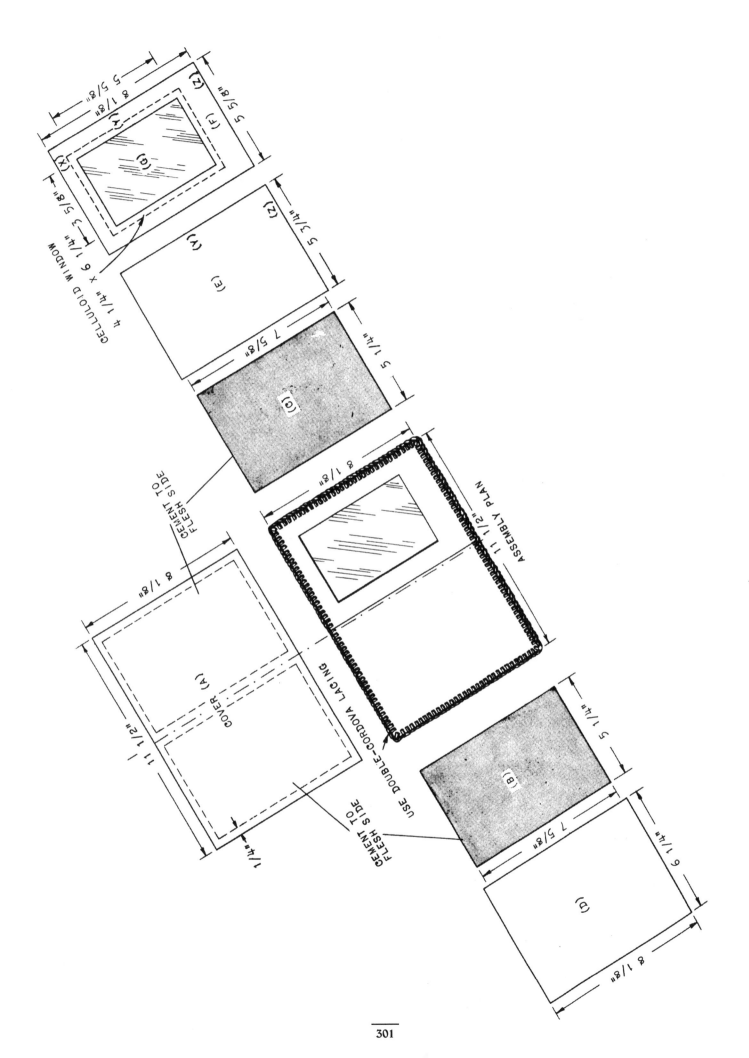

5 5/8"

8 1/8"

(Z)

(F)

(G)

5 5/8"

(X)

6 1/4" x 3 5/8"

CELLULOID WINDOW

(Y)

5 3/4"

(E)

(Z)

7 5/8"

5 1/4"

(C)

CEMENT TO FLESH SIDE

8 1/8"

11 1/2"

ASSEMBLY PLAN

8 1/8"

COVER (A)

11 1/2"

1/4"

USE DOUBLE-CORDOVA LACING

CEMENT TO FLESH SIDE

5 1/4"

(B)

7 5/8"

6 1/4"

(D)

8 1/8"

Picture Frame

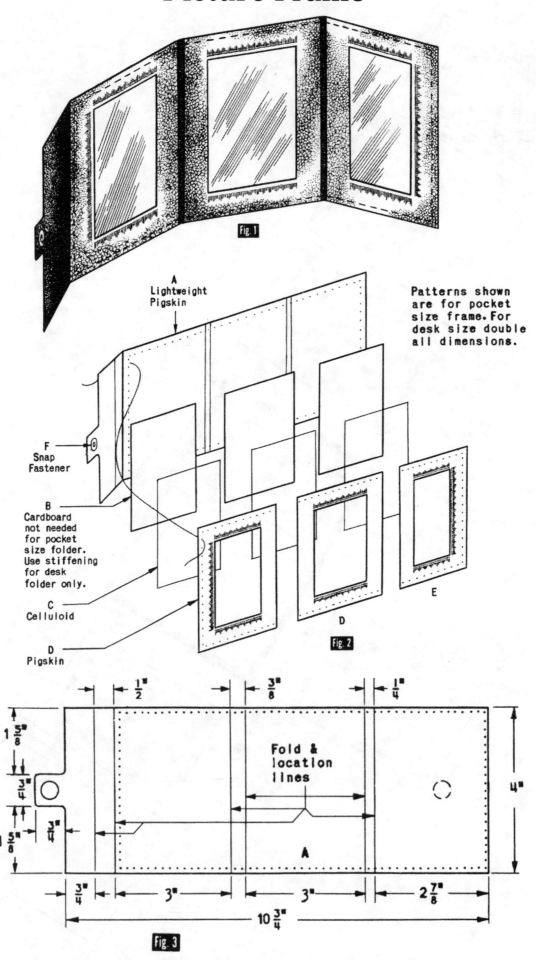

Fig. 1

A
Lightweight
Pigskin

Patterns shown
are for pocket
size frame. For
desk size double
all dimensions.

F
Snap
Fastener

B

Cardboard
not needed
for pocket
size folder.
Use stiffening
for desk
folder only.

C
Celluloid

D
Pigskin

D

E

Fig. 2

Fold &
location
lines

A

$\frac{1}{2}$" $\frac{3}{8}$" $\frac{1}{4}$"

$1\frac{5}{8}$" $\frac{3}{4}$" $1\frac{5}{8}$" $\frac{1}{4}$"

4"

$\frac{3}{4}$" 3" 3" $2\frac{7}{8}$"

$10\frac{3}{4}$"

Fig. 3

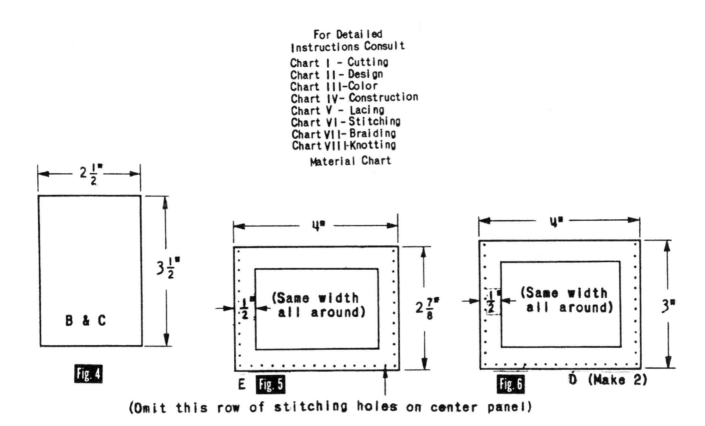

For Detailed
Instructions Consult
Chart I – Cutting
Chart II – Design
Chart III – Color
Chart IV – Construction
Chart V – Lacing
Chart VI – Stitching
Chart VII – Braiding
Chart VIII – Knotting
Material Chart

2 1/2"

3 1/2"

B & C

Fig. 4

4"

(Same width all around)

2 7/8"

1/2

E Fig. 5

4"

(Same width all around)

3"

1/2

Fig. 6   D (Make 2)

(Omit this row of stitching holes on center panel)

PROCEDURE: (CONSULT LEATHER CRAFT PROCESSING CHARTS)

1. Cut and prepare parts (A), (C), (D), (E). Figs. 3, 4, 5, 6.

2. Crease along folding lines of (A) with edge creaser. Fig. 3.

3. Attach cap of snap fastener (F) to tab of (A). Figs. 2, 3. (Fold (A) to determine position of post of snap fastener. Insert post.)

4. Cement parts (D) and part (E) to part (A), $\frac{3}{16}$" along all edges to be stitched. Fig. 2.

5. With spacing wheel mark stitching holes $\frac{1}{7}$" apart on all cemented edges. Fig. 2.

6. With awl, punch stitching holes. Figs. 2, 3, 5, 6.

7. Sew with saddle stitch. Figs. 1, 2.

8. Insert (C) through side openings of sectional frames.

MATERIALS:

Light weight pigskin (toolable)

Celluloid

Snap fastener, $\frac{7}{16}$" dia.

Heavy linen thread

Rubber cement

Cardboard (desk model only)

TOOLS:

(1), (5), (6), (12), (21), (25), (41), (43), (15 No. 4).

Photo Album

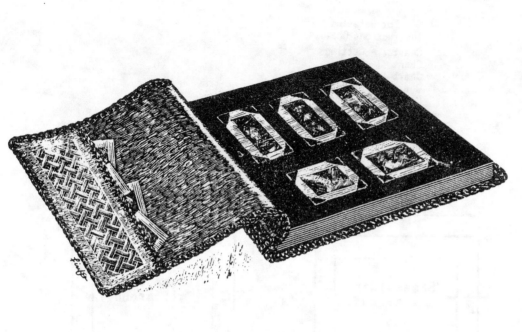

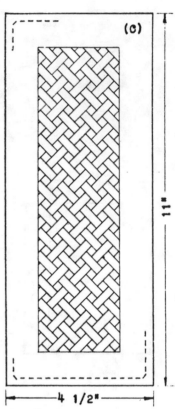

(C)

11"

4 1/2"

PROCEDURE:
HAVING PREPARED TWO EACH OF (A)(B)(C)...
(1) TOOL OR CARVE DESIGN AS SHOWN.
(2) CEMENT (B) TO BACK OF (A)
(3) PUNCH 1/8" THONG SLITS 3/16" FROM
    EDGES OF ALL PIECES (A)(B)(C)
(4) LACE OPEN EDGE OF (C), CEMENT TO END
    OF (A) REVERSE SIDE - SEE ILLUSTRATION.
(5) LACE EDGES OF FRONT AND BACK.
(6) PUNCH TWO 1/4" HOLES IN FRONT AND BACK
    COVER. TIE WITH FOUR OUNCE STEERHIDE
    3/16" X 36". USE 10" X 13" FILLER.

TOOLS: (1)(4)(6)(8)(9)(13)(17)

MATERIALS: CONSULT LEATHER CHARTS,
           RUBBER CEMENT

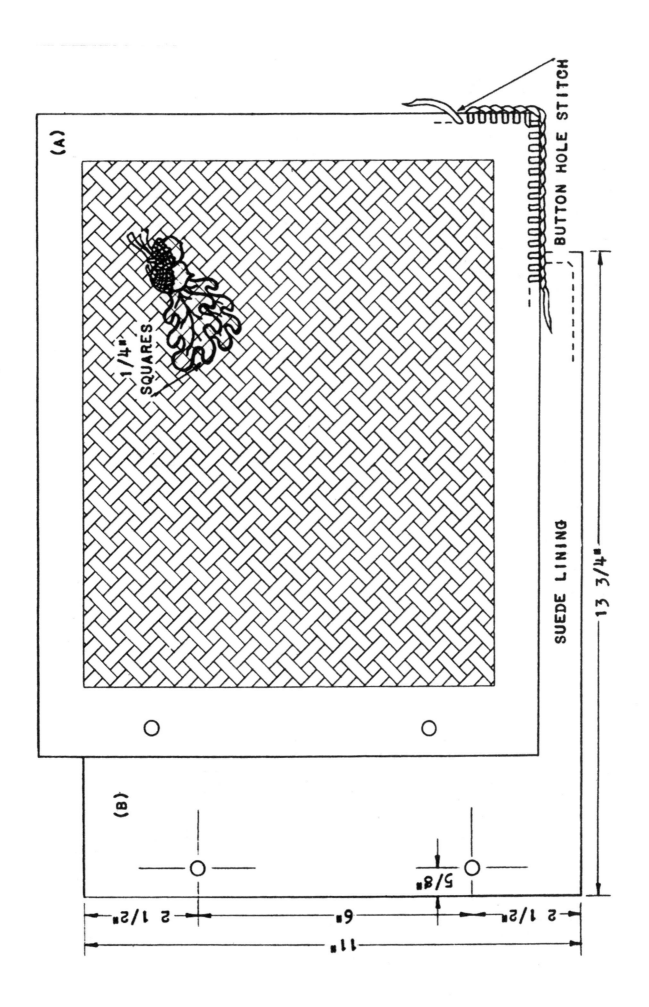

BUTTON HOLE STITCH

(A)

1/4" SQUARES

SUEDE LINING

13 3/4"

(B)

2 1/2"

6"

5/8"

2 1/2"

11"

Photo Frame

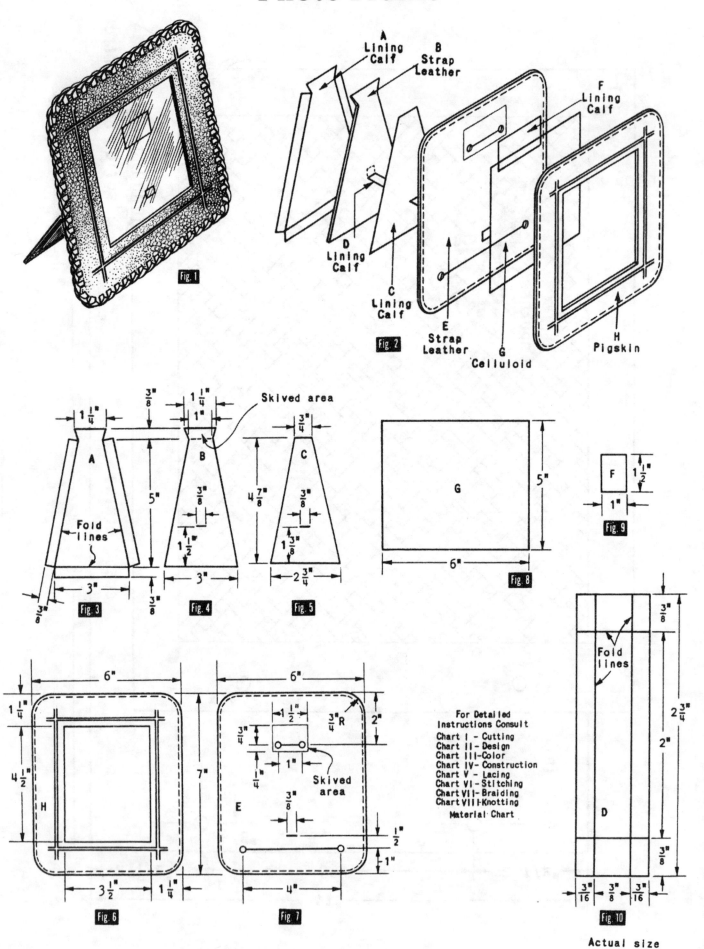

Fig. 1

A — Lining Calf
B — Strap Leather
C — Lining Calf
D — Lining Calf
E — Strap Leather
F — Lining Calf
G — Celluloid
H — Pigskin

Fig. 2

Skived area

Fold lines

Fig. 3
Fig. 4
Fig. 5

Fig. 8

F

Fig. 9

Skived area

Fig. 6
Fig. 7

For Detailed
Instructions Consult
Chart I - Cutting
Chart II - Design
Chart III - Color
Chart IV - Construction
Chart V - Lacing
Chart VI - Stitching
Chart VII - Braiding
Chart VIII - Knotting
Material Chart

Fold lines

D

Fig. 10

Actual size

306

PROCEDURE: (CONSULT LEATHER CRAFT PROCESSING CHARTS)

1. Cut and prepare parts (A), (B), (C), (D), (E), (F), (G), (H), including slits in (B), (C), (E). Figs. 3,4,5,6,7,8,9,10.

2. Fold and cement (D). Fig. 10.

3. With cemented edges underneath, run (D) through (C) and (B) and cement 3/8" tab of (D) to flesh side of (B). Figs. 2, 4, 5.

4. With edge creaser, mark folding lines on (A). Fig. 3.

5. Cement (A) to (B) flesh sides together. Fold over edges of (A) and cement to skin side of (B). Fig. 2.

6. Cement (C) to skin side of (B) to cover edges of (A). Fig. 2.

7. On flesh side of (E) skive bed for tab of (AB) where shown. Fig. 7.

8. Taper tab of (AB) (exposed by (C)) by skiving. Fig. 4.

9. Insert tab of (AB) into slit in (E) and cement against skived bed. Fig. 2.

10. Run (D) through (E) and cement 3/8" tab of (D) to flesh side of (E). Fig. 2.

11. Cement (F) to (E) flesh sides facing. Fig. 2.

12. Place flesh sides of (E) and (H) together. With awl punch 3/32" thong slits through (E) and (H). Figs. 6, 7.

13. Lace (E) to (H) with triple overlay stitch. Insert celluloid (G) before lacing bottom edges. Fig. 2.

MATERIALS:

Pigskin

Strap leather

Lining calf, 10 oz.

Celluloid

Goatskin lace 3/32" x 13'

Rubber cement

TOOLS:

(1), (4), (5), (6), (17), (18), (19), (26), (33), (40).

Photo Album Covers

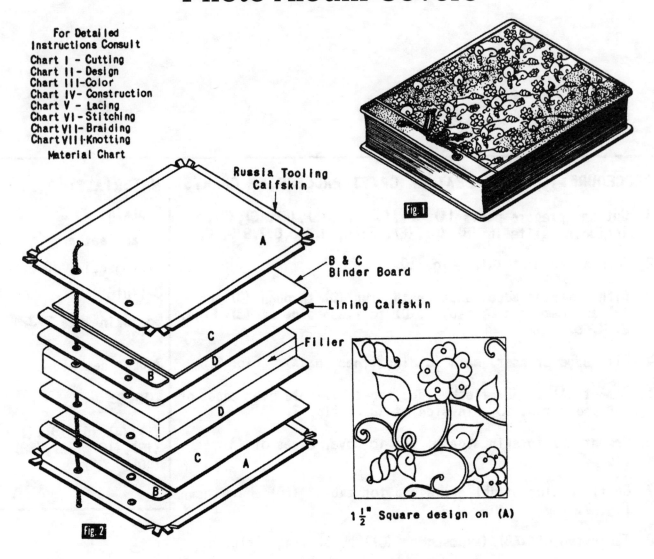

Russia Tooling Calfskin

Fig. 1

A

B & C
Binder Board

Lining Calfskin

Filler

C

D

B

D

C

A

B

Fig. 2

$1\frac{1}{2}"$ Square design on (A)

PROCEDURE: (CONSULT LEATHER CRAFT PROCESSING CHARTS)

1. Cut and prepare parts (A), (B), (C) and (D). Figs. 3, 4, 5, 6.

2. Cement (B) and (C) to flesh side of (A) leaving 1/4" space between (B) and (C). Fig. 2.

3. Fold over edges of (A); cement to (B). Fig. 2.

4. Cement flesh side of (D) to (ABC). Fig. 2.

5. Punch holes for eyelets through (ABCD) with drive punch. Figs. 2, 5, 6.

6. Insert eyelets. Fig. 2.

7. Braid a 4-plait round diamond pattern cord from craft strip. Fig. 2. and Leather Chart VII.

8. Insert cord through eyelets. Figs. 1, 2.

MATERIALS:

Russia tooling calfskin, 2 oz.

Lining calfskin

4 – Eyelets, No. 6K

Craft strip, 3/32", brown

Hard-rolled binder board

Pliobond plastic adhesive

TOOLS:

(1), (3-No. 7), (6), (14), (20)

See Leather Chart VII for braiding

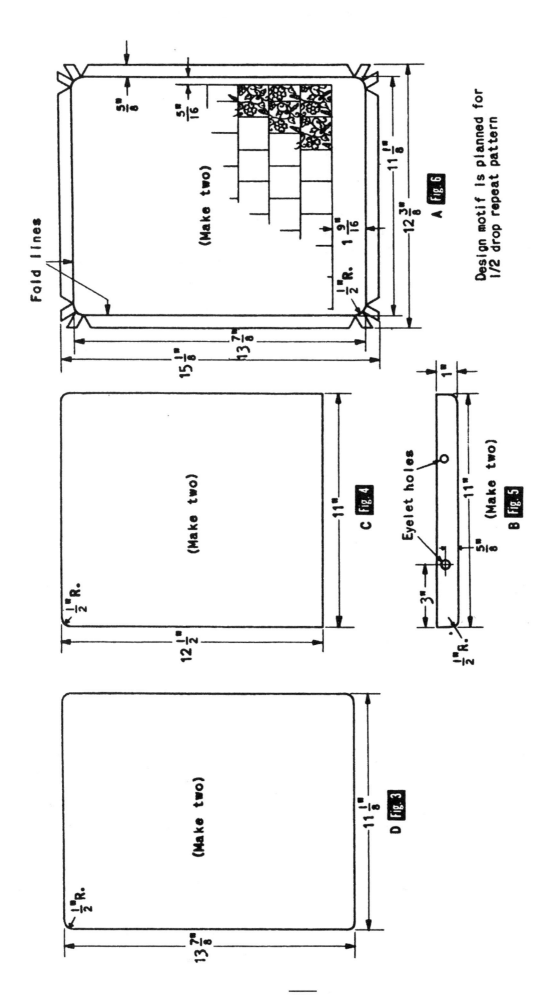

Fold lines

(Make two)

$\frac{5"}{8}$

$\frac{5"}{16}$

$1\frac{9"}{16}$

$\frac{1"}{2}$ R.

$11\frac{1"}{8}$

$12\frac{3"}{8}$

A **Fig. 6**

Design motif is planned for
1/2 drop repeat pattern

$15\frac{1"}{8}$

$13\frac{7"}{8}$

(Make two)

$\frac{1"}{2}$ R.

$11"$

$12\frac{1"}{2}$

C **Fig. 4**

Eyelet holes

$1"$

$11"$

$\frac{5"}{8}$

$3"$

$\frac{1"}{2}$ R.

(Make two)

B **Fig. 5**

(Make two)

$\frac{1"}{2}$ R.

$11\frac{1"}{8}$

$13\frac{7"}{8}$

D **Fig. 3**

Photo Book Ends

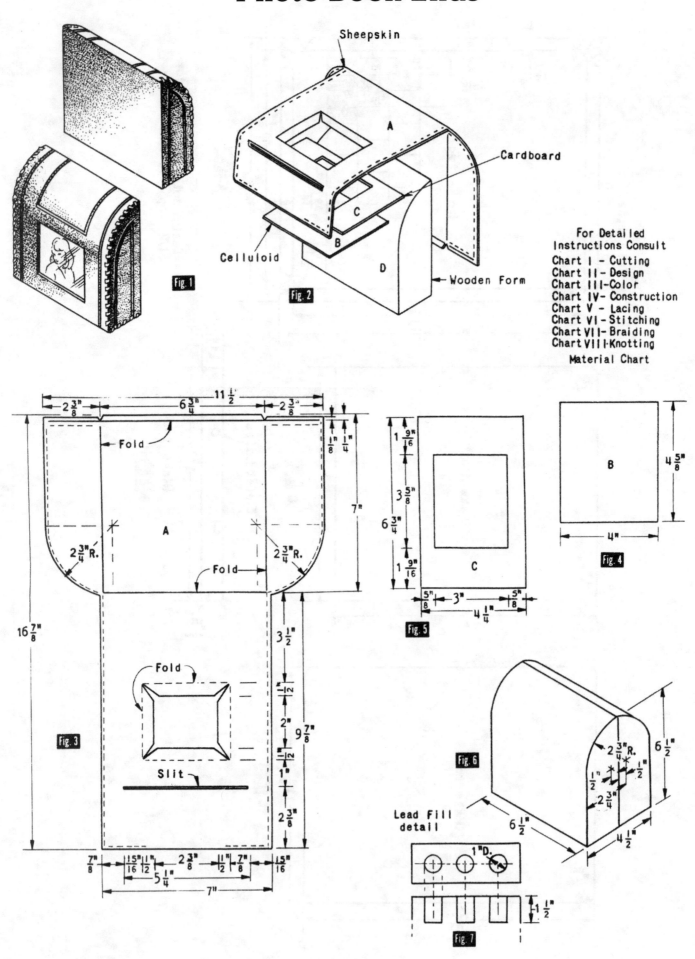

Sheepskin

A

Cardboard

C

B

Celluloid

D

Wooden Form

Fig. 1

Fig. 2

For Detailed
Instructions Consult
Chart I – Cutting
Chart II – Design
Chart III – Color
Chart IV – Construction
Chart V – Lacing
Chart VI – Stitching
Chart VII – Braiding
Chart VIII – Knotting
Material Chart

Fold

7"

Fold

$2\frac{3}{4}$" R.

A

$2\frac{3}{4}$" R.

Fold

Slit

Fig. 3

$16\frac{7}{8}$"

$3\frac{1}{2}$"

$9\frac{7}{8}$"

$2\frac{3}{8}$"

$2\frac{3}{8}$" $6\frac{3}{4}$" $2\frac{3}{8}$" $11\frac{1}{2}$"

Fig. 5

C

$6\frac{3}{4}$"

$1\frac{9}{16}$

$3\frac{5}{8}$

$1\frac{9}{16}$

$\frac{5}{8}$" 3" $\frac{5}{8}$"

$4\frac{1}{4}$"

Fig. 4

B

$4\frac{5}{8}$"

4"

Fig. 6

$2\frac{3}{4}$" R.

$6\frac{1}{2}$"

$6\frac{1}{2}$"

$4\frac{1}{2}$"

Lead Fill
detail

1"D.

$1\frac{1}{2}$"

Fig. 7

310

PROCEDURE: (CONSULT LEATHER CRAFT PROCESSING CHARTS)

1. Cut and prepare parts (A),(B), and (C). Figs. 3, 4, 5.

   Note: Construct weighted wooden forms.

2. Mark all fold lines in (A) with edge creaser. Fig. 3.

3. Cement cardboard (C) to flesh side of (A). Figs. 2, 3.

4. Turn down flap edges of photo cutout of (A) and cement to (C). Figs. 2, 3.

5. Mark guide line for thong slits 1/8" from edges of (A) to be laced. Fig. 3.

6. Punch matching thong slits with awl on guide lines of (A).

7. Lace front edges of (A) with whip stitch. Do not terminate thongs at bottom corners. Fig. 2.

8. Slip (A) over wooden form (D). Cement back bottom 1/4" flap of (A) to back bottom edge of (D). Then cement bottom piece of (A) to bottom of (D) leaving slit in (A) open for insertion of photo. Fig. 2.

9. Finish lacing bottom side edges. Fig. 2.

10. Insert celluloid (B) in slot. Fig. 2.

MATERIALS:

Pinseal tooling sheepskin

Cardboard, lightweight

Celluloid

Calfskin lace, 3/32", 6'

Rubber cement

TOOLS:

(1), (4), (5), (6), (9), (18), (40).

Easel Picture Frame

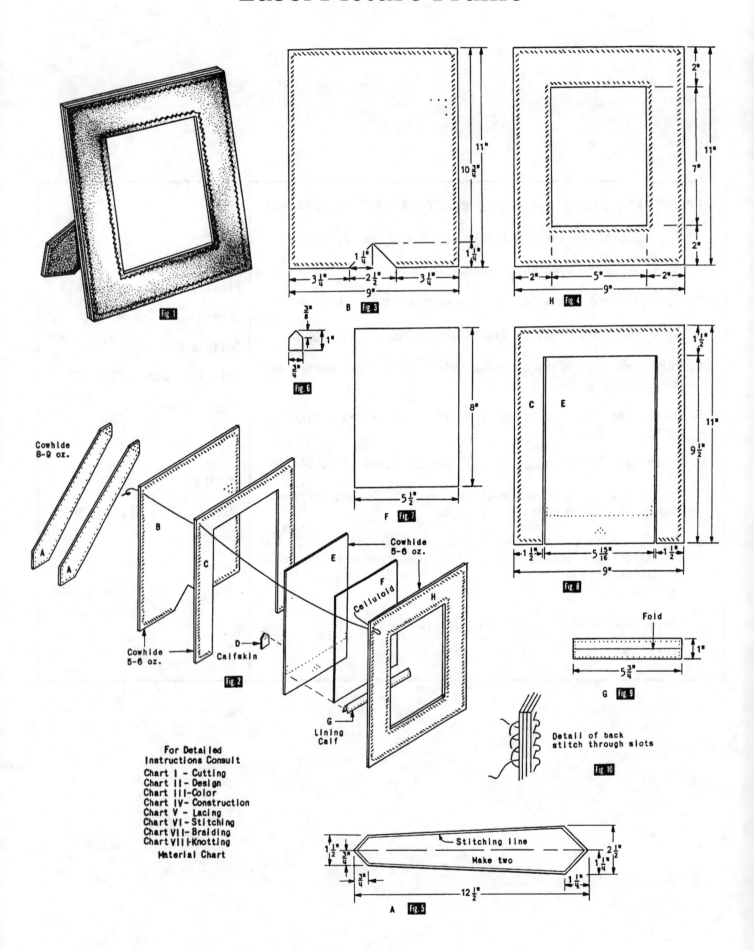

Fig. 1

Fig. 3   B

Fig. 4   H

Fig. 6

Fig. 7   F

Fig. 8

Cowhide
8-9 oz.

Cowhide
5-6 oz.

Cowhide
5-6 oz.

Calfskin

Lining
Calf

Celluloid

Fig. 2

Fold

G   Fig. 9

Detail of back
stitch through slots

Fig. 10

For Detailed
Instructions Consult
Chart I – Cutting
Chart II – Design
Chart III – Color
Chart IV – Construction
Chart V – Lacing
Chart VI – Stitching
Chart VII – Braiding
Chart VIII – Knotting
Material Chart

Stitching line

Make two

A   Fig. 5

PROCEDURE:(CONSULT LEATHER CRAFT PROCESSING CHARTS)

1. Cut parts (A), (B), (C), (D), (E), (F), (G) and (H). Figs. 3, 4, 5, 6, 7, 8, 9.

2. Skive flesh side of triangular area only of parts (A) to be attached to (B). (Skive so that 2 thickness of (A) will equal 1 thickness of original leather.) Figs. 2, 5.

3. Cement (A) to (A), flesh sides together, and triangular area only of (D) to (E). Figs. 2, 6, 8.

4. Mark stitching lines with edge creaser around all edges of (AA). Fig. 5.

5. Mark stitching holes on crease line of (AA) with 1/7" spacing wheel. Fig. 2.

6. Punch stitching holes with awl in all edges of (AA) not to be attached to (B). Fig. 2.

7. Sew edges of (AA) with saddler's stitch. Fig. 2.

8. Cement triangular area of (AA) to (B). Figs. 2, 3.

9. Punch stitching holes with awl through cemented area of (AA) and (B). Figs. 2, 3.

10. Sew (AA) to (B) with saddler's stitch. Fig. 2.

11. Skive flesh side of (B) to match area of (E). (Skive sufficient depth for insertion of photo and celluloid). Fig. 2.

12. Fold and cement (G). Fig. 9.

13. Cement 1/8" along cut edges of (G) to (E). Figs. 2, 8, 9.

14. Mark stitching holes with 1/7" spacing wheel, 1/8" from cut edges of (G), and triangle of (D) on (E). Fig. 2.

15. Punch stitching holes through (G) and (D) on (E). Fig. 2.

16. Sew (G) to (E) with saddle stitch and (D) to (E) with saddler's stitch. Fig. 2.

17. Mark stitching guide line 1/8" from inner and outer edges of (H). Figs. 2, 4.

18. Punch 3/32" thong slits, 1/4" apart, at 45° angle to guide line, along inner edge of (H). Fig. 4.

19. Sew inner edge with variation of back stitch. Figs. 1, 2, 4, 10.

20. Cement (C) to flesh side of (H). Fig. 2.

21. Cement (CH) to flesh side of (AB). Fig. 2.

22. Repeat steps (18) and (19) on outer edge of assembled parts. Figs. 1, 2, 4.

23. Insert photo and celluloid (F) in pocket between (G) and (E). Then insert (E) in space cut out of (C). Fig. 2.

24. Sandpaper to smoothness all raw edges of leather with No. 00 sandpaper. Figs. 1, 2.

25. Apply beeswax to cut edges and rub until glossy. Fig. 1.

MATERIALS:

Cowhide, 8-9 oz.

Cowhide, 5-6 oz.

Calfskin (scrap), 2 oz.

Lining calf, 1 oz.

Celluloid

Heavy linen thread

Casco flexible cement

TOOLS:

(1), (6), (17), (19), (27), (28), (40), (41).

Five-View Photo Frame

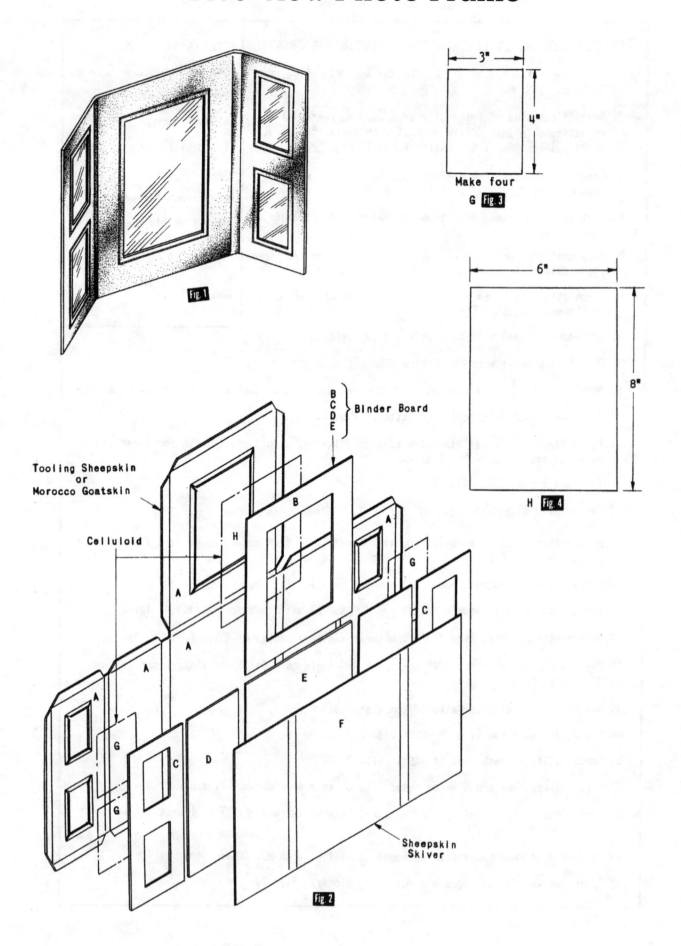

Fig. 1

3"
4"
Make four
G Fig. 3

6"
8"
H Fig. 4

B C D E } Binder Board

Tooling Sheepskin
or
Morocco Goatskin

Celluloid

A B A

H

A

A

A

G

C

E

F

G

C D

G

Sheepskin
Skiver

Fig. 2

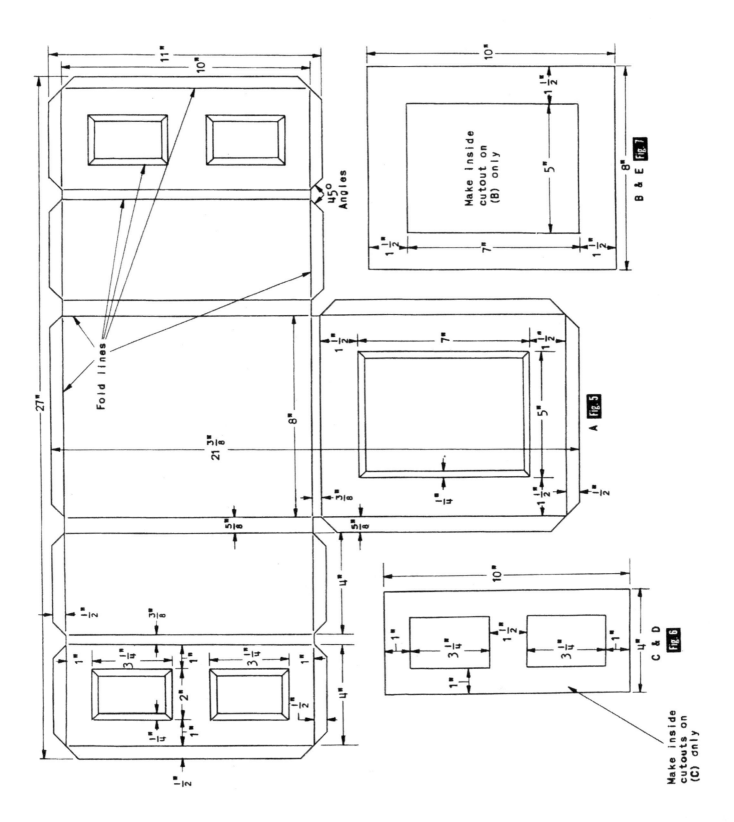

11"

10"

45°
Angles

Fold lines

27"

21 3/8"

8"

5/8"

5/8"

4"

1/2"

3/8"

1"

3 1/4"

1"

3 1/4"

2"

1"

1/2"

1 1/4"

1"

4"

1/2"

10"

Make inside
cutout on
(B) only

5"

7"

1/2"

1/2"

1/2"

8"

B & E **Fig. 7**

1/2"

7"

1 1/2"

5"

3/8"

1 1/4"

1 1/2"

1 1/2"

1/2"

A **Fig. 5**

10"

1"

3 1/4"

1 1/2"

3 1/4"

1"

1"

1"

4"

C & D **Fig. 6**

Make inside
cutouts on
(C) only

315

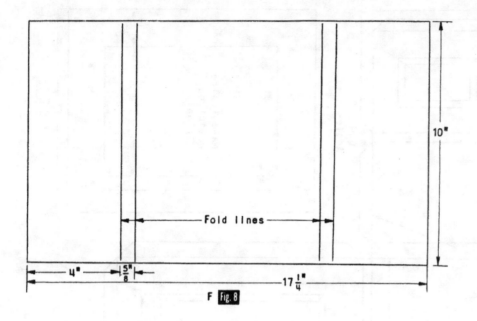

10"

Fold lines

4" | 5/8" | 17 1/4"

F Fig. 8

For Detailed
Instructions Consult
Chart I - Cutting
Chart II - Design
Chart III - Color
Chart IV - Construction
Chart V - Lacing
Chart VI - Stitching
Chart VII - Braiding
Chart VIII - Knotting
Material Chart

PROCEDURE: (CONSULT LEATHER CRAFT PROCESSING CHARTS)

1. Cut and prepare parts (A), (B), (C), (D), (E), (F), (G) and (H). Figs. 3, 4, 5, 6, 7, 8.

2. Skive all edges to be cemented. Fig. 2.

3. Mark all fold lines in (A) and (F) with edge creaser. Figs. 5, 8.

4. Cement parts (B), (C), (D) and (E) to flesh side of (A). Fig. 2.

5. Fold back all flap edges of (A) on (B), (C) and (D). Fig. 2.

6. Cement (F) over parts (D) and (E) on (A). Fig. 2.

7. Fold back and cement (AC) on (ADF); (AB) on (AEF). Leave inside edges uncemented for insertion of celluloid (G) and (H) and photos as shown. Fig. 2.

8. Insert parts (G) and (H). Fig. 2.

MATERIALS:

Tooling sheepskin or Morocco goatskin, 1 oz.

Binder board .062"

Sheepskin skiver

Celluloid

Rubber cement

TOOLS:

(1), (6), (15-6), (19).

316

Woman's Saddle Purse

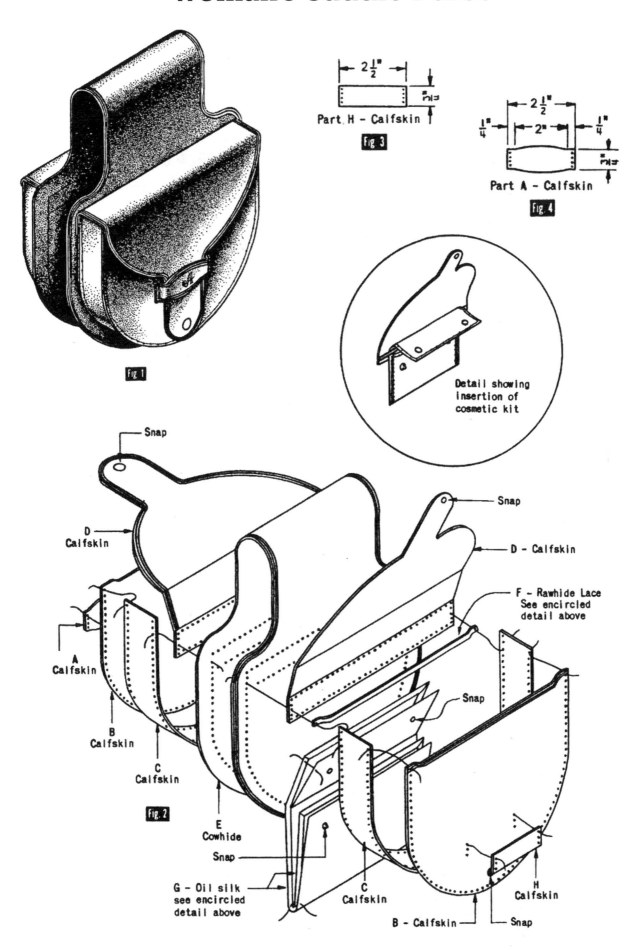

Part H — Calfskin

Fig 3

Part A — Calfskin

Fig. 4

Detail showing insertion of cosmetic kit

Snap

D Calfskin

Snap

D — Calfskin

F — Rawhide Lace See encircled detail above

A Calfskin

B Calfskin

C Calfskin

Snap

Fig. 2

E Cowhide

Snap

G — Oil silk see encircled detail above

C Calfskin

H Calfskin

B — Calfskin

Snap

Fig 1

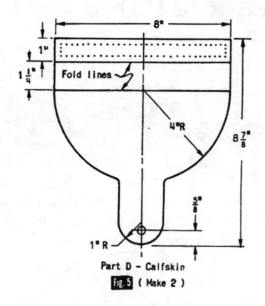

8"

1"

1¼"

Fold lines

4"R

8⅞"

⅝"

1"R

Part D – Calfskin

Fig. 5 (Make 2)

For Detailed
Instructions Consult
Chart I – Cutting
Chart II– Design
Chart III–Color
Chart IV– Construction
Chart V – Lacing
Chart VI– Stitching
Chart VII– Braiding
Chart VIII–Knotting
Material Chart

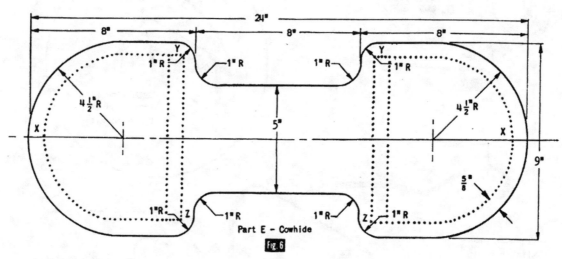

24"

8"

8"

8"

Y

1"R

1"R

1"R

Y

1"R

4½"R

4½"R

5"

X

X

9"

1"R

Z

1"R

1"R

Z

1"R

⅝"

Part E – Cowhide

Fig. 6

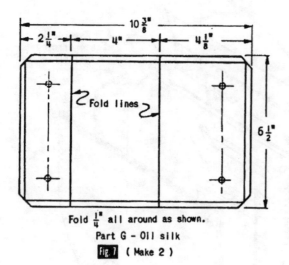

10⅜"

2¼"

4"

4⅛"

Fold lines

6½"

Fold ¼" all around as shown.

Part G – Oil silk

Fig. 7 (Make 2)

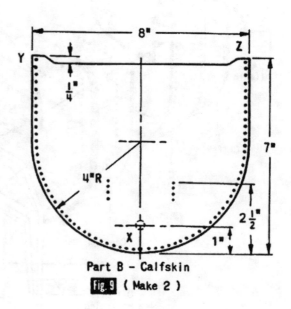

8"

Y

Z

¼"

7"

4"R

2½"

X

1"

Part B – Calfskin

Fig. 9 (Make 2)

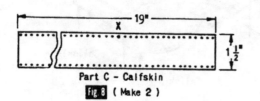

19"

X

1½"

Part C – Calfskin

Fig. 8 (Make 2)

318

PROCEDURE: (CONSULT LEATHER CRAFT PROCESSING CHARTS)

MATERIALS:

Case cowhide, 5 oz., natural

Heavy calf, 3 oz., natural

Oil silk

4 snap fasteners

Heavy linen thread

Rubber cement

Rawhide lace, $\frac{3"}{16}$ 8" long

TOOLS:

(1), (5), (6), (8), (12), (17), (22), (25), (27), (28), (41), (43).

1. Cut and prepare parts (A), (B), (C), (D), (E), (G) and (H). Figs. 3, 4, 5, 6, 7, 8, 9.

2. With double edge creaser, crease all edges of (A), (D) and (E) and unsewn top edge of (B). Figs. 1, 2.

3. Place (A) and (H) in positions on (B). With awl, punch stitching holes $\frac{1"}{8}$ apart, $\frac{1"}{8}$ from ends of (A) and (H) simultaneously through matching parts of (A), (H) and (B). Figs. 2, 3, 4, 9.

4. Sew (A) and (H) to (B) with saddler's stitch. Fig. 2.

5. Attach cap of snap fastener to tab of (D), and post and spring of snap to (B). Figs. 2, 5, 9.

6. With edge creaser, crease (D) on folding lines. Fig. 5.

7. Cement (D) in position on (E). With $\frac{1"}{7}$ spacing wheel, mark stitching holes $\frac{1"}{4}$ from edges and fold, on flesh side of (D). Figs. 2, 5, 6.

8. With awl, punch stitching holes as marked. Fig. 2.

9. Sew (D) to (E) with saddler's stitch. Fig. 2.

10. With $\frac{1"}{7}$ spacing wheel, mark stitching holes $\frac{1"}{8}$ from edge on long edges of (C). Fig. 8.

11. On section of bag with (H), cement ends of (F) to points on (DE) where (C) will be stitched to (DE). Fig. 2.

12. Place point (X) of (C) on point (X) of (E). Using marked stitching holes on (C) as guide, mark an equal number of holes on matching parts of (E). Mark from points (X) to (Y); then (X) to (Z). Punch stitching holes in (C) and (E). Figs. 2, 6, 8.

13. Sew (C) to (E) with saddler's stitch. Fig. 2.

14. Place point (X) of (C) on point (X) of (B). Using marked stitching holes on (C) as guide, mark an equal number of holes on matching parts of (B). Mark from points (X) to (Y); then (X) to (Z). Punch stitching holes in (C) and (B). Figs. 2, 8, 9.

15. Sew (AB) and (HB) to (CDE) with saddler's stitch. Fig. 2.

16. Turn back all sides of (G). Cement edges. Fig. 7.

17. Place (G) to (G) with cemented edges facing. Sew (G) to (G), $\frac{1"}{8}$ from edge of (G), on sewing machine. Fig. 7.

18. Fold (GG) on folding lines. Figs. 2, 7.

19. Attach snap fasteners to (GG). Figs. 2, 7.

20. Sew folded ends of (GG), $\frac{3"}{16}$ from edge, on sewing machine. Figs. 2, 7.

21. Insert flap of (GG) between (F) and (D). Turn down flap and snap. Fig. 2.

Riding Crop

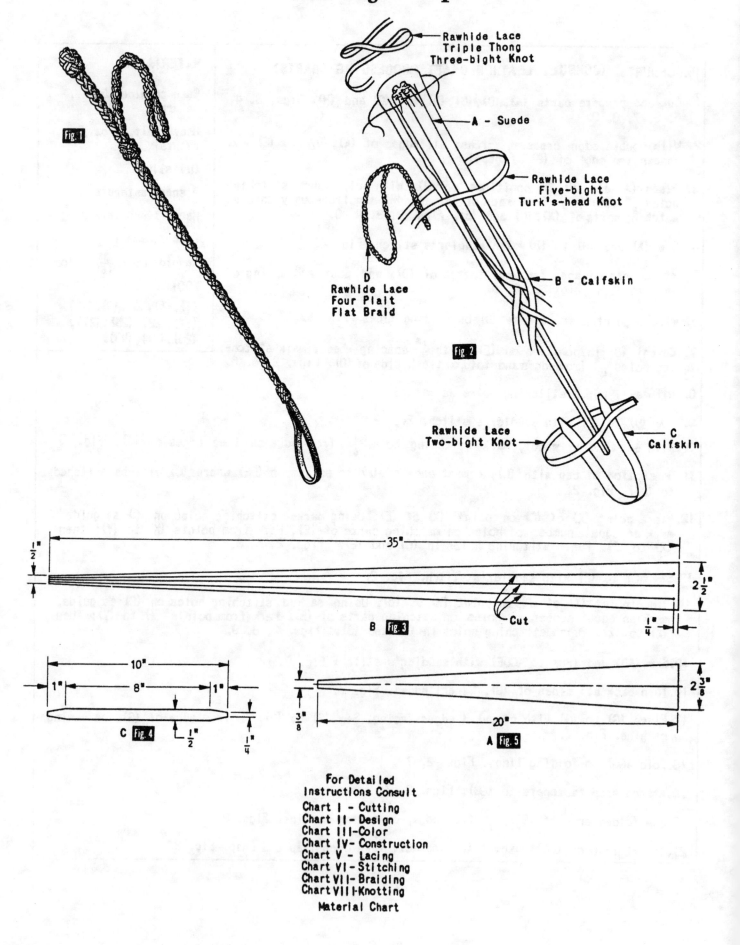

Fig. 1

Rawhide Lace
Triple Thong
Three-bight Knot

A – Suede

Rawhide Lace
Five-bight
Turk's-head Knot

B – Calfskin

D
Rawhide Lace
Four Plait
Flat Braid

Fig. 2

Rawhide Lace
Two-bight Knot

C
Calfskin

35"

½"

2½"

¼"

B Fig. 3

Cut

10"

1"

8"

1"

½"

¼"

C Fig. 4

3/8

2 3/8

20"

A Fig. 5

For Detailed
Instructions Consult
Chart I – Cutting
Chart II – Design
Chart III – Color
Chart IV – Construction
Chart V – Lacing
Chart VI – Stitching
Chart VII – Braiding
Chart VIII – Knotting
Material Chart

PROCEDURE: (CONSULT LEATHER CRAFT PROCESSING CHARTS)

1. Cut parts (A), (B) and (C). Figs. 3, 4, 5.

2. Fold core (A) in half lengthwise, with wrong side out. Place 25" tape or firm cord lengthwise within fold. Sew end of cord between folded edges at pointed end of (A). Fig. 5.

3. Stitch long edges of (A) together on sewing machine, keeping cord away from stitching edge. Fig. 5.

4. Pull cord so that (A) will turn inside out with seam edges inside. Cut away cord at tip of (A). Fig. 2.

5. Fill core (A) with birdshot. Sew up open end of (A) with short running stitch used as drawstring to close (A). Fig. 2.

6. Cement uncut end of (B) around wide end of (A). Tie firmly. Figs. 2, 3.

7. Braid strands of (B) around core (A) with four-plait braid. Fig. 2.

8. End strands of (B) in terminal Turk's-head knot at end of (A). Fig. 2.

9. Fold end strap (C) and cement narrowed ends around tip of (AB) with an overlap of 1". Tie firmly. Figs. 2, 4.

10. Make a two-bight knot, using double thong structure, over junction of (C) on (AB). Fig. 2.

11. Make a four-plait flat braid for hand strap (D). Tie to (AB) with twine. Figs. 1, 2.

12. Make a five-bight Turk's-head knot to cover joint of (D) on (AB). Figs. 1, 2.

13. Make a triple-thong three-bight knot on upper end of (AB). Figs. 1, 2.

MATERIALS:

Suede

Calfskin, 2 oz., natural

1/8" Rawhide lace, natural

Linen thread

Birdshot

Twine

Tape or cord, 25" long

Rubber cement

TOOLS:

(1), (6), (20), (21), (26), (41).

See Leather Charts VII and VIII for braiding and knotting.

Desk Letter Rack

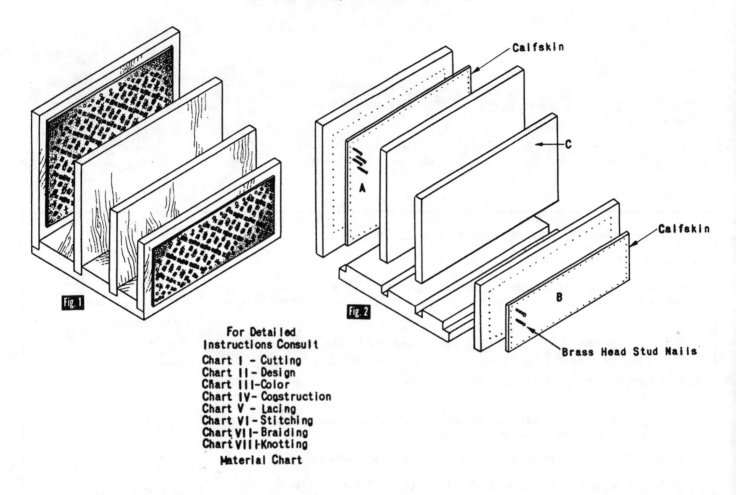

Fig. 1

Fig. 2

Calfskin

C

Calfskin

B

Brass Head Stud Nails

For Detailed
Instructions Consult
Chart I - Cutting
Chart II - Design
Chart III - Color
Chart IV - Construction
Chart V - Lacing
Chart VI - Stitching
Chart VII - Braiding
Chart VIII-Knotting
Material Chart

PROCEDURE: (CONSULT LEATHER CRAFT PROCESSING CHARTS)

1. Cut and prepare parts (A) and (B). Figs. 3, 4.

   Note: Make rack (C) of 1/4" three-ply wood. Finish in desired color. Attach (A) before assembling and (B) after assembling.

2. Outline all edges of (A) and (B) with double-edge creaser. Figs. 3, 4.

3. Skive all edges of (A) and (B) on flesh side. Figs. 3, 4.

4. Cement (A) and (B) to (C). Fig. 2.

5. Mark tack holes at 1/4" intervals in space between 2 creased lines around (A) and (B) on (C).

6. Hammer brass stud nails along all edges of (A) and (B). Figs. 1, 2.

MATERIALS:

Russia tooling calfskin, 2 oz., to harmonize with rack

10 doz. small brass head stud nails

Rubber cement

TOOLS:

(1), (6), (17), (27).

Design tools: (15, No. 7), (38, No. 8).

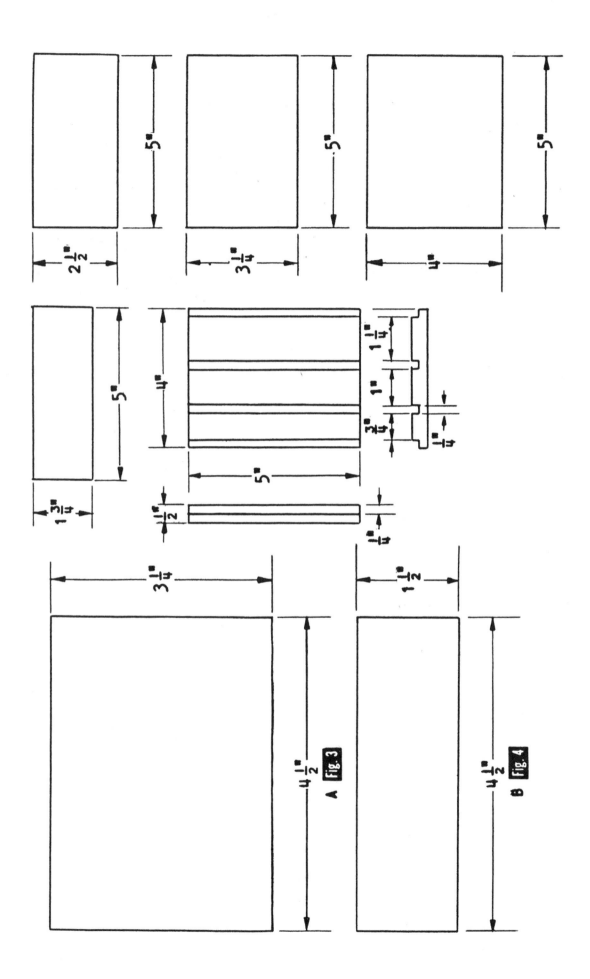

5"

5"

5"

$2\frac{1}{2}$"

$3\frac{1}{4}$"

4"

5"

4"

$1\frac{3}{4}$"

$1\frac{1}{4}$"

1"

$\frac{3}{4}$"

$\frac{1}{4}$"

5"

$\frac{1}{2}$"

$\frac{1}{4}$"

$3\frac{1}{4}$"

$1\frac{1}{2}$"

$4\frac{1}{2}$" A **Fig. 3**

$4\frac{1}{2}$" B **Fig. 4**

Desk File

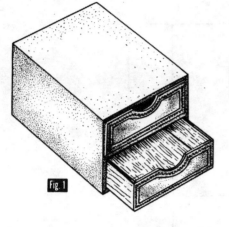

Fig. 1

All Leather Parts
Morocco Goatskin

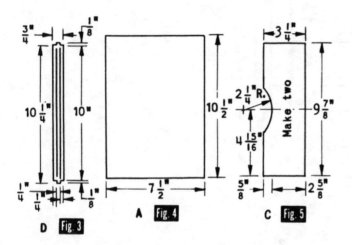

Fig. 2

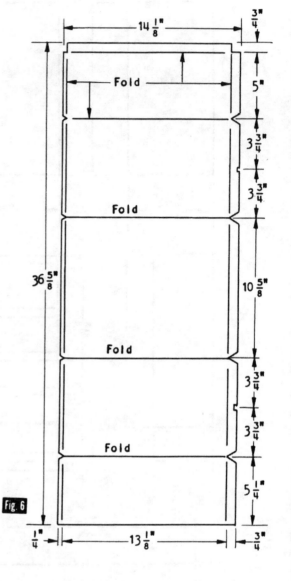

D Fig. 3

A Fig. 4

C Fig. 5

B Fig. 6

PROCEDURE: (CONSULT LEATHER CRAFT PROCESSING CHARTS)

1. Cut and prepare parts (A), (B), (C) and (D). Figs. 3, 4, 5, 6.

   Note: Construct wooden box (EFG) with 2 drawers of 1/4" plywood. Paint inside any color desired.

2. Skive all edges to be cemented. Fig. 2.

3. Cement (D) to edge of (F), with folds cemented to top and bottom of (F), and 1/8" flaps extending over (E). Fig. 2.

4. Cement (B) around (E) with ends of (B) overlapping on center bottom of (E). Cement 3/4" notched flap edges of (B) to inside edge of drawer opening of (E) and 1/4" notched flap edges to back end of (E). Fig. 2.

5. Cement (A) to back end of (E). Fig. 2.

6. Cement parts (C) to parts (G). Fig. 2.

MATERIALS:

Morocco goatskin, toolable
Rubber cement

TOOLS:

(1), (6), (15-1 and -6), (19).

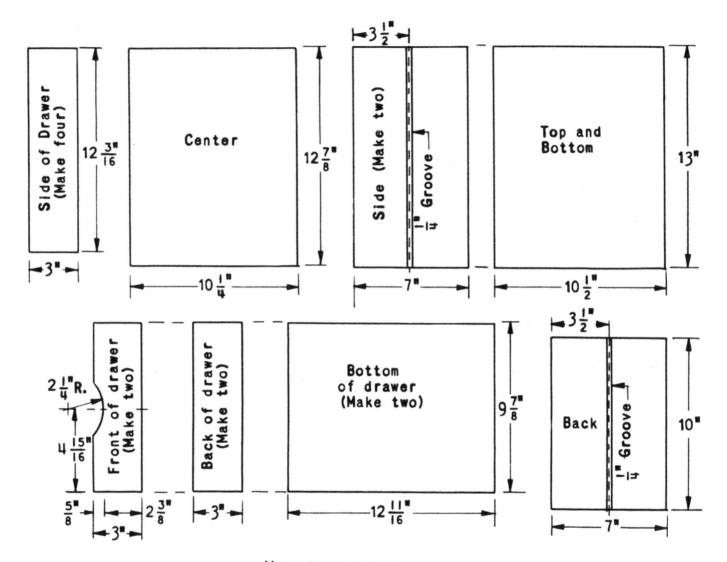

Wood Box Details

For Detailed
Instructions Consult
Chart I - Cutting
Chart II- Design
Chart III-Color
Chart IV- Construction
Chart V - Lacing
Chart VI- Stitching
Chart VII- Braiding
Chart VIII-Knotting
Material Chart

Traveling Sewing Kit

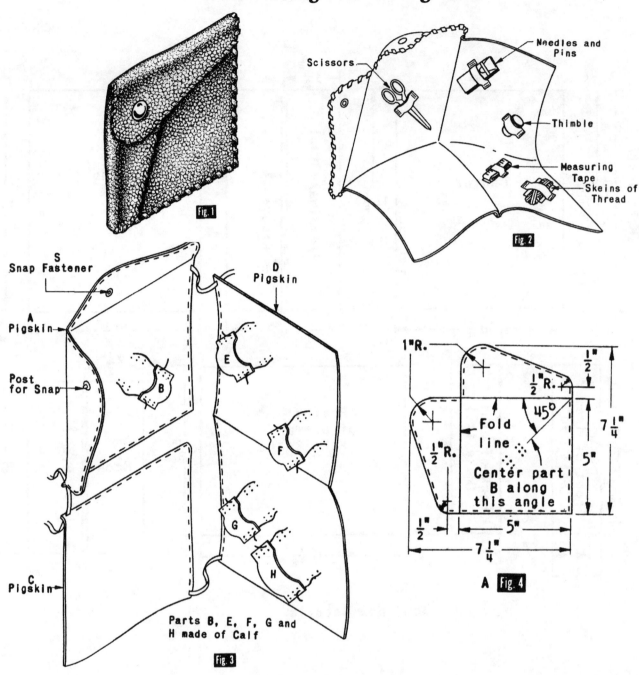

Fig. 1

Fig. 2
- Scissors
- Needles and Pins
- Thimble
- Measuring Tape
- Skeins of Thread

Fig. 3
- S Snap Fastener
- A Pigskin
- Post for Snap
- D Pigskin
- B
- E
- F
- G
- H
- C Pigskin

Parts B, E, F, G and H made of Calf

Fig. 4
- 1"R.
- $\frac{1}{2}$"R.
- $\frac{1}{2}$"
- 45°
- Fold line
- Center part B along this angle
- $\frac{1}{2}$"R.
- $\frac{1}{2}$"
- 5"
- 5"
- $7\frac{1}{4}$"
- $7\frac{1}{4}$"
- A

PROCEDURE: (CONSULT LEATHER CRAFT PROCESSING CHARTS)

1. Cut parts (A), (B), (C), (D), (E), (F), (G) and (H). Figs. 4, 5, 6, 7.

2. Place parts (B), (E), (F), (G) and (H) on (A) and (D). With awl, punch 1/8" stitching holes simultaneously through all matching parts as shown. Figs. 3, 4, 7.

3. Sew (B), (E), (F), (G) and (H) to (A) and (D) with saddler's stitch. Fig. 3.

4. With metal edge creaser, mark folding line on (D). Outline with creaser all edges of (C) and (D) not to be laced. Figs. 3, 5, 7.

5. With awl, punch 3/32" thong slits simultaneously through matching parts of (A), (C) and (D) and on flaps of (A) as shown. Figs. 3, 4, 5, 7.

6. Lace (A), (C) and (D) with whip stitch. Fig. 3.

7. Attach snap fastener (S) to (A). Fig. 3.

MATERIALS:

Pigskin

Lining calf (for straps)

Goatskin lacing, 3/32", 6-1/2' long

Matching heavy linen thread

Snap fastener

TOOLS:

(1), (4), (6), (12), (17), (18), (25), (26), (27), (40), (41), (43).

For Detailed
Instructions Consult
Chart I - Cutting
Chart II - Design
Chart III - Color
Chart IV - Construction
Chart V - Lacing
Chart VI - Stitching
Chart VII - Braiding
Chart VIII - Knotting
Material Chart

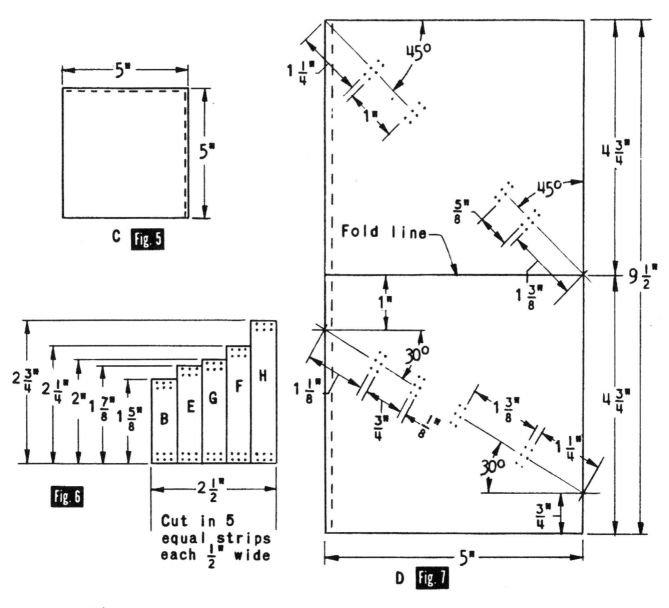

Fig. 6 and Fig. 7 drawn proportionately twice size.

Sewing Box

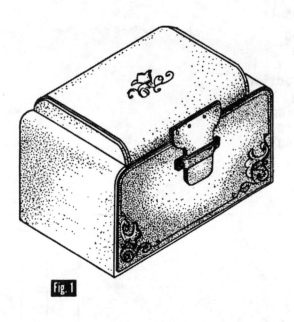

Fig. 1

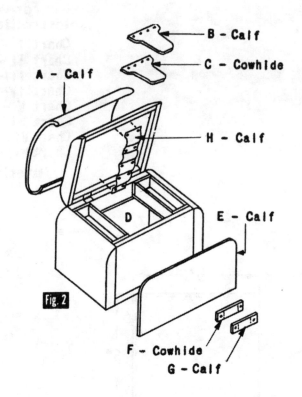

B – Calf

C – Cowhide

A – Calf

H – Calf

D

E – Calf

Fig. 2

F – Cowhide

G – Calf

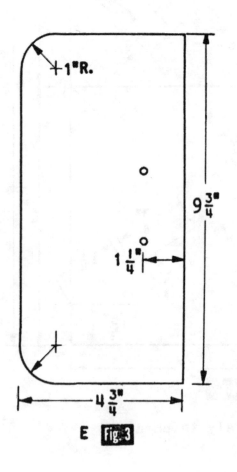

+ 1"R.

9 $\frac{3}{4}$"

1 $\frac{1}{4}$"

4 $\frac{3}{4}$"

E Fig. 3

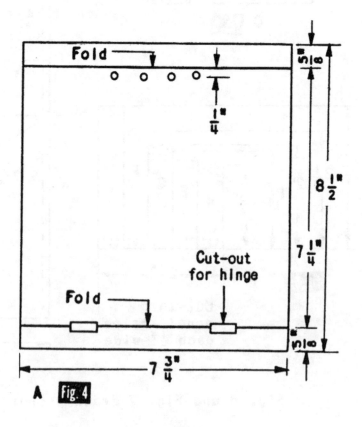

Fold

$\frac{5}{8}$"

$\frac{1}{4}$"

8 $\frac{1}{2}$"

7 $\frac{1}{4}$"

Cut-out
for hinge

Fold

$\frac{5}{8}$"

7 $\frac{3}{4}$"

A Fig. 4

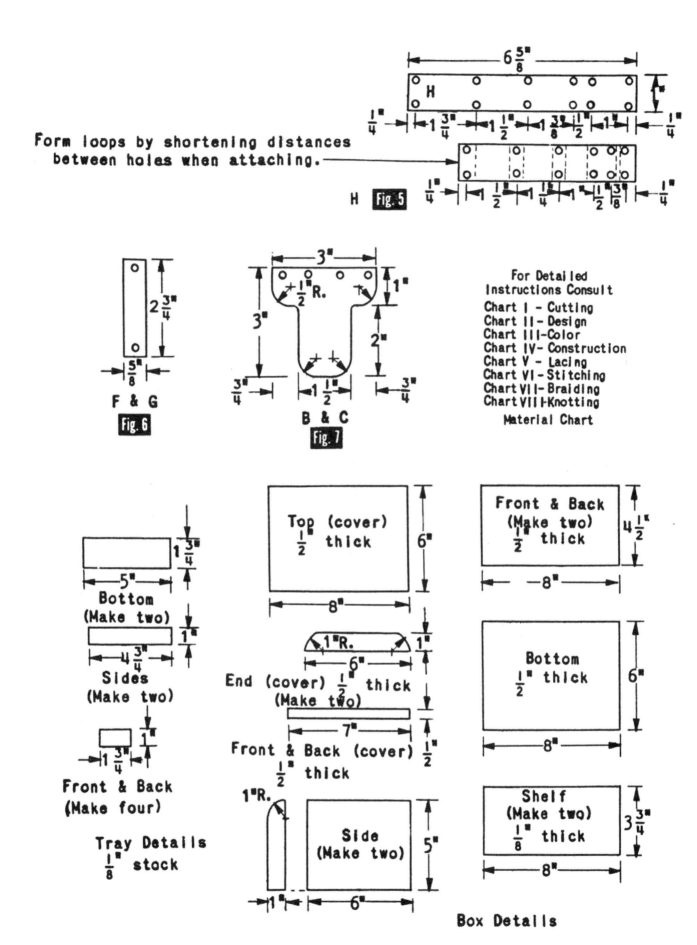

Form loops by shortening distances between holes when attaching.

H **Fig. 5**

F & G
Fig. 6

B & C
Fig. 7

For Detailed
Instructions Consult

Chart I – Cutting
Chart II – Design
Chart III – Color
Chart IV – Construction
Chart V – Lacing
Chart VI – Stitching
Chart VII – Braiding
Chart VIII – Knotting
Material Chart

Bottom
(Make two)

Sides
(Make two)

Front & Back
(Make four)

Tray Details
⅛" stock

Top (cover)
½ thick

End (cover) ½" thick
(Make two)

Front & Back (cover) thick
½

Side
(Make two)
1"R.

Front & Back
(Make two)
½" thick

Bottom
½" thick

Shelf
(Make two)
⅛" thick

Box Details

Tray and box details drawn proportionately ½ size.

329

PROCEDURE: (CONSULT LEATHER CRAFT PROCESSING CHARTS)

1. Cut and prepare parts (A), (B), (C), (E), (F), (G) and (H). Figs. 3, 4, 5, 6, 7.

   Note: Construct wooden box (D) with two removable spool trays of pine wood. Stain walnut.

2. Skive edges of (A) and (E). Figs. 3, 4.

3. Cement (E) to (D). Cement (A) to (D) with front edge of (A) under front edge of cover of (D), and back edge of (A) under back edge of cover of (D). Fig. 2.

4. Cement (B) to (C), and (G) to (F) flesh sides together. (Stain raw edges to match color of calfskin). Fig. 2.

5. Outline (B), (G) and (H) with edge creaser. Figs. 5, 6, 7.

6. Cement edge of (BC), ends of (FG), and ends of (H) to (D) as shown. Figs. 1, 2.

7. Hammer brass head nails across edge of (CB), ends of (FG), and at specified distances on (H). Figs. 1, 2, 5.

8. Apply Johnson's paste wax to both wood and leather surfaces. Rub to a glossy finish. Fig. 1.

MATERIALS:

Russian tooling calf, 2 oz.

Cowhide case leather, 5-6 oz.

Rubber cement

Brass head nails

Johnson's paste wax

TOOLS:

(1), (6), (17), (19).

Stationery Folder

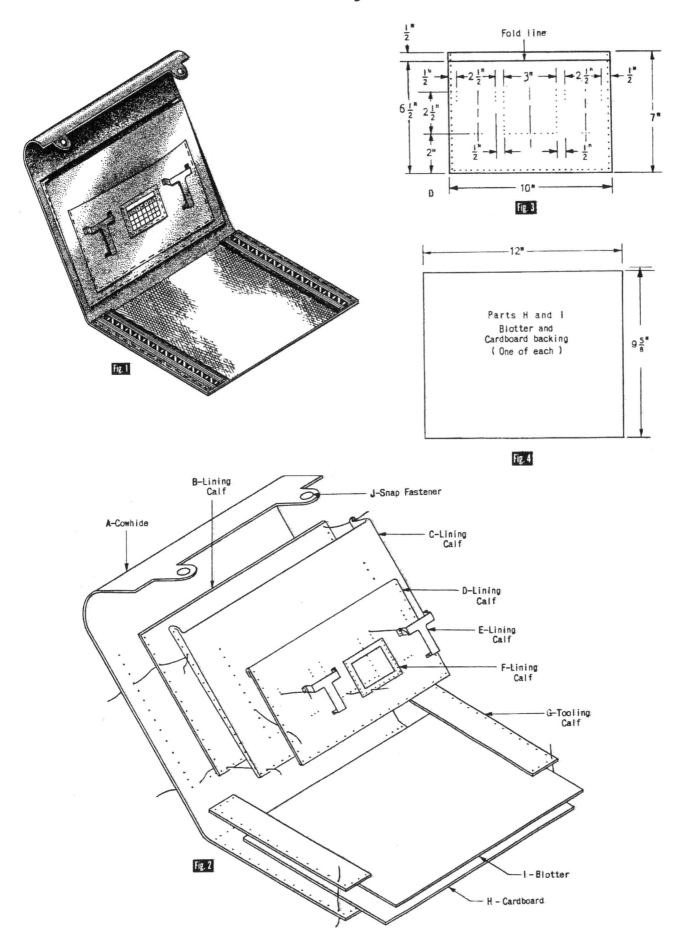

Fig. 1

Fig. 3

Fold line

1/2"

1/2"

2 1/2"

3"

2 1/2"

1/2"

6 1/2"

2 1/2"

7"

2"

1/2"

1/2"

D

10"

Fig. 4

12"

Parts H and I
Blotter and
Cardboard backing
(One of each)

9 5/8"

Fig. 2

B-Lining
Calf

A-Cowhide

J-Snap Fastener

C-Lining
Calf

D-Lining
Calf

E-Lining
Calf

F-Lining
Calf

G-Tooling
Calf

I-Blotter

H - Cardboard

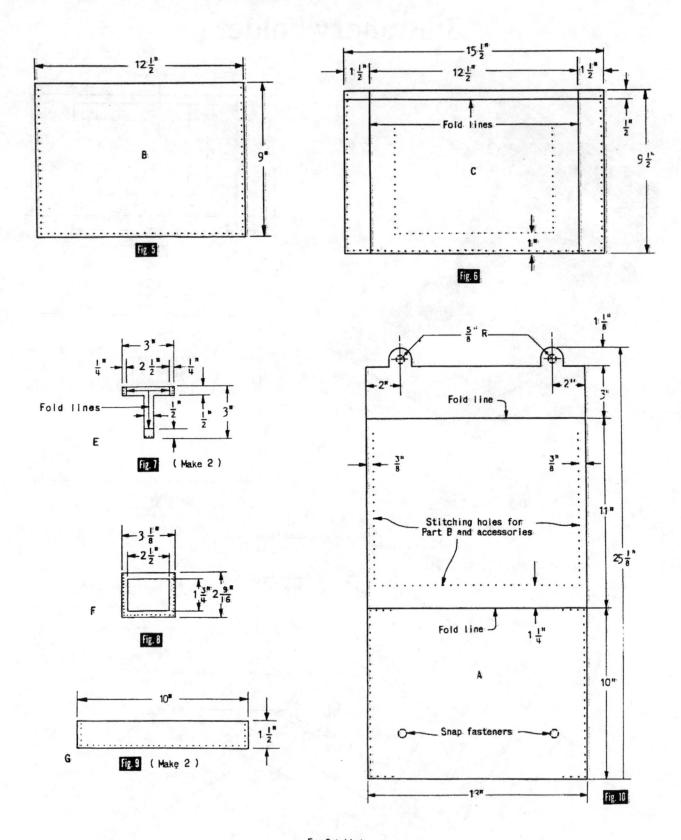

Fig. 5

Fig. 6

Fold lines

E   Fig. 7   (Make 2)

F   Fig. 8

G   Fig. 9   (Make 2)

Fold line

Fold line

Stitching holes for
Part B and accessories

Fold line

A

Snap fasteners

Fig. 10

For Detailed
Instructions Consult
Chart I - Cutting
Chart II - Design
Chart III - Color
Chart IV - Construction
Chart V - Lacing
Chart VI - Stitching
Chart VII - Braiding
Chart VIII - Knotting
Material Chart

332

PROCEDURE: (CONSULT LEATHER CRAFT PROCESSING CHARTS)

1. Cut and prepare parts (A), (B), (C), (D), (E), (F), (G), (H), (I). Figs. 2, 3, 4, 5, 6, 7, 8, 9, 10.

2. Attach two snap fasteners in part (A). Figs. 1, 2, 10.

3. Fold down tops of (C) and (D) $\frac{1}{2}$" and cement. Figs. 3, 6.

4. Punch stitching holes with awl, $\frac{1}{7}$" apart, in parts (E) and (F), Figs. 2, 7, 8. Punch matching holes in part (D).

5. Saddle stitch (E) and (F) to (D).

6. Punch stitching holes in (D) and (C), simultaneously, $\frac{1}{7}$" apart. Figs. 3, 6.

7. Saddle stitch part (D) to (C). Figs. 1, 2.

8. Cement (B) to (A). Figs. 1, 5, 10.

9. Punch stitching holes in (AB) and (C), simultaneously, $\frac{1}{7}$" apart. Figs. 2, 5, 6, 10.

10. Saddle stitch (AB) to (C). Figs. 1, 2.

11. Punch stitching holes in parts (G) and part (A), simultaneously, $\frac{1}{7}$" apart. Figs. 2, 9, 10.

12. Saddle stitch parts (G) to part (A), Figs. 1, 2.

13. Insert parts (H) and (I) under parts (G). Fig. 2.

MATERIALS:

Tooling cowhide, 5 oz.

Lining calf

Tooling calf

Blotter

Cardboard

2 snap fasteners

Heavy linen thread

Rubber cement

Calendar, optional

TOOLS:

(1), (5), (6), (8), (12), (17), (22), (25) (29) (41) (43).

Stationery Case

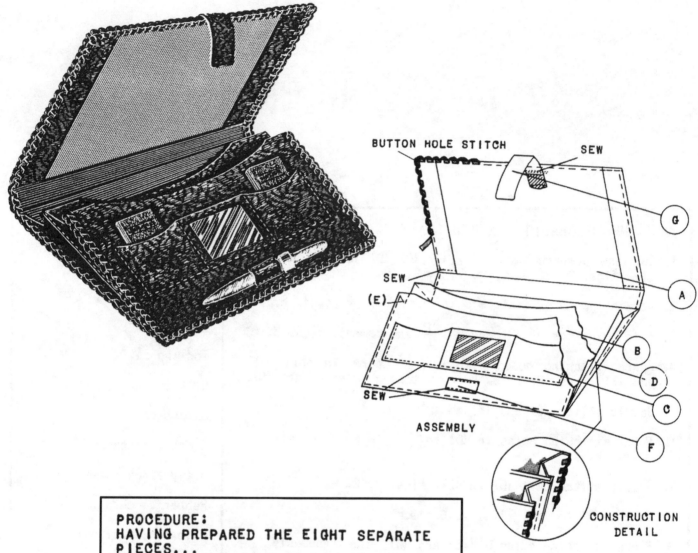

BUTTON HOLE STITCH

SEW

G

SEW

(E)

A

B

D

C

F

ASSEMBLY

CONSTRUCTION DETAIL

PROCEDURE:
HAVING PREPARED THE EIGHT SEPARATE PIECES...
(1) LOCATE AND SEW (C)&(F) ON (A), FINISHED SIDE.
(2) INSERT (G) THRU SLIT, CEMENT AND SEW TO FLESH SIDE OF (A).
(3) INSERT (H) INTO SLITS AND CEMENT TO FLESH SIDE OF (A).
(4) FOLD OVER FLAPS OF (A), FLESH SIDES TOGETHER AND SEW ENDS INDICATED IN ASSEMBLY.
(5) SEW (D)&(E) TO (B), FINISHED SIDES OUT, AS IN CONSTRUCTION DETAIL AND ASSEMBLY.
(6) LOCATE (B) ON (A), CEMENT EDGES TO BE LACED. SLIGHTLY ROUND CORNERS.
(7) PUNCH 3/32" THONG SLITS 1/8" IN FROM EDGES OF (A)(B)(D)&(E), LACE
(8) INSERT CELLOPHANE WINDOW.

TOOLS: (1)(2)(4)(6)(16)(17)

MATERIALS: CONSULT LEATHER CHARTS, RUBBER CEMENT, AND CELLOPHANE.

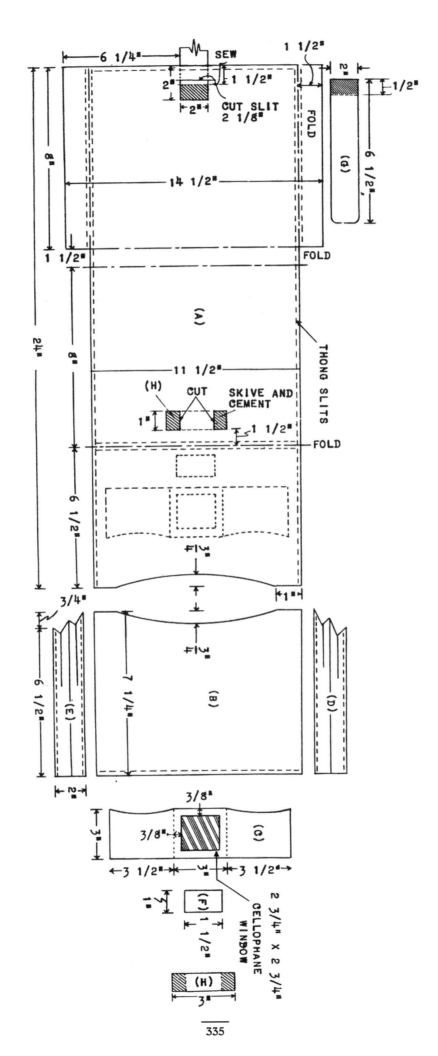

SEW

6 1/4"

1 1/2"

2"

1/2"

2"

1 1/2"

CUT SLIT
2 1/8"

2"

FOLD

(G)

6 1/2"

8"

14 1/2"

24"

1 1/2"

FOLD

(A)

THONG SLITS

8"

11 1/2"

(H)

CUT

SKIVE AND
CEMENT

1"

1 1/2"

FOLD

6 1/2"

3"
4

3"
4

1"

3/4"

(E)

6 1/2"

7 1/4"

(B)

(D)

2"

3/8"

3"

3/8"

(C)

3"

3 1/2"

3"

3 1/2"

CELLOPHANE WINDOW

2 3/4" X 2 3/4"

1"

(F)

1 1/2"

(H)

3"

335

Stuffed Dog

PROCEDURE:
(1) LAY OUT THE PARTS AS INDICATED ON YOUR PRE-
PARED TEMPLATE PAPER AND CUT THEM OUT.
(2) CUT TEMPLATE SHAPES OUT OF THE LEATHER YOU
HAVE CHOSEN (SMOOTH OR FURRY).
(3) INSERT TONGUE (T) THRU (M) AND CEMENT TO
FLESH SIDE OF (W)- SEW EYES IN PLACE.
(4) SEW (Y)&(Z), FLESH SIDES OUT, FROM POINT (A)
TO (B), SEW (W) TO (X) AS INDICATED.
(5) SEW (W) TO (Y)&(Z) FROM POINT (A) TO (D),
FLESH SIDES OUT.
(6) SEW (WX) TO (Y)&(Z) FROM POINT (D) TO (C).
(7) TURN RIGHT SIDE OUT AND STUFF- SEALING BY
SEWING FROM POINT (C) TO (B).
(8) CUT TWO STRIPS 1/2" WIDE, 9" LONG FOR COLLAR
AND BELT. ASSEMBLE REMAINING PARTS ACCORDING
TO FIGURE 1.

TOOLS: (1)(6)

MATERIALS: CONSULT LEATHER CHARTS, RUBBER CEMENT,
TWO BUTTON EYES, LINEN THREAD.

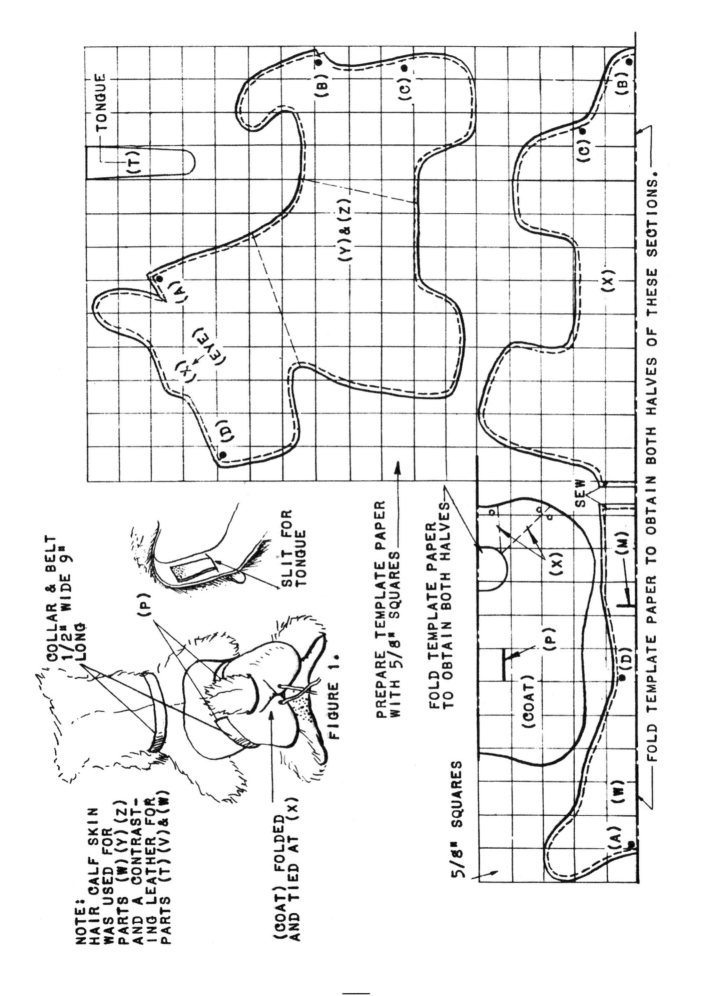

TONGUE

(T)

(B)

(C)

(Y) & (Z)

(A)

(X) (EYE)

(D)

NOTE:
HAIR CALF SKIN
WAS USED FOR
PARTS (W)(Y)(Z)
AND A CONTRAST-
ING LEATHER FOR
PARTS (T)(V)&(W)

COLLAR & BELT
1/2" WIDE 9"
LONG

(P)

SLIT FOR
TONGUE

(COAT) FOLDED
AND TIED AT (X)

FIGURE 1.

PREPARE TEMPLATE PAPER
WITH 5/8" SQUARES

FOLD TEMPLATE PAPER
TO OBTAIN BOTH HALVES

5/8" SQUARES

(A)

(W)

(COAT)

(P)

(D)

(X)

(P)

SEW

(B)

(C)

(X)

(M)

FOLD TEMPLATE PAPER TO OBTAIN BOTH HALVES OF THESE SECTIONS.

Giraffe

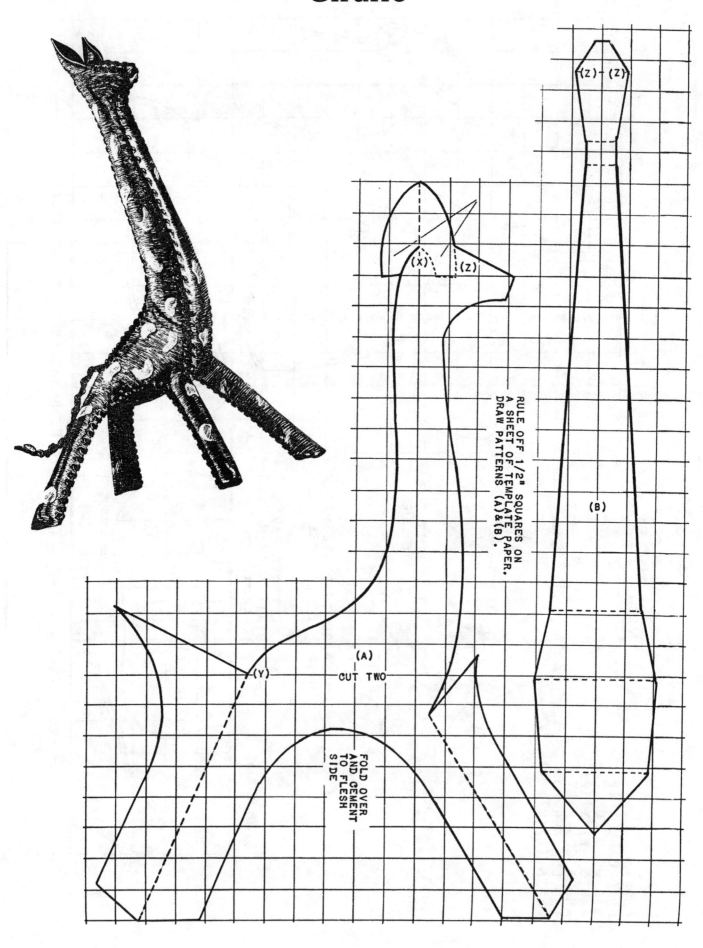

(Z) - (Z)

(X)

(Z)

RULE OFF 1/2" SQUARES ON
A SHEET OF TEMPLATE PAPER.
DRAW PATTERNS (A) & (B).

(B)

(A)
CUT TWO

(Y)

FOLD OVER
AND CEMENT
TO FLESH
SIDE

PROCEDURE:
HAVING PREPARED THE THREE SEPARATE PIECES...
(1) PUNCH 3/32" THONG SLITS 1/8" IN FROM ALL
    EDGES, EXCEPT AROUND THE EARS.
(2) LACE THE PIECES (A) FROM (X) TO (Y), FLESH
    SIDES TOGETHER. THEN LACE THE LEGS AND STUFF
    WITH COTTON.
(3) STARTING AT (Z), LACE DOWN ON BOTH SIDES OF
    (B)&(A) AND STUFF WITH COTTON DURING THIS
    FINAL OPERATION. BRAID TAIL.

TOOLS: (1)(2)(4)(6)(16)(17)(18)(21)

MATERIALS: CONSULT LEATHER CHART,
           TEMPLATE PAPER, AND COTTON.

Stuffed Elephant

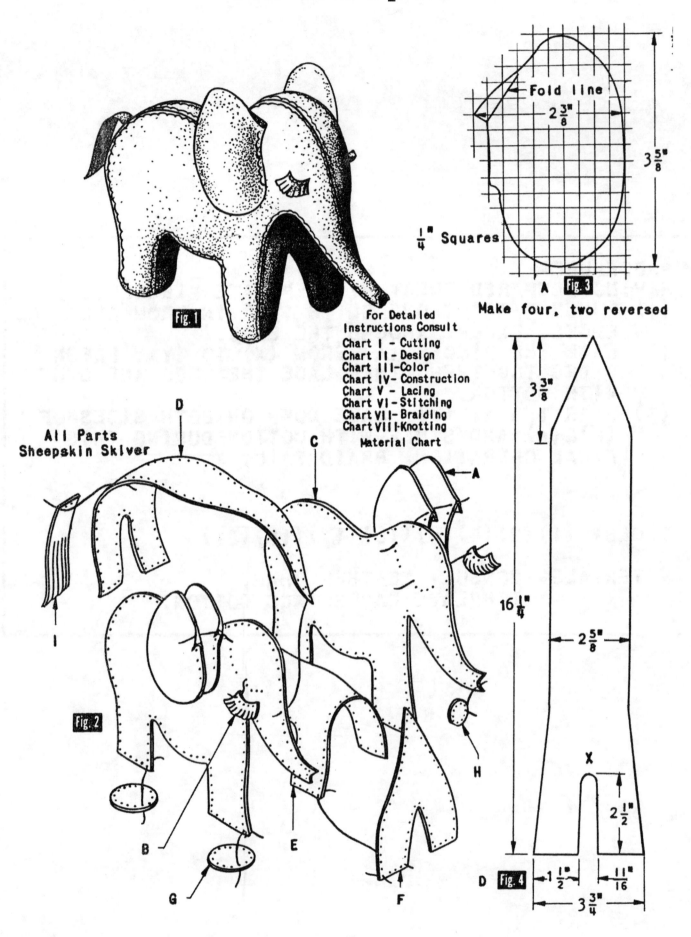

Fig. 1

Fig. 3

Fold line

$2\frac{3}{8}$"

$3\frac{5}{8}$"

$\frac{1}{4}$" Squares

A

Make four, two reversed

For Detailed
Instructions Consult

Chart I – Cutting
Chart II – Design
Chart III – Color
Chart IV – Construction
Chart V – Lacing
Chart VI – Stitching
Chart VII – Braiding
Chart VIII – Knotting

Material Chart

All Parts
Sheepskin Skiver

D

C

A

I

Fig. 2

B

G

E

F

H

$3\frac{3}{8}$"

$16\frac{1}{4}$"

$2\frac{5}{8}$"

X

$2\frac{1}{2}$"

$1\frac{1}{2}$"

$\frac{11}{16}$"

$3\frac{3}{4}$"

D **Fig. 4**

340

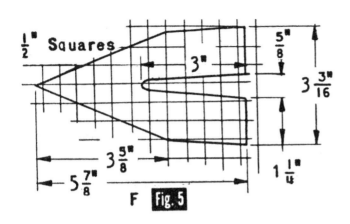

$\frac{1}{2}$" Squares

3"

$\frac{5}{8}$"

3$\frac{3}{16}$"

3$\frac{5}{8}$"

5$\frac{7}{8}$"

1$\frac{1}{4}$"

F **Fig. 5**

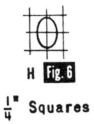

H **Fig. 6**

$\frac{1}{4}$" Squares

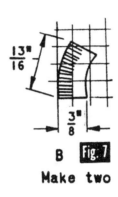

$\frac{13}{16}$"

$\frac{3}{8}$"

B **Fig. 7**

Make two

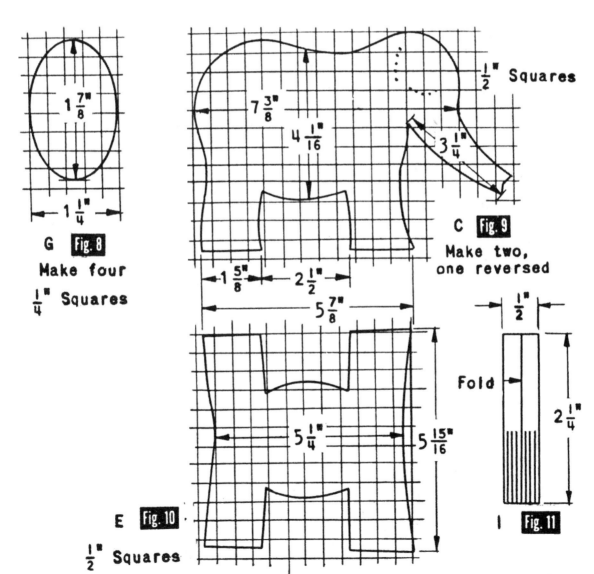

1$\frac{7}{8}$"

1$\frac{1}{4}$"

G **Fig. 8**

Make four

$\frac{1}{4}$" Squares

7$\frac{3}{8}$"

4$\frac{1}{16}$"

$\frac{1}{2}$" Squares

3$\frac{1}{4}$"

C **Fig. 9**

Make two,
one reversed

1$\frac{5}{8}$"

2$\frac{1}{2}$"

5$\frac{7}{8}$"

$\frac{1}{2}$"

Fold

2$\frac{1}{4}$"

I **Fig. 11**

5$\frac{1}{4}$"

5$\frac{15}{16}$"

E **Fig. 10**

$\frac{1}{2}$" Squares

PROCEDURE: (CONSULT LEATHER CRAFT PROCESSING CHARTS)

1. Cut parts (A), (B), (C), (D), (E), (F), (G), (H) and (I). Figs. 3, 4, 5, 6, 7, 8, 9, 10, 11.

2. Cement (A) to (A), flesh sides together. Fig. 2.

3. Fold (AA) as indicated. Sew parts (AA) and parts (B) to parts (C) where shown. Figs. 2, 3, 9.
   Note: Use closely spaced saddle stitching for all sewing, with 1/8" seam allowance.

4. Fold and cement tail (I). Cement top end to skin side of (D) at point (X). Figs. 2, 4, 11.

5. Sew outside edges of (D) to parts (C), beginning at hind legs. Fig. 2.

6. Sew (F) to (DC). Figs. 1, 2.

7. Sew (E) to (DCF). Figs. 1, 2.

8. Stuff elephant with cotton batting through foot and trunk openings.

9. Sew parts (G) to foot openings. Fig. 2.

10. Sew edges of (C) together at back of trunk line, beginning where point of (F) terminates; then sew at front of trunk line, beginning where point of (D) terminates. Fig. 2.

11. Finish stuffing trunk. Sew (H) to end of trunk. Fig. 2.

MATERIALS:

Sheepskin skiver, 1 oz., contrasting colors

Cotton batting

Linen thread

TOOLS:

(1), (21), (41).

Stuffed Horse

Fig. 1

Saddle and
Bridle Optional

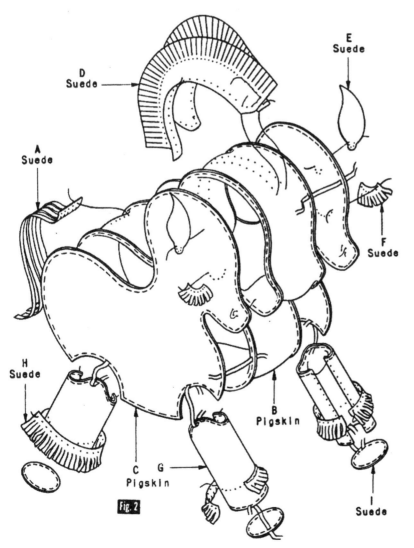

D
Suede

E
Suede

A
Suede

F
Suede

H
Suede

B
Pigskin

C
Pigskin

G

Suede

Fig. 2

For Detailed
Instructions Consult

Chart I – Cutting
Chart II – Design
Chart III – Color
Chart IV – Construction
Chart V – Lacing
Chart VI – Stitching
Chart VII – Braiding
Chart VIII Knotting
    Material Chart

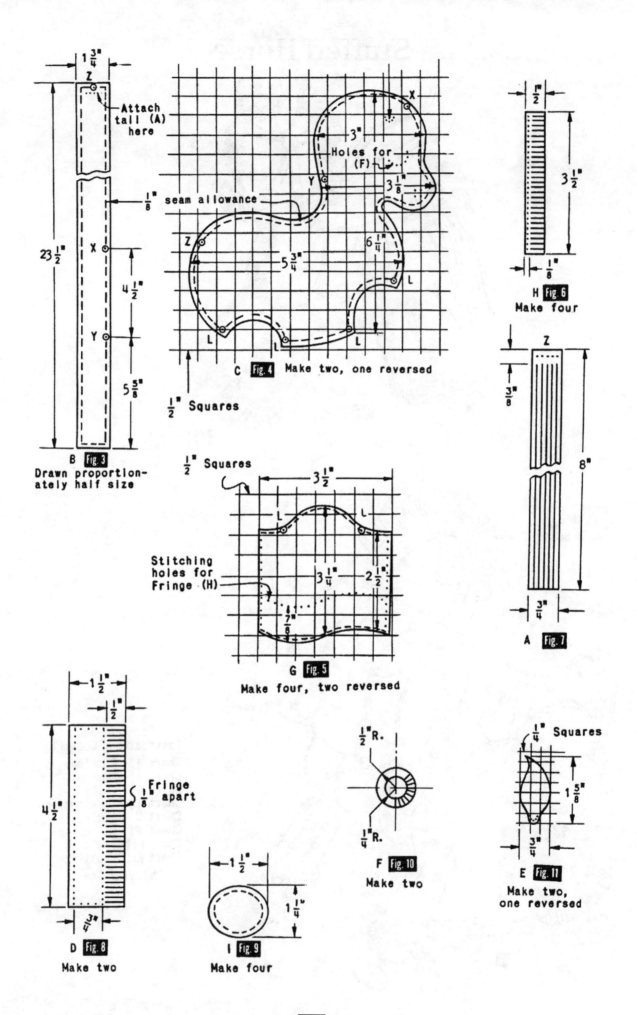

$1\frac{3}{4}$"

Z

Attach
tail (A)
here

$\frac{1}{8}$"

seam allowance

$23\frac{1}{2}$"

X

Y

$4\frac{1}{2}$"

$5\frac{5}{8}$"

B **Fig. 3**
Drawn proportion-
ately half size

Holes for
(F)

3"

$3\frac{1}{8}$"

$6\frac{1}{4}$"

$5\frac{3}{4}$"

Z

L

L

L

L

C **Fig. 4** Make two, one reversed

$\frac{1}{2}$" Squares

$\frac{1}{2}$"

$3\frac{1}{2}$"

$\frac{1}{8}$"

H **Fig. 6**
Make four

$3\frac{3}{8}$"

Z

8"

$\frac{3}{4}$"

A **Fig. 7**

$\frac{1}{2}$" Squares

$3\frac{1}{2}$"

L   L

Stitching
holes for
Fringe (H)

$3\frac{1}{4}$" $2\frac{1}{2}$"

$\frac{1}{8}$"

$\frac{7}{8}$"

G **Fig. 5**
Make four, two reversed

$1\frac{1}{2}$"

$\frac{1}{2}$"

$4\frac{1}{2}$"

Fringe
$\frac{1}{8}$"
apart

$\frac{3}{4}$"

D **Fig. 8**
Make two

$1\frac{1}{2}$"

$1\frac{1}{4}$"

I **Fig. 9**
Make four

$\frac{1}{2}$"R.

$\frac{1}{4}$"R.

F **Fig. 10**
Make two

$\frac{1}{4}$" Squares

$1\frac{5}{8}$"

$\frac{3}{4}$"

E **Fig. 11**
Make two,
one reversed

344

PROCEDURE: (CONSULT LEATHER CRAFT PROCESSING CHARTS)

1. Cut and prepare parts (A),(B),(C),(D),(E),(F),(G),(H), and (I) using patterns. Figs. 3, 4, 5, 6, 7, 8, 9, 10, 11.

2. Place (E) and (F) in position on (C). Punch with awl closely spaced stitching holes through matching parts. Figs. 2, 4, 10, 11.

3. Sew (E) and (F) to (C) with saddler's stitch. Fig. 2.

4. Punch four stitching holes with awl on (C) for nostrils. Fig. 4.

5. Make cross stitch with contrasting colored heavy linen thread for nostrils on (C), using four holes. Figs. 1, 2.

6. Place (D) to (D), flesh sides facing. Sew (D) to (D) with closely spaced saddle stitch 1/16" from inner cut of fringe. Figs. 2, 8.

7. Unfold (DD). Place seam of (DD) on center line of (B) between points (X) and (Y). Cement (DD) to (B). Figs. 2, 3.

8. Mark stitching holes with 1/7" spacing wheel, 3/32" from edge on ends of (DD), and on line indicated on (G) for (H). Figs. 5, 8.

9. Punch stitching holes, as marked, simultaneously through matching parts (DD) and (B). Fig. 2.

10. Place point (Z) of (A) on point (Z) of (B). Punch with awl closely spaced stitching holes 1/8" from edge, through matching parts (B) and (A). Figs. 3, 7.

11. Saddle stitch (DD) to (B), (BD) to (A), and (H) to (G) 1/16" from edge of (H), using stitching holes on (G) as guide. Figs. 2, 5, 6.

12. Punch with awl 3/32" thong slits, 1/8" from edge, on all sides of (B), on foot end of (GH), and on matching parts of (I). Figs. 3, 5, 9, and Leather Chart V.

13. Punch with one-prong awl 3/32" thong slits 1/8" from edge, simultaneously through curves (LL) on (C) and curve (LL) on (GH). Figs. 4, 5.

14. Lace (GH) to (C), flesh sides facing, with whip stitch. Fig. 2.

15. Place straight edges of (GH) together, flesh sides facing. Mark stitching holes 1/8" from edge with 1/7" spacing wheel. Fig. 5.

16. Punch stitching holes with awl simultaneously through matching edges of (GH). Fig. 5.

17. Sew seam of (GH) with saddler's stitch. Fig. 2.

18. Place end of (B) opposite point (Z) of (C), flesh sides facing. Using thong slits punched in (B) as guide, punch thong slits with one-prong awl through (C) where edges match those of (B). For smooth contour, allow sufficient fullness on curved edges of (C) to fit straight edge of (B). Between points (L) on (C), punch thong slits through (GH) and (B) simultaneously. Between points (X) and (Y) on (C), include (DD) in punching slits. Fig. 4.

19. Lace one entire side of (B) to (C) with whip stitch, including inner span of leg between points (L) on (GH). Figs. 2, 5.

20. Lace the other side from point (Z) through (Y) and (X) to the first point (L) on (C). Figs. 2, 4.

21. Without terminating thong, stuff head of horse with tightly packed cotton.

22. Continue to lace (B) and (GH) to (C) through last point (L) on rear leg. Fig. 4.

23. Without terminating thong, stuff body with cotton.

24. Finish lacing to point (Z). Fig. 4.

25. Lace ends of (B) at point (Z). Fig. 4.

26. Braid strips of (A) in three double strands for 3/4". Knot strands. Cut in uneven lengths. Figs. 1, 2, 7.

27. Stuff (GH) with cotton.

28. Lace (I) to (GH) with whip stitch. Figs. 2, 5, 9.

MATERIALS:
Pigskin, white
Goatskin lace, 3/32", brown or natural
Suede, brown
Heavy linen thread

TOOLS:
(1),(4),(6),(17),(18),(21), (25),(28),(33),(40),(41).

See Leather Chart V for punching thong slits.

Thermos Protector

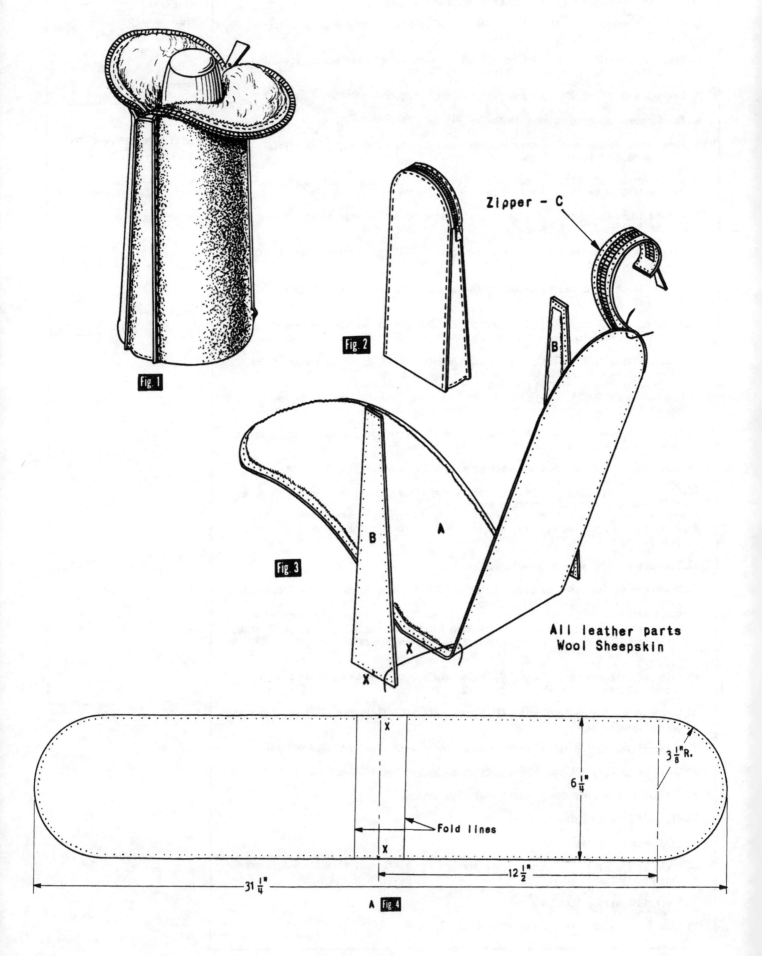

Fig. 1

Fig. 2

Zipper - C

B

Fig. 3

B

A

X

X

All leather parts
Wool Sheepskin

X

$3\frac{1}{8}"$R.

$6\frac{1}{4}"$

Fold lines

X

$12\frac{1}{2}"$

$31\frac{1}{4}"$

A Fig. 4

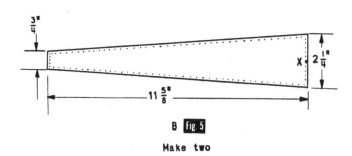

3/4"

X 2 1/4"

11 5/8"

B Fig. 5

Make two

For Detailed
Instructions Consult
Chart I - Cutting
Chart II - Design
Chart III - Color
Chart IV - Construction
Chart V - Lacing
Chart VI - Stitching
Chart VII - Braiding
Chart VIII - Knotting
Material Chart

PROCEDURE: (CONSULT LEATHER CRAFT PROCESSING CHARTS)

1. Cut parts (A) and (B). Measurements are for pint size. Figs. 4, 5.

2. Trim off wool on all stitching edges, including zipper edge. Fig. 3.

3. Place gussets (B) in position with (A), points (X) coinciding, wool sides facing. Fig. 3.

4. Sew edges of (B) to (A) with saddler's stitch, 1/8" from edge. Whip stitch edges if additional reinforcement is desired. Fig. 3.

5. Baste zipper (C) in position on (AB). Fig. 3.

6. Sew (C) to (AB) with saddler's stitch. Remove basting threads. Fig. 3.

MATERIALS:

Wool sheepskin

Zipper, 3/16" teeth, 10" long

Heavy linen thread

TOOLS:

(1), (6), (21), (41).

347

Cigarette Box

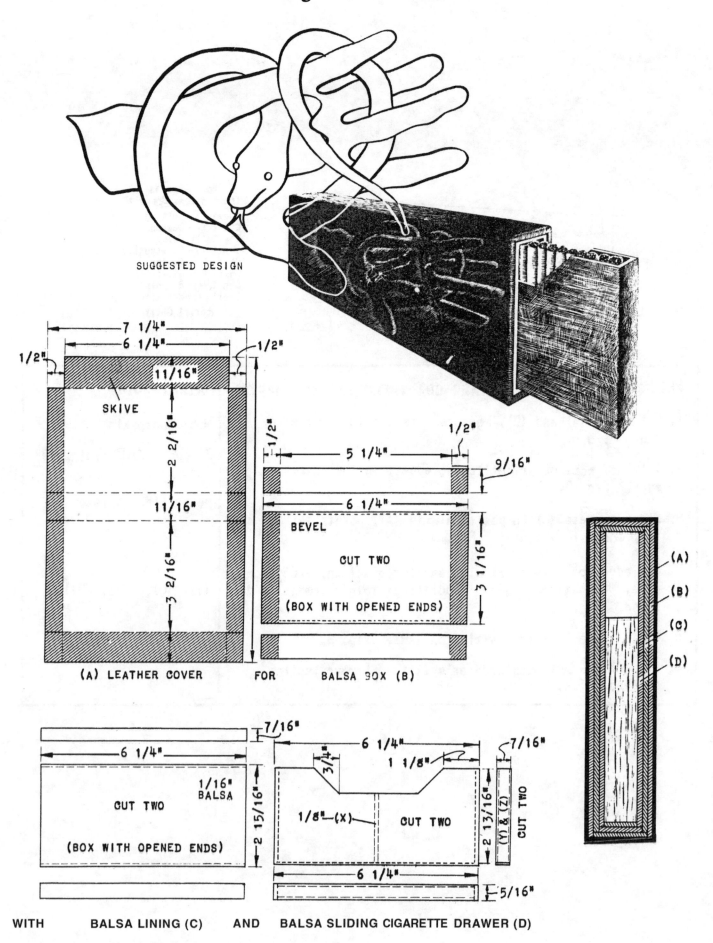

SUGGESTED DESIGN

7 1/4"
6 1/4"
1/2"
1/2"
11/16"
SKIVE
2 2/16"
11/16"
3 2/16"

(A) LEATHER COVER

1/2"
5 1/4"
1/2"
9/16"
6 1/4"
BEVEL
CUT TWO
(BOX WITH OPENED ENDS)
3 1/16"

FOR   BALSA BOX (B)

(A)
(B)
(C)
(D)

7/16"
6 1/4"
1/16" BALSA
CUT TWO
(BOX WITH OPENED ENDS)
2 15/16"

WITH   BALSA LINING (C)

7/16"
6 1/4"
3/4"
1 1/8"
1/8" (X)
CUT TWO
2 13/16" (Y) & (Z)
CUT TWO
6 1/4"
5/16"

AND   BALSA SLIDING CIGARETTE DRAWER (D)

PROCEDURE:
HAVING PREPARED THE COVER (A) - TOOLED DESIGN AND SKIVED EDGES....
(1) CUT OUT PARTS FOR (B) (C)&(D) OF 1/16" BALSA, (EXCEPT FOR (X)(Y)
    & (Z) WHICH WILL BE OF 1/8" STOCK).
(2) GLUE PARTS OF (B) TOGETHER AS SHOWN BY DOTTED LINE AND SECTION
    DRAWING. USE PINS TO HOLD PARTS TOGETHER WHILE DRYING. WHEN DRY,
    SMOOTH ROUGH SURFACES WITH SANDPAPER.
(3) CEMENT FLESH SIDE OF (A). ALSO OUTSIDE AND BEVELED SURFACES OF
    (B). THEN PUT THEM TOGETHER, FOLDING FLAPS OF (A) OVER BEVELED
    EDGES OF (B) LAST.
(4) LINE (B), BY GLUEING IN PARTS (C).
(5) GLUE PARTS (D) TOGETHER. WHEN DRY, COVER OUTSIDE SURFACES OF (D)
    WITH SILKSPAN AND PAINT WITH OLD ROSE LACQUER. HOWEVER, FIRST
    TRY (D) FOR SIZE AND, IF NECESSARY, SANDPAPER SURFACES FOR
    TOLERANCE.

MATERIALS:

CONSULT LEATHER CHARTS, BALSA WOOD 1/8" AND 1/16" SHEETS, COMMON
PINS, LEPAGES GLUE, RUBBER CEMENT, SILKSPAN, OLD ROSE LACQUER,
COTTON FOR BACKING TOOLED DESIGN.

TOOLS:

(1)(6)(9)(10)(11)(13)

349

Crayon Case

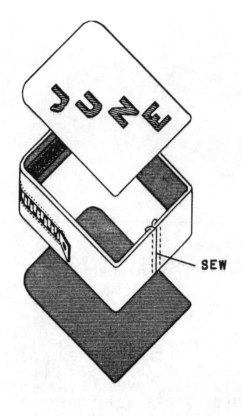

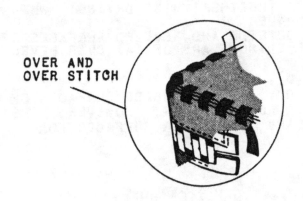

OVER AND
OVER STITCH

(NOTE)

NAME OF PERSON OR INITIALS
CAN BE CUT OUT OF CONTRAST-
ING LEATHER AND APPLIQUED
TO COVER OR TOOLED. THIS
MUST BE DONE BEFORE ASSEMBLY.

SEW

PROCEDURE:
HAVING PREPARED THE THREE SEPARATE PIECES...
(1) PUNCH 3/32" THONG SLITS 1/8" FROM EDGES
    AS SHOWN IN DRAWINGS.
(2) SEW 4 1/2" ZIPPER INTO (B).
(3) LACE (A) (B) & (C) TOGETHER.

TOOLS: (1) (2) (4) (6) (13) (17)
FOR TOOLING ADD (9) (10) (11)

MATERIALS: CONSULT LEATHER CHARTS, 4 1/2" ZIPPER

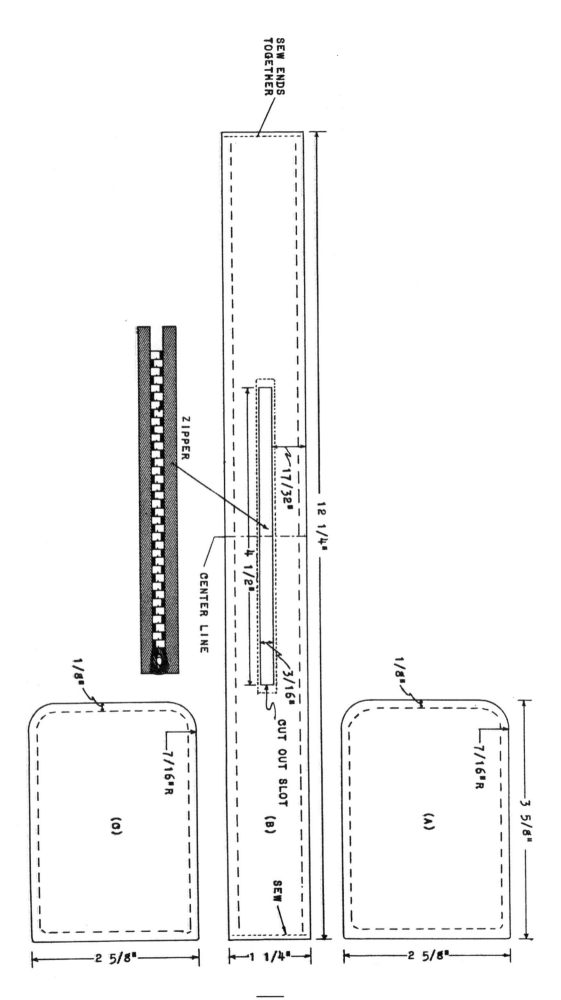

SEW ENDS TOGETHER

12 1/4"

ZIPPER

CENTER LINE

17/32"

4 1/2"

3/16"

CUT OUT SLOT

SEW

(B)

1/8"

7/16"R

(C)

2 5/8"

1 1/4"

1/8"

7/16"R

(A)

3 5/8"

2 5/8"

Combination Case

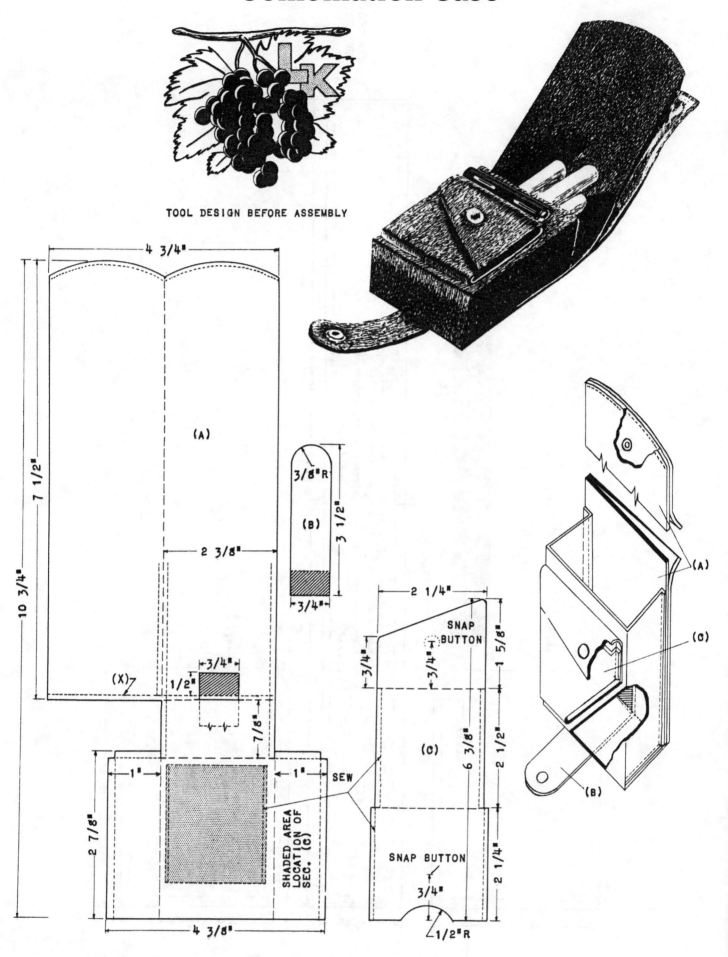

TOOL DESIGN BEFORE ASSEMBLY

(A)

3/8"R

(B)

3 1/2"

3/4"

4 3/4"

7 1/2"

10 3/4"

2 3/8"

(X)

1/2"

3/4"

7/8"

1"

1"

SEW

SHADED AREA
LOCATION OF
SEC. (C)

2 7/8"

4 3/8"

2 1/4"

SNAP
BUTTON

3/4"

3/4"

1 5/8"

6 3/8"

(C)

2 1/2"

2 1/4"

SNAP BUTTON

3/4"

1/2"R

(A)

(C)

(B)

PROCEDURE:
HAVING PREPARED THE THREE SEPARATE PIECES...
(1) LOCATE AND SET SNAP BUTTON IN (C), CEMENT
    EDGES TO BE SEWN TOGETHER, THEN LOCATE ON
    FINISHED SIDE OF (A) AND SEW TOGETHER.
(2) SET SNAP BUTTON IN (B), THEN INSERT (B)
    THRU SLIT IN (A) AND CEMENT TO FLESH SIDE.
(3) FOLD OVER WALLET END OF (A), FLESH SIDES
    TOGETHER, AND SEW ALONG DOTTED LINE (X).
(4) SEW SIDES OF COMPARTMENT TO WALLET, FLESH
    SIDES IN, AS IN ASSEMBLY.
(5) FILL POCKETS WITH ITEMS, FOLD WALLET FLAP
    OVER THREE SIDES TO LOCATE SNAP BUTTON.
    SET BUTTON AND SEW END OF WALLET.

TOOLS: (1)(6)(9)(10)(11)(12)(13)

MATERIALS: CONSULT LEATHER CHARTS,
           RUBBER CEMENT.

Pipe & Tobacco Pouch

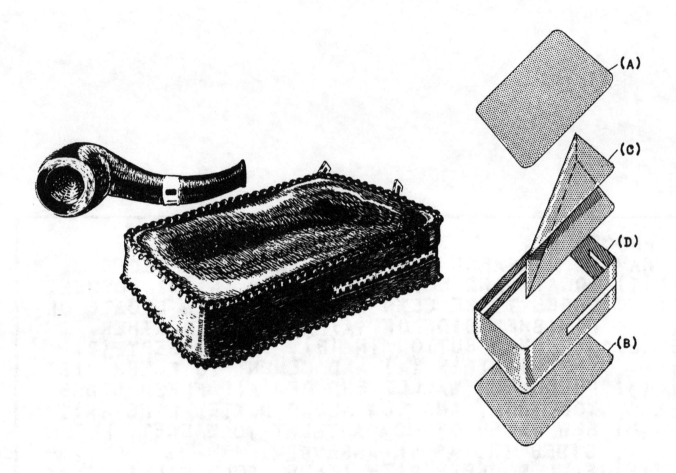

PROCEDURE:
HAVING PREPARED THE FOUR SEPARATE PIECES...
(1) SEW 5" ZIPPERS INTO (D). SKIVE AND CEMENT
    ENDS OF (D) TOGETHER.
(2) LOCATE (C) OVER (A), AND (D) OVER (C).
    CEMENT EDGES TO FACILITATE PUNCHING 3/32"
    THONG SLITS 1/8" IN FROM EDGES.
(3) LACE (D)(C)&(A) TOGETHER.
(4) SEW ENDS (V)&(W) TO (D).
(5) IN THE SAME MANNER, LOCATE AND CEMENT EDGES
    OF (B)(C)&(D) TOGETHER. PUNCH THONG SLITS AND
    LACE.

TOOLS: (1)(2)(4)(6)(16)(17)(18)(19)

MATERIALS: CONSULT LEATHER CHARTS, RUBBER CEMENT,
           AND TWO 5" ZIPPERS.

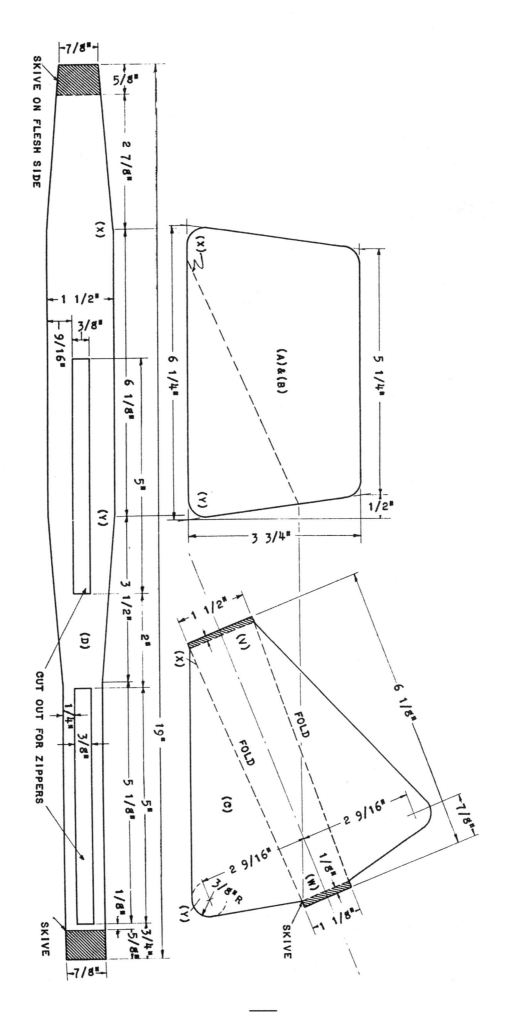

SKIVE ON FLESH SIDE

7/8"

5/8"

2 7/8"

(X)

1 1/2"

3/8"

9/16"

6 1/8"

5"

(Y)

3 1/2"

(D)

2"

CUT OUT FOR ZIPPERS

1/4"

3/8"

5 1/8"

5"

1/8"

SKIVE

5/8"

3/4"

7/8"

19"

(X)

6 1/4"

(A)&(B)

5 1/4"

(Y)

1/2"

3 3/4"

1 1/2"

(X)

(V)

6 1/8"

FOLD

FOLD

(C)

2 9/16"

7/8"

2 9/16"

1/8"

(W)

3/8" R

(Y)

SKIVE

1 1/8"

355

Combination Pouch Roll

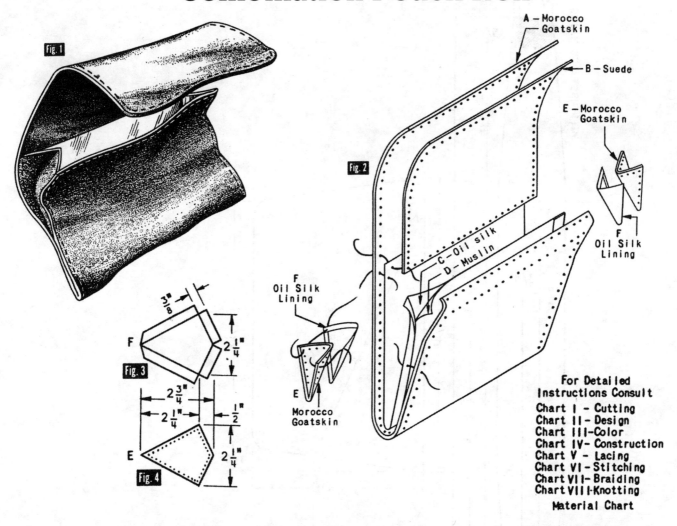

Fig. 1

Fig. 2

A — Morocco Goatskin
B — Suede
E — Morocco Goatskin
C — Oil silk
D — Muslin
F Oil Silk Lining
F Oil Silk Lining
E Morocco Goatskin

Fig. 3
F
3/8"
2 1/4"

Fig. 4
E
2 3/4"
2 1/4"
1/2"
2 1/4"

For Detailed Instructions Consult
Chart I – Cutting
Chart II – Design
Chart III – Color
Chart IV – Construction
Chart V – Lacing
Chart VI – Stitching
Chart VII – Braiding
Chart VIII – Knotting
Material Chart

PROCEDURE: (CONSULT LEATHER CRAFT PROCESSING CHARTS)

1. Cut parts (A), (B), (C), (D), (E), (F). Figs. 3, 4, 5, 6, 7, 8.

2. Mark fold lines in part (A), using edge creaser. Fig. 6.

3. Fold back long sides of part (C) 1/4", and all edges of parts (F) 3/8", as indicated. Figs. 3, 8.

4. Cement part (B) to part (A), leaving 1/2" free to cover top edge of part (C). Cement edges of (D) under folded edges of (C). Fig. 2.

5. With 1/7" spacing wheel, mark stitching holes around four sides of (A), on edges of (E), and on edge of (B) covering part (C). Figs. 2, 4, 5, 6.

6. With awl, punch all stitching holes, matching parts (AB) and (E). Figs. 1, 2.

7. Lay parts (DC) on part (A) (folds inside) with top edge under part (B), and bottom edge under fold of (A). Fig. 2.

8. Lay parts (F), (with folds inside) on part (E). Fig. 2.

9. Saddle stitch top edges of parts (EF) from front to back. When corner is reached, stitch along matching edges of (ACD) and (EF) to point of gusset; then stitch front and back folds of (ACD) together. Figs. 1, 2.

10. Saddle stitch (AB) and finish stitching front opening (ACD) and (EF). Figs. 1, 2.

MATERIALS:

Morocco goatskin

Suede

Oil silk

Unbleached muslin

Heavy linen thread

Rubber cement

TOOLS:

(1), (5), (6), (21), (25), (41).

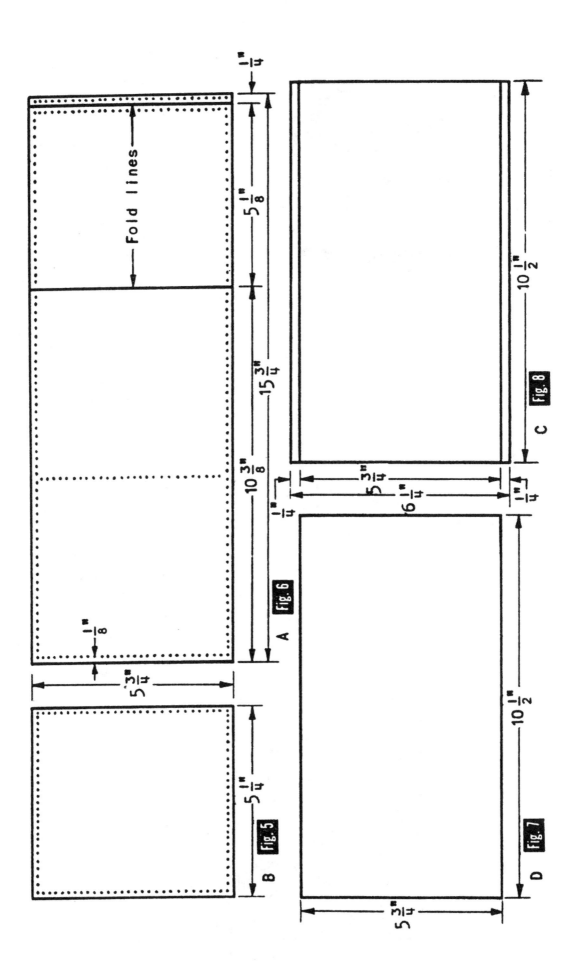

Fold lines

Fig. 5

Fig. 6

Fig. 7

Fig. 8

A

B

C

D

$\frac{1}{4}$"

$\frac{1}{8}$"

$5\frac{1}{8}$"

$15\frac{3}{4}$"

$10\frac{3}{8}$"

$5\frac{3}{4}$"

$5\frac{1}{4}$"

$10\frac{1}{2}$"

$5\frac{3}{4}$"

$6\frac{1}{4}$"

$\frac{1}{4}$"

$\frac{1}{4}$"

$10\frac{1}{2}$"

$5\frac{3}{4}$"

Crayon Case

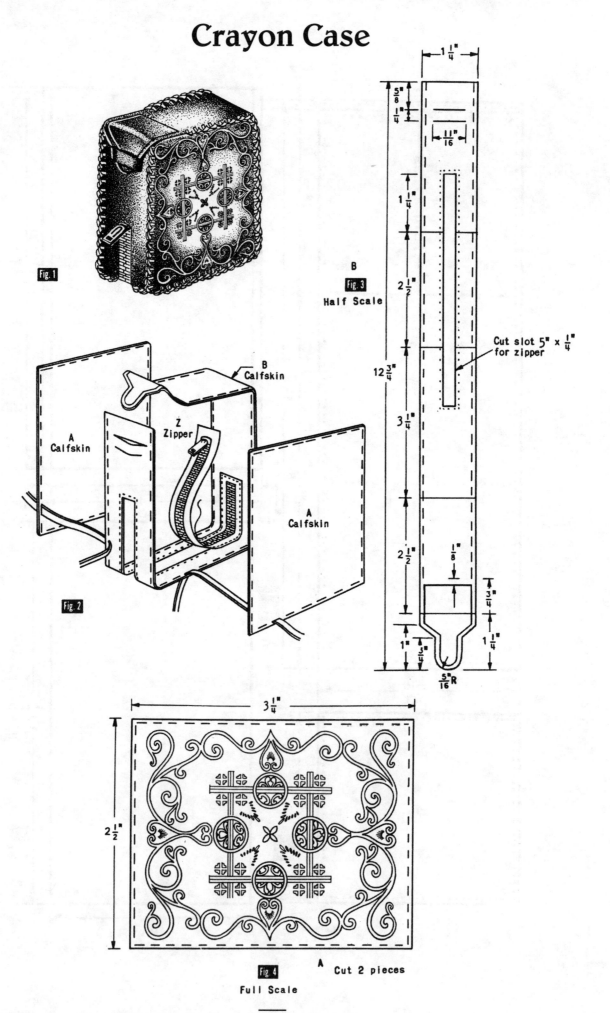

Fig. 1

Fig. 2

A Calfskin

B Calfskin

Z Zipper

A Calfskin

B

Fig. 3

Half Scale

$1\frac{1}{4}''$

$\frac{5}{8}''$

$\frac{1}{4}''$

$\frac{11}{16}''$

$1\frac{1}{4}''$

$2\frac{1}{2}''$

Cut slot 5" x $\frac{1}{4}''$ for zipper

$12\frac{3}{4}''$

$3\frac{1}{4}''$

$2\frac{1}{2}''$

$\frac{1}{8}''$

$3\frac{1}{4}''$

$1''$

$1\frac{1}{4}''$

$\frac{5}{16}''$R

$3\frac{1}{4}''$

$2\frac{1}{2}''$

Fig. 4

Full Scale

A Cut 2 pieces

358

PROCEDURE: (CONSULT LEATHER CRAFT PROCESSING CHARTS)

1. Cut and prepare parts (A) and (B). Figs. 3, 4.

2. With edge creaser, mark folding and edge line on tab of (B) as shown. Figs. 2, 3.

3. Cut slits for tapered end of (B) in straight-cut end of (B). Figs. 2, 3.

4. Cut slot for (Z) in (B). Fig. 3.

5. With $\frac{1}{7}"$ spacing wheel, mark stitching holes $\frac{3"}{32}$ from edge of slot, around all edges of slot in (B). Fig. 3.

6. With awl, punch stitching holes in (B) as marked. Fig. 3.

7. Cement edges of (Z) under slot. With sewing awl, lock stitch (Z) to (B). Figs. 2, 3.

8. With awl, punch $\frac{3"}{32}$ thong slits, $\frac{1}{8}"$ from edge, simultaneously through all matching edges of (A) and (B) as shown.

9. Lace (A) to (B) with double overlay stitch.

MATERIALS:

Russia tooling calfskin ($2\frac{1}{2}$ oz.)

Calfskin lace $\frac{3"}{32}$, 16'

Placket style zipper, 5" long

Heavy linen thread

TOOLS:

(1), (4), (6), (17), (18), (23), (25), (26), (27), (28), (33), (40).

For Detailed Instructions Consult
Chart I – Cutting
Chart II – Design
Chart III – Color
Chart IV – Construction
Chart V – Lacing
Chart VI – Stitching
Chart VII – Braiding
Chart VIII – Knotting
Material Chart

Pipe Rack

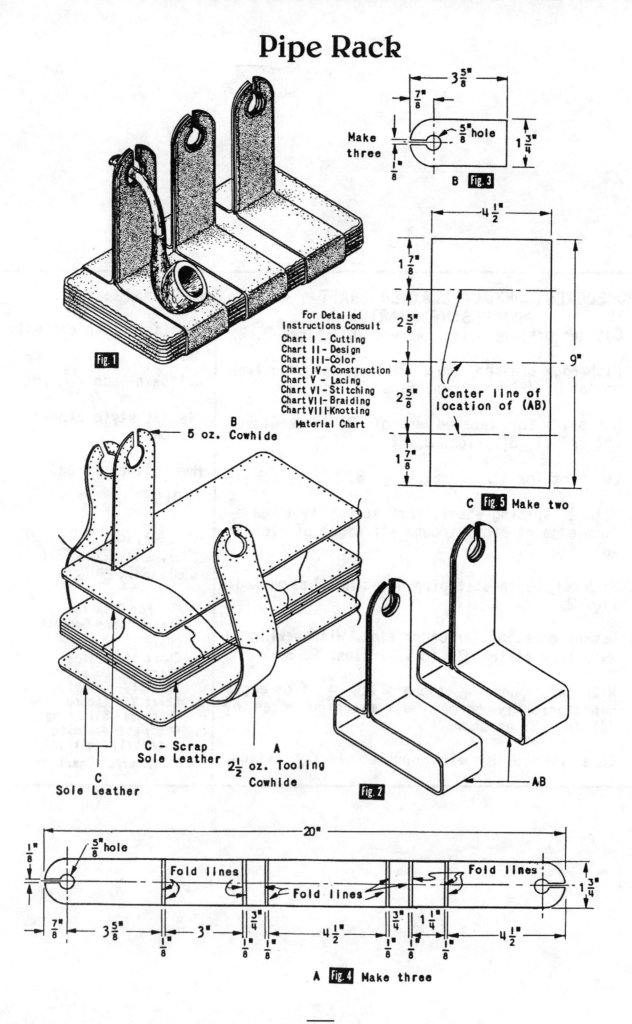

$3\frac{5}{8}$"

$\frac{7}{8}$"

Make three

$\frac{5}{8}$"hole

$1\frac{3}{4}$"

$\frac{1}{8}$"

B   Fig. 3

Fig.1

For Detailed
Instructions Consult
Chart I - Cutting
Chart II- Design
Chart III-Color
Chart IV- Construction
Chart V - Lacing
Chart VI- Stitching
Chart VII- Braiding
Chart VIII-Knotting
Material Chart

$4\frac{1}{2}$"

$1\frac{7}{8}$"

$2\frac{5}{8}$"

9"

$2\frac{5}{8}$"

Center line of
location of (AB)

$1\frac{7}{8}$"

C Fig. 5 Make two

B
5 oz. Cowhide

C – Scrap
Sole Leather

A
$2\frac{1}{2}$ oz. Tooling
Cowhide

C
Sole Leather

AB

Fig. 2

20"

$\frac{1}{8}$"

$\frac{5}{8}$"hole

Fold lines

Fold lines

Fold lines

Fold lines

$1\frac{1}{4}$"

$\frac{7}{8}$"

$3\frac{5}{8}$"

3"

$\frac{1}{8}$"

$\frac{3}{4}$"

$\frac{1}{8}$"

$4\frac{1}{2}$"

$\frac{1}{8}$"

$\frac{3}{4}$"

$1\frac{1}{4}$"

$\frac{1}{8}$"

$4\frac{1}{2}$"

A Fig. 4 Make three

PROCEDURE: (CONSULT LEATHER CRAFT PROCESSING CHARTS)

1. Cut and prepare parts (A),(B) and top and bottom layers of (C). Figs. 3, 4, 5.

2. Cut up scraps of leather to form inside layers of (C). Build up (C) to a height of 3/4" by piecing together, jig-saw fashion, tightly fitted leather scraps of same thickness. Fig. 2.

3. Sandpaper all skin surfaces to be cemented. Fig. 2.

4. Assemble and cement inside layers of (C), to outer layers of (C), with skin side exposed on top and bottom surfaces. Place under weight and allow to dry 18-24 hours. Fig. 2.

5. Sandpaper all cut edges of (C) to a smooth surface. Apply successive coats of Johnson's paste wax, rubbing thoroughly to achieve a smooth, waxed finish. Figs. 1, 2.

6. Mark stitching holes on (C) with 1/5" spacing wheel, 3/16" from edges. Fig. 2.

7. Drill 1/6" stitching holes with hand drill as marked. Fig. 2.

8. Sew through edges of (C) with saddler's stitch. Figs. 1, 2.

9. Cement (B) to flesh side of one end of (A). Figs. 2, 3, 4.

10. Place (AB) in position around (C) to determine placement of horizontal stitching holes through (AB). Mark stitching line on both sides. Figs. 2, 5.

11. Remove (AB) from (C). Using stitching line as guide, punch stitching holes 1/8" apart through (AB) and free end of (A). Fig. 2.

12. Mark stitching holes with 1/7" spacing wheel, 1/8" from edge of vertical part of (AB). Fig. 2.

13. Cement (AB) to (C) so that punched stitching holes coincide 1-1/4" from back edge of (C). Then cement unattached end of (A) to (AB). Fig. 2.

14. Punch stitching holes with awl through edges of (AB) as marked. Fig. 2.

15. Sew (AB) with saddler's stitch. Start with horizontal line across (AB) on (C); continue around (AB). Figs. 1, 2.

MATERIALS:

Sole leather
Tooling cowhide, 2-1/2 oz.
Cowhide, 5 oz.
Pliobond plastic adhesive
Heavy linen thread

TOOLS:

(1),(6),(17),(25),(28),(30),(33).
1/16" hand drill

Multi-Purpose Pouch

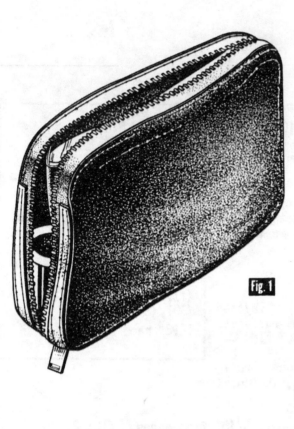

Fig. 1

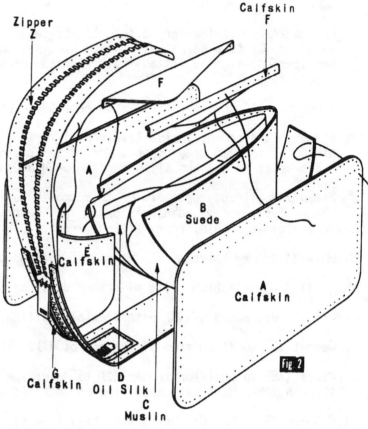

Zipper
Z

Calfskin
F

F

A

B
Suede

A
Calfskin

E
Calfskin

G
Calfskin

D
Oil Silk

C
Muslin

Fig 2

For Detailed
Instructions Consult
Chart I - Cutting
Chart II - Design
Chart III - Color
Chart IV - Construction
Chart V - Lacing
Chart VI - Stitching
Chart VII - Braiding
Chart VIII - Knotting
Material Chart

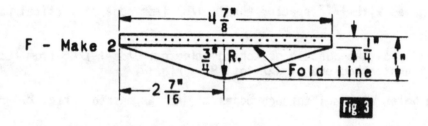

F - Make 2

$4\frac{7}{8}$"

$\frac{3}{4}$" R.

$\frac{1}{4}$"

1"

Fold line

$2\frac{7}{16}$"

Fig. 3

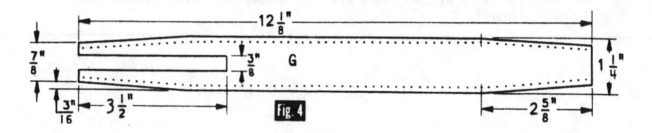

$12\frac{1}{8}$"

$\frac{7}{8}$"

$\frac{3}{8}$"

G

$1\frac{1}{4}$"

$\frac{3}{16}$"

$3\frac{1}{2}$"

$2\frac{5}{8}$"

Fig. 4

362

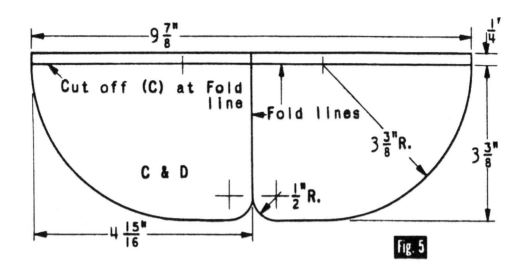

9 7/8" | 1/4"

Cut off (C) at Fold line

Fold lines

3 3/8"R.

3 3/8"

C & D

1/2"R.

4 15/16"

Fig. 5

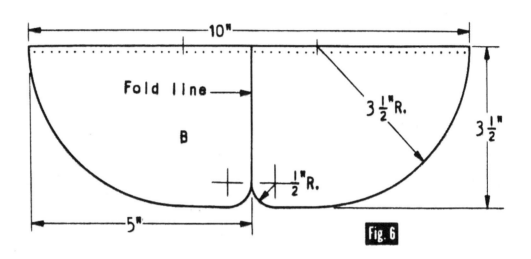

10"

Fold line

3 1/2"R.

3 1/2"

B

1/2"R.

5"

Fig. 6

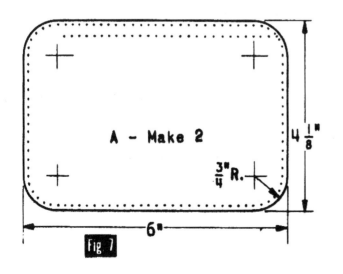

A — Make 2

3/4"R.

4 1/8"

6"

Fig. 7

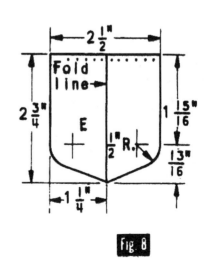

2 1/2"

Fold line

2 3/4"

E

1/2"R.

1 15/16"

13/16"

1 1/4"

Fig. 8

PROCEDURE: (CONSULT LEATHER CRAFT PROCESSING CHARTS)

1. Cut and prepare parts (A), (B), (C), (D), (E), (F) and (G). Figs. 3, 4, 5, 6, 7, 8.

2. Fold (B), flesh sides facing. On sewing machine stitch together all sides except top opening. Figs. 2, 6.

3. Place folded (C) around matching sides of folded (D). On sewing machine, stitch (C) and (D) together on all sides except top opening. Figs. 2, 5.

4. Turn down 1/4" edge of (D) over raw edge of (C) and cement folded edge in place. Fig. 2.

5. Insert (CD) in (B). Cement 1/4" edge of (D) to (B). Fig. 2.

6. With edge creaser, mark folding line and outline curved edge of (F) and edge of (E). Figs. 3, 8.

7. Cement flesh side of straight edge below fold of (F) to outside top edge of (BCD). Figs. 2, 3.

8. Cement flesh side of top edge of (E) to matching edge of (F) on (BCD). Fig. 2.

9. Place (BCDEF) in position on (A) with skin side of (F) flat against flesh side of (A). With awl, punch 1/8" stitching holes simultaneously through (A) and (BCDEF), 3/8" from top edge of (A) as shown. Figs. 2, 7.

10. Sew (A) to (BCDEF) with saddler's stitch. Fold down curved edge of (F) inside opening of (BCD). Fig. 2.

11. With edge creaser, outline all edges of (A) and (G) where zipper (Z) will be attached. Figs. 2, 4, 7.

12. Using creased lines for stitching guide, sew (Z) to (A) and (G) on sewing machine. Figs. 2, 4, 7.

13. Place (ZG) and (A) in final position. With 1/7" spacing wheel, mark stitching holes 1/8" from edge of (ZG) on (A). Figs. 2, 4, 7.

14. With awl, punch stitching holes simultaneously through matching edges of (ZG) and (A). Figs. 2, 4, 7.

15. Sew (ZG) to (A) with saddler's stitch. Fig. 2.

MATERIALS:

Calfskin, 2-1/2 oz.
Suede, 2 oz.
Unbleached muslin
Oil silk
Heavy linen thread
Zipper, 10"
Casco flexible cement

TOOLS:

(1), (6), (17), (21), (25), (27), (41).

Tobacco Humidor

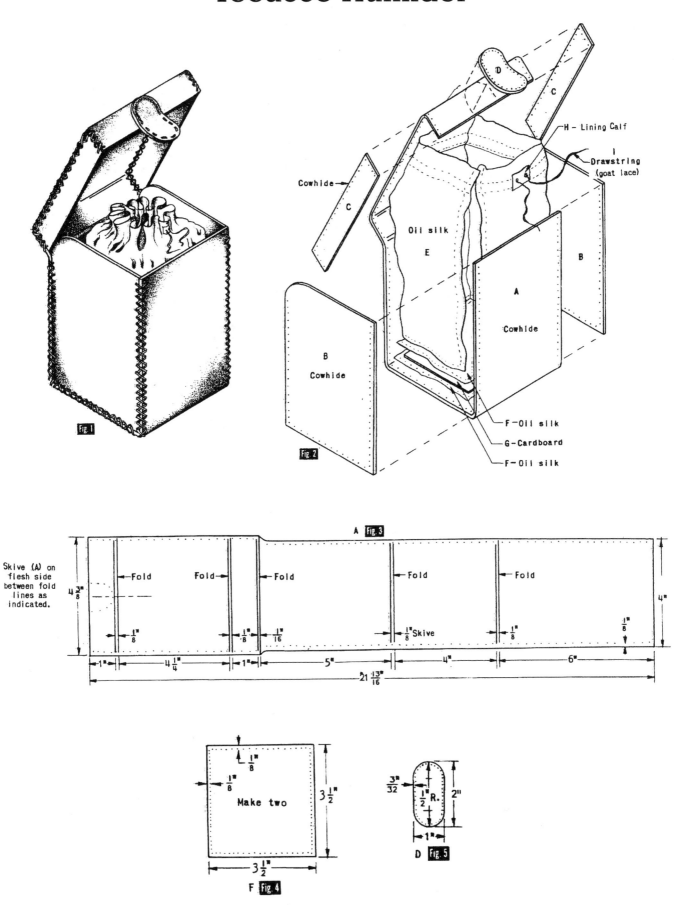

Fig. 1

Cowhide→

Oil silk
E

H – Lining Calf

I
Drawstring
(goat lace)

B

A

Cowhide

B
Cowhide

F – Oil silk
G – Cardboard
F – Oil silk

Fig. 2

A Fig. 3

Skive (A) on
flesh side
between fold
lines as
indicated.

4 3/8"

Fold   Fold   Fold   Fold   Fold

4"

1/8"   1/8" 1/16"   1/8" Skive   1/8"   1/8"

1"   4 1/4"   1"   5"   4"   6"

21 13/16"

1/8"

Make two

3 1/2"

1/8"

3 1/2"

F Fig. 4

3/32"   1/2" R.   2"

1"

D Fig. 5

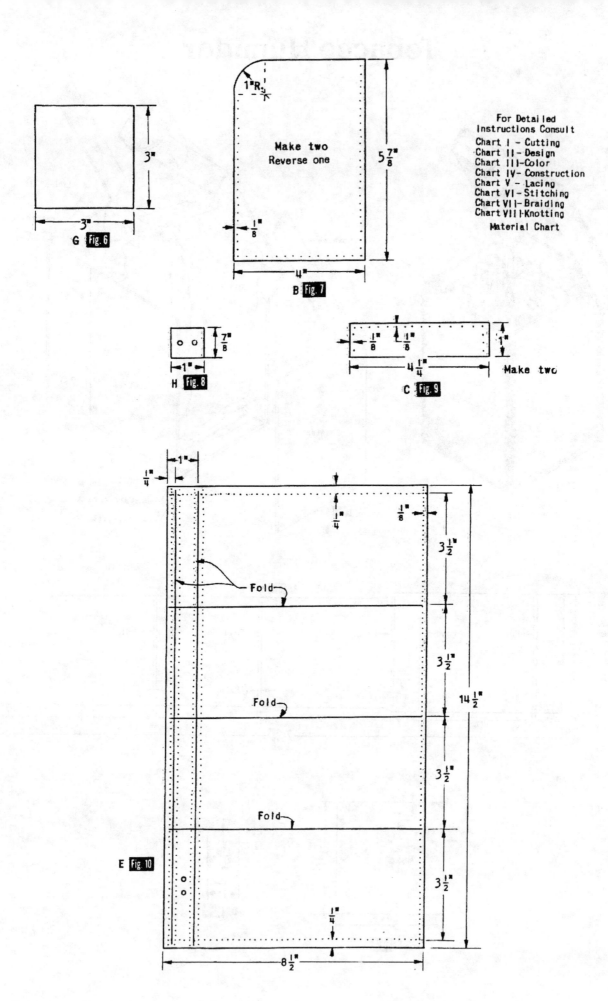

3"

3"

G **Fig. 6**

1"R

Make two
Reverse one

5 7/8"

1/8"

4"

B **Fig. 7**

For Detailed
Instructions Consult
Chart I – Cutting
Chart II – Design
Chart III – Color
Chart IV – Construction
Chart V – Lacing
Chart VI – Stitching
Chart VII – Braiding
Chart VIII – Knotting
Material Chart

7/8"

1"

H **Fig. 8**

1/8" 1/8"

1"

4 1/4"

Make two

C **Fig. 9**

1"

1/4"

1/4" 1/8"

3 1/2"

Fold

3 1/2"

Fold

14 1/2"

3 1/2"

Fold

3 1/2"

E **Fig. 10**

1/4"

8 1/2"

PROCEDURE: (CONSULT LEATHER CRAFT PROCESSING CHARTS)

1. Cut parts (A), (B), (C), (D), (E), (F), (G), (H). Figs. 3, 4, 5, 6, 7, 8, 9, 10.

2. Mark deep fold lines with edge creaser in (A), skiving between lines, and outline unstitched edges of (A), (B) and (C). Figs. 3, 7, 9.

3. Mark parallel thong holes 1/4" apart, 1/8" from edge, on matching edges of (A), (B) and (C). Where corners are laced, allow for equal number of holes in (A) and its matching part. Figs. 2, 3, 7, 9.

4. Punch all thong holes with No. 1 tube. Fig. 2.

5. Punch with awl closely spaced stitching holes 3/32" from edge of (D), simultaneously through (A) and (D). Figs. 3, 5.

6. Stitch around loose end of (D) with saddle stitch. Finish stitching (D) to (A) with saddler's stitch. Fig. 2.

7. Lace all matching edges of (B) and (C) to (A) with cross stitch. Fig. 2.

8. Sew long edge of (E) to (F) on sewing machine, 1/8" from edge, starting and ending at corner. Finish by stitching vertical seam of (E). Fig. 2.

9. Turn (EF) with raw seam inside. Stitch turned and flattened seam 1/8" from inverted seam line, concealing all raw edges. (French seam.) Fig. 2.

10. Cement (H) to (E). Fig. 2.

11. Punch drawstring holes through (HE) with No. 3 tube. Fig. 2.

12. Turn down 1" for hem at top of (EF). Turn under 1/4" of raw edge and hem on sewing machine. Leave 3/8" space for drawstring (I) and stitch again. Fig. 2.

13. Insert (I) through holes in (EH). Fig. 2.

14. Cement (G) to second (F). Fold over edges of (F) and cement to (G). Fig. 2.

15. Cement cardboard side of (GF) to base of (EF). Fig. 2.

16. Insert oil silk pouch in humidor. Fig. 2.

MATERIALS:

Cowhide, extra heavy, 8-9 oz.
Scrap of cowhide, 5-6 oz. (for tab)
Oil silk
Cardboard
Casco flexible cement
Goat lacing, 3/32"
Heavy linen thread

TOOLS:

(1), (6), (8), (17), (21), (25), (26), (27), (41).

Crayon Case

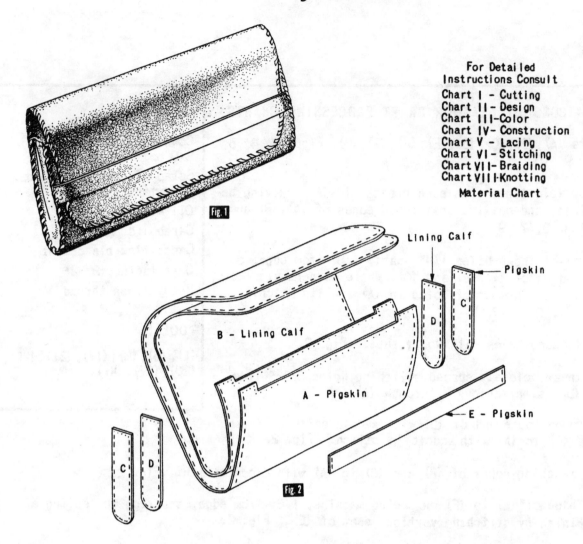

Fig. 1

For Detailed
Instructions Consult
Chart I - Cutting
Chart II- Design
Chart III-Color
Chart IV- Construction
Chart V - Lacing
Chart VI - Stitching
Chart VII - Braiding
Chart VIII-Knotting
Material Chart

Lining Calf
Pigskin
B - Lining Calf
A - Pigskin
E - Pigskin
C   D
Fig. 2

PROCEDURE: (CONSULT LEATHER CRAFT PROCESSING CHARTS)

1. Cut parts (A), (B), (C), (D) and (E). Figs. 3, 4, 5.

2. Cement (B) to (A) and (D) to (C). Fig. 2.

3. Mark stitching holes with 1/7" spacing wheel 1/8" from top edge of (CD) and notched edge of (AB). Figs. 3, 5.

4. Punch stitching holes with awl as marked. Figs. 3, 5.

5. Sew with saddler's stitch. Fig. 2.

6. Mark guide line with awl for thong slits on all edges of (AB) and (CD) not already stitched. Figs. 2, 3, 5.

7. Punch 3/32" thong slits around all edges of (AB) including ends of (E) where attached to front of (AB). Punch thong slits in (CD) to correspond to matching edges of (AB). Fig. 2 and Leather Chart V.

8. Assemble all parts and lace with whip stitch. Figs. 1, 2.

MATERIALS:

Pigskin, 2-1/2 oz.

Lining Calf

Goat lacing 3/32", 7-1/2"

Linen thread

Rubber cement

TOOLS:

(1), (4), (6), (17), (18), (25), (28), (40), (41).

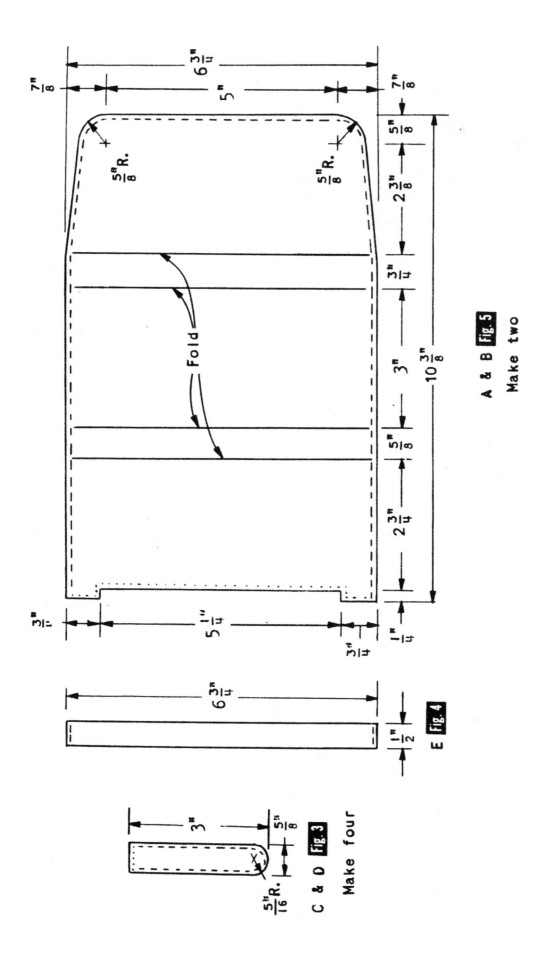

$\frac{7"}{8}$ $6\frac{3"}{4}$ $\frac{7"}{8}$

$5"$

$\frac{5"}{8}$ R. $\frac{5"}{8}$ R.

$\frac{5"}{8}$

$2\frac{3"}{8}$

$3\frac{"}{4}$

Fold

$3"$ $10\frac{3"}{8}$

$\frac{5"}{8}$

$2\frac{3"}{4}$

$\frac{1"}{4}$

$1\frac{"}{1}$ $\frac{3"}{4}$

$5\frac{1"}{4}$

A & B **Fig. 5**

Make two

$6\frac{3"}{4}$

$\frac{1"}{2}$

E **Fig. 4**

$3"$

$\frac{5"}{8}$

$\frac{5"}{16}$ R.

C & D **Fig. 3**

Make four

369

Decorative Pottery Base

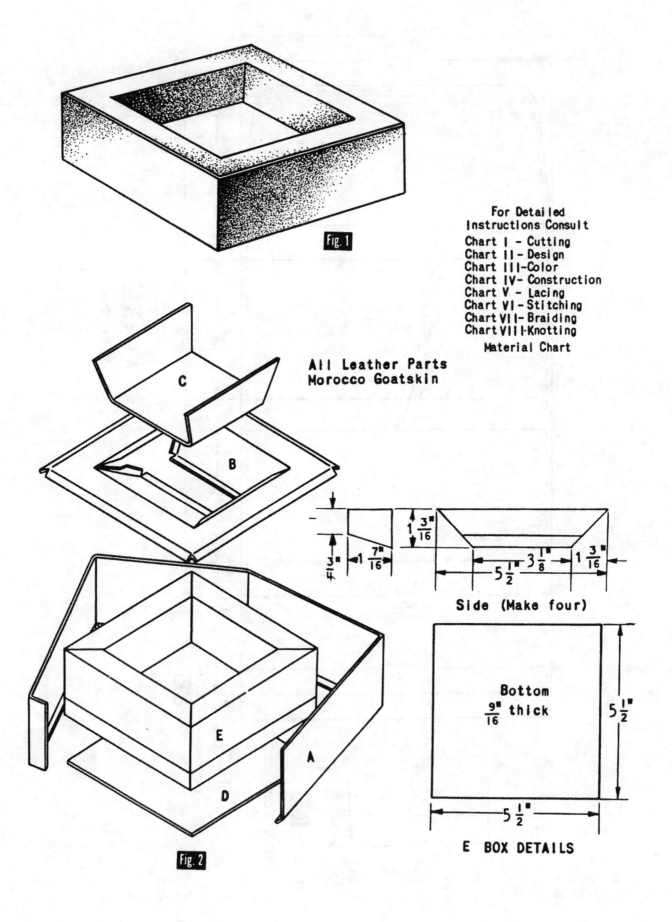

Fig. 1

For Detailed
Instructions Consult
Chart I - Cutting
Chart II - Design
Chart III - Color
Chart IV - Construction
Chart V - Lacing
Chart VI - Stitching
Chart VII - Braiding
Chart VIII - Knotting
Material Chart

All Leather Parts
Morocco Goatskin

Side (Make four)

Bottom
$\frac{9}{16}$" thick

$5\frac{1}{2}$"

$5\frac{1}{2}$"

E BOX DETAILS

Fig. 2

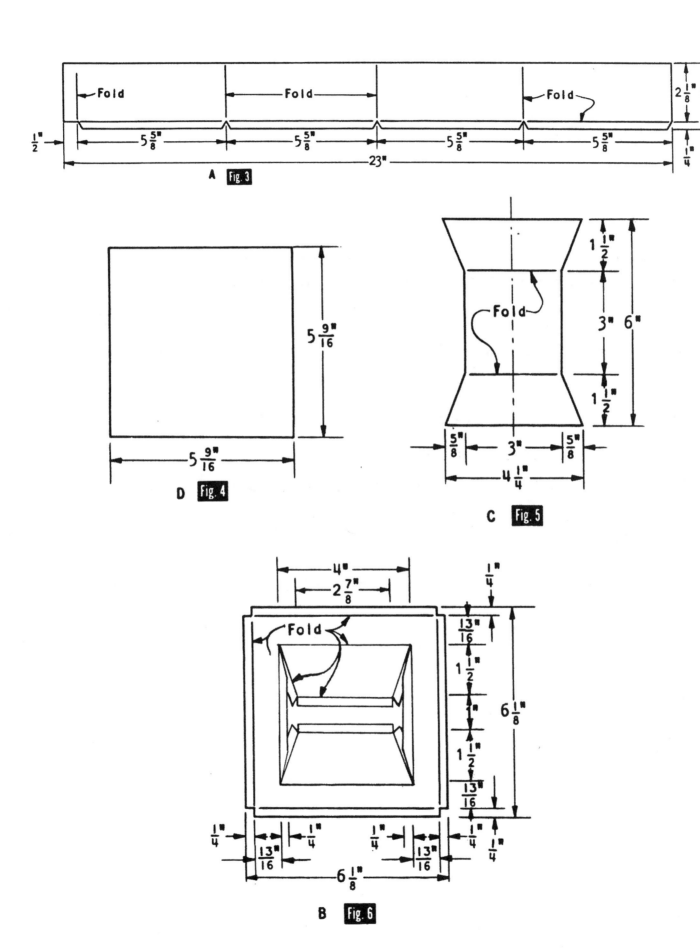

A **Fig. 3**

D **Fig. 4**

C **Fig. 5**

B **Fig. 6**

PROCEDURE: (CONSULT LEATHER CRAFT PROCESSING CHARTS)	MATERIALS:
1. Cut parts (A),(B),(C) and (D). Figs. 3, 4, 5, 6.	Morocco goatskin
Note: Construct wooden base (E).	Rubber cement
2. Skive all edges to be cemented. Fig. 2.	
3. Mark all fold lines with edge creaser. Figs. 3, 5, 6.	
4. Cement (B) to wooden base (E). Fig. 2.	TOOLS:
5. Cement (C) within (E), covering flap edges of (B). Fig. 2.	(1), (6), (19).
6. Cement (A) around sides of (E), covering flap edges of (B) and extending under base of (E). Overlap ends of (A) at corner. Fig. 2.	
7. Cement (D) to base of (E) covering flap edges of (A). Fig. 2.	

Cosmetic Traveling Kit

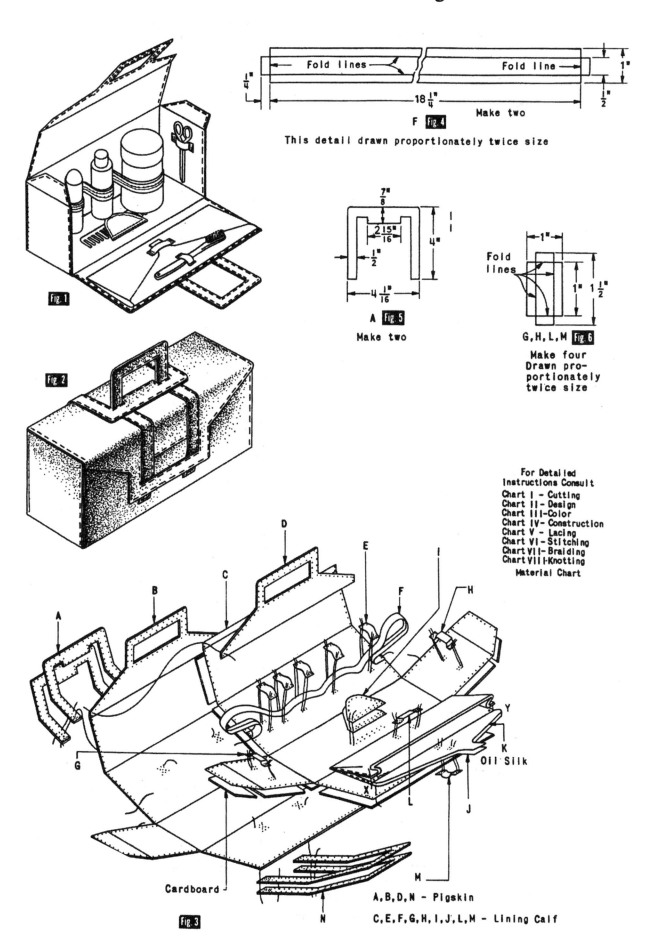

Fold lines

Fold line

1"

4½"

18¼"

½"

Make two

F **Fig. 4**

This detail drawn proportionately twice size

7/8"

2 15/16"

½"

4 1/16"

4"

A **Fig. 5**

Make two

1"

Fold lines

1"

1½"

G, H, L, M **Fig. 6**

Make four
Drawn pro-
portionately
twice size

For Detailed
Instructions Consult
Chart I – Cutting
Chart II – Design
Chart III – Color
Chart IV – Construction
Chart V – Lacing
Chart VI – Stitching
Chart VII – Braiding
Chart VIII – Knotting

Material Chart

Fig. 1

Fig. 2

D

C

B

A

E

F

I

H

Y

K

Oil Silk

G

X

L

J

Cardboard

M

N

Fig. 3

A, B, D, N – Pigskin

C, E, F, G, H, I, J, L, M – Lining Calf

373

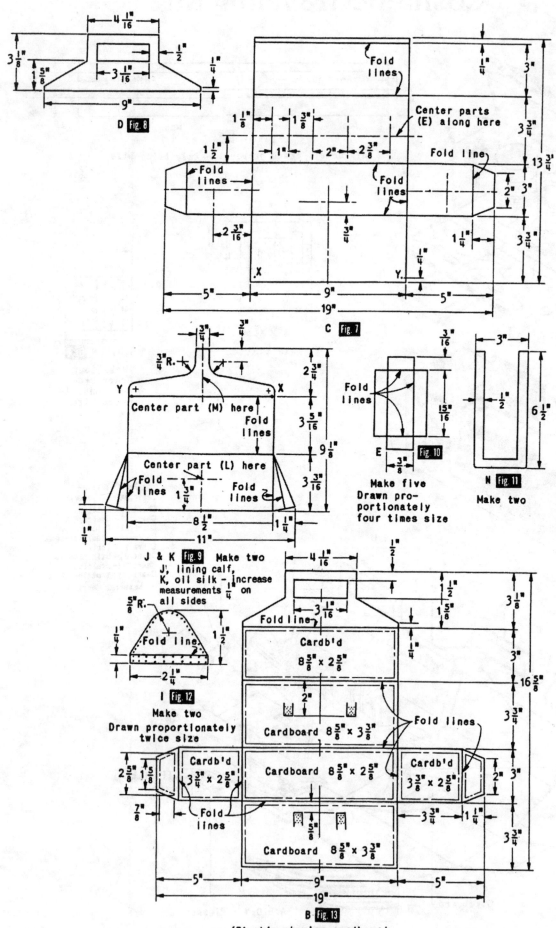

D **Fig. 8**

Center parts (E) along here

Fold lines

Fold line

Fold lines

Fold lines

.X

Y.

C **Fig. 7**

Center part (M) here

Fold lines

Center part (L) here

Fold lines

Fold lines

J & K **Fig. 9** Make two
J', lining calf,
K, oil silk - increase
measurements ¼ on
all sides

Fold lines

E **Fig. 10**

Make five
Drawn pro-
portionately
four times size

N **Fig. 11**

Make two

Fold line

I **Fig. 12**

Make two
Drawn proportionately
twice size

Fold line

Cardb'd
$8\frac{5}{8}$" x $2\frac{5}{8}$"

Cardboard $8\frac{5}{8}$" x $3\frac{3}{8}$"

Cardb'd
$3\frac{3}{4}$" x $2\frac{5}{8}$"

Cardboard $8\frac{5}{8}$" x $2\frac{5}{8}$"

Cardb'd
$3\frac{3}{8}$" x $2\frac{5}{8}$"

Fold lines

Cardboard $8\frac{5}{8}$" x $3\frac{3}{8}$"

Fold lines

B **Fig. 13**

(Pigskin showing cardboard
represented by dotted lines.)

374

PROCEDURE: (CONSULT LEATHER CRAFT
PROCESSING CHARTS)

1. Cut parts (A), (B), (C), (D), (E), (F), (G), (H), (I), (J), (K), (L), (M), (N). Figs. 4 through 13.

2. Cement (A) to (A) and (N) to (N) flesh sides together. Figs. 5, 11.

3. Mark 1/7" stitching holes 1/8" from all edges of (AA) and (NN). Fig. 3.

4. Punch stitching holes with awl. Where (AA) and (NN) are attached to (B) punch holes through all matching parts simultaneously. Fig. 3.

5. Sew (AA) and (NN) with saddle stitch. Then sew both parts to (B) with saddler's stitch. Figs. 3, 13.

6. Cement all cardboards to flesh side of (B), allowing 3/16" between edge of cardboard and all cut edges of leather or fold lines. Fig. 13.

7. Turn all edges of (E), (F), (G), (H), (L), and (M) on fold lines. Cement each edge. Figs. 4, 6, 10.

8. Stitch edges of (F) on sewing machine. Fig. 4.

9. Place (E) on center line position of (C) as shown. Allowing adequate width for insertion of (F), stitch each end of (E) to (C) on sewing machine. Insert (F). Figs. 3, 7.

10. Place (G), (H), (L) and (M) on center line positions of (C) and (J) as shown. On sewing machine, stitch ends of (G), (H), (L) and (M), allowing sufficient fullness for insertion of nail file, scissors, closing tab of (J), and toothbrush, respectively. Figs. 3, 7, 9.

11. Cement (I) to (I), flesh sides together. Fig. 12.

12. Stitch rounded edges of (II) on sewing machine. Fig. 3.

13. Place (II) on center line position of (C). Punch with awl double row of stitching holes through matching parts of (II) and (C) as shown. Figs. 3, 7.

14. Sew (II) to (C) with saddler's stitch. Fig. 3.

15. Turn back 1/4" on all edges of (K). Fig. 9.

16. Cement turned edges of (K) against flesh side of (J). Fig. 3.

17. Fold (JK). Stitch gusset ends and flap of (JK) on sewing machine. Figs. 3, 9.

18. Stitch (JK) to (C) on sewing machine from points (X) to (Y). Figs. 3, 9.

19. Cement (C) with its assembled parts to cardboard reinforcement on (B). Fig. 3.

20. Lightly press cemented lining (C) against (B) in spaces between cardboard with round end of embossing tool. Trim any edges of (C) that might extend beyond (B). Fig. 3.

21. Cement (D) to top flap of (B) flesh sides together, overlapping (C) 1/4". Fig. 3.

22. Mark stitching holes with 1/7" spacing wheel, 1/8" from edge, on all edges of (B), cut-out for strap in (B) and matching edge of (D). Mark matching stitching holes on edges of 2 back corner seams, including ends of (F) in seams. Fig. 2.

23. Punch stitching holes with awl. Fig. 3.

24. Sew 2 back corner seams with saddler's stitch. Figs. 2, 3.

25. Sew along entire remaining edge of (BC) and around cut-out for strap, with saddle stitch. Figs. 2, 3.

MATERIALS:

Pigskin, 2-1/2 oz.

Lining calf, dark brown, 1 oz.

Oil silk

Cardboard

Rubber cement

Heavy linen thread, brown

TOOLS:

(1), (6), (17), (21), (25), (28), (30), (33), (41).

Man's Traveling Case

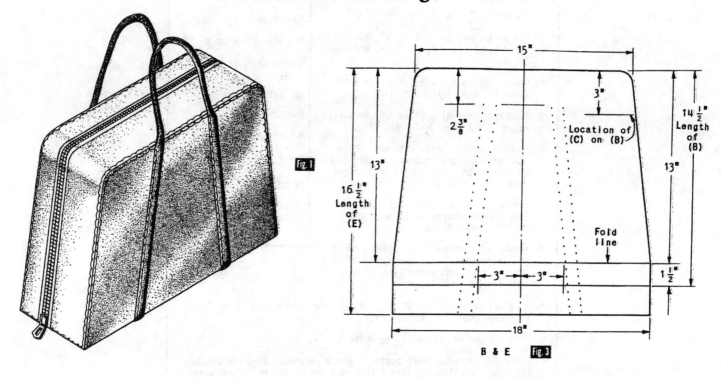

Fig. 1

Fig. 3

B & E

15"

2 3/8"

3"

Location of
(C) on (B)

14 1/2"
Length
of
(B)

13"

13"

16 1/2"
Length
of
(E)

Fold
line

3"   3"

1 1/2"

18"

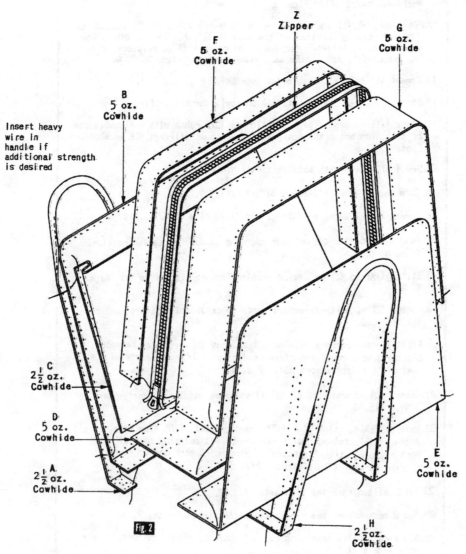

Fig. 2

Z
Zipper

F
5 oz.
Cowhide

G
5 oz.
Cowhide

B
5 oz.
Cowhide

Insert heavy
wire in
handle if
additional strength
is desired

C
2 1/2 oz.
Cowhide

D
5 oz.
Cowhide

A
2 1/2 oz.
Cowhide

E
5 oz.
Cowhide

H
2 1/2 oz.
Cowhide

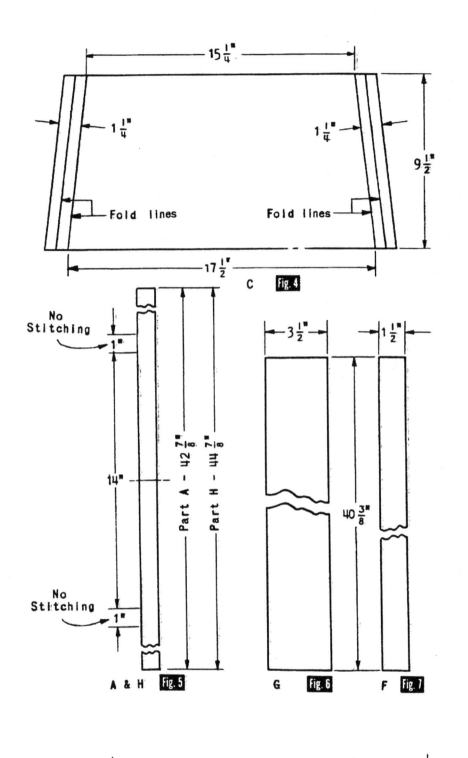

15 ¼"

1 ¼"   1 ¼"

9 ½"

Fold lines   Fold lines

17 ½"

C   Fig. 4

No
Stitching
1"

No
Stitching
1"

14"

Part A – 42 ⅞"

Part H – 44 ⅞"

A & H   Fig. 5

3 ½"   1 ½"

40 ⅜"

G   Fig. 6   F   Fig. 7

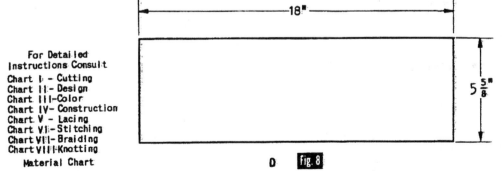

18"

For Detailed
Instructions Consult
Chart I – Cutting
Chart II – Design
Chart III – Color
Chart IV – Construction
Chart V – Lacing
Chart VI – Stitching
Chart VII – Braiding
Chart VIII – Knotting
Material Chart

5 ⅝"

D   Fig. 8

PROCEDURE:(CONSULT LEATHER CRAFT PROCESSING CHARTS)

MATERIALS:

Cowhide, $2\frac{1}{2}$ oz.

Cowhide, 5 oz.

Zipper, 40"

Heavy linen thread

Casco flexible cement

TOOLS:

(1), (5), (6), (17), (19), (22), (23), (25), (28), (30), (41).

1. Cut parts (A), (B), (C), (D), (E), (F), (G) and (H). Figs. 3, 4, 5, 6, 7, 8.

2. Mark fold lines on (A), (B), (C), (E) and (H). Figs. 3, 4.

3. Skive flesh side of (A), (B), (E) and (H) on fold lines for a width of 1/4". Figs. 3, 5.

4. Skive 1/4" of all edges of (A), (B), (E), (F), (G) and (H) to make a more flexible stitching edge. Figs. 3, 4, 5, 6.

5. Mark 1/5" stitching holes, 1/8" from edge, on all edges of (A) and (H) except short span indicated. Mark stitching holes on handle length parallel for stitching together. Figs. 2, 5.

6. Punch stitching holes in (A) and (H) on edges of handle length. Figs. 2, 5.

7. Fold (A) and (H) for handles. Stitch folded (A) and (H) with saddler's stitch. Fig. 2.

8. Cement strap ends of (A) to (B) and (H) to (E) in folded position. Figs. 2, 3.

9. Punch stitching holes through (A) and (B), and (H) and (E). Fig. 2.

10. Stitch (A) to (B) and (H) to (E) with saddler's stitch. Fig. 2.

11. Fold (C) on fold lines. Fig. 4.

12. Mark stitching holes 1/8" from all stitched edges, on (C) with 1/7" spacing wheel. Fig. 2.

13. Cement edges of (C) in position on (B) and punch stitching holes through bottom edge of (C) on (B) only. Fig. 2.

14. Stitch bottom edge of (C) with saddler's stitch. Fig. 2.

15. Mark 1/5" stitching holes 3/16" from edge, on edges of (F) and (G) to be stitched to (BC), (D) and (E). Mark corresponding stitching holes on (BC) and (E) respectively. Fig. 2.

16. Mark stitching holes with 1/7" spacing wheel, 1/8" from edges of (F) and (G) to be stitched to zipper (Z). Fig. 2.

17. Punch stitching holes, with awl, in all edges of (B), (E), (F) and (G). Fig. 2.

18. Stitch (Z) to (F) and (G) with sewing awl. Fig. 2.

19. Stitch (F) to (B) and (G) to (E) with saddler's stitch. Fig. 2.

20. Cement (D) with flesh side up in position on folded ends of (B) and (E), within the bottom of case. Fig. 2.

21. Mark 1/5" stitching holes, 3/8" from folded edges of (B) and (E) over (D) and 1/4" from all cut edges of (B) and (E) over (D). Fig. 2.

22. Punch stitching holes through (B), (E) and (D) as marked, including ends of (A) and (H) already cemented and stitched to (B) and (E). Fig. 2.

23. Cement tape ends of (Z) to flesh side of (D). Fig. 2.

24. Punch double row of closely spaced stitching holes for reinforcement through (D) and cemented ends of (Z). Fig. 2.

25. Stitch (D) to (B), (E), (F), (G) and ends of (Z) with saddler's stitch. Fig. 2.

Man's Unfitted Traveling Case

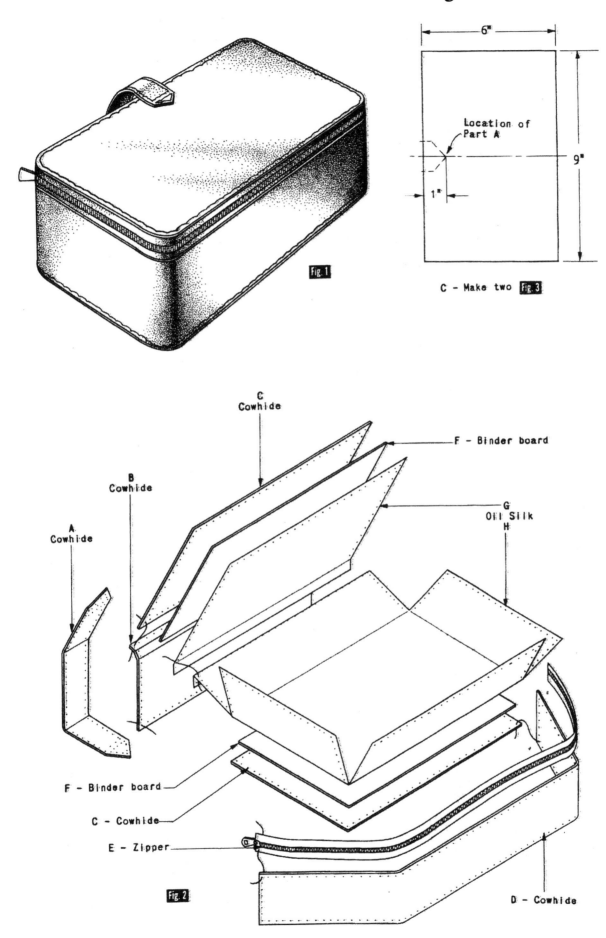

6"

9"

Location of
Part A

1"

C - Make two **Fig.3**

Fig.1

C
Cowhide

F - Binder board

B
Cowhide

G
Oil Silk
H

A
Cowhide

F - Binder board

C - Cowhide

E - Zipper

D - Cowhide

Fig.2

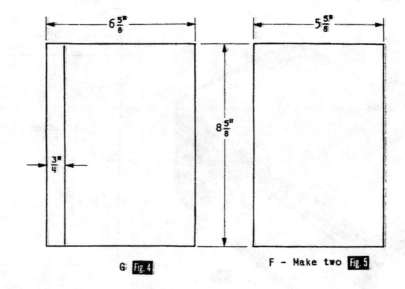

6 5/8"

5 5/8"

8 5/8"

3/4"

G: Fig. 4

F - Make two Fig. 5

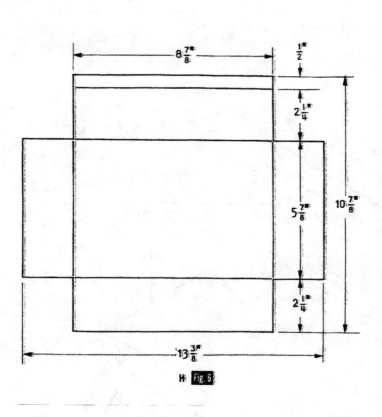

8 7/8"

1/2"

2 1/4"

10 7/8"

5 7/8"

2 1/4"

13 3/8"

H: Fig. 6

5/8"

Fold lines

9"

3"

B Fig. 7

2 3/8"

6 1/8"

9 1/4"

6 1/8"

D Fig. 9

1 1/4"

6"

A Fig. 8

(This detail drawn proportionately 1/3 larger)

For Detailed
Instructions Consult
Chart I - Cutting
Chart II - Design
Chart III - Color
Chart IV - Construction
Chart V - Lacing
Chart VI - Stitching
Chart VII - Braiding
Chart VIII - Knotting
Material Chart

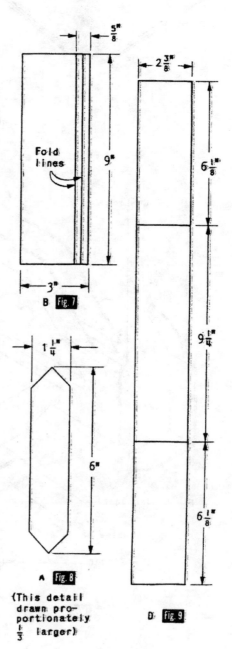

PROCEDURE: (CONSULT LEATHER CRAFT PROCESSING CHARTS)

1. Cut (A), (B), (C), (D), (F), (G) and (H). Figs. 3, 4, 5, 6, 7, 8, 9.

2. Skive all stitching edges except zipper edges. Fig. 2.

3. Outline all edges of (A), (B), (C) and (D) with edge creaser, and mark hinge lines on skin side of (B). Figs. 3, 7, 8, 9.

4. Mark stitching holes with 1/7" spacing wheel on crease lines marked on (A), (B), (D) and corresponding stitching holes on edges of (C). Fig. 2.

5. Punch stitching holes with awl on all edges as marked. Fig. 2.

6. Sew long edges of (B) to matching edges of parts (C) with saddler's stitch. Fig. 2.

7. Sew long edges of (A) with saddler's stitch. Do not terminate threads. Figs. 1, 2.

8. Cement pointed ends of (A) in position on parts (C). Using holes already punched in (A) as a guide, punch through (AC). Figs. 2, 3.

9. Finish sewing (A) to (C) with saddler's stitch. Figs. 1, 2.

10. Sew (D) to (B) and bottom (C) with saddler's stitch. Start at vertical corner of (B) and short end of (D). Stitch along bottom edges of (D) and (C); finish by sewing other vertical corner of short end of (D) to (B). Fig. 2.

11. Sew corners of oil silk (H) to form lining for (BCD), and cement 1/2" fold of (H) at back edge. Fig. 2.

12. Cement parts (F) to parts (C). Fig. 2.

13. Cement edges of (G) to (CF) with hinge edge of (G) overlapping hinge edge of (B). Fig. 2.

14. Cement top edges of (H) within top edges of (BCD) with folded edge overlapping (G) at hinge edge of (B). Fig. 2.

15. Cement tape edges of zipper (E) to edges of (CG) and to edges of (DH) on the lining side. Fig. 2.

16. Sew (E) to (CG) and (DH) with back stitch, using holes punched in (C) and (D) as guide. (Step 4). Finish sewing back top edge of (GH) to (B). Fig. 2.

MATERIALS:

Cowhide, 4-5 oz.

Oil silk

Hard-rolled binder board (millboard) .093"

Rubber cement

Linen thread

Zipper, 1/4" tooth span, 21" long.

TOOLS:

(1), (6), (17), (19), (25), (27), (28), (41).

Crayon Case

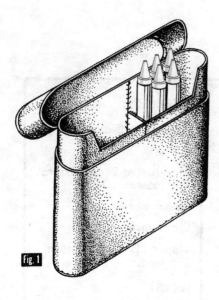

Fig. 1

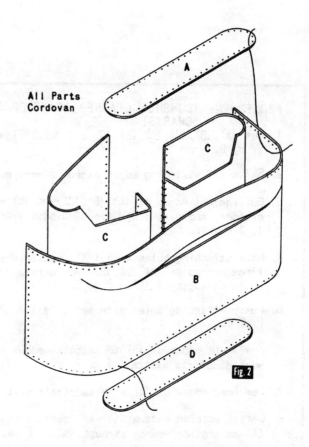

All Parts
Cordovan

Fig. 2

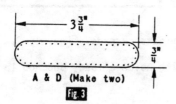

$3\frac{3}{4}"$

$\frac{3}{4}"$

A & D (Make two)

Fig. 3

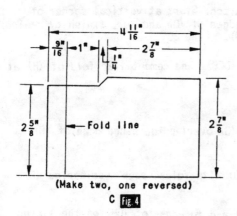

$4\frac{11}{16}"$

$\frac{9}{16}"$ $1"$ $2\frac{7}{8}"$

$\frac{1}{4}"$

$2\frac{5}{8}"$ $2\frac{7}{8}"$

← Fold line

(Make two, one reversed)

C **Fig. 4**

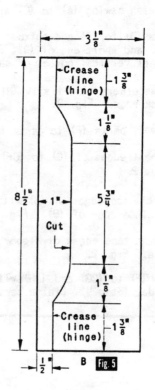

$3\frac{1}{8}"$

Crease line (hinge) — $1\frac{3}{8}"$

$1\frac{1}{8}"$

$8\frac{1}{2}"$ $1"$ $5\frac{3}{4}"$

Cut

$1\frac{1}{8}"$

Crease line (hinge) — $1\frac{3}{8}"$

$\frac{1}{2}"$

B **Fig. 5**

For Detailed
Instructions Consult
Chart I – Cutting
Chart II – Design
Chart III – Color
Chart IV – Construction
Chart V – Lacing
Chart VI – Stitching
Chart VII – Braiding
Chart VIII – Knotting
Material Chart

PROCEDURE: (CONSULT LEATHER CRAFT PROCESSING CHARTS)

Note: This case to be made of thin, stiff leather such as Cordovan (horse hide). Measurements vary with thickness of leather.

1. Cut parts (A), (B), (C) and (D). Figs. 3, 4, 5.

2. Outline edges of all parts and mark fold lines in (C) and hinge line on (B) with edge creaser. Figs. 3, 4, 5.

3. Mark parallel stitching holes with 1/7" spacing wheel on crease lines of both vertical edges of parts (C) and all outside edges of (B). Fig. 2.

4. Punch stitching holes in (C) and (B). Fig. 2.

5. Fold parts (C), with short vertical edge forming corner at back with long vertical edge. Fig. 2.

6. Sew corner of parts (C) with parallel butt edge stitch. Do not cut thread of last corner sewn.

7. Cement together partition ends of (C); finish sewing extended edges of high ends with parallel butt edge stitch. Fig. 2.

8. Place (B) around parts (C) to test correct tight fit. Trim short ends of (B) if too long. Remove (C) and sew short ends of (B) with parallel butt edge stitch. Fig. 2.

9. Cement parts (C) inside (B), allowing 1/8" of (B) to fall below (C) for stitching (B) to (D). Dry thoroughly. Fig. 9.

10. Mark stitching holes on crease lines of (A) and (D) to correspond to stitching holes on top and bottom edges of (B) respectively. Figs. 2, 3.

11. Punch stitching holes in (A) and (D). Fig. 3.

12. Sew (A) and (D) to (B) with saddler's stitch. (Skive stitching edges of (A), (D) and (B) if leather is too stiff for flexible stitching edge). Fig. 2.

MATERIALS:

Cordovan leather (horse-hide)

Note: A stiff thin leather must be used for this case

Rubber cement

Linen thread

TOOLS:

(1), (6), (17), (25), (27), (28), (41).

See Leather Chart V for marking holes on curves and for butt edge parallel stitching.

Umbrella Cover

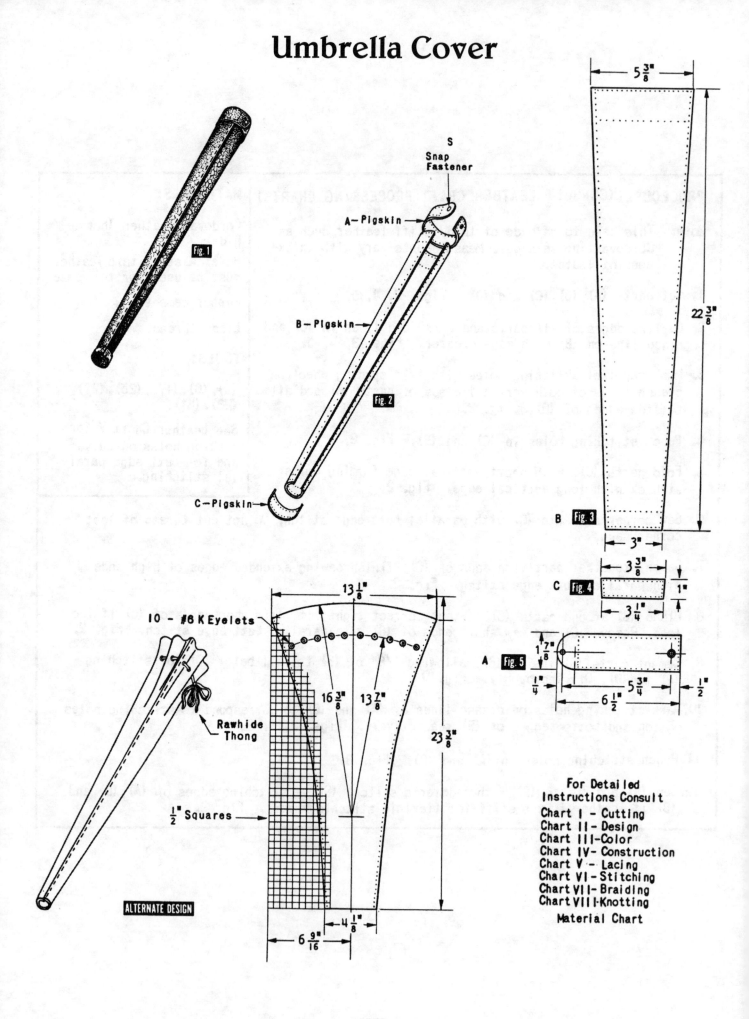

Fig. 1

S
Snap
Fastener

A—Pigskin

B—Pigskin

Fig. 2

C—Pigskin

5 3/8"

22 3/8"

B Fig. 3

3"

3 3/8"
C Fig. 4   1"
3 1/4"

1 7/8"
A Fig. 5
1/4"   5 3/4"   1/2"
6 1/2"

10 - #6 K Eyelets

Rawhide
Thong

1/2" Squares

13 1/8"

16 3/8"   13 7/8"

23 3/8"

4 1/8"

6 9/16"

ALTERNATE DESIGN

For Detailed
Instructions Consult
Chart I - Cutting
Chart II- Design
Chart III-Color
Chart IV- Construction
Chart V - Lacing
Chart VI - Stitching
Chart VII- Braiding
Chart VIII-Knotting
Material Chart

384

PROCEDURE: (CONSULT LEATHER CRAFT PROCESSING CHARTS)

1. Cut and prepare parts (A), (B), and (C). Figs. 3, 4, 5.

2. Match edges of (B) lengthwise. Hold edges together with clamp. Fig. 2.

3. Punch stitching holes with awl, 1/7" apart, 1/8" from edge, simultaneously through matching edges. Figs. 2, 3.

4. Attach snap fastener (S) to (A). Figs. 2, 5.

5. Place (A) and (C) in position on (B). Punch stitching holes with awl 1/7" apart, 1/8" from edge, simultaneously through matching parts. Figs. 2, 4, 5.

6. Attach (A) and (C) to (B) with saddle stitch. Fig. 2.

7. Overlay long edges of (ABC) 1/4" beginning at narrow end. Fig. 2.

8. Sew long seam with saddle stitch, using matching holes. Figs. 1, 2.

MATERIALS:

Pigskin, lightweight

Snap fastener

Heavy linen thread

TOOLS:

(1), (6), (12), (17), (25), (28), (41).

Umbrella Cord

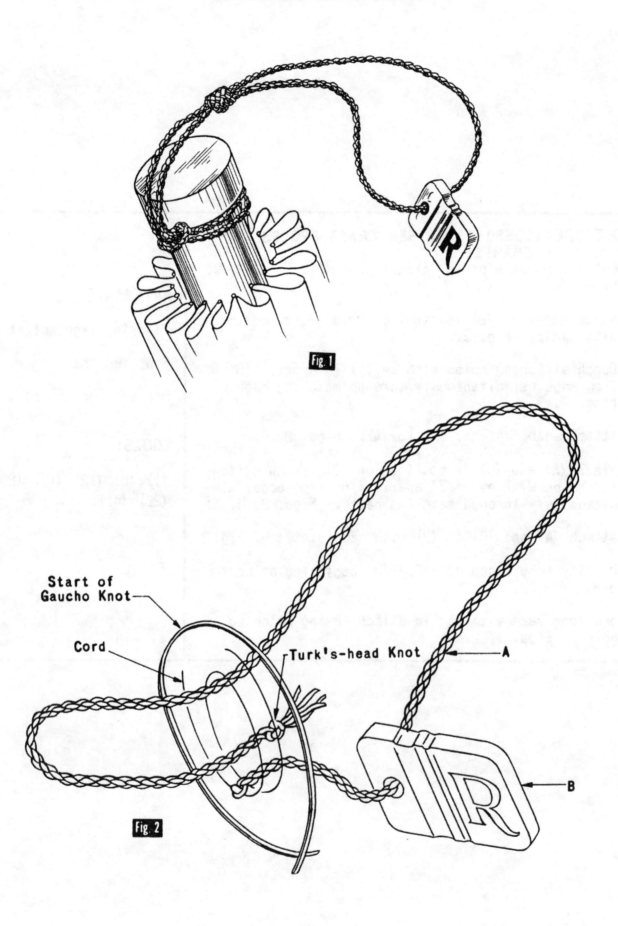

Fig. 1

Start of
Gaucho Knot

Cord

Turk's-head Knot

A

B

Fig. 2

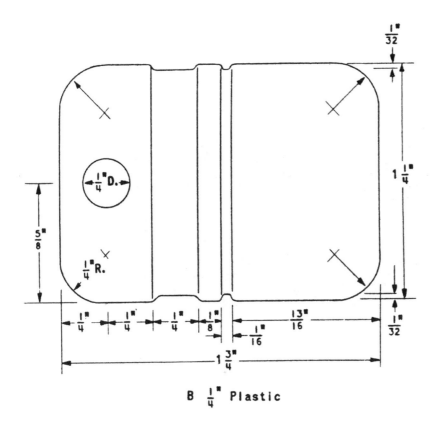

For Detailed
Instructions Consult
Chart I - Cutting
Chart II - Design
Chart III - Color
Chart IV - Construction
Chart V - Lacing
Chart VI - Stitching
Chart VII - Braiding
Chart VIII - Knotting
Material Chart

B $\frac{1}{4}$" Plastic

PROCEDURE: (CONSULT LEATHER CRAFT PROCESSING CHARTS)

1. Braid lace (A) in four-plait round, diamond pattern (2 colors) to a length of 22". Fig. 2.

2. Terminate braid with a terminal Turk's-head knot. Fig. 2.

3. Slip monogram plate (B) over braid. Figs. 1, 2.

4. Overlap ends of braid 1/2", forming 2 loops. One loop is 4-1/2" long, and the hand grasp loop with monogram in position, takes up the remaining braid. Fig. 2.

5. Tie ends of braid, with loops formed, securely with cord. Fig. 2.

6. Form single Gaucho knot, basket weave pattern over junction of ends. Figs. 1, 2.

7. Attach 4-1/2" loop on umbrella handle. Fig. 1.

MATERIALS:

Craft strip plastic lace, 3/32"

TOOLS:

(20), (21).

See Leather Charts VII and VIII for Braiding and knotting.

Watch Band

PROCEDURE:
HAVING PREPARED THE 3 SEPARATE PARTS...
(1) CEMENT FLESH SIDES OF (A), FOLD FLESH
    SIDES TOGETHER AND PUNCH NO.OO HOLES
    AS INDICATED. LACE.
(2) CEMENT FLESH SIDE OF (B).
    CEMENT (C) TO (B), AS INDICATED.
    INSERT BUCKLE, FOLD OVER ENDS OF (B)
    FLESH SIDES TOGETHER, AND SEW ENDS.
    PUNCH NO.OO HOLES AND LACE.
(3) PUNCH NO.O HOLES IN (A) AS INDICATED.

TOOLS. (1)(6)(8)(17)

MATERIALS: CONSULT LEATHER CHARTS, BUCKLE,
           RUBBER CEMENT.

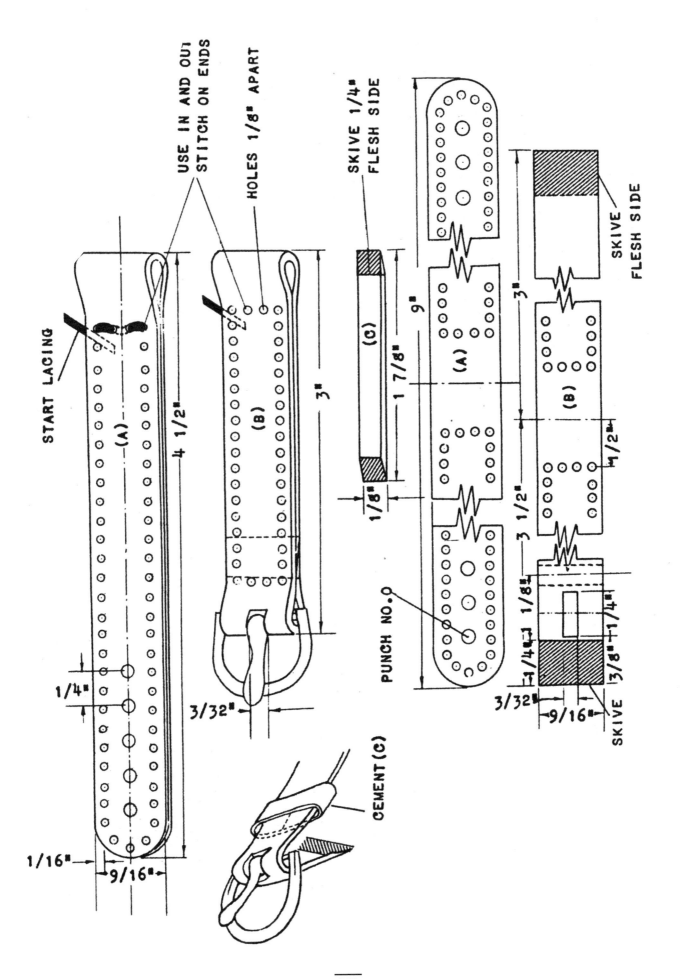

START LACING

USE IN AND OUT
STITCH ON ENDS

HOLES 1/8" APART

SKIVE 1/4"
FLESH SIDE

(A)

(B)

(C)

4 1/2"

3"

9"

1 7/8"

1/8"

3"

3 1/2"

(A)

(B)

SKIVE
FLESH SIDE

1/2"

1/4"

1/4"

1/16"

1/4"

9/16"

3/32"

PUNCH NO. 0

CEMENT (C)

3/32"

3/4"

1/8"

3/8"

9/16"

SKIVE

Man's Watch Strap

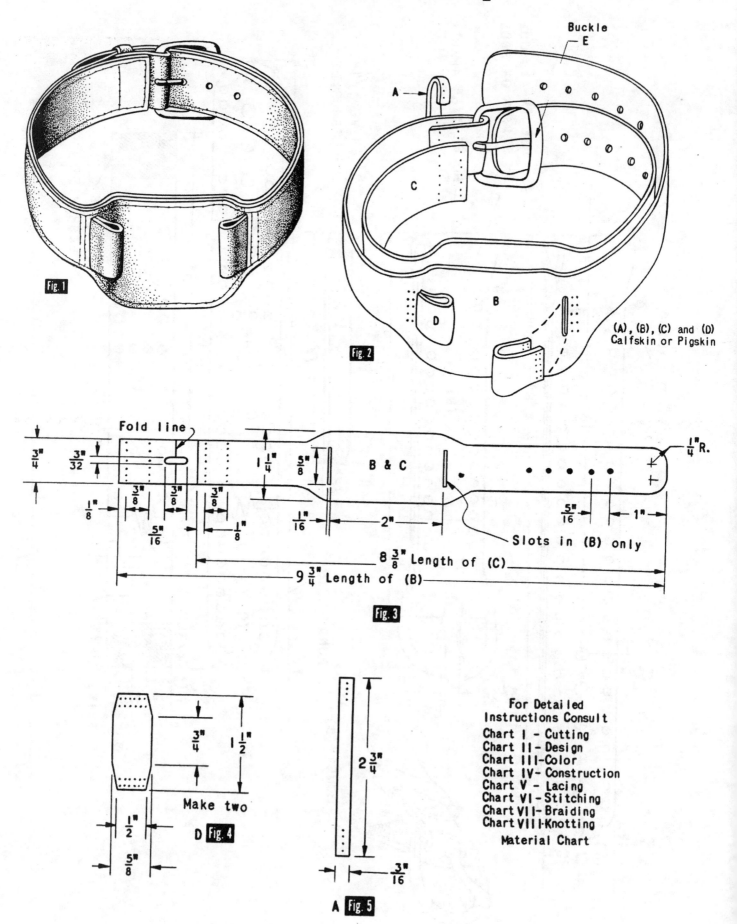

Buckle E

A

C

(A), (B), (C) and (D)
Calfskin or Pigskin

D   B

Fig. 1

Fig. 2

Fold line

3/4"   3/32"

B & C

1 1/4"   5/8"

1/4" R.

Slots in (B) only

1/8"   3/8"   3/8"   3/8"

1/8"

1/16"   2"

5/16"   1"

5/16"

1/8"

8 3/8" Length of (C)

9 3/4" Length of (B)

Fig. 3

3/4"   1 1/2"

Make two

D Fig. 4

1/2"

5/8"

2 3/4"

3/16"

A Fig. 5

For Detailed
Instructions Consult
Chart I - Cutting
Chart II - Design
Chart III - Color
Chart IV - Construction
Chart V - Lacing
Chart VI - Stitching
Chart VII - Braiding
Chart VIII - Knotting
Material Chart

PROCEDURE:(CONSULT LEATHER CRAFT PROCESSING CHARTS)

1. Cut parts (A),(B),(C) and (D). Figs. 3, 4, 5.

2. Skive ends of (A) and (D) and square end of (B). Figs. 3, 4, 5.

3. Fold parts (D) and insert ends in slits of (B). Figs. 2, 3, 4.

4. Punch with awl, double row of closely spaced stitching holes, 1/16" and 3/16" from slits, through (B) and (D) as shown. Figs. 2, 4.

5. Sew parts (D) to (B) with saddler's stitch. Figs. 1, 2.

6. Cut slot in square end of (B) for prong of buckle (E). Fig. 3.

7. Fold (A) over (B) with skived ends overlapping 3/8" on flesh side of (B). Fig. 2.

8. Punch row of closely spaced stitching holes through overlapping ends of (A) on (B). Fig. 5.

9. Sew (A) to (B) with saddler's stitch. Fig. 2.

10. Insert buckle (E) in (B). Cement folded end of (B) over (A) on (B). Fig. 2.

11. Cement (C) to (ABDE). Fig. 2.

12. Punch holes for prong of (E) in end of (BC). Fig. 3.

13. Punch closely spaced stitching holes with awl through folded end of (B) 1/8" and 1/2" from end of (C). Fig. 3.

14. Sew with saddler's stitch. Fig. 2.

15. Mark stitching line with edge creaser around assembled parts. Figs. 1, 2.

16. Stitch on sewing machine. Figs. 1, 2.

MATERIALS:

Pigskin or calfskin

Buckle, 3/4"

Rubber cement

Linen thread

TOOLS:

(1), (6), (8), (17), (25), (27), (33), (41), (43).

Wastebasket

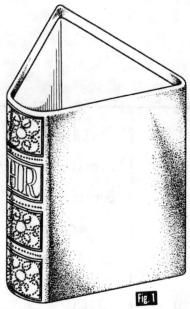

Fig. 1

Fold over to cover wood

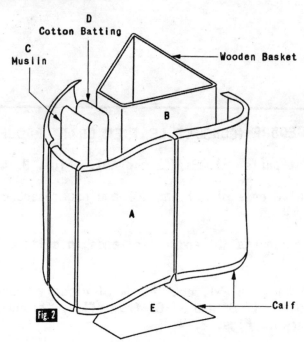

C Muslin

D Cotton Batting

Wooden Basket

B

A

E

Calf

Fig. 2

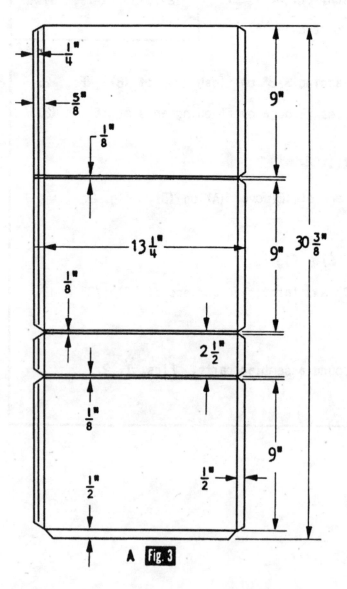

$\frac{1}{4}$"

$\frac{5}{8}$"

$\frac{1}{8}$"

9"

$13\frac{1}{4}$"

9"

30$\frac{3}{8}$"

$\frac{1}{8}$"

2$\frac{1}{2}$"

$\frac{1}{8}$"

9"

$\frac{1}{2}$"

$\frac{1}{2}$"

A Fig. 3

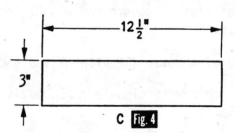

12$\frac{1}{2}$"

3"

C Fig. 4

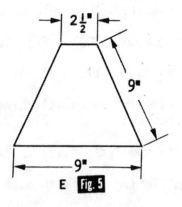

2$\frac{1}{2}$"

9"

9"

E Fig. 5

For Detailed
Instructions Consult
Chart I - Cutting
Chart II - Design
Chart III - Color
Chart IV - Construction
Chart V - Lacing
Chart VI - Stitching
Chart VII - Braiding
Chart VIII - Knotting
Material Chart

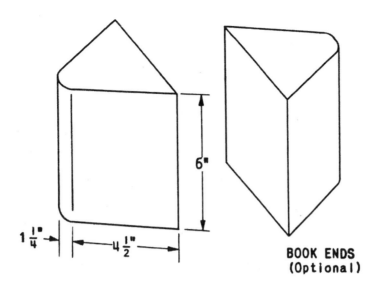

6"

1 1/4"   4 1/2"

BOOK ENDS
(Optional)

Wood Basket Details
(For bottom see Fig. 5.)

2 1/2" x 11 3/4"

Back

8 1/2" x 11 3/4"

Side (Make two)

9" x 11 3/4"

Front

PROCEDURE: (CONSULT LEATHER CRAFT PROCESSING CHARTS)	MATERIALS:
1. Cut and prepare parts (A), (C) and (E). Figs. 3, 4, 5.	Tooling calf, 2 oz., color optional
Note: Construct wastebasket form of 1/4" plywood. Bookend forms to be of weighted wood. Both to be covered with leather.	Cotton batting
2. Skive all edges of (A) and (E). Figs. 3, 5.	Unbleached muslin
3. Place a strip of cotton batten (D), about 1/4" thick, on 2-1/2" plane of basket (B). Fig. 2.	Rubber cement
4. Cement edges of muslin (C) over (D) on (B), entirely covering (D) to hold it in place. Fig. 2.	Wooden basket
5. Cement (A) to (B), with edges turned down within top edges and under base of (B). Overlap ends of (A) and cement at back corner. Fig. 2.	TOOLS:
6. Cement (E) to base of (B). Fig. 2.	(1), (6), (19).

Wastebasket

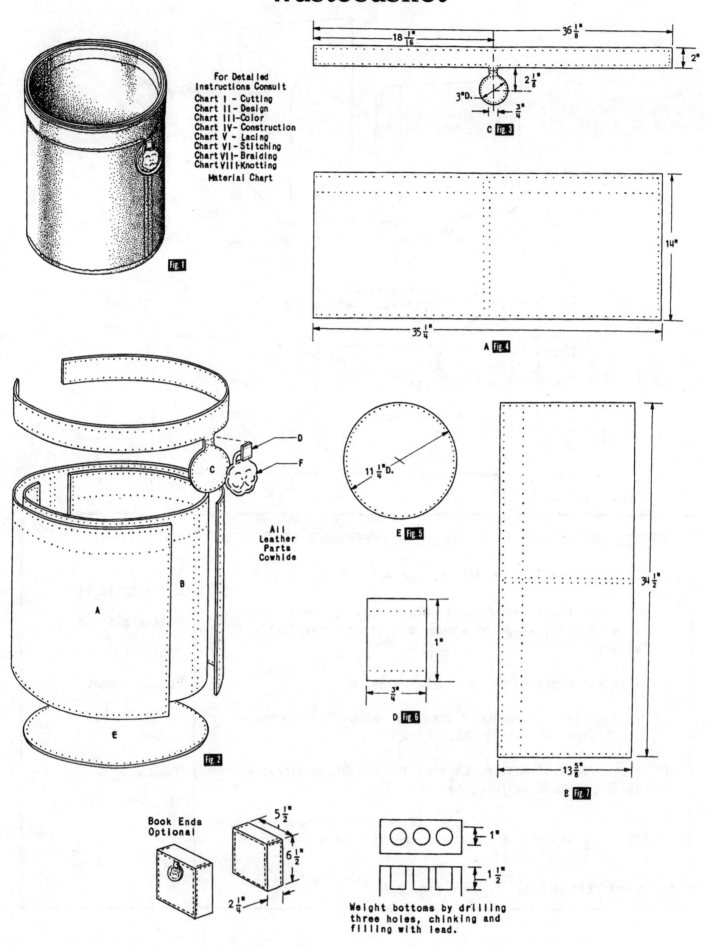

For Detailed
Instructions Consult
Chart I – Cutting
Chart II – Design
Chart III – Color
Chart IV – Construction
Chart V – Lacing
Chart VI – Stitching
Chart VII – Braiding
Chart VIII – Knotting
Material Chart

All
Leather
Parts
Cowhide

Fig. 1

C Fig. 3

18 $\frac{1}{16}$"   36 $\frac{1}{8}$"   2"

3"D.   2 $\frac{1}{8}$" $\frac{3}{4}$"

A Fig. 4

14"

35 $\frac{1}{4}$"

E Fig. 5

11 $\frac{1}{4}$" D.

D Fig. 6

1" $\frac{3}{4}$"

B Fig. 7

34 $\frac{1}{2}$"

13 $\frac{5}{8}$"

Fig. 2

Book Ends
Optional

5 $\frac{1}{2}$"   6 $\frac{1}{2}$"   2 $\frac{1}{4}$"

1"   1 $\frac{1}{2}$"

Weight bottoms by drilling
three holes, chinking and
filling with lead.

394

PROCEDURE: (CONSULT LEATHER CRAFT PROCESSING CHARTS)

MATERIALS:

Heavy cowhide, 6-8 oz., natural
Heavy linen thread, white
Rubber cement

TOOLS:

(1), (6), (17), (19), (25), (41).

1. Cut parts (A), (B), (C), (D) and (E). Figs. 3, 4, 5, 6, 7.

2. Skive on flesh side of ends and bottom edges of (A) and (B) and entire edge of (E), to a width of 1/4". (Skive at an angle to facilitate sewing of a vertical piece to a horizontal piece.) Fig. 2.

3. Punch parallel stitching holes with awl, 1/8" from vertical edges of (B), at about 2" intervals. Fig. 7.

4. Bring edges of (B) together temporarily with flesh side out by tying the matching holes with string. Fig. 2.

5. Place rounded (B) over a large can or cylindrical object as near the size of the basket as possible. Fig. 2.

6. Cement (A) to (B) flesh sides together, with ends of (A) on opposite side of ends of (B). Set top edges of (A) and (B) flush to allow additional 3/8" of (A) for stitching to (E). Use cylindrical form within (AB) to achieve rounded contour while cementing Fig. 2.

7. Tie string in spiral fashion around (AB) from top to bottom to prevent springing of cemented edges. Allow to dry thoroughly. Fig. 2.

8. Remove cylindrical form. Place (AB) over long block of wood for punching stitching holes.

9. Mark stitching guide line 1/8" from each cemented vertical edge and bottom edge of (A) and 1/4" from edge of (E). Mark double row of stitching holes, 1/4" apart, on (A), 1/8" to either side of ends of (B) cemented within (A). Fig. 2.

10. Mark stitching holes 1/4" apart on all guide lines. Mark holes on (E) to correspond with stitching holes on bottom edge of (A). Fig. 2 and Leather Chart V

11. Punch all stitching holes with awl. Fig. 2.

12. Snip exposed ends of strings temporarily tied to edges of (B). Fig. 2.

13. Stitch (E) to (AB) and vertical seams of (AB) with saddler's stitch. Fig. 2.

14. Mark stitching guide line 1/8" from edge, around circular tab on (C), and 1/4" from edge on all other edges of (C). Fig. 3.

15. Mark stitching holes 1/4" apart on all edges of (C). Fig. 3.

16. Punch stitching holes on circular tab and neck of (C). Fig. 3.

17. Stitch tab and neck with saddler's stitch. Figs. 1, 2.

18. Place (D) in position on (C), leaving 1/4" fullness to accomodate ring of metal ornament (F). Figs. 2, 3.

19. Punch closely spaced stitching holes 1/8" from ends of (D) through matching parts of (C) and (D). Fig. 2, 6.

20. Insert ring of (F). Sew (D) to (C) with saddler's stitch. Fig. 2.

21. Cement (C) around (AB), centering circular tab on seam of (A). Figs. 1, 2.

22. Punch stitching holes through (ABC) as marked. Fig. 2.

23. Stitch with saddler's stitch. Figs. 1, 2.

Weaving

Introduction

The art of weaving grew out of the need for protection. It is possible that birds provided early humans with the inspiration to weave. This birdwatching led to the possibility of interweaving strands of grasses, shreds of bark, dried animal intestines and long hair of animals into mats and garments, after observing the intricate manner in which birds intertwined twigs and hairs in making their nests. Spinning developed when humans sought to produce strands longer than the longest hairs and vegetable fibers available to them.

It is difficult to determine whether a fully developed form of weaving with threads had its origin in the Far East or Egypt. Scenes of Egyptian life, pictured in tombs that date back to 4500-2475 B.C., show weavers at work. The embalming procedure of these Egyptians required the body to be wrapped in long strips of fine linen, which indicates that the method of weaving was well advanced. The garments of the Egyptians were made almost entirely of linen because the Nile valley provided flax in abundance.

Wool Weaving Perfected

The manufacture of silk fabrics dates back to 2640 B.C. Chinese myths attribute the invention of the first silk weaving loom to the empress of W-Hang, but silk culture and its weaving were not understood in Europe until 3,000 years later, so carefully did the Chinese guard their secret.

India is the oldest known cotton-producing country. Regulations concerning its weaving appear in the laws of Manu, 1000 B.C., indicating that the weaving processes were well established there 3000 years ago.

Woolen fabrics were woven by the Persians, Greeks and Romans. The weaving of wool reached perfection in Europe during the latter part of the ninth century in Flanders. After the Norman Conquest, the Anglos and Saxons wore wool, but its manufacture did not become extensive until 1331.

Established During Revolution

Fabrics were woven right in the homes. Many who earned their livelihood by it formed draper's or cloth guilds. Much weaving was also carried on in monastaries.

This manual production in the home, and by small guild units, gradually shifted to large scale manufacture and became an established industry during the Industrial Revolution.

Weaving

Modern Loom Developed from Primitive Methods

However complicated modern looms appear today, they are essentially the same in principle as the most primitive type.

To weave the simplest fabric, there must be a framework upon which the *warp* threads for the ground of the material are stretched; one round bar on which unwoven *warp* threads are attached, and one on which the finished material is rolled. Both vertical and horizontal looms were used by the primitives.

The earliest vertical loom consisted of a wooden beam or bar suspended between trees. One end of each *warp* thread was wound on the beam; the other end was tied to a small stone, the weight of which held the warp thread taut. The *weft* thread, or horizontal thread of a fabric, was wound on a stick that was drawn under and over the *warp* threads to interlock the vertical threads with the horizontal.

This manner of weaving was used by some Native Americans.

Method Devised To Raise Threads

The primitive horizontal loom was a frame with the warp threads stretched taut from one end to the other. Small articles could be woven on the frame in a horizontal position, or a large frame could be tilted against a wall or tree to weave larger articles. The simple frame looms used in primary grades are based on this horizontal principle.

A method was finally devised by which groups of warp threads could be raised alternately to permit the insertion of the *weft* threads, without the tedious process of going under and over one warp thread at a time. Odd-numbered threads, 1, 3, 5, 7, etc., were attached to one bar (harness) while even-numbered threads, 2, 4, 6, 8, etc., were attached to the other harness.

Each harness carries a series of *heddles* (cords or wires) that have "eyes" through which the warp threads are strung. This keeps the warp unentangled and simplifies the numbering of the threads as the loom is being strung, or "dressed."

Use of Two-Harness Looms

Two-harness looms produce the simplest type of weave: under one, or over one, called a "plain" or "tabby" weave. The first harness, carrying the odd-numbered threads, is raised to produce a separation from the second harness, carrying the even-numbered threads.

This separation creates a space called a *shed*. The *shuttle*, a device on which the weft thread is wound, is *shot* or passed through the shed under the threads on harness (1), and over the threads on harness (2). The second harness is then raised, reversing the positions of the warp threads, and creating a new shed. The weft is shot back through the shed, now over the threads on harness (1), and under the threads on harness (2). This alternation of harnesses continues for the length of the fabric.

Origin Of 'Treadling'

A plain weave can be strung on a four-harness loom, such as the Structo looms. Odd-numbered threads are strung in their numerical sequence on harnesses (1) and (3), while even-numbered threads are strung in their numerical sequence on harnesses (2) and (4). When harnesses (1) and (3) are raised, all odd-numbered threads are separated from the even-numbered threads on harnesses (2) and (4).

This manipulation of the harnesses is known as *treadling.* The term originates from the fact that large floor looms are controlled by foot pedals or "treadles." Table looms, such as the Structo eight-inch, 20-inch, and 26-inch four-harness looms, are controlled by levers manipulated by hand. Treadling refers to this manipulation of the harnesses, on all weaving projects described in this book.

The looms used for craft weaving usually have two or four harnesses. However, a few carry as many as 16. The manipulation of this loom would require treadling similar to that which an organist uses to operate the pedals of an organ.

TYPES OF WEAVING

Craft weaving falls into four main classifications: Plain, or Tabby Weave, Twill Weave, Pattern Weave and Tapestry Weave.

PLAIN WEAVE was described in the foregoing discussions to illustrate the principles of weaving. Variations of plain weave can be achieved in the following ways:

(a) Use a heavy weft with light warp to create a ribbed or corded effect.

(b) Use groups of threads rather than a single thread in sequence on each harness. For example: warp threads 1, 2, 3, on harness (1); 4, 5, 6 on harness (2); 7, 8, 9 on harness (3); 10, 11, 12 on harness (4). Introduce weft three times in the same shed, interlocking weft around the warp on each selvage before reversing weft through same shed. Otherwise the weft will come out of shed on tracing its route. This alternation of three warp and three weft produces a *block* effect, called basket weave.

TWILL WEAVES, as woven by the craftsman, are usually woven on four-harness looms. The harnesses are threaded as for a plain weave. The treadling sequence is one of progression rather than alternation.

Harnesses (1) and (2) are raised; the weft passes over warp threads on harnesses (3) and (4). Harnesses (2) and (3) are raised, the weft passes over warp threads on harnesses (2) and (4). Harnesses (3) and (4) are raised; the weft passes over warp threads on harnesses (1) and (2). Harnesses (4) and (1) are raised, the weft passes over warp threads on harnesses (2) and (3). Thus, the treadling sequence is noted as 1 and 2, 2 and 3, 3 and 4, 4 and 1; continue 1 and 2, 2 and 3, etc.

Diagonal Effect Created In Fabric

The weft shoots over two warp, under two; in the next treadling it shifts either to the left or right by one warp only, going over two warp, under two, etc.

This succession of shifting over one warp at a time creates a diagonal effect in the fabric. The "Woman's Scarf," in this book, is an example of a one-way twill.

A twill may be varied in the following ways:

(a) The progression or sequence of treadling can be reversed at regular intervals. Treadle 1 and 2, 2 and 3, 3 and 4, 4 and 1, 1 and 2. Then reverse sequence, with 1 and 2, as the turning point each time, treadling 4 and 1, 3 and 4, 2 and 3, 1 and 2. Then repeat the forward progression, etc. This type of reversed twill produces a zig-zag effect, known as *herringbone.* The "Knitting Bag," shown in this book, is an example of the reverse twill.

(b) The regularity of a twill can be changed by threading 2 or 3 heddles side by side on the same harness. This produces a long shot of weft over the warp. Such varied group threading is found in the "Man's Muffler."

PATTERN WEAVES are woven on looms of four harnesses or more. The four-harness loom provides hundreds of possible designs. For this reason the average craft weaver works with a four-harness loom, and this discussion will be confined to patterns for that loom.

Drafts patterns are achieved through a variety of both treading and treadling. The diagram for threading the harness is called a *draft.*

Drafts are drawn on graph (squared) paper. A horizontal row of squares represents one harness. The bottom row represents the front or first harness; the one next to the bottom represents the second; the one next to the top, the third; the top one represents the fourth harness. Any one square filled in on any one of the rows, represents a warp thread on one heddle on that particular harness. A harness may carry several warp side by side, but never one above the other on other harnesses.

Planning Of Patterns

Drafts are usually read from *right* to *left*. In cases where the draft for the entire fabric has been given, it has seemed advisable to arrange it to read from *left* to *right*.

A pattern weave is usually planned so that a 1-3 or 2-4 treadling (or both) produces a plain (tabby) weave to be shot between a treadling that produces a pattern shot; for instance a 3-4. See "Table Runner."

Some patterns are not planned with this treadling, and it may be necessary to interlock the last warp on each selvage with the weft, so that the next shot of weft will not "back out" of the shed. This is necessary when a warp on the selvage is shot under or over two or more times, exposing a span of "unlocked" warp. See "Floor Mat."

In some cases, the treadling of one harness only will result in a plain weave. One-half of all warp threads are strung on that harness, with the remaining half divided between the other three harnesses. See "Table Cloth."

Many pattern weaves can be woven, with just one weft, without shifting shuttles when introducing a plain weave shot, if such is included in the draft. See "Muffler."

Heavier Weft Emphasized

Many standard patterns, however, make use of two shuttles, one wound with a fine thread (usually the same as warp), and one wound with a heavier colored yarn, wool or cotton. The shuttle with the colored yarn is used for the pattern shots, and the shuttle with the fine thread is used for the plain weave shots, to alternate with the pattern shots. This change in weft minimizes the plain weave weft, and emphasizes the heavier weft in the pattern block.

Early American coverlets were woven in this manner. For examples, see "Manual of Instructions" for Structo looms.

TAPESTRY WEAVES are woven on two- or four-harness looms that are strung as for a plain weave, except that the warp threads are spaced further apart, usually one warp for every other *dent* (space between wires in the reed of the beater).

The shuttle, instead of going across the entire width of the warp, covers only those warp threads where that particular color is desired. Each color is wound on a different shuttle or a large needle in the case of small color areas.

Alternating warp threads are raised; a weft of each color appearing in that line is introduced. As one color area ends and another begins the two colored wefts join by encircling the same warp thread. Now the harnesses are shifted and the warp threads that were under are now up. The colored wefts are again introduced. When a specific color area is completed the weft is drawn to the back and clipped, but not so close as to unravel.

The weft threads in a tapestry weave are packed close together with the beater, so that all warp threads are hidden. This is made possible by the wide spacing of the warp threads mentioned previously.

Examples of the tapestry method are found in the "Woman's Envelope Purse" and "Rug or Wall Hanging" (Navajo design).

Tapestry weave was the only method by which a pattern could be introduced into weaving when the loom was in its primitive stage.

Indian Tapestry Weaving

Examples of tapestry weave are found among the upholstery fabrics woven by the early Egyptians. The Native Americans provide some of the most outstanding examples of this type of weave in their blankets and mats. The highest achievements in the tapestry method were reached during the Middle Ages and Early Renaissance, when the wall cloths (tapestries) of the period became pictorial representations of the times.

Entire families or guilds were employed in weaving a single tapestry over a period that often extended into many decades. Every gradation of color in the flesh tones, the clothing, animals, trees, flowers and buildings in these pictorial wall hangings represents a change of the weft color. When it is realized that dozens of people, all elaborately dressed, appear in these tapestries, a boundless admiration is developed for the skill and patience of the artist-weavers involved.

DRESSING THE LOOM

The preparation of the loom for the actual weaving of a fabric is called *dressing* the loom.

The various stages in the dressing process are illustrated and described briefly in the Weaving Instructions. However, it is necessary to amplify on the more intricate details.

WARPING BOARD: The wall-type board illustrated in the instructional poster can be made of 3/4 inch thick plywood. The pegs, slightly tapered, are made of 1/2-inch dowels usually cut from four inches to five inches long.

The warping board illustrated prepares warp six yards long. Longer board, thus increasing the length of the route covered by the warp. A much longer route can be arranged by driving a long nail or peg into the baseboard directly below the center of the board. The warp should then be taken from peg (2) at the left, down to the pen on the baseboard, and up to peg (3) at the right, etc. (See Weaving Instructions, pages 404-407).

WARPS: Ready-warped spools can be purchased. Because the range of color and material may not afford the color desired for a specific article, it is advisable to know how to prepare your own warps.

Directions for setting up a loom with ready-warped spools are found in manufacturer's catalogues.

The method of determining the number of warp threads per article is described in the Weaving Instructions. Each article described also lists the number of warp needed. For those who wish to weave articles not described, determine the warp count according to:

(1) The weight of the yarn used

(2) The coarseness of the desired fabric

Most looms are equipped with a reed that has 15 dents (slits) to an inch. A fine, closely woven fabric, with a fine cotton or linen warp, would call for 30 warp per inch, or two warp per dent.

A course, loosely woven fabric, with a heavier cotton or linen warp, would call for 15 warp per inch or one warp per dent. Most woolen items, such as mufflers and baby blankets, call for 15 warp per inch, or one warp per dent. Many rugs and heavy tapestry weaves skip every other dent, thus creating a wider space in the warp.

WEAVING OPERATIONS
(Refer to Weaving Instructions, pages 404-407, for details.)

The actual weaving of an article is more simple than the preparation of the warp. The amateur should be cautioned to maintain a straight selvege (edge) by not drawing the weft too tight before beating. Neither should it be left so loose as to form a row of loops on the edge.

BEATING: Beating of the weft should be done with consistent pressure, so that a regular spacing of weft creates an even tone to the fabric.

Do not weave the fabric to a point near the beater where it is difficult to insert the shuttle in the shed. Release tension on the cloth beam and then the warp beam by adjusting the ratchets, when the cloth has to be rolled on the cloth beam.

Unroll a few inches of warp, and slowly roll the woven fabric on the cloth beam. Adjust the ratchets to obtain the same tension to the warp as when weaving was started. Do not roll so much of the cloth on the beam that the beater cannot function.

WEAVING YARNS: In addition to the standard weaving yarns used in the articles, many unusual textural effects can be achieved with a variety of materials.

Modern weavers have successfully introduced cellophane, strands of spun glass and sinuous vegetable fibers, such as palm-leaf strands, for borders and block designs in table mats and drapery fabrics. Care should be taken when cleaning such articles.

Jute, a sturdy yarn of vegetable fibers, is popular for rug weaving. A cotton carpet warp

is used when jute is used for the weft.

Weavers, after some experience, will be able to plan their own drafts and arrive at individual textural effects.

GLOSSARY

TERMS	EXPLANATION
Beam, Breast	The front, horizontal part of frame nearest to weaver, on which warp must lie as it is tied to the metal bar of the cloth beam.
Beam, Cloth	The front revolving cylinder to which warp ends are tied, and on which the finished fabric is rolled.
Beam, Warp	The back revolving cylinder on which the warp is rolled.
Beater (also called Batten)	The movable frame with a comb-like strip of metal through which warp threads are drawn. Used to pack weft together.
Board, Warping	The multi-pegged wall board on which warp is measured and prepared for stringing on the loom.
Cone	The conical-shaped spool on which some cotton yarns are wound.
Crank	Used to adjust tension of warp; to unroll warp; and to wind woven fabric on cloth beam.
Dent	The slit between the wires in the reed of the beater, through which warp threads are drawn.
Draft	The threading scheme, drawn on graph paper, indicating the sequence of warp threads on each harness. Each square represents a warp thread in a heddle.
Drawing-In	The process of pulling warp threads in their proper sequence through the eyes of the heddles on each harness.
Filler	The heavy cotton yarn used as weft to establish correct spacing of warp threads preliminary to weaving the final fabric.
Ground	The warp threads which form the "backing" for the material before the horizontal or weft threads are woven in.
Hank	Two or more skeins of wool yarn tied together.
Harness	The frame to which the heddles for carrying warp threads are attached; in a "draft" a single horizontal row of squares represents one harness.
Heading	The 3/4, span of weaving between the "filler" and the final weaving. The weft in the heading is usually same weight as warp.
Heddles	Narrow metal strips, suspended on harnesses, with small eye-like openings through which warp threads are drawn.
Hook	Used for drawing warp threads through heddles and dents in the reed.
Latch	The device which "catches" the levers that regulate the manipulation of the harnesses.
Leases	The sticks that are used to separate the "under" from the "over" warp threads in dressing the loom.
Levers	The hand controls that regulate the manipula-

tion of the harnesses.

Pattern .... The classification of weaving which introduces a design into a fabric by means of varied thread and treadling of the harnesses.

Plain (also .... The classification of
called Tabby) weaving which results in a simple under-and-over effect in the threads of the fabric.

Ratchet .... The tooth-edged disc at the end of each warp and cloth beam, that holds the beam stationery or effects its release.

Reed .... The comb-like metal strip in the beater through which the warp threads are drawn to regulate the width and spacing of the warp.

Shed .... The space between threads that is created by the separation of harnesses, for the insertion of the weft.

Shot .... The insertion of a weft through a shed.

Shuttle .... The device on which the weft is wound to simplify the insertion of a weft in the shed.

Sleying .... The process of drawing the warp threadsthrough the dents in the reed.

Tabby .... See Plain Weave.

Tapestry .... A classification of weaving where the warp is strung as for a plain weave, but the weft is changed as often as the design calls for a change in color.

Tension .... The tautness of the warp. Even tension produces a regular weave; uneven tension produces a ripply quality.

Treadle .... The manipulation of the harnesses: raising and lowering them according to the weave.

Tying-In .... The process of tying the warp ends to the metal bar on the cloth beam after the sleying process.

Warp .... The longitudinal threads of the fabric; those that form the ground of the fabric and determine its pattern by their threading.

Weft .... The horizontal threads of the fabric; threads that are wound on shuttles to facilitate their insertion into the shed created by raised and lowered harnesses.

EQUIPMENT AND SUPPLIES

Order the following items from any supply firm for weaving materials.

(1) Looms, four-harness, eight-inch, 20 inches, 26 inches, table models,

(2) Shuttles, wood, large, medium, small,

(3) Hooks, threading,

(4) Ready-warped spools (Order sample card of warp available on spools, if warp is not to be prepared on warping board. Complete directions for assembling spools on special hexagonal steel warp beam will be found in manufacturer's manual of instructions).

WEAVING, KNOTTING, BRAIDING
Weaving, Knotting, Braiding Tools and Equipment Materials

Item No.	Materials
1	Looms Weaving 24" 4 Harness 5526
2	Looms Weaving 14" 4 Harness 5523

3	Each Loom with Beam, Spools, Shuttles, Hook Draw in Reeds, Shuttles Speed- O-Weave Frame
4	Craft Strip 7/64" Gimp Blue 103 Yd. Balls
5	Craft Strip 7/64" Gimp Dk. Green 100 Yd. Balls
6	Craft Strip 7/64"GimpTan 100 Yd. Balls
7	Craft Strip 7/64"Gimp Dk. Brown 100 Yd. Balls
8	Craft Strip 7/64" Gimp Black 100 Yd. Balls
9	Craft Strip 7/64" Gimp Red 100 Yd. Balls
10	Craft Strip 7/64" Gimp White 100 Yd. Balls
11	Craft Strip 7/64" Gimp Gold 100 Yd. Balls
12	Craft Strip 7/64" Gimp Silver 100 Yd. Balls
13	Craft Strip 7/64" Gimp Orange 100 Yd.
14	Pyro-cord 1/16 Diam.100 Yd. Balls Black
15	Pyro-cord 1/16 Diam.100 Yd. Balls White
16	Pyro-cord 1/16 Diam. 100 Yd.Balls Red
17	Pyro-cord 1/16 Diam.100 Yd.Balls Green
18	Pyro-cord 1/16 Diam.100 Yd.Balls Orange
19	Pyro-cord 1/16 Diam.100 Yd.Balls Blue
20	Pyro-cord 1/16 Diam. 100 Yd.Balls Brown
21	Pyro-cord 1/16 Diam.100 Yd.Balls Yellow
22	Belfast Cord Dark Green (Ball)
23	Belfast Cord Brown (Ball)
24	Belfast Cord Navy Blue (Ball)
25	Belfast Cord Red (Ball)
26	Belfast Cord Black (Ball)
27	Belfast Cord White (Ball)
28	Ready Warped Spools Cotton White 20 Yds. 60 Ends
29	Ready Warped Spools Egyptian Nat. 10 Yds. 60 Ends
30	Ready Warped Spools Mercerized Cotton 10 Yds. 60 Ends 28 Ready Warped Spools Linen Nat. 10 Yds. 60 Ends
31	Variegated Imitation Fibres 4/32 Green (Lb.)
32	Tulip Carpet Warp 1327 Red (Tube)
33	Tulip Carpet Warp 1325 Lt. Blue (Tube)
34	Tulip Carpet Warp 1326 Dk. Blue (Tube)
35	Tulip Carpet Warp 841 Yellow (Tube)
36	Tulip Carpet Warp 845 White (Tube)
37	Tulip Carpet Warp 1332 Wine (Tube)
38	Tulip Carpet Warp 1331 Dk. Brown (Tube)
39	Tulip Carpet Warp 836 Black (Tube)
40	Weaving Wool W-67 Grn. Gold 2 Oz. Skeins
41	Weaving Wool W-1 White 2 Oz. Skeins
42	Weaving Wool W-28 Navy 2 Oz.Skein
43	Weaving Wool W-95 Red 2 Oz.Skein
44	Weaving Wool W-46 Rose Pin 2 Oz.Skein
45	Weaving Wool W-36 Turquois 2 Oz. Skein
46	Weaving Wool W-80 Orchid 2 Oz. Skein
47	Weaving Wool W-26 Lt. Blue 2 Oz.Skein
48	Weaving Wool W-30 Dk. Blue Oz. Skein
49	Weaving Wool W-2 Black 2 Oz. Skein
50	Weaving Wool W-5 Peach 2 Oz. Skein
51	Tulip 3-Strand Soft Twist K-1 Bleach 2 Oz. Tubes
52	Tulip 3-Strand Soft Twist K-47 Coral Pink 2 Oz. Tubes
53	Tulip 3-Strand Soft Twist K-26 Lt. Blue 2 Oz. Tubes
54	Tulip 3-Strand Soft Twist K-27 Skipper Blue 2 Oz. Tubes
55	Tulip 3-Strand Soft Twist K-95 Red 2 Oz. Tubes
56	Tulip 3-Strand Soft Twist K-2 Black 2 Oz. Tubes
57	Tulip 3-Strand Soft Twist K-60 Green 2 Oz. Tubes
58	Tulip 3-Strand Soft Twist K-61 Medium Green 2 Oz. Tubes
59	Tulip 3-Strand Soft Twist K-10 Yellow 2 Oz.Tubes
60	Tulip 3-Strand Soft Twist K-70 Lavender 2 Oz. Tubes
61	Tulip 3-Strand Soft Twist K-124 Dk. Brown 2 Oz. Tubes
62	Tulip 3-Strand Soft Twist K-36 Turquoise 2 Oz. Tubes

Weaving Instructions

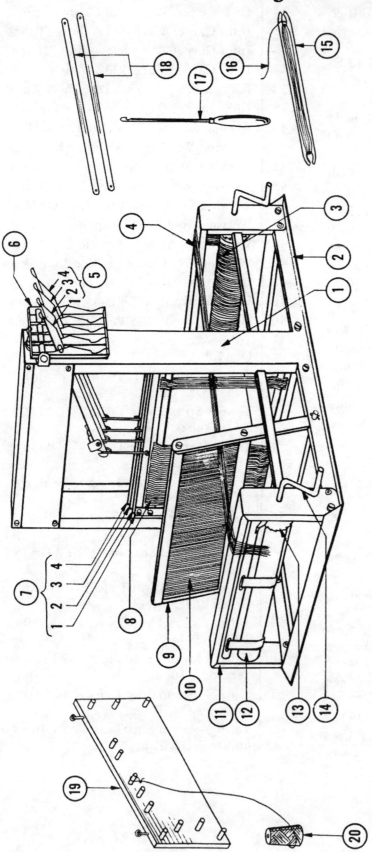

PARTS INDEX

1. MAIN FRAME
2. BOTTOM FRAME
3. WARP BEAM
4. WARP
5. LEVERS — 1, 2, 3, 4
6. LATCH
7. HARNESSES — 1, 2, 3, 4
8. HEDDLES
9. BEATER
10. REED
11. BREAST BEAM
12. CLOTH BEAM
13. RATCHET
14. CRANK
15. SHUTTLE
16. WEFT
17. THREADING HOOK
18. LEASE STICKS
19. WARPING BOARD
20. CONE OF YARN
    (SPOOL OR BALL ALSO)

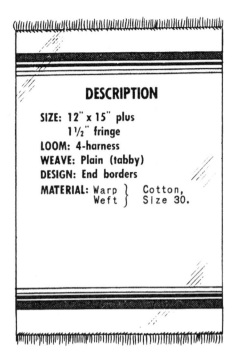

DESCRIPTION

SIZE: 12" x 15" plus
      1½" fringe
LOOM: 4-harness
WEAVE: Plain (tabby)
DESIGN: End borders
MATERIAL: Warp } Cotton,
            Weft } Size 30.

TRAY CLOTH

"DRESSING" THE LOOM

DRAFT   Harness

4) 90
3) warp
2) on each
1) harness

30 warp threads per inch
x 12", width of fabric
360, total No. of warp threads
÷4, No. of harnesses
90, warp on each harness

I. COUNT WARP THREADS

1. Count warp as shown. (All in one color or as specified in drafts).
2. Measure length of warp needed. (8 times length of fabric to be woven; depends also on span of loom frame).

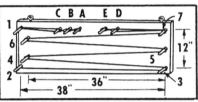

II. USING A WARPING BOARD

1. This route provides 2 warp, 6 yds. each.
2. Tie end of warp from spool to peg (A); carry it over (B), under (C), around pegs (1) to (7), over (D), under (E), around and over (E), under (D), around numbered pegs back to (1), over (C), under (B), around (A).
3. Repeat route for specified no. of warp.
4. Keep colored yarns in correct sequence if mixed colors are used in warp. Separate in groups as shown at (B) and (C) in Fig. III.

CHAIN CONSTRUCTION

III. REMOVING WARP FROM WARPING BOARD

1. Warp is more easily spaced if tied with cord in equal groups (or colors) separating loop (B) from (C), and loop (D) from (E) while warping is in progress. Knot firmly.
2. First remove warp from pegs (A), (B), (C). Hold strands of warp quite taut. Start forming a chain. As chain progresses, release warp from numbered pegs.

3. Tie last loop of chain near point (D).
4. Remove all warp from board.
5. Remove warp stick tied to warp beam.
6. Insert stick (X) through loops (E).
7. Pass a cord through loops (D) and knot cord ends through holes in ends of (X).
8. Remove cords tied at (D) and (E) in step (1). Retain cord tying chain at (D).

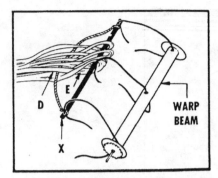

IV. TYING WARP TO WARP BEAM

1. Space warp on (X); tie (X) to warp beam.
2. Remove cord tying loop of chain at (D).
3. Wind warp on beam; slowly release chain.
4. Insert lease sticks in loops (B) and (C) between harnesses and warp beam. (Fig. VI).

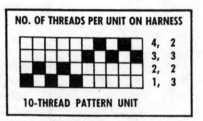

NO. OF THREADS PER UNIT ON HARNESS	
	4, 2
	3, 3
	2, 2
	1, 3
10-THREAD PATTERN UNIT	

V. COUNT HEDDLES PER HARNESS

15 warp threads per inch
x 8", width of muffler
120, total no. of warp threads
÷10, no. of threads per unit
12, no. of complete units
$3 \times 12 = 36$, heddles on H-1
$2 \times 12 = 24$, heddles on H-2
$3 \times 12 = 36$, heddles on H-3
$2 \times 12 = 24$, heddles on H-4

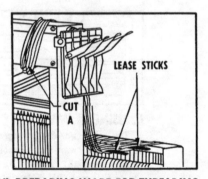

VI. PREPARING WARP FOR THREADING

1. Unroll enough warp to hang over loom.
2. Cut cord of one group of warp at (B), (C).
3. Pull group on top of loom. Cut warp at (A).
4. Draw warp through heddles.
   See Fig. VII. Repeat with all groups.

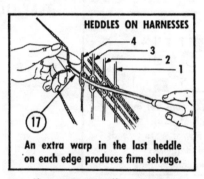

An extra warp in the last heddle on each edge produces firm selvage.

VII. "DRAWING-IN" THE WARP

1. Use hook with slotted end down.
2. Draw warp thread through heddle eye with threading hook (17).
3. Tie warp to avoid unthreading.

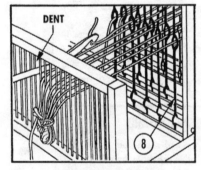

VIII. "SLEYING" THE WARP

1. Center width of fabric on reed.
2. Draw 2 warp through each dent.
   (15 dents per inch; 30 warp per inch).
3. Tie warp to prevent slipping.

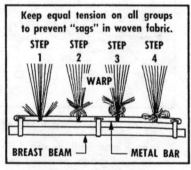

Keep equal tension on all groups to prevent "sags" in woven fabric.

IX. "TYING-IN" THE WARP

1. Raise metal bar over breast beam.
2. Tie center group of warp first.
3. Then tie one on each side until all groups are tied as in Step (4).

WEAVING PROCEDURE

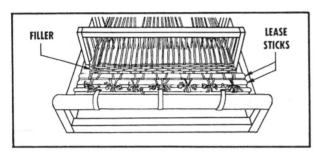

I. INTRODUCTION OF WEFT

1. Press levers 1 and 3; insert a lease stick. Press levers 2 and 4; insert other lease stick. Use beater after each insertion.
2. Continue alternate treadling and insert 5 rows of heavy cotton filler.
3. Weave next a ¾" "heading" with same weft as to be used for fabric.

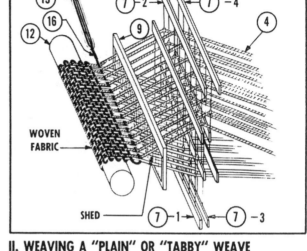

II. WEAVING A "PLAIN" OR "TABBY" WEAVE

1. A plain weave consists of pressing alternately (treadling) levers 1 and 3; 2 and 4. This results in a simple under-and-over-weave.
2. Press levers 1 and 3 to raise harnesses 1 and 3. Warp on harnesses 2 and 4 are lowered. This creates a "shed".
3. Insert weft (a "shot") in shed. Pack weft with beater before changing levers. Use short sharp "beats".
4. Press levers 2 and 4. Beat weft again. Insert weft in new "shed". Beat weft. Continue treadling and beating.
5. Change weft for colored borders.

III. BROKEN THREADS

1. Knot one end of new warp to end of broken warp.
2. Wind other end around pin placed in fabric opposite break. Create equal tension.
3. Remove pin after fabric is off loom. Weave loose end of warp in and out of fabric with needle.
4. Knots should not appear in weft. Overlap ends of weft under and over 4 warp threads when new weft has been added to shuttle, or when introducing new color in weft.

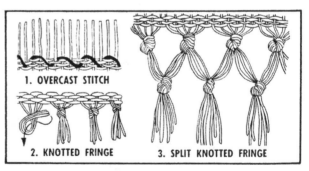

IV. REMOVING FABRIC

1. Complete fabric.
2. Insert cotton filler to width of length of fringe specified.
3. Release warp.
4. Cut warp a few at a time. Tie in bunches in front of reed to prevent unthreading if same warp is to be used for further weaving.

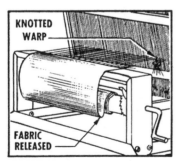

5. Remove fabric from cloth beam.
6. Cut warp to fringe length desired.
7. Remove carefully "heading" and filler. Do not unravel weft.

V. TREATMENT OF WARP ENDS

Reinforce weft edge at warp ends to prevent unravelling. Additional methods are suggested on Job Sheets.

Tray Cloth

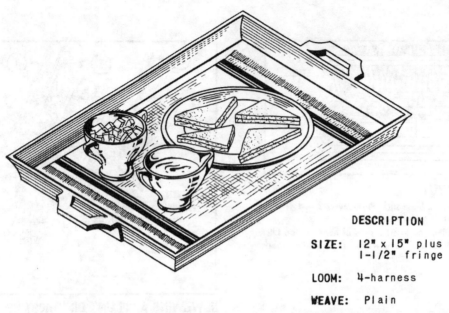

DESCRIPTION

SIZE: 12" x 15" plus 1-1/2" fringe

LOOM: 4-harness

WEAVE: Plain

DESIGN: End bordering

MATERIAL:

Warp } Cotton,
Weft } Size 30.

COLOR LEGEND:

☐ Yellow Warp
⊠ Yellow Weft – A
◉ Green Weft – B ⎫
⊘ Brown Weft – C ⎬ Borders
◻ Rust Weft – D ⎭

30 Warp per inch;
2 Warp per dent.

Harnesses
4
3 } 90 warp
2 } on each
1 } harness

Weft
⊠ →

Treadling
2-4
1-3
2-4
1-3
2-4

Repeat Alternate Treadling.

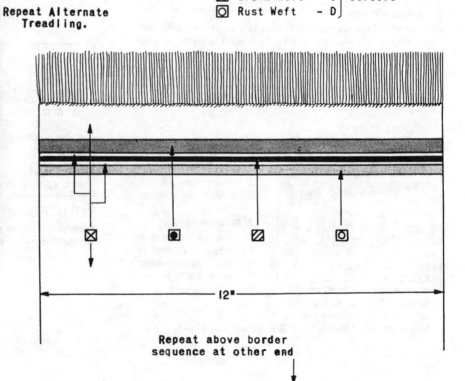

12"

Repeat above border sequence at other end

PROCEDURE:

1. Consult Weaving Instructions.

2. Thread the warp for a 12" wide tray cloth, as indicated in draft, on a 20", 4-harness loom.

3. Wind yellow (A), green (B), brown (C) and rust (D) weft threads on separate, medium sized shuttles.

4. Weave entire cloth in plain weave. Alternate treadling 1 and 3 with 2 and 4. Introduce borders with weft as follows: weave 1" (A), 3/8" B, 1/8" (A), 1/8" (C), 1/8" (A) and 1/4" (D).

5. Weave 11" of (A). Repeat border as in step (4).

6. Allow for 1-1/2" fringe at each end. Cut warp threads.

7. Reinforce weft at each fringe edge with an overcast stitch in contrasting color, (B), (C) or (D).

Man's Muffler

DESCRIPTION

SIZE: 12"x50", plus 1½" fringe

LOOM: 4-harness

WEAVE: Plain

DESIGN: Stripes

MATERIAL:
Warp } Wool
Weft } Fine, 2-ply

COLOR LEGEND:
Gray (A)
Purple (B)
Blue (C)
Black (D)
Red (E)

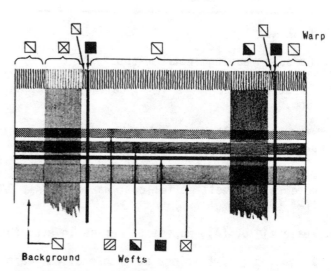

Warp

Background

Wefts

Follow this threading sequence, including no. of colored warp specified.
Colors will not necessarily fall on harness indicated.

15 Warp per inch; 1 Warp per dent.

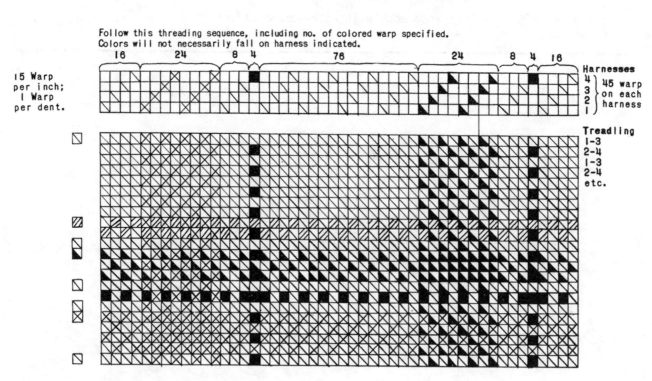

16   24   8 4   76   24   8 4 16

Harnesses
4
3   45 warp
2   on each
1   harness

Treadling
1-3
2-4
1-3
2-4
etc.

410

PROCEDURE:

1. Consult Weaving Instructions.

2. Thread the warp for a 12" wide muffler, as indicated in draft, on a 20", 4-harness loom.

3. Wind gray (A), purple (B), blue (C), black (D) and red (E) on separate, medium sized shuttles.

4. Weave entire piece in plain weave. Alternate treadling 1 and 3 with 2 and 4. Introduce borders with weft as follows: weave 2" (A), 1/2" (B), 1/4" (A), 3/4" (C), 1/4" (A), 1/4" (D), 1/4" (A) and 1" (E).

5. Weave 39-1/2" of (A). Repeat border as in step 4, reversing sequence of colors if desired.

6. Allow for 1-1/2" fringe at each end. Cut warp threads.

7. Reinforce weft at each fringe edge with an overcast stitch, using (A).

Man's Muffler

DESCRIPTION

SIZE: 12" x 50" plus 1½" fringe

LOOM: 4 - harness

WEAVE: Plain

DESIGN: Check plaid

MATERIAL:
Warp } Wool
Weft } Fine, 2-ply

COLOR LEGEND:
■ Brown – A
⊡ Aqua – B
⊠ Gray – C

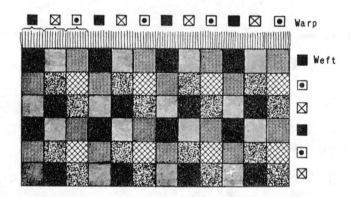

Warp

Weft

Note: Colors will not necessarily fall on harnesses indicated. Follow threading sequence.

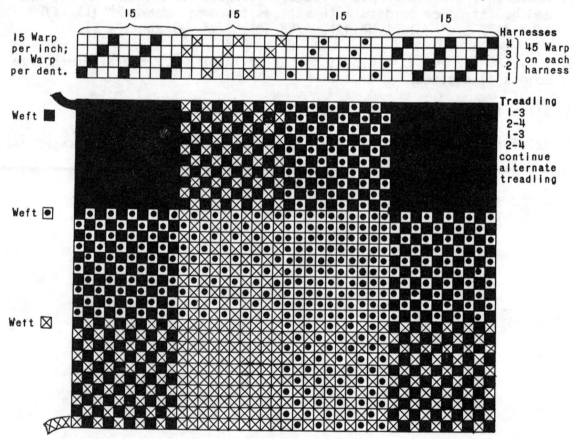

15 Warp per inch;
1 Warp per dent.

Harnesses
4
3
2
1
} 45 Warp on each harness

Weft ■

Weft ⊡

Weft ⊠

Treadling
1-3
2-4
1-3
2-4
continue alternate treadling

PROCEDURE:

1. Consult Weaving Instructions.

2. Thread the warp for a 12" wide muffler, as indicated in draft, on a 20", 4-harness loom.

3. Wind brown weft (A), aqua weft (B) and gray weft (C) on separate, medium sized shuttles.

4. Weave entire piece in plain weave. Alternate treadling 1 and 3 with 2 and 4. Introduce check plaid with weft as follows: insert weft (A) 14 times; insert weft (B) 14 times; insert weft (C) 14 times.

5. Repeat sequence in step (4) until muffler is approximately 50" long.

6. Allow for 1-1/2" fringe at each end. Cut warp threads.

7. Reinforce weft at each fringe edge with an overcast stitch, using (A).

Bath Mat

DESCRIPTION

SIZE: 20" x 30" plus 2" fringe

LOOM: 4-harness

WEAVE: Plain

DESIGN: Stripes, vertical and horizontal

MATERIAL:
Warp: Carpet warp
Weft: Rug yarn

COLOR LEGEND:
Gray or natural
Green or other color
White

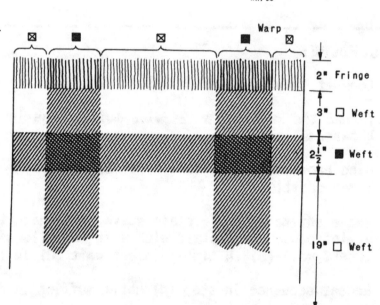

Warp

2" Fringe

3" □ Weft

2½" ■ Weft

19" □ Weft

15 Warp per inch; I Warp per dent. 303 Warp for 20"-mat.
Repeat each unit the no. of times specified, in sequence given.

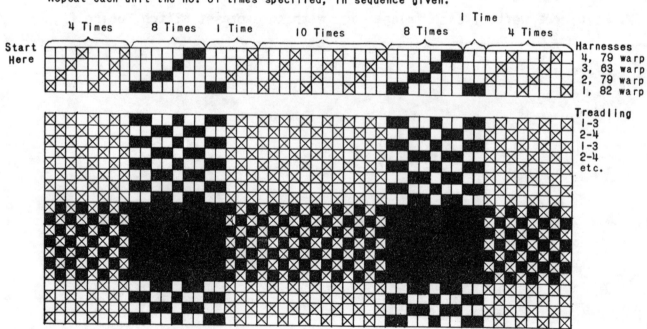

Start Here

4 Times   8 Times   I Time   10 Times   8 Times   I Time   4 Times

Harnesses
4, 79 warp
3, 63 warp
2, 79 warp
I, 82 warp

Treadling
1-3
2-4
1-3
2-4
etc.

414

PROCEDURE:

1. Consult Weaving Instructions.

2. Thread the warp for a 20" wide mat, as indicated on draft, on a 20", 4-harness loom.

3. Wind gray cotton weft (A) (same as used for warp), heavy, white cotton weft (B) and heavy, colored cotten weft (C) on separate large shuttles.

4. Weave entire piece in plain weave. Alternate treadling 1 and 3 with 2 and 4, as follows: insert weft (A) 6 times to form a reinforced edge on mat. Insert weft (B) to a width of 3".

5. Insert weft (C) to form a border 2-1/2" wide.

6. Insert weft (B) for 19".

7. Repeat step (5). Insert weft (B) to a width of 3".

8. Insert weft (A) 6 times.

9. Allow for 2" fringe at each end. Cut warp threads.

10. Knot warp threads in groups of approximately 12 threads per knotted fringe.

Place Mat

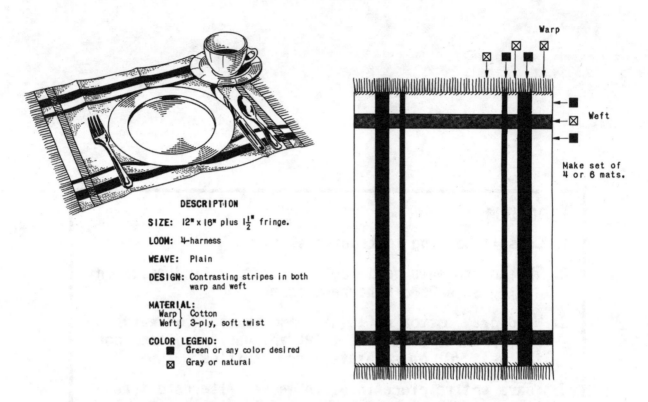

DESCRIPTION

SIZE: 12" x 16" plus 1½" fringe.

LOOM: 4-harness

WEAVE: Plain

DESIGN: Contrasting stripes in both warp and weft

MATERIAL:
Warp ⎱ Cotton
Weft ⎰ 3-ply, soft twist

COLOR LEGEND:
■ Green or any color desired
⊠ Gray or natural

Warp

Weft

Make set of 4 or 6 mats.

Follow color sequence in numbers indicated. Colors may not necessarily fall on same harness.

20   10   10   5   90

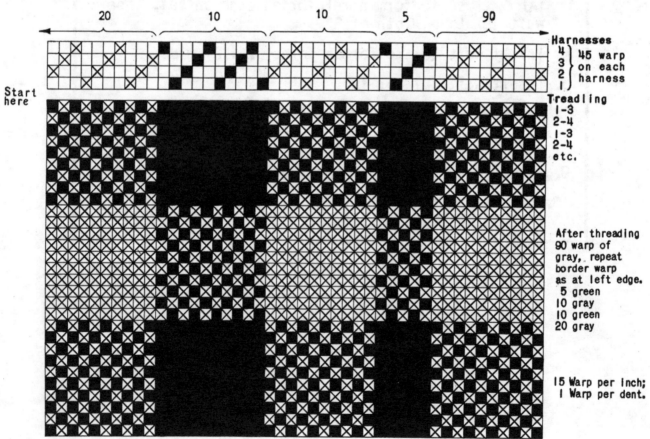

Start here

Harnesses
4
3   45 warp
2   on each
1   harness

Treadling
1-3
2-4
1-3
2-4
etc.

After threading 90 warp of gray, repeat border warp as at left edge.
5 green
10 gray
10 green
20 gray

15 Warp per inch; 1 Warp per dent.

416

PROCEDURE:

1. Consult Weaving Instructions.

2. Thread the warp for a 12"-wide place mat, as indicated in draft, on a 20", 4-harness loom.

3. Wind green (A) and gray (B) weft threads on separate, medium sized shuttles.

4. Weave entire mat in plain weave. Alternate treadling 1 and 3 with 2 and 4. Introduce border with weft as follows: insert (A) 31 times; insert (B) 20 times.

5. Continue to weave background with (A) for 14".

6. Insert (B) 20 times; insert (A) 31 times.

7. Allow for 1-1/2" fringe at each end. Cut warp threads.

8. Reinforce weft at each fringe edge with an overcast stitch in (A).

Place Mat and Napkin

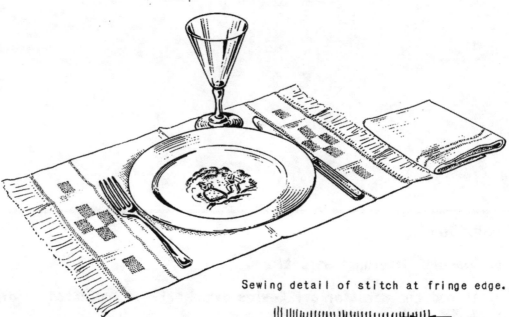

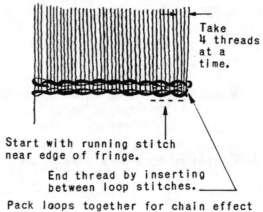

Sewing detail of stitch at fringe edge.

Take 4 threads at a time.

Start with running stitch near edge of fringe.

End thread by inserting between loop stitches.

Pack loops together for chain effect

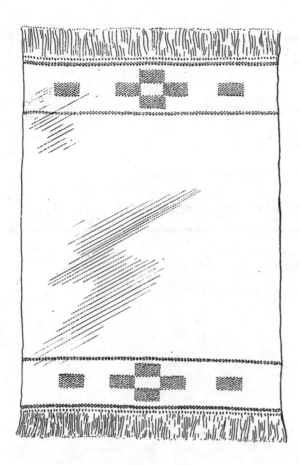

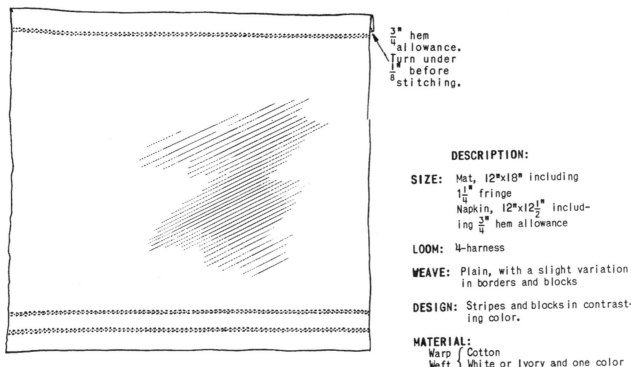

$\frac{3}{4}$" hem
allowance.
Turn under
$\frac{1}{8}$" before
stitching.

DESCRIPTION:

SIZE: Mat, 12"x18" including
$1\frac{1}{4}$" fringe
Napkin, 12"x12$\frac{1}{2}$" including $\frac{3}{4}$" hem allowance

LOOM: 4-harness

WEAVE: Plain, with a slight variation
in borders and blocks

DESIGN: Stripes and blocks in contrasting color.

MATERIAL:
Warp { Cotton
Weft { White or Ivory and one color
{ for border

COLOR LEGEND:
⊠ White or natural
■ Any color desired

30 Warp per inch;
2 Warp per dent.

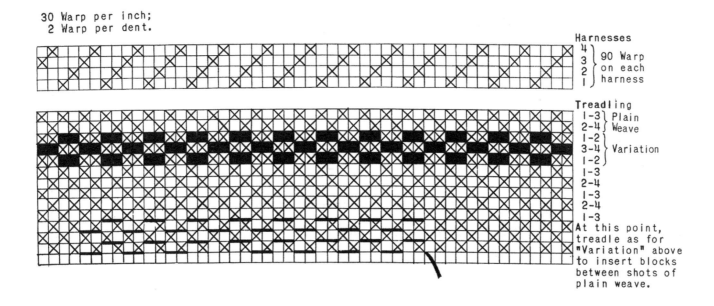

Harnesses
4
3 } 90 Warp
2 } on each
1 } harness

Treadling
1-3 } Plain
2-4 } Weave
1-2 }
3-4 } Variation
1-2 }
1-3
2-4
1-3
2-4
1-3
At this point,
treadle as for
"Variation" above
to insert blocks
between shots of
plain weave.

PROCEDURE:

1. Consult Weaving Instructions.

2. Thread the warp for a 12" wide mat, as indicated in draft, on a 20", 4-harness loom.

3. Wind white weft (A) on one medium sized shuttle, and blue weft (B) on one medium sized shuttle and 4 small shuttles or 4 large darning needles.

4. Weave as follows:

   Insert 2 rows of (A), using alternate treadling I and 3; then 2 and 4.

5. Insert 3 rows of (B) using alternate treadling I and 2; 3 and 4; I and 2.

6. Insert 5 rows of (A) using alternate treadling of a plain weave I and 3; 2 and 4.

7. Treadle I and 2; insert (B) on a small shuttle to form bottom center block in border design. Span 32 warp threads in all (over 2, under 2) 16 times. Do not cut thread (B).

8. Treadle 2 and 4; insert one weft (A).

9. Treadle 3 and 4; insert second weft of (B) in block design, not cutting thread.

10. Treadle I and 3; insert one weft (A).

11. Repeat steps (7), (8), (9) and (10) until block consists of 12 wefts of (B).

12. Treadle I and 3; insert one weft (A).

13. Repeat steps (7), (8), (9) and (10) to form 4 blocks of 12 wefts of (B). See design on mat. Use 4 small shuttles, one for each block.

14. Treadle I and 3.

15. Repeat steps (7), (8), (9), and (10) to form top center block of 12 wefts of (B).

16. Insert 5 rows of (A) using alternate treadling of a plain weave I and 3; 2 and 4.

17. Insert 3 rows of (B) using alternate treadling I and 2; 3 and 4; I and 2.

18. Continue to weave mat for 10-1/2" with alternate treadling of plain weave I and 3; 2 and 4.

19. Repeat border design.

20. Insert 2 rows of (A), using alternate treadling I and 3; 2 and 4.

21. Allow for 1-1/4" fringe at each end. Weave in cotton filler before starting to weave napkin.

22. Weave napkin with alternate treadling of plain weave, I and 3; 2 and 4.

23. Insert 3 rows of (B), using alternate treadling of I and 2; 3 and 4; I and 2. See spacing of borders on design of napkin.

24. Weave desired number of mats and napkins. Cut warp threads.

25. Finish mats by reinforcing fringe edge with stitch as shown.

26. Hem napkins as shown.

Hot Dish Mat

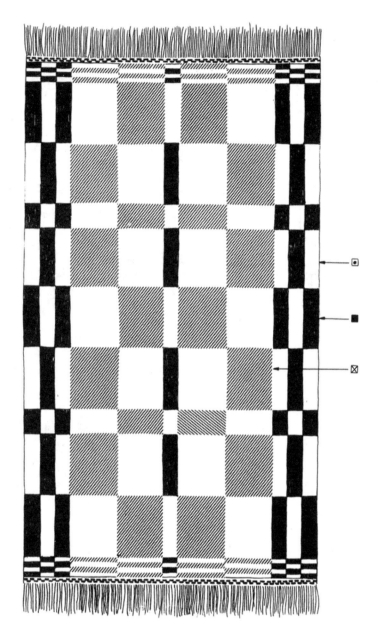

Make set of 3 or 4 mats

DESCRIPTION

SIZE: $6\frac{1}{4}"$ x $10\frac{1}{2}"$ plus $\frac{3}{4}"$ fringe

LOOM: 4-harness

WEAVE: Plain

DESIGN: Bars and checks; reversible, due to inter-
change of colors in warp.

MATERIAL:
   Warp: Cotton, carpet warp, 3 colors
   Weft: (1) Same as lightest color used in warp
          (2) Rug yarn, Cotton

COLOR LEGEND:
   ■   Black or any dark color
   ⊠   Rust or any medium dark color
   ◉   Yellow or any medium light color

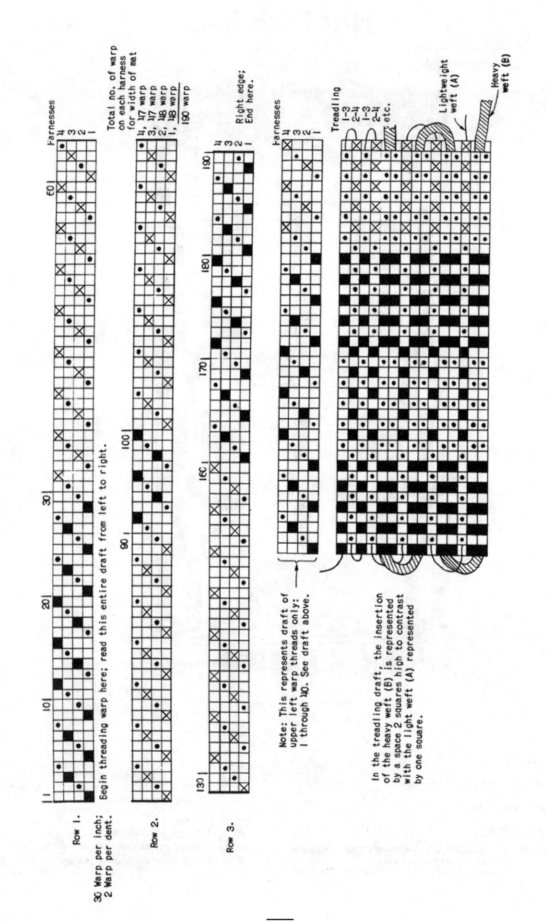

Harnesses

Total no. of warp
on each harness
for width of mat

4, 47 warp
3, 47 warp
2, 48 warp
1, 48 warp

190 warp

Right edge;
End here.

Harnesses

Treadling

1-3
2-4
1-3
2-4
etc.

Lightweight
weft (A)

Heavy
weft (B)

Row 1.

Begin threading warp here; read this entire draft from left to right.

30 Warp per inch;
2 Warp per dent.

Row 2.

Row 3.

Note: This represents draft of
upper left warp threads only;
1 through 40. See draft above.

In the treadling draft, the insertion
of the heavy weft (B) is represented
by a space 2 squares high to contrast
with the light weft (A) represented
by one square.

PROCEDURE:

1. Consult the Weaving Instruction Poster.

2. Thread the warp for a $6\frac{1}{4}$" mat, as indicated in draft, on an 8", 4-harness loom.

3. Wind colored weft (A), using any one thread used in warp, and heavy white weft (B) on separate, medium sized shuttles.

4. Treadle 1 and 3, 2 and 4 alternately, 2 times each, inserting (A) in each shed.

5. Treadle 1 and 3; 2 and 4; 1 and 3; 2 and 4; inserting (B) in each shed.

6. Treadle 1 and 3, insert (B).

7. Treadle 2 and 4, insert (A).

8. Repeat step (6) then (7), repeating alternately until 5 wefts of (B) have been woven. End sequence with step (6).

9. Treadle 2 and 4, insert (B).

10. Treadle 1 and 3, insert (A).

11. Repeat step (9) then (10), repeating alternately until 5 wefts of (B) have been woven. End sequence with step (9).

12. Treadle 1 and 3, insert (B).

13. Treadle 2 and 4, insert (A).

14. Repeat step (12) then (13).

15. Treadle 2 and 4, insert (B).

16. Treadle 1 and 3, insert (A).

17. Repeat step (15) then (16), repeating alternately until 5 wefts of (B) have been woven. End sequence with step (15).

18. Repeat step (8).

19. Repeat step (17).

20. Repeat steps (12), (13) and (14).

21. Repeat step (17).

22. Repeat step (8).

23. Treadle 2 and 4; 1 and 3; 2 and 4; 1 and 3; inserting (B) in each shed.

24. Treadle 2 and 4; 1 and 3; alternately 2 times each, inserting (A) in each shed.

25. If a set of 3 or 4 mats is to be made, weave in cotton filler between mats.

26. Allow for 3/4" fringe at both ends. Cut warp threads.

27. Stitch across warp fringe at edge of weft on sewing machine.

Place Mat

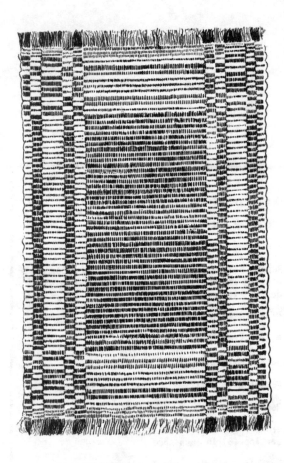

DESCRIPTION

SIZE: $11" \times 15\frac{1}{2}"$ plus $\frac{3}{4}"$ fringe

LOOM: 4-harness

WEAVE: Plain

DESIGN: Bars and stripes

MATERIAL:
Warp: Cotton, Carpet Warp
      White and one color
Weft: Cotton, White Carpet Warp and
      Rug Yarn, white

COLOR LEGEND:
◨ White   ■ Any color

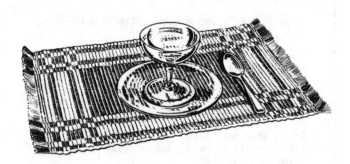

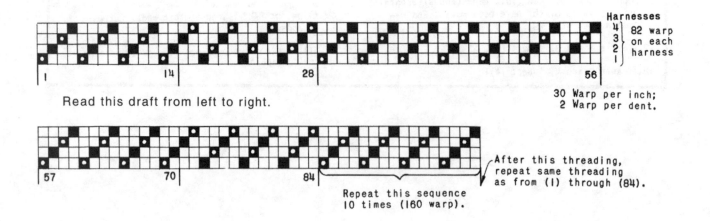

Harnesses
4
3
2
1
} 82 warp on each harness

Read this draft from left to right.

30 Warp per inch;
2 Warp per dent.

After this threading, repeat same threading as from (1) through (84).

Repeat this sequence 10 times (160 warp).

PROCEDURE:

1. Consult Weaving Instructions.

2. Thread the warp for an 11" mat, as indicated in draft, on a 20", 4-harness loom.

3. Wind weft threads on separate large shuttles, using same white thread as used for warp (A) and heavy white weft (B).

4. Treadle 1 and 3, 2 and 4, alternately, 5 times in all, inserting (A) in each shed.

5. Treadle 2 and 4, insert (B).

6. Treadle 1 and 3, insert (A).

7. Treadle 2 and 4, insert (B).

8. Treadle 1 and 3, insert (B).

9. Treadle 2 and 4, insert (A).

10. Treadle 1 and 3, insert (B).

11. Treadle 2 and 4, insert (B).

12. Treadle 1 and 3, insert (A).

13. Repeat steps (11) and (12) 2 times.

14. Treadle 2 and 4, insert (B).

15. Treadle 1 and 3, insert (B).

16. Treadle 2 and 4, insert (A).

17. Treadle 1 and 3, insert (B).

18. Treadle 2 and 4, insert (B).

19. Treadle 1 and 3, insert (A).

20. Treadle 2 and 4, insert (B).

21. Treadle 1 and 3, insert (B).

22. Treadle 2 and 4, insert (A).

23. Repeat steps (21) and (22), 44 times in all.

24. Repeat steps in sequence from (5) through (20).

25. Repeat step (4).

26. Allow for 3/4" fringe. Cut warp threads.

27. Stitch across warp fringe at edge of weft on sewing machine.

Bath Mat

DESCRIPTION

SIZE: 23" x 40" plus 4½" fringe

LOOM: 4-harness

WEAVE: Plain

DESIGN: Bars, checks and stripes

MATERIAL: Warp – Carpet warp
Weft – Cotton, Size 4/4

COLOR LEGEND: ■ Any color   ⊠ White

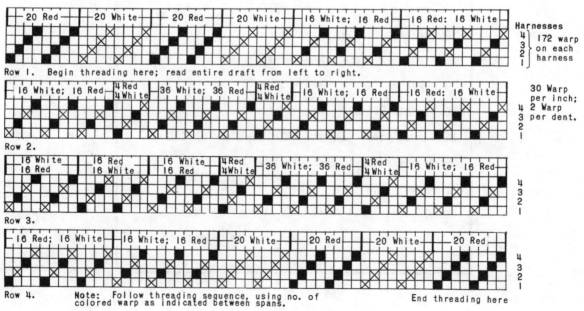

Row 1. Begin threading here; read entire draft from left to right.

Row 2.

Row 3.

Row 4.   Note: Follow threading sequence, using no. of colored warp as indicated between spans.   End threading here

Harnesses
4
3
2
1
} 172 warp on each harness

30 Warp per inch;
2 Warp per dent.

PROCEDURE:

1. Consult Weaving Instructions.

2. Thread the warp for a 23"-wide mat, as indicated in draft, on a 26", 4-harness loom.

3. Wind one weft thread on large shuttle, using same white thread as used for warp (A).

4. Wind other weft thread on large shuttle, using heavy white cord (B).

5. Treadle 1 and 3, 2 and 4 alternately, 6 times in all, inserting (A) in each shed.

6. Treadle 1 and 3, insert (B) in shed.

7. Treadle 2 and 4, insert (A) in shed.

8. Repeat steps (6) and (7), 6 times in all.

9. Treadle 1 and 3, insert (A) in shed.

10. Treadle 2 and 4, insert (B) in shed.

11. Treadle 1 and 3, insert (A) in shed.

12. Repeat steps (10) and (11), 6 times in all.

13. Treadle 2 and 4, insert (A) in shed.

14. Continue to weave, repeating steps (6) through (13), until desired length of mat is reached.

15. Repeat step (5).

16. Allow for 4-1/2" fringe. Cut warp threads.

17. Knot warp threads in groups of approximately 8 threads per knotted fringe.

Woman's Scarf

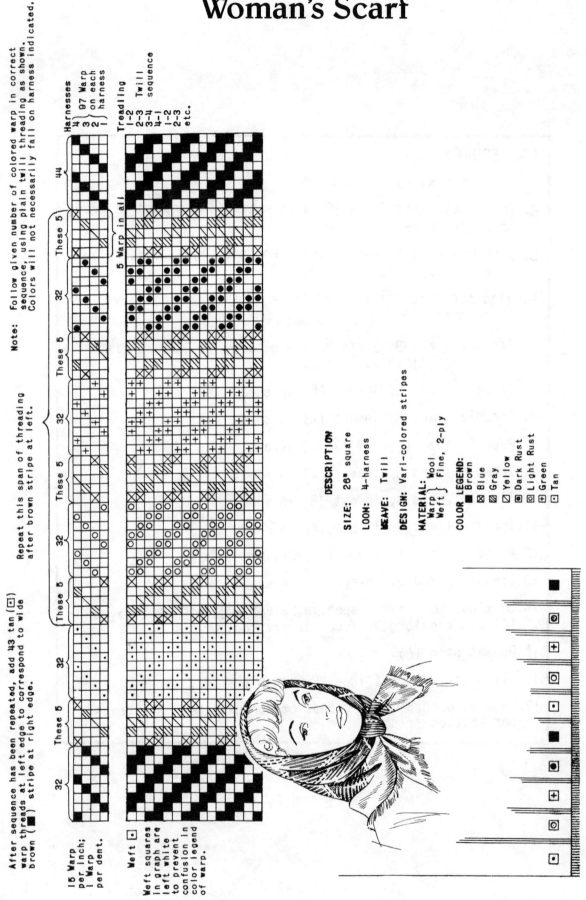

Note: Follow given number of colored warp in correct sequence, using plain twill threading as shown. Colors will not necessarily fall on harness indicated.

Repeat this span of threading after brown stripe at left.

After sequence has been repeated, add 43 tan (⊡) warp threads at left edge to correspond to wide brown (■) stripe at right edge.

Harnesses

4 }
3 } 97 Warp
2 } on each
1 } harness

Treading

1-2 }
2-3 } Twill
3-4 } sequence
4-1 }
1-2 }
2-3 }
etc.

5 Warp in all

These 5 | 32 | These 5 | 32 | These 5 | 32 | These 5 | 32 | 32 | 32 | These 5 | 32 | These 5

44

15 Warp per inch; 1 Warp per dent.

Weft ⊡

Weft squares in graph are left white to prevent confusion in color legend of warp.

DESCRIPTION

SIZE: 26" square

LOOM: 4-harness

WEAVE: Twill

DESIGN: Vari-colored stripes

MATERIAL:
Warp } Wool
Weft } Fine, 2-ply

COLOR LEGEND:
■ Brown
⊠ Blue
⊘ Gray
⊿ Yellow
◉ Dark Rust
⊙ Light Rust
⊕ Green
⊡ Tan

PROCEDURE:

1. Consult Weaving Instructions.

2. Thread the warp for a 26"-wide scarf, as indicated in draft, on a 26", 4-harness loom.

3. Wind brown weft (A) and tan weft (B) on separate large shuttles.

4. Weave the entire scarf in twill weave, treadling as follows: 1 and 2; 2 and 3; 3 and 4; 4 and 1; 1 and 2; etc.

5. First insert 10 rows of weft (A), packing them close together with the beater, to form a firm edge.

6. Then weave remaining length of scarf with weft (B), using a looser weave.

7. Pack together the last 10 rows of weft (B) with the beater to form a firm edge.

8. Allow for 1/2" fringe at both ends. Cut warp.

Woman's Bag

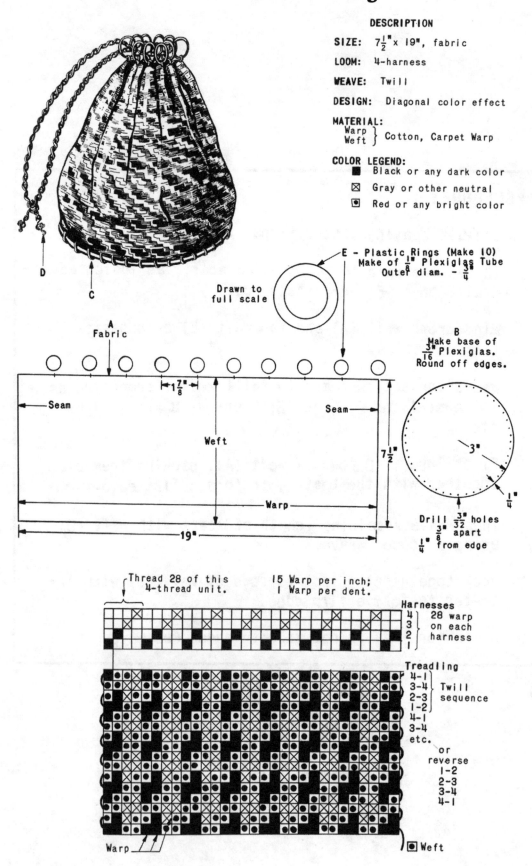

DESCRIPTION

SIZE: $7\frac{1}{2}$" x 19", fabric

LOOM: 4-harness

WEAVE: Twill

DESIGN: Diagonal color effect

MATERIAL:
Warp
Weft } Cotton, Carpet Warp

COLOR LEGEND:
■ Black or any dark color
⊠ Gray or other neutral
⊡ Red or any bright color

E - Plastic Rings (Make 10)
Make of $\frac{1}{8}$" Plexiglas Tube
Outer diam. — $\frac{3}{4}$"

Drawn to full scale

A
Fabric

B
Make base of
$\frac{3}{16}$" Plexiglas.
Round off edges.

Seam

Seam

$1\frac{7}{8}$"

Weft

$7\frac{1}{2}$"

Warp

19"

3"

$\frac{1}{4}$"

Drill $\frac{3}{32}$" holes
$\frac{3}{8}$" apart
$\frac{1}{4}$" from edge

Thread 28 of this
4-thread unit.

15 Warp per inch;
1 Warp per dent.

Harnesses
4
3
2
1

28 warp
on each
harness

Treadling
4-1
3-4 } Twill
2-3 } sequence
1-2
4-1
3-4
etc.

or
reverse
1-2
2-3
3-4
4-1

Warp

⊡ Weft

430

PROCEDURE:

1. Consult Weaving Instructions.

2. Thread the warp for a 7-1/2" wide panel, as indicated in draft, on an 8", 4-harness loom.

3. Wind weft thread on a small shuttle.

4. Weave entire fabric with twill, treadling as follows: 4 and 1; 3 and 4; 2 and 3; 1 and 2. Repeat sequence. Sequence may be reversed; treadle 1 and 2; 2 and 3; 3 and 4; 4 and 1. Repeat.

5. Allow for 1" fringe at both ends. Cut warp.

6. Reinforce weft at fringe edges by sewing back and forth on sewing machine. Cut excess fringe.

7. Sew fringe edges together on sewing machine, with 1/4" seam on inside of bag (A). Reinforce seam edges with overcast stitch.

8. Attach (A) to base (B) with black Plastik lace, stitching through selvage edge and holes drilled in (B).

9. Sew plastic rings (E) to top selvage edge at 1-7/8" intervals.

10. Braid a spiral cord 24" long of black carpet warp for drawstring (D). Knot ends of braid to prevent raveling.

11. Insert (D) through rings (E) and tie ends in simple knot.

Man's Muffler

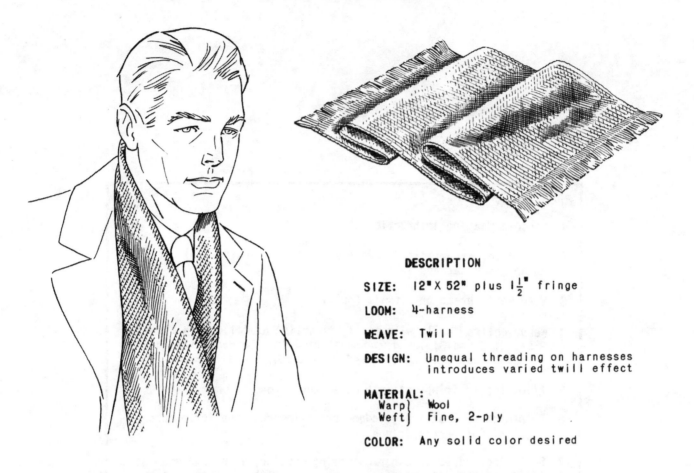

DESCRIPTION

SIZE: 12" X 52" plus $1\frac{1}{2}$" fringe

LOOM: 4-harness

WEAVE: Twill

DESIGN: Unequal threading on harnesses introduces varied twill effect

MATERIAL:
  Warp⎱ Wool
  Weft⎰ Fine, 2-ply

COLOR: Any solid color desired

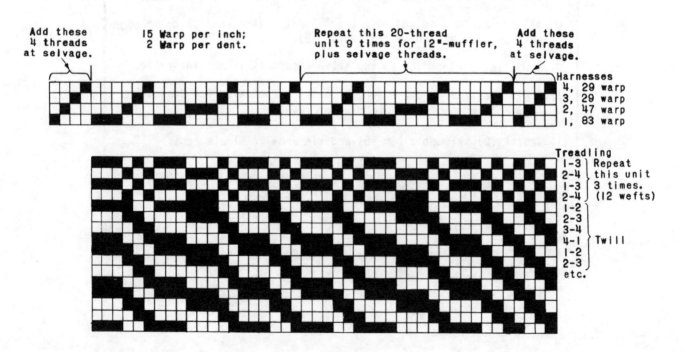

Add these 4 threads at selvage.

15 Warp per inch; 2 Warp per dent.

Repeat this 20-thread unit 9 times for 12"-muffler, plus selvage threads.

Add these 4 threads at selvage.

Harnesses
4, 29 warp
3, 29 warp
2, 47 warp
1, 83 warp

Treadling
1-3 ⎫ Repeat
2-4 ⎬ this unit
1-3 ⎪ 3 times.
2-4 ⎭ (12 wefts)
1-2 ⎫
2-3 ⎪
3-4 ⎪
4-1 ⎬ Twill
1-2 ⎪
2-3 ⎭
etc.

432

PROCEDURE:

1. Consult Weaving Instructions.

2. Thread the warp for a 12" wide muffler, as indicated in draft, on a 20", 4-harness loom.

3. Wind weft on a medium sized shuttle.

4. Weave firm edge on end of muffler in plain weave. Alternate treadling 1 and 3 with 2 and 4. Insert weft 12 times.

5. Weave the remainder of scarf in twill weave, treadling as follows: 1 and 2; 2 and 3; 3 and 4; 4 and 1; 1 and 2; etc.

6. Repeat step (4).

7. Allow for 1-1/2" fringe at both ends. Cut warp.

8. Reinforce weft at each fringe edge with an overcast stitch if desired.

Knitting Bag

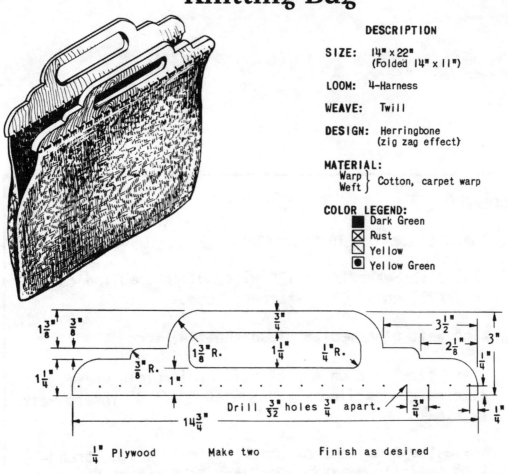

DESCRIPTION

SIZE: 14" x 22"
(Folded 14" x 11")

LOOM: 4-Harness

WEAVE: Twill

DESIGN: Herringbone
(zig zag effect)

MATERIAL:
Warp } Cotton, carpet warp
Weft }

COLOR LEGEND:
■ Dark Green
⊠ Rust
◹ Yellow
⊙ Yellow Green

1⅜" ⅜" ¾" 3½" 3"
1¾" R. 1⅜" R. 1¼" ¼" R. 2⅛" ¼"
1¼" ⅜" R. 1" Drill 3/32" holes ¾" apart. ¾" ¼"
14¾"

¼" Plywood   Make two   Finish as desired

Follow this warp threading
in this color sequence. Repeat
this 4-thread unit 105 times.

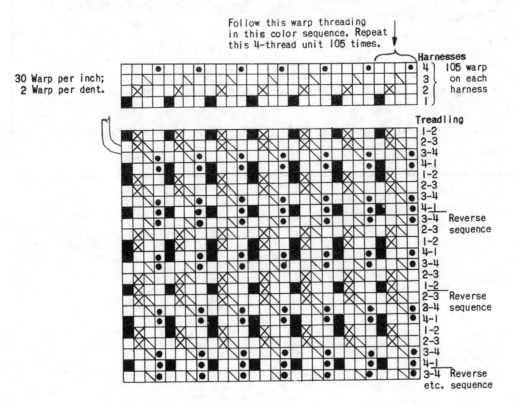

30 Warp per inch;
2 Warp per dent.

Harnesses
4 } 105 warp
3   on each
2 } harness
1

Treadling
1-2
2-3
3-4
4-1
1-2
2-3
3-4
4-1 ── Reverse
3-4   sequence
2-3
1-2
4-1
3-4
2-3
1-2
2-3 ── Reverse
3-4   sequence
4-1
1-2
2-3
3-4
4-1
3-4 ── Reverse
etc. sequence

434

PROCEDURE:

1. Consult Weaving Instructions.

2. Thread the warp for a 14" wide fabric, as indicated in draft, on a 20", 4-harness loom.

3. Wind yellow weft on a medium-sized shuttle.

4. Weave the entire fabric in a herring-bone twill, beginning the fabric as follows: treadle 1 and 2; 2 and 3; 3 and 4; 4 and 1; 1 and 2; 2 and 3; 3 and 4; 4 and 1.

5. Now reverse treadling: 3 and 4; 2 and 3; 1 and 2; 4 and 1; 3 and 4; 2 and 3.

6. Repeat step (4), then (5), alternately, until 22" of fabric are woven..

7. Allow for 1" fringe at both ends. Cut warp.

8. Reinforce weft at fringe edge by sewing back and forth on sewing machine.

9. Cut fringe quite close. Turn under raw edges and sew a 1/2" hem.

10. Fold fabric to form bag, approximately 14" x 10-1/2". Line bag if desired.

11. Sew selvage edges of bag together with overcast stitch, leaving 3-1/2" free at top corners of bag.

12. Construct pair of handles as per measurements.

13. Attach bag to handles with an overcast stitch, sewing through drilled holes, and hemmed edges.

Table Runner

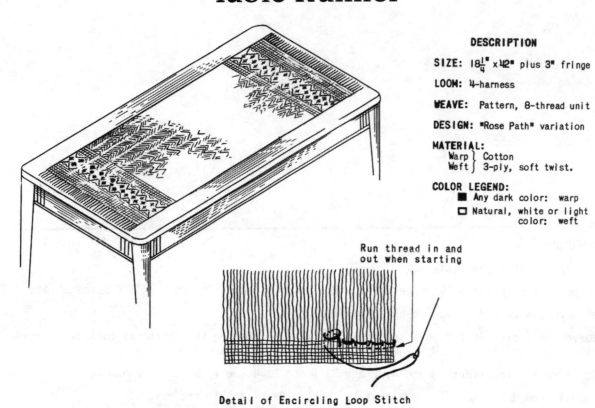

DESCRIPTION

SIZE: $18\frac{1}{4}$" x 42" plus 3" fringe

LOOM: 4-harness

WEAVE: Pattern, 8-thread unit

DESIGN: "Rose Path" variation

MATERIAL:
Warp } Cotton
Weft } 3-ply, soft twist.

COLOR LEGEND:
■ Any dark color: warp
□ Natural, white or light color: weft

Run thread in and out when starting

Detail of Encircling Loop Stitch

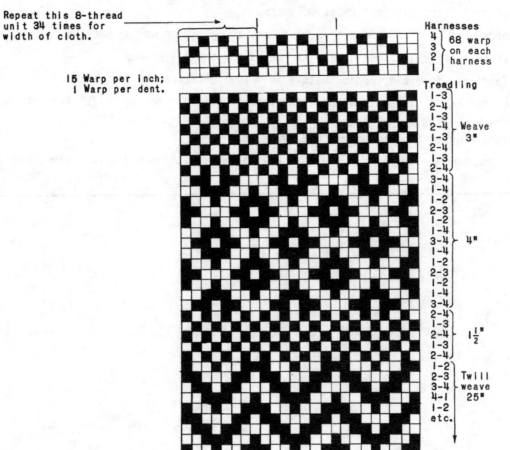

Repeat this 8-thread unit 34 times for width of cloth.

Harnesses
4
3
2
1
} 68 warp on each harness

15 Warp per inch; 1 Warp per dent.

Treadling
1-3
2-4
1-3
2-4 } Weave
1-3   3"
2-4
1-3
2-4
3-4
1-4
1-2
2-3
1-2
1-4
3-4 } 4"
1-4
1-2
2-3
1-4
3-4
2-4
1-3
2-4 } $1\frac{1}{2}$
1-3
2-4
1-2
2-3 } Twill
3-4 } weave
4-1   25"
1-2
etc.

PROCEDURE:

1. Consult Weaving Instructions.

2. Thread the warp for an 18" wide runner, as indicated in draft, on a 20", 4-harness loom.

3. Wind natural weft thread on a large shuttle.

4. Weave runner for 3" as follows: treadle 1 and 3; 2 and 4 alternately, as in plain weave. End sequence with 2 and 4.

5. Weave diamond border for approximately 4" as follows: treadle 3 and 4; 1 and 4; 1 and 2; 2 and 3; 1 and 2; 1 and 4; 3 and 4. Repeat in same sequence, ending 4" border with 3 and 4.

6. Introduce plain weave for 1-1/2" as follows: treadle 2 and 4; 1 and 3 alternately, ending sequence with 2 and 4.

7. Weave twill background for 25" as follows: treadle 1 and 2; 2 and 3; 3 and 4; 4 and 1; 1 and 2, etc. End sequence with 1 and 2.

8. Repeat step (6).

9. Repeat step (5).

10. Repeat step (4) beginning sequence with 2 and 4.

11. Allow for a 3" fringe at each end. Cut warp.

12. Secure fringe to edge of weft, with an encircling loop stitch, taking 4 threads at a time. See detail.

Floormat

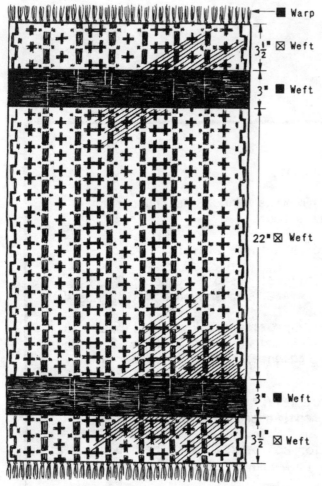

■ Warp
⊠ Weft
3½"
■ Weft 3"
22" ⊠ Weft
3" ■ Weft
3½" ⊠ Weft

DESCRIPTION

SIZE: 20"x35" plus 2½" fringe

LOOM: 4-harness

WEAVE: Pattern, 14-thread unit

DESIGN: Cross and bar with border

MATERIAL:
   Warp: Carpet Warp
   Weft: Cotton Rug Yarn
          or Cotton Filler
          Size 4/4

COLOR LEGEND:
   ■ Black or dark color
   ⊠ Rose or medium dark color

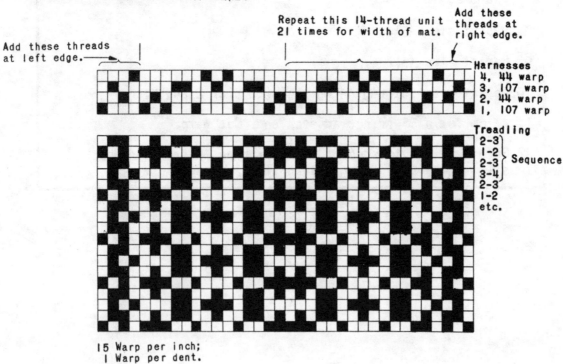

Add these threads at left edge.

Repeat this 14-thread unit 21 times for width of mat.

Add these threads at right edge.

Harnesses
4, 44 warp
3, 107 warp
2, 44 warp
1, 107 warp

Treadling
2-3
1-2
2-3 } Sequence
3-4
2-3
1-2
etc.

15 Warp per inch;
I Warp per dent.

PROCEDURE:

1. Consult the Weaving Instructions.

2. Thread the warp for a 20"-wide mat, as indicated in draft, on a 20", 4-harness loom.

3. Wind some black (A) (same as used for warp), rose (B) and black (C) weft threads on separate large shuttles.

4. Weave entire mat with the same treadling, as follows: 2 and 3; 1 and 2; 2 and 3; 3 and 4. Repeat sequence.

5. Introduce (A), (B) and (C) as follows: weave 8 wefts of (A) to create a firm edge.

6. Weave 3-1/2" with (B) weft.

7. Weave 3" with (C) weft.

8. Weave 22" with (B) weft.

9. Repeat step (7), then (6), ending with (5).

10. Allow for 2-1/2" fringe at each end. Cut warp.

11. Knot warp threads in groups of approximately 6 threads per knotted fringe.

Child's Muffler

DESCRIPTION

SIZE: 8" x 36" plus 2" fringe

LOOM: 4-harness

WEAVE: Pattern, 10-thread unit

DESIGN: "Huck" pattern

MATERIAL:
Warp } Wool
Weft } Fine, 2-ply

COLOR:
Warp: Any bright color
Weft: White or natural

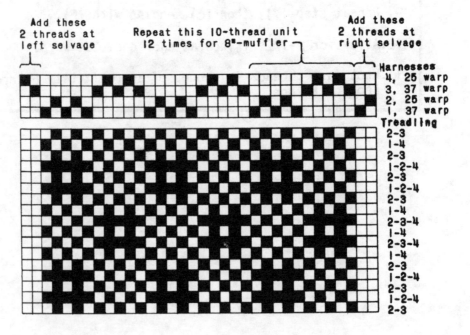

Add these 2 threads at left selvage

Repeat this 10-thread unit 12 times for 8"-muffler

Add these 2 threads at right selvage

15 Warp per inch;
1 Warp per dent.

Harnesses
4, 25 warp
3, 37 warp
2, 25 warp
1, 37 warp

Treadling
2-3
1-4
2-3
1-2-4
2-3
1-2-4
2-3
1-4
2-3-4
1-4
2-3-4
1-4
2-3
1-2-4
2-3
1-2-4
2-3

PROCEDURE:

1. Consult Weaving Instructions.

2. Thread the warp for an 8"-wide muffler, as indicated in draft, on an 8", 4-harness loom.

3. Wind weft thread on small shuttle.

4. Weave scarf for 2-1/2" as follows: treadle 2 and 3, 1 and 4, alternately, ending sequence with 1 and 4.

5. Weave pattern area for 31" as follows: treadle 2 and 3; 1, 2 and 4; 2 and 3; 1, 2 and 4; 2 and 3; 1 and 4; 2, 3 and 4; 1 and 4; 2, 3 and 4; 1 and 4. Repeat preceding sequence for length needed.

6. Repeat step (4).

7. Allow for a 2" fringe at each end. Cut warp.

8. Reinforce weft at each fringe edge with an overcast stitch in warp color.

Baby's Blanket

DESCRIPTION

SIZE: 40" square (2 panels sewed together)

LOOM: 4-harness

WEAVE: Pattern, 12-thread unit

DESIGN: Variation of "Dornick"

MATERIAL:
Warp } Wool
Weft } Fine, 2-ply

COLOR LEGEND:
■ Any color, warp
□ White, weft

Alternate warp color for each 12-thread unit of design if desired. For example: pink, blue, pink, etc.

Thread 25 of this 12 thread unit

15 Warp per inch; 1 Warp per dent.

Harnesses
4
3 } 75 warp on each harness
2
1

Treadling
3-4
2-3
1-2
1-4
3-4
2-3
1-2
1-4
3-4
2-3
1-2
1-4
3-4
2-3
1-2
2-3
3-4
1-4
3-4
2-3
1-2
2-3
3-4
1-4
3-4
2-3
1-2 Plain
2-3 twill
3-4 tread-
1-4 ling
1-2
2-3
etc. to
borders on
opposite end.

442

PROCEDURE:

1. Consult the Weaving Instruction Poster.

2. Thread the warp for a 20" panel (2 panels sewed together for blanket), as indicated in draft, on a 20", 4-harness loom.

3. Wind weft thread on large shuttle.

4. Weave twill edging of panel for 3" as follows: treadle 3 and 4; 2 and 3; 1 and 2; 1 and 4. Repeat sequence as needed for 3", ending with 1 and 2.

5. Weave approximately 4" of the diamond pattern as follows: treadle 2 and 3; 3 and 4; 1 and 4; 3 and 4; 2 and 3; 1 and 2. Repeat sequence as needed for 4", ending with 1 and 2.

6. Weave approximately 26" of the center background twill of panel as follows: treadle 2 and 3; 3 and 4; 1 and 4; 1 and 2. Repeat sequence as needed for 26". End sequence with 1 and 2.

7. Repeat step (5).

8. Weave twill edging of panel for 3" as follows: 2 and 3; 3 and 4; 1 and 4; 1 and 2. Repeat sequence as needed for 3".

9. This completes 1 panel for blanket. Insert heavy cotton filler for 4".

10. Weave second panel. Space borders equally, so that all horizontal patterns will correspond when 2 panels are sewed together.

11. Allow for 2" fringe. Cut warp. Remove cotton filler between panels.

12. Sew panels together with overcast stitch in white yarn. Reinforce weft at each fringe edge with overcast stitch.

Tablecloth

DESCRIPTION

SIZE: 4' square: two 24" panels sewed together

LOOM: 4-harness

WEAVE: Pattern, 24-thread unit

DESIGN: "Bronson" weave

MATERIAL:
Warp } Cotton
Weft } Size 30

COLOR LEGEND:
■ Any dark color for warp
White, natural or light color for weft, or vice versa

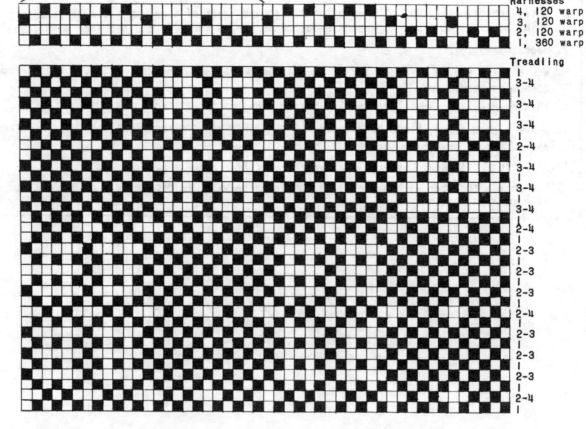

Repeat this 24-thread unit 30 times.

30 Warp per inch; 2 Warp per dent.

Harnesses
4, 120 warp
3, 120 warp
2, 120 warp
1, 360 warp

Treadling
3-4
3-4
3-4
2-4
3-4
3-4
3-4
2-4
2-3
2-3
2-3
2-4
2-3
2-3
2-3
2-4

PROCEDURE:

1. Consult Weaving Instructions.

2. Thread the warp for a 24" panel (2 panels sewed together for cloth .), as indicated in draft, on a 26", 4-harness loom.

3. Wind weft on large shuttle.

4. Weave entire cloth as follows:

   (a) Treadle 1; then 3 and 4; 3 times each
   (b) Treadle 1; then 2 and 4;
   (c) Treadle 1; then 3 and 4; 3 times each
   (d) Treadle 1; then 2 and 4.
   (e) Treadle 1; then 2 and 3; 3 times each
   (f) Treadle 1; then 2 and 4.
   (g) Treadle 1; then 2 and 3; 3 times each
   (h) Treadle 1; then 2 and 4.

   The above treadling constitutes one complete repeat of unit.

5. Repeat step (4) successively to complete one 48" panel.

6. Insert heavy cotton filler for 4".

7. Weave second panel.

8. Allow for 2" fringe. Cut warp. Remove cotton filler between panels.

9. Sew panels together with short overcast stitch.

10. Reinforce weft at each fringe edge with overcast stitch. Cut fringe and hem.

Shoulderette

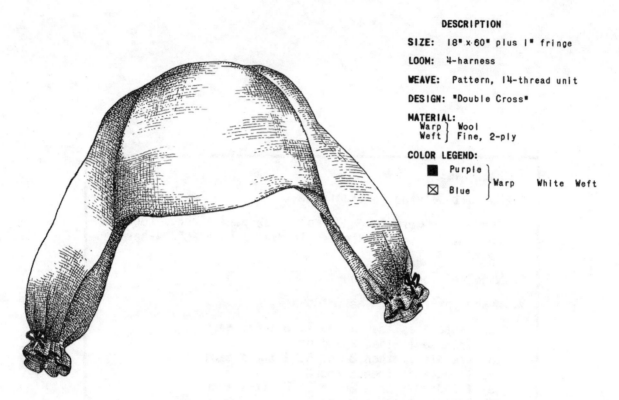

DESCRIPTION

SIZE: 18" x 60" plus 1" fringe

LOOM: 4-harness

WEAVE: Pattern, 14-thread unit

DESIGN: "Double Cross"

MATERIAL:
Warp } Wool
Weft } Fine, 2-ply

COLOR LEGEND:
■ Purple
⊠ Blue } Warp   White Weft

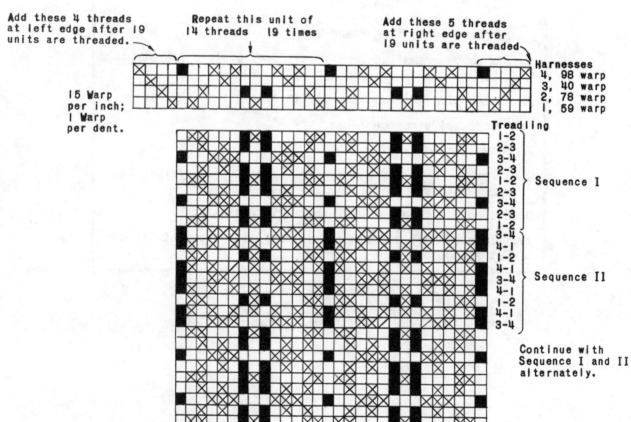

Add these 4 threads at left edge after 19 units are threaded.

Repeat this unit of 14 threads   19 times

Add these 5 threads at right edge after 19 units are threaded

15 Warp per inch; 1 Warp per dent.

Harnesses
4, 98 warp
3, 40 warp
2, 78 warp
1, 59 warp

Treadling
1-2
2-3
3-4
2-3
1-2   } Sequence I
2-3
3-4
2-3
1-2

3-4
4-1
1-2
4-1   } Sequence II
3-4
4-1
1-2
4-1
3-4

Continue with Sequence I and II alternately.

PROCEDURE:

1. Consult Weaving Instructions.

2. Thread the warp for an 18" panel, as indicated in draft, on a 20", 4-harness loom.

3. Wind white weft thread on a large shuttle.

4. Start weaving by treadling 2 and 3.

5. Then proceed with first unit of design as follows: treadle 1 and 2; 2 and 3; 3 and 4; 2 and 3; 1 and 2; 2 and 3; 3 and 4; 2 and 3; 1 and 2.

6. Weave second unit of design as follows: treadle 3 and 4; 4 and 1; 1 and 2; 4 and 1; 3 and 4; 4 and 1; 1 and 2; 4 and 1; 3 and 4.

7. Repeat steps (5) and (6), alternating the units of design for the remainder of the panel.

8. End weaving by treadling 2 and 3.

9. Allow for a 1" fringe. Cut warp.

10. Reinforce weft at fringe edge with an overcast stitch in purple yarn.

11. Sew selvage edges of ends of panel together for 18" or 20" to form sleeves.

12. Insert 1/8" ribbon in-and-out of fabric, 1" from edge of sleeve opening, to act as drawstring at cuff.

Muffler

DESCRIPTION

SIZE: $13\frac{1}{4}"\times44"$ plus 1" fringe

LOOM: 4-harness

WEAVE: Pattern, 36-thread unit

DESIGN: Variation of "M and O" pattern

MATERIAL:
Warp } Wool
Weft } Fine, 2-ply

COLOR: All white, or solid color

15 warp per inch;
1 warp per dent.

Group 3
8 warp

Group 2
8 warp

Group 1
20 warp

Harnesses
4, 54 warp
3, 46 warp
2, 54 warp
1, 46 warp

From Right to Left thread warp repeating Groups 1, 2 and 3 in following sequence:
1, 2, 3, 2, 3, 2, 1, 2, 3, 2, 3, 2, 1, 2, 3, 2, 3, 2, and 1.

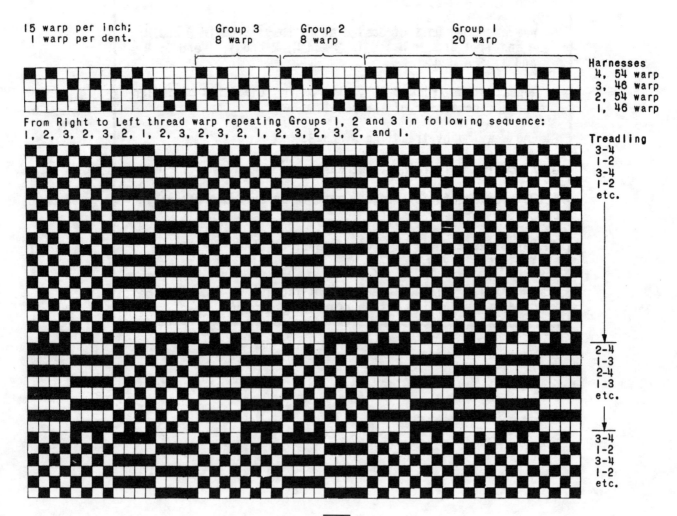

Treadling
3-4
1-2
3-4
1-2
etc.

2-4
1-3
2-4
1-3
etc.

3-4
1-2
3-4
1-2
etc.

PROCEDURE:

1. Consult Weaving Instructions.

2. Thread the warp for a $13\frac{1}{4}"$ wide muffler, as indicated in draft, on a 20", 4-harness loom.

3. Wind weft thread on a medium sized shuttle.

4. Weave large blocks and vertical bars as follows: treadle 3 and 4, with 1 and 2 alternately, inserting weft 18 times in all. End sequence with 1 and 2.

5. Weave small blocks and horizontal bars as follows: (steps (5) through (9)) treadle 2 and 4, with 1 and 3 alternately, inserting weft 8 times in all. End sequence with 1 and 3.

6. Treadle 3 and 4, with 1 and 2 alternately, inserting weft 6 times in all. End sequence with 1 and 2.

7. Repeat step (5).

8. Repeat step (6).

9. Repeat step (5).

10. Repeat steps (4) through (9) as needed for a 44" muffler. End weaving with step (4).

11. Allow for a 1" fringe at both ends. Cut warp.

12. Reinforce weft at each fringe edge with an overcast stitch in matching yarn.

Woman's Envelope Purse

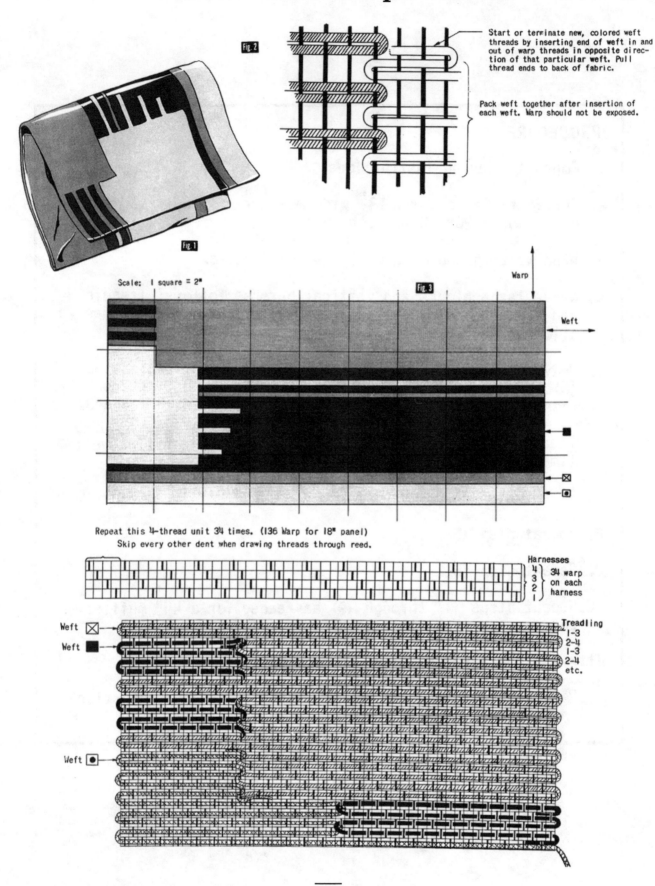

Fig. 2

Start or terminate new, colored weft threads by inserting end of weft in and out of warp threads in opposite direction of that particular weft. Pull thread ends to back of fabric.

Pack weft together after insertion of each weft. Warp should not be exposed.

Fig. 1

Scale: I square = 2"

Fig. 3

Warp

Weft

Repeat this 4-thread unit 34 times. (136 Warp for 18" panel)
Skip every other dent when drawing threads through reed.

Harnesses
4
3
2
1
34 warp on each harness

Weft ⊠
Weft ■
Weft ⊙

Treadling
1-3
2-4
1-3
2-4
etc.

DESCRIPTION

SIZE: 8"x18" panel. 6"x8" when
       folded to purse size

LOOM: 4-harness

WEAVE: Tapestry (Plain weave treadling)

DESIGN: Modern motif

MATERIALS:
  1. Weaving;
       Warp - Cotton, Carpet Warp
       Weft - Wool, Sport Yarn, 4-ply

  2. Miscellaneous:
       Lining, rayon, black, $8\frac{1}{2}$"x$18\frac{1}{2}$"
       Snap fastener
       Sewing thread, black, cotton
       Needle

COLOR LEGEND:
  ■ Black or any dark color
  ⊠ Aqua or any medium dark color
  ◉ Yellow or any light color

PROCEDURE:

1. Consult Weaving Instructions.

2. Thread the warp for an 18" wide panel, as indicated in draft, on a 20", 4-harness loom.

3. Wind aqua (A), black (B) and dark yellow (C) weft
   threads on separate small shuttles.

4. Enlarge the design shown to 8" x 18" by scaling or
   photography. Sketch final drawing on tracing paper,
   blocking in the design areas with colored crayons,
   as indicated in the design. Use the colored en-
   largement for a weaving guide. Fig. 3.

5. Weave entire panel with alternate treadling of 1 and 3 with 2 and 4.
   This treadling is always used for a "tapestry" weave, in which the
   background of the fabric is broken up into varied colors.

6. Pack weft close together after insertion of each weft. The warp
   threads are never exposed in a "tapestry" weave. Fig. 2.

7. Introduce colors as indicated in design. First weave 3/4" of (C); terminate (C). Weave 1/2" of (A); terminate (A). Weave 1/4" of (B). Do
   not terminate (B). Introduce one weft of (C) for span of block shown.
   Do not terminate (C). Introduce weft of (B), and encircle (B) and (C)
   around same warp thread at corner of block of (C). Fig. 2. Continue to
   insert (C) and (B), one weft at a time, encircling them around same
   warp at each meeting point. Introduce other colors as specified in en-
   larged, crayon sketch of design.

8. In beginning or terminating weft threads, always insert end of thread
   in and out of warp threads in opposite direction of that particular
   weft. Fig. 2.

9. Allow for 2" fringe. Cut warp.

10. Knot warp ends, 2 threads to a knot, close to edge of weft. Trim warp
    ends.

11. Fold panel, wrong side out, into 3 equal parts. (The top flap may be
    a bit narrower than pocket section. Fig. 1.

12. Sew knotted edges of pocket section together with a close, tight over-
    cast stitch.

13. Turn purse right side out, with side seams hidden. Turn down to wrong
    side and hem knotted edges and selvage edge of flap section.

14. Fold lining into 3 parts, to correspond to purse. Sew edges of pocket
    section.

15. Place lining within purse. Turn down to wrong side the edge of lining
    at pocket edge of purse.

16. Sew lining to edge of pocket section, concealing all raw edges.

17. Turn under edges of lining on flap of purse. Sew lining to flap.

18. Sew a snap fastener to flap and corresponding location on front of
    pocket section.

Rug or Wall Hanging

COLOR LEGEND
- ■ Black (A)
- ☐ Gray (B)
- ▥ Mustard (C)
- ▧ Tan (D)
- ▨ Orange (E)
- ☐ White (F)

DESCRIPTION

SIZE: 24" x 23" plus 2" fringe.

LOOM: 4-harness

WEAVE: Tapestry.

DESIGN: Navajo

MATERIAL:
Warp — Cotton carpet warp.
Weft —"WOOLY DOWN" yarn (Heavy)

Detail showing weft threads packed together with all warp threads hidden.

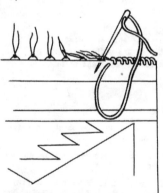

Detail of overcasting warp ends.

Thread warp for entire rug in this sequence.
180 warp for 24" rug; I warp for every other dent.

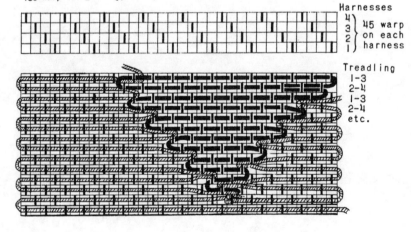

Harnesses
4
3 } 45 warp
2 } on each
1 } harness

Treadling
1-3
2-4
1-3
2-4
etc.

PROCEDURE:

1. Consult Weaving Instructions.

2. Thread the warp for a 24" wide rug, as indicated in draft, on a 26", 4-harness loom.

3. Wind black (A), gray (B), mustard (C), tan (D), orange (E) and white (F) on separate medium-sized shuttles.

4. Enlarge the design shown to 24" x 23".

5. Follow instructions given for "tapestry" weaving in steps (4) through (8) on page 242.

6. Introduce colors as indicated in rug design, or substitute other colors for the six suggested.

7. Allow for 2" fringe. Cut warp.

8. Knot warp ends, 2 threads to a knot, close to edge of weft.

9. Finish edges in either of 2 ways:
    a. Cut warp ends to about 1". Turn under to wrong side, about 1/2" of edge of rug. Tuck knotted warp ends under folded edge. Hem edge firmly with black yarn. Overcast selvage edges of rug with same yarn.
    b. Cut warp ends to about 1". Sew weft edge, felling and covering knotted warp ends with an overcast stitch. See detail. Continue to overcast selvage edges with same yarn.

10. Form a knotted tassel of heavy black yarn at each corner, while proceeding with overcasting, if desired.

Woman's Belt

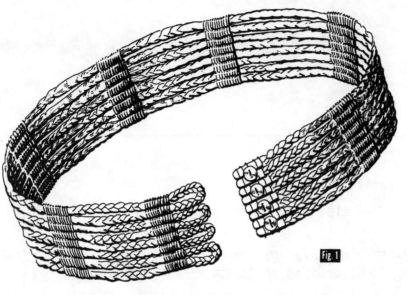

Fig. 1

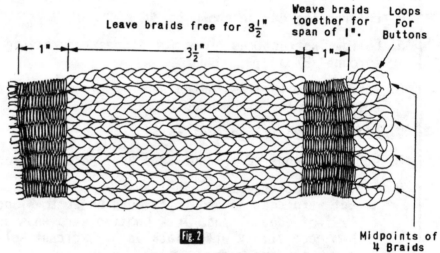

Leave braids free for 3½"

Weave braids together for span of 1".

Loops For Buttons

|← 1" →|←——— 3½" ———→|← 1" →|

Fig. 2

Midpoints of 4 Braids

Detail of combining braids to form belt.

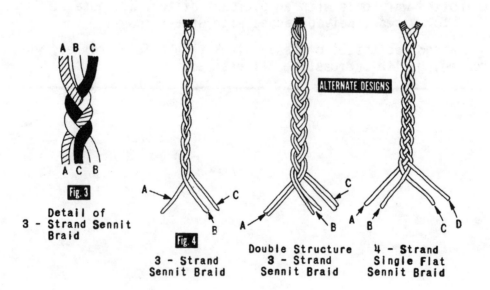

A B C

A C B

Fig. 3

Detail of
3 - Strand Sennit
Braid

A ↗   C ↖

B ↘

Fig. 4

3 - Strand
Sennit Braid

ALTERNATE DESIGNS

C ↖

A ↗   B ↘

Double Structure
3 - Strand
Sennit Braid

A ↗ B ↘   C ↗ D ↘

4 - Strand
Single Flat
Sennit Braid

454

PROCEDURE:

1. Cut 12 strands, 4 each of (A), (B), (C), of raffia for braiding 4 braids twice the desired length of belt. (6-1/2" strand shortens to 5" when braided.) Fig. I.

2. Use 3 different colored strands for each braid, or 3 strands of the same color for each braid , or all one color.

3. Secure ends (A), (B), (C) to edge of table with scotch tape in sequence shown. Fig. 3.

4. Lead (C) down and across (B) to the left.
   Lead (A) down and across (C) to the right. Continue, alternating the outside strands as they are led over the center strand. Fig. 3.

5. Complete 4 braids. Tape ends to prevent unravelling.

6. Locate midpoint of each braid length, fold and flatten side by side to form 4 loops for buttons. Fig. 2.

7. Attach the 8 braided lengths together by weaving in and out with heavy linen thread (or raffia). Leave loops free to accomodate size of button desired. Figs. I, 2.

8. Weave 8 braided lengths together at sides and back of belt. Fig. I.

9. Remove tape from cut ends of braids. Stitch extreme ends firmly. Complete by weaving braids for same span as at loop end.

MATERIALS:

Raffia or colored cotton rug yarn
Heavy linen thread
4 buttons

Woman's Belt

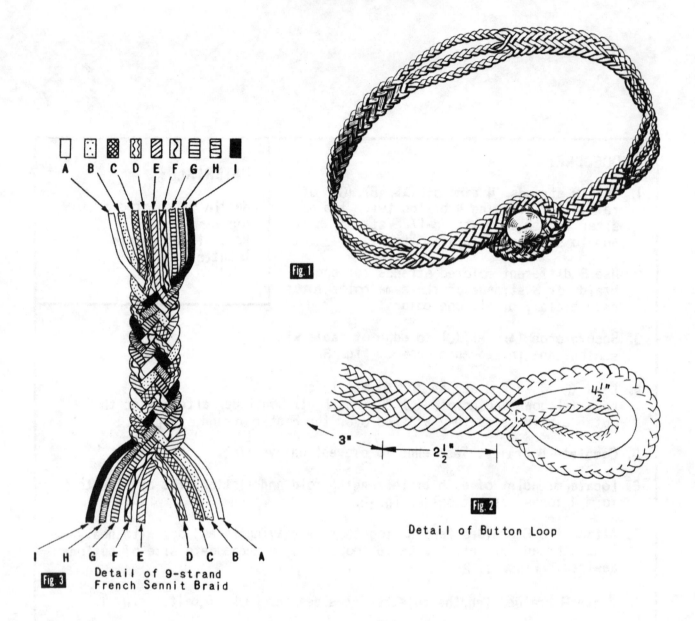

A B C D E F G H I

Fig. 1

Fig. 3

I H G F E D C B A

Detail of 9-strand
French Sennit Braid

Fig. 2

Detail of Button Loop

4½"

3"

2½"

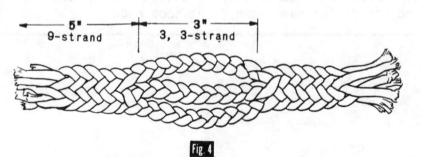

5"
9-strand

3"
3, 3-strand

Fig. 4

Detail of 9-strand Sennit Braid
Separating into three, 3-
strand Sennit Braids

PROCEDURE:

1. Cut 9 strands (A through I) of cord for braiding 9-strand French Sennit Braid. (4" cord shortens to 3" when braided.) Figs. 1, 3.

2. Select colors as desired.

3. Secure ends (A through I) to edge of table with Scotch tape, in sequence shown, with 4 strands on one side and 5 on the other. Fig.3.

4. Lead strand (I) (odd-numbered strand on extreme edge) across the front; going over (H) and (G); then under (F) and (E) toward opposite side.

5. Lead strand (A) (now the extreme strand on odd-numbered side) over (B) and (C); then under (D) and (I) toward opposite side.

6. Continue for 7 inches, always leading odd-numbered strand over two, then under two strands toward opposite side. Figs. 2, 3.

7. Divide the 9-strand braid into 3 groups of 3 strands each, after 7 inches of 9-strand braid is completed. Braid each group in the 3-strand Sennit method for a length of 3 inches. Fig. 4.

8. Alternate 9-strand braid with length of 3-strand braids until the desired length of belt is reached. Terminate the button end of belt with 9-strand braid. Figs. 1, 2.

9. Secure ends of strands by sewing firmly.

10. Loop 7" length of 9-strand braid to form button hole. Fig. 2.

11. Sew on button.

MATERIALS:

Choice of:
1. Bag cord, rayon, 1/8" dia.
2. Metallic tubing cord, 1/8" dia.
3. Cotton rug yarn
4. Raffia
Heavy linen thread
1 button

Beach Bag

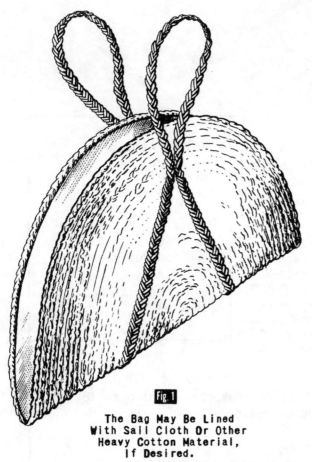

Fig. 1

The Bag May Be Lined
With Sail Cloth Or Other
Heavy Cotton Material,
If Desired.

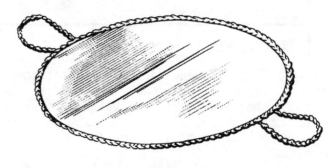

Fig. 2

Beach Bag In Open Position
Used As Beach Seat. (Lined)

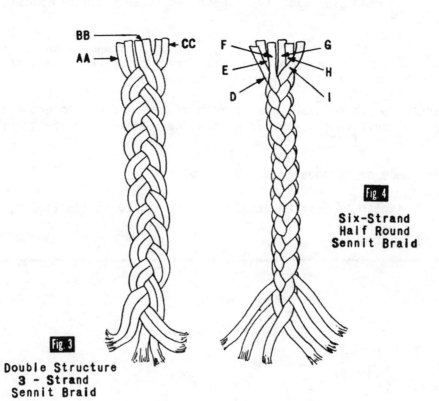

BB ——
AA ——
—— CC

Fig. 3

Double Structure
3 - Strand
Sennit Braid

F
E
D
G
H
I

Fig. 4

Six-Strand
Half Round
Sennit Braid

PROCEDURE:

1. Cut 6 strands (2 each of (A), (B), (C)) of rug yarn for braiding double structure, 3-strand Sennit braid for handles. Double strands are used. (3" strand shortens to about 2" when braided.) Figs. 1, 3.

2. Select colors as desired.

3. Secure ends (AA), (BB), (CC) to edge of table with scotch tape, in sequence shown. Fig. 3.

4. Braid a 38" length for handle strap. Fig. 1.

5. Cut 6 strands (D through I) of rug yarn for braiding 6-strand Half-Round Sennit braid, out of which the bag is constructed. (52 yards of braid requires strands 70 yards each. Figs. 1, 4.

6. Secure ends (D through I) to edge of table with scotch tape, in sequence and grouping shown. Fig. 4.

7. Start with strand (D) down and under from left to right and up between (G) and (H), over (G), then across to left group.

8. Lead strand (I) down and under from right to left and up between (F) and (D), then over to the right group.

9. Bring strand (E) down and over left to right and up between (I) and (G), then over (I) to the left group, etc.

10. Continue braiding, always in same sequence; down and under from first one side and then the other; then under 2 and over I and back to own side. Complete 52 yards.

11. Sew ends of strands to prevent unravelling.

12. Form circular loop at one end to form center of bag. Sew loop and continue to sew braid as for a braided mat. 52 yards of braid forms a circular mat, approximately 24" in diameter. Fig. 2.

13. Pin handle braid in position on bag. Sew firmly. Fig. 1.

14. When bag is in open position, it may be used as beach seat. Fig. 2.

MATERIALS:

Cotton rug yarn
Heavy linen thread

Spiral Cord

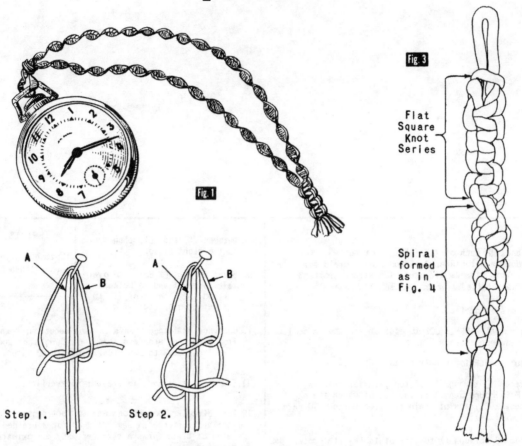

Fig. 1

Fig. 3

Flat
Square
Knot
Series

Spiral
formed
as in
Fig. 4

A B

Step 1.   Step 2.

Fig. 2

Formation of Square Knot
Step (1) shows beginning. Step (2) shows
the complete square knot. A series of
square knots in the same four strands of
(A) and (B) forms the "flat", shown in
Fig. 3. The "flat" makes a good beginning
for a spiral-knotted watch chain, dog
leash, etc.

Fig. 4

Make only one half
the knot made in
Fig. 2, step (2) to
obtain spiral effect.

B

A

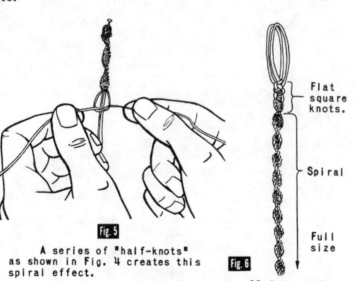

Fig. 5

A series of "half-knots"
as shown in Fig. 4 creates this
spiral effect.

Fig. 6

Flat
square
knots.

Spiral

Full
size

Linen thread, No. 20, forms this
sized spiral cord for watch chain.

Use for neck cords, watch chains, umbrella cords, dog leashes, lamp pulls or window shade pulls.

PROCEDURE:

I. Cut strand of cord (A) about twice the desired length of final cord; cut (B) about 4 times the length of (A). (4" of cord reduces to I" when knotted.) Figs. 2, 4.

2. Loop mid points of 2 cords over a nail. Fig. 2.

3. Form square knots for about I/2", following steps in fig. 2.and fig. 3.

4. Knot remaining cord for length desired, using spiral knot procedure. Figs. 3, 4, 5.

5. End cord with square knot as in step (2) if desired.

6. Give a cord a "finish":
   a. Silk or nylon thread does not knot very tightly. Prevent loosening by drawing finished cord through a cloth moistened with a solution of 25 grains of ordinary resin in 2 oz. of rectified spirits of turpentine.

   b. Stiffen a cord by dipping into a pan of melted paraffin, or a solution of varnish diluted with turpentine. Allow to dry for a week.

   c. Knot ends of cord and paint with clear nail polish or cellulose cement to prevent unravelling, when no stiffening or entire cord is desired.

MATERIALS:

Cotton, rayon, silk or linen
Selection of weight of thread depends on diameter of spiral cord needed for specific purpose. For example:
Use No. 20 linen thread for a watch chain about 3/32" diameter.

Woman's Belt

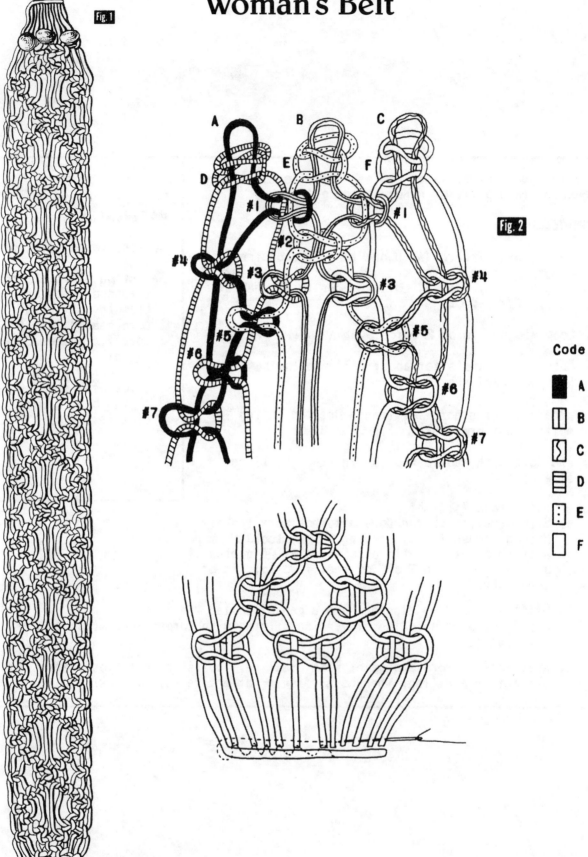

Fig. 1

Fig. 2

Code

A
B
C
D
E
F

PROCEDURE:

1. Cut 6 strands (A) through (F) of cord 5 yards each. Locate mid-point of each.

2. Form individual loops with (A), (B) and (C) as shown in fig. 2.

3. Form knots (#1) between (A) and (B) and (B) and (C). Fig. 2.

4. Bring one end of (D), (E) and (F) down through knots (#1) as shown.

5. Loop free ends of (D), (E) and (F) to form knots around (A), (B) and (C).

6. Now all three doubled strands have been knotted together and there are twelve free ends.

7. One free end of (E) and (F) is brought through knots (#1).

8. Form knot (#2) with both ends of (E) and draw both ends of (B) through it.

9. Form knots (#3) between (D) and (B) and (B) and (F). Draw one end of (E) through each knot.

10. Form outside knots (#4) with (A) and (D) and (C) and (F). Draw ends of (A) and (C) through them.

11. Form knots (#5), (#6) and (#7) with (E) and (A) and (E) and (C); (D) and (A) and (C) and (F); and (A) and (D) and (C) and (F), respectively. Draw ends (D) and (F), (A) and (C), and (A) and (C) through knots (#5), (#6) and (#7), respectively.

12. Proceed as before, until desired length of belt is reached. Follow pattern of belt as shown in figs. 1 and 2.

13. Terminate ends of strands by sewing as in fig. 2.

MATERIALS:

Choice of:
1. Bag cord, rayon, 1/8" diameter
2. Tubing cord, metallic (gold or silver) 1/8" diameter

463